SIXTH EDITION

FAMILIES, PROFESSIONALS, AND EXCEPTIONALITY

Positive Outcomes Through Partnerships and Trust

ANN TURNBULL
The University of Kansas

RUD TURNBULL
The University of Kansas

ELIZABETH J. ERWIN
Montclair State University

LESLIE C. SOODAK
Pace University

KARRIE A. SHOGREN
The University of Illinois, Urbana-Champaign

Boston   Columbus   Indianapolis   New York   San Francisco   Upper Saddle River
Amsterdam   Cape Town   Dubai   London   Madrid   Milan   Munich   Paris   Montreal   Toronto
Delhi   Mexico City   Sao Paulo   Sydney   Hong Kong   Seoul   Singapore   Taipei   Tokyo

Vice President and Editor in Chief: Jeffery W. Johnston
Executive Editor: Ann Castel Davis
Editorial Assistant: Penny Burleson
Vice President, Director of Marketing: Quinn Perkson
Marketing Manager: Erica DeLuca
Senior Managing Editor: Pamela D. Bennett
Project Manager: Sheryl Glicker Langner
Senior Operations Supervisor: Matthew Ottenweller
Senior Art Director: Diane C. Lorenzo
Text Designer: Candace Rowley
Cover Designer: Ali Mohrman
Photo Coordinator: Carol Sykes
Cover Art: Ali Mohrman
Full-Service Project Management: Christian Holdener, S4Carlisle Publishing Services
Composition: S4Carlisle Publishing Services
Printer/Binder: Edwards Brothers
Cover Printer: Lehigh-Phoenix Color
Text Font: Berkeley-Book

Credits and acknowledgments borrowed from other sources and reproduced, with permission, in this textbook appear on appropriate page within text.

Every effort has been made to provide accurate and current Internet information in this book. However, the Internet and information posted on it are constantly changing, so it is inevitable that some of the Internet addresses listed in this textbook will change.

Library of Congress Cataloging-in-Publication Data

Families, professionals, and exceptionality : positive outcomes through partnerships and
  trust / Ann Turnbull . . . [et al.]. — 6th ed.
     p. cm.
  Includes bibliographical references and index.
  ISBN 978-0-13-707048-0
  1. Parents of exceptional children—United States.   2. Exceptional children—Family relationships—United
States.   3. Counselor and client—United States.   I. Turnbull, Ann P.
  HQ759.913.F36 2011
  649'.15—dc22   2010003107

10 9 8 7 6 5 4 3 2

www.pearsonhighered.com

ISBN 10:   0-13-707048-9
ISBN 13: 978-0-13-707048-0

DEDICATION

RUD and ANN TURNBULL dedicate this edition to their son, Jay, who died in January 2009. He was the inspiration for their work, the centrifugal force in their lives, and, with their daughters, Amy and Kate, the delight of their years together.

ELIZABETH dedicates this book to Mom for teaching her about love; to Alyssa, Dad, and Bill for teaching her about family; and to Rick for teaching her about partnership.

LESLIE dedicates this book to her husband, Ian, and her daughter, Gaby, for their never-ending love, and in remembrance of her mother and father, Jeanne and George, for their love and guidance.

KARRIE dedicates this book to her Aunt J., who taught her about grace, love, the dignity of risk, and the amazing possibilities of support and community for people with and without disabilities.

PREFACE

:: THE FAMILIES

We could not have written this book without the families whom we feature. They allowed us to enter their lives by telling us their stories. By telling their stories, they became our and our readers' teachers. They are forces for "the disability cause." But they are more than that: They are exemplars of all that is good, decent, generous, steadfast, and optimistic.

:: THE ORGANIZATION

Part I introduces the reader to the family systems theory. That theory undergirds our book because it not only explains the complexity of the lives of families affected by disability but it also simplifies our understanding of those families.

Part II sketches the history of family-professional relationships and thereby provides the context for our discussion of today's relationships—what they are and what they should and can be. Part II also describes the two federal laws that govern special education services, emphasizing the special education law (Individuals with Disabilities Education Act). As the history chapter hints and the law chapter makes clear, disability is a civil rights issue, and IDEA is more than "just" a law about education: It is a law about equal opportunity for a full, enviable life.

Part III introduces the seven principles that constitute the construct called partnership. It then emphasizes communication, one of the principles, and, in each of the following chapters, illustrates how educators should apply the principles. In a word, part III provides both theory (chapter 7) and practice (chapters 8 through 12); moreover, it does so in light of the family systems theory (part I) and consistent with the most recent stage of history and the law (part II).

:: NEW TO THIS EDITION

Although this, the sixth edition, is similar in many ways to the previous edition, it differs in some significant respects.

It is similar in that it describes the family systems theory (part I), the history and current status of policy (part II),

and the principles of partnership and their application by teachers and other professionals (part III). It is also similar in that it cites the most recent research; we have brought the text and references to date (2009).

It is unlike the previous edition in other respects.

- It features six families, not four. These families are, themselves, different than the families in the fifth edition; they are "fresh faces."
- Recognizing the extraordinary times in which we live and the role of the armed forces in our times, this book highlights a Marine Corps family, the Nelms family.
- The sixth edition has an increased emphasis on the older individual with a disability and the role families continue to play in their lives. Unlike the previous edition, this book features three students who have graduated from secondary school. They appear in chapter 12, where we discuss the outcomes of special education. These students differ in at least two respects, thus adding variety to the chapter. Two (Lanz Powell, in chapters 3 and 4, and Ryan Frisella, in chapters 11 and 12) have just entered college.
- Also unlike the previous edition, this book portrays a family's entire life span. The youngest child is Eric Lindauer (preschool and kindergarten); the elementary school child is Chad Nelms; the middle-school student is Maria Hernandez; the secondary and postsecondary school students are Lanz Powell and Ryan Frisella; and the adult is our son, Jay Turnbull.
- Like the previous edition, this book features cultural diversity. There is one African American family, Lanz and Xenia Powell; one Hispanic American family, Maria, Eloisa, and Henrique Hernandez; and four white families. But unlike the previous edition, one of these families is a single-parent family (Lanz and Xenia Powell).
- This edition portrays more disabilities than the previous edition. Here, you will find students with physical, intellectual, other developmental, and multiple disabilities.

ACKNOWLEDGMENTS

Of course we acknowledge the families whom we have featured: Without them, this book would lack the human face that research so desperately and constantly needs.

Once again, Rud and Ann are deeply indebted to Lois Weldon, their all-purpose assistant, for her diligence, patience, and great skills in preparing the manuscript and sleuthing the references. Lois has "been with us" for all editions of this book. She is invaluable. We also appreciate the assistance of Heather Aldersey, a graduate student at the Beach Center, in helping us and Lois prepare the final manuscript for submission to the publisher.

A special thank you is due to Gaby Kirschner, a high school student, and Grace Wuertz, a graduate student, who diligently checked and compiled countless references for Elizabeth and Leslie.

All the authors bow to Ann Davis, our editor at Pearson. She knows the market and the strategies for making this book the leading text in its particular market; she has a powerful way of shaping, directing, encouraging, and rewarding us for our work; and she has become our dear friend and indispensable colleague for her work in this book and another, *Exceptional Lives.*

Others at Pearson who have assisted us and earned our gratitude are our editor, Ann Davis, and her wonderful editorial assistant, Penny Burleson. Sheryl Langner, Production Manager, and Carol Sykes, Photo Editor, have, as in the past, provided expert support. We could also not have completed this edition without the assistance of Cindy Durand, copy editor extraordinaire. Finally, we are continually grateful to Jeff Johnston, Editor in Chief, for his long-standing support of us through the years.

We have benefited from the constructive critiques of reviewers of the previous edition. They helped us significantly as we wrote this edition. They are Rachelle Bruno, Northern Kentucky University; Melissa Olive, Texas State University; Alec Peck, Boston College; and Doug Sturgeon, University of Rio Grande.

Most importantly, we all recognize and honor the life of Jay Turnbull. It is our hope that his legacy will continue to live on in the pages of this book.

BRIEF CONTENTS

CONTENTS

:: chapter eight ::

Families as Partners in Communication and Collaboration 159

:: chapter nine ::

Families as Partners in Evaluating a Student 183

:: **chapter ten** ::

Families as Partners in Developing Individualized Plans 209

:: **chapter eleven** ::

Meeting Families' Basic Needs 233

:: **chapter twelve** ::

Professionals and Families as Partners for Student Outcomes 257

The Family Systems Perspective

As you will soon learn from chapters 1 through 4 and indeed throughout the entire book, it is best to enter into trusting partnerships with families by understanding that families are systems. Whatever happens to one of the family members happens to all of them. The metaphor we use to describe the family systems perspective is a mobile.

If you put one part of a mobile into action, you create motion in all of the other parts. That is how it is with families. The characteristics of family members (chapter 1), their ways of interacting with each other (chapter 2), the functions they perform for each other (chapter 3), and how they move through various stages of their lives set the family system into motion, just like a mobile (chapter 4).

Family Characteristics

LUKE, CHRISTINE, AND ERIC LINDAUER

"Luke is just a fluke," says his mother, Christine Lindauer. Disregard the lilting rhyming and consider the reason behind her statement.

Luke is 3½ years old. He is already a charmer of teenage girls and adults who cannot help but notice then disregard his low muscle tone and speech limitations. What's the source of those limitations? A definitive answer was available only after Luke was a year old.

Until then, Christine wondered whether Luke's delays could have had anything to do with the fact that her older sister, Stacy, has an intellectual disability. Genetic testing and genetic counseling ruled out any connection between Christine, her sister, and Luke's father, Eric—indeed, between any family member—and Luke. So, Luke's anomaly is indeed a fluke.

But Luke's diagnosis and his parents' genetic workups did not occur until Luke was a year old. Would an earlier diagnosis have made any difference? Here, too, the answer is unclear. "I would have changed the way I interacted with Luke, but whether that would have made a difference, who knows," says Christine. "But I was clueless, a new mom. I had worked with preschoolers when I taught in Taiwan, but I had no experience with babies. I thought, 'Is it just me?' that Luke didn't respond. Eric and I are introverts, laid-back, and weren't exactly animated or interested in singing 'Old MacDonald' to Luke. When I made attempts it felt so unnatural and fake, but I didn't understand the real reason why. Luke's low muscle tone and perhaps poor vision prevented him from engaging with me the way a typically developing baby would. He didn't respond back, so of course it felt awkward making funny faces to what appeared to be an uninterested baby. If I had understood this, I would have attempted to engage him more."

Luke is not just a fluke. He is a mystery. Why does he have this anomaly? And what difference does he make in his family? Undoubtedly, he makes a difference, but just how much of one is the still-to-be-answered puzzle.

Let's take a closer look at Luke's family. Both of his parents are graduates of the Massachusetts Institute of Technology. Christine trained as a chemical engineer and became a manager of a start-up technology company in New York City. Eric trained as a computer scientist and mathematician and worked in the finance

industry. Financially successful in the city, they grew tired of the fast-paced lifestyle and migrated to San Diego.

Luke was born there, but San Diego did not satisfy their taste. Free to live anywhere in the country and seeking a community of friends, they followed some of their MIT friends and bought a home in Pittsboro, a few miles south of Chapel Hill, North Carolina.

Once there, they realized that neither wanted to be a stay-at-home, full-time parent. That had nothing to do with Luke; each had a personality that would not be satisfied by that role. So, they enrolled Luke in a day-care center at the Frank Porter Graham Child Development Institute, a research center of The University of North Carolina focused on normal and atypical child development.

Pleased with the program, they then enrolled him in its preschool. Both programs serve children with and without disabilities. Having taught preschoolers in Taiwan for a while, Christine became involved as a volunteer and now is a part-time employee at the center. Luke has begun to affect her career. Not so with Eric.

The grandparents are too far away to be involved in Luke's everyday life, but wish they could play a bigger role. Asked to characterize her family, Christine talks about Luke's grandparents. Her mother and her two aunts own and operate a golf course and restaurant in Harmony, Pennsylvania; they live next door to each other. It is a tightly knit extended family, where Christine says "Her cousins feel more like brothers and sisters, and her aunts like second mothers."

By contrast, Eric's parents are divorced and remarried, so there are two sets of grandparents along with several great-grandparents. One side in Detroit, Michigan, and the other in Battle Creek, Michigan; it can make holiday travel quite extensive. That said, Eric's father and stepmother have bought a second home near them and will spend half the year there when his stepmother retires.

How to sum up the Lindauer family? By definition, Eric, Christine, and Luke are family by reason of marriage and blood. Their size is three; there are no immediately involved grandparents, uncles, or aunts. Their form is nuclear; they live together. Their cultural background is German American. Their socioeconomic status is mixed: They are highly educated, they were professionally and financially successful in New York, but they live modestly now.

think about it

Now that you've "met" the Lindauer family, think about them and their relevance to your potential partnerships with them.

- What single trait do they have that is most likely to make them want to be a partner with you and other educators?
- What trait is most likely to challenge you, and other educators, as you seek to be a partner with them?
- What partnerships with professionals have Christine and Eric already had, and what can you learn about them from their previous partnerships with professionals?

:: INTRODUCTION

This chapter focuses on the first component of the family systems framework: the family's characteristics. Family characteristics are *inputs* into the family system. Figure 1.1 shows you the family systems framework, highlighting family characteristics. These include (1) the characteristics of the family as a whole, (2) the characteristics of individual members, and (3) unique circumstances. The characteristics of the family as a whole include its cultural background, socioeconomic level, and geographic location. In addition, each member of the family varies in individual characteristics related to exceptionality, coping styles, and health status. Finally, many families face unique circumstances such as economic hardships, homelessness, addiction to alcohol or drugs, abuse and neglect, exposure to violence and other fearful experiences, imprisonment, chronic illness, teenage parenting, and parenting with a disability. Every family is a distinct mixture of diverse characteristics.

To develop trusting partnerships with families, you need to understand the distinct mixture of diverse characteristics that makes each family unique. You may begin that understanding by focusing on the family's characteristics.

FIGURE 1.1   **Family systems framework: emphasis on family characteristics.**

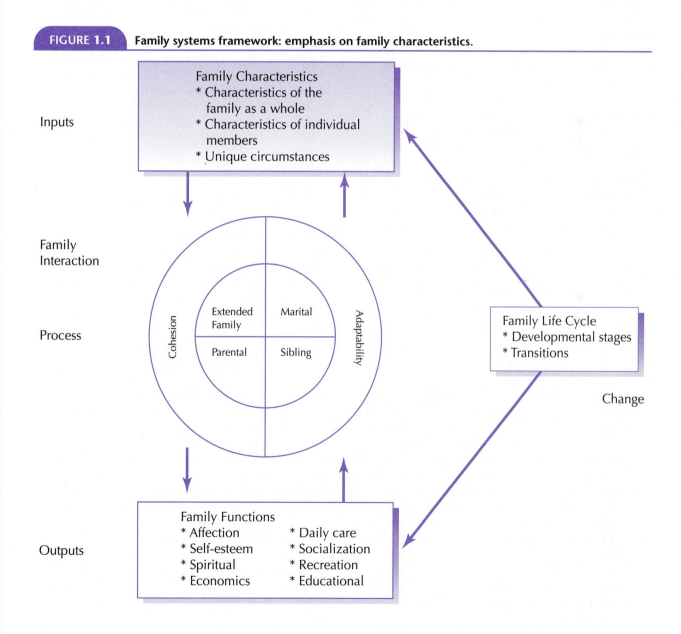

:: CHARACTERISTICS OF THE FAMILY AS A WHOLE

A family shares many characteristics as a single entity. Some of these characteristics are the family's size and form, cultural background, socioeconomic status, and geographic location. To build a trusting partnership with each family, you will want to understand and take each characteristic into account.

Family: Definition, Size, and Form

Before discussing family size and form, let's think about a definition for the term *family*. Before we do, answer these questions: Who are the members of your family? How do you define your family?

Your definition is a starting point, at least for our work together in this book. The U.S. Census Bureau defines family as a group of two or more people related by birth, marriage, or adoption who reside together (Iceland, 2000). Does this definition fit how you define your own family? It does not fit our experiences with families. As a professional, you will encounter people who define *family* by including individuals who do not share the same household or are not related by blood, marriage, or adoption. Do all of your family members live in the same household? Are all the members of your family related by blood, marriage, or adoption?

We define family as follows (Poston et al., 2003):

Families include two or more people who regard themselves as a family and who carry out the functions that families typically perform. These people may or may not be related by blood or marriage and may or may not usually live together. Which definition is a better match for your family?

Each family's size and form depends on its own definition of family. Family size and form can be as exclusive as the Census Bureau's definition or as inclusive as ours. Family size and form refer to the number of children, number of parents, presence and number of stepparents, number of live-in family members who are unrelated by blood or marriage, and the involvement of the extended family.

Data from the 2000 Census reveal that over 20 million families or about 30% of families in the United States had at least one member with a disability (Wang, 2005). The impact of a child's disability on the family can vary, depending on the family's size and form. In large families, more people are often available to help with chores and specialized supports and resources needed by the child with a disability. Other children in the family can remind parents that their child with a disability is more like than unlike his or her brothers and sisters and that all children have various combinations of strengths and needs.

It is often assumed that a child with a disability creates severe strain in most marriages. However, this is not necessarily the case. Risdal and Singer (2004) analyzed all the research on marital adjustment in parents of children with disabilities and found that the research does not support the assumption that children with disabilities "cause severe family strain in almost all families" (p. 101). They note that marital challenges do exist in some families, and advocate for improved individualized family support for all families. You will learn more marital interactions and the impact of a child with disability in chapter 2.

You are certain to have students in your class whose parents are single. A father of two young children who had only seen his own father once every year or so when he was growing up described his decision to be the primary caregiver of his children:

The day my baby was born, I said, "I gotta find a better life." I had always said that I was not going to be like my daddy. I mean, I had the idea, the dream, as a kid because of some of the things my mother went through. I said, "I don't want my kids to go through any of this shit. I'm going to get married the right way." But, of course, that didn't happen as far as the marriage. But I just said I was not going to abandon my kids . . . because I never had the opportunity to be with my dad. I just did not want to be like my father. (Coles, 2003, p. 255)

Although households headed by fathers are growing in number, approximately one third of youth with disabilities live in a single-parent household where the parent is their biological mother. The poverty rate among families headed by a single mother is almost 40% when a child in the family has a disability (Fujiura & Yamaki, 2000). Of the 3.2 million single-parent households that experience poverty, approximately one in five has a member with a disability. And, single-parent households headed by a single mother are more likely than any other family type to have a child with a disability (Wang, 2005). In a study examining material hardship in American families with children with disabilites, Parish and colleagues (2008) found that single-parent, female-headed households were at the greatest risk for living in poverty. However, Cauthen and Fass (2009) suggest that although single-parent households are at greater economic risk, largely because of the lack of potential for two incomes, even two-parent families cannot protect against economic uncertainty. They report that more than one in four children with disabilities in two-parent households live in poverty. (In 2008 and 2009, Americans experienced an economic recession that undoubtedly exaccerbated economic challenges for families who have children with disabilities. As this book goes to press, data on the effects of the recession on those families are not yet conclusive. You should, however, be prepared to work with families who have experienced recent significant economic challenges.)

Clearly, two of the characteristics that contribute to the likelihood that families will experience poverty are single-parent, female-headed households and the presence of children (particularly more than one child) who have a disability. According to some recent data, there are over 8 million women and children in the United States receiving WIC (Supplemental Nutrition Program for Women, Infants, and Children) (Children's Defense Fund, 2008). There remains a critical need to implement more effective and long-term support for single mothers of children with disabilities who are living in poverty. Birenbaum (2002) suggests that "mothers on welfare roles, compared to those who have managed to get off and stay off public assistance, are themselves at a higher risk of disability, perhaps because they themselves have grown up under the same biological and environmental circumstances as their children" (p. 217).

If the major characteristics of single-parent families are that they are headed by females, face economic challenges,

---

TOGETHER WE CAN

Marie Manning—Possibilities for Partnership

"I need $6 for a shirt for school, Mom," my 11-year-old son, Zack, declared. For the first time in 4 years, he was participating in a field trip. With a lot of support, Zack had finally overcome the behavioral challenges associated with his autism. The celebration was bittersweet for me, however. There was no doubt that he deserved a team shirt; but money is always in short supply for a single mother with two children. Moreover, the personal anxiety of caring for Zack's every single need, maintaining every single appointment for him, and putting out every single fire with the school while juggling every financial burden often seemed insurmountable. Zack's aggressiveness was erratic at times and required many teacher conferences, IEP meetings, and appointments with behavior specialists and psychiatrists to regulate his behavior and monitor his medication. I found myself leaving work early at least once a week to take him to appointments or attend conferences with the school. Ensuring that my son's needs were met forced me to be in two places at once: he needed me, and I had to work to support us. . . . Financially, we were quickly falling behind in our obligations. My only option was to continue my education full-time. . . . Not only would going to school full-time accelerate my career, but it also would allow me to take advantage of a full scholarship at a local university and free me up to help ensure that Zack's needs were met. . . . When he left school early for an appointment (with an agency that would provide us with financial support), he lost class time and was assigned additional homework, creating havoc with his nightly routine. . . . My stomach would churn with anxiety when any additional costs arose, including the much-needed extracurricular activities and even the $6 shirt. . . . My anxieties about soccer were answered when he played his first game with the team. "That's the most fun I ever had

losing!" Zack exclaimed as he ran off the soccer field. My heart was overfilled with joy, and tears trickled down my face. I was overwhelmed with his success and completely understood his exuberance. Although I am fighting a losing battle financially and the daily stresses drain the energy out of me, being a parent of such a dynamic child overshadows all of it. His spirit and personality shine through everything else. . . . In a world where daily struggles are a fact of life, the simple celebrations of minor achievements can be of major importance. There is nothing more exciting to me than when someone else tries to grasp the complexities of a life as a single parent who has a child with special needs. The teachers who have had the most success with Zack have overlooked inconsequential issues, such as whether he uses a pen or pencil on an assignment, and instead celebrated the fact that he completed his assignment and turned it in on time. It is better to celebrate than criticize, especially when a family has only one parent and few resources other than themselves.

Marie Manning,
University of North Texas

Take Action!

- When you teach a child whose parent(s) have so many financial burdens, focus on the "big picture" of the child's education. You will demonstrate that you respect the parents.
- Also, try to understand the complexities of the family's life. You will become more like an equal partner if you can see life from their perspective.
- When the child makes progress, let the child's parent(s) know. You will show that you can communicate in a positive way.

and may be short on time and energy, then surely Marie Manning and her family are typical. Read the Together We Can box on the previous page for a glimpse into her family.

A different pattern of family size and form—more than two parents—exists when one or both parents in the original family have remarried. The new blended family may include children and extended family members from two or more marriages. Children may have to abide by different rules in two different households, adapt to two different lifestyles, or surrender the adult roles they may have assumed while their custodial parent was single. Stepparents may be uncertain about their authority and children may regard their acceptance of a stepparent as a sign of disloyalty to their biological parent. Because they have a ready-made family from the first day of their marriage, parents may not have the privacy or time to establish their new relationship. Finally, negotiations among all the adults—the former and current spouses—may be necessary to resolve conflicts over the children and visitation schedules, discipline, lifestyle, and so on. On the positive side, a wide circle of interested family members may be able and willing to support each other and the member with the disability. As a result, a blended family can offer an expanded and rich pool of resources and support.

There are over half a million children in the foster care system and over 2.5 million grandparents raising their grandchildren (Children's Defense Fund, 2008). Be sure to take into account how these families, as well as single-parent, cohabitating-partner, or remarried families, make decisions about a child's education. When the adults convene, they may engage in an amiable discussion about the child's best interests. Or, they may create a family power struggle, requiring you or other professionals to mediate differences and state what you believe is best for the child. You may want to consult the school social worker or school counselor for suggestions on how to be most supportive in especially challenging situations.

Cultural Background

Cultural and Microcultural Characteristics. Just as your own cultural background influences what you value, how you think, and how you behave, each student and family will also be highly influenced by their cultural backgrounds.

The term *culture* refers to the foundational values and beliefs that set the standards for how people perceive, interpret, and behave within their family, school, and community. Sometimes people refer to culture as consisting only of a person's race or ethnicity (generally defined to include one's national origin, religion, and race) (Gollnick & Chinn, 2002). Although race and ethnicity are major influences in one's culture, many other factors constitute one's cultural identity. These multiple influences are *microcultures* (Gollnick &

Chinn, 2002). Figure 1.2 illustrates microcultures that can shape a person's overall cultural identity.

Each of these microcultures can influence family/professional partnerships in many different ways.

- *Religion,* as well as religious beliefs and customs, influences the holidays that families celebrate and thus the appropriateness of your communication with them concerning holiday events, schedules, and rituals.
- *Language* influences all aspects of communicating with families, especially when families do not speak English at all or are unable to read in English or any other language.
- *Gender* influences beliefs about the roles that various family members should take in communicating with professionals.
- *Race* influences the likelihood that people will experience discrimination if they are of the nonmajority culture; the racism in turn fosters skepticism about trusting others of a different race.
- *Ethnicity* influences whether people think they belong or whether they perceive themselves as outsiders in schools, particularly when they are of diverse ethnicity.
- *Age* influences the experiences parents have, as in the case of teenage mothers who suddenly find themselves with parental responsibilities.
- *Geography* poses certain opportunities and barriers to partnerships, such as in rural settings when families live a long distance from school without public transportation.
- *Income* influences the resources available to families and the extent to which their housing, medical care, and nutrition are adequate.

Microcultures shape the particular cultural beliefs of families. For example, a white man from the Midwest who attends a fundamentalist Christian church and is the father of a child with a learning disability may have worldviews—especially those related to disability—that differ from an African American man from New York City who attends a mosque and is the father of a child who is deaf. Similarly, the African American man may have worldviews different from those of a newly immigrated Vietnamese family whose members are highly paid professionals and leaders in their Roman Catholic church and whose child with autism has extraordinary mathematical talents. Despite the differences among families, do not assume that any one "type" of family values their child or the child's education any more or less than any other "type" of family. Make no assumptions; treat all families as you would want to be treated and treat them consistently with the law (chapter 6) and best practices (chapters 7 through 12).

FIGURE 1.2 Cultural identity shaped through microcultural groups.

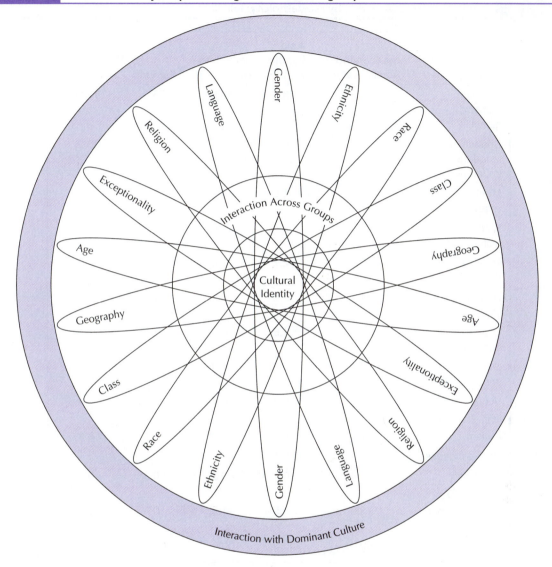

Different cultural attributes (not just racial or ethnic) exist in each of these three families. These attributes may change over the family's life span. You will learn more about the changes in a family's life span in chapter 4. One family may change its religion or choose atheism; another family's economic status may improve or decline precipitously. Still another family may be influenced by racial or religious intermarriage. Disability status also can influence one's cultural affiliations, such as the strong group identity known as *Deaf culture* (Scheetz, 2004).

Racial/Ethnic Composition of Special Education. In the United States children with disabilities represent approximately 9% of the school-aged population (U.S. Department of Education, 2007). The number of children receiving special education under the Individuals with Disabilities Education Act (IDEA) continues to grow. For example, from 1995 to 2004 the total number of students with disabilities from ages 6 to 21 receiving special education and related services jumped from almost 5 million to more than 6 million (U.S. Department of Education, 2007). Figure 1.3 sets out the percentages of students receiving special education services according to different racial/ethnic groups and categories of disability. Compare and contrast the information in this table.

As you will see from the data, learning disabilities is the largest disability category across all race and ethnic groups.

| FIGURE **1.3** | Disability distribution of students ages 6 through 21 receiving special education and related services under IDEA, Part B, by race/ethnicity: fall 2004. |

Disability	American/Indian Alaska Native	Asian/ Pacific Islander	Black (non-Hispanic)	Hispanic	White (non-Hispanic)
Specific learning disability	53.3	38.4	44.8	56.6	44.1
Speech or language impairments	16.3	26.2	14.4	18.6	20.2
Mental retardation	7.4	8.6	14.9	7.6	7.9
Emotional disturbance	8.0	4.4	11.0	4.9	7.9
Multiple disabilities	2.0	2.7	2.2	1.7	2.3
Hearing impairments	1.0	2.8	0.9	1.5	1.1
Orthopedic impairments	0.7	1.6	0.8	1.2	1.1
Other health impairments	6.4	5.8	6.9	4.7	10.1
Visual impairments	0.3	0.8	0.4	0.5	0.4
Autism	1.3	6.6	2.0	1.7	3.1
Deaf-blindness	!	0.1	!	!	!
Traumatic brain injury	0.4	0.4	0.3	0.3	0.4
Developmental delay	3.0	1.5	1.3	0.6	1.3
All disabilities[a]	100.0	100.0	100.0	100.0	100.0

Source: U.S. Department of Education, Office of Special Education Programs, Data Analysis System (DANS), OMB #1820-0043: "Children with Disabilities Receiving Special Education Under Part B of the *Individuals with Disabilities Education Act*," 2004. Data updated as of July 30, 2005.

[a]Total may not sum to 100 because of rounding.

! Percentage is <0.05.

What other trends do you notice? Take careful note of the disproportionate representation of certain groups. African American children are approximately twice as likely to receive special education and related services under the label of mental retardation (*intellectual disability* is the preferred term) than students in all other racial/ethnic groups (U.S. Department of Education, 2007). In addition, these data show that they also are more likely to be identified as having emotional disturbance than other students. Overall, American Indian/Alaska Native and Black (non-Hispanic) students are more likely to be identified as having a disability and served under IDEA Part B than students in all other racial/ethnic groups combined.

There has been a history of exclusion, disproportionality, and discrimination within the system of special education for students with disabilities who are from culturally and linguistically diverse backgrounds and their families. Exclusion refers to barring or banishing a student from school; disproportionality refers to enrolling more students of a minority/diverse background in special education than the percentage of those students in the entire school population; and discrimination refers to denying equal opportunities to education solely on the basis of disability.

Unfortunately, disproportionality and discrimination continue to be the case (Fiedler et al., 2008; Harry & Klinger, 2006; McHatton, 2007). In a study of cultural beliefs and practices with families (Eberly, Joshi, & Konzal, 2007), one African American teacher noted,

> As a Black child, I was told I was stupid by teachers. Sometimes teachers say some ignorant things to parents, and they don't even realize it. I didn't realize that my son was getting so many negative messages from that school. He came out thinking terrible stuff about Black people, and he's Black. (p. 17)

Stereotyping and discrimination may very well be linked to the overrepresentation of students from culturally and linguistically diverse backgrounds referred for special education and related services.

To address the issue of disproportionality within the special education system, Fiedler and colleagues (2008) suggest using a checklist to promote the use of culturally responsive practices school-wide and in inclusive classrooms—those in which students with and without disabilities are educated together. They suggested asking "has the principal established an attitude among staff that 'all students are our students' as opposed to an attitude of 'my students and your students' and 'do teachers (e.g., general education, ESL, special education) work collaboratively to support all children in the classrooms?'"

An analysis of trends related to the disproportionate representation of African American students receiving special education services reveals a great deal about the socioeconomic status of these students. The poorer the family, the greater the chance the student will receive special education services. Compared to white or Asian/Pacific Islander students, a higher percentage of African American, Latino, and American Indian/Alaskan Native students attend high poverty schools (Planty et al., 2009). Further, families who experience poverty often live in communities that lack resources for schools (National Research Council, 2002; Silverstein, Lamberto, De Peau, & Grossman, 2008).

Immigration and Limited English Proficiency. Immigration trends strongly influence diversity in schools. The 2000 U.S. Census revealed that approximately 10% of the population had recently immigrated. This percentage represents approximately 28.5 million individuals, including approximately 8.5 million school-age children. The number of school-age children who are immigrants is predicted to double in the foreseeable future (Camarota, 2001). Over half of immigrant families in the United States experience poverty. Douglas-Hall and Chau (2008) report that 35 percent of children whose parents were born in the United States are considered low-income compared to 58 percent of children whose parents were not born in the United States.

One Chinese mother of a child with disabilities who had recently immigrated to the United States reported that the language difficulties she experienced caused her to withdraw from school activities:

> Because your English is not good, perhaps when you speak, he could not understand you. But perhaps when he answered your questions, you could not understand him. Then you become shy and withdrawn, because you could not overcome that handicap. (Lai & Ishiyama, 2004, p. 103)

Slightly more than 2.5 million students recently have received instruction to improve English proficiency (U.S. Department of Education, 2001). Of these, 5.5% or approximately 145,000 were students with disabilities. In the 2003–2004 school year, the number of students receiving English as a second langague instruction jumped to 3.8 million (U.S. Department of Education, 2006). Of these 3.8 million students, 12%—or over 460,000 students—also received special education services.

There are visible roadblocks in the educational system facing students and families from culturally and linguistically diverse backgrounds. "Racial disproportionality is not the only cultural challenge in special education; disproportionality is also associated with language proficiency" (Turnbull, Turnbull, & Wehmeyer, 2010, p. 79).

Many families of children with disabilities who have limited English proficiency identify communication as a huge barrier to developing trusting partnerships. Research with Latino parents has consistently revealed that limited English proficiency strongly affects the extent to which educators provide appropriate supports and information to students and families (Lian & Fontánez-Phelan, 2001; McHatton, 2007; Salas, 2004; Shapiro, Monzo, Rueda, Gomez, & Blacher, 2004). Research with Chinese (Lai & Ishiyama, 2004; Lo, 2008) and Korean families (Kim, Lee, & Morningstar, 2007) reached similar conclusions. A Korean mother of a student receiving special education services described this challenge as follows:

> A bunch of papers are coming from the school. I don't know what is important and what is not. So, I always stack them on the table, hoping my husband can read them to find really important papers. My child often

misses field trips because I could not read the directions and the papers. English is such a problem. (Park & Turnbull, 2001, p. 137)

In addition to langauge proficiency, one overlooked issue is loss of language—the discontinued use of a native language. The "loss" phenomenon has affected Native American students and their families more than any other racial or cultural group (Turnbull, Turnbull, & Wehmeyer, 2010). Clearly, there are multiple and complex issues that impact language proficiency and partnerships.

To foster trusting partnerships, some special education professionals will need to be multilingual or have access to interpreters (Al-Hassan & Gardner, 2002). But you and indeed all professionals need to honor cultural diversity and work to develop cultural competence. Cultural competence extends far beyond merely using interpreters although this is one helpful resource. Cultural competence is about fostering a self-awareness as well as an understanding and respect for the cultural community in which the family belongs.

When communicating with parents who do not speak English, do not use jargon and technical terminology unless absolutely necessary (e.g., when referring to a particular assessment procedure or professional support service or device). When communicating through interpreters, limit your comments to a few sentences so there is ample time for the interpreter to translate your ideas to the family. Periodically "check in" with the family to ascertain their understanding as well as to determine the accuracy of the translation. Lynch and Hanson (2004) provide additional useful suggestions for working with families who are immigrants and do not speak English through using interpreters.

- Learn proper protocols and forms of address (including a few greetings and social phrases) in the family's primary language
- Introduce yourself and the interpreter, describe your respective roles, and clarify mutual expectations and purpose of the meeting
- During the interaction with family members, address your remarks and questions directly to them (not the interpreter)
- Speak clearly and somewhat more slowly but not more loudly
- Limit your remarks and questions to a few sentences between translations and avoid giving too much information at once

Differences in Cultural Values. Language and communication challenges are not the only factors that affect your relationships with families. Cultural values also play a huge role. In this section, we will address two fundamental values that may come into play as you work with families from different cultures. Some families will adopt an *individualistic perspective,* and other families will adopt a *collective perspective.* Some families will have less confidence in *system-centered solutions* than in *relationship-centered solutions.*

Individualism Versus Collectivism. The most dominant racial/ethnic microculture in the United States is European American. This microculture typically values individualism, self-reliance, early achievement of developmental milestones, and competition with others (Hanson, 2004; Harry, 2008).

The individualistic perspective is a fundamental premise of special education (Kalyanpur & Harry, 1999). As you will learn in chapter 6, federal policy requires that special education instruction focuses on *individual* outcomes. Students with disabilities have individualized education programs that identify their current individual levels of performance and then specify future goals and objectives. Likewise, a state-of-the-art curriculum emphasizes self-determination, fostering autonomy and individual decision making (Wehmeyer, 2002); but that curriculum may be countercultural for some families while also being highly culturally valued by others. Culture will influence not only what the family wants for their child's curriculum, but also, as we point out in chapter 11, whether the family chooses to be a partner with professionals or to defer to professionals.

By contrast, some racial/ethnic microcultures emphasize *collectivism,* which values the group more strongly than the individual (Frankland, Turnbull, Wehmeyer, & Blackmountain, 2004; Kalyanpur & Harry, 1999). Within the African American culture, a group orientation is often valued over private gain (Logan, 2001; Willis, 2004). One African American immigrant father shared his thoughts about the community's responsibility for children's well-being

In a childcare center, there are many people who are always keeping an eye on your child, and this is similar to what happens back home where every adult in a neighborhood is responsible for the well-being of the children in that neighborhood. (Obeng, 2007, p. 262)

Similarly, in Asian cultures, individuals are often expected to have family as a central focus of their lives and to engender ". . .primary loyalty, mutual obligation, cooperation, interdependence, and reciprocity" (Chan & Lee, 2004, p. 252). Similar expectations exist among Middle Eastern families (Sharifzadeh, 2004, p. 391).

What is the relevance of individualism and collectivism for developing trusting partnerships with families? There are two implications—one affecting process and the other affecting curriculum and outcomes. With respect to process, some families may regard individualized education programs as contradictory to their orientation of collective, cooperative, and mutually reciprocal priorities. With respect to curriculum, some families may not be interested in their child's accomplishing developmental milestones or specific academic tasks if the accomplishment singles out their child for special attention, acclaim, or recognition. Similarly, some families may be far more interested in having their children learn to take care of the home and elderly family members rather than acquiring job skills in a competitive industry (Frankland et al., 2004).

System-Centered Versus Relationship-Centered Approaches.

Members of the dominant racial/ethnic group—European Americans—typically expect solutions for disability-related problems to be system based; that is, they expect solutions to be guided by federal and state policy and to be implemented at the state and local levels. This viewpoint emphasizes two contrasting theories of normalcy: the pathological model from medicine and the statistical model from psychology.

The pathological model seeks to identify the "pathology" within the child and to "fix" it through technological and knowledge-based solutions. The statistical model seeks to identify an individual's deviations from those projected on the normal curve and to provide remediation to the individual to make up for the deviation (Kalyanpur & Harry, 1999; Turnbull & Stowe, 2001). It is no surprise that this value is reflected in the legal underpinnings of special education and that the vast majority of families who participate in policy-reform advocacy are European American, middle- and upper-middle-class families (Turnbull & Turnbull, 1996; Zirpoli, Wieck, Hancox, & Skarnulis, 1994). Families from culturally and linguistically diverse backgrounds may not be adequately or equally represented in policy reform and advocacy efforts, but that situation is beginning to change. Take note of this parent's perspective, which other Korean parents are adopting as they acculturize to more traditional American mores:

> There is a Korean saying, "do not pour water into a broken pot"; many Korean parents and families regard people with disabilities as the broken pot. I do not agree on that. We, as parents, should not give up helping our children; rather we should make more effort to help them. We should be an advocate for our children. I consider myself as a pioneer to open a door for Monica. I think that we should teach our children how to fish, not give fish to them. (Kim, Lee & Morningstar, 2007, p. 257)

Members of many diverse racial/ethnic groups regard personal relationships, not policies and procedures, as the bases of decision making (Lynch & Hanson, 2004; Shapiro

et al., 2004). In an inve[...]
Native families who ha[...]
wanted professionals t[...]
life (Ryan et al., 2006[...]

> In the Unupiaq cu[...]
> sisters, as well as e[...]
> parents (often eld[...]
> sionals are not m[...]
> his or her parent[...]
> the people who [...]

Similarly, native Hawaiian culture emphasizes relationships with other people but also with the community at large, the land, and the spiritual world (Mokuau & Tauili'ili, 2004). And Native American cultures strongly prize relationships with nature, especially those that promote a sense of harmony (Joe & Malach, 2004).

What does this mean as you seek to develop partnerships with families? For one thing, the legal and bureaucratic referral and evaluation process to determine whether a student has a disability, and the educational implications of that finding and of individualizing special education services (chapters 9, 10, and 12), may be culturally uncomfortable or inappropriate for families who approach their child's education from a relationship orientation.

You may need to spend significant time establishing genuine relationships before you and the family begin making educational decisions. This has major implications for your time—a rare commodity for many professionals—and your willingness to establish personal familiarity as the basis for trust. Whereas many European American professionals and families may be eager "to get to the bottom line" in a meeting, many families from culturally diverse backgrounds may prefer to spend much more time, especially up-front time, on building relationships.

In addition, people with an established personal relationship with the family can be part of their circle of support in collaborating with you and other professionals. Not all encounters need to be two-way (between an educator and a parent only); rather, the family's other trusted partners—members of the family's cultural communities and tribes—can make valuable contributions to family-professional partnerships (Frankland et al., 2004; Zuniga, 2004).

We have discussed two ways that cultural values may differ, but many other variations occur within and across microcultures and cultures (Kalyanpur & Harry, 1999; Lynch & Hanson, 2004; Zhang & Bennett, 2003). You will learn about other cultural variations in chapters 2 through 12.

To appreciate the significance of a cultural variation, reflect on how your brothers or sisters, cousins, or other family members are like or unlike you. Are you sometimes

...e who are members of the same micro-... even share family experiences can have ...erent values?

...e it is essential to honor families' cultural diver-... der to be partners with them, we will repeatedly ...t how you can develop trusting partnerships with ...ilies who have diverse cultural traditions. Bear in mind ...hat assumptions about cultural values of families (that is, what values the family "should" have because they are from specific microcultures) are not always accurate. Some families defy stereotypes. They may display traits from their own cultural traditions, as well as personal traits not strongly associated with their cultural traditions. We caution you against pigeonholing a family solely on the basis of certain microcultures; that is too simplified an approach.

Socioeconomic Status

A family's socioeconomic status (SES) includes its income, the level of family members' education, and the social status associated with the occupations of its wage earners. Here, disability and SES interact with each other quite dramatically. Many stereotypes about poverty exist. The National Center for Children in Poverty (Cauthen & Fass, 2009) recently noted:

> The most commonly held stereotypes about poverty are false. Family poverty in the U.S. is typically depicted as a static, entrenched condition, characterized by large numbers of children, chronic unemployment, drugs, violence and family turmoil. But the realities of poverty and economic hardship are very different. Americans often talk about "poor people" as if they are a distinct group with uniform characterisitcs and somehow unlike the rest of "us". In fact, there is great diversity among children and families who experience economic hardship. (Cauthen & Fass, 2009, p. 3)

What assumptions do you make regarding families facing poverty? Recognize your own biases so they don't interfere with building partnerships with families. It bears repeating: Don't make assumptions about families and their deep interest in their children.

According to the National Center for Children in Poverty, over 13 million children in the United States live in families that are considred low income. Low income is often defined as income two times below the federal poverty level. The number of children living in low-income families continues to increase. (As we noted previously, the 2008–2009 recession has had a huge effect on families; data on its effect on families who have children with disabilities are not conclusive.) According to rather recent data, however, more than half of children who live in low-income families have at least one parent who works full time and year-round (Douglas-Hall & Chau, 2007). Between 2000 and 2007, the number of children of all ages living in poverty increased by 15%. Poverty rates for young children are the highest with about 21% of children under the age of 6 years living in poverty compared to 15% or children 6 years and older (Fass & Cauthen, 2008).

As you learned when reading about cultural diversity, a strong relationship exists between the identification of children as having a disability and some racial/ethnic groups. Poverty also affects this relationship. The National Research Council (2002) documented that children from racially/ethnically diverse backgrounds are much more likely to be members of families with low income. The rates of child poverty are 34% among children who are black and 29% among Latino children compared to only 10% among Caucasian children (Fass & Cauthen, 2008). Given the higher rate of African American students placed in the special education system, it is noteworthy that African Americans have been approximately 2.5 times more likely than European Americans to experience poverty (Fujiura & Yamaki, 2000; U.S. Department of Education, 2007). The higher disability rate among children from diverse racial groups appears to be primarily associated with a higher incidence of families who experience poverty and who are headed by a single parent.

Although a child is born into poverty every 33 seconds and there are over 13 million American children who live in poverty (Children's Defense Fund, 2008), the poverty rate is even higher for families who have children with disabilities (Fujiura & Yamaki, 2000; Wang, 2005). Wang (2005) notes that the poverty rate is even higher in families with more than one child with a disability.

The number of children a family has can have an impact on parents' employment. For many parents, it is not possible to work and also take care of their children with disabilities. For others, working, parenting, and being partners with their children's teachers presents a triple whammy. There are, however, teachers and parents—especially those from diverse or impoverished backgrounds—who establish partnerships around children's behavior and, in doing so, make parenting and working more manageable, as you will read in the Change Agents Build Capacity box on the next page.

According to the U.S. Department of Education (2002), the odds that a child will receive special education services are 1.5 times greater if the child lives in poverty than if the child does not. In every state across the country, families who have a member with a disability are more likely than other families to live in poverty (Wang, 2005). Poverty typically does not occur in isolation; it is associated with a number of other demographic characteristics related to the parents' education and the family structure (single- or two-parent

CHANGE AGENTS BUILD CAPACITY

Jessica Hannebaum—The White Church Approach

White Church Elementary School in Kansas City, Kansas, begins every school year with "family advocacy days." Consider that title. It's not just a new name for "teacher-parent conferences." It's a signal that the entire faculty will advocate for not just the child but also the child's family.

That's certainly how Jessica Hannebaum worked with the families of two third graders who had significant behavioral challenges. The children were from families that differed by race and socioeconomic status. What made the families more like than unlike each other was their children's extreme noncompliant behavior and the fact that each child used prescribed medication to help stabilize their moods and behaviors.

Recognizing that the parents of each child were well-educated professionals, she communicated often and directly, holding "Student Improvement Team (SIT) meetings" every four to six weeks, sending home daily "behavior logs," and asking them if she and they agreed on priorities for their children. By making that inquiry, she demonstrated that she regarded them as equals—as people who knew about their children and could contribute to their education.

Although she was in her first year as a teacher, she proved her professional competence at the SIT meetings by quoting her mother, a special education teacher with over 20 years' experience: "Begin each day with a positive outlook because every day starts with a clean slate." Then she proved her competence by developing and making clear her policies, curriculum, interventions, and expectations.

And, finally, she earned their respect by saying, "I will do my best to help your child succeed in the classroom through behavior plans, but it takes your child's and your cooperation outside the classroom to truly make an impact."

To prove she was committed to the children and their parents, she spent extra time before and after school with the children and their parents. "I wanted to give extra attention to the students and prove to the parents I was committed to helping their children succeed." She then added: "That's how I gained their trust." Of course, it's also how she built the children's and parents' capacities to overcome very challenging student behavior.

Take Action!

- To the maximum extent possible, bring the parents into the child's education (as Jessica does). Parents and children have their own interactions at home; a child's behavior at school is not always identical to his or her behavior at home.
- To bring parents into the child's education, pay attention to how you communicate; encourage your colleagues to create a school-based culture of advocacy; prove you are professionally competent by using evidence-based approaches to resolve behavior challenges; respect the child and their parents by talking about expectations and outcomes; take the extra step to prove your commitment; and expect their trust.

families). For example, parents who have lower levels of education are at greater risk for living in poverty. Over 80% of children whose parents have less than a high school diploma live in low-income families, and more than 50% of children whose parents have only a high school degree are low income (Cauthen & Fass, 2009).

The impact of family income occurs not only at the student and family level but also at the school level. Schools are often characterized as low SES or high SES schools; as you will learn in chapter 6, the federal No Child Left Behind Act characterizes low SES schools as Title 1 or disadvantaged schools. The National Research Council (2002) reported that schools with a high concentration of children from low-income backgrounds have lower per-student expenditures and fewer experienced, well-trained teachers than schools with a high concentration of children from middle-income and upper-middle-income backgrounds. The Council also reported that parent advocacy is less likely to occur in schools with a high concentration of students from low-income backgrounds.

In every relationship with families, including those from low-income backgrounds, we encourage you to demonstrate respect, be nonjudgmental, and recognize their unique strengths and important contributions. In chapter 8, you will learn more about communicating with families, including those who experience poverty; in chapter 11, you will learn how to help families connect with community agencies that can assist them in meeting their basic needs.

The theory that families at lower SES levels may be less interested in educational partnerships may hold true for some families. But for others, the theory simply does not apply—nor should it. In our experience, a family's SES is not a reliable indicator of its motivation or knowledge/skills to develop family-professional partnerships. Your role as a professional is to encourage predictable, nonjudgmental, and trusting partnerships that convey to all families regardless of SES that you respect them and recognize their strengths. You will learn more later in this chapter about unique circumstances associated with homelessness, and you will learn in all chapters how to establish trusting partnerships with families from all socioeconomic levels.

Geographic Location

As a result of the rapid growth of technology and increased mobility in most segments of society, regional differences in family values and forms are receding. Yet regional patterns remain: Southern hospitality, Yankee stoicism, Midwestern conformity, and Western independence remain attributes of many families (McGill & Pearce, 1996). Rural and urban factors also significantly influence service delivery and family life (Butera, 2005; Darling & Gallagher, 2004; Ridgley & Hallam, 2006).

According to the U.S. Census Bureau, more families in rural areas have a member with a disability than do families not living in rural areas (Wang, 2005). In addition, families living in the South are more likelty to have a member with a disability as well as experience poverty than are families from other parts of the country. Further data from the U.S. Department of Education (2007) indicate that more students with disabilities receive special education services in rural school districts than do students in urban or large town districts. As compared to their peers in urban areas, students in rural areas tend to experience more poverty over a longer period of time. In addition, the availability and quality of special education services may differ in rural areas. The population of rural areas may fluctuate as local industries close, reducing the tax base and talent base simultaneously.

It is often difficult for educators to provide appropriate services in the least restrictive environment when students are geographically far apart. Many school districts create consolidated (jointly operated) special education programs and transport students to them rather than dispersing the specialists across the school district's entire, widespread area. Distance impedes opportunities for teachers and families to enter into face-to-face partnerships.

Life in a rural environment also hinders the recruitment and retention of highly qualified teachers and other specialists.

For many families, just accessing the necessary services and supports can create hardships. In a study on low-income families from rural areas (Ridgley & Hallam, 2006), one mother noted "we have mostly what we need, except when [our car broke down]. Our car messed up on us" (p. 137). Another family from the same study indicated challenges getting her daughter to the cardiologist explaining that the family had to "come up with the gas money to get her to the doctor" (p. 137). Another family had to rely on bus service to get to a faraway city to see a specialist but often did not have the $5 bus fare to get there.

On the other hand, rural areas can often provide social support from informal networks such as neighbors, churches, and civic/social organizations. Some school districts use video- and teleconferencing to link teachers, specialists, and parents. (You will learn more about how to communicate with families when you read chapter 8.)

Urban areas have their own set of challenges and resources. Among families living in an urban area, 22% were raising a child with a disability, compared to 13% of all families in nonurban areas (Wang, 2005). Also, families who lived in an urban area and had a member with a disability were more likely to live in poverty than families without a member with a disability. It is sometimes difficult to evaluate whether urban students have a disability, given the complicated effects of poverty, race/ethnicity, and limited English proficiency.

Urban school districts often struggle to recruit and retain qualified personnel, especially those skilled in working with families from diverse or minority backgrounds. Further, living in a complex, energy-filled urban environment can make parent-professional partnerships difficult to create.

Jonathan Kozol, the well-respected advocate and activist on public education, visited 60 urban public schools for his book, *Shame of a Nation*, and found that conditions for inner-city children had actually grown worse since the Supreme Court's ruling in 1954 in *Brown v. Board of Education*. (In that case, the Court held that segregation in schools solely on the basis of race violates the federal constitution and its provisions that states must assure the "equal protection" of the law to all people in the state.)

Kozol (2005) noted the inexcusable conditions in urban public schools such as the absence of basic school supplies, serious overcrowding, and inhumane physical conditions, among others. There were ". . .computer classes where, according to one student, "we sit there and talk about what we would be doing if we had computers" (Kozol, 2005, p. 171). Kozol suggested that discrimination in public schools is visible and blatant: "(W)hat is happening right now in the poorest communities of America—which are largely black communities . . . is the worst situation black America has faced since slavery" (p. 313). Kozol has a valid point. But you should also bear in mind that, although urban areas face complex challenges, they also may offer valuable resources for families. These include a wide variety of accessible and affordable services and a widely used system of public transportation.

Military families, migrant farm workers, construction workers, corporate executives, and others have jobs that require them to relocate frequently. How can you minimize the worries that often accompany a family's relocation? Communicate with and secure records from the student's previous school. Avoid asking routine family and medical history questions except when the information you need is not in the records or when families want to retell their story. Offer relocated families a tour of the school their child will attend, describe its programs, and introduce the family and student to the staff and other families in the program. When working with families who have immigrated into the United States, determine how much English they know and, if their English is limited, what their native language is; some families may not be literate in their native language and may try to conceal that from you. Work to facilitate a smooth relocation for the family.

In describing family characteristics, we have emphasized how families are the same yet different. Their size and forms, cultural backgrounds, socioeconomic levels, and geographic locations each present unique challenges. We cautioned that you should not make assumptions about families based solely on their characteristics. And we pointed out that the constant and underlying common themes in your effort to build partnerships with them: (1) respect their values; (2) try to understand the many issues they face, in addition to their child's disability; (3) be creative as you try to capitalize on their strengths and resources; and (4) be open to forming partnerships that address their greatest expectations.

:: CHARACTERISTICS OF INDIVIDUAL MEMBERS

The commonality and diversity of families persist when we take into account the individual characteristics of each member of the family. These personal characteristics include the child's disability, each family member's skills in managing life, mental and physical health, communication style, and motivation. These characteristics can either strengthen or limit the family as a whole. They affect the family's response to the disability of one of its members and the family's inclination and ability to be partners with professionals. Let's now address the characteristics of the child's disability and the life management skills of family members.

Characteristics of a Child's Disability

The family as a whole and each of its members respond to a family member's characteristics related to a disability. These characteristics include (1) the nature of the disability (for example, is the student visually impaired?) and (2) the extent or degree of the disability (for example, what types and intensities of support will the student need over time?).

Nature of the Disability. The nature of the disability influences the family's response to it. For example, the families of children who have medically complex needs often have to adapt their routines to provide continuous care. They often have special needs for illness-specific information, equipment, and financial assistance (Batshaw, 2002). A child with a hearing impairment needs communication accommodations that may include interpreters or equipment such as special telephones and captioned television (Jackson & Turnbull, in press). Likewise, the primary concerns of parents of children with emotional disorders, attention deficit/hyperactivity disorder, head injury, and autism often relate to the child's problem behavior and appropriate responses to it (Baker et al., 2003; Fidler, Hodapp, & Dykens, 2000; Hastings & Brown, 2002; Stein, Efron, Schiff, & Glanzman, 2002).

Regardless of the type of disability, if the child has a problem behavior or the parents perceive children's behavior as challenging, the family undoubtedly will benefit from a supporting partnership to minimize the problem behavior and to teach their child appropriate behavior (Fenning, Baker, Baker, & Crnic, 2007; Turnbull & Ruef, 1997).

There is no clear-cut evidence that the particular nature of the disability alone can predict how parents, siblings, or extended family will respond and adapt to the disability (Blacher & Hatton, 2001). Each child and each disability creates unique circumstances, including the need to form partnerships with specialists and with other families similarly affected.

If you assume that a disability invariably burdens a family, you would be wrong. Children and youth with disabilities continue to make their own positive contributions to their families (Hastings & Taunt, 2002; King, Baxter, Rosenbaum, Zwaigenbaum, & Bates, 2009; Scorgie & Sobsey, 2000; Turnbull & Turnbull, 1978). Indeed, many families have affirmed that their children with disabilities are sources of happiness and fulfillment. Moreover, they have reported stress and well-being levels similar to those of adults in the general population. Skeptical? Here's a typical affirmation of the research results, from the mother of a child with a disability:

> I've had by-pass surgery, three husbands, a son who left for the army and never came back, a pile of bills that never got paid and Colin, who was born with micro-cephaly. I've had lots of troubles in my life but Colin sure hasn't been one of them. Troubles with doctors, neighbors, late SSI payments, wheelchairs that won't move, and funny questions I never felt like answering. But never had any trouble with Colin. Churches that never came through, relatives that never came by, one grandbaby I've yet to meet, and heartburn—must be since the day I was born. And Colin, he was my sweet-boy. Light my day with that funny smile, and how he'd wake up to me when I came to get him in the morning. Why, if it weren't for Colin, I'd have thought life had pulled a dirty trick. (Blue-Banning, Santelli, Guy, & Wallace, 1994, p. 69)

Almost 15 years later, families still herald the positive contributions that their children with disabilities have on their lives. One parent commented, "I think he's just helped us become more rounded, more acccepting, more aware . . . that life out there is a challenge and different, and to appreciate the little things" (King et al., 2009, p. 57). In a study examining mothers' experiences having a child with Down syndrome, Lalvani (2008) suggests that mothers often resist society's negative messages about disability. One parent explained:

> [People] think you're overwhelmed, yor're running around and I think they think you just don't have fun. . . They think if you're a family with a disabled kid that you, your family, doesn't have fun. . .I disagree totally. We have a lot of fun. (p. 441)

Extent and Age of Onset of the Disability. You might assume that a severe disability always has a greater impact, but again you would be wrong. The extent of the child's disability and when the child acquired the disability—the age of onset—are often highly related. For example, the diagnosis of a severe disability in a newborn requires the parents to deal immediately with what typically is an unexpected shock. When, however, a disability such as an emotional disorder or a learning disability manifests itself later in a child's life, the parents may feel a sense of relief—the diagnosis may affirm that they have been justified to be concerned about their child.

These families may have to cope with a complex set of mixed emotions. Some families of a child with a learning disability, for example, may be confused and frustrated upon learning that their child, who appears capable in so many ways, indeed has a disability (Shapiro, Church, & Lewis, 2002). Others may be relieved to learn that there are reasons for the problems they have observed in their child and yet feel guilty for not identifying their child's disability earlier. Wang and colleagues (2004) found that the severity of a young child's disability is associated with both mother and father's satisfaction with their family's quality of life.

Another factor can be the gradualness or suddenness of onset. Often the families of children with learning disabilities have a gradual awareness that the child has unique needs. A very different circumstance occurs with a sudden onset such as a head injury resulting from an adolescent's diving accident. In those circumstances, families are thrust immediately into the world of trauma and rehabilitation units and often receive highly ambiguous prognoses (Michaud, Semel-Concepcíon, Duhaime, & Lazar, 2002). These families often have to make a series of ongoing readjustments as their child's characteristics fluctuate.

Severe disabilities or exceptional and early-blooming talent are often more apparent than less severe disabilities or average or latent talent. An obvious disability may enable family members to accommodate readily to the child's unique needs; however, it may stigmatize the entire family and result in their social rejection. By contrast, when disabilities are invisible, parents, siblings, or extended family members may feel confused since the child may not "look" like he or she has a disability. A family may develop a more definitive understanding of the child's support needs when their child has a severe disability because the disability is more noticeable. When, however, a child has a milder disability, the family may find its hopes for the future alternately raised and dashed as the child progresses or falls back.

The nature of the student's disability and the age of onset greatly influence when a student receives special education services and the type of services schools provide. As you develop partnerships with families, we encourage you to be sensitive to how students' individual characteristics shape families' priorities, resources, and concerns. We also encourage you to highlight the student's strengths and preferences, to prevent the child's disability from obscuring these and other characteristics.

Life Management Skills

The term *life management skills* refers to the techniques that people use to solve their problems (Scorgie et al., 1999). Olson et al. (1983) categorized the skills as follows: reframing, passive appraisal, spiritual support, social support, and professional support. We briefly define each skill here and provide examples highlighting how families apply these skills to having a child with a disability. As you read about these life management skills, consider how they apply to professionals as well as families. How do you use these skills to solve your own problems?

1. *Reframing:* changing how you think about a situation in order to emphasize its positive aspects over its negative ones (Hastings & Taunt, 2002; Lin, 2000).

   > "Picking up the pieces of our life's puzzle and reworking it into a different" picture. (Bailey, Skinner, & Sparkman, 2003)

2. *Passive appraisal:* setting aside your worries.

   > "I try not to worry about where Eric will get a job after he graduates from high school. I try not to think about what his adult life will be. It works best for me to just take a day at a time. There is no use getting all upset over something that is years away." (Poston & Turnbull, 2004)

3. *Spiritual support:* deriving comfort and guidance from your spiritual beliefs (Poston & Turnbull, 2004; Skinner, Correa, Skinner, & Bailey, 2001).

   > "We are told that love conquers all. This is so, even death. But faith makes bearable the otherwise unbearable." (Turnbull et al., 2009, p. 37)

4. *Social support:* receiving practical and emotional assistance from your friends and family members (Brown, Anand, Fung, Isaacs, & Baum, 2003).

   > "My parents—especially my mom—are supportive. Both of them have taken the time to learn more about the diagnosis, which I think has helped in their acceptance of it." (Hutton & Caron, 2005, p. 187)

5. *Professional support:* receiving assistance from professionals and agencies (Romer, Richardson, Nahom, Aigbe, & Porter, 2002; Soodak & Erwin, 2000; Zionts, Zionts, Harrison, & Bellinger, 2003).

   > "The best IEP was my most recent IEP for my son. What made it my best IEP meeting was that my son's new teacher was very open to discussion and willing to hear out my concerns for my son's educational progress and needs." (Beach Center, 2000)

We want to add a caveat about the term *life management strategies*. The professional literature typically uses the term *coping strategies* instead of *life management strategies*. Families, however, talk about *coping* less often than professionals. Also, coping typically refers to dealing with a crisis situation; many family challenges, however, occur daily and weekly (Scorgie et al., 1999). The words you use

in your work—your professional terminology—can be barriers to your partnerships with families. You will want to use terms that do not stigmatize families or suggest that they or their children "suffer" from some kind of pathology or that *coping* always is an heroic act, though in fact it sometimes is.

Family members vary in the number of life management strategies they use and in the quality or effectiveness of each strategy (Bailey et al., 1999; Lin, 2000; Scorgie et al., 1999). Within the same family, some members may have strong life management capabilities, and others may need much more support because their own capabilities have not yet developed fully.

Think of life management capacity metaphorically: For each member of the family, "The end of the rope is the end of the rope, regardless of how long the rope is" (Avis, 1985, p. 197). Individual family members have ropes of differing lengths.

You will want to avoid judging one family member in relation to another or wondering why one finds a situation so problematic that another finds so benign. Remember, the length of everyone's rope varies and depends on all the situations they are handling in their life. As a partner, regard yourself as a "rope lengthener," supporting everyone involved (families, professionals, friends, and community citizens) so that they will increase their capacity to address and resolve their priority concerns.

:: UNIQUE CIRCUMSTANCES

Families face challenges over and above a child's disability. Indeed, the presence of a disability may not be the family's most significant challenge. A family may experience addiction to alcohol or drugs, abuse and neglect, exposure to violence and other fearful experiences, imprisonment, and chronic illness. In this section, we will address some unusual circumstances such as homelessness and parenting with a disability. We use the term *unique circumstancesss* to refer to the experiences or conditions, separate from the disability, that are also influencing how family members interact (chapter 2), carry out their functions (chapter 3), and change across the life cycle (chapter 4).

Homelessness

Earlier in this chapter you learned that poverty is closely associated with students receiving special education services and more with single-female-headed households than with two-parent families (Fujiura & Yamaki, 2000; Parish,

Rose, Grinsteim-Weiss, Richman, & Andrews, 2008; Wang, 2005).

The National Coalition for the Homeless (2002) documented that children are the fastest-growing group of the nation's homeless population. More than 1.3 million children are homeless and 40% of the homeless population are families of young children (National Law Center of Homelessness and Poverty, 2009). Becoming homeless can often affect families who have not been living in poverty. As Gargiulo (2006) notes, "some economically advantaged families may also confront a loss of housing. A medical crisis, job termination or unexpected bills could easily push a family into homelessness" (p. 358).

Homelessness has devastating effects on children's well-being, including their education. That is why the federal special education law (chapter 6) emphasizes that state and local education agencies should take specific steps to inlcude homeless children with disabilities in schools [20 U.S.C. Sec. 1400(c)].

Children who are homeless often move from shelter to shelter, disrupting their school attendance (Institute for Children and Poverty, 2001). One study reported that approximately one half of children who are homeless have developmental delays compared to 16% of children who experience poverty but who have stable housing (Kelly, Buehlman, & Caldwell, 2000). These children also experience emotional and behavioral problems three to four times more frequently than children in the general school population. Chronic situations homeless children often face include health hazards, emotional stress, and unhygenic and overcrowded living conditions; each may increase the risk that the child will receive special education services (Jackson, 2004).

Developing partnerships with parents who are homeless poses unique challenges, but these are not insurmountable. A highly successful program in Tennessee provides training to parents, after-school tutoring at shelters, convenient and safe places where students can play, clothing, and school supplies (Davey, Penuel, Allison-Tant, & Rosner, 2000). Read one single mother's perspective about being homeless in the My Voice box below. As a teacher, you might wonder how you will ever find the time to be an advocate, start a new program, or meet the unique needs of families who are homeless. You can start by considering who among your professional colleagues could best address these special challenges. You might begin by enlisting the help of school counselors (Strawser, Markos, Yamaguchi, & Higgins, 2000) and school social workers (Markward & Biros, 2001).

MY VOICE

On Being Homeless, Latina, and a Single Parent

". . . and you are sitting there and it's like your whole world is flashing right before your eyes and you say things that you don't mean to say and you try to say them in a proper way, but it just don't come out that way. I walked out there crying, literally, eating my tears because here I am no money, homeless, and I knew [my child] needed to be stable, somehow. And it took me so long to get where I am now, and if I didn't go back and talk to the head supervisor of the program and give him a piece of my mind, I wouldn't have gotten my section eight [subsidized housing]. They literally treat you like you're garbage. I'm not the first one to come out of that office crying. I've seen women come out of that place crying. . ."

Take Action!

- Consider accompanying mothers such as this one to the welfare office to support them.
- If you do accompany them, you will demonstrate that you respect them and are willing to advocate for them. Respect and advocacy are two of the seven elements of an effective partnership, as you will learn in chapter 7.
- If you cannot accompany them, refer them to a school social-services professional who might accompany them or refer them to agencies or people who would.

Source: Excerpted from McHatton (2007, p. 243–244).

Parents with Disabilities

As people with disabilities are increasingly being integrated into their communities, people with disabilities may choose to become parents. Of course, parents who have disabilities also have strengths, just as their children who have disabilities have strengths. Often the disability itself does not interfere with how the family functions. The disability may actually enhance the parent's understanding of the child as, for example, when deaf parents raise deaf children (Jackson & Turnbull, in press). "In many ways they could not be happier than they are now. . .what to others might seem a world of terrible isolation is in fact a world of contentment with its own vibrant language and culture" (Hewitt, 2000, p. 138).

When a parent has a physical disability, the effects on your relationship with him or her primarily involve such logistics as providing accessible meeting rooms or perhaps communicating through the most accessible and convenient means. The child of a parent who is deaf sometimes is the parent's communication link. That is the reality for a student, Jeannie, her deaf mother, and her teacher:

> We didn't have anybody who had sign language because our district's deaf education teacher was strictly from the oral school. So I asked Jeannie to interpret at our conference, since I knew she was very good at sign language. Unfortunately, what I needed to tell Jeannie's mother was that I had some concerns about her behavior in class. . . . The mother just nodded and smiled. I didn't understand her reaction. . . . It was only later that I discovered that Jeannie had not, to say the least, translated accurately what I was saying! (Beach Center, 2000)

Although it might have been convenient to involve Jeannie, doing so presented obvious problems.

What happens when adults with intellectual disability (formerly called mental retardation) have children? Researchers estimate (based on U.S. Census data) there are approximately 1.4 million parents with mental retardation in the United States who have children under the age of 18 (Holburn, Perkins, & Vietze, 2001). Typically, more women than men with intellectual disability are parents, and typically these parents tend to have two to three children. Holburn and colleagues (2001) reached the following conclusions (based on their comprehensive review of the research on parents with intellectual disability):

- Approximately one quarter of the children of parents with an intellectual disability will have an intellectual disability. When both parents have an intellectual disability, the risk doubles.

- Challenges in parenting tend to increase as children get older.
- Mothers with intellectual disability rarely abuse their children; most mothers with intellectual disability provide adequate care, although some may unintentionally neglect their children.
- A parent's competence is influenced by their background and current life circumstances; particular strengths, needs, and future plans; and style of interacting with his or her children.
- The most successful programs for increasing parenting skills are home based, long term, and based on a partnership between the parent and a professional in which the professional teaches the parent how to plan and make decisions.
- Parents with intellectual disability often have other challenges, such as unemployment or underemployment, substandard housing, inadequate health care, and problems with money management.

Researchers have interviewed 30 adults who had been raised by at least one parent with an intellectual disability (Booth & Booth, 2000) and concluded that the children generally demonstrated resilience as adults. The availability of friends and family to assist the parent with intellectual disability was a key factor in achieving positive outcomes. The children had a close emotional bond with their parents, but a lack of services and supports often contributed to challenges and limitations experienced by the family.

To increase the likelihood of successful parenting by adults with intellectual disability, successful programs have broken down each step of a child-care task and created line drawings illustrating each of the steps of the task analysis, manuals written at a the third-grade reading level or below, or audiotapes of the manuals. These programs also included home visits to facilitate parents implementing the training materials. When these steps were used, parents with intellectual disability learned 96% of the child-care skills they were taught and maintained 80% of those skills after the study ended (Feldman, 2004).

Teenage Parents

Although the pregnancy rate for young women ages 15 to 19 years in the United States is at its lowest in 30 years, annually more than 750,000 American teenagers become parents (Alan Guttmacher Institute, 2006). The United States has the highest rate of live births to teenagers in the postindustrialized world; the rate is 55 per 1,000 females between the ages of 15 and 19. In addition to taking on the responsibilities of parenting, teenage mothers often experience low income, single parenthood, low educational levels, and poor health outcomes associated with pregnancy (Furstenberg, 2003).

Parenting programs aimed at teenage mothers may be delivered in a group or on a one-to-one basis. They also vary in the intensity and duration (Barlow & Coren, 2000; Barlow & Stewart-Brown, 2000; Coren, Barlow, & Stewart-Brown, 2003). Programs are offered in schools, homes, health clinics, and family support centers.

Overall, researchers conclude that parent programs for teenage mothers have produced positive changes in both parent and child outcomes. The most typical programs appear to be group based and offered over a 12- to 16-week span. Researchers speculate that a group setting enables teenage mothers to benefit from peer perspectives and support. A concern in many programs is the high dropout rate, ranging from about one third to nearly one half. If you are working with teenage mothers, be sure to partner with them to identify the barriers they encounter. Structure programs and interactions to facilitate their involvement.

Almost all of the literature related to teenage parents of children with disabilities focuses on mothers, and very little attention is given to teenage fathers (Coren et al., 2003). You will want to develop successful partnerships with teenage parents of children with disabilities. Many strategies apply to both mothers and fathers. DeJong (2003) suggests several ways to build trust with teenage parents:

- Work to ensure consistency in the professionals interacting with young children so that teenage parents can experience consistency and have someone to communicate with on a regular basis
- Address the teenage parent's individual needs and concerns by scheduling regular opportunities to communicate
- Provide teenage parents with the power and choice to increase the likelihood that they have some control in their lives
- Assist teenage parents in practicing and managing their responsibilities to support them in developing more independence
- Help teenage parents make plans and set goals to foster their child's enhanced development and well-being
- Provide opportunities for teenage parents to be reflective, to enhance the likelihood that they learn to be sensitive, responsive caregivers

We encourage you to read first-person accounts written by teenage mothers. Excellent sources include Gill (1997), Leff and Walizer (1992), Miller (1994), and Rose and Gallup (1998).

REVISITING LUKE, CHRISTINE, AND ERIC LINDAUER

What will preschool, elementary, middle, and secondary school and then adulthood be like for Luke Lindauer? How will Christine and Eric and the Lindauer "family mobile" move over time? How will their family interactions, the functions they perform for each other, and how they move through the various stages of their lives change over time? These questions beg an answer, one that awaits the future. There have been plenty of questions for the Lindauer family in the past; and each has been answered. So the only safe answer for questions about the future is to let the future unfold as the past has unfolded, bit by bit. As it does, a family's views about disability and special education will shape and be shaped by events that the family can control and by some that the family cannot control.

Think about Eric and Christine's perspective of Luke's disability. How is this similar and different from the perspective you might hold as a professional?

When Eric discovered just how rare Luke's chromosomal abnormality was, he said, "We hit the lottery. No, I really mean that. We hit the lottery with this kid."

Christine concurs. "As Luke develops into this beautiful person, we adore every aspect of him. He wouldn't be the same without those little slips in his genetic code. Parents always talk about how fast their children grow up, and, oh, how to cherish those younger years while they last. Well, our son is developmentally delayed, so we feel like we get to have a little extra time in the moment. I again think about my sister Stacy, and how she never really went through those rebellious teenage years. How lucky would I be if Luke turns out to be the boy who always loves his mother! Being a parent of a child with special needs is challenging, but I'm not in a position to say that it's harder than parenting any other child. It's different, and my guess is there are pluses and minuses on both sides."

SUMMARY

You have just started to learn about families and how to be an effective partner with them. The first step in being an effective partner is to understand about the characteristics of the family, the characteristics of its individual members, and the unique circumstances facing a family. We described those for you and suggested (in the three boxes featuring a family) how you could take action to be a partner, using your understanding about the characteristics we set out.

CHARACTERISTICS OF THE FAMILY AS A WHOLE

- Definition, size, and form of family
- Cultural background

- Socioeconomic status
- Geographic location

CHARACTERISTICS OF INDIVIDUAL MEMBERS

- The child's disability
- The family's life management skills

UNIQUE CIRCUMSTANCES

- Homelessness
- Parenting with a disability

LINKING CONTENT TO YOUR LIFE

One way to gain a greater understanding of family characteristics is to reflect on your own family. By recognizing the family patterns that you have experienced, you are more likely to understand how your own values can influence ways in which you interact with other families.

FAMILY CULTURE

Describe the culture of your family of origin to a classmate. Explain how cultural values were embedded in the ways you celebrate holidays, your spirituality/religion or lack of it, and the foods that you ate as a child. What advice did you hear repeatedly from the adults in your family? How did your family's cultural values influence the nature of this advice?

LIFE MANAGEMENT SKILLS

You read about five life management skills—reframing, passive appraisal, spiritual support, social support, and professional support. What one or two life management skills were most frequently used in your family? Which were rarely used and why?

UNIQUE CIRCUMSTANCES

Either in your family of origin or in the family that you have established as an adult, reflect on at least one unique challenge and how it affected your family. In what ways did your family seek assistance? Overall, was your family strengthened by the experience or weakened by it? Describe why you think your family was strengthened or weakened.

Family Interaction

LUKE, CHRISTINE, AND ERIC LINDAUER

There's something about Christine and Eric Lindauer that suggests "systems." She graduated with a degree in chemical engineering and worked as a management consultant and software project manager. He earned his degree in mathematics, worked as a java developer in the finance industry, and now makes money as an online poker player. Engineering, management, programming, and poker—each involves systems.

There's something else about the Lindauer family that suggests "systems." What does *systems* mean when the concept applies to families?

It means that whatever happens to one of them happens to all of them. Luke's disability affects where he attends school, and that in turn affects Eric's drive to earn funds to pay for day care and preschool. And, Luke's disability has begun to shape Christine's career.

As a whole, there are four "Lindauer" families: Luke, Christine, and Eric; Eric's father and stepmother; Eric's mother, stepfather, and brother; and Christine's mother, sisters, and extended family.

Christine is candid about herself and her family. At this point in time, summer 2009—just 11 years after graduating from college—she and Eric have already passed through several stages of their lives. They were children, adolescents, college students, friends, and professionals; and now they are married and have their son, Luke. What were their developmental stages? That's not hard to detect; just read the previous sentence. What were their big transitions? Home to college was one; college to the workforce another; marriage still another; and parenthood the most recent one. When Luke leaves his day-care program and enters preschool in the fall of 2009, he and they will experience yet another transition. Luke will not be in the infant-toddler category any longer; he'll be a preschooler. Change has been a constant in their lives; it is inevitable.

How Luke, Christine, and Eric handle these changes will depend in large part on how they relate to each other.

And, they already have a pattern. Are they affectionate? "Yes!!" She emphasizes her answer. Do she and Eric regard themselves positively? By all means. "We have plenty of self-esteem and confidence, especially Eric. He has no problems going against the norm."

Are they spiritual? As children, they were raised in different churches. At MIT, they were agnostics. Now, they acknowledge that "we are all connected." They are on a spiritual journey, arising from an interest in yoga, Buddhism, Hinduism, and quantum physics. This journey has helped to shape their mission in life, as individuals and as a family—to live in the moment and be happy where they are. They hope to pass this message on to Luke.

What about their family's economics? Eric and Christine both had high-salaried jobs in New York; at the ages of 29 and 30, they were in a "better than average financial position." Now, having scaled back from their time in New York, they live a modest lifestyle. "We no longer have that drive to make a lot of money, but of course if a need was there, a family member in trouble or some other financial crisis, we'd quickly step up to the plate."

They have struggled to figure out daily care for Luke. They "have gone back and forth on the division of labor" between themselves, and they finally have settled on seeking outside help with child care and preschool.

They socialize with their friends from MIT and the new friends they have made in Pittsboro and Chapel Hill. Luke, however, is not social with children his own age; he tends to play alone and is more likely to engage with adults.

"We are homebodies," Christine says when asked about her family's recreation. Luke likes the community pool and the beach at nearby Jordan Lake, in Raleigh. Beyond that, it is dinner parties once a week.

As for education, two MIT degrees speak for themselves: Education is a value they share. They also value this for Luke; the day-care and preschool programs at the Frank Porter Graham Child Development Institute include children with and without disabilities and bring researchers and their evidence-based interventions together with caring practitioners.

Think of the Lindauer family as a system with subsystems. Now you're thinking in the "family systems" way. That's a good way to think.

think about it

- What are the subsystems within a family and how does a child's disability influence them?
- How can family-professional partnerships support marital, parental, sibling, and extended family subsystems?
- How can teachers increase the likelihood that families will have balanced levels of cohesion and adaptability?

:: INTRODUCTION

Imagine a baby in a crib. She looks up and sees a toy above her. It is a mobile. She reaches out, touches one arm, and watches, fascinated, as each piece moves, not just the one she touched.

The baby has learned a lesson about mobiles, families, and systems. All pieces of the mobile are connected to each other, just as members of a family are connected to each other. What happens to one happens to all: that describes a "system."

Who are the all? And how is it useful to describe them and their relationships, their connections with each other, their "mobile-ness"? Family-theory literature gives us two frameworks to answer those questions.

One framework describes relationships according to the subsystems of a family. Thus, members are related through marriage and they interact with each other as spouses—this is Christine and Eric, forming the marital subsystem. Family members also are related and interact with each other as parents and children—this is Luke, Christine, and Eric, forming the parental subsystem. Brothers and sisters have relationships with each other; but since Luke is an only child, there is no sibling subsystem in the Lindauer family. Grandparents, relatives, and friends have relationships with each other—this is Luke and Christine's parents and relatives, forming the extended family subsystem.

As we pointed out in chapter 1, the term *family* refers to two or more people who regard themselves as family and who perform some of the functions that families typically perform. Family, then, can be people who are not related by blood or marriage if they function as family members. To describe these four subsystems—marital, parental, sibling, and extended—does not, however, suffice to portray how family members relate and interact with each other. Two questions remain. First, are the family members "close" with each other—do they experience cohesion? The second question is whether the family is adaptable. Can the family adapt to meet changing life circumstances, including the presence of a disability?

When you begin to work with families, you will notice how families (perhaps like your own) create subsystems; are more or less cohesive; and adapt well, poorly, or not at all to changing life circumstances. Just remember to look at them as the baby in a crib looked up at the mobile: An inert mobile is not nearly as fascinating as one whose every part moves when one part is activated.

:: FAMILY SYSTEMS THEORY

In this chapter you will learn about family members' interactions within the family and how the relationships within the family come into play as you develop partnerships with them. Here, as in chapter 1, we define *family* according to the functions that various people play.

The family systems framework (the circle within Figure 2.1) shows four basic types of interactions or relationships—marital, parental, sibling, and extended family. We display the types of relationships in the inner quadrants of the framework and their qualities—cohesion and adaptability—in the outer ring.

During the past several years, special educators, particularly early childhood special educators, have shifted from focusing primarily on the child or the parental subsystem (especially the mother and child subsystem) to focusing more broadly on the family as a whole (McWilliam, Snyder, Harbin, Porter, & Munn, 2000; Turnbull, Turbiville, & Turnbull, 2000).

> In a mobile all the pieces, no matter what size or shape, can be grouped together and balanced by shortening or lengthening the strings attached or rearranging the distance between the pieces. So it is with a family. None of the family members is identical to any other; they are all different and at different levels of growth. As in a mobile, you can't arrange one without thinking of the other. (Satir, 1972, pp. 119–120)

A single mother of several children, one of whom is an elementary-age son with attention-deficit/hyperactivity disorder, further elaborates on this metaphor:

> Quality of life for me is being happy and that means doing what makes me feel happy, because if I'm happy, then it comes across and falls into my children's lives. If I'm not happy, then it creates a whole lot of chaos, and a negative, negative environment. So I've learned to let go of things, and concentrate on what makes me happy, so in turn, my kids will be happy. And it's working. (Beach Center, 1999)

Yolanda, a mother of a young child with Down syndrome, discusses how having a child with a disability has enhanced her family in ways they did not imagine:

> I think my life is more rich—more rich than I would have imagined . . . I always felt as if our life was going to be good. I never felt like it was going to be this good. And I think that this good is because of the all the enriching experiences of being around people with special needs . . . he just opened up a whole world to us. (Lalvani, 2009, p. 36)

Family systems theory provides a framework for understanding what a family is and how it functions (chapters 1 through 4) and shows you how to establish trusting partnerships with families (chapters 5 through 12). Family systems theory rests on three assumptions relevant to your partnership with families. These assumptions relate to (1) the input/output configuration of systems, (2) the concepts of wholeness and subsystems, and (3) the role of boundaries in defining systems (Whitechurch & Constantine, 1993).

Input/Output

The first assumption of family systems theory is that family characteristics (chapter 1) are inputs into the system. The system then responds to these inputs, and the interaction produces outputs. Systems theory focuses on "what happens

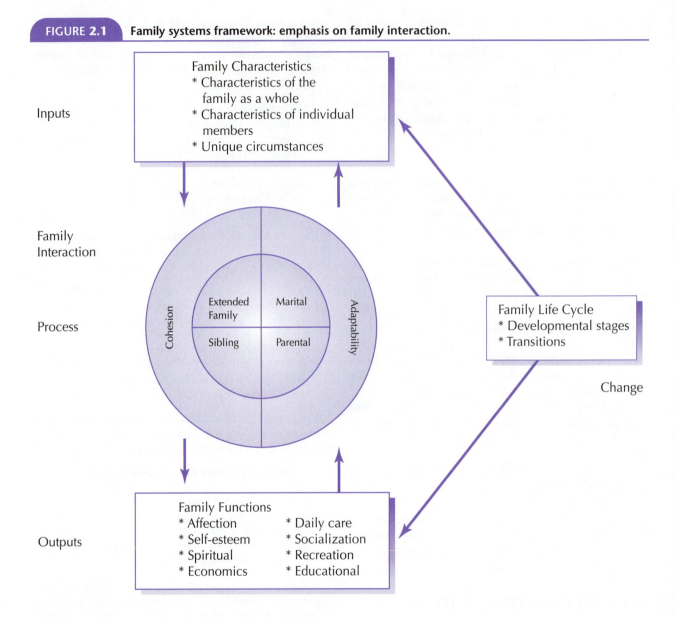

FIGURE 2.1   **Family systems framework: emphasis on family interaction.**

Inputs

Family Characteristics
* Characteristics of the
  family as a whole
* Characteristics of individual
  members
* Unique circumstances

Family
Interaction

Process

Cohesion

Extended
Family

Marital

Sibling

Parental

Adaptability

Family Life Cycle
* Developmental stages
* Transitions

Change

Outputs

Family Functions
* Affection   * Daily care
* Self-esteem   * Socialization
* Spiritual   * Recreation
* Economics   * Educational

to the *input* as it is processed by the system on its way to becoming an *output*" (Broderick & Smith, 1979, p. 114, italics added).

Accordingly, and as Figure 2.1 shows, a family's characteristics are the inputs into the family interaction. The family interaction occurs as families perform roles and interact with each other. The output of these roles and interactions are family functions, which we discuss in chapter 3. Thus, inputs interact with the system and produce outputs, and the outputs relate to how the family

functions. This chain of input, interaction, output, and functions resembles a mobile: A slight push (input) on one part of the family system produces an effect (output), with a change in the movement of the entire mobile. Every part of the mobile—every family member and their roles and interactions—moves whenever any part of the mobile moves. In this chapter, you will learn how a family's characteristics influence family members' roles and how family members interact with each other and with others outside the family.

Wholeness and Subsystems

The second assumption of family systems theory is that the system is a whole, must be understood as a whole, and cannot be understood through only one or more of its parts, namely, its members (Whitechurch & Constantine, 1993). Simply understanding the child with a disability does not mean that you will understand the family, yet understanding the family is necessary for understanding much about the child.

Many professionals assume that they can establish trusting family partnerships if they know only the mother or the student perspective. This is a mistake because a family consists of the sum of its members' interactions with each other. You should focus on the aggregated inputs into the family and the resulting combined interactions within the family and with people outside it.

Boundaries

The third and last assumption in family systems theory is that boundaries exist between family members and subsystems, resulting from the interaction of family members with each other and from the interaction of the family unit with outside influences. You probably acknowledge boundaries between yourself and your parents and between yourself and your siblings, if you have siblings. Boundaries also exist between family members on the one hand and the educators who work with their children on the other. These boundaries may often differ from those between family and friends, family and leaders of religious/spiritual communities, and other people with whom the family interacts.

Families vary in the degree to which their boundaries are open or closed to educators or other nonmembers. Whether a family is more or less open affects how much the family will want to collaborate with educators or others. Some boundaries are porous; others are not. "You should keep in mind that any interaction with the child or other member ripples throughout the whole family" (Zuna, Turnbull, & Turnbull, in press, p. 35).

The boundaries within a family also define its members' roles with respect to each other. In some families, extended family members may take on the parents' roles because the boundary between the two subsystems (extended family and parental) is open. In other families, grandparents may meet resistance when they make suggestions about child rearing. In those families, the boundary between parental and extended family subsystems is closed.

In this chapter, you will learn about family subsystems (marital, parental, sibling, and extended) and two "operating rules" of family systems and subsystems. We call these rules *cohesion* and *adaptability*.

∷ FAMILY SUBSYSTEMS

Within the traditional nuclear family, there are four major subsystems (see Figure 2.1):

1. *Marital subsystem:* interactions between husband and wife or same-sex or domestic partners
2. *Parental subsystem:* interactions between parents and their children
3. *Sibling subsystem:* interactions between children in a family
4. *Extended family subsystem:* interactions between members of the nuclear family, relatives, and others who are regarded as relatives.

Interactions within one family will, of course, differ from those within another family; interactions also vary according to the subsystems within each family and the membership within each subsystem. For example, a family with only one child has no sibling subsystem. Similarly, a single parent does not have a formal marital subsystem but may have the equivalent if the parent has a long-term partner.

You should simply ask the student's parent or parents to tell you about their family and listen carefully to the people they mention. These people are candidates for a partnership between yourself and the family. You do, however, need to ask the parent or parents about involving these extended family members, because the federal special education law grants rights to parents, not grandparents or uncles or aunts, to make decisions about the child's education (see chapter 6).

Marital Subsystem

Interactions within the marital subsystem involve people who are married to each other or individuals who function as though they were married to each other. Whether married or not married but functioning as parents, all adults functioning as parents of a child with a disability are influenced by the child. The question is: How?

Impacts: Negative, Positive, and Mixed. Are marriages strengthened, weakened, or unaffected by the presence of the child with a disability? As confusing as it seems, research says the answer to each of these questions is yes.

Popular belief has been that a child with a disability has a negative impact on a marriage; however, recent research suggests this is not always the case. Early research suggested that the rate of divorce, marital disharmony, and desertions by husbands was higher in marriages where there was a child or youth with a disability (Gath, 1977; Hodapp & Krasner, 1995; Murphy, 1982).

Those findings mirror other research. One group of researchers assessed marital harmony in couples soon after the birth of a child with spina bifida and again nearly a decade later (Tew, Payne, & Lawrence, 1974). The researchers maintained contact with these couples as well as with comparison couples who did not have a child with spina bifida. The couples with a child with spina bifida were found to have lower marital harmony and twice the divorce rate. As Helen Featherstone (1980), the parent of a child with a disability, noted: "A child's handicap attacks the fabric of a marriage in four ways. It excites powerful emotions in both parents. It acts as a dispiriting symbol of shared failure. It reshapes the organization of the family. It creates fertile ground for conflict" (p. 91).

However, recent studies have shown that the divorce rate is not necessarily higher when a family has a child with a disability (Benson & Gross, 1989; Urbano & Hodapp, 2007). Indeed, some husbands and wives report higher levels of marital satisfaction resulting from their shared commitment to their child (Brobst, Clopton, & Hendrick, 2009; Risdal & Singer, 2004; Scorgie & Sobsey, 2000; Stoneman & Gavidia-Payne, 2006). However, this does not mean that there cannot be serious or insurmountable problems in the marriage. The question is whether or not these problems are related to having a child with a disability.

In a meta-analysis on marital adjustment in parents of children with disabilities, Risdal & Singer (2007) found that even though some families do experience marital strain when they have a child with a disability, the "impact is small and much lower than would be expected given earlier assumptions about the supposed inevitability of damaging impacts of children with disabilities on family well-being" (p. 101). Thus, it appears that strain on marriages as a result of having a child with a disability has a much smaller effect than once thought—and is often influenced by other factors. Elsie Helsel (1985) reflected on the impact of her son, Robin, on her marriage:

> Professionals are constantly probing and asking questions concerning how Robin's constant presence and problems affect our marriage. Once again, there are pluses and minuses. From my point of view, Robin has added more strength than strain. My husband and I will not have a footloose, carefree, romantic retirement lifestyle, but we will have something else—the opportunity to feel needed. (pp. 85–86)

In a study examining mothers' experiences and perceptions about having a child with Down syndrome, many women talked about the positive transformation that occurred in their personal lives. One parent described feeling "more connected" with her spouse (Lalvani, 2008). Her statement reflects other research about the positive impact a child with a disability can have on a marriage (Green, 2007). Studies have found that women report greater marital satisfaction when their partners use more problem-focused strategies in dealing with stress associated with daily and routine challenges (Stoneman & Gavidia-Payne, 2006). You will learn more about how families use coping and problem-solving strategies later in this chapter.

Other research has found no impact of having a child with a disability on the family system (Abbott & Meredith; 1986; Singer & Nixon, 1996; Young & Roopnarine, 1994). Overall, you should remember that each family system is unique and how a child with a disability affects the family system and the marital subsystem will vary based on family characteristics and interactions. Once again, we caution you: Make no assumptions about the effect of the child on the marital subsystem.

The child with a disability is not the only input into a marital relationship; other characteristics are also inputs into the family system. Reflect on what you have already learned about the many ways family characteristics vary (chapter 1). Multiple characteristics within families, not just the child with a disability, influence the stability of a marriage. Among the influencing factors are the family's cultural values. Those in turn are shaped by how each member identifies and perceives his or her own cultural identity and by how each perceives the other's cultural beliefs and practices.

Marital Stability. A strong marriage affects a family's overall well-being (Simmerman, Blacher, & Baker, 2001). In a study of the significant and positive changes that occurred in the lives of parents of children with disabilities, a parent underscored the critical importance of marital stability to the family's quality of life: "Your marriage is foundational to everything. It was our love that carried us through" (Scorgie & Sobsey, 2000, p. 202). At the same time, a strong marriage is not the only way to achieve positive family outcomes. Many single parents of children with a disability also experience strong family well-being.

Brobst, Clopton, and Hendrick (2009) conducted a study comparing 45 couples who had children with autism spectrum disorders and 45 who did not. They discovered that although parents of children with autism did report greater parenting stress and lower relationship satisfaction than parents of children without autism, both groups had similar perceptions of their partner's support, respect, and commitment to the marriage. Within any marriage, each partner has specific needs and roles to fulfill for their partner (such as affection, socialization, and self-esteem). It makes good sense to respect and support the marital relationship as you form partnerships with parents and the significant others who are part of the marital subsystem such as cohabitating partners or stepparents. Figure 2.2 provides tips on how to support interactions between parents and their significant others.

Some couples can benefit from marital counseling or related services from psychiatrists, marriage counselors,

FIGURE 2.2 **Supporting interactions between parents and significant others.**

- Communicate with parents and ask them what preferences they have regarding how and when they communicate with you.
- Encourage parents to consider activities they may wish to engage in separate from their child or children.
- Ask parents what kinds of information or resources they would find most helpful. Make information available to them based on their preferences.
- Consider time and other implications of home-based, educational activities on the needs of the parents to spend quality time together as a couple.
- Seek ways to offer flexible scheduling or other alternatives if a planned school activity or meeting conflicts with a couple's schedule.

psychologists, and clinical social workers. If you believe that a family might benefit from marital counseling or therapy, determine which issues are appropriately handled by you in your professional role and which are more appropriately handled by professionals who specialize in family counseling or therapy.

If the issues are better handled by specialized professionals, ask the family whether they would like you to suggest names of qualified professionals whom they may contact and even whether they want you to make the referral on their behalf.

If you are unsure how to proceed, you should discuss your perspective about the family with the school social worker or counselor, withholding the name of the family and the student so as to ensure their privacy and earn trust in your ability to honor any confidentiality they have asked for or may expect to have. If you do consult with other qualified people in your school, it is best to limit your request for help by asking for advice on how best to proceed; it is not advisable to ask them to intervene unless the family already has given you their permission to ask for intervention. In some cases, the social worker or counselor might take the lead and have an initial conversation with the family.

Parental Subsystem

The parental subsystem consists of interactions between parents or other couples acting as parents and their children. Couples can consist of biological, step, adoptive, or foster parents. Some couples stay married to each other, some never marry, some divorce, and some remarry.

Impacts. Just as with marital satisfaction, the impact of a child with a disability on the parental subsystem varies and

is based on the family's characteristics. Some parents of children with disabilities report greater stress and more challenges than parents who do not have children with disabilities (Baker-Erizcen, Brookman-Frazee, & Stahmer, 2005; McMahon, Malesa, Yoder, & Stone, 2007; Olsson & Hwang, 2001; Warfield, Krauss, Hauser-Cram, Upshur, & Shonkoff, 1999). Other parents do not report differences in stress (Gowen, Johnson-Martin, Goldman, & Appelbaum, 1989; Harris & McHale, 1989) or depression levels (Singer, 2004). In this section, we will discuss issues associated with (1) foster parents, (2) adoptive parents, (3) gay and lesbian parents, (4) fathers, and (5) mothers.

Foster Parents. The word *foster* means to help someone develop. Foster parents take care of children who are not their biological children, by providing a safe and welcoming home for them. Foster parents often have permanent or temporary custody of children who are in the care or custody of a state's child protection agency because they have been abused, neglected, or otherwise maltreated by their biological parents.

Foster parents do not have the same legal status as a child's biological parents or as parents who legally adopt a child. Their authority is limited by the state agency or by the order of the court that places a child into foster care. You should always determine the legal status of a foster parent before you rely on that person's authority with respect to the child's education. One parent shares her perspectives on being a foster parent:

> We became foster and adoptive parents in the early 1980s and have continued caring for children for almost 20 years. We have cared for about 25 children through foster placements. Most of these children have had special needs. . . . We have had many social workers, medical providers, and other professionals involved in our lives and the lives of our children over the years. We have watched policies and funding change, and for the changes that improved our lives, I am grateful. However, some changes made no sense or are too complicated. Many of us who parent special needs kids are, frankly, too tired at the end of the day to send e-mails or call our representatives. (Reeves, 2005/2006, p. 20)

Earlier in the first decade of the twenty-first century, approximately 600,000 children were in foster care in the United States (Emerson & Lovitt, 2003). Alarmingly, infants and young children who have physical, cognitive, and health-related disabilities constitute the fastest-growing population of children in need of foster care (Benton Foundation, 1998). One study of children in foster care identified nearly half as needing mental health services (Leslie et al., 2000) and another study found that 75% to 80% of school-age children in foster care had emotional or behavior disorders (Clausen, Landsverk, Ganger, Chadwick, & Litrownik, 1998). It is more likely that a child will be in foster care when the child's parents abuse alcohol or drugs, have mental health challenges, abuse and neglect their children, have other children who are adjudicated to be juvenile delinquents, or are poor (Humphrey, Turnbull, & Turnbull, 2006; Moore & Vandivere, 2000).

During the school years, children and youth in foster care tend to have high rates of absenteeism, midyear changes from one school to another, discipline-related suspensions from school, and a need to repeat one or more grades (Emerson & Lovitt, 2003). Consider the story of Carolyn Johnson, an African American woman who entered the foster care system at age 7:

> Throughout my childhood and teenage years, I was in over seven foster care and group home placements. . . . One of the most difficult parts of foster care was not knowing what was to going to happen to me. There was always a sense of uncertainty and confusion. I often felt scared and alone. . . . Being separated from my siblings was another painful part of being in foster care . . . Some of my experiences in the foster care system were positive. When I was eight years old, I was placed in a wonderful and nurturing foster home. This foster mom showed us love, patience, and kindness—all of the things a child needs. It felt like a real home to me. (Hall-Laude, 2005/2006, pp. 1, 36)

Children of non-European ethnic descent make up approximately two thirds of the foster care population (Behrman, 2004). Of all racial groups, African American children and youth have the highest representation in foster care, constituting 38% of the foster care population. Given that African American students are also disproportionately represented in the special education system, you are likely to teach and work with foster parents of African American students who are in foster care and frequently move from school to school.

Approximately one fourth of children and youth in foster care are placed with relatives and approximately half are placed with nonrelatives. The remaining children and youth are placed in group homes or institutions (Behrman, 2004). Children typically spend an average of 33 months in foster care, and the longer children stay in foster care, the greater the likelihood that they will experience many different foster care placements ("foster care drift").

What happens after foster care? More than half of children return to their birth families, about one fifth are adopted, and one tenth live with relatives. Other post-school outcomes for youth in foster care are also causes for great concern.

- Approximately 25% of children in foster care are homeless and approximately one third are on welfare 1 to 1.5 years after leaving foster care at age 18.
- Only 40% of youth in foster care had held a job for at least one year up to four years after leaving foster care (Child Welfare League of America, 2002; Emerson & Lovitt, 2003).

We encourage you to make special efforts to develop trusting partnerships with foster parents. Typically they are either left out of the educational decision-making process or included at only a superficial level (Altshuler, 1997). Emerson & Lovitt (2003) suggest collaborating with the social worker and/or counselor at your school who can provide important information about legal arrangements that govern foster care placements. You will want to share with the foster parents the nature of the student's educational program, just as you would for parents who do not have foster children, and direct them to resources and support services, particularly if they have had limited experience with children with disabilities.

Adoptive Parents. Research with mothers who have adopted children with disabilities shows that adoptive families typically experience a high level of well-being (Glidden, 1989; Glidden, Kiphart, Willoughby, & Bush, 1993; Lazarus, Evans, Glidden, & Flaherty, 2002; Todis & Singer, 1991). One study followed families for 12 years who had adopted children with developmental disabilities (Glidden & Johnson, 1999). The study concluded that adoptive mothers were generally positive about the outcomes for themselves and their children and that the adopted children experienced good outcomes. The mothers reported that the strongest benefits were giving and receiving love, feeling pride in the child's achievements, and happiness. Mothers did report anxiety, worry, and guilt around the children's developmental delays. However, mothers consistently reported that benefits were much greater than the problems. Interestingly, 50% of the families had adopted at least one additional child with developmental disabilities.

Research has found more similarities than differences in the coping strategies used by adoptive and birth parents of children with developmental disabilities (Glidden, Billings, & Jobe, 2006). Lazarus and colleagues (2002) found that adjustment levels and short- and long-term positive outcomes were similar for transracial adoption (adopting a child of another race or ethnicity) and interracial adoption (adopting a child from a similar race or ethnicity). They suggest that "ethnicity and race differences of parents and children do not generally diminish the positive outcomes reported by parents" (p. 21).

Gay and Lesbian Parents. Gay and lesbian parents have been growing in number (Lamme & Lamme, 2001); however, the exact number of gay or lesbian parents is difficult to determine. Societal barriers and discrimination inhibit many people from disclosing their sexual orientation. Estimates are that the number of children and youth in the United States who have gay parents ranges from 6 million to 12 million

(Lamme & Lamme, 2003). It is estimated that same-sex couples raise 4% of all adopted children and 3% of foster children in the United States. The foster care system would need an additional $130 million if there was a ban on gay and lesbian parents serving as foster families (Gates, Badgett, Macomber, & Chambers, 2007). Children enter gay families in many different ways, including through adoption, surrogacy, artificial insemination, foster parenting, and birth to parents previously in heterosexual relationships.

Two comprehensive reviews of research conducted over the last two decades have concluded children raised by gay and lesbian parents do not significantly differ from children raised by heterosexual parents with respect to their gender roles and social and emotional development (Fitzgerald, 1999; Tasker, 1999). Both reports do, however, point to the much greater likelihood that these children will experience stigma, bullying, and societal discrimination. Positive outcomes of growing up with gay and lesbian parents can include greater exposure to diversity, a more open climate about sexuality, and less emphasis on gender-defined roles within the family.

Australian researchers interviewed more than 100 gay and lesbian parents and 48 children and youth with gay or lesbian parents (Ray & Gregory, 2001). Their findings document the societal discrimination that these parents and students faced.

- Seventy-three percent of parents said their most common concern was whether their children would be teased or bullied.
- Sixty-two percent were concerned that there would be no discussion in the preschool or school curriculum about gay and lesbian families.
- Slightly more than half of the parents worried that their children would have to answer difficult questions.

The experiences reported by the children in this study were particularly revealing. Bullying was a major problem. According to the students, bullying usually started around grade 3 and became harsher as students proceeded through middle and high school. Slightly less than half of the students had experienced bullying by grade 6. Elementary students who were bullied generally sought teacher intervention, but many teachers did not take sufficient action to stop the bullying.

From grades 7 to 12, bullying was also common, although it seemed to subside in grades 11 and 12. When bullying did occur, it escalated more than at the elementary level, as described by one girl: "I had apple cores and banana peels and rocks thrown at me every time I walked past them. 'Dyke, dyke, dyke' they'd call at me. I used to get very scared; very frightened" (Ray & Gregory, 2001, p. 32). High school students expressed disappointment that their teachers did not provide any kind of discipline for homophobic taunting.

They also underscored the benefits of being raised in gay and lesbian families, including having a greater appreciation of diversity, participating in events for gay people such as gay pride events, and feeling special.

There is, however, research that documents the benefits of gay-lesbian marriage. Research has shown that gay and lesbian parents who adopt children are able to respond well to the responsibilities and tasks that are necessary for healthy family functioning (Enrich, Leung, Kindle, & Carter, 2005). Beyond the research, there are powerful narratives, such as the one you will read in the My Voice box on page 34.

Figure 2.3 includes tips on how you can help create a respectful school environment for students who have gay or lesbian parents. These suggestions will assist you in creating strong partnerships with gay and lesbian parents.

FIGURE 2.3 Creating a respectful school climate for gay and lesbian parents and their children.

- Seek out experiences where you interact with people who have diverse sexual orientation, and enhance your own comfort level in being with others who are different from you.
- Just as you would celebrate Black, Hispanic, and women's history months, also celebrate Gay Pride week. Encourage parents and other community citizens who are gay to speak at an assembly, provide audiovisual resources about gay issues, and highlight famous gay and lesbian people (Walt Whitman, Oscar Wilde, Alexander the Great, Billie Jean King, Gertrude Stein) in the curriculum.
- Encourage students to do book reports and research projects on gay issues.
- Point out gender stereotypes in books and encourage students to recognize diversity within gender roles.
- At middle and high school levels, encourage activism in combating harassment.
- Encourage students who appear to be the target of discrimination and harassment related to homophobic language to receive support from school counselors. Provide discipline to students who harass or bully others in a homophobic way.
- Find out about local support groups, and encourage students who are dealing with their own sexual orientation issues or those of their parents to consider attending these support groups.
- Display gay-affirmative symbols in the school such as rainbow stickers.

MY VOICE

Gay and Lesbian Partners—The Fears of Intolerance

When our daughter first started preschool, we were scared. We were in a somewhat unusual situation. My partner had been the one to officially adopt our daughter, even though we were both involved in the process every step of the way. And, while we had started the process of solidifying my legal rights, it was taking longer than we wanted it to. Plus, we had had some bad experiences; once my partner had been out of the country and our daughter needed a medical procedure and I could not consent for it. We spent a crazy night trying to coordinate legalities from opposite sides of the earth, while my daughter lay there just wanting her mommy to take care of her.

So when preschool was starting we were very, very anxious; we knew that both of us would need to be involved every step of the way because of our daughter's special needs. Even though we viewed ourselves as equal partners, would the school? Would we run into issues with them listening to my ideas? Would my partner have to bring everything to them? How could we handle that? Should we try to figure out some way to expedite the adoption process, even if it cost a great deal of money?

Luckily, our worst fears never materialized. We were both treated as full partners in our daughter's education. There were a few legal things we had to deal with—paperwork so I could pick her up and talk to the school about certain things—but the school facilitated all of this. And, there was never a question about both of us being equal partners on her team. Now, as we transition to elementary school, the legal issues are taken care of, but we still worry about if we can re-create the level of trust and collaboration we had with the preschool program.

Take Action!

- Think about the roles that each of these parents play in their daughter's life and how you can understand these roles and build trusting partnerships.
- Think about what legal issues you might need to be aware of and how you can respect these issues while also building trusting partnerships.
- Think about the anxiety that this family experienced and how you could address these anxieties in building partnerships.

Fathers. How do the outcomes experienced by fathers of children with disabilities compare to those experienced by mothers? The research is mixed:

- Some studies report more favorable outcomes for fathers (Trute, 1995).
- Other studies report more favorable outcomes for mothers (Kazak & Marvin, 1984; Olsson & Hwang, 2001; Veisson, 1999).
- Studies report that mothers and fathers experience similar outcomes although their stress comes from different sources (Hastings, 2003; Roach, Orsmond, & Barratt, 1999; Saloviilta, Italinna, & Leinonen, 2003).
- Still other studies indicate no differences in outcomes or in the sources of stress (Ainge, Colvin, & Baker, 1998; Dyson, 1997; Hastings Kovshoff, Ward, Espinosa, Brown, & Remington, 2005; Keller & Honig, 2004).

As you learned in chapter 1, many family characteristics influence how a family adjusts to having a child with a

disability. One of those characteristics is the type of disability. Research has shown that fathers (and mothers) of children with Down syndrome experience less stress from child-related factors than fathers of children whose disabilities are not associated with a particular etiology (Ricci & Hodapp, 2003). Another study found that fathers and mothers of children with Down syndrome and autism spectrum disorders held similar beliefs about having a child with a disability but differed in the strategies they used to meet their priorities (King, Baxter, Rosenbaum, Zwaigenbaum, & Bates, 2009). Studies have shown, however, that stress experienced by fathers of children with disabilities is strongly influenced by their partner's depression (Hastings et al., 2005) and the personal and/or social acceptance of the child (Keller & Honig, 2004; McHatton, 2007; Saloviita, Italinna, & Leinonen, 2003). In one study, Mexican and Puerto Rican mothers of children with disabilities described the father's reaction to having a child with a disability: "He didn't accept her [the child]" and "He just couldn't handle it" (McHatton, 2007, p. 243).

The cause and nature of a disability makes a difference for fathers.

The father-child relationship has many potentially positive outcomes for children and youth. Fathers positively influence their children's cognitive, personal-social, and sex-role-identification development (Grossman et al., 2002; Roggman, Boyce, Cook, Christiansen, & Jones, 2004). Recent research shows that when fathers are involved with children at age 7, the children have better psychological adjustment in their teenage years (Flouri & Buchanan, 2003). Furthermore, when fathers are involved when their children are 16 years old, the youth have fewer psychological problems when they are in their 30s. Clearly, fathers' involvement provides psychological protection for their children.

Fathers who are highly involved with their children also report developing greater self-awareness. The father of a son with autism described the discovery of his own "inner child" as he parented his son:

> I'm a little kid too. I like to have fun. I try to go to places that my son likes and also that I like. Neither of us like to play Little League baseball, so we go to amusements parks and have fun together. To give you an example, we'll go into the gate and he'll start to run and I'll run right behind him to get to the first ride. So, I guess the engineer [i.e., professional persona] leaves me a little bit . . . and I act more like a kid. (Rieger, 2004, p. 206)

Research has examined the types of activities that fathers do with their children. Data from longitudinal study of a national sample of children with developmental disabilities suggested that fathers of children with and without developmental disabilities did not differ in the level of involvement with their children (Dyer, McBride, Santos, & Jeans, 2009). Another study that focused only on families of children with severe disabilities found that fathers primarily were involved with their child with a disability in the areas of playing, nurturing, discipline, and deciding on services (Simmerman et al., 2001).

Research has identified how fathers in low-income families want to be involved in Early Head Start and Head Start programs. Both programs are designed for low-income families with preschool children and both emphasize the child's early development. Approximately half of the fathers participate in the programs in one way or another (Fagan, 1999). Interviews with 575 men whose children attended Early Head Start revealed that juggling work and other demands is the primary barrier to their involvement in a child's educational program (Summers, Boller, & Raikes, 2004). Fathers also said they need information about parenting and expressed their preferences for receiving information through parenting classes, written information, or a telephone hotline. A typical comment was:

> Yeah, I could use help with everything. I could probably use some classes. I don't know what kind of classes are there, but I'd certainly be willing to go to a few to get some pointers on working with kids and how to raise them up as good as you can. . . . I could use some hints on how to get them to do what you want. How to make discipline more . . . of a forethought than an afterthought, if you know what I mean. And I just need help with day-to-day operations. (Summers et al., 2004, p. 70)

Another group of fathers also responded that there were no barriers to their participation in their child's educational program, and they were not interested in any resources. When one father was asked if there is anything that human service agencies could do to help him as a father, he replied, "I don't ever go to any of that stuff. I'm on my own. I'll [take care] of my child on my own. I'd rather do it on my own instead of letting them people tell me what to do with my child. I do it on my own" (Summers et al., 2004, p. 71).

Because fathers have been traditionally perceived as the less involved parent, professionals should make an extra effort to establish partnerships with them (Frieman & Berkeley, 2002; Rump, 2002). Rump (2002) suggests strategies educators might use to reach out to fathers:

- Include information about the importance of men in children's lives in mission statements, family handbooks, and family communications.
- Involve the father during family/child program intake. If a father is not present, inquire about him or other significant male figures in the child's life, and stress their important roles in the family.
- Talk with the father as well as the mother when telephoning a family at home.
- Ensure that program print materials communicate to men as well as women by monitoring the choices of paper color, graphics, topics, and language.

There can be a number of significant men in the lives of children who do not have a traditional father figure. Grandfathers and nonpaternal males such as male partners of mothers, teachers, men from religious communities, brothers, and neighbors can bring an important male presence into the lives of children. If you develop trusting partnerships with only one parent or with only one of several family members, it will probably fall short of being a true family partnership. Be inclusive; reach out to all parents and to all family members if you have permission to do so.

Mothers. Although the trend is for mothers and fathers to share parenting roles, mothers have traditionally assumed a larger part of the responsibility for tending to family needs (Renwick, Brown, & Raphael, 1998; Simmerman et al., 2001; Traustadottir, 1995; Voydanoff & Donnelly, 1999). What are the consequences of this disproportionate responsibility?

Singer (2006) conducted a meta-analysis of studies that focused on maternal depression and found that the majority of mothers (approximately 68% of mothers of children with disabilities) did not show elevated symptoms of depression. However, 18% of mothers of children without disabilities and 32% of mothers of children with disabilities scored over the cutoff for minor depression. He noted that there is a far more pessimistic view of how mothers function when they have children with disabilities than their real-life experiences warrant. To address mothers who have symptoms of minor depression, he urges responsive services, supports, and resources to alleviate the additional challenges these mothers face.

Other research on maternal stress and depression has suggested that stress experienced by mothers of children with disabilities has been associated with behavior challenges with their children (Hastings & Brown, 2002; Hastings et al., 2005; Saloviita, Italinna, & Leinonen, 2003) as well as the care demands of taking care of their child (Keller & Honig, 2004). Data from a longitudinal study examining the stress of mothers with children with intellectual disability revealed that maternal distress led to children's increased behavior challenges and the child's behavior challenges promoted maternal distress (Hastings, Daley, Burns, & Beck, 2006).

The number of children with disabilities in a family may also affect maternal stress. In a study of mothers of children with autism, mothers who had another child with a disability (other than the child with autism) experienced more depressive symptoms and anxiety and lower family adaptability than mothers who had only their child with autism (Orsmond, Ling-Yi, & Seltzer, 2007).

It is important for you to recognize the sources of stress for mothers if you are intent on building a partnership with the family. Your early interactions with mothers and other family members are the foundations for your later relationships with them. Unfortunately, mothers' initial experiences with professionals are not always positive.

Lalvani (2008) reported that mothers of young children with Down syndrome consistently received negative messages about having a child with a disability, most of which came from the medical community. One parent recalled, "What were not helpful were visits to my OB. He was Dr. Doom and Gloom. Instead of celebrating that we were having a baby, he'd always say 'How are you?' in a pitiful way" (p. 440). Another

mother shared her experience: "None of the nurses had mentioned anything about the baby. Nothing. No congratulations, nothing. Really no one. I feel like they were trying to avoid my room" (p. 440).

These voices are representative of the findings from a study that examined over 1,200 mothers of children with Down syndrome after the birth of their child (Skotko, 2005). Findings suggest that the majority of mothers felt anxious or frightened after the diagnosis. Few if any positive aspects of Down syndrome were shared with mothers, and they reported receiving limited or no resources to support them. Read about policy responses to newborns with disabilities in the Change Agents box on page 37.

Researchers who examined stress in Latina mothers whose infants were in the neonatal intensive care unit reported they had higher levels of stress related to caregiving roles and communication than English-speaking mothers (Denny, Okamoto, Singer, Brenner, & Barkley, 2006). These researchers suggested that limited opportunities for Spanish-speaking mothers to communicate in their native language likely contributed to this stress. Understanding the early experiences of mothers (and fathers) is particularly useful for learning about and supporting family interactions.

It is important to note that despite early negative messages about disability, mothers often experience personal, positive transformations and come to view having a child with Down syndrome positively (Lalvani, 2008). Lalvani suggests that mothers "acknowledged that there were definitely many difficulties and stressful moments that arise when raising a child with a disability; however, they attributed these to be a part of motherhood, or quite simply, another aspect of parenting [any child]" (p. 442).

There is growing interest about the impact of a child's disability in different cultural and ethnic groups (Harry, 2008; Zhang & Bennett, 2003). In a study of mothers of children with autism spectrum disorders, Bishop, Richelr, Cain, and Lord (2007) found that African American mothers had lower levels of negativity about having a child with a disability than Caucasian mothers. Discovering how a family perceives the child's disability is an important part of understanding family interactions.

Sibling Subsystem

The sibling subsystem consists of the interactions between brothers and sisters. One of the most obvious interactions relates to socializing; brothers and sisters often provide the first peer relationships for each other. Through their interactions, brothers and sisters give each other opportunities to experience sharing, companionship, loyalty, rivalry, denial, and other feelings. As with all family relationships,

CHANGE AGENTS

Build Capacity—Genes Are Destiny?

Genes are destiny. True? Yes, in some ways. No, in others.

Genes influence the biology of family members. A person's biology is inherent until medically altered; traits are passed down from a parent. But genes need not shape families' lives. Why? Because everyone's life is malleable, and not just medically. Indeed, nothing has so changed the lives of most individuals with disabilities and their families as public policy and professional practice.

That's so because public policy reflects the past even as it is a beacon into the future. It's also so because professional practice reflects the past even as it equips a person and family for the future.

At least two different but similar policy statements have shaped the interactions of family members affected by disability, including those whose genetic characteristics appear in their children.

The Principles of Treatment of Disabled Infants, issued in 1983 by leading professional and medical associations in the fields of intellectual and physical disabilities, condemned the withholding or withdrawing life-sustaining treatment from newborns with birth anomalies solely because they have disabilities. It presumed they have a moral and legal right to treatment and called on federal, state, and nonprofit agencies to support the babies and their parents. Congress codified the Principles when it amended the Child Abuse Prevention and Treatment Act. Interactions among family members that include withholding and withdrawing of life-sustaining medical procedures, food, and water now are disallowed. (Authors' note: Rud Turnbull, a coauthor of this book, was one of the principal draftsmen of the Principles.)

The Principles of End-of-Life Treatment, adopted in 2006 by a large number of family-driven and professionally based disability organizations, tracked the "baby" principles, condemned withholding and withdrawing life-sustaining treatment of any child and adult solely because of disability, and presumed in favor of treatment. Although these have not been adopted as part of federal law, some elements of them are in state guardianship and medical-practice laws, affecting family members' interactions with each other. (Authors' note: Rud Turnbull also was a member of the consortium of disability policy leaders who drafted these Principles.)

Take Action!

- When you consider how family members interact with each other, bear in mind that they often face difficult decisions and may appreciate your guidance so long as it is based on well-received principles about treating members who are at the edges of their lives.
- Be careful not to impose your judgment on them when they face hard decisions; instead, offer them support or, if your conscience does not permit you to do so, refer them to individuals and agencies from which they can receive support.

the nature of the brother-sister bond is culturally rooted. Different cultures have different expectations for siblings. Stoneman (2005) suggests that in many cultures, caretaking is a paramount role in the daily life of the family, and siblings' roles can reflect that expectation. Other influences that can shape sibling relationships are age, birth order, gender, and disability.

Although siblings can be socialization agents (Gallagher et al., 2000) and even tutors (Tekin & Kircaali-Iftar, 2002) during their younger years, they often are increasingly responsible for providing care and coordinating services for their brother or sister with a significant disability. These roles increase as their parents age. In fact, research on families whose members with a disability have lived with their parents well into adulthood shows that siblings, especially sisters, tend to provide caregiving and companionship when their parents are in the later stages of life (Orsmond & Seltzer, 2000). Consider this sibling's perspective about her 17-year-old brother with cerebral palsy:

> I think [Paul's] going to need a lot of support for living on his own, working on vocational skills and things like that. And I think that, my hope is that, he would call me and ask me for help. . . . When you get to be that age, you can't tell your parents everything. So, I'd be the one for him to call. Most of the time, if there was something that went wrong, whatever, I'm pretty sure he would call me instead of them. (Marks, Matso, & Barraza, 2005, p. 210)

Brothers or sisters with a disability influence their siblings in many different ways (Fisman, Wolf, Ellison, & Freeman, 2000; Lardieri, Blacher, & Swanson, 2000). Siblings can derive many benefits from the relationship, including enhanced maturity, self-esteem, social competence, insight, tolerance, pride, vocational opportunities, advocacy, and loyalty. Others sometimes experience negative effects, including embarrassment, guilt, isolation, resentment, increased responsibility, and pressure to achieve. Still others regard having a brother or sister with a disability as a neutral experience. Like all sibling relationships, positive and negative reactions can also occur simultaneously. There is no single definitive impact; impact depends on the size of the family, birth order, gender, the nature of the disability, cultural beliefs, coping styles, and other unique circumstances occurring within the family. For a perspective on siblings and their partners, read the Together We Can box below and go to http://www.siblingsupport.org/sibshops/index_html for more information.

TOGETHER WE CAN
Tara Kosieniak—Denying and Affirming a Brother's Influence

If honesty is the best policy, then Tara Kosieniak is a leader. Ask her about her brother, Nick, five years younger than she and affected by cerebral palsy, significant intellectual disability, and muscular dystrophy, and Tara will tell you she can remember only two happy memories:

> I was a very sad and lonely child. I pretty much played by myself, not with my sib, not with my parents. The two that I have are when one time I taught Nick to play with one of his toys and the other was when he stood up in my wedding.

Ask her about problematic interactions, and, again, she'll be candid:

> My interactions were limited. For a good part of his life, he was sick . . . then just kind of frail. . . . I was not taught how to play with him. We did not do things as a family so it was almost like I was an only child with this sort of cloud hanging over my head.

Put a question to her about "lessons" and "impacts" that Nick taught or had, and you'll confront some complexity. When asked to be a "Santa's helper" for a child in special education, Tara declined:

> I did not want to do it because I lived this daily and I wanted to interact with someone normal. These were first graders, and I was only asked because I had a brother with a disability. I felt guilty about it but still decided not to.

Then listen to what she tells you about herself as she grew older:

> Nick actually chose the direction I was going to go to with my career and has pretty much shaped it ever since. I started working with kids with disabilities when I was 16, providing respite to families. Again, I was asked to do this because I had a sib. This time, I gave in but ended up loving it. In college, my focus was all about disabilities/human services. . . . Because I was so profoundly affected, I was looking to validate my feelings and looking not to feel so alone. . . . Respite had an impact on my choice to get involved with sibling issues because . . . there were other sibs around. We connected and I learned what life was like for them and that it was similar to what I was feeling. I no longer felt alone.

What does Tara do now? After having worked in agencies serving people with developmental disabilities, she established a statewide sibling support network, SIBS: Supporting Illinois Brothers and Sisters (www.sibsnetwork.org), and is a member of the national sibling support network. Because of Nick and together with professionals and other siblings, she is a national leader.

She's journeyed a long way: "no" to being a helper and "yes" to being a supporter. She has both denied and affirmed Nick's influences.

Take Action!

- Embrace the complexities that Tara describes, how she once rejected her sibling role when asked to be Santa's helper and then affirmed it.
- When working with any member of a family, assume that there is no single interaction between each member and the person with a disability.
- Instead, be open to paradoxes (denial becomes affirmation)—the mixture of sadness and loneliness with the delight of a brother's standing up (against all odds) at a wedding.

Early research and false assumptions often stated there were predominately negative outcomes and experiences for siblings of persons with disabilities (Dykens, 2005; Hodapp, Glidden, & Kaiser, 2005; Stoneman, 2005). However, in a recent review of the research on siblings of children with disabilities, Stoneman (2005) identified the following themes:

- There is no difference in self-esteem in siblings of children with and without disabilities.
- Most sibling relationships are positive, rich, and satisfying.
- Having a sibling with a disability does not cause pathology or maladaption in children.
- Parents do tend to focus more attention to their children with disabilities than typical siblings.

Research supports the notion that having a sibling with a disability is generally a positive experience. Of course, there can be many challenges just as in any family interaction. Here is one parent's perspective on the positive relationship between her son, Jamal (who has a disability), and his siblings:

> It's just normal to them. This is who he is. I have always appreciated that in them . . . They like to go in his room and watch movies—but they watch them with him, they don't ignore him. They all eat popcorn together. During football games, Jamal's older brother, Donnell, will play rough house with the Nerf football. Jamal just breaks out in uncontrollable laughter. I think that's what I like the most—seeing them do things that typical siblings do. (Zuna, Turnbull, & Turnbull, in press, p. 39)

Even given the positive outcomes and experiences associated with having a sibling with a disability, some siblings may be interested in support or resources. There may also be specific life cycle stages where siblings want information or interactions with other siblings who have similar experiences.

Don Meyer, a national leader in creating support programs for siblings of children with disabilities, has created a model known as "Sibshops." Sibshops provide information and emotional support that "reflect a belief that brothers and sisters have much to offer one another—if they are given a chance. Sibshops are a spirited mix of new games (designed to be unique, offbeat, and appealing to a wide ability range), new friends, and discussion activities" (Sibshops, 2009). The Sibshops curriculum has been used throughout the world including the United States, Canada, England, Iceland, Japan, New Zealand, and Mexico. If your community does not sponsor Sibshops, you might collaborate with families, educators, people with disabilities, and other community citizens to start one.

Can siblings be helpful in promoting the successful inclusion of their brother or sister with a disability? Yes, according to one research study (Gallagher et al., 2000). Siblings offer valuable perspectives on how to include their brother or sister with a disability in school and other activities. The child with a disability often wants to emulate his or her brother or sister or at least be in the same school. Brothers and sisters can ensure that their sibling with a disability receives opportunities and encouragement at school and in community activities. Siblings can serve as a conduit of information between the school and their parents.

Because brothers and sisters carry out important roles within a family, it behooves professionals to include them in family partnerships. Read first-person narratives for additional insight into sibling perspectives (Gans, 1997; Meyer, 2009; Meyer & Vadasy, 2007).

Extended Family Subsystem

Think of each person in your extended family and then total how many there are. Reflect on the role that they have had in your life, beginning when you were a young child until the present. What factors have either increased or decreased their availability and support?

The Role of Culture. The answers to these questions may depend on your cultural background. Cultures tend to define the composition of extended family and the frequency of contact between the nuclear and extended families (Lynch & Hanson, 2004). Consider these two examples:

> In most American Indian families, the concept of family is defined broadly to include extended family members and fictive kin (i.e., nonfamily members incorporated into the family network) in addition to the immediate family (Malach et al., 1989). Other members of the family's tribe may be included as well. In many cases, extended family members rather than the biological parents may hold primary responsibility for care of the children. Often, grandparents or other extended family members willingly assume child-rearing responsibilities so parents of young children can be employed. Furthermore, parents may seek the advice and assistance of older family members and elders in the larger family network, given the value placed on age and life experiences. In interventions, these extended family members may act as service coordinators for child and family to obtain needed services. (Joe & Malach, 2004, pp. 117, 119)

> Latinos, as a whole, adhere to a collective sense of family, often resulting in extended family configurations that offer valuable support services (Vega et al., 1983). Moreover, the godparent or *compadre* system offers support by adding to the family via marriage and the use of godparents at baptism, confirmation, and the *quinceañeras*, the coming-out celebrations for 15-year-old girls. (Zuniga, 2004, p. 196)

Although many cultures value the support of extended family members, there is great diversity in the presence, frequency, and type of support that extended family members provide. You should not assume that every family from a culturally or linguistically diverse background gains support from extended family members.

From the outset, ask parents to define which family members they want to involve as they work with you and other professionals. Only after they identify these extended family members should you try to identify culturally sensitive ways for including them in partnerships.

Grandparents. Grandparents can often provide a unique and important source of support and yet there is limited information about their role and outcomes in families of children with disabilities. When 120 mothers of a child with moderate to profound intellectual disability were asked to describe the grandparents' role, 45% said they received help with child care from grandparents, 40% received advice and encouragement, 16% received help with household tasks, and 15% received financial assistance (Heller, Hsieh, & Rowitz, 2000). A study of the extent of grandparent support (Heller et al., 2000) reported that parents of children with a disability received less practical help with everyday tasks than parents of children without disabilities; however, both groups received the same amount of emotional support. Another study suggested that in single-parent families, grandparents were more likely to provide support and were more likely to provide weekly help to families of children with disabilities than other relatives or friends (Green, 2001). One study, however, documented that support as well as stress can be associated with grandparent presence (Hastings, Thomas, & Delwiche, 2005). These researchers found that within the same family, grandparent support and conflict was associated with mothers' (but not fathers') stress.

A different kind of stress occurs when the child is diagnosed with a genetic condition (Bailey, Skinner, & Sparkman, 2003). Typically, parents receive genetic counseling and then must explain these findings to grandparents, uncles, aunts, or other members of their extended family. One study investigated the perspective of parents who had children with the genetic condition known as Fragile X syndrome (Bailey, Skinner, & Sparkman, 2003). Nearly all of the parents reported that either they or their spouse informed extended family members of the genetic test results. Approximately two thirds of the parents described this experience as either somewhat stressful or very stressful since extended family members needed to consider the meaning of the results for themselves. This was especially true for siblings of the parent who was the genetic carrier of the condition.

Grandparents and other extended family members of children with disabilities need information and support to deal with their own feelings and to know how to provide care for the rest of the family (Janicky, McCallion, Grant-Griffin, & Kolomer, 2000). Grandparents' or family members' ideas about people with disabilities may be more traditional than those of the child's parents. For example, a Latino mother of a young child with a disability described how her own mother agreed to make a *mandos* (bargain) related to her grandchild. She promised the Virgin of Guadalupe (Mexico) that she would visit the basilica and wear the colors of the Virgin every day if the Virgin would heal her grandchild. The child's own mother did not subscribe to her mother's approach; the differences were more generational than spiritual.

Sometimes extended family members may share their negative perceptions about children with disabilities. For example, one mother shared that her uncle commented "this is a tragedy" (Lalvani, 2008, p. 441), and another shared that her great-aunt remarked, "if you had known, you could have started over again and gotten, you know, had another baby" (Lalvani, 2008, p. 441). Conversely, grandparents and other family members can be very helpful in dealing with the new reality of life with a child with a disability.

Up until this point, we have focused on grandparents as part of the extended family; however, many grandparents assume the parenting role. The number of grandparents who are care providers for their grandchildren has increased substantially over the last 10 years (Janicky et al., 2000). Some of the reasons include teenage parents, unemployment, poverty, substance abuse, maternal incarceration, and child abuse and neglect. A study of 164 grandparents providing primary care to grandchildren with disabilities in New York revealed that 96% were female and 80% were African American (Janicky et al., 2000). Grandparents identified two reasons for assuming caregiving duties: to cope with substance abuse by the child's mother and to prevent the child from being placed in foster care because of parental child abuse and neglect. Approximately three fourths of the grandparents reported that the children experienced problems in school, and two thirds said the children had challenging behavior and developmental delays. The researchers concluded:

- Caregiving was an all-consuming role in their lives.
- Their days were fraught with uncertainty because they generally could not access proficient formal and informal supports.
- They were constantly worried about remaining alive long enough to provide care for their grandchildren into adulthood (Janicky et al., 2000, p. 49).

FIGURE 2.4 **Assisting extended family members.**

- Provide parents with information to help them better understand the needs and reactions of extended family members.
- Provide parents with information about the disability, needs of children and priorities of families that can be shared with extended family members.
- Encourage the development of grandparent or extended family member support groups. Those groups might be facilitated by school social workers, psychologists, PTA volunteers who are grandparents, or extended family members of a child with a disability.
- Find individuals in the community or at school who can be matched with an extended family member to share positive reflections and perspectives on life with a child with a disability.
- Encourage extended family member participation in IEP or IFSP conferences, classroom visits, school events, and family support programs.
- Provide library materials, community resources, or Internet sources for extended family members.

A comparison of grandparents who were raising a grandchild with a disability and those raising a child without a disability revealed that both groups were caring for an average of two children (Force et al., 2000). Although grandparents raising children with and without disabilities had many similarities, they also differed. Grandparents who had a child with a disability reported a greater need for help from schools, a greater need for transportation, and greater use of speech therapy services. Additionally, only about 10% of the grandparents raising a grandchild with a disability had contact with disability service agencies. It is important for schools or other service-providing agencies to reach out to grandparents who are the primary care provider, especially since both groups of grandparents had symptoms of depression. Figure 2.4 includes suggestions on providing information and resources that can assist extended family members to support the child and family.

:: COHESION AND ADAPTABILITY

You have just learned about the subsystems—the people who interact in the family. Now it is time to consider how they interact. You will learn about two elements of family interaction—cohesion and adaptability. Cohesion and adaptability in a family describe (1) the emotional bonding

that members of family subsystems have and (2) the quality and nature of boundaries, organization, and negotiations among family subsystems (Olson, Gorall, & Tiesel, 2007).

The rules governing family interaction are unique to each family and are influenced by their culture. The families you interact with will vary in cohesion, adaptability, and what works for them (Lynch & Hanson, 2004).

Because many of the early studies on families of children with disabilities have been conducted by European American researchers with European American research participants, some professionals think that the level of cohesion and adaptability acceptable to European American families is the level to which all families should adhere. As you learned in chapter 1, however, culture and other characteristics significantly affect families, and professionals must honor each in developing partnerships.

Cohesion

You have already learned that certain boundaries serve as lines of demarcation between people who are inside and outside a subsystem. The roles that members of a subsystem play often define these boundaries. For example, the two adult members in a traditional nuclear family may interact with each other in the roles of husband and wife and with their children as father and mother.

Boundaries may be open or closed; that is, they may or may not be accessible to interaction with people outside the subsystem. From a European American perspective, subsystems are typically open enough to allow individual autonomy and closed enough to provide support for each family member (Summers, 1987).

These boundaries also help define families' bonding relationships. Family members typically feel closer to each other than to those outside the family. This element of family bonding relates to cohesion (Olson, Sprenkle, & Russell, 1979).

Family cohesion refers to family members' close emotional bonding with each other and to the level of independence they feel within the family system (Olson et al., 1980; Olson, 1988). Cohesion exists across a continuum, with high disengagement on one end and high enmeshment on the other. One author used the physical metaphor of "the touching of hands" to describe cohesion in the family:

> The dilemma is how to be close yet separate. When the fingers are intertwined, it at first feels secure and warm. Yet when one partner (or family member) tries to move, it is difficult at best. The squeezing pressure may even be painful. . . . The paradox of every relationship is how to touch and yet not hold on. (Carnes, 1981, pp. 70, 71)

Another parent described how cohesion is fostered in the family through the use of humor. "We would tell this joke in our family . . . because that is part of our culture. We all know that joke. So, as a family [we] can connect on some level [by using it]. It is part of our family" (Rieger, 2004, p. 202). Most families operate somewhere in the center of the cohesion continuum.

Range of Cohesion. When families are highly cohesive, boundaries among their subsystems are blurred or weak (Minuchin & Fishman, 1981). For example, a mother of a child who is deaf and blind and has many physical care needs may delegate some of the responsibilities to an older daughter. The daughter may have fewer parent-child and sibling interactions because she has been drawn into the parental subsystem. Her own needs as a child and a sibling may be overlooked or subordinated.

Your challenge is to identify the appropriate extent of cohesion according to each family's cultural beliefs. What may appear to be overprotection in one culture may be appropriate protection, nurturance, and affection in another. For example, Latino families may find it acceptable for preteens or even adolescents to sit on their mother's lap or for preschoolers to drink from a baby bottle long after European American parents would consider those actions inappropriate (Zuniga, 2004). When you honor families' cultures, you provide the context for trust to evolve in your partnerships with them.

What happens when families have low degrees of cohesion, even to the point that children with disabilities are isolated from other family members? Limited interaction leaves children without the support, closeness, and assistance needed to develop independence. Low cohesion—sometimes called disengaged family interaction—can involve limited involvement of family members in each other's lives, few shared interests or friends, excessive privacy, and a great deal of time apart (Olson, 2006, 2007). Few decisions are made with family input and involvement. For all family members, particularly the member with a disability, low cohesion can be both lonely and difficult.

Disengaged relationships can take place within and among subsystems (Olson, 2006, 2007). For example, disengagement within a subsystem exists when a father denies the child's disability and withdraws from parental and marital interactions. Disengagement among subsystems occurs when the members of the extended family cannot accept the child and that part of the family subsystem is excluded from family celebrations.

Implications of Cohesion. Positive outcomes accrue for families when family cohesion is balanced (Dyson, 1993;

Gavidia-Payne & Stoneman, 1997; Lightsey & Sweeney, 2008; Margalit, Al-Yagon, & Kleitman, 2006; Olson, Gorall, & Tiesel, 2007). A balanced level of cohesion is an early predictor of children's growth and communication, social skills, and daily living skills (Hauser-Cram et al., 1999).

By contrast, low family cohesion is a predictor of greater parenting and child-related stress at important transition points, such as leaving early intervention programs and entering kindergarten (Warfield et al., 1999). Low family cohesion is a much stronger predictor of parent and child stress than the child's age or type of disability.

In a study examining stress in families with a child with a disability, researchers found that "the level of harmony in the family seems to be the most crucial factor influencing stress" (Keller & Honig, 2004, p. 346). Over the years studies on the positive contributions that individuals with disabilities make to their families have revealed that parents especially value the increased family unity and closeness that often comes from having a child with a disability (Behr & Murphy, 1993; Lalvani, 2008; Stainton & Besser, 1998; Summers, Behr, & Turnbull, 1989; Turnbull, Guess, & Turnbull, 1988).

There are two reasons you should work with families to establish a comfortable level of cohesion. First, by recognizing the levels of cohesion between and within subsystems, you can create a context that supports the family as a whole to meet its needs as well as the child's (Zuna, Turnbull, & Turnbull, in press).

Second, by considering the degree of family cohesion, you can provide appropriate services and supports or refer the family to those services (Margalit, Al-Yagon, & Kleitman, 2006; Taanila, Järvelin, & Kokkonen, 1999). For example, you will know to ask whether a particular program encourages a culturally appropriate level of cohesion. Or you will be competent to make appropriate early education recommendations. Mothers who are highly involved in early childhood programs are sometimes unintentionally reinforced for establishing highly cohesive relationships with their young children. They are encouraged to spend considerable time in the classroom, attend mothers' groups, provide home teaching, and transport children to various services (Turnbull et al., 2000). When they spend all this time with the child, what happens to their own needs and the needs of other family members? Obviously, you will want to be sensitive to the implications of your professional recommendations.

Adaptability

Adaptability refers to the family's ability to change in response to situational and developmental stress (Olson et al., 1980; Olson, 1998) and to the leadership, organization, and negotiations families demonstrate (Olson, Gorall, & Tiesel, 2007).

As with a family's cohesion, adaptation is influenced by family values and cultural background. Adaptability can be viewed on a continuum. At one end are families who may be unable or unwilling to change in response to stress. At the other end are families who are constantly changing, so much so that they create significant confusion within the family system (Olson et al., 1979). Again, most families fall somewhere in the center.

Ranges of Adaptability. At one end of the adaptability continuum, families demonstrate a high degree of control and structure, and their interactions involve many strictly enforced rules. These families firmly delineate the hierarchy of authority along with the roles that each person plays. In this structure, negotiating authority and roles is rare and usually intolerable. For example, consider a family with a son who sustains a brain injury and accompanying physical disability. If in the past, the child's mother was primarily responsible for meeting the child's needs; the added caregiving demands may be more than she can handle. However, if the family is not comfortable with sharing responsibilities with new collaborators outside of the family, the added demands can create stress for the mother as well as all other family members. Research suggests that there is a relationship between parental adaptation to their child's disability and the quality of relationships they have (Wade, Stancin, Taylor, Drotar, & Yeates, 2004).

There are two reasons to consider the degree of adaptability in the family as you propose educational programs. First, many families gradually adapt their power hierarchies to support their child or adolescent to become a self-determined adult. As you will learn in chapter 4, self-determination is culturally rooted. Some families place great value on their children's increasing autonomy, whereas others emphasize family interdependence (Brotherson, Cook, Erwin, & Weigel, 2008; Kalyanpur & Harry, 1999; Shogren & Turnbull, 2006). You need to be sensitive to family and student preferences while negotiating the degree of student decision making that the family considers appropriate.

Second, it is helpful to identify the person or persons who have primary control over family decisions and rules. For example, if you ask a mother to try a home-based language program but do not take into account the husband's decision-making power and possible rejection of your request, it is unlikely that the program will be effective. Indeed, if the mother carries out the intervention against her husband's wishes, the program may create marital and parental conflict. You should examine how any recommendation for home-based programs will affect each family member. Work with the family to develop options consistent with its values, goals, and ability and willingness to adapt.

By contrast, other families demonstrate a low degree of control and structure. Their interactions often are characterized by few rules, and even these are seldom enforced. Promises and commitments are often not respected and family members may learn that they cannot depend on one another. Frequently, there is no family leader, negotiations are endless, and roles are unclear and often changing.

All families can experience periods of chaos during stressful life events. But when chaos is a consistent way of life, the consequences can be negative for the family and the student with a disability. Consider a mother whose son has attention-deficit/hyperactivity disorder and is struggling academically and socially. The mother has a live-in boyfriend who is the family's primary source of financial support. During the last two years, the boyfriend has begun to drink heavily and has become physically abusive. When the boyfriend begins to drink, existing rules are suddenly harshly interpreted for the child. When the fighting escalates, the rules change and survival becomes the main concern. Later the remorseful boyfriend becomes extremely indulgent, creating a third set of rules. The cycle repeats and the child experiences instability and chaos. Because of his disability, the child also experiences difficulty interpreting social cues and his ever-revolving family lifestyle exacerbates his problems.

Implications of Adaptability. As you learned, most families strike a balance between the high and low extremes of adaptability and flexibility (Olson et al., 1980). The ability to be flexible and to adapt to life changes is a key factor contributing to positive adjustment (Glidden, Billings, & Jobe, 2006; Lustig & Akey, 1999). Family members often value identifying a range of options when life changes occur and negotiating the best option for the family (adaptability and flexibility) while also maintaining a strong commitment to each other and the family (cohesion). However, research indicates that "families who face competing demands may become less flexible in their ability to accommodate everyone's needs" (Orsmond, Lin, & Sletzer, 2007, p. 265).

You can use any one or more of three effective ways to support those families who are dissatisfied with their current level of adaptability and flexibility. First, help families plan for positive change. If possible, discuss schedule changes and transitions well in advance. Ask yourself: Is this change too sudden or radical for this family's current level of adaptability? Does the family have the flexibility to handle the change given current family roles? Some students and families may benefit from gradual transitions. When a student will be changing classrooms or school buildings, start with a gradual transition, one day a week, before making the complete transition. If a child needs to learn how to ride the bus, intermediate steps may be reassuring to the student and his or her family. Initially, the student may only ride part of the way or ride along with a friend or another family member. Also, invite the bus driver to be part of the planning team.

Second, encourage families to examine alternatives. Many families who lack flexibility and adaptability may not know how to examine alternatives (Shank & Turnbull, 1993; Summers, Templeton-McMann, & Fuger, 1997). They may benefit from learning problem-solving skills. One mother described how using humor to solve problems made all the difference in her family:

> Humor is a problem-solving tool. I think humor is the best way to talk about the things that bother you. I have a choice of how you look at it. I choose to use the lighter

side of it, because I see humor as an alternative solution to my problems. (Reiger, 2005, p. 201)

Third, if a family may be interested in receiving services from the school counselor, school social worker, or other community professionals, collaborate with the school counselor or social worker on how to approach the family and suggest these alternatives. If a family asks you about possible resources, refer members to those resources. Remember, however, that family dynamics are complicated and often require highly specialized professionals to provide the most appropriate and personalized supports. Knowing when to refer a family is critical for all professionals in special education.

REVISITING LUKE, CHRISTINE, AND ERIC LINDAUER

The Lindauer family has several subsystems. Within Luke's immediate family, there are three quite distinct individuals: a young boy with a disability and two MIT graduates pursuing different careers. Christine and Eric form the marital subsystem—and each has different characteristics and levels of adaptability, flexibility, and cohesion. Each parent is introverted—at least that's how Christine describes herself and Eric. And they have worked to adapt to having a child with a disability yet maintain cohesion within their marital subsystem.

Christine and Eric's relationship with Luke forms the parental subsystem. Christine and Eric are flexible in the roles they adopt as parents, sharing household responsibilities and using outside sources (e.g., day care and preschool) to meet Luke's needs. Since Luke is an only child, there is no sibling subsystem. In terms of the extended family subsystem, Christine and Eric's parents and stepparents in Eric's case and relatives are involved in their lives and play defined roles. Also, Christine and Eric are

seeking a community in Pittsboro. That was what motivated them to move from San Diego to just south of Chapel Hill.

Remember, just like a mobile, what happens to one family member or in one family subsystem affects the entire family system. And, changes will continue to happen in the Lindauer family system as each member grows and develops. But, is change just a temporal thing for the Lindauer family—something that happens as time goes by? So far, yes.

The Lindauer's fundamental characteristics have not changed. Two of them are still and always will be well educated and bright. One—Luke—is an unknown at this point. True, he has a disability. But what does that mean for him, Christine, and Eric? There is no way to predict; we know only that he has a special challenge but we don't yet know what he will achieve in his life. Much will depend on how his parents, researchers, and practitioners become partners with each other.

SUMMARY

We focused in this chapter on the interactions family members have with each other, continuing our description of the family-systems approach. A family's characteristics are the inputs (chapter 1); a family's interactions are the outputs (chapter 2). There are four subsystems within a family; the interactions within each are the topic of this chapter.

FAMILY SYSTEMS THEORY AND FOUR SUBSYSTEMS

- Marital—husband and wife or other partners functioning as if they were married
- Parental
- Sibling
- Extended family

THE MARITAL SUBSYSTEM

- Impacts of disability
- Stability of marital system

THE PARENTAL SUBSYSTEM

- Impacts of disability
- Foster parents

- Adoptive parents
- Gay and lesbian parents
- Fathers
- Mothers

THE SIBLING SUBSYSTEM

The Extended Family Subsystem

- Role of culture
- Grandparents
- Genetic issues

Cohesion and Adaptability

- Family cohesion—the emotional attachment that family members have toward each other and the level of independence each feels within the family
- Adaptability—the ability to change in response to circumstances within or outside the family

LINKING CONTENT TO YOUR LIFE

As you reflect on your own family's interactions, think about what has worked well for you and what has not. Families with whom you develop partnerships will have their own style of family interaction. What can you learn from your personal experiences to support families in experiencing the most positive interactions possible?

FAMILY SUBSYSTEMS

- Think about the different subsystems in your family. Can you identify all the different subsystems? How would you characterize your family members' interactions within each subsystem?
- What role does culture play in how your family interacts with one another?

COHESION

- How would you describe your family's cohesion during the years when you were a young child, and how

did that cohesion change or not change over your family's life cycle? How did your family's cohesion affect you in establishing more independence as a young adult?

ADAPTABILITY

- Did your family ever face a stressful situation that required every member to adapt to change? Could your family be adaptable under these circumstances? What helped your family be successful with change? What were the barriers? How will your own experiences with adaptability enable you to understand the stress that your students' families face?

Family Functions

LANZ AND XENIA POWELL

What if you wore five hats every day? One as a sister of a person with a disability, one as the single-parent mother of a person with a disability, one as the aunt of three children who have disabilities, one as a teacher in special education, and one as a teacher in general education. No doubt you would have some interesting perspectives about families, their many functions, and their interactions with professionals in special and general education. You might as well be Xenia Powell, for she wears each hat.

Xenia's brother, Phillip, has an intellectual disability. Now 45, he has lived in a group home since he was 3. Xenia's son, Lanz, is 18. Although he has Asperger's syndrome, he is academically talented and has just graduated from the Lindbloom Math and Science Academy, a Chicago magnet school; he is headed to college next year at National Louis University, near Chicago.

Xenia's sister, Geneva, has three children—one has an intellectual disability and the other two have learning disabilities and are enrolled in college near Chicago. Xenia has taught both special education and general education classes in Chicago's public schools and plans to earn her master's degree in special education.

Two of Xenia's five hats are professional: special education teacher and general education teacher. The other three are familial: sister, mother, and aunt. Because Xenia lives with only Lanz, not her mother or sister, let's leave that one hat on—her mother hat—and learn about how she and Lanz function as a family.

"Oh, we're affectionate, Lanz and I. No doubt!" That's a good characteristic, but not without its challenges. "Now that Lanz is headed to college, he's thrilled. But when he leaves, it will break the rhythm of our family. I cling so hard to him."

How's her and Lanz's self-esteem? It's rock solid. "As I've raised Lanz, I never thought 'Oh, woe is me.' Never. You do what you have to do." And she had to do a lot, challenging the school system that hired her to provide Lanz an appropriate education (read more in the "Change Agent" feature in this chapter).

Spirituality is a big part of Xenia's life. When talking about Lanz leaving home for college, Xenia admits she clings so hard to Lanz. Why? "I don't want to tell my father I failed," she explains, referring to her belief in God. As a member of the Capernium church, a "full-gospel" church on Chicago's south side, Xenia applauds Lanz for

"walking this journey with me." He watches the TV Bible quiz show *Virtual Memory* and has his own Bible, which he studies regularly.

Xenia's candid about her family's economics. "We were well cared for by our mother. I didn't know we were poor until I went to college." Lanz does not receive any federal benefits, and Xenia has worked full time since 1997, some of the time in day care but most in the city's schools.

Daily care is simple enough, with only one challenge. "Lanz can do everything he needs to but has poor time management skills. I constantly have to tell him, 'Lanz, it's time to do this or that.'"

Xenia and Lanz live close enough to her mother, Mercedes, and sister, Geneva, that they are the core of their social circles. They don't go out much for recreation. "We're homebodies. We play games, watch TV, and sometimes go to movies with Lanz's Auntie Geneva."

Education is important. Having been admitted to Howard University in Washington, DC, but knowing she couldn't afford to go there, Xenia attended and graduated from Huron College in Huron, South Dakota. "I went where I got money." She has battled the schools for Lanz, and now she's seeing him off to college. Her niece, Arianne, is in college in Jackson, Mississippi, and her nephew, Giovanni, is in college in Mitchell, South Dakota. Education is a family imperative. Next up for Xenia: her master's degree in special education.

think about it

- Assuming you are Lanz's teacher, which of the many roles she has played in Lanz's life would be most likely to contribute to your partnership with her?
- Which of the many roles she has played would you most want to support her to carry out?
- And what aspect of Xenia's family life is most likely to challenge you as you try to build a partnership with her?

:: **INTRODUCTION**

In chapter 1, we defined *family* as two or more people who regard themselves as a family and who perform some of the functions families typically perform. In this chapter, we focus on the second part of that definition, the functions that families typically perform.

The tasks that families perform to meet the individual and collective needs of their members are referred to as family functions. We identify eight categories of family functions: (1) affection, (2) self-esteem, (3) spiritual, (4) economics, (5) daily care, (6) socialization, (7) recreation, and (8) education (Turnbull, Summers, & Brotherson, 1984). The family systems framework calls these the family's *outputs* (see Figure 3.1). You will learn about each of the eight family functions, their common themes, and implications for you as a potential partner with families who have children with disabilities.

A family generally tries to engage in activities that reasonably satisfy its members' wants and needs. One role of the family is to show the younger members how to meet those needs and perform these functions so that responsibilities can be transferred from the older to the younger generation, consistent with the cultural values and traditions of the family.

As you will learn in chapter 4, a family's life cycle stage strongly influences a family's activities and the contributions of individual family members. Additionally, the family's characteristics (chapter 1), interactions among its members (chapter 2), and life cycle stage (chapter 4) influence how functions are addressed within the family.

Because the family is an interacting system, it is impossible for you to consider family functions (outputs) without taking the other portions of the family system into account. Likewise, you are more likely to create a trusting partnership

FIGURE 3.1 Family systems framework: emphasis on family functions.

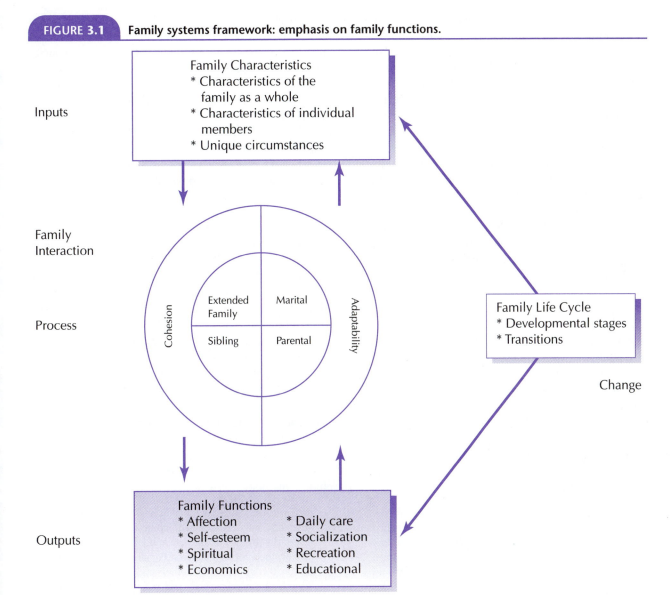

with families when you understand the way that they address these eight functions and the impact of their cultural values and personal preferences.

:: IMPACT OF DISABILITY ON FAMILY FUNCTIONS

Each category of family functions is distinct; however, assets or challenges in one family function usually affect other functions. For example, economic difficulties can have a negative effect on family members' social or recreational activities. Likewise, stress related to financial worries can

have a negative impact on affection and self-esteem. Alternatively, a child's positive contributions to household chores (that is, daily care) can enhance self-esteem, affection, and recreational outcomes.

Each of the family functions is affected by every family member, including the member with a disability. This influence may be positive, negative, or neutral (Blacher & Hatton, 2001; Brown, Anand, Fung, Isaacs, & Baum, 2003; Singer, 2006; Turnbull, Turnbull, Agosta, Erwin, Fujiura, Singer et al., 2004). Many people erroneously assume that a child or youth with a disability has a negative impact on the family. However, research has documented many positive contributions that children with disabilities make to their families (Bayat, 2007; Blacher & Baker, 2007; King, Baxter, Rosenbaurm, Zwaigenbarum, & Bates, 2009; Hastings, Beck, & Hill, 2005; Scorgie & Sobsey, 2000). For you to fully understand the impact of a child's disability on the family, you must consider both the child's contributions to the family as well as the challenges they may encounter. What positive contributions can you identify so far in the Powell family?

As you read this chapter, consider the following questions. What are the family's priorities for achieving balance in carrying out family functions? What cultural values and personal preferences influence these priorities? The more you respond to each family's priorities, the more likely you are to develop a trusting partnership with them. To answer these questions and apply the answers as you work with families, think about your family's priorities. What cultural values and preferences most significantly influence your family's priorities?

Affection

Studies report that families who consider themselves successful emphasize positive family interaction, including sharing affection (Poston, 2002). Affection can be characterized in many different ways, but especially important are (1) exchanging verbal and physical affection and (2) exchanging unconditional love (Poston, 2002; Summers, 1987).

Exchanging Verbal and Physical Affection. Families have many different ways of exchanging affection. Consider this example of affection:

> After finishing dinner with my husband, Allen, and my son, it was just [my son] and I left sitting at the kitchen table. I was so tired (after all it was 7pm!) that I put my head down on the arm of his wheelchair. I positioned his hand and fingers on my head and hair so he would have that "sensory" experience of feeling my hair as his fingers would move (and I would get a gentle head massage!). The armrest was actually quite soft and comfortable, and we stayed in silence like this for at least five minutes. I probably even dozed off! All of a sudden I heard a voice . . . [My son's] digitized voice from his communication device: "I LOVE YOU." I looked up at him stunned, and as the tears formed in my eyes (as they are as I retell the story), he just started smiling and laughing. [He] knew what my reaction was going to be to what he said, even before he saw the look on my face. He knew how happy he made me with those three words. (Wolfbiss, 2009, p. 58)

Exchanging verbal and physical affection relates to the attachment that family members have between and among each other. Research has particularly focused on the bond between mothers and children (Osofsky & Thompson, 2000). From a family systems perspective, attachment between and among family members is a priority and consists of encouraging interactions between parents and children that deepen their emotional commitments to each other. "Human development occurs in the context of an escalating psychological ping-pong game between two people who are crazy about each other" (Bronfenbrenner, 1990, p. 31). As you learned in chapter 2, attachment usually occurs in families when emotional-bonding relationships are balanced.

Cultural influences strongly affect how families display affection. For example, Asian families may be in close physical contact with infants, carrying them during naps and having infants and toddlers sleep in the same room or bed with parents and other siblings until they are school age or older (Chan & Lee, 2004). The same is usually true of Middle Eastern families: "Middle Eastern mothers . . . are much more permissive than their Western counterparts in allowing their infants and young children to be kissed, held, or hugged" (Sharifzadeh, 2004, p. 394).

A major but natural issue for families is their child's evolution from expressing physical affection within the family to expressing physical affection and sexuality with one or more chosen partners (see chapter 4).

Exchanging Unconditional Love. All children have basic needs for acceptance, appreciation, and love. Exchanging unconditional love is an essential ingredient of family affection, as Harriet Rousso (1984), a social worker with a physical disability, noted:

> In particular, disabled children need to have their bodies, disability and all, accepted, appreciated, and loved. Especially by significant parenting figures. This will solidify the sense of intactness. For all children, disabled or not, the "gleam in the mother's eye" in response to all aspects of the child's body and self is essential for the development of healthy self-esteem. This includes the parent's ability to show pride and pleasure in the disabled part of the body, as one valid aspect of the child, and to communicate appreciation and respect for the child's unique, often different-looking ways of doing things. . . . Parents too often communicate to their child, directly and indirectly, that the disability should be hidden or altered; if (the disability is) not purged, the child should strive toward appearing as "normal" and nondisabled as possible. This attitude can put the child into an identity crisis, causing him or her to push that feeling of intactness way underground. (Rousso, 1984, pp. 12–13)

Families and professionals may need to examine their own values. What are their expectations about a child's achievement, normalcy, success, attractiveness, or progress as prerequisites for unconditional acceptance, appreciation, or love? Within a family, unconditional love for all members, whatever their respective characteristics, cannot be taken for granted, nor can it be underestimated. A number of families have described their child as a major catalyst for enhancing family love (Bayat, 2007; Behr & Murphy, 1993). Dr. Donald Rosenstein, clinical director of the National Institute of Mental Health and the father of a son with autism, spoke of his family's journey and connections:

> I believe that "reframing a problem" can help to overcome it. But adaptation is not the same as becoming tolerant of or inured to something. Adaptation allows for creative possibilities. [Our son] has adapted to us and we to him, and through this process our family has discovered deep and meaningful connections with each other—connections we never thought possible. (Rosentein, 2008)

No family role is more important than the expression of love and affection. Figure 3.2 provides tips for supporting families

| FIGURE 3.2 | **Addressing families' affection needs.** |

- ■ Recognize the needs that all family members have for affection. For example, if a parent-child home teaching program each night interferes with a busy family's only opportunities to catch up on the day's events, play games, or snuggle on the couch together, reconsider the plan to achieve a balance in meeting affection needs, not just educational needs.
- ■ Work with students to be able to express verbally and in writing their affectionate feelings toward their family. Students might make up stories, poems, or even a family portfolio that includes writing and other related projects focusing on affection.
- ■ Provide materials in a resource library and arrange discussion groups involving resource persons who can help parents and students with an exceptionality gain a better understanding of sexuality and affection. Young adults or adolescents, depending on age, type, and severity of exceptionality, benefit from accurate and sensitive information about sexuality and affection.
- ■ Help parents identify their child's positive contributions to affection as well as other family functions. Encourage family members to discuss what positive contributions each makes. For example, at dinner encourage family members to share at least two things they appreciate about each of the other members. They can also highlight the similarities and differences in each person's list.

to express love and affection. And, the more you express unconditional love for a child, the more likely you are to encourage high-quality affection within the family.

One family member's disability can have an impact on the self-esteem of all. For example, new parents may have anticipated raising children with typical abilities. When they learn that their child has unique abilities and challenges, they may feel less secure in their own ability to parent (Kuhn & Carter, 2006).

Parents of children with disabilities may have self-esteem challenges, such as feelings of guilt, if they believe their own genetic makeup or their personal misconduct caused the disability (Bailey, Skinner, & Sparkman, 2003). Likewise, their self-esteem may be affected when their infants do not respond readily to soothing or stimulation or when they deal with existential issues of why the child has a disability. Many parents draw on their strengths and optimism to rebound emotionally:

> I learned that the only good reason to have a child is to raise a decent human being—the underachievers as well as the overachievers—and if you're counting on producing an athlete or scholar, you better think again. Three quarters of young couples in a recent survey said they would choose abortion if told their fetus had a 50 percent chance of growing up to be obese. If you're one of them, don't take the risk.
>
> I learned to expect the unexpected, a good reminder for anyone considering parenthood. On what should have been one of the happiest days of my life, I received the worst possible news, and here's the part worth noting: I survived. I pieced back together my broken heart and found a way to enjoy life anyway. I tossed out the old yardsticks for measuring success and created new ones. In a culture that turns athletes into heroes and defines beauty as perfection, I learned to love a child who is slow, clumsy and imperfect. I built a new life with different expectations. And I learned a new definition of what it means to have something in the family: the courage it takes to let go of the child you want to embrace the child you get. (Herbert, 2009)

A different dilemma occurs for families who have faced multiple challenges and low levels of self-esteem for much of their lives. Many parents (especially mothers, according to the research) who experience poverty, substance abuse, and mental health challenges are highly vulnerable to demoralization, depression, and low expectations for the future (Belle, 2003; Furstenberg, 2003). Self-esteem is susceptible to many challenges across the life span (including the special challenges we described in chapter 1). Professionals who have trusting partnerships with parents facing multiple challenges typically affirm and build on the parents' strengths.

One such strength can be a family's persistence. Professionals are genuinely respectful of and impressed by families' abilities to endure in the face of events that the professionals did not believe they, themselves, could survive. A journalist recalled being encouraged by a therapist to write about a retreat that had been held for mothers of children with disabilities:

> These women are not saints or martyrs. But they see gifts where others might see only hardships. "Write this column for *them*," [The therapist and founder of the retreat] told me, as the mothers packed their cars to head back to their families. They are not looking for pity or praise, just acceptance of their challenges. "We're not special," she said. "We're just human beings, doing what we do with love." (Banks, 2009)

A family's self-esteem can depend on whether its members see the connections between their actions and good things that happen. A mother of a child with autism described how she felt when extended family members and professionals celebrated her son's accomplishments: "The [preschool] providers always notice and comment on [his] progress and our efforts. Their positive reinforcement and support validates that we are doing our best for our son" (Beach Center, 2000). Sometimes you may need to help family members see that their actions have made a difference. Think about how your family members have helped you see that your actions make a difference.

The self-esteem of students with learning disabilities has been the focus of considerable research. Some studies have found that children with learning disabilities have lower self-concept than their peers without learning disabilities (Lackaye, Margalit, Ziv, & Ziman, 2006; Nowicki, 2003); other studies have found there to be no difference in self-concept among students with and without learning disabilities (Gans, Kenny, & Ghany, 2003; Zeleke, 2004).

Most research on the self-concept of students with learning disabilities has been carried out in schools. A study of the self-concept, academic self-perception, social competence, and behavioral problems of children with learning disabilities and their siblings without learning disabilities found no significant differences in self-concept or academic self-perception between the two groups (Dyson, 2003). Parents did, however, rate their children with learning disabilities as having lower social competence and more behavioral problems compared to their siblings without learning disabilities. Parents who were more stressed themselves tended to rate their children as having less social competence. When family-professional partnerships are strong and families get the support that they need, they are more likely to enhance the social competence of their children.

A study comparing the self-esteem of students before and after they were identified formally as having a learning disability found that students reported higher levels of self-esteem following diagnosis (MacMaster, Donovan, & MacIntyre, 2002). Merely receiving the diagnosis enabled students to see that their learning problems were not as extensive as the students originally feared and could be easily remediated (MacMaster et al., 2002). Undoubtedly, it is important for the family and student to understand the diagnosis and to be involved in the process of how that diagnosis is shared and used. Remember Xenia Powell and read about her experiences with labels and the law, and how she advocated for change in the Change Agents Build Capacity box on page 53.

Judith Heumann, an adult with a physical disability and a national policy leader in special education and rehabilitation, shared her perspective about diagnosis:

> The most significant goal for parents of disabled students is assuring that their children maintain the sense of self-esteem with which we are all born. Parents are their children's most important role model. If disabled children know their parents have great expectations for them, they will have great expectations for themselves. (Heumann, 1997)

How might you support parents of children with physical disabilities and mild cognitive impairments to enhance their children's self-esteem? You might consider offering a program that was successful for parents. The program included six weekly lessons in which parents met as a group. Through presentations, discussions, and individual and group activities, they learned how to help their children develop independence, participate in leisure activities, interact with peers, be assertive, cope with tough situations, and practice self-advocacy (Todis, Irvin, Singer, & Yovanoff, 1993). As a result of the training, parents' self-esteem increased; children gained self-care skills, completed chores more often, and became more assertive; and the parents became more likely to support their child's request for autonomy and independence.

What are the implications of these self-esteem issues for family-professional partnerships? A family's and student's self-esteem can be influenced by how you recognize their strengths. Sadly, many families and students are much more accustomed to having their weaknesses pointed out. You can, instead, affirm their strengths. Take the time to recognize when family members' actions lead to positive outcomes for children. Let them know that they have made a difference. Affirm the students' strengths by encouraging them to identify their preferences, make choices, and develop and act on their interests. When you support students in achieving greater independence, you

CHANGE AGENTS BUILD CAPACITY

Xenia Powell—Labels and Law Inside the School

Lanz Powell is academically talented but has a disability. Xenia didn't learn that until she took in-service classes offered by the Chicago Public Schools for prospective special education teachers.

"That's when they labeled Lanz as having an emotional-behavioral disorder. They misdiagnosed him. I asked them to reclassify him, I had all kinds of data about his behaviors, I got a new evaluation and paid for it myself, and told them he doesn't have an emotional-behavioral disorder." In response, the schools dropped the "EBD" label and categorized Lanz as having Asperger's syndrome and a specific learning disability.

Why was Xenia so adamant about Lanz's EBD label? "I know the schools from the inside. I know the law from inside the school building. With that EBD label, they put limits on my son."

After she was successful in persuading the school system to remove that diagnosis, she faced another challenge. Lanz had acquired the specific-learning disability diagnosis. That was wrong, too. "Lanz has an IQ of 125. I never told him the school labeled him 'LD' because he is so strong that he doesn't even recognize the possibility of failure."

When a teacher told Lanz he had a specific learning disability, Xenia was "furious." "I asked her, 'Why did you tell him that, you just gave him a crutch to lean on.' I did not want Lanz to have any excuses. I didn't want him to think it is OK to fail. I told him, 'You are the one responsible for your success or failure.' I was thrilled when the schools removed his LD label and left him with only the autism label. But now he didn't have a dual diagnosis so he lost his one-on-one support in school."

Take Action!

Assume you are a teacher of a student like Lanz and that student's mother, like Xenia, told you she was furious for giving her child a crutch. Consider these responses.

- Determine the criteria your state or local educational agency uses to classify a student as having an EBD, a specific learning disability, or Asperger's syndrome.
- Justify your decision to the student's mother on the basis of your professional qualifications; appeal to her on an educator-to-educator basis.
- Be open to reexamining your conclusions.
- Explain how you will support the student to learn; make it clear you are not limiting him but, instead, giving him the support he needs.
- Try to understand the mother's perspective and how a "crutch" may impact different family functions, especially the self-esteem function.

are also sending a message that you recognize and value their strengths.

Often, students without disabilities comment on their peers who do have disabilities. Sometimes, the comments are negative; sometimes, not. When students comment on other students, you have a chance to shape their attitudes and share with the parents of the students with disabilities the positive comments. That's what Lanz Powell's teacher did when she sent the poem in the My Voice box on the following page to Xenia Powell, his mother; she sent it to us, obviously appreciative of the student who wrote it and the teacher who gave it to her.

Spirituality

We use the term *spiritual* to refer to beliefs associated with spirituality and religion. Spirituality usually refers to how people find meaning in their lives; how they respond to the sacred; and how they perceive the connections between themselves, others, and the universe (Canda, 1999; Gaventa, 2001). For example, many Native American belief systems are highly spiritual and link human beings to the larger universe.

> The Hopis (a Pueblo tribe in northern Arizona), believe that the original spiritual "being" shared with the Hopi people certain rules of life and placed spiritual helpers, the Kachinas, near the tribe to protect and help them maintain that way of life. The Kachinas, therefore, help teach and guide the Hopis through their songs, prayers, and ceremonies (Titiev, 1972). Among the Apaches, the Mountain Spirits have a similar role to that of the Kachinas. Appropriate members of the respected tribes impersonate these deities during special ceremonies. (Joe & Malach, 2004, p. 122)

MY VOICE
Lanz—A Poem by His 12th-Grade Classmate

I think he called me his "Purple Power Ranger."
And at the time, Lance, he was a stranger,
So, naturally, as anyone would when someone tells
    them that,
I felt my immediate safety in danger;
however, as I grew to know him, I became accustomed
    to his magic.

I go to school with a boy named Lanz,
And he's autistic and he's big and can be annoying
    at times,
And he sometimes whines when he doesn't get his way.
But, still, he's pretty alright
Lanz is loud and slightly oblivious to the walls people place
    around them
(I think it's called personal space),
And teens and young adults who attend my school
Seem to lack empathy for the autistic,
A combination that doesn't breed an understanding
    environment.
Hell, he may be socially awkward, but why yell at him for
    what he cannot control.
His scars may not be visible to the naked eye,
But I know words like "Retard," "Slow," and "Stupid"
    do open deep wounds.
But, Lanz, he is beautiful in his retort,
And while he may whine for a while, he'll eventually
    forgive and smile
And call them friend once again.

Lanz performs magic spells.
Lanz pulls pennies from the air
And casts them into wishing wells,
Wishing only to make us teens and young adults smile.

And he made me his "Purple Power Ranger" one day
Because I said "hi" in the hallway when no other teens or
    young adults would.

I happened to be wearing a purple shirt that day
Lucky Me . . . no,
Lucky me (I'm serious)
That 'Power Ranger' bond built an intimacy between us.
I did and still do learn from him on a daily basis
(Even after someone informed him society sees purple
    as a 'girl' color.
I do not know who now has my former title.)

Lanz, with him, lunch is a trip,
Either entertaining or melancholic.

Entertaining Scenario:
He'll pop on his iPod and play either
"Whacha Know About Me" or "My Milkshake Brings
    All the Boys to the Yard,"
And he'll dance, putting on a public show for everyone in
    the lunchroom.
Some people will cheer him on, others join in on the fun,
    get up, and dance.
Lanz knows how to bust a move or cut a rug or
    get down
Or whatever new word to call dancing the kids
    have found.
By the end, we are all smiling.

A More Melancholic Turn:
He'll go a table filled with those he sees as friends
    and ask,
"Hey guys, Can I sit here? I won't be a bother."
His 'friends' will say, "No Lanz, not today"
And before he even gets the chance to walk away,
They'll call him a hurtful name, as if deafness was a side
    effect of autism. (It's not)
But, Lanz, is beautiful in his retort,
And while he may whine for a while, he'll smile
And dependent on the pigment of their shirt,
He'll assign them a color and call them his
    power ranger.

I've seen Lanz, I've seen him do it.
I've seen him perform his magic spells,
I've seen his joy put Santa to shame and
His creative ideas out-do those of Keebler Elves.

Now I know what you're thinking,
"Magic isn't real"
Well, I hate to spill the beans as there are still many hungry
    tummies in the world
But I have to be honest:
He didn't do magic in the way you think of it.

People treat Lanz less than his worth, less than human,
Yet he keeps smiling,
Keeps genuinely smiling his contagious smile.
His ability to be happy is his magic.
Lanz places his happiness in people, yet he is not dependent
    on people.
He teaches me how to forgive and smile on a
    daily basis
And that, to me, is magic.

Not all spirituality is religious. Religion is typically defined as the organized patterns of beliefs, rituals, and social structures to which people adhere in fulfilling their spiritual quest (Canda, 1999; Fitzgerald, 1997). People explore the spiritual meaning of their lives and achieve a sense of spirituality through a broad range of activities, one of which may relate directly to their religious beliefs and activities.

Although spirituality and religion are manifested in multiple ways across different cultures (Gollnick & Chinn, 2002; Lynch & Hanson, 2004), a common theme is the role of the family in transmitting spiritual beliefs from one generation to another (Roehlkepartain, King, & Wagener, 2005). A family's spiritual perspectives can vastly impact their values, beliefs, and rituals. Consider how Confucianism affects family life through its strong emphasis on filial piety:

> Filial piety consists of unquestioning loyalty and obedience to parents and concern for and understanding of their needs and wishes. It also includes reverence for ancestors whose spirits must be appeased. Filial piety further extends to relations with all authority figures and defines a social hierarchy of allegiance and reciprocal moral obligations characterized by the "five relations": 1) king/justice, subject/loyalty; 2) father/love, son/filiality; 3) elder brother/brotherly love, younger brother/reverence; 4) husband/initiative, wife/obedience; and 5) friends/mutual faith. (Chan & Lee, 2004, pp. 225–226)

Research consistently finds that children with disabilities are a catalyst for a family's increased spirituality (Bayat, 2007; Poston & Turnbull, 2004). A parent of a child on the autism spectrum described how his family's conviction of their faith had intensified: "For my family, it has brought us closer, closer to God, closer to each other. We are there for each other" (Bayat, 2007, p. 711).

The spiritual function of the family often comes into play in terms of (1) interpreting the meaning of the child's disability and (2) having a religious community that provides concrete and emotional support.

The spiritual function of the family is critically important as a basis for interpreting the meaning of disability (Poston & Turnbull, 2004; Skinner, Bailey, Correa, & Rodriguez, 1999; Zhang & Bennett, 2001). Interviews with Latino mothers about their spiritual interpretations of disability revealed that approximately three fourths believed that their child was a blessing or a gift from God (Skinner et al., 1999; Skinner, Correa, Skinner, & Bailey, 2001). These mothers felt they were the recipient of God's blessing or gift because they were worthy or because God was trying to teach them to be better people through the experience of raising their child. These mothers also tended to have higher levels of faith than fathers, and parents who were not as acculturated in the majority culture had higher levels of faith than those who are more acculturated.

Another study interviewed 137 parents of children with and without disabilities. The researchers found that parents of children with disabilities frequently emphasized that their child was a gift from God and that their spiritual/religious faith played a major role in understanding the meaning of their child's life and in having hope for the future (Poston & Turnbull, 2004).

> I have to say for all parents that have kids with disabilities, or exceptionalities, I think you have to look at that as a gift from God as a blessing, as a test of your faith. If you have faith, it's going to work out. (Poston & Turnbull, 2004, p. 16)

Kalyanpur and Harry (1999) described the experiences of a Hmong family with a 7-year-old child, Kou. Social workers brought a suit against Kou's parents for refusing corrective surgery on his two clubfeet. Consistent with their spiritual beliefs, Kou's parents interpreted his condition as a "sign of good luck" and as an indication that "a warrior ancestor whose own feet were wounded in battle could be released from a sort of spiritual entrapment" (p. 16). As families interpret disability positively and within a spiritual framework, opportunities will occur for their beliefs to be sources of comfort and motivation. How might you react if you were Kou's teacher and his parents refused corrective surgery? What spiritual/religious interpretations of disability may influence your reaction? (In chapter 8, you will learn techniques for resolving conflict when team members have different beliefs and priorities.)

Alternatively, some families may adopt spiritual interpretations that disability is a punishment for past sins or transgressions.

> . . . a Korean mother of two boys with mental retardation claimed that the spirit of a dead horse that had entered her sons' bodies during her respective pregnancies caused their "sickness." She, in turn, sought the cure for their affliction by resorting to daily prayer and meditation. Another mother (Chinese) insisted that her daughter with severe developmental delays was possessed by a ghost and would regularly bring her to a monk who sang chants (a series of repetitive choruses), gave offerings to appease the spirits, and provided the mother with a "lucky charm" made from special herbs to hang around the child's neck. (Chan & Lee, 2004, p. 267)

As you develop a reliable alliance with families by honoring their cultural traditions, we encourage you to be open to their interpretations of their child's disability. Their religious/spiritual beliefs do not necessarily have to be consistent with yours. Your role is to seek to understand how they bring meaning to their life experiences.

Many families derive tremendous instrumental and emotional support from their religious communities. They experience pride and satisfaction in having their children participate in valued religious rituals. For example, in the Jewish religion, a religious ceremony called a bar mitzvah (for boys) or bat mitzvah (for girls) marks the rite of passage from childhood to adulthood. Parents of children with developmental disabilities who participated in this ceremony described the experience in terms of their heightened sense of connectedness and enhanced self-image (Vogel & Reiter, 2004).

> The service was quick. Jarrett was wheeled to the Torah, helped by family to touch the Torah and, at the end, to cover the Torah. [The rabbi] spoke of "a bar mitzvah where we get a chance to look at the big picture," and [Jarett's dad] mentioned "learning to accept Jarrett exactly as he is." Mostly, it was music and dancing. The men danced in a circle around Jarrett. At one point, [Jarett's dad] hoisted his son from the wheelchair, held him up from behind, and the two swayed together to the Hasidic classics. (Winerip, 2008)

Many families, however, have trouble finding a religious community that can respond to their child's needs (Poston & Turnbull, 2004; Vogel, Polloway, & Smith, 2006).

> When my son was 18 months or so, before I thought of having him evaluated, I was sitting in the service and an older woman asked me to remove my disruptive toddler. She had this tone that I soon become immune to, of condemnation of my parenting. I took my children . . . to the nursery and cried my eyes out. . . . A few weeks later, I tried to take my children to the service again, but my son was just as disruptive. When I stood up to leave, the pastor stopped me. In the middle of her sermon, she told me to sit down. She told the rest of the congregation that my son was a member of the church and that it was all of our responsibility to raise and teach him the ways of God. The tears I am shedding as I write this story are ones of gratitude in contrast to those I shed seven years ago in the nursery of my church. (Gaventa, 2008, p. 66)

When families find an accepting spiritual or religious community, many positive experiences can accrue.

> Church experience is just wonderful. I mean, it just takes over. I don't know. I mean, once you walk through the door, that's it. And well, she loves music, so, that's it. Once she walks in the door . . . she goes straight to the front, she can sit on the organ. She doesn't touch the keys or nothing. But she just sits there, long as the organ's playing, she sitting there. She gets up once it stops and get up and go and sit down. And, you know, that's the most, best place I think she's not being, not just tolerated. (Poston & Turnbull, 2004, p. 103)

FIGURE 3.3	Addressing families' spiritual/ religious needs.

- Encourage families who are interested in spiritual/religious support to set aside time for this family function, ask for support from their spiritual/religious community, and ask for support from professionals with whom they work.
- Encourage churches in your community to provide support for individuals with disabilities and their families, which might mean including the young person in religious education and social activities.
- Invite the individuals who are responsible for religious education to the student's IEP meeting if this is agreeable with the student and parent.
- Encourage special education teachers who may be interested to take an active part in the religious education program that they attend to promote inclusion for individuals with disabilities.
- Inquire whether religious organizations in the community have accommodations and programs that are particularly geared to the needs and interests of your students.

Figure 3.3 provides tips for supporting spiritual/ religious organizations to include children and youth with disabilities and their families.

Some people mistakenly assume that children and youth with intellectual disabilities might not be interested in religious or spiritual participation because of their inability to comprehend abstract concepts. On the contrary, research has shown that adults with mild and moderate disabilities report that religion is a very important part of their lives (Shogren & Rye, 2004). Researchers found that adults with mild and moderate disabilities indicated that they regularly attended religious services. And, participation in the religious organization was their most frequent community-oriented activity. However, although the individuals regularly attended worship services, they were not as likely to be included in social or educational activities of the church, perhaps because of inadequate accommodations for people with disabilities. The majority of participants said they thought about God on a regular basis, believed in God, and prayed to God. An intellectual disability does not preclude individuals having clear conceptions of religion as well as identifying symbols associated with their beliefs (Swinton, 2004; Turnbull, 2009).

Much has been written about the role of the church in the lives of African American families (Willis, 2004). Many African American churches currently provide educational, recreational, and social service supports for families in addition to religious/spiritual support. Later in this chapter, you will learn how the Men's Fellowship of an African American Baptist church in Ohio launched an after-school program to provide tutoring, recreation, and moral/social skill development for children while their parents were working (p. 60).

Given the constitutional separation of church and state, you may ask whether it is your role to help families address their spiritual/religious needs. We believe many families benefit from their beliefs and derive concrete and informational support from their religious communities (Poston & Turnbull, 2004; Zhang & Rusch, 2005). You can help families if you collaborate within their spiritual/religious communities to create the adaptations and accommodations they need to participate in their community. In chapter 10, you will learn in more detail about conducting comprehensive IFSP/IEP conferences. These conferences could be ideal opportunities for family contacts with spiritual/religious programs to learn about adaptations and accommodations for children and youth with disabilities.

Economics

Nearly all families need to earn money; only a few have the luxury of being supported by unearned income. Many families of children with disabilities qualify for government benefits because of the presence of disability. In chapter 11, you will learn more about family support programs that provide financial subsidies—Supplemental Security Income (SSI) and the Home and Community-Based Services (HCBS) Waiver Program. One of your professional roles is to know about available financial resources and where to refer families for more information.

Whatever their sources of income, all families must decide how to handle their money. Family resources vary tremendously, and finances affect how families respond to the challenges of their children's disability. Do not assume that families who cannot pay for certain activities or services are less committed to their children than more affluent families. In one study, Mexican and Puerto Rican single mothers of children with disabilities, 92% of whom were receiving public assistance, described their interactions with school personnel and social service workers as particularly demeaning (McHatton, 2007). The mothers believed the professionals discriminated because they had made negative assumptions about the families' culture, because the mothers were single parents, and because the professionals had low expectations for their children.

Because advocacy is one of the seven elements of partnership, you should value and advocate for all families. Take the time to understand how disability affects each family and then advocate for supports for the family. Bear in mind that families often spend more money on their children with disabilities than on their other children. A child's disability—especially autism, intellectual disability (mental retardation), spina bifida, cerebral palsy, and health conditions requiring technology support—can create excess costs (Shattuck & Parish, 2008).

These excess expenses may include food (specialized diets and adaptive feeding equipment), transportation (to service providers), recreation, clothing (specially adapted or tailored garments), medical care and medications, specialized services and therapies, home modifications (such as specially designed furniture), adaptive equipment (such as hearing aids, adaptive seating equipment, adapted toys), and mobility devices (such as walkers and crutches, and personal care) (Parish & Cloud, 2006). Private insurance and public funding typically do not cover all of a family's disability-related expenses (Parish, Rose, Grinstein-Weiss, Richman, & Andrews, 2008). The burden of these expenses can significantly affect families. The out-of-pocket health care expenses for families with children with disabilities typically are twice that of other families (Newacheck & Kim, 2005). In addition, out-of-pocket expenses were greater for families living in states with lower-median incomes (Shattuck & Parish, 2008).

Sometimes even families fortunate enough to have otherwise adequate health insurance coverage find the costs of accessing and maintaining specialized adaptive equipment and medical services are not fully covered:

> Isabella is a very active girl; she enjoys participating in many outdoor activities and P.E. class with her peers. Isabella will be 9 years old soon, and we feel she would be a good candidate for a power wheelchair; however, our insurance company will only pay for a manual chair. Even with multiple requests and notes from her doctor, our insurance company refuses to pay for a power chair at her age. We desperately want her to keep up with her friends at school and a power chair would give her more independence. We know she has the determination to learn to use a power chair, but we struggle to pay our bills some months, and purchasing a chair is only an option for rich people. (Zuna, Turnbull, & Turnbull, in press)

The economic impact of raising a child with disabilities varies by the child's age, the nature and extent of the child's disability, and family composition (Parish & Cloud, 2006; Parish et al., 2008). For example, it may be more costly to care for a child with significant medical challenges than for a child with mild learning disabilities. Not surprisingly, low-income families have the most difficulty meeting the economic demands of raising a child with disabilities (Parish et al., 2008). You will learn more about community resources to help families ease their financial burden in chapter 11.

There is a second economic impact of disability that many families experience. Not only may families encounter greater expenses, but the presence of a family member with a disability may also affect parents' employment status. Many parents of children with disabilities, particularly mothers, do not take a job or reduce their work hours to provide the level of care and supervision needed by their child.

- I had a career before my child's diagnosis. Now all that doesn't seem important anymore. I work a part-time job so I can be home with my son (Hutton & Caron, 2005, p. 186).
- I substitute teach, I taught part-time, I tried being a realtor, I tried to do all those rounds . . . It's just all these jobs that were just too demanding to try to hold things together at home, because I'm the one who holds things together . . . (Parish, 2006, p. 399).
- I have found it literally impossible to work. Isabella has had several surgeries related to her contractions due to her severe cerebral palsy. You can't say to [an employer] 'I'd like to work, but I need Tuesday afternoons and every other Friday off, so Isabella and I spent all the time going to doctors and therapy and I just have never gone back to work (Zuna, Turnbull, & Turnbull, in press).

The experiences of these mothers are not uncommon:

- Nearly 24% of families with children who have special health care needs either end or cut back on their employment (National Survey of Children with Special Health Care Needs, 2005/2006).
- The employment rate of family households raising children with disabilities was 73.5% compared to an employment rate of 83.3% for households raising children without a disability (Wang, 2005).
- A survey of 349 parents of children with serious emotional and behavioral disorders found that 48% of parents had quit a job to care for their children, and 27% had been terminated due to work disruptions resulting from the needs of their child with a disability (Rosenzwieng & Huffstutter, 2004).
- Analysis of data from 22,000 children and their families indicated that having a child with an unstable health condition increases the likelihood of a mother reducing her hours of work by two and a half times (Leiter, Krauss, Anderson, & Wells, 2004).

In many families, the impact of disability on employment continues throughout the life span. One study reported that approximately half of mothers with adult children with disabilities worked outside the home, compared to three fourths of the mothers of adult children without disabilities. Further, of the mothers with adult children with disabilities who worked outside the home, each mother worked an average of 9 hours per week, compared to 22 hours per week for mothers of adult children without disabilities who worked outside the home (Einam & Cuskelly, 2002).

The primary reason for the unemployment of the mothers of adult children with multiple disabilities was the caregiving demands associated with their child's condition. However, mothers who worked outside the home reported better mental health; this finding suggests that work may provide a break from caretaking responsibilities.

Interestingly, fathers of adult children with multiple disabilities tended to fall into one of two groups: one group worked fewer hours than fathers of young adults without disability while the other group worked more hours. The wives of the husbands who worked longer hours said they believed their husbands had retreated from caretaking and immersed themselves in more intensive work outside the home (Einam & Cuskelly, 2002).

Consistent with previous research on the positive contributions of children with disabilities to their families (Blacher & Baker, 2007; Hastings, Beck, & Hill, 2005; Scorgie & Sobsey, 2000), some parents find that their career is enhanced because of issues associated with their child's disability.

> It is actually because of Salma's disability that my career has been enhanced. You get involved, because parents should be educating themselves, and that's where you as a person can grow and benefit. Despite a disability or difficulty, you can strengthen yourself in different ways, and that's how I became a special education teacher. (Brown et al., 2003, p. 221)

A major consideration for family employment can be finding satisfactory child-care arrangements. Mothers of young children with developmental disabilities encounter more difficulty finding quality child care, and it is particularly challenging for mothers of children with more severe disabilities and behavior problems (Carnevale, Rehm, Kirk, & McKeever, 2008; Rosenzweig, Brennan, Huffstutter, & Bradley, 2008). Further, parents of preschool children with developmental disabilities often rely on family members and other in-home caregivers rather than formal care providers (Booth-LaForce & Kelly, 2004). These parents found that there were multiple barriers to accessing formal child care, including the costs of child-care programs, transportation, and lack of access to specialized services and therapy. Moreover, children with disabilities in low-income families received lower quality of care in formal child care than children without disabilities at age 3 (Wall, Kisker, Peterson, Carta, & Jeon, 2006).

Not surprisingly, parents of children with disabilities have a difficult time finding adequate care providers across the life span. Older children with disabilities may need intermittent or continuous support from a formal provider much longer than typically developing children (Parish, 2006). Mothers often state that there are inadequate options for support and supervision of their adolescent children with disabilities.

> I cut back my work to three-quarter time when Evie was in I guess 7th grade . . . I just couldn't find sitters that were reliable . . . it's very stressful, you just never know when a sitter is going to fall through, or you're going to get a call to pick up your child, or you know, same thing if your kid is sick or whatever, you can just leave them at home if they're 14, but I can't leave her at home. There have been so many times that I have missed work because of whatever careprovider arrangements falling through, or just no careproviders. (Parish, 2006, p. 398)

One might assume that mothers who are employed full-time and have children with disabilities experience higher levels of stress than mothers who work part-time or are unemployed. Yet one study found no differences in child demands, family support, or stress based on whether or not the mother was employed (Warfield, 2001). However, the research focused on mothers of 5-year-old children, and most of the children were in school for a portion of the day. Parents whose children needed more assistance with basic caregiving and who had children with problem behavior experienced more absenteeism from work.

Think about how you might support families to find successful child-care arrangements. How could you collaborate with child-care providers to support students with disabilities? And, remember to provide families with general information about financial benefits to which they might be entitled or to at least refer them to a source from which they can get that information. You will learn about these resources in chapter 11.

Daily Care

Another basic function of families consists of meeting their members' physical and health needs. This includes the day-to-day tasks of living: cooking, cleaning, laundry, transportation, obtaining health care when needed, and so forth. A substantial portion of family life is devoted to attending to these needs. Meeting daily needs is one of the significant outputs of family interaction. Family members often work together to carry out their roles and responsibilities in meeting physical and health needs.

Nearly 22% of households have one or more children under 17 with special health care needs (National Survey of Children with Special Health Care Needs, 2005/2006). During the 2000–2001 school year, approximately 292,000 children and youth ages 6 to 21 were identified as having a health impairment. This number had grown to more than 500,000 children and youth by the fall of 2005 (U.S. Department of Education, 2006). A health impairment is any condition that limits strength, vitality, and alertness due to acute or chronic asthma, attention-deficit disorder, diabetes, epilepsy, a heart condition, or other similar conditions (IDEA regulations, codified at 34 Code of Federal Regulations, Sec. 300.7(c)(9)). Health impairments of children, in addition to other types of disabilities, can greatly increase daily caregiving needs (Carnevale et al., 2008; Shattuck & Parish, 2008). Daily care needs may include toileting, bathing, grooming, and medical monitoring. In addition, families of children who are medically fragile may experience crises requiring extraordinary intervention.

These daily care issues frequently manifest themselves in everyday routines such as sleeping and eating. Consider a family whose child has chronic health needs and requires special assistance while eating.

> [My son] was now two and a half years old, was not self-feeding, and was only eating pureed food. We had begun making his diet ourselves and were having to cook separate meals for him because it all had to be pureed and mixed together. We could not separate the food out, or he would scream and refuse to eat . . . The stress this puts on a family is unimaginable. . . . My husband and I would eat when we could and argue on who was going to feed [him], knowing that each mealtime would bring more crying, screaming, and kicking. There were times, I have to admit, that I would go in the shower or outside just to be out of earshot. (Mortorana, Bove, & Scarcelli, 2008, p. 58)

Another significant daily care issue for parents of children with health needs is often dealing with medical equipment, specialized procedures, and medical appointments (Carnevale et al., 2008).

> Yea, getting home late at night and just being able for her to go to bed. You know, normally when we get home late, we still have to connect her tubing machines, we have to fill up the bottles, you know. She can't bathe herself, so I always have to be there for her, where I see my sister's kids . . . they can put themselves to bed, and she can't. (Rehm & Bradley, 2005, p. 814)

In addition to managing the logistical tasks associated with caregiving, families must also deal with health insurance policies (if they have insurance) to access needed services and secure reimbursement of expenses. A national study of more than 2,200 parents of children with special health care needs in 20 states revealed that approximately half reported problems with accessing services, especially home health and mental health services (Krauss, Wells, Gulley, & Anderson, 2001).

> The most important need is more home nursing so that I can get some sleep at night. Insurance companies claim "custodial" care is not covered. She requires "skilled nursing." Her traech needs to be changed often, ventilator alarms throughout the night, etc., yet I must work in order to provide the things she needs. (Krauss et al., 2001, p. 176)

Aside from health issues, some extraordinary care considerations can arise for children with disabilities. Some self-help skills are age related; as children with disabilities grow and develop, most gain in the ability to independently carry out such activities. Daily living skills can be a part of a student's IFSP/IEP if those goals are appropriate for the student's strengths, preferences, and needs. Brothers and sisters can also be collaborators. School-age children can support their brothers or sisters with disabilities to carry out and develop basic self-help skills.

Although some children have a need for greater support with daily living skills, others do not. In fact, children with disabilities can make many positive contributions by helping with housekeeping, yard work, laundry, or the needs of younger siblings.

> Of my three children, the one with autism is my lifesaver when it comes to housework. He believes that everything has a place and belongs in it. His room would pass any army inspection. He organizes drawers and pulls weeds out of the flowerbeds. On the other hand, the clutter and mess in the bedrooms of my normal kids is shameful. When I ask for their help, they consider it an infringement on their social life. (Beach Center, 1999)

Given the increasing number of children who are home alone after school, including those who have disabilities, some schools are teaming up with community organizations to provide self-care instruction for parents and children. The goal of these programs is to prepare children to handle emergencies, prevent accidents and sexual abuse, manage their time, learn leisure skills, and practice good nutrition.

Staying home alone or with other siblings can be particularly challenging for students who experience disabilities that make it more challenging to make quick decisions in threatening circumstances or to use their time in a constructive way. Moreover, students who experience specific health conditions such as asthma, epilepsy, or diabetes need to know how to respond to an emergency situation, as do brothers and sisters and other people who may be available to provide assistance (Eisenberg, 2000; Roberts, 2000).

After-school programs are especially important in low-income neighborhoods where parents are less likely to have money to pay for child care and where neighborhood crime is often higher (Halpern, 2002; Woodland, 2008). As a result of a partnership between Columbus Public Schools and The Ohio State University College of Education, the members of the Mt. Olivet Baptist Church Men's Fellowship donated their time and money to start an after-school program for young, urban at-risk students (Gardner et al., 2001). The program emphasized academic skill instruction, homework completion, recreation, and moral/social skill development. An evaluation of the program outcomes indicated that the students made substantial gains in academic skills.

Socialization

Socialization is vital to overall quality of life for most individuals. Persons of all ages need opportunities to experience both the joys and disappointments of friendships (Meyer, Park, Grenot-Scheyer, Schwartz, & Harry, 1998). Many families experience stress in meeting the socialization needs of their child or youth with disability. In one study, a majority of parents of children, youth, and adults with problem behavior expressed disappointment and a lack of hope about their son's or daughter's development of meaningful friendships (Turnbull & Ruef, 1997). In another study, parents of young children with Asperger's syndrome placed a strong priority on their children's social interactions and friendships (Brewin et al., 2008). In a third study, mothers of school-age children with a wide range of disabilities were interviewed (Overton & Rausch, 2002). One mother in this study noted how her entire family was affected by her son's interactions with other children:

> I think sometimes the parents are more thrilled than the child. Some time ago, if he would get a phone call, I would just be elated. He was kind of like, "Okay." He was happy, but I was just, call my husband. I mean, it's a big thing. (Overton & Rausch, 2002, p. 16)

Many individuals with disabilities have concerns about their lack of friends or the motives that people have in being friends with them. Students with learning disabilities have reported more loneliness, greater isolation, and lower peer acceptance than their peers whose school achievement is in the average range (Jones, Pearl, Van Acker, Farmer, & Rodkin, 2008).

On the issue of motivation for friendship, individuals with disabilities have pointed out that friendship is not always the outcome of relationships where people are paid helpers or when people regard the friendship as a "special friendship" rather than a real one (Van der Klift & Kunc, 2002). Some families and professionals may welcome your encouragement and guidance on developing friendships. Families may welcome collaboration with school personnel because they recognize the importance of teaching social skills in the environments in which these skills are likely to be used:

> She really needs social skills . . . and the problems with doing social skills with kids with Asperger's or other disabilities outside of school time is that you're at home, and you know, what good is doing social skills sitting in the living room with nobody around? (Brewin et al., 2008, p. 248)

Often, families and professionals focus on other important areas of the child's development and unwittingly ignore the social dimensions. One way to address this need is to include socialization goals on students' IEPs. Fortunately, there have been a growing number of studies conducted on social interventions to guide educators in developing meaningful social goals for students (Kroeger, Shultz, & Newsom, 2007; Matson, Matson, & Rivet, 2007; Owen-DeSchryver Carr, Cale, & Blakley-Smith, 2008).

The Circle of Friends approach has been successful with many students with disabilities (Falvey, Forest, Pearpoint, & Rosenberg, 2002; Turnbull, Pereira, & Blue-Banning, 1999). Professionals or parents typically initiate a Circle of Friends by inviting peers to form a support network to provide advice, insight, and opportunities for a child with a disability who would like to have more friends. Members of the circle emphasize the child's strengths and preferences. They and the child work together with an adult to set and implement goals that will increase both the quantity and quality of friendships.

The Circle of Friends approach seems to enhance the social acceptance of children with emotional and behavioral disorders in elementary school classes (Frederickson & Turner, 2003; Frederickson, Warren, & Turner, 2005). However, this approach did not have an effect on the social behaviors of the children who were the focus of the intervention.

Another approach to increase children and youth's social networks is peer modeling. One excellent peer modeling program is called Peer Buddies (Hughes & Carter, 2006). This service-learning program matches a student with a disability with a typically developing student for mutual support and friendship. Hughes and Carter (2006) offer suggestions for implementing a peer buddy program in your school, including ways to gain student interest in the program, effectively match peers and buddies, and prepare students to provide effective and appropriate supports.

You can also connect students through Best Buddies, a nonprofit organization that strives to enchance the lives of people with intellectual disabilities through one-to-one friendships with peers who do not have disabliiies (www .bestbuddies.org). Best Buddies offers four programs: College, High School, Middle School, and Citizens. A study of the College Best Buddies Program found that both college students and individuals with disabilties benefit from their partipation in the program (Hardman & Clark, 2006). The experiences of participants of one high school Best Buddies program were reported in a story that appeared in their high school newsletter.

> [My buddy] and I hang out a lot. We go out for ice cream, we went to a play. I went to his basketball game and he's coming to my orchestra concert, which I'm excited about. It's great to hang out with him. (Lyer & Mitchell, 2009, p. 13)

Some teachers have found that a very successful strategy is to encourage participation in extracurricular activities so that students with disabilities have more opportunities for informal interaction. A different strategy used by an urban school district was to provide a tutor/mentor for students with significant emotional and behavior problems who did not have positive peer interaction (Turnbull et al., 2000). One of the major roles of the tutor/mentor was to help students meet new peers involved in sports and other positive activities.

There are many ways that families and professionals can facilitate relationships (Gordon, Feldman, & Chiriboga, 2005; Taub, 2006):

- Create opportunities. Bring students together so they will have an opportunity to know each other.
- Make accommodations. Adapt the physical environment so individuals with disabilities have a greater opportunity to interact with their peers in a meaningful way.
- Support positive interactions. Recognize when students interact positively and develop friendships and mentoring relationships.

Figure 3.4 highlights research-based strategies that families have used to facilitate friendships between their children with disabilities and children who do not have disabilities (Turnbull, Pereira, & Blue-Banning, 1999). You may share these with the parents of your students.

| FIGURE 3.4 | Friendship strategies. |

Foundational Theme

■ Accepting the child/youth unconditionally (for example, loving the "disabled portion" of the child/youth and perceiving her or him as "whole" rather than "broken")

Creating Opportunities

■ Advocating for inclusion in the neighborhood school (for example, working to have the child/youth attend the neighborhood school rather than be bused to a school across town)
■ Supporting participation in community activities (for example, enrolling the child/youth for a First Communion class and supporting the instructor to engage in comfortable interaction)
■ Initiating and facilitating a Circle of Friends (for example, starting a Circle of Friends to encourage friendships within the school and community settings)
■ Setting sibling-consistent expectations (for example, in light of how siblings call their friends on the phone, encouraging the child/youth and his or her friends to call each other)

Making Interpretations

■ Encouraging others to accept the child/youth (for example, discussing their child's/youth's strengths and needs with others and supporting others to know how to communicate comfortably)
■ Ensuring an attractive appearance (for example, ensuring that the child/youth is dressed and groomed in a way that is likely to draw positive and appropriate attention)

Making Accommodations

■ Advocating for partial participation in community activities (for example, encouraging an instructor of community activities to know how to adapt expectations to enable partial participation in completing them)

Many families believe they don't have the time or energy to facilitate friendships. But you and other individuals involved in the child's life can do that work for and with them by involving general and special education teachers, related service providers, paraprofessionals, family members, community members, and classmates (Calloway, 1999; Meyer et al., 1998; Turnbull, Pereira, & Blue-Banning, 2000). Oftentimes classmates and peers may have some of the best ideas for facilitating friendships in a natural way.

Recreation

Recreation, play, and enjoying leisure time are important aspects of a good life for individuals with disabilities and their families (Mactavish & Schleien, 2004; Mahon, Mactavish, & Bockstael, 2000). Recreation includes sports, games, hobbies, or play that can be done outdoors or indoors as a spectator or a participant; and in an independent, cooperative, or competitive manner. Families' recreation activities tend to involve small combinations of family members in activities such as swimming, walking, or bike riding (Mactavish & Schleien, 2004); outdoor recreation benefits families of children with developmental disabilities (Scholl, McCovy, Rynders, & Smith, 2003).

A family's culture influences its views about the role of recreation and leisure. An African American cultural scholar describes play as necessary for promoting children's well-being:

Play is seen as important for both social (to have friends and fun) and physical (to have a strong body) well-being. In contrast with cultures that push children toward early adulthood, in African-American families there is a belief that a child should be a child; and getting "grown" too soon is frowned on, especially if older family members live in the home or have influence in the family. (Willis, 2004, p. 162)

Other cultures may not emphasize "age-appropriate" play or recreation separate from family members. A Middle Eastern woman describes her perspective on this issue:

Middle Eastern parents, particularly mothers, rarely have social and recreational activities separate from their children. Family gathering, picnics, cinemas, and, to a lesser extent, sports events are among the most common social events in the Middle East; children are usually included in all of them. Most Middle Eastern boys do not start to have activities of their own until after puberty; for unmarried girls, this may come even later. (Sharifzadeh, 2004, p. 334)

Depending on the nature of the child's disability, the family's recreational role may be expanded, unaffected, or curtailed (Schleien & Heyne, 1998). Some children and youth have special gifts or interests related to sports, athletics, or games (e.g., chess or bridge), and a significant portion of family time may be devoted to supporting their interests and involvement. The priority given to recreation may be a positive experience not only for the child with disabilities but also for the family's overall interaction. One parent spoke of how her family was affected when her older daughter, who had a severe reading disability, took up swimming:

When she showed an interest in swimming, I encouraged her. She took swimming lessons at the YWCA, and we all started swimming a lot as a family. Now she swims on a team for the city during the summer, and next year she's decided to try out for the swim team at her high school. She has a lot of confidence in this area. She swims circles around most of her friends and all of her family! But I'm a lot better swimmer today than I would have been without her influence. (Beach Center, 1999)

Some families' recreation is curtailed because of the nature of their child's disability, the unavailability of community resources, disapproving public reactions to their son or daughter, or general lack of accommodations. Families have experienced substantial limitations in recreational activities outside the home such as eating in a restaurant, taking a vacation, and shopping (Jackson, Traub, & Turnbull, 2008; Rehm & Bradley, 2005; Potvin, Prelock, & Snider, 2008). Parents of children who are deaf have avoided community playgrounds and restaurants that tended to have too much background noise (Jackson et al., 2008). One single-parent mother spoke of how she avoided the negative reaction of strangers to her child's disability:

> I go out less. I try to bother the others as little as possible . . . They made faces. They got mad. Because they don't understand about a disabled child. They get upset and they think she must be dumb, or he must be stupid and I try to avoid this. (McHatton, 2007, pp. 244–245)

Recreational activities can often require a great deal of planning for families of children with disabilities. Planning can help ensure that all family members have a good time. However, for some families, the time needed to plan activities may limit the family's spontaneity (Mactavish & Schleien, 2004).

> I am always aware of things in the environment that set my son off, which takes a lot of planning and thinking ahead before I go anywhere with him. We can never just pick up and leave. (Hutton & Caron, 2005, p. 186)

Family vacations can be particularly daunting for families of children who may have medical or behavioral issues. For example, a mother of a 9-year-old spoke of her hesitation to fly on an airplane with her child because of the likelihood that her child would need a change of clothes during the flight (Rehm & Bradley, 2005). Family vacations can also bring families great joy. Sometimes the experience of a family traveling together is well worth the effort it takes to make it happen.

Families and professionals alike have sponsored "special populations" recreation programs rather than include children and youth with disabilities in typical community opportunities. A mother of a daughter with an intellectual disability (mental retardation) shared how she purposely abandoned special programs in favor of inclusive ones:

> A long time ago I stopped looking at newspaper listings of special programs. . . . Now I just notice what Kathryn

might like. All kinds of courses are given by community schools, YMCAs, or churches. Grandparents and teenagers, beginners, or those with some familiarity with the subject all take the same course. Though there may be beginning, intermediate, or advanced levels, nobody would notice or care if someone took the same course several times. For most of us . . . taking enough time is more important than special techniques. (Bennett, 1985, p. 171)

Consistent with this mother's philosophy, many parents and professionals emphasize natural learning opportunities that occur as part of family, neighborhood, and community routines and traditions (Dunst, Bruder, Trivette, Humby, Raab, & McLean, 2001; Dunst, Hamby, Trivette, Raab, & Bruder, 2000; Dunst, Trivette, Hamby, & Bruder, 2006). Many recreational activities provide excellent opportunities for children and families to socialize, learn important skills, and build social networks.

- Family outings—shopping, going to restaurants, going to friends' houses.
- Play activities—playgrounds, ball fields, gyms.
- Community activities—fairs, libraries, recreational centers.
- Recreation activities—swimming, softball, horseback riding.
- Children's attractions—petting zoos, parks, pet stores.
- Art/entertainment activities—music activities, art centers, children's theater.

Leaders in early intervention also advocate for a natural learning orientation:

- Identifying the settings that most interest a child and family.
- Identifying the learning opportunities that are most consistent with the child's strengths and preferences and that provide a source of strong motivation.
- Providing supports and services from the early intervention program to enable the child and family to be successful in that setting.
- Encouraging the family to provide naturally occurring learning opportunities in the same settings.

Sometimes it is necessary to use adaptations to facilitate a child's participation in naturally occurring activities at home, school, and in the community. Assistive technology—the use of off-the-shelf, adapted, or specially made devices—enlarges a student's opportunities for recreation and play (Judge & Parette, 1998). However, parents underutilize assistive technology (Dugan, Campbell, & Wilcox, 2006), sometimes choosing low-tech, off-shelf toys for their child with disabilities even when high-tech toys were available to them (Hamm, Mistrett, & Ruffino, 2006). (You will learn more about strategies for increasing a family's use of assistive devices for their children with disabilities in chapter 12.)

One approach to facilitating a child's participation in activities and routines that includes both environmental changes and assistive technology is called adaptive interventions (Campbell, Milbourne, & Wilcox, 2008). For example, you can adapt the environment by repositioning furniture to allow greater mobility or you can use adaptive equipment, such as a stander—a device that supports a student to stand in an upright position when the student cannot do so independently.

Leisure and recreation should be an important part of each child's curriculum; as you will learn in chapter 6, the federal special education law, Individuals with Disabilities Education Act, provides that recreation, including therapeutic recreation, is a "related service" to which a student is entitled if it is necessary for the student to benefit from special education (20 U.S.C. Sec. 1402(26)). So, you will want to find out from families what hobbies and interests they and their child particularly enjoy and where in the community they would especially like to pursue these activities. Then you can consider how to teach the skills the student needs to participate successfully or how to adapt the recreation setting and equipment to foster the student's participation. As a student participates in various recreation and leisure activities, the student acquires greater self-esteem and the family's caregiving responsibilities may diminish.

Education

Families generally place a strong emphasis on education. Within the European American culture, education is typically seen as the key to success in employment, financial, and quality-of-life opportunities (Hanson, 2004). A similar perspective appears in this Chinese proverb:

> If you are planning for a year, sow rice; if you are planning for a decade, plant trees; if you are planning for a lifetime, educate people. (Chan & Lee, 2004, p. 253)

Families from diverse cultural and linguistic backgrounds often encounter educational and social barriers in attaining equal opportunities for their children (Kalyanpur & Harry, 1999; National Research Council, 2001). In one study, researchers interviewed professionals on child study teams in nine schools who were responsible for determining whether students who were English language learners were eligible for special education services. The researchers concluded:

> We are very concerned about the pervasive negative attitude toward parents and the lack of effort to build on family strengths. At times, school personnel were barely able to conceal a distinct contempt, which seemed to be based on a combination of racial and socioeconomic stereotyping, along with the tendency to base a view of a family on one piece of negative information. This tendency was observed in teams of various ethnicities, with ethnic minority school personnel being just as likely as their White counterparts to denigrate families. Though there were notable exceptions to this pattern, in general parents were marginalized and their input undervalued. In addition, this negativity toward parents actually put some children at greater risk of special education placement. (Klingner & Harry, 2006, p. 2277)

Parents of children with disabilities are often highly involved in their child's education. A study of parents of middle and high school age students with disabilities found that 82% of the families regularly talk to their children about school, 75% help their children with homework at least once a week, and 93% report that they participate in at least one school-based activity (Newman, 2005a). According to this study, parents' involvement in and out of school equaled and at times exceeded the involvement of parents of their peers in the general population.

A second analysis, which included parents of both elementary and secondary students with disabilities, explored parents' satisfaction with their child's schooling (Newman, 2005b). Most parents of children with disabilities reported that they were satisfied with their child's schooling, although parents of secondary students tended to be less satisfied than parents of elementary students. In addition, parents of students with disabilities were less satisfied with their child's schooling than parents of students in general education across all grade levels.

Throughout this book, you will learn about families' roles in meeting their children's educational needs. Here we will emphasize the importance of maintaining balance in family functions rather than overemphasizing education to the detriment of other functions. In chapter 4, we will describe two educational tasks that many families assume at four different life cycle stages. One of the fundamental premises of a family systems approach is the importance of maintaining balance in carrying out family roles.

As we will discuss in chapter 5, professionals sometimes emphasize the role of parents as teachers or tutors. That emphasis is appropriate if it is consistent with a family's values, priorities, and available time. If it is not, the differences in the focus at school, other service agencies, and home can impair the development of trusting partnerships. Many parents and students with disabilities respond negatively to professional overemphasis on educational needs. Professionals should remember that educational needs are only one of eight functions that families must address. As Maddux and Cummings (1983) warned:

> If academic learning is required in both the home and the school, a child who has difficulty learning gets very little relief. The home ceases to be a haven from scholastic pressures. Imagine how most of us would feel if the most frustrating, least enjoyable, and most difficult thing about our work were waiting for us when we came home each day. (p. 30)

Beware of the "fix it" approach where children and youth with disabilities are almost continuously placed in quasi-teaching situations by well-intentioned teachers, family, and friends. These perpetual educational efforts to make the child "better" may have a negative impact on the child's self-esteem. Children and families seek acceptance and normalcy; not all activities need to be viewed as educational:

> Sam, as a 4-year-old, has a life almost as scheduled as mine—and I'm a lawyer. Needless to say, he's exhausted by everything else that he's programmed into . . . so although we think that activities that help him work on basic skills are beneficial. . . . just as important to use, and probably more important to him, is that he gets to escape back to the life of a 4-year-old. (Mactavish & Schleien, 2004, p. 134)

Professionals and families need to be keenly aware of a child and family's perspective on disability and educational programming. Although participation and learning are shared goals, each individual holds their own perspective on their meaning (Hammel, Magasi, Heinemann, Whiteneck, Bogner, & Rodriguez, 2008). Taking the time to learn about a family's belief, values, and everyday life ensures that you develop strategies to support the family's daily routine (Bernheimer & Weisner, 2007). Adults with disabilities can be valued mentors, role models, and consultants in assisting professionals, families, and children and youth with disabilities to gain a vital and genuine perspective (Klein & Kemp, 2004).

:: TIME AS A FACTOR IN MEETING FAMILY FUNCTIONS

Undoubtedly, time is a major issue for all families. Approximately two thirds of all employed parents with children under 18 report that they do not have enough time to meet their children's needs, that they often leave their children unattended at home, and that they rely on their children to be occupied by watching television (Families and Work Institute, 2002). Given that this report is mainly from parents who have children without disabilities, what impact do you think having a child with a disability has on a family's time?

In chapter 2, we discussed how mothers and fathers distribute household duties. Traditionally, attending to the daily care needs of family members has been "women's work," and female caring roles often expand when the child has a disability (Parish, 2006; Traustadottir, 1995). Mothers have expressed a commitment to maintain an ordinary family life by simply being able to carry out their daily routines. Rather than assessing the severity of their child's disability according to traditional standards, they more frequently interpret severity according to the limitations and constraints placed on family life. As one mother described, "Once he's home [after school], I have to watch him continually just to keep him and [his younger sister] safe . . . it's exhausting. I simply can't deal with anything else" (Benson, Karlof, & Siperstein, 2008, p. 58).

Family members of children with disabilities see their responsibilities extending beyond those of daily caregiving.

> No, you are not targeting him to sit at home, you're targeting him to have jobs, and a home, and a life, and friends, and just getting that done is full-time and depressing work. . . . there's no one else can give that to . . . it goes beyond just hiring help, it goes to the work of . . . creating lives for these kids that are as big as they can be, or as full as they can be. Who is going to do that work other than mom? (Parish, 2006, p. 400)

What role do you have in helping to realize a family's dreams for their child? How can you advocate for the family and child? Read the Together We Can box on the next page and think about how the professionals in Betsy's life helped her and her family realize their dreams.

The impact of having a child with a disability is unique to each family. It all depends on the family's characteristics, interactions, functions, and life span issues. Clearly, a significant factor is the family's level of adaptability, as you learned in chapter 2. Consider two families—one that maintains a very strict schedule and is quite frustrated by any change, and another that has a balanced level of adaptability characterized by flexible rules and routines. If these two families had children with identical characteristics, the family with more balanced adaptability probably would have less difficulty carrying out family functions than the family whose roles and routines are strictly implemented.

TOGETHER WE CAN

Betsy's Journey to Independence

My name is Betsy. I am a 25-year-old woman. I live in my own apartment, which is great because it gives me the privacy I want and a place to express myself. I can relax in my comfortable black leather lounge chair while I watch my favorite TV shows or pretend I am a rock star. By the way, I have Down syndrome.

From the time I was born, my parents had a vision for me like they had for my four siblings. The vision was that I would have a happy childhood—growing, playing, and going to school with the other kids in my neighborhood. When I was two-and-a-half-years-old, I went to the nursery school around the corner from my house. Now we call this "Inclusive Education," but at the time it just seemed like the right thing to do.

By the end of middle school, I had a "Circle of Friends" that was made up of family, teachers, classmates, and friends. I loved when we met because I could share my dreams for my future. The Circle would help me figure out how I could make those dreams a reality. One time in eighth grade, I was asked to speak at a conference about my dreams for the future. I discovered I liked speaking to groups of people and soon I was being asked to share my experiences with others. I have traveled as far as San Francisco; Baltimore; Seattle; and Washington, DC, giving keynote addresses and participating in conferences. I tell people about how successful it can be to live an inclusive life—in your own school and community—when you have people who support and believe in you.

High school was great. I had some wonderful educators who believed in inclusive education and helped me with the transition from school to adult life. I had great support when I was in general education classes, like aides, books on tape, peer buddies, and adapted tests. Also during high school, I had an amazing teacher who helped facilitate the vision my family and I had of being fully included into all aspects of school and community life. My "inclusion facilitator" helped me explore many jobs in my community to find out what kind of work I liked to do. I learned how to plan meals and grocery shop—though to tell you the truth, I really don't like to cook. If my budget would allow, I would eat out or order food in most of the time.

How grateful I am that my parents never lost their inclusive vision that has led me to a life of independence. I am also grateful to all the fine people who listened to what I felt was important in my life and continue to support me on my journey. It is a great journey, and I am enjoying my life.

Take Action!

- Make sure you understand and support a family's vision for their child.
- Consider how, in partnership with a family, you can:
  - Support families to use community resources for recreation and learning.
  - Facilitate friendships among children.
  - Modify instruction so that each student can learn.
  - Teach students to use self-advocacy skills.

Source: Adapted from: Smith, B. Journey toward independence: how a young woman with down syndrome became an independent adult, Inclusive Communities, PBS Parents. Retrieved from http://www.pbs.org/parents/inclusivecommunities/independence.html

There are at least four barriers facing families who want to use their time efficiently and effectively (Brotherson & Goldstein, 1992, p. 518):

- The inability of professionals to coordinate their activities among themselves
- The overwhelming number of tasks parents were asked by professionals to complete
- The lack of local and accessible services
- A lack of flexible and family-centered scheduling of services

This father refers to many of these barriers in his description of the demands on his family's time:

> I attend all of the meetings for my son. There has been an enormous amount of paperwork and hours and hours of therapy each week—not to mention a lot of travel involved, which is stressful on our family because it disrupts home schedules and meal times. Our time and our home is not our own because we are always going to meetings or having people in our home. (Hutton & Caron, 2005, p. 185)

You can make a significant contribution to the quality of family life by helping to remove time barriers and by facilitating the effective and efficient use of time. For example, be certain that you are teaching naturally occurring activities that are meaningful to children and families and consider the family's resources when scheduling appointments.

One of the greatest lessons you can derive from understanding family functions is to understand how busy family life is. Educational issues are only one of eight family functions. Families may or may not be able to devote the time to educational issues that you, as an educational professional, might deem desirable. As you pursue your career and your own family life, it is likely that you will experience these same time crunches.

Particularly for families who have a child with a severe disability, it is critical to recognize that they are dealing with lifelong issues that require the endurance of a marathon runner, not a sprinter. Professionals, however, often are tempted to urge the parents to make substantial investments of time over the short term (like a sprinter) to enhance what the child might be able to learn. "Parents think of time as daily routine, they also see the care of their child as an ongoing, life long, ever-evolving commitment, not a short-term education or therapeutic contact. This is a significant difference in time orientation that should be highlighted for professional understanding of families" (Brotherson & Goldstein, 1992, p. 523).

REVISITING LANZ AND XENIA POWELL

Think back to the Xenia Powell and her five different hats. Imagine wearing so many different hats with so many different responsibilities and then imagine completing all the tasks associated with each of the family functions you have learned about in this chapter.

Now think about how Xenia and Lanz function as a family and how each of the functions also acts to satisfy and nurture them. Xenia and Lanz show each other affection and support each other's self-esteem. They draw significant support from their faith and their extended family spiritually, economically, and socially. They have clear activities they enjoy—including relaxing at home! When Lanz requires support with managing his time, Xenia is able to provide this for him even if it means just saying, "Lanz, it's time to go do your homework." And, just as one of the purposes of family functions is to transfer knowledge of how to perform these functions to younger family members, consistent with the cultural values and traditions of their family, Lanz has learned to value education and both he and Xenia will soon be off to college!

Xenia and Lanz have found a way to perform the tasks associated with their family functions in ways that are consistent with their family characteristics. Now, how they have performed these tasks has changed over time. The things Xenia focused on to build her and Lanz's self-esteem were very different when he was a young child. Now that Lanz is reaching adulthood, she celebrates the value he places on education and his being accepted to college. In the past, however, she celebrated him just getting through the school year.

Now think about how you, as a professional, could impact Xenia and Lanz as they perform their family functions. If Xenia did not have all of her "hats" and the knowledge that comes with each "hat," how might this have impacted the Powell's family functions and your role in supporting all the functions? But given all of Xenia's "hats," what could you do as a professional to support the efficient and effective use of time? Think about all the time that Xenia spent advocating for Lanz. Always keep in mind that families, like the Powells, are running a marathon, and you are fortunate to be able to run one leg of the marathon with them—but this does not mean you have to sprint! If you try to force them to sprint, this will overwhelm them and limit them in successfully completing the rest of the marathon.

SUMMARY

Families exist to meet the individual and collective needs of their members. The tasks they perform to meet those needs are influenced by families' culture and are referred to as family functions; in a family systems framework, they are the *outputs*. There are eight categories of family system functions or outputs:

- **Affection.** verbal and physical affection, and unconditional love
- **Self-esteem.** self-image and feelings about yourself
- **Spirituality.** beliefs that shape a family's understanding of the meaning of life
- **Economics.** the impact of disability on a family's financial resources and the management of those resources
- **Daily care.** the tasks of daily living, such as cooking, cleaning, transportation, and securing access to health care
- **Socialization.** making friendships for the family and its member with a disability
- **Recreation.** engaging in leisure activities, either alone or with others
- **Education.** securing a free, appropriate (individualized) public education

LINKING CONTENT TO YOUR LIFE

As you think about your own experiences in carrying out the eight family functions, bear in mind that the families with whom you develop partnerships may attend to their functions in ways that may not be the ones you have used or would recommend. All families are different.

- **Affection.** As you were growing up, who were the members of your family who expressed verbal and physical affection to you? Was the exchange of affection in your family excessive, about the right level, or insufficient? How do your own experiences affect your beliefs about the role of families in expressing affection?
- **Spirituality.** What are your religious/spiritual values and beliefs? How do you rely on religious/spiritual values and beliefs when you face particularly challenging situations? How do your values and beliefs influence the extent to which you are comfortable conversing with families about their spirituality?
- **Daily care.** Have you ever encountered a situation with families of children with disabilities in which you felt that, given similar circumstances, you would not be able to handle the daily care requirements? What supports and services might be provided to enable a family to carry out their daily care responsibilities in a reasonable and effective way?
- **Education.** What one or two educational activities or experiences helped improve family functions within your own family? How might the education that you provide to students also enable them to be more successful with one or more family functions?

CHAPTER 4

Family Life Cycle

LANZ AND XENIA POWELL

Xenia Powell grew up in Chicago, on the rough and tumble "south side," and attended schools there. Bright enough to be admitted to one of the nation's most prestigious all-black institutions of higher education, Howard University in Washington, DC, but too poor to attend, she accepted a scholarship offer from Huron University in Huron, South Dakota.

"Attending Huron totally changed me. It gave me a different outlook on life. I thought chaos was normal, all the noises of the city, the police-car sirens, the things that don't work. But Huron was calm, and the calm was really weird. I didn't even know that calm was supposed to be the way things should be. I needed that calm. Chicago was just too much for me."

Just too much for her, indeed. "I was a trouble-maker, especially in junior high school, there on the south side. Always in trouble."

Then there was high school, her realization she was bright and her blunted ambition to attend Howard. And then there was Huron. And while she was there, she had Lanz.

"Lanz became my constant, my steady in life. Without him, I could have had a breakdown." Xenia does not explain that last statement, but it is clear Lanz made a huge difference as she became a teacher.

"Because of Lanz, I see what's not being done for my students. Without him, I would have judged my students' parents; I would have seen their faults."

And she might have given up on many of her students, but she didn't. No more than she gave up on Lanz, now headed to college.

"Some students don't accept me as a parent. Some reject me. Some are hungry for me to be like a parent. I tell them, Lanz is my child. And you are too. I'll call you on Saturday morning, I'll knock on your door, I'll call you on your cell phone and here's my number so you can call me."

What motivates Xenia? What makes her want to wear all those hats?

"I'm attracted to the neediest kids. This is Lanz's gift to me. It's my assignment. I wouldn't have chosen the at-risk and special ed kids. But God gave me Lanz and the equipment to do that job, and so I'm doing it the best I can."

think about it

- If you had to identify Xenia's life cycle, what stages would you identify?
- What life cycle stages has Lanz experienced?
- What stage lies ahead for him?
- If you were a teacher trying to partner with a mother like Xenia, what would you learn from knowing her life cycle and her characterizations of each cycle?

:: INTRODUCTION

In chapter 1, you learned about families' characteristics. In chapter 2, you learned about families' interactions. In chapter 3, you learned about families' functions. These chapters emphasized that each family is unique and each is a system—whatever happens to one member affects all members. You have learned nearly everything you need to know about the family system theory. There is, however, one final part of the family systems theory you need to learn. It relates to how a family changes across its life cycle (Carter & McGoldrick, 2005). The life cycle element of the family systems theory is the focus of this chapter.

The first three elements of the family systems theory—family characteristics (chapter 1), interactions (chapter 2), and functions (chapter 3)—provide only a snapshot of what should more accurately be portrayed as a full-length motion picture. All families transition through different stages as members are born, grow up, leave home, bring in new members through marriage or other permanent relationships, retire, and die. Families may also experience unexpected or sudden changes that drastically alter their lives; these include divorce, death, separation by military service or other job-related relocations, job transfers, unemployment, immigration, or natural catastrophes. Whether the change is expected and "on cycle," or unexpected and "off cycle," the family changes. And so do its characteristics (chapter 1), interactions (chapter 2), and functions (chapter 3). In Figure 4.1, you can see how the four components of the family system, including family life cycle changes, relate to each other.

:: FAMILY LIFE CYCLE THEORY

Family life cycle theory explains how a family changes over time (Carter & McGoldrick, 1999; Rodgers & White, 1993). The theory is that each family experiences certain predictable stages. As a family moves from one stage to the next, it enters an interim phase known as transition. For example, families typically experience a childbirth and child-raising stage. The parents learn to care for the child and understand what parenthood entails, and the child typically learns how to talk, walk, and explore the environment of home and perhaps preschool.

Leading family theorists have identified six typical individual life cycle states; not unexpectedly, these stages vary somewhat within and across cultures (Carter & McGoldrick, 2005):

- Leaving home as single young adults
- Marriage and the new couple
- Families with young children
- Families with adolescents
- Launching children
- Families in later life

A family's life cycle encompasses the interactions among the changes that each member of the family experiences (Carter & McGoldrick, 2005; Olson, 1988). For example, a father who was simultaneously caring for his 81-year-old mother, 21-year-old son with a developmental disability, and 13-year-old daughter while also working 50 hours a week commented: "I felt whipsawed. No matter how much I did for one generation, there was always

FIGURE 4.1 Family systems framework: emphasis on family life cycle.

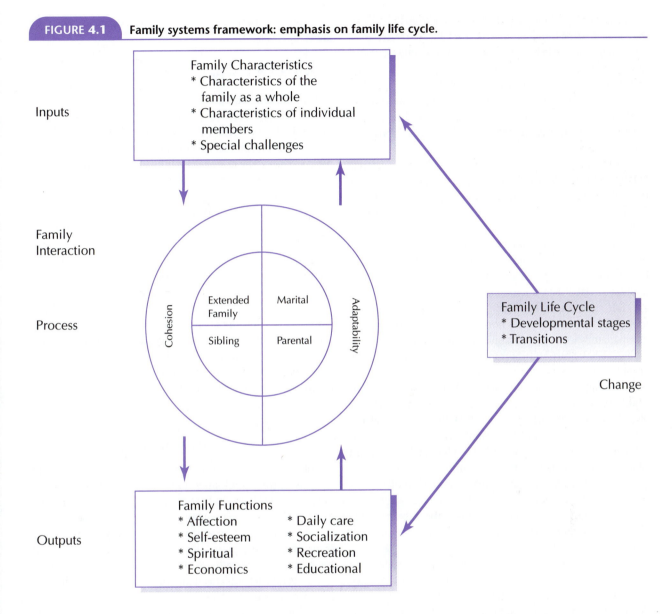

another whose needs cried out to me with such fervor that I felt I couldn't fulfill all of them. In a sense, my mother had become my son, because she had the greater disability and because he was becoming more independent" (Beach Center, 2000).

The functions the family and its individual members must accomplish at each stage occur when a family is fully inside a life cycle stage; they have "arrived," as it were. But to "arrive," a family must first transition from one stage to another. Transitions are the periods between stages; they are times when the family adjusts its interactions and roles to prepare for the next developmental stage (Carter & McGoldrick, 2005; Rodgers &

White, 1993). For example, a transition occurs when an infant leaves the birth and early childhood stage and enters the childhood stage. With any transition come changes in the following:

- *Family characteristics.* For example, the personal characteristics of the child change.
- *Family interactions.* For example, the parental subsystem changes as the child matures and communicates with the parents in a different way.
- *Family functions.* For example, the child spends more time in school and on homework and contributes more to daily tasks.

When the transition is complete—and the transition itself may take a while—the family has reached—"arrived" at—the next stage. The family then begins performing tasks and having interactions appropriate for that stage.

Transition periods are usually briefer than the stages to which they relate. But because transitions can result in confusion and conflict, transitions are almost always times of heightened stress (Carter & McGoldrick, 2005; White & Klein, 2008).

Using life cycle theory to understand family change (1) highlights similar family rhythms over time and (2) illustrates the continuity of a family's life. As you partner with a family, you may learn that they have a long-term commitment to school and community inclusion; in turn, you will understand why they want certain kinds of services for their child—namely, to assure integration in school and community. They have a history of commitment; they are not likely to change it; and you need to take it into account.

Life cycle theory has been criticized for not sufficiently taking into account varying norms across different cultural groups, family forms, and disability-related factors (Rodgers & White, 1993; Turnbull, Summers, & Brotherson, 1986). Some ethnic groups, for example, value interdependence among family members; for them, independence, as exemplified by an adult child's leaving the family home and living elsewhere may be non-negotiable (Kalyanpur & Harry, 1999; Turnbull & Turnbull, 1996). That fact alone will influence the family's approach to the child's education and plans for the child to transition to adulthood.

In remarried families, particularly those with older children from a previous marriage, several life cycle stages may occur simultaneously as children from the first marriage approach adulthood while the newly married couple gives birth to or adopts their own children.

In this chapter, you will learn about the four life cycle stages during which the family is most likely to experience contact with schools: birth and early childhood, childhood, adolescence, and young adulthood. You will also learn about the transition from one stage to another and how disability can affect the family's ability to adjust to change. As you read, keep in mind the energy and persistence that families need as they run the marathon of life cycle stages and face the hurdles of life cycle transitions.

:: LIFE CYCLE STAGES

To illustrate how family functions and priorities change as the family moves through its life cycle, we will highlight two educational issues many families encounter during each of the four life style stages. In highlighting the educational issues, we teach you about one of the eight family functions (chapter 3)—education—across each of the four life span stages.

Birth and Early Childhood

During the early childhood years, the typical family is likely to be intensely focused on its inner workings (Carter & McGoldrick, 2005). A childless couple probably has explored the parameters of their relationship. The couple also has begun to blend the norms of their two families of origin (their own parents and siblings) into one and to respond to each other's needs.

When the couple has a child, the couple's attention shifts from the two of them and their families of origin to their child and their new roles as parents. Even as the couple faces the task of nurturing their child, they also must learn how to meet their needs as a couple; they now have two "subsystems" to nourish: the marital and the parental.

A family that has a member with a disability can confront a number of educational challenges during this early parenthood stage. Three of these challenges are (1) discovering and coming to terms with the disability and its implications, (2) participating in early childhood services, and (3) parenting to foster self-determination.

Discovering and Coming to Terms with Disability

Infants with severe and multiple disabilities, in contrast to those with mild disabilities, typically are identified at birth as having special needs. In several states, screening currently exists for 30 or more metabolic and genetic diseases at birth (Bailey, Skinner, & Sparkman, 2003). Early identification sometimes occurs prenatally, with fetal therapy possible in the first 3 or 4 months of pregnancy (Schonberg & Tifft, 2002). With such advanced identification, some families use advanced diagnostic information to prepare for the birth of a child with special needs and others choose to terminate the pregnancy (Bell & Stoneman, 2000; Roberts, Stough, & Parrish, 2002).

Recent advances in genetic testing have made detection of some conditions, including Down syndrome, possible and safer earlier in a woman's pregnancy (Benn, 2002; Benn & Chapman, 2009). In 2007 the American College of Obstetricians and Gynecologists recommended for the first time that all women, regardless of age, be screened for Down syndrome (ACOG, 2007).

Controversy surrounds the merits of expanded prenatal testing. On the one hand, early detection enables parents to access psychological or therapeutic supports earlier and is consistent with families' preferences for information (Bailey,

Skinner, & Warren, 2005). On the other hand, many professionals and family members have argued that expanding newborn screening can be problematic: if the fetus is correctly diagnosed to have a genetic-linked disability, there may be pressure to terminate the pregnancy. The pressure itself, and certainly the abortion of the fetus, devalues the child solely because of disability and can lead to reduced funding for research and services for individuals with disabilities (Benn & Chapman, 2009; Place, 2008). The Change Agents Build Capacity box below casts a different light on the matter of devaluation; it is a joint statement from the American College of Obstetrics and Gynecology, the Down Syndrome Society, and the National Down Syndrome Congress affirming the value of children with Down syndrome.

Some children will be diagnosed with a disability during their early childhood years. Often, parents or other adults will recognize atypical behaviors in their children that lead them to seek further screening or assessment. A study of parents of children with autism and parents of children with other developmental disabilities found that the first concern of both

groups of parents was their child's language development (Coonrod & Stone, 2004). Interestingly, parents of children diagnosed with autism in this study spoke of concerns about their child's social deficits only when asked specifically about these behaviors, suggesting that service providers may need to elicit information about various aspects of a particular disability by asking parents specific questions.

Regardless of whether the diagnosis occurs prenatally, at birth, or during the early years, some professionals have argued that families may experience a grief cycle. These professionals compare the "disability grief cycle" to the "death grief cycle"—the so-called stages that family members encounter after a beloved family member dies. The "disability" and "death" grief cycles arguably include shock, denial, guilt and anger, shame and depression, and acceptance (Kübler-Ross, 1969; Leff & Walizer, 1992; Moses, 1983; Vyas, 1983). Largely based on clinical case studies in the 1960s and 1970s, some research has concluded that mothers of children with disabilities do experience grief solely because of their child's disability. That research, however, has been described

---

CHANGE AGENTS BUILD CAPACITY
Genetics, Disability, and Public Policy

You read in chapter 2 that controversy surrounds the procedures that enable physicians to diagnose a disability in a fetus and the decisions that parents legally may make concerning a course of action after the diagnosis. Like other "hot" social controversies, this one has entered the public arena, with parents, physicians, and policy makers acting together to build capacities for families and physicians.

In 2008, Congress enacted Public Law 110-374, the so-called Kennedy-Brownback Act (formally titled Prenatally and Postnatally Diagnosed Conditions Awareness Act). It authorizes the federal public health service to assist physicians and women by providing them accurate information about the physical, developmental, educational, and psychosocial outcomes for the babies, to strengthen networks to support the women, and to ensure that they receive up-to-date and accurate information about the accuracy of medical tests that detect prenatally diagnosable conditions.

Soon after Congress enacted the Kennedy-Brownback Act, the Down Syndrome Society, National Down Syndrome Congress, and American College of Obstetricians and Gynecologists issued a joint statement (2009) affirming the value of the lives of individuals with prenatally diagnosable conditions; disavowing withholding and withdrawal of

treatment solely because of the child's disability; and calling on federal, state, and nongovernmental agencies to support the children and their families.

Take Action!

- Remember that, although genes are destiny, they are not the entirety of destiny. Public policy and professional practice also shape families' and individuals' destiny.
- When you are working with a family whose unborn child has or may have a prenatally diagnosable disability, give them a copy of the Kennedy-Brownback law and refer them to the department of health in the state where they live. You may download a copy of the law by googling "Kennedy-Brownback Act of 2007."
- If the family has an unborn child with Down syndrome, give them a copy of the statement and refer them to a state or local chapter of either the Down Syndrome Society or the National Down Syndrome Conference. You may download a copy by going to the websites of these two organizations.

as lacking empirical rigor (Blacher, 1984a, 1984b). That is not to say, however, that some parents do not experience grief, for indeed some do (Moses, 1983; Vyas, 1983).

Although some research continues to emphasize the disability grief cycle that families undergo, other research questions whether parents must pass through sequential stages to reach the stage commonly known as "acceptance" (Blacher & Hatton, 2001; Gallagher, Fialka, Rhodes, & Arceneaux, 2001; Hastings & Taunt, 2002). Clinical descriptions of parental grief also have failed to document how and what "grieving" parents were initially told about the nature of their child's disability (Lee, 1994).

One study interviewed parents about how the prenatal diagnosis of Down syndrome was shared with them. Six of the ten mothers interviewed felt that their obstetrician or obstetrical nurse communicated negative perspectives of Down syndrome when discussing the diagnosis with them (Helm, Miranda, & Angoff-Chedd, 1998). One mother said the obstetrician commented, "This child will not accomplish anything. Everyone [in my practice] has aborted" (Helm et al., 1998, p. 57).

The same mothers discussed how professionals should deliver information to parents who undergo prenatal testing. They suggested that professionals (1) discuss test results with parents in person, (2) avoid making judgments or assumptions about the parents' decision regarding the pregnancy, (3) provide current and accessible information to families, and (4) recognize the parents' feelings without displaying pity (Helm et al., 1998). This advice is just as applicable to families hearing a diagnosis after the child is born.

In one study, parents shared their interpretations of "being in denial." One of the authors, the parent of a child with a disability, described her husband's reaction when she asked him to recall his early impressions of their son, who is now a teenager. Her husband remembered a much more optimistic view of their child's development than she did. "She asked her husband if during those early years, he was 'in denial.' He paused and replied, 'No, I wasn't in denial. I was in hope'" (Gallagher, Fialka, Rhodes, & Arceneaux, 2001, p. 14). Think about how you can work to affirm parents' dreams and hopes for their child.

A study comparing the experiences of parents of children diagnosed with Down syndrome in 1970 and in 2003 found that mothers' feelings of guilt and stress have become less prevalent in recent years. Further, mothers tend to receive greater support and respect than in the past (Lenhard et al., 2007). However, mothers in the 2003 cohort also reported a stronger sense of segregation in their communities because of their child with disabilities.

The effect of the initial diagnosis on families from diverse (non-European/American) cultures is not yet well understood. However, cultural beliefs and values may impact how families react to having a child with a disability. For example, in Native American culture:

> When a family member has a disability or illness, traditional ceremonies are conducted to begin the healing process and to protect the individual and the rest of the home from further harm. For that reason, an Indian family may want to complete traditional ceremonies before they become involved in a regimen recommended by physicians or other service providers. (Joe & Malach, 2004, p. 125)

Developmental milestones also have cultural variations. In a European American culture, beginning to walk is considered a major milestone, whereas a first laugh, first hunt, first dance, or ear piercing may have similar priority for some Native American tribes (Joe & Malach, 2004; Sipes, 1993).

In chapter 9, you will learn strategies for informing parents about the presence of a disability and working to foster a trusting partnership. At this point, just remember that discovering the disability and coming to terms with it are part of a major life cycle task for many families, especially during the early childhood years. The task is no less significant for families when their children are older. That is often the case for families whose children have learning and behavioral challenges that are not precisely identified until they are in elementary school and unsuccessfully face the demands that their schools impose on them.

Participation in Early Childhood Services. Learning about the child's disability is the first of a lifelong series of interactions families will have with professionals. Families with young children whose disabilities have already been identified are likely to enter the world of early intervention and preschool education. Early intervention is often described as "Part C programs." As you will learn in chapter 6, Part C of the Individuals with Disabilities Education Act (IDEA) authorizes services for infants and toddlers, ages birth to 3 (sometimes called "zero to three"). In 2007, approximately 321,000 infants and toddlers were served in early intervention programs nationwide. Approximately 58% of children served are White, 23% Hispanic, 13% Black, 5% Asian/Pacific Islander, and 1% American Indian/Alaskan Native (U.S. Department of Education, 2006).

Part C requires states to provide early intervention services in the child's natural environments. These include the child's home, a community-based setting with children who do not have disabilities, or a community-based setting that serves only (or primarily) children with disabilities (20 U.S.C. Secs. 1432(4)(G) and 1436(d)(5); Dunst, Bruder, Trivette, & Hamby, 2006; Dunst et al., 2001; Stowe & Turnbull, 2001). More than three quarters of all early intervention services took place in the home during the 2003–2004 school year. Only 8% of the children were served in specialized programs for children with disabilities (U.S. Department of Education, 2006).

The U.S. Department of Education sponsored a national study that included over 2,500 parents in 20 states to document the progress of infants and toddlers in early intervention programs. The final report of the National Early Intervention Longitudinal Study (NEILS) was published in 2007 (Hebbeler et al., 2007). Findings suggest that early intervention supports children's developmental progress and that families are generally satisfied with the services they receive. Children receiving early intervention services tend to experience substantial progress in key developmental areas—motor, self-help, communication, and cognition. Families report that early intervention services have a significant impact on their child's development and that they are satisfied with the quality and quantity of the services. Parents also feel greater confidence in their parenting roles, their ability to support their child to learn and develop, and their capacity to work with professionals to advocate for their child's needs.

In contrast, parents report feeling far less comfortable addressing their child's behavioral problems. As a professional in early intervention or early education programs, you will want to use some of the practices we identify in chapters 8 through 12 to support parents to develop skills to address their children's behavioral challenges (Crnic, Hoffman, Gaze, & Edelbrock, 2004).

Researchers using NIELS data have reported that families from culturally and linguistically diverse backgrounds, families with low incomes, and families in which the mother had less formal education tended to be less satisfied with early intervention services (Bailey, Hebbeler, Scarborough, Spiker, & Mallik, 2004; 2005). In chapters 8 through 12, you will learn about effective practices for working with families from diverse ethnic, cultural, and linguistic backgrounds, and you already know, from chapter 1, that culture powerfully affects families and their responses to disability and disability professionals.

When children reach the age of 3, they often transition from Part C early intervention programs to Part B early childhood preschool programs. This transition is a significant one. Early intervention programs focus on family-centered services, as reflected in the individual family service plan (IFSP) (20 U.S.C. Sec. 1436(d)(8); Dunst, 2002; Hanson et al., 2000). Preschool programs tend to be more school focused than early intervention programs.

Families from culturally or linguistically diverse backgrounds may experience additional challenges during the transition because of differences between the family's cultural values, which may not emphasize education so much as other developmental aspects of the child, and the practices of the early childhood preschool program. (Rous, Schroeder, Stricklin, Hains, & Cox, 2007)

A recent review of 50 studies of children or families in transition provided information about the transition experiences of children and families during the early childhood years (Rosenkoetter, Schroeder, Hains, Rous, & Shaw, 2008):

- High-quality child care and developmentally appropriate preschool and kindergarten classrooms were associated with better academic and social outcomes and adjustment in the next environment.
- Preschool and kindergarten teachers considered social development and social communication to be stronger indicators of school readiness than academic skills.
- Teaching young children with disabilities the skills that directly relate to what is required in the next environment was associated with more successful adjustment to and positive outcomes in the next setting.
- Positive relationships and transition support activities make transition less stressful for families.

Research is beginning to shed light on the specific supports and relationships that facilitate positive transitions for young children with disabilities and their families. A study of 22 families geographically dispersed throughout the United States reported their experiences when they transitioned from early intervention to preschool services (Hanson et al., 2000). Although some families reported positive experiences, the majority cited a number of significant problems all related to a lack of clarity of what to expect in the next environment. One parent described the information void as follows:

> What the teacher did was she just rang me up. She said, "We need it. We're going to do a transition meeting. Can you make Thursday afternoon?" And I said, "Yes." And, you know, I never thought to say, "Oh, what does that exactly mean?" . . . So, I didn't know what it [the meeting] was about. (Hanson et al., 2000, p. 285)

The recommendations from this research study include (1) viewing transition as a process that starts early with planning and collaboration, (2) exchanging information with families in advance of meetings, (3) visiting preschools that might be options for placement, and (4) identifying a key person or guide to facilitate the process and ensure that parents are told the full range of options available (Hanson et al., 2000).

One study explored how parents and teachers participated in a comprehensive set of transition activities that began when the children entered preschool and continued through their entry into kindergarten (La Paro, Kraft-Sayre, & Pianta, 2003). The activities included parent meetings, kindergarten visits, linking preschoolers to kindergarten "buddies," and holding interschool curriculum meetings. The vast majority of parents participated in many of the activities and found the activities in which they participated to be helpful (La Paro et al., 2003).

In another study, focus groups of administrators, parents, and early childhood practitioners provided information about effective transition supports, especially around two aspects of transition (Rous, Myers, & Stricklin, 2007). The first related to the presence of interagency collaborations; these supported positive transitions by having clearly articulated interagency agreements and transition policies as well as effective communication and collaboration among individuals within the agencies. One participant in this study noted, "What we are hearing from families is their positive experience is directly related to how the partners come together at the community level to support their transition effort" (p. 13). The second related to the specific transition supports that were provided to children and families. Supports identified as effective by the focus groups included providing families with information, including families in the development of the child's IEP, and arranging for family and child visits to the next environment (Rous et al., 2007).

Fostering Self-Determination in Young Children

Freedom, choice, and control over one's life are at the heart of understanding self-determination in children with disabilities and their families. Self-determination means, among other things, living one's life consistent with one's values, preferences, strengths, and needs (Turnbull & Turnbull, 2001). Researchers have identified four essential characteristics of self-determination: autonomy, self-regulation, psychological empowerment, and self-realization (Wehmeyer, 2007; Wehmeyer, Abery, Mithaug, & Stancliffe, 2003).

Research on self-determination has primarily involved adolescents and adults (Test, Fowler, Brewer, & Wood, 2005; Wehmeyer & Palmer, 2003). However, there is growing understanding of the critical importance of providing a solid foundation for self-determination during early childhood (Brotherson, Cook, Erwin, & Weigel, 2008; Erwin, Brotherson, Palmer, Cook, Weigel, & Summers, 2009; Erwin & Brown, 2003; Shogren & Turnbull, 2006). Self-determination develops across the life span (Turnbull & Turnbull, 2006), yet it will not easily emerge unless supported early in life (Erwin & Brown, 2003; Shogren & Turnbull, 2006).

A young child's family plays an important role in supporting, or not supporting, a child to be self-determined. Young children spend most of their time in the home. It is within the home that young children may be given opportunities

to practice the skills that underlie self-determination, such as expressing their preferences, making choices, and exercising control over their environments (Brotherson et al., 2008). It is through these opportunities that children learn that they are causal agents in their own lives (Brotherson et al., 2008).

Researchers have identified several strategies that professionals and families can use to provide opportunities for young children to develop self-determination (Brotherson et al., 2008; Erwin et al., 2009; Shogren & Turnbull, 2006). Many of the recommended strategies focus on enhancing opportunities for the child's engagement by arranging or modifying natural environments. For example, these strategies may include: (a) creating a "kid space" in the main living area; (b) placing toys where the child can access them without assistance; (c) setting up predictable and consistent routines; (d) creating a private area the child can call his or her own; (e) displaying photos and artwork at the child's eye level; (f) allowing the child to decide what to do, eat, or wear; and (g) being careful to avoid overprotecting the child by supporting age-appropriate risk taking (Brotherson et al., 2008; Erwin et al., 2009: Shogren & Turnbull, 2006).

It is imperative for you to consider families' values and priorities related to self-determination. The concept of self-determination represents a value with Anglo-European roots and may not be always consistent with values embraced by other cultural perspectives (Kalyanpur & Harry, 1999; Lynch & Hanson, 2004; Zhang, 2005). Kalyanpur and Harry (1999) have suggested that the self-determination concept reflects Western society's value that children are individuals with rights who should have opportunities to exert those rights to maximize their potential. However, the value ascribed to self-determination in one culture may conflict directly with values of other cultural groups, such as the Hmong, who deeply value group identity and would reject freedom of choice, particularly for children. Moreover, not all families from the same cultural or ethnic backgrounds share the same values.

You should have open conversations with families about the meaning and importance of self-determination in their child's life. Families exercise their choice in many different ways. Some emphasize harmony over progress; others value community over individualism (Lynch & Hanson, 2004). We encourage you to ask families how important values such as choice making, independence, and personal control are to them and to observe how their values are enacted in their child-rearing practices.

Ideally, early intervention professionals collaborate with families as they prepare for the marathon ahead, namely, the full life cycle of the family. By focusing on long-range needs, professionals enable families to enhance their quality-of-life outcomes and avoid the burnout that can occur when families exert all their efforts during the "100-yard dash" of an early intervention program (Turnbull, 1988). Professionals can help families develop resilience and pace to attain their goals over a lifelong marathon. You have learned how you can provide resources and support to families by helping them identify their strengths, meet their basic needs, establish balance and equity in their lives, and plan for their family's future.

Childhood

Entry into elementary school typically widens children's and families' horizons. When their children enter elementary school, families may have their first encounter with many of the issues we discuss in this book, including acquiring a vision for their child's future and a perspective on the appropriateness of inclusion.

Developing a Vision for the Future

Parents of children with a disability typically want the same things that all parents want for their children: a home, friends, happiness, and a chance to contribute to their community (Hughes, Valle-Riestra, & Arguelles, 2008; Turnbull & Turnbull, 1999). The question that you should ask yourself is simply this: How can I support families and the professionals who work with them to develop a vision for the future? Start by being skeptical about the traditional desires of special educators, other professionals, and families to "be realistic." Janet Vohs, the mother of a young adult with multiple disabilities, made just that point in writing about her family:

> Families of children with disabilities are not allowed—or at least not encouraged—to have a dream or a vision for their children's future. What the past has given as possible outcomes for people with disabilities is far less than inspiring. If all we have to look forward to is an extension of the past, I should think we would want to avoid the pain of that future as long as possible. But I have a motto: Vision over visibility. Having a vision is not just planning for a future we already know how to get to. It is daring to dream about what is possible. (Vohs, 1993, pp. 62–63)

What's your role when working with the family? Start by realizing the power of a shared vision: "A shared vision is not an idea. . . . It is rather a force in people's hearts, a force of impressive power . . . Few, if any, forces in human affairs are as powerful as shared vision" (Senge, 1990, p. 206). Susan Rocco, a parent of a son with autism, learned early about the benefits of shared visions:

> As the parent . . . I had experienced most points on the power continuum. The unequal power relationship with

Jason's teachers and therapists generally put the burden on me to wheedle, cajole, threaten, flatter—in essence, work harder at the relationship than anyone else—to get the desired outcome. The few times I have experienced true synergy, when we partners are working from our strengths and shared values, the burden has fallen away. The beauty of the synergistic model is that there is no more "them" and "us." "We" pool our resources and our creative juices, and "we" all celebrate in the success. (Turnbull, Turbiville, & Turnbull, 2000, p. 645)

As a professional in early education or elementary school programs, you often will be parents' initial source of information about their child's special needs. You will have the opportunity to talk with them about their child's near-term academic experiences and expectations and the long-term outcomes that those experiences should produce. (You will learn about academic experiences and expectations, as well as about long-term outcomes, in chapter 6, and about how to be a partner in achieving academic progress and long-term outcomes in chapters 7 through 12.) You can offer to be a partner with families in developing a vision for themselves and their child. As you make that offer, bear in mind the difficulties Xenia Powell describes in the My Voice box on the next page, and remember that negative thinking by professionals and other families and outdated public attitudes impede visions of what can be (Ivey, 2004; Mutua, 2001).

Developing a Perspective on Inclusion. As you will learn in chapter 6 and have already read, IDEA creates a presumption in favor of educating students in the least restrictive environment. It provides that students with disabilities must be educated with students who do not have disabilities to the maximum extent appropriate for the student and that the student may be removed from that type of education only when the nature and extent of the student's disability is such that education of the child in regular classes with supplementary aids and services cannot be achieved satisfactorily (20 U.S.C. Sec. 1412 (a) (5)). We will describe IDEA's provisions in greater detail in chapter 6.

Before we do, however, you will benefit by knowing just how extensively students with disabilities are included in the general curriculum and regular education classrooms. Figure 4.2 provides that information for the most recent school year (2003–2004). What are your predictions about changes in the degree to which students with disabilities are placed in general education classrooms as they age? Do you think it is more, less, or about the same?

Based on the most current data available, the highest percentage of students ages 6 through 11 – 62% are in general education classrooms for 80% or more of the school day (U.S. Department of Education, 2006). However, as students

MY VOICE

Xenia Powell—Educating Students and Mopping the Floor

As angry as Xenia was at the teacher who told her son, Lanz, that he had a learning disability—because she thought the teacher was giving him a crutch or a reason to fail—she is determined not to do as that teacher did.

"I tell my students to stop making excuses. I tell them, 'Don't use your home situation as an excuse for what you do here in my classroom. Use it as a reason to do better.' I know all about excuses."

How can Xenia be so sure of herself? It's because she was the troublemaker as a young teenager. Because she lived a college experience so entirely different than her life in Chicago. Because she had Lanz while in college.

"I've had to advocate especially hard for Lanz. He's easy to like. So some teachers don't believe he has special needs. They think he's lazy. Other teachers gave him the wrong labels. Whatever. A lot of them give him—and other students—just enough, nothing more. They don't really push their students."

Is that Xenia's way? Is that how she treats her students when she wears her general or special educator hat? No way. She's gone through enough life stages to know that shortchanging students is wrong, and blaming their parents is also wrong.

"We've got to push our students. You know, you can put a mop on the floor, but if you don't have soap and water, you're just pushing the dirt from one place to another, you're not cleaning the floor. Education is like that. That's what I've learned. Put down that soap and water, and then push the mop. I offer myself to my students, and then I push them."

Take Action!

- When you talk with your students' parents, let them know about your own education and your own family. Let them see you as a person, not a distant professional. Let them know you have experiences in life that you can bring to bear for them and their children.
- And then let them know about mops, soap, and water. You might even tell them what a teacher of one of the authors of this book told him when he was a ninth grader: "Learning is hard work."
- How can you model Xenia's high expectations for her students and be a positive force for change in your school and in the lives of the students and families you work with?
- Why do you think Xenia feels so strongly that blaming parents and shortchanging students is wrong? If you encounter other professionals who tend to blame parents or shortchange students, what can you do to change their perspective and support them to develop more trusting partnerships with families?

age, fewer are placed in general education classrooms. Only 44% of students with disabilities aged 12 to 17 were served in general education classrooms for 80% or more of the school day.

Students with speech or language impairments and students with specific learning disabilities are most likely to be served for the greatest percentage of time in the general education classroom (U.S. Department of Education, 2006). Students with intellectual disability (also known as mental retardation), deaf-blindness, autism, and emotional disturbance are least likely to spend time in general education classrooms. It is unclear as to whether the relative lack of inclusive placements for some students with disabilities represents parental and student choice or the availability of resources within a school or district (Turnbull, Zuna, Turnbull, Poston, & Summers, 2007).

Educational placement also varies by the students' racial or ethnic background. Although nearly 57% of white students with disabilities are educated in general education classrooms for more than 80% of the school; only 41% of black students with disabilities are (U.S. Department of Education, 2006).

Until now, you have learned about where students with disabilities are placed for their education. However, an appropriate education is about much more than just placement. Inclusive education focuses on including students in typical, age-appropriate environments—the general education classroom—as well as building resources and supports

FIGURE 4.2 **Percentage of students ages 6 through 21 in different education environments during the 2003–2004 school year.**

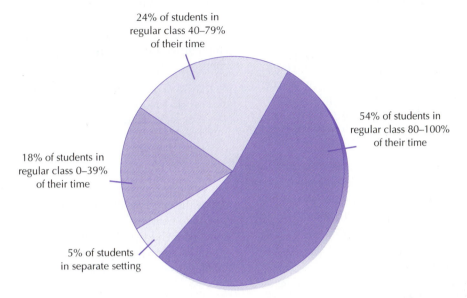

24% of students in regular class 40–79% of their time

54% of students in regular class 80–100% of their time

18% of students in regular class 0–39% of their time

5% of students in separate setting

Source: U.S. Department of Education. (2006). *Twenty-eighth annual report to Congress on the implementation of the Individuals with Disabilities Education Act.* Washington, DC: Author.

to promote success for all students in that setting. Indeed, there are four key characteristics of inclusive education:

- All students receive their education in the school they would have attended if they had no disability.
- Students are placed into classrooms according to the principle of natural proportions; assuming that approximately 12% to 15% of all students in a school have disabilities, then no more than 12% to 15% of all students in any classroom will have disabilities.
- Teaching and learning is restructured for all students so that special education supports exist within general education classes.
- School and general education placements are age- and grade-appropriate (Turnbull et al., 2004, p. 66).

As children with disabilities enter elementary school, many parents begin to weigh the benefits and drawbacks of inclusion. Most families strongly favor inclusion (Leyser & Kirk, 2004; Peck, Staub, Galluci, & Schwartz, 2004; Soodak et al., 2002) and actively pursue inclusive experiences for their school-age children. Some families even pursue inclusion during early intervention and the early childhood years (Erwin & Soodak, 1995; Erwin, Soodak, Winton, & Turnbull, 2001).

Several studies have analyzed families' perspectives on inclusion (Fredrickson, Dunsmuir, Lang, & Monsen, 2004;

Gallagher et al., 2000; Leyser & Kirk, 2004; Palmer, Fuller, Aurora, & Nelson, 2001). The research reveals these key themes:

- Although parents vary in their opinions, most parents are generally positive about inclusive placements.
- Most parents, regardless of the type or severity of the child's disability, perceive that general education classrooms, contrasted to more specialized settings, do a better job of (1) enhancing their child's self-esteem, (2) enabling their child to have more friendships and peer role models, (3) improving their child's academic and functional skills, and (4) preparing their child for life in the real world.
- Parents have concerns related to (1) the qualifications of teachers, (2) availability of individualized supports or services in general education settings, and (3) the need to intensively advocate for inclusive programs.

Many families lament how hard they must work for inclusion despite it being one of their child's educational rights (Erwin et al., 2001; Soodak et al., 2002). In one study, 27 families participated in focus groups in which they spoke of their efforts to obtain the best educational outcomes for their children (Hess, Molina, & Kozleski, 2006). Most parents wanted their children to receive special education services within general education and were willing to work to make it happen. One mother described her son as being "scarred" by his experience in a self-contained class. Another parent in this study spoke of her son's inclusive schooling in this way:

> The school, the whole atmosphere, you know, when you're in a school that has a lot of special needs kids . . . the entire staff has a different kind of [outlook]. It a fairer idea of how to look at those children, I guess. It's part of the school culture. So we fought really hard to get him here, and, you know, we were thinking of moving, but we won't move till he's too old to go here anymore. (Hess et al., 2006, p. 15)

Parents sometimes have to advocate for their children when the services to which their children are entitled are not forthcoming. For example, one mother was willing to "fight for services" by "go[ing] over [the principal's] head" if her child was placed in a self-contained class:

> I looked for another supervisor, and I made a big commotion. And they didn't leave her out. Because it is necessary to do it [be assertive] here in this country. Because being a Latino, they think that one needs other things—or what do I know—and they have to pay attention to me. (McHatton, 2007, p. 244)

Even after inclusive education is made available to children, parents often find that they must monitor its implementation (Soodak & Erwin, 1995).

Parents of children with disabilities have wide-ranging opinions on every topic, including the appropriateness of inclusion (Lindsay & Dockrell, 2004). As one parent said:

> I have a fear of security and safety, and I felt that he needed to be in a more confined, limited environment where he could get the attention that he needed. (Poston, 2002, p. 293)

Another group of parents often express strong opinions about inclusion—the parents of children who do not have disabilities. Obviously, they have a stake in the quality of education provided in general education classrooms. Based on a review of the research, Duhaney and Salend (2000) found that parents of children without disabilities:

- Felt that general education classrooms were meeting their children's educational needs with greater acceptance of diversity when children with disabilities were included.
- Perceived that the presence of children with disabilities in classrooms had benefits for their own children, including being more sensitive, being more helpful, having a greater acceptance of diversity, displaying fewer behavior problems, and having a more positive self-concept.

In a later survey of almost 400 parents of children without disabilities, researchers found similar support for inclusive education (Peck, Staub, Gallucci, & Schwartz, 2004). Only a small group of parents expressed concerns that teacher time and attention was unfairly given to children with disabilities. One parent, in expressing her concerns, said:

> My second grade daughter had a child who disrupted her class 2–3 times per hour. And it took the teacher three to five minutes to get the child back on task each time. I feel that this was a disservice to the other children in the class. (Peck et al., 2004, p. 140)

We encourage you to consider how you would respond to this parent's viewpoint. How might you go about differentiating the concepts of fairness and sameness? What might you do to build trust with parents having similar concerns about their children? You will be better able to answer these questions after reading chapters 8 through 12; don't expect to have answers "at the ready" right now.

Adolescence

Adolescence is the next life cycle stage in the family's development. Perhaps more than any of the life cycle stages, adolescence is strongly influenced by cultural values (Preto, 1999). For example, many European Americans generally think of their children becoming adults at around the age of 18; other cultures, such as some American Indian cultures, may perceive adulthood as starting immediately after puberty (Deyhlę & LeCompte, 1994).

In addition to various ethnic/racial interpretations of adolescence, many religions have adolescent-related rituals to signal increasing maturity. Christening is one example; bar mitzvah and bat mitzvah (for Jewish boys and girls, respectively) is another. Still another is la Quinceañera, a celebration of a Mexican girl's 15th birthday, representing her passage from childhood into womanhood:

> The Quinceañera celebration has two parts a mass and reception. Various cultural traditions are part of this event. For example, the "changing of the shoes" occurs when the young girl enters the church wearing flat shoes and her father (or significant person in her life) changes the flats to high heeled shoes symbolizing the transition into womanhood. Then the young woman will have a tiara placed signifying in front of God and the community her triumph over childhood and her ability to face challenges ahead. At the reception the young woman performs a traditional waltz/dance symbolizing once again this transition and that the community and her family will now treat her as a young woman (Department of Child and Family Services, 2009).

Adolescence can be stressful for youth and other family members. In a national study conducted with more than 1,000 families in the general population, parents reported that the life cycle stages of adolescence and young adulthood were the two stages with the highest amount of overall family stress (Olson et al., 1983). A disability may mitigate or compound some of the typical adolescent stressors for families. For example, parents might experience only minor rebellion and conflict because their children may have fewer peers after whom to model such behaviors, fewer opportunities to try alcohol and drugs, or decreased mobility and fewer chances to take dangerous risks. In other cases, adolescence may bring greater isolation, a growing sense of difference, and confusion and fear about emerging sexuality. Some pertinent educational issues during the adolescent stage include (1) sexuality education and (2) self-determination skills.

Sexuality Education. Many adolescents with disabilities have the same desires and hopes for marriage, children, and sexual intimacy as do all teens (Murphy & Elias, 2006). Approximately one half of high school students are sexually active (U.S. Department of Health and Human Services, 2006). In addition, children under 14 are increasingly reporting sexual activity (Petosa & Wessinger, 1990).

A large percentage of female adolescents with developmental disabilities reported being sexually active and using contraceptives (Scotti et al., 1997). Similarly, research has documented that adolescents with chronic health problems (for example, diabetes or asthma) and disabilities (for example, cerebral palsy or muscular dystrophy) are similar to their peers in sexual activity, patterns of contraceptive use, and pregnancy rates (Surís, Resnick, Cassuto, & Blum, 1996).

Is sexuality education necessary or desirable for students with disabilities? Some would answer, "Yes." As one teacher explained: "We see sexual problems among our students all of the time and, although we gossip about them, we do nothing to help students understand their feelings or drive. Really, we avoid getting involved. It's easier for us that way" (Brantlinger, 1992, pp. 9–10).

> A professional who works with adolescents with disabilities commented: The classic word around here is "redirect" to be interpreted as "you can't do it here" or "that is not appropriate here." The problem is there is nowhere where sex is appropriate. "Redirect" sounds objective, but it is really oppressive. The administrators talk out of both sides of their mouth. They sound like they are for normalization but, in truth, they're not. At least they're not when it comes to sexual behavior. (Brantlinger, 1992, p. 11)

However, you or some families might answer the question whether sexuality education is necessary or desirable for students with disabilities by saying "no." Your answer would conform with the data: Sexuality education is generally unavailable in schools. Indeed, only about 5% of all students receive sexuality education throughout their public school career. Only 21 states require sexuality education (Alan Guttmacher Institute, 2009). And viewpoints vary on the appropriate focus of sexuality education. Some advocate for an abstinence-only approach, whereas others advocate for an abstinence-plus sexuality curriculum that explores birth control. Research studies have shown that an abstinence-plus sexuality program of instruction results in more positive long-term outcomes while not increasing sexual intercourse rates among adolescents (Kirby, 2000).

Researchers have reviewed sexuality curriculum guides recommended by the Sexuality Information Education Center of the United States (SIECUS) for use with students with disabilities, concentrating on those available through the SIECUS library (Blanchett & Wolfe, 2002). The curriculum content covered in these programs included (1) biological and reproductive concepts, (2) health and hygiene, (3) relationships, and (4) self-protection and advocacy.

These researchers found that just 2 out of the 12 curricula included suggestions for parent-professional communication related to sexuality education. It is especially important for teachers to have a solid grasp of sexuality content to teach the subject effectively, but they also must be comfortable talking to students and families about the topic.

In chapter 2, you learned about some of the issues with establishing partnerships with gay and lesbian parents. You also read about the taunting that some children of same-sex parents face at school. Sexuality education needs to be appropriate for each student's sexual orientation. Approximately 10% of students who have a disability are gay, lesbian, or bisexual (Blanchett, 2002). There are barriers to teaching them about sexuality, as this teacher commented:

> I am a gay teacher who has noticed the lack of tolerance and support for students with any [disabilities, race, sexual orientation, etc.] difference from the average student and I'm trying to arrange a forum/support service in my middle school to support these students. Of course, in trying to make this happen, I must overcome all of the obstacles involved in initiating something like this. (Blanchett, 2002, p. 84)

We encourage you to consider carefully your role in preparing all students to live in a diverse society. Just what is your obligation to teach tolerance of all kinds of differences—those related to disability as well as sexuality?

Nearly all parents worry that their child—especially one who has a disability—may be a victim of sexual abuse. As many as 83% of females and 32% of males with developmental disabilities are victims of sexual abuse, and their abuse often goes unreported (Horner-Johnson & Drum, 2006; Petersilia, 2001; Protection and Advocacy, 2003). Approximately one fourth of the incidents of abuse occurred in institutions specifically for people with developmental disabilities; another fourth occurred in group homes for people with disabilities; and the remaining incidents occurred in the victim's own home, a work setting, or a vehicle. In the vast majority of cases, the victim knew the perpetrator; this is also true for people without disabilities who are victims of sexual abuse (Furey, 1994). Many families may expect abuse from a stranger or in an unsupervised situation in a public place, but research suggests that sexual abuse is far more likely to be perpetrated by a person in a position of trust and authority, such as a support provider, attendant, or family member (Collier, McGhie-Richmand, Odette, & Pyne, 2006).

Youth and their families need accurate information about sexual abuse, its likelihood, and strategies to prevent it (Lesseliers & Van Hove, 2002). The skills and knowledge to prevent sexual abuse should be a key topic in sexuality training during the adolescent years (Lee & Tang, 1998).

Expanding Self-Determination Skills. As you learned earlier in this chapter, the foundation for self-determination begins during the early childhood years (Brotherson et al., 2008; Erwin et al., 2009). Promoting self-determination often receives more focused attention during adolescence as this is a time, in most cultures, when older children are given more responsibility over their daily activities and for setting and attaining life goals.

Child development theory (Marvin & Pianta, 1992) and research (Algozzine et al., 2001; Field & Hoffman, 2002; Wehmeyer, 2002) show that building on a student's interest and direction is fundamental to the development of self-determination. Research has shown that student self-determination is associated with improvements in classroom behavior, including on-task and communication skills (Copeland & Hughes, 2002; Test et al., 2005), and academic performance (Fowler, Konrad, Walker, Test, & Wood, 2007). In addition, students who are more self-determined when they exit high school tend to achieve better post-school outcomes related to employment, access to health care, financial security, and independent living (Wehmeyer & Palmer, 2003). In a study of the support young adults with disabilities received from their families in their transition to adulthood, researchers concluded that "by allowing opportunities for exploration and even failure, parents . . . promoted self-determination and allowed independent decision making" (Lindstrom et al., 2007, p. 360).

Several research studies have found that teachers view self-determination as important for students with disabilities, but lack the skills or the opportunities to teach self-determination skills (Grigal, Nueber, Moon, & Graham, 2003; Mason, Field, & Sawilowsky, 2004; Wehmeyer, Agran, & Hughes, 2000). Parents of adolescents with disabilities also report viewing self-determination as important for their children, and support the teaching and practice of self-determination in secondary schools (Grigal et al., 2003).

Several frameworks for teaching the skills associated with self-determination exist. One model of instruction is the Self-Determined Learning Model of Instruction (SDLMI). The SDLMI is a process for teaching students goal-setting and problem-solving skills and consists of three phases—setting a goal, taking action, and adjusting the goal or plan. For each of these phases, student questions, educational supports, and teacher objectives are specified (Wehmeyer, Agran, Palmer, Martin, & Mithaug, 2003; Wehmeyer, Palmer, Agran, Mithaug, & Martin, 2000). Figure 4.3 illustrates phase 1, which focuses on goal setting.

As illustrated in Figure 4.3, the SDLMI is a framework for teaching students a set of questions to ask themselves as they are identifying and working toward a goal. Educational supports are specified for teachers; the supports are skills that can be taught to students to enable them to answer the questions specified in the model. The first phase (shown in Figure 4.3) focuses on identifying a goal. The second phase supports students to develop an action plan for attaining their goal and the third phase focuses on the steps to evaluate the success of the action plan and to modify the action plan or goal, as needed.

Research on the SDLMI has reported encouraging findings. Approximately 80% of students made progress toward their self-selected goal and 55% achieved their goal (Wehmeyer et al., 2000). Studies have shown that students with a range of disabilities gain academic, social, and behavioral skills after learning the SDLMI (Agran, Blanchard, Wehmeyer, & Hughes, 2002; Palmer & Wehmeyer, 2003).

Teaching self-determination skills can also provide students with disabilities with access to the general education curriculum. Researchers have found that middle school students who use the SDLMI in general education classes to develop problem-solving and study skills achieved educationally relevant goals and increased their self-determination (Palmer, Wehmeyer, Gipson, & Agran, 2004).

Parents can be involved in promoting their child's self-determination (Palmer & Wehmeyer, 2002). Earlier in this chapter we provided examples of strategies families can use to facilitate self-determination in young children. Families can also promote decision-making, problem-solving, and goal-setting skills at home. One approach is to involve the student actively and meaningfully in decisions pertaining to their lives. We will discuss this concept, as it relates to individualized education program (IEP) development, more in chapter 10.

FIGURE 4.3   **The self-determination model of instruction—phase 1.**

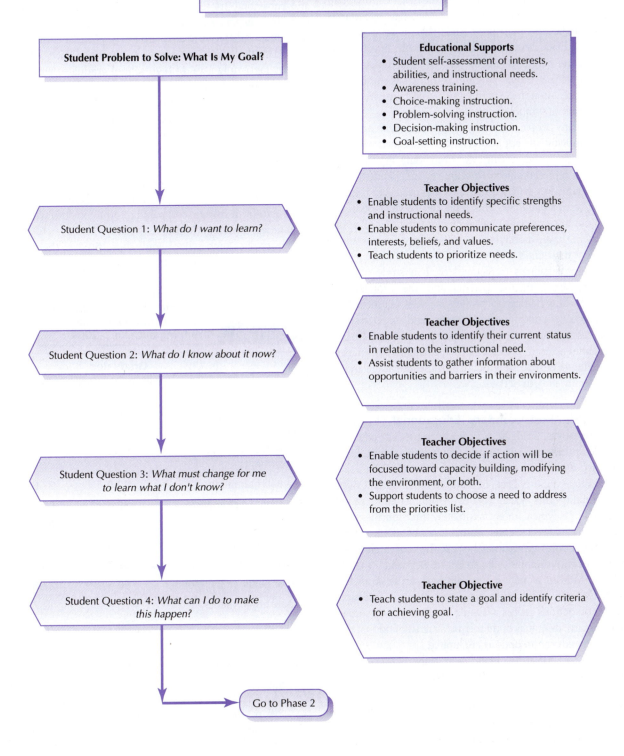

Phase 1: Set a Goal

Student Problem to Solve: What Is My Goal?

Educational Supports
- Student self-assessment of interests, abilities, and instructional needs.
- Awareness training.
- Choice-making instruction.
- Problem-solving instruction.
- Decision-making instruction.
- Goal-setting instruction.

Student Question 1: *What do I want to learn?*

Teacher Objectives
- Enable students to identify specific strengths and instructional needs.
- Enable students to communicate preferences, interests, beliefs, and values.
- Teach students to prioritize needs.

Student Question 2: *What do I know about it now?*

Teacher Objectives
- Enable students to identify their current status in relation to the instructional need.
- Assist students to gather information about opportunities and barriers in their environments.

Student Question 3: *What must change for me to learn what I don't know?*

Teacher Objectives
- Enable students to decide if action will be focused toward capacity building, modifying the environment, or both.
- Support students to choose a need to address from the priorities list.

Student Question 4: *What can I do to make this happen?*

Teacher Objective
- Teach students to state a goal and identify criteria for achieving goal.

Go to Phase 2

Adulthood

Adulthood can be regarded as having three dimensions: autonomy, membership, and change (Ferguson & Ferguson, 2006). The autonomy dimension emphasizes the individual's arrival into adulthood. Membership includes community connectedness and affiliation. And, change acknowledges each individual's capacity for ongoing growth. According to Ferguson and Ferguson (2006), each of these dimensions is associated with "symbols" of adulthood, such as employment (a symbol of autonomy), voting (a symbol of membership), and marriage (a symbol of change).

For many people, especially those of European American descent, moving into adulthood is often associated with finding employment and moving away from home. For the young adult, this represents achieving greater independence and responsibility. For parents, it means a process of letting go of their son or daughter. This stage can be difficult in any family, but it is especially challenging for families with young adults who have disabilities. It is often hard for parents to "let go" of their child with a disability. It is also sometimes hard for professionals to "let go" of their student with a disability. For both the parents and the professionals, transition—and "letting go"—often includes (1) identifying postsecondary educational programs and supports and (2) accessing supported employment options. Trusting partnerships among professionals and families can increase the likelihood of success, as defined by the individual and his or her family, in both of these areas.

Identifying Postsecondary Educational Programs and Supports. Students pursue postsecondary education for at least these reasons: to gain better employment, higher earnings, and a successful adult life (Getzel, Stodden, & Briel, 2001; Gilmore, Bose, & Hart, 2001; National Council on Disability and Social Security Administration, 2000). Although it is typical for approximately three fourths of high school graduates to enter some type of postsecondary education, only approximately one third of high school graduates with disabilities do so (Horn, Berktold, & Bobbit, 1999). Without a high school diploma or its equivalent, students with disabilities may find that postsecondary education options are not available. And even those students who do have diplomas or their equivalent still find that postsecondary education options are limited.

For the 2003–2004 school year, only 54% of students with disabilities graduated with a standard diploma (U.S. Department of Education, 2006). However, there is wide variability in the graduation rate across disability categories. Figure 4.4 reports the percentage of students with disabilities graduating with a standard diploma or dropping out. As you

review the data, what can you learn about the likelihood of graduation for students with different disabilities? What group is least likely to graduate? What group is most likely to drop out? Note that the dropout rate for youth with emotional and behavioral disorders is about twice as high as any other disability category. Additionally, approximately 11% of youth with disabilities received an alternative credential rather than a standard diploma (Government Accounting Office, 2003).

In 1987 only 15% of high school graduates with disabilities enrolled in postsecondary education. By 2003, however, the enrollment of students with disabilities in postsecondary programs had more than doubled to 32% (National Longitudinal Transition Study [NLTS2], 2005). One third of college students who report having a disability have a learning disability (Mull, Sitlington, & Alper, 2001). But, researchers have found that five years after high school, 80% of the students with learning disabilities had not graduated from college, compared to 56% of youth without disabilities (Murray, Goldstein, Nourse, & Edgar, 2000). Ten years after high school graduation, 56% of the youth

FIGURE 4.4 Percentage of students age 14 and older with disabilities graduating with a standard diploma or dropping out, 2003–2004.

	Graduated with a Standard Diploma	Dropped Out
Specific learning disabilities	59.6	29.1
Speech or language impairments	61.3	29.4
Mental retardation	39.0	27.6
Emotional disturbance	38.4	52.3
Multiple disabilities	48.1	22.2
Hearing impairments	67.6	16.7
Orthopedic impairments	62.7	16.5
Other health impairments	60.5	27.8
Visual impairments	73.4	12.7
Autism	58.5	13.2
Deaf-blindness	51.6	17.5
Traumatic brain injury	61.9	23.0
All disabilities	54.5	31.1

Source: U.S. Department of Education. (2006). *Twenty-eighth annual report to Congress on the implementation of the Individuals with Disabilities Education Act.* Washington, DC: Author.

with learning disabilities still had not graduated compared to 32% of individuals without disabilities.

Across disability categories, only 29% of all students with disabilities who enroll in postsecondary education programs graduate or complete their programs (Newman, Wagner, Cameto, & Knokey, 2009). However, only a third of students who were identified as having a disability in high school informed the postsecondary program of their disability. Perhaps most importantly, less than a quarter of the students received accommodations or supports from their post-secondary school, although more than 80% had received some type of accommodation or support while in high school.

Disparities also exist in the graduation rates of students with disabilities from diverse racial, ethnic, and linguistic backgrounds. Figure 4.5 shows the number and percentage of students with disabilities from diverse backgrounds graduating with a standard diploma and dropping out. What patterns do you see? What factors do you think contribute to the range in student outcomes?

For a long time many people assumed that a postsec-ondary education was inappropriate or impossible for students with significant intellectual disabilities. But this perspective has changed, and leaders in the field now refer to a new paradigm for postsecondary educational opportunities for students with severe and multiple disabilities (Stodden & Whelley, 2004). There are three model approaches in post-secondary education for these students:

- A substantially separate-program model in which students with significant intellectual disabilities attend an entirely different and separate program on a college campus (much like a separate class in an elementary or secondary school).

- A mixed program model that includes a combination of separate programs to learn life skills and opportunities to be integrated into campus courses.
- An individualized support model where supports and services are based on each student's educational and career goals.

A number of postsecondary programs exist for students with autism and intellectual and developmental disabilities (Alpern & Zager, 2008; Carroll, Blumberg, & Petroff, 2008; Hart, Mele-McCarthy, Pasternack, Zimbrich, & Parker, 2004; Zafft, Hart, & Zimbrich, 2004). These programs vary in their approaches. However, each program provides the supports needed for students to participate in college classes, engage in social activities with their age peers, and gain independence.

Because the Individuals with Disabilities Education Act (IDEA) provides that every student with a disability must have an individualized plan for transition from secondary education to postsecondary opportunities, including postsec-ondary education, vocational education, or continuing and adult education (20 U.S.C. Sec. 1402(34)), you should support students and families to identify appropriate postsec-ondary career goals, ensure that students develop requisite skills, and teach students to complete applications and access services consistent with their support needs. (In chapters 11 and 12, you will read about students with disabilities who have entered postsecondary programs.) Parents and students need advice about scholarship opportunities, loans, work-study programs, and disability-related funding opportunities (such as Social Security and Vocational Rehabilitation bene-fits). Resource guides in a school or local library and work-shops on college planning and academic and financial issues can be helpful for families and high school students.

FIGURE 4.5 Number and percentage of students age 14 and older with disabilities graduating with a standard diploma or dropping out, by race/ethnicity 2003–2004.

Race/Ethnicity	Graduated with Standard Diploma		Dropped Out	
	Number	Percentage	Number	Percentage
American Indian/Alaska Native	3,052	47.8	2,850	44.6
Asian/Pacific Islander	4,297	63.5	1,486	22.0
Black	32,507	39.1	31,843	38.3
Hispanic	25,925	47.6	19,438	35.7
White	148,291	61.3	66,444	27.5

Source: U.S. Department of Education. (2006). *Twenty-eighth annual report to Congress on the implementation of the Individuals with Disabilities Education Act.* Washington, DC: Author.

Students and families will also need your support in learning about the disability supports available at postsecondary institutions. There are several questions you and the student and the student's parents or other family members should try to answer: Does the postsecondary institution provide special assistance, such as tutoring programs for students with learning disabilities? How accessible is the campus for wheelchair users? Does the state vocational rehabilitation program provide financial assistance for personal care attendants while the student is attending college? Does the postsecondary institution have an office that oversees the provision of reasonable accommodations for students with disabilities? Is there a published and well-enforced plan for complying with the Americans with Disabilities Act? In a word, does the postsecondary institution provide appropriate and reasonable accommodations for the student? Read Piper's story in the Together We Can box below to learn how family members and professionals

---

TOGETHER WE CAN
Piper Goes to College

Transition from high school to college raises students' hopes and anxieties. That is true for Piper (a pseudonym for a real person who does not want to reveal her identity). She is a 17-year-old high school student in Illinois. Piper's dream—indeed, her family's, too—was to attend the local university. Like many people with Asperger's syndrome, she and her family were particularly anxious about the often "unspoken" expectations of the university environment.

Piper was an excellent student, quickly picked up new material, and performed well on assignments and activities where she worked alone. But she struggled to understand social interactions.

To prepare Piper for this transition, her high school transition team convened to develop a plan. The team included Piper and her parents, a transition specialist from the school, her teacher, adult service providers, and a representative from the disability services office at the local university.

The team recommended that Piper audit at least one college course before enrolling in the university; auditing would allow her to learn about the expectations in university courses and about social interactions at the university before enrolling full time.

However, being able to audit the courses was only the first step. The second was to develop a system of support. The team talked about putting in place supports from Piper's high school from the local adult service provider—people from either agency who would attend classes with her. She and her family questioned whether that plan was age-appropriate and whether it would stigmatize Piper.

Their concerns caused the team to abandon that plan and adopt a different one, namely, to use "peer mentors" to support her. That approach had two advantages: It addressed the family's concern about the stigmatizing nature of school- or service provider–based supports, and it created an opportunity for Piper to socialize with other university students. Piper's parents and the transition specialist would partner on identifying peer mentors and educating them about Piper's gifts and needs.

Piper's team posted flyers throughout the university and advertised through its disability services office. The team, including Piper, screened volunteers.

With mentors on board, Piper audited courses, made friends other than just her peer mentors, and learned more about the expectations around social interactions. Her parents said that this experience was beneficial not just in preparing her for college, but also in preparing her to develop friends as an adult.

Take Action!

- Build on your students' and their families' vision for the future.
- Be creative; devise several plans; adopt the one most likely to satisfy the student's preferences and meet the student's needs.
- When the student is 16 years old, start the planning for transition, as required by the Individuals with Disabilities Education Act. (You will learn about that law in chapter 6.)
- Include both the student and the family in planning for transition. Listen to their concerns, talk about them (communicate), and work with them to address the concerns (advocate for them—treat them as equals, treat them with respect). Remember the adages: "Nothing about me without me. Nothing about us without us." It's about equality.

collaborated to support one young woman's successful transition to college.

Although families are often their children's primary advocates during the elementary and secondary school years, colleges and universities expect the students themselves to advocate for themselves. After all, they are likely to have reached the age of legal maturity, usually 18, and to be emancipated from their parents. Certainly, that is the approach under IDEA: The rights of the student's parents transfer to the student when the student reaches the age of legal maturity (20 U.S.C. Sec. 1414(d)(1)(A)). One of the best preparations for postsecondary educational success is to prepare students and families during the elementary and secondary years to learn the skills that will be necessary to meet disability and educational needs in adulthood.

Accessing Supported Employment. According to the 2007 Annual Disability Status Report published by Cornell University:

- Of all working-age people with disabilities (ages 21 to 64), only about 37% are employed full or part time compared to 80% of working-age people without disabilities. This gap is very problematic.
- Employment rates vary by disability; 46% of individuals with a sensory disability reported being employed compared to 31% of individuals with a physical disability and 28% of individuals with a mental disability.
- The median yearly income of individuals with disabilities who worked full time was approximately $34,000 compared to $40,000 for individuals without disabilities (Erickson & Lee, 2008).

Obviously, employment is the area where individuals with disabilities experience the widest gap between themselves and those who do not have a disability.

Individuals with severe disabilities face particular challenges. The traditional employment option for them has been a sheltered workshop. A sheltered workshop usually is a large, segregated work center exclusively operated for people with disabilities. The average wage for individuals in sheltered workshops is $2.40 an hour. The lowest wages typically are earned by individuals with intellectual disability; they average around $52 a week (Wehman et al., 2004). Almost three fourths of individuals served in rehabilitation programs are either in segregated nonwork day programs or sheltered workshops (Braddock, Rizzolo, & Hemp, 2004).

The most frequently cited reason for individuals remaining in segregated day services is they are "not ready" for more complex employment settings. The theory behind sheltered employment is, among other things, that if the individuals stay in a sheltered workshop long enough to learn work skills and habits, they might "become ready" for nonsheltered work. The theory is flawed if only because there is a strong push for inclusion of individuals with disabilities across all sectors of society. Yet state and federal funding continues to be primarily devoted to supporting segregated employment (Braddock et al., 2004). According to a recent study however, more than half of the 52,954 individuals participating in Community Rehabilitation Programs in 2004 were served in segregated programs (Inge, Wehman, Revell, Erickson, Butterworth, & Gilmore, 2009).

Supported employment developed in the early 1980s as a way to provide long-term support for individuals with severe disabilities in integrated work settings. The goal of supported employment is to support the development of independent work skills and the ability to earn competitive wages in an inclusive job market (Wehman, Bricout, & Kregel, 2000). People with disabilities who engage in supported employment frequently have a job coach who provides direct training and assistance to enable them to fully carry out the job responsibilities.

The average hourly wages in supported employment are at least 2.25 times the average hourly wage in sheltered employment (Kregel & Dean, 2002). Long-term studies have clearly documented the benefits of supported over sheltered employment for individuals with disabilities, their families, and taxpayers. Accordingly, the number of people in supported employment increased by more than 200% from 1998 to 1999. Approximately 32,400 individuals were in supported employment in 1988, whereas approximately 107,800 were in supported employment just 10 years later (Wehman et al., 2004).

The findings of research on factors associated with successful supported employment include:

- Employees with disabilities are more likely to earn higher wages and to be more integrated when they have similar work roles to other employees and when the initial training and orientation of supervisors and co-workers is positive.
- People with disabilities in supported employment have more inclusive participation in social activities when co-workers receive training by supported employment personnel (Mank, Cioffi, & Yovanoff, 1997).
- Employees with more severe disabilities have better outcomes when they have positive co-worker relationships and when they have fewer hours of job coaching support from supported employment personnel outside of the employment setting (Mank, Cioffi, & Yovanoff, 1998).
- Employees with disabilities have better outcomes when co-workers and supervisors receive

specific information about providing support to the employee early on (Mank, Cioffi, & Yovanoff, 1999).

- Employees with disabilities have better outcomes when they have a combination of job coaching and when their co-workers are trained to provide support to them. Without co-worker training, greater hours of job coaching does not lead to outcomes that are as positive (Mank, Cioffi, & Yovanoff, 2000).
- The field of supported employment is growing. More people with severe disabilities are in supported employment, and improvements in job acquisition, job roles, job orientation, and relationships with co-workers have been shown (Mank, Cioffi, & Yovanoff, 2003).

Another form of employment is self-employment (Wehman et al., 2004). Self-employment enables adults with disabilities to retain government benefits they may lose under other employment options. It also can be individualized to their particular strengths, interests, talents, and marketplace demands. Some disability organizations provide assistance with start-up costs to enable adults with disabilities to launch a business.

What can you do to support families who are seeking employment for their son or daughter with a disability? Start by providing families with comprehensive information about the benefits of employment. Information about employment options may be particularly useful to individuals in lower-income families who may be less able to focus on the career needs of their adolescent and adult children (Lindstrom, Doren, Metheny, Johnson, & Zane, 2007). Also, provide assurances about job security and safety to family members and individuals with disabilities, as families have reported these issues are of particular concern (Magliore, Grossi, Mank, & Rogan, 2008). Families can be major resources in locating employment options. One study revealed that approximately 80% of jobs secured by former special education students were obtained through a family connection (Hasazi, Gordon, & Roe, 1985). Just as people without disabilities find jobs through family and friendship networks, so do people with disabilities.

:: LIFE CYCLE TRANSITIONS

As we noted at the beginning of this chapter, life cycle stages are like the plateaus between the peaks and valleys of the transition from one life cycle to another (Carter & McGoldrick, 2005). Transitions are often the most challenging periods for families because they are characterized by change (Falicov, 1988).

Two factors tend to reduce the amount of stress most families feel during a transition. First, the roles and expectations of the new life cycle stage are typically fairly well defined. As we noted earlier in this chapter, the transition may be marked by some kind of a ritual, like a wedding, a bar or bat mitzvah, a graduation, or a funeral. These ceremonies serve as signals to the family that their relationships and roles are changing. And the expected interactions and roles for the new stage are often familiar to a family because they have known or heard about other families that have passed through that stage. Second, the timing of transitions is typically understood within various cultural contexts. In European American culture, for example, children are often expected to leave home after they graduate from high school. In Latino culture, however, it is typical for children, especially daughters, to live with their parents until they marry (Falicov, 1996). As one Latino mother stated:

> I have never said that to my daughter. I told her, "When your own daughters are grown, never tell them to leave, because that is very Anglicized." And among Latino families, no, on the contrary, my father used to tell me, "Why do you want to be going out all the time? You have your house here." (Rueda, Monzo, Shapiro, Gomez, & Blacher, 2005, p. 406)

The expected roles for and the future of a family member with a disability, however, may not be clear, and rituals to mark transitions may be different or absent. Life cycle transitions are often more stressful when they are not expected. In this section, you will learn about (1) the implications of uncertain futures and (2) unexpected transitions.

Uncertainty About the Future

For many families of children and youth with disabilities, the future is a frightening unknown. There are at least three reasons why this is so. First, the families may not know other families whose children with disabilities have transitioned from one stage to another; or, if they know those families, they may find that their child's disability is significantly different from the disability of those other families. Second, the families may have followed the usual admonition to "take things one day at a time." They may have welcomed and adhered to that common wisdom not only because more than enough responsibilities confront the family in the present but also because the future is so ambiguous.

Third, rituals marking transitions for youth without disabilities may be blurred or nonexistent for youth with disabilities. The time when a transition occurs—or should occur—may be marked not with a celebration but with chronic frustration that supports are not in place. Not only is the family uncertain about how and when their interactions will change, but they may lack cues that interactions will change. In a follow-up study of the life management strategies of parents of children with disabilities one mother noted:

> You know, there's deep hurts, I think. It's hard to deal with especially when you see your friends' kids at the same age who are going to university or getting engaged or, you know, they have the empty nest already, and they have the freedom to come and go as they please, and we don't. (Scorgie & Wilgosh, 2008, p. 107)

Families of children with disabilities identify times of transitions as being the most challenging (Rous et al., 2007; Winn & Hay, 2009; Ytterhus, Wendelborg, & Lundeby, 2008). Earlier in this chapter we discussed families' experiences in the transition from early intervention to preschool and from preschool to kindergarten. For many families, transition to adulthood poses unique and complex challenges. A study of the perspectives of students with disabilities revealed a lack of attention to future planning (Morningstar, Turnbull, & Turnbull, 1995). The majority of high school students had only a vague sense of possible futures. They reported that their families were the major source of support in developing a vision for the kinds of jobs that they would like to have and where they would like to live. Only a very small percentage of these students said their school-based vocational training had been helpful in planning for the future.

Yet these students and their families clearly need vocational and transitional services (Bambara, Wilson, & McKenzie, 2007; Mank, 2007). According to the National Longitudinal Transition Study-2, students with disabilities often rely on the support of family members and friends when making decisions, and parents are most likely to access information about post-school options from their child's school (Wagner, Newman, Cameto, Levine, & Marder, 2007). As a teacher, you will support your students and their families by providing them with information about community resources, services, and opportunities and by involving them earlier than later in planning for their transitions from secondary schools (Ankeny, Wilkins, & Spain, 2009).

> It's been hard to go through all these different steps, but the social service people and the school people have continually reinforced, "Have I done these things yet?" "Are you remembering that this happens when he turns this age?" Things like that. So they are constantly prompting and educating us as we go these different phases of his life. (Ankeny et al., 2009, p. 33)

Students from culturally and linguistically diverse families and those living in underserved areas can encounter special challenges during transitions. Culturally diverse parents report they experience a lack of understanding and respect for their values, particularly when the family's transition goals differ from those of the dominant culture (Kim & Morningstar, 2005; Rueda, et al., 2005). It is important to remember that not all cultures emphasize individualism and independent living as a goal for their adult children (Bambara et al., 2007). Sometimes language differences and the overuse of special education jargon prevent culturally and linguistically diverse parents from meaningfully participating in the transition process (Kim & Morningstar, 2005; LandAdam, Zhang, & Montoya, 2007).

The lack of availably of post-school opportunities in some areas is also extremely problematic. A follow-up study of students who left school on the Fort Apache Indian reservation revealed that less than one third of the graduates were employed, two thirds experienced substance abuse, and nearly half had been arrested, mainly for driving while intoxicated (Shafer & Rangasamy, 1995). The authors pointed out the catch-22: Economic opportunity comes at the cost of leaving the reservation; so students were forced to choose between economic self-sufficiency and confronting ". . . a world for which they are not prepared" with different cultural values (Shafer & Rangasamy, 1995, p. 64).

As you learned earlier in this book, IDEA requires that transition services be offered to families at two different life span stages. First, it requires transition planning as part of the individualized family support plan (IFSP) for toddlers who, at age 3, are moving from early intervention to early childhood services (20 U.S.C. Secs. 1412(a)(9) and 1436). The child's IFSP must include the steps that early intervention and preschool staff will undertake to support the child's transition. Second and as we noted previously, IDEA requires transition planning for students leaving secondary school (20 U.S.C. Sec. 1414(d)(1)(A)). The student's individualized education plan (IEP) must contain a transition plan that consists of

> . . . a coordinated set of activities for a student, designed with an outcome-oriented process that promotes movement from school to post-school activities, including postsecondary education, vocational training, integrated employment (including supported employment), continuing in adult education, adult services, independent living, and/or community participation (20 U.S.C. Sec. 1402(34)).

The *coordinated set of activities* must be based on the student's preferences, strengths, and needs (20 U.S.C. Sec. 1414(d)(A); Garay, 2003; Thoma, Rogan, & Baker, 2001). As you will learn in chapter 10, IDEA requires that the IEP include a statement of transition services when the student is 16 years old. The IEP must also state the interagency requirements and linkages needed to implement the transition plan when the student is 16. Teachers have the benefit of the full IEP committee, including representatives from multiple agencies, to implement these requirements (Certo et al., 2003).

We encourage you to develop trusting partnerships with families and students that will enable you to pinpoint educational goals and objectives that best propel the student toward a desirable future. Visits to new classrooms, colleges/ universities, or places of employment; meetings with future teachers, adults with disabilities, and parents of older children with similar exceptionalities can all help to reduce the fear of the future. Figure 4.6 offers some suggestions for easing the transitions between each of the life cycle stages discussed in this chapter.

Unexpected Transitions

Families with a member who has a disability are likely to experience a life cycle transition at unexpected or unusual times—certainly not at the always-typical times that are part of the lives of students who do not have disabilities.

They also are likely to experience transitions in atypical ways (not just at atypical times). For example, a young adult might remain at home well into his or her parents' elderly years (Kim, Greenberg, Seltzer, & Krauss, 2003; Magaña, 1999).

Although European American culture generally regards this type of living arrangement as an "off-time transition," research indicates positive outcomes for elderly parents who have provided care. A study of more than 200 aging mothers of adults with intellectual disability who were living at home led the researchers to the following conclusion: "Specifically, the women in our sample were substantially healthier and had better morale than did other samples of caregivers for elderly persons and reported no more burden and stress than did other caregivers" (Seltzer & Krauss, 1989, pp. 309–310). Within the Puerto Rican culture, the role of familism (direct caregiving provided by family members) is extremely strong, and families expect to take care of their members over the life span (Magaña, 1999).

Some transitions may occur earlier than the expected time. For instance, researchers have found that placing a child in a living situation outside the home can create a range of emotions that include stress and burden as well as relief

---

| FIGURE 4.6 | Enhancing successful transitions. |

Early Childhood

- Advise parents to prepare for the separation of preschool children by periodically leaving the child with others.
- Gather information and visit preschools in the community.
- Encourage participation in Parent-to-Parent programs. (Veteran parents are matched in one-to-one relationships with parents who are just beginning the transition process.)
- Familiarize parents with possible school (elementary and secondary) programs, career options, or adult programs so they have an idea of future opportunities.

Childhood

- Provide parents with an overview of curricular options.
- Ensure that IEP meetings provide an empowering context for family collaboration.
- Encourage participation in Parent-to-Parent matches, workshops, or family support groups to discuss transitions with others.

Adolescence

- Assist families and adolescents to identify community leisure-time activities.
- Incorporate into the IEP skills that will be needed in future career and vocational programs.
- Visit or become familiar with a variety of career and living options.
- Develop a mentor relationship with an adult with a similar exceptionality and an individual who has a career that matches the student's strengths and preferences.

Adulthood

- Provide preferred information to families about guardianship, estate planning, wills, and trusts.
- Assist family members in transferring responsibilities to the individual with an exceptionality, other family members, or service providers as appropriate.
- Assist the young adult or family members with career or vocational choices.
- Address the issues and responsibilities of marriage and family for the young adult.

(Baker & Blacher, 2002). Another off-time transition is death of a child (Turnbull, 2009). Illness and death may be expected parts of life for an older person; when they happen to a child, they can be regarded as cruel twists of fate. The loneliness and scale of the loss of a child is reflected by this parent:

> Freedom is not all it's cracked up to be! I miss her. The touch of her. She was full of life and she was my life! I'd do the housework around her. I did everything around her. It was my whole life. All that pain from the day she was born 'til the day she died? I wouldn't want to be without it. I still want her back. A part of me went with her! I don't know what to do with myself. (Todd, 2007, p. 642)

Another mother poignantly commented about the lack of understanding other people had of her grief:

> I felt a lack of opportunity to speak and pressure to carry on as normal. Someone said—"Well now you carry on with your life. You can start being normal people again." But that's not how I saw it. I was normal, and Marie was just Marie to me! How could they say that? They didn't understand what it was like for us when Marie was alive and they understood even less after she died! I think we never really had support to deal with Marie's death really. (Todd, 2007, p. 643)

Regardless of the reason that children make off-time transitions, families deserve your support and assistance. They deserve your allegiance in creating a trusting partnership that can help them get what they want in dealing with the unexpected.

REVISITING LANZ AND XENIA POWELL

Xenia Powell knows more than a little bit about life cycle changes and transition points: high school to college, college to motherhood, and one job to another. She's also well versed in the typical life cycle changes of being a mother: raising Lanz from birth through high school.

What's next? Barring bad health, she and Lanz can expect him to earn his degree, find his first job, change jobs (as nearly everyone does), and become a middle-aged man. She herself can expect to accompany him along those stages, as she has done throughout his life. She can expect to retire and then enter her old age years.

Many families can make pretty safe assumptions about their lives; that is so because many do not have a child with a disability. But Xenia is not among the many.

For her, it is safest not to make any assumptions. That's what disability can do: It can cause a family to put aside its assumptions about the future.

Perhaps it is best for Xenia and the professionals who work with her to abide by a single rule: Make no assumptions.

If they adopt this rule, then they should adopt still another: Have high expectations. Xenia had them for herself; Lanz had them for himself.

What professional would dare not have high expectations for them, even as that same professional would be inclined to make no assumptions? Not one who knows about life cycle stages and the surprising effects of disability.

SUMMARY

The changes over a family's life cycle typically occur during four stages—birth and early childhood, childhood, adolescence, and adulthood. Sometimes these events happen "on cycle." Sometimes they are "off cycle." In this chapter, we highlighted issues related to the family function of education at each of these four life cycle stages:

BIRTH AND EARLY CHILDHOOD

- Discovering and coming to terms with disability
- Participating in early childhood services
- Parenting to foster self-determination

CHILDHOOD

- Developing a vision for the future
- Developing a perspective on inclusion

ADOLESCENCE

- Providing sex education
- Expanding self-determination skills

ADULTHOOD

- Identifying postsecondary educational programs and supports
- Accessing supported employment opportunities

LINKING CONTENT TO YOUR LIFE

What stages and transitions have you experienced? How does your family cope with transitions? How can you use this knowledge about yourself and your family to build partnerships with your students' families?

EARLY CHILDHOOD

- How can you support families when their child is diagnosed with a disability prenatally, at birth, or in early childhood?
- What are your beliefs about genetic testing and abortion?
- How can you ensure parents get access to up-to-date nonbiased information about their child's disability and what to expect?

ELEMENTARY

- What are some of the most important things to consider when working with families to build a vision for the future?

- How can you work with families to learn about their cultural beliefs and practices to develop culturally responsive services?
- What would you do if another professional you worked with was not responsive to the family's vision or had low expectations for a child?

ADULTHOOD

- How can you work to prepare students with disabilities for the transition to adulthood?
- Given the lack of individualized, appropriate services available to many individuals with disabilities in adulthood, how can you as an educator work with families to develop resources and strategies to enable students and their families to achieve their vision?
- How can you support families who are experiencing stress because of unexpected transitions and work with them to identify positive strategies for addressing the life changes?

INTRODUCTION TO PART II

History and Public Policy Related to Partnerships

Obviously, families are not the only people who are involved in their children's education. The most important other people are teachers, administrators, providers of specialized services in the schools, and other professionals.

In chapter 5, we describe the roles that families have played. We focus on how those roles relate to their children's education and to the professionals who are involved with their children.

In chapter 6, we describe the two federal education policies that are the backbone of efforts to reform America's schools and that provide the structure within which families and professionals enter into partnerships with each other.

Historical and Current Roles of Parents and Families

JAY, RUD, AND ANN TURNBULL

Jay Turnbull was born June 24, 1967, some five years before the civil rights revolution on behalf of citizens with disabilities blossomed. As a baby, his disability was apparent; he was not attaining the developmental milestones that characterized babies without disabilities, and physicians soon determined that he had mental retardation (now known as intellectual disability) and recommended that his parents place him in an institution. Indeed, Jay did live in two privately operated facilities between the ages of three and seven. By then, his parents had divorced and his father, Rud, had remarried, this time to Ann. "Now, we'll bring Jay home," she said, and so they did, in the summer of 1974.

No one blamed Rud or Jay's biological mother for his disability; they escaped the charge that they caused his disability. But, after Rud and Ann married, neither they nor Jay were free from the expectations that society placed on them, expectations that they would play certain roles in caring for Jay. Indeed, Rud and Ann soon lived out those roles.

They were officers of local, state, and national/international associations of parents committed to individuals with intellectual and other developmental disabilities. To assure that Jay would not spend his life idly, they organized special education, respite, summer camp, group home, and sheltered workshop programs to benefit him and others in their community and state in Chapel Hill, North Carolina, and, later, Lawrence, Kansas.

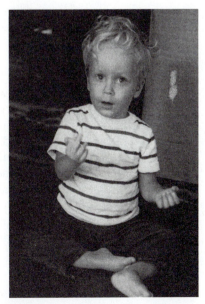

They sought, received, and often acted on the advice of physicians, psychiatrists, special educators, psychologists, applied behavior analysts, positive behavior support specialists, speech-language therapists, music therapists, massage therapists, and yoga instructors, always seeking to mitigate Jay's disabilities, for, when he was 13, he was determined to have autism and, when he was in his early 20s, he was determined to have a rapid cycling bipolar disorder and, in his 30s, an irregular heart rhythm. When they learned about the most recent scientifically based interventions, they used them. Often, they had to develop ways of supporting Jay when there was little, if any, science to tell them what to do for him. Sometimes, they had to battle professionals to prevent Jay from being subjected to interventions that were patently harmful and yet represented the normal practice of the time.

They became advocates not just for their son but also for the entire disability community, writing laws and regulations; authoring proclamations

calling for new laws and approaches to enhancing families' and individuals quality of life; testifying in state legislatures and Congress to persuade policy makers to change laws; serving on local, state, and national commissions in which parents and professionals were collaborating to change policy and practice; and using their own research and others' as well as the foundations for their advocacy. When they had the law on their side, they argued the law; when they had the facts but not the law, they argued the merit of the facts; and when they had neither, they screamed until someone in power responded.

Because they understood the law and science of interventions, they often made decisions about Jay's supports without consulting with or being bound by professional practices that thwarted them and Jay in obtaining the quality of life they sought. More often, however, they found or taught and groomed professionals who would join them in launching new ways to support Jay. Always, they sought partnerships with professionals who knew and practiced the state-of-the-art and shared their values, knowing they could not act alone and still support Jay as he wanted and deserved to be supported.

Even as young children, Jay's sisters, Amy (just a bit more than 7 years younger than Jay) and Kate (10 years younger), supported and often joined Ann and Rud as they played these many roles. Like so many other families, Jay's "cause" enlisted not just his parents but also his sisters and, in turn, others who entered the Turnbull family, not just as people related by blood, marriage, or partnership, but as extended family members.

That was the life that Rud, Ann, Amy, Kate, and other family members played from the day, in August, 1974, when Rud and Ann brought Jay home to live with them, until January 7, 2009, the day Jay died, taken by a massive heart attack, suddenly, instantly, and unexpectedly ripped out of the lives of his family and a community of friends that stretched far beyond the confines of Lawrence, Kansas.

think about it

- How have the roles of parents varied over the last 100 years? What roles did Jay's family play?
- From parents' and professionals' perspectives, what were the beneficial and not so beneficial consequences of the various roles parents and families played? What advantages accrued to Jay's family? What disadvantages?
- What are parents' and families' current roles and how do those roles influence professionals in providing scientifically based, peer-reviewed special education services? What relationships with the research and practice communities did Jay's family have?

:: INTRODUCTION

Why do you need to know about the roles parents and families played as they carried out their awesome responsibilities of raising their children and securing their education? First, history helps you understand what professionals, especially general and special educators, do today. The actions of professionals are often legacies from the past. Second, the lessons of history may assist parents, families, and professionals to overcome today's challenges. And third, history teaches that today's approaches may seem as improbable to the next generation as earlier approaches seem now. (We will use the words *families* and *parents* interchangeably in the rest of the chapter.)

Parents have played eight major roles over time, roles that Jay's parents and then his sisters and extended family members played: (1) they have been regarded as the source or cause of their child's disability, (2) they have organized themselves into voluntary associations, (3) they have developed services for their children, (4) they have been the recipients and beneficiaries of professionals' decisions, (5) they have been their children's teachers, (6) they have been political advocates, (7) they have made education decisions, and (8) they have been partners with professionals. These roles do not represent discrete eras, each with a clear beginning and end. Rather, the roles overlap. There is, however, a general chronological trend to them.

:: PARENTS AS SOURCE OR CAUSE OF THEIR CHILD'S DISABILITY

The leaders of America's eugenics movement (1880–1930)—a movement to improve the health of Americans by, among other things, preventing people with disabilities from marrying or procreating—often accused parents of being the source or cause of their child's disability (Barr, 1913). To eliminate or reduce the number of "unfit" parents, the eugenicists argued, would improve the human race through selective breeding. The eugenics movement was heavily influenced by (1) often-flawed genealogical investigations such as Goddard's (1912) study of the Kallikak family, tracing a family's history through multiple generations of individuals who were identified at that time as "feeble-minded" when in fact they were simply poor; (2) Mendel's laws of heredity, which held that various traits, such as disability, are passed from one generation to another, within a family; and (3) studies (MacMurphy, 1916; Terman, 1916) that argued that delinquent behaviors were strongly associated with "feeble-mindedness" (Scheerenberger, 1983).

As we just noted, the eugenics movement resulted in laws that limited the ability of people with intellectual disability and other disabilities to marry and required them to be sterilized and institutionalized so they could not have children (Ferguson, 1994). In upholding a compulsory sterilization law, Justice Oliver Wendell Holmes, Jr., wrote for the Supreme Court: "Three generations of imbeciles are enough" (*Buck v. Bell,* 1927). Gould (1981) and Smith (1985) have documented that the eugenics movement was misdirected; it was not so much about preventing another generation of "imbeciles" as about controlling the ability of people who were poor to have children. Wehmeyer (2003) pointed out that the movement resulted in the involuntary sterilization of more than 50,000 Americans with an intellectual disability. A California law reflected the attitude toward sterilization during this period. The statute authorized the board of trustees of a state institution, on the recommendation of the superintendent, a clinical psychologist, and a physician, to sterilize involuntarily institutionalized "feeble-minded, chronic manic and demented people, with or without their consent, before discharging them" (Landman, 1932, p. 59).

The eugenics movement also justified the institutionalization of persons with an intellectual disability (formerly called idiots, morons, mental defectives, or mentally retarded). In 1900, only 9,334 persons with an intellectual disability were institutionalized in 1900, but by 1930, 68,035 were in institutions (Scheerenberger, 1983). Professionals were the primary advocates for institutionalization and took upon themselves the role of convincing parents that their children would be better off in institutions. An educational leader provided the following testimony to a New York State Commission in 1915 regarding her efforts to convince parents of "feeble-minded" children to be placed in institutions:

> The point that I think is most interesting in connection with that is that out of 100 cases, I was only able to persuade the parents to send twenty children, and of those twenty children only fifteen remained a year, and at the present time, so far as I know, three more have come out of the institutions and there are now only two . . . which seems to be to point to the fact that until we have some law by which the parents can be made to put the children there, or until we have some law that will compel them to keep them there once they are there, that the public school is the place in which these children have to be educated. (New York State Commission, 1915/1976, p. 114; Ferguson, 2008, p. 52)

During this era, professionals placed strong emphasis on convincing parents to institutionalize their children, although there were some parents who clearly resisted this push. This resistance is exemplified in the following quote from a mother who regretted her decision to institutionalize her son and for 10 years wrote to the institution's superintendent asking that her son be released:

> Now Dr., please stop and think one minute. Doesn't a mother's love go to (*sic*) deep for her children to be separated from them the way I have from Albert. Now please let us hear a kind answer as soon as you can for Dr. if I had only made a visit to the institution first, I do not think I would have been willing to place him there. Please let us know right away what we can do. (Ferguson, 2008, p. 55)

Interestingly, the file for her son identified this mother as "retarded" and the superintendant required the family to post $1,000 bond before they could take their son home for a short vacation. In the end, the superintendent advised the mother that she could visit him occasionally but that the ". . . boy needs institutional care, and it is far better that he remain here" (Ferguson, 2008, p. 56). The number of institutionalized adults and children grew steadily until the mid-1980s, when the movement known as deinstitutionalization finally took hold and caused states to reduce the number of people in institutions (Braddock, Hemp, & Rizzolo, 2008).

The parents-as-cause perspective extended beyond intellectual disability to autism (Bettelheim, 1950, 1967), asthma (Gallagher & Gallagher, 1985), learning disabilities (Oliver, Cole, & Hollingsworth, 1991; Orton, 1930; Thomas, 1905), and emotional disorders (Caplan & Hall-McCorquodale, 1985). Nowhere has professional blame been more directed to parents than with autism. In the 1940s and 1950s, professionals typically described parents of children and youth who had autism as rigid, perfectionist, emotionally impoverished, and depressed (Kanner, 1949; Marcus, 1977). A leading professional, Bruno Bettelheim (1950, 1967), contended that a child who had autism and who exhibited severe withdrawal from his or her parents and other people was responding to the stress created by the parents' "extreme and explosive" hatred of the child. Bettelheim even advocated a "parentectomy"— namely, institutionalizing the child and thereby replacing natural parents with institutional staff and professionals who allegedly would be more competent and caring.

By contrast, in 1977 the National Society for Autistic Children issued a definition of autism that states "no known factors in the psychological environment of a child have been shown to cause autism." In response to this new definition, Frank Warren (1985), the father of a young man with autism and a national disability advocate, pushed for the rejection of Bettelheim's position (see the My Voice box below). Today, autism refers to a developmental disability that significantly affects a student's verbal and nonverbal communication, social interaction, and educational performance; it generally occurs before a child is three years old; and it is not the result of any factors in the child's psychological environment (American Psychiatric Association, 2000).

Some disabilities in children can arise from their parents' behavior. Fetal alcohol syndrome can occur when a pregnant women uses alcohol (Haffner, 2007). The use of illicit drugs such as cocaine and heroin can lead to newborns experiencing withdrawal symptoms at birth and possible long-term developmental issues, including learning and behavior problems (Batshaw, Pellegrino, & Roizen, 2007). Likewise, pregnant women who use illegal intravenous drugs put their children at risk for HIV, the cause of AIDS. Approximately 25% of infants whose mothers are infected with HIV will also become infected if they do not receive intervention (Bell, 2007). However, some children

---

MY VOICE
Frank Warren—Shame on You!

That means we didn't do it . . . We, the parents of autistic children, are just ordinary people. Not any crazier than others. Not "refrigerator parents" any more than others. Not cold intellectuals any more than others. Not neurotic or psychopathic or sociopathic or any of those words that have been made up. It means, Dr. Bettelheim, that you,

and all those others like you who have been laying this incredible guilt trip on us for over 20 years, you are wrong and ought to be ashamed of yourselves.

Source: Warren, F. (1985). A society that is going to kill your children. In H. R. Turnbull & A. P. Turnbull (Eds.), *Parents speak out: Then and now* (2nd ed., p. 217). Upper Saddle River, NJ: Merrill/Prentice Hall.

who are exposed to detrimental conditions early in life develop relatively unscathed, whereas other children fail to thrive and experience developmental delays (Sameroff, 2009; Werner & Smith, 1992).

Our best advice to you is this: Avoid blaming parents. If you need to know the cause of a disability, investigate it. If you learn that parents may have been a cause, as, for example, in instances of child abuse or alcohol or drug abuse during pregnancy, use that information to design supports for the family. Identify and affirm the family's positive contributions to their child. You may be able to help prevent disabilities in their other children and avoid exacerbating their child's existing disability. Blaming can create a barrier to trusting partnerships between you and the family. Without a partnership, you will be less effective in supporting the family, and they will derive less benefit from you.

∷ PARENTS AS RECIPIENTS OF PROFESSIONALS' DECISIONS

As recently as the 1970s, professionals generally expected parents to comply passively and gratefully with decisions about the programs in which their children should participate. As Kolstoe (1970), an author of an early leading textbook on the methods of educating students with disabilities, wrote:

> Should it be judged that special class placement will probably be of most benefit to the child, then placement should be made without delay. Both the child and his parents should be told that the child is being transferred into the special class because the class is special. . . . The entire program should be explained so the parents will understand what lies ahead for the child and so they can support the efforts of the teachers with the child. (p. 42)

As we will point out later in this chapter and throughout the book, some professionals still believe that they know what is best for a student, so they expect families to defer to professional judgment, especially regarding the student's evaluation, individualized program, and educational placement. These expectations place professionals at the center of the decision-making team, directing parents and families about the child's education. (Later in the chapter, we will contrast professionally centered decision-making teams with family-centered decision-making teams and with family-professional partnership decision-making teams.)

Professionals who believe that they are the center of the decision-making team can create a psychological barrier to effective family-professional partnerships by inadvertently (or sometimes deliberately) intimidating parents or even angering them by being so authoritative (Bezdek, Summers, & Turnbull, in press; Turnbull, Turbiville, & Turnbull, 2000). This barrier can be particularly problematic for families from diverse backgrounds whose culture clashes with that of the professionals (Harry, 2008; Kalyanpur & Harry, 1999). Try to be an equal partner with families when making decisions, and try not to expect them to be the passive recipients of your decisions. Throughout this book, you will learn how you can establish trusting partnerships. Understanding and applying these principles will give you the ability to assist parents in significant ways.

∷ PARENTS AS ORGANIZATION MEMBERS

Parents and other family members of children with disabilities began to organize on a local level in the 1930s and on the national level in the late 1940s and 1950s (see the Change Agents Build Capacity box on page 100). They were motivated by (1) their belief that public and professional responses to their children's educational and other needs were inadequate and (2) their desire to share emotional support with others who were facing similar challenges.

Parents created The Arc of the United States in 1949, originally naming it National Association for Retarded Children. The United Cerebral Palsy Association (UCPA) was founded in that same year, largely through the efforts of Leonard H. Goldenson, the father of a child with cerebral palsy. Here is how he described UCPA's beginnings:

> One day, realizing the cost of driving our child into New York City from Westchester, my wife said to me, "Leonard, I know we can afford to do this but what about the poor people? How can they afford to do it?" And she added, "Why don't we look into the possibility of trying to help others in this field?"
>
> It was on that basis that I started to investigate the whole field of cerebral palsy.
>
> Upon investigation, I found there were probably only twenty-some-odd doctors in the entire United States who knew anything about cerebral palsy. I found there were only a few local parents groups in the country that were trying to do something about it. But the parents were so involved with their own children and had to take so much time with them, they could not get out to raise money and inform the public about the subject. (Goldenson, 1965, pp. 1–2)

CHANGE AGENTS BUILD CAPACITY

The History of The Arc of the United States

To name the time and place of the beginning of this movement is like trying to isolate the first growth of grass. For truly, this is a grassroots movement.

The Council for the Retarded Child in Cuyahoga County (Cleveland, Ohio) holds the record in seniority. This group was founded in 1933 to assist children of the area who had been excluded from public schools. More than 10 other organizations were established in the 1930s and one in 1942.

After World War II, the next new organization seems to have appeared in 1946, and each succeeding year recorded an increasing number of groups. A survey published by Woodhull Hay in August 1950, revealed . . . 19,300 dues-paying members, located in 19 states. . . .

In 1950, two sessions were planned, with parent participation, at the American Association on Mental Deficiency meeting in Columbus, Ohio, to plan future directions to help "retarded children." Following these sessions, a handful of parents from east coast to west coast met and the drama started to unfold. In the words of a parent who was there:

> "Imagine it! Practically every parent there thought his group was the pioneer. Most of us were strangers to each other—suspicious of everyone's motives and jealous of their progress."

But the strange atmosphere soon changed. A steering committee was established and planned a convention for later that year in Minneapolis. Ninety persons registered at the convention. Of these, 42 were delegates from 23 organizations in the states of: California, Connecticut, Illinois, Massachusetts, Michigan, Minnesota, Missouri, New Jersey, New York, Ohio, Texas, Vermont, Washington, and Wisconsin.

A masterful statement of purposes emanated from the labors of that first convention. These were parents with a purpose. No money, no precedent, no policy to follow. The officers and directors, in most instances, were strangers to one another—but strangers with a common goal—to help ALL "retarded children" and their parents. In installing officers on that memorable Saturday night (September 30) Luther W. Youngdahl, then governor of Minnesota, said: "Our great democracy can be measured best by what it does for the least of its little citizens." He turned a small hotel auditorium into a cathedral as the hearts and souls of misty-eyed parents echoed those words.

Take Action!

- Recognize the power of organizations in bringing people together collectively to be change agents as contrasted to people having to work in isolated fashion.
- Go to the website of The Arc of the U.S. (www.thearc.org) to review its current mission, projects, and publications.
- Consider your own willingness to join current efforts to advance quality-of-life opportunities for all students with exceptional needs.

Source: NARC. (1954). *Blueprint for a crusade. Publicity and publications manual.* Washington DC: The ARC.

Other parent groups include the National Society for Autistic Children, founded in 1961 and now called Autism Society of America; the Association for Children with Learning Disabilities, founded in 1964; Children and Adults with Attention-Deficit/Hyperactivity Disorder, founded in 1987; and the Federation of Families for Children's Mental Health, founded in 1988 with a firm commitment to including minority families in leadership roles. Note that each of these organizations focuses on a particular type of disability.

Nowadays, families tend to coalesce around specific disability conditions, preferring the smaller disability-specific associations to those that address more than one type of disability. For example, early on The Arc of the United States was the organization for families who had children with intellectual disability, regardless of the particular type of intellectual disability. In the past two decades, however, parents and professionals have created organizations that address discrete and narrow categories of disabilities, for example, the National Down Syndrome Congress and the National Down Syndrome Society, and the National Fragile X Foundation. Both Down syndrome and Fragile X are conditions that are largely associated with an intellectual disability.

The obvious advantage of a tightly focused disability-specific organization is that it offers highly particularized support and information to its members and can secure policy and practices that specially favor its members and their children. A disadvantage is that it can be easily marginalized and irrelevant to larger disability-policy advocacy.

Despite their impact on service delivery and political advocacy, parent organizations cannot be all things to all parents. The late Elizabeth Boggs, one of the founding members of The Arc of the United States, wrote the following concerning her role as a parent advocate:

> I am proud to be the only person who has been continuously active in some volunteer capacity with the National Association for Retarded Citizens [now called The Arc of the United States] since I participated in its founding in 1950. . . . The cause has taken me to 44 states, plus Puerto Rico and 10 foreign countries. It is hard to put a job title on the role I've played. One could say that I've been a social synergist with a predisposition toward communication and collaboration rather than confrontation. (Boggs, 1985, pp. 39–40)

Janet Bennett, also a parent, described organizational membership in a much different light:

> My first phone call to my local unit produced a pleasant enough response from the office secretary and a promise of some information to be mailed. This material consisted of a short summary of the unit's programs and services and a long questionnaire on which I could indicate areas in which I would be delighted to volunteer. . . . The message was clear: a parent in my circumstances, trying to cope with a trauma of uncertain dimensions, should marshal her forces, muster her energies, and get out and work for the cause. . . .
>
> If I had had an unretarded baby, I'd never in a million years have thought of volunteering for anything during that period. Now that I had Kathryn, why in the world would I be expected to do anything of the kind? Yet in the face of minimal help from the organization, it was telling me I should help it. And numb from shock and diminished self-confidence, I did my best to comply. (Bennett, 1985, pp. 163, 164)

Some parents, not all, find it helpful to belong to parent organizations. You should share information with parents about appropriate local, state, and national organizations and encourage them to determine the level and type of their own participation. In every state, there is a Parent Training and Information Center (PTI), funded by the U.S. Department of Education. Each PTI is led by parents who have school-aged children with disabilities; each offers training, materials, consultation, and advocacy for parents; and each is cross-disability, meaning that it responds to parents without respect to the nature or severity of their child's disability. You will learn more about PTIs and other parent resources in chapter 9.

⁜ PARENTS AS SERVICE DEVELOPERS

Parents have played a major role in developing services for individuals with disabilities at all life stages. During the 1950s and 1960s, they and the organizations they created established education programs for children who were excluded from public schools solely because of their disabilities. These parents organized classes in community buildings and church basements, solicited financial support from charitable organizations, and did the job the schools should have been doing (Scheerenberger, 1983). In all of these endeavors, parents have assumed five jobs: creating public awareness, raising money, developing services, operating services, and advocating for others to assume responsibility for service operations. Even today, parents continue to operate services for their children, usually through the organizations to which they belong.

More than two decades ago, Samuel Kirk (1984), a distinguished special education pioneer, described the profound impact of parent organizations:

> I found a satisfaction in associating with many intelligent and knowledgeable parents in these organizations. I found that through association with other parents they learned what the best programs were for their children. If I were to give credit to one group in this country for the advancements that have been made in the education of exceptional children, I would place the parent organizations and parent movement in the forefront as the leading force. (p. 41)

Although some family members prefer to develop, operate, and control the services their children receive, you should not expect them to start and maintain services that are the professionals' responsibility. For example, you should not expect parents of students with autism to start transition programs that prepare students with autism to live their adult lives in an inclusive fashion. After all, parents of children without disabilities are not expected to start and maintain a college-preparatory curriculum in their local high school. Families should have full opportunities to partner with professionals in creating educational, vocational, and recreational programs; but they should not have to assume full responsibility. There is one very good reason for this: Many parents simply do not have the time to develop and operate services. As you learned in chapter 3, parents often devote an extraordinary amount of time to meeting their family functions and satisfying the demands of their for-pay jobs. You should support parents to be parents, first and foremost, not service providers. For parents, service development should be an option, not an expectation.

:: PARENTS AS TEACHERS

The role of parents as teachers emerged during the 1960s, peaked during the 1970s, and was moderated during the mid- to late 1980s. At the root of the parent-as-teacher role was a large body of evidence showing that a family's environment influences their children's intelligence (Hunt, 1972). In particular, data showed that families from economically deprived home environments lacked the opportunities typically available in middle- and upper-class homes (Zigler & Muenchow, 1992). Thus, President Kennedy's New Frontier and President Johnson's Great Society initiatives (for example, Head Start and, later, Early Start) included programs that trained parents to teach their children. The children were expected to make more progress because of their enriched home environments.

As you will learn in the next chapter, the federal special education law, Individuals with Disabilities Education Act, declares that the education of all children with disabilities can be made more effective when the federal government assists state and local education agencies to strengthen the roles and responsibilities of parents and ensure that parents have meaningful opportunities to participate in their children's education (20 U.S.C. Sec. 1401 (c)(5)(B)). That is one reason IDEA gives parents the rights you will learn about in the next chapter and why the law also authorizes and supports the PTIs we mentioned earlier in this chapter.

By providing various rights to parents and supporting capacity-development activities for them, such as the PTIs, Congress acknowledges a theory called environmental enrichment. The theory is largely credited to researcher Urie Bronfenbrenner:

> Bronfenbrenner's notion of parent involvement and the ecological (environmental-influence) model of child development emerged from two sources—his own childhood and his cross-cultural research. Born in Moscow, he emigrated to the United States in 1923. His father, a physician, took a job as director of an institution for the "feeble-minded" in Letchworth Village, New York.

> From time to time, Bronfenbrenner's father would anguish over the institutionalization of a person who did not have mental retardation. Sadly, after a few weeks there, these people of normal intelligence would begin to mimic the mannerisms of the residents who inarguably had a cognitive limitation. When one of the nondisabled "patients" came to work in the Bronfenbrenners' household, however, she gradually resumed a "normal" life, accidentally teaching young Urie an important lesson in how family and community expectations and environments influence human behavior. (Zigler & Muenchow, 1992, pp. 16–17)

Bronfenbrenner's approach—called ecological because it linked family environment to human development—was the basis on which professionals prepared parents for increasing their children's progress and achievement. In the 1970s, professionals, convinced by research showing that parents can be effective teachers of their children (Bricker & Bricker, 1976; Shearer & Shearer, 1977), urged parents to use behavioral principles and child development techniques. Believing that they knew best what the children needed (Turnbull et al., 2000), they praised parents who became coeducators, at-home teachers. By contrast, they withheld praise from those who did not, believing that good parents were those who frequently acted as teachers, not "just" parents. Here is what a mother of a child with Down syndrome had to say about her role and professionals' expectations:

> The message to me as a mother that was pervasive in early intervention's emphasis on development milestones was that we needed to "fix" James. The harder I worked, the more he would achieve . . . I readily became James' teacher. His playtime at home became "learning time" . . . Any free time we had was to be spent on his therapy or to be spent feeling guilty that we weren't doing his therapy. I remember one developmental milestone that he never achieved—stacking three. I modeled for him, prompted him, and finally held his hand while we did it together. Inevitably, when left to attempt it on his own, James would pick up the blocks and throw them. He found this hysterically funny. His early intervention teacher thought he was noncompliant. (Turnbull, Blue-Banning, Turbiville, & Park, 1999, p. 164)

James is now 31 years old and has an inclusive life in his community. His mother looks back on the years of working with him so intensely at home and laments that she has no memories of truly enjoying him as a baby; being under so much pressure to educate him, she lost much of the joy of simply being with him.

Given the optimism that the research data justified (Baker, 1989), it was only natural for early childhood special education programs to insist that parents should be teachers of their own children (Shearer & Shearer, 1977). During the height of the parent-training era, Karnes and Teska (1980) identified the competencies that parents needed to acquire to fulfill their "teacher" role:

> The parental competencies required for direct teaching of the handicapped child at home involve interacting with the child in ways that promote positive behavior; reinforcing desired behavior; establishing an environment that is conducive to learning; setting up and maintaining a routine for direct teaching; using procedures appropriate for teaching concepts and skills; adapting lesson plans to the child's interests and needs; determining whether the child has mastered knowledge and skills; keeping meaningful records, including notes on child progress; participating in a staffing of the child; communicating effectively with others; and assessing the child's stage of development. (p. 99)

These are fewer than half of the skills the authors regarded as essential to the parent-as-teacher role. Compare these skills to the ones you have to master in your own professional training program. Is it realistic to expect parents to develop so many teaching skills?

Some parents find teaching to be very satisfying. Others say it produces guilt and stress if they cannot constantly work with their son or daughter with a disability. Another unintended consequence is the impact that instruction from parents, provided even within the context of typical routines, can have on the self-esteem of children and youth with disabilities. Diamond (1981) described her experiences with her parents as a child with a physical disability:

> Something happens in a parent when relating to his disabled child; he forgets that they're a kid first. I used to think about that a lot when I was a kid. I would be off in a euphoric state, drawing or coloring or cutting out paper dolls, and as often as not the activity would be turned into an occupational therapy session. "You're not holding the scissors right," "Sit up straight so your curvature doesn't get worse." That era was ended when I finally let loose a long and exhaustive tirade. "I'm just a kid! You can't therapize me all the time! I get enough therapy in school every day! I don't think about my handicap all the time like you do!" (p. 30)

Many of today's parents of children and youth with disabilities, unlike parents during the 1970s and early 1980s, seem to balance their roles as teachers with their other roles (Turnbull, Blue-Banning, Turbiville, & Park, 1999; Turnbull et al., 2005). Indeed, as you will learn in chapter 9, many families want more information (not necessarily formal training sessions) on various topics including available services/resources, helping with homework, and future planning.

We encourage you to partner with the families of the students you teach by asking them to let you know what information would be helpful to them in becoming a more informed educational decision maker. Remember to find out informational preferences from not only mothers—but also fathers, brothers and sisters, and extended family members. In situations in which parents are helping their children learn, partnerships will do everyone more good than a professional-knows-best approach.

:: PARENTS AS POLITICAL ADVOCATES

Parents have been successful advocates at the federal, state, and local levels and in legislatures, courts, and executive agencies. Because educational services for most students with disabilities were woefully inadequate throughout 1950 to 1970, parents took on a new role as political advocates. In the early 1970s, parents of students with intellectual disabilities and the Pennsylvania Association for Retarded Children won a lawsuit against the state to obtain a free, appropriate education for children with mental retardation (*Pennsylvania Association for Retarded Citizens (PARC) v. Commonwealth of Pennsylvania,* 1971, 1972).

Within a year after the court's decision in *PARC,* parents and their organizations had brought 27 right-to-education suits in 21 states, usually successfully (Melnick, 1995). Buoyed by their success, parents sought federal legislation to implement the courts' decisions (Turnbull, Stowe, Agosta, Turnbull, Schrandt, & Muller, 2007; Turnbull, Stowe, & Huerta, 2007). Parent organizations representing all areas of disability, particularly The Arc, joined forces with professionals, particularly the Council for Exceptional Children, and successfully advocated for comprehensive federal legislation requiring the states to provide all students with disabilities a free appropriate public education.

> While there was a national agenda in the 1970s to enact special education legislation, at the grassroots level, parents were at the core of the power of the advocacy movement. For parents, advocacy is characterized by "politics of passion," as the stakes are high and a decision has direct impact on the well-being of the child and the family. . . . Most disability advocacy organizations started as local parent groups. . . . (Itkonen, 2007, p. 9)

The parent groups were immensely successful as political advocates and convinced Congress to pass the federal special education law that you will learn about in the next chapter. It is a tribute to parent advocacy—always greatly aided by and sometimes sparked by professional organizations—that Congress passed these laws, that the parent organizations were able to form coalitions with each other and professional groups, and that all of this has been accomplished in a continuous and consistent manner. Lowell Weicker (1985), a former U.S. senator and the father of a son with Down syndrome, played an important role in the advocacy movement and noted the role parents played to preserve and then improve federal policy. In the mid-1980s, he described the impact of political advocacy on attempts by the Reagan administration to de-emphasize the federal role in special education, attempts that he and the parent advocacy movement thwarted:

> The administration did not get its way. Why? Because the disabled people in this country and their advocates repudiated a long-held cliché that they were not a political constituency, or at least not a coherent one. It was assumed that in the rough and tumble world of politics they would not hold their own as a voting block or as advocates for their cause. But that assumption was blown to smithereens in the budget and policy deliberations of 1981, 1982, and again in 1983. In fact, I would be hard-pressed to name another group within the human service spectrum that has not only survived the policies of this administration but has also defeated them as consistently and as convincingly as the disabled community has. Indeed, it has set an example for others, who were believed to be better organized. (p. 284)

A comprehensive analysis of parent and professional organizations' advocacy in advancing special education policy from 1975 to the present highlighted the most effective advocacy strategies (Itkonen, 2009). Families were particularly effective as advocates because of their diligence and their high personal stakes in what happened to their children.

Having been effective as advocates to persuade the courts and then Congress to create rights to education for their children, parents had hardly completed their work. Indeed, they soon took on a new role, one that the federal law fostered and one that many parents wanted.

∷ PARENTS AS EDUCATIONAL DECISION MAKERS

As you will learn in chapter 6, IDEA was revolutionary when it was enacted because it granted—and still grants—parents a right to participate with educators in making decisions about their children, recognizing the critical role that families play in their children's development, the desirability of fostering parent-professional partnerships, and the necessity of subjecting schools to parental oversight.

In granting these rights to parents, Congress adopted—and still affirms—the basic premise that families of children and youth with disabilities could make no assumptions that the public schools would enroll their children, much less educate them appropriately (Turnbull, Turnbull, & Wheat, 1982). Congress regarded—and still regards—parents as monitors of educators' work. This view reflected—and still reflects—a major reversal in expectations about parents' roles. No longer were parents expected to passively receive professionals' decisions. Now, they were and still are expected to make educational decisions and to monitor professionals' decisions.

There is little that is static about being an education decision maker; the role is dynamic and changed since 1975, when Congress enacted IDEA (Erwin & Soodak, 2008). Although parents' relationships with professionals may have become more equal than two decades ago, the majority of parents participate in educational decision making in a more passive than active style, as you will learn in chapter 11. Sometimes parents do not have the time to be educational decision makers. As you learned in chapter 3, many families have no unclaimed time to add more responsibilities. Other families do not have the motivation to be educational decision makers. Still others have the motivation but do not have the knowledge and skills. Even those who have time, motivation, knowledge, and skills face an educational context that inhibits rather than facilitates their role as partners. This is particularly so for parents from culturally and linguistically diverse backgrounds (Harry, 2008; Kalyanpur & Harry, 1999).

In the field of early childhood education, the role of parents as decision makers took a new direction in the 1980s with the introduction of a family-centered model. The role of parents as the recipients of professionals' decisions is professionally centered. Over time, however, practitioners, policy leaders, and researchers, especially those in early education, began to move from professional-centeredness to family-centeredness (Dunst, Trivette, & Deal, 1988; Epley, Summers, & Turnbull, in press; Turnbull et al., 2000).

Five key elements of family-centeredness are (1) building on family choice by ensuring that families are the ultimate decision makers, (2) capitalizing on families' strengths, (3) making the family the unit of services and support, instead of centering services and support on only the child or the child and mother, (4) building positive relationships with families, and (5) providing individualized family services (Allen & Petr, 1996; Epley, Summers, & Turnbull, in press).

The first characteristic, family choice, is especially notable. The ideal in family-centered services is for professionals to defer to the family in decision making regarding the nature and extent of services and supports for the young child and for other family members. Yet, family-centeredness is stronger as a philosophy than as a practice in early intervention services (Dunst, 2002; Epley et al., in press). Furthermore, family-centered practices diminish as the child grows older (Dunst, 2002).

:: FAMILIES AS PARTNERS

In this book, we focus on the role of families as partners. An important word in that sentence is *families*. As we stated earlier, until early intervention developed a family-centered approach, almost all emphasis was on parents and not on families. Under family-centered approaches, the whole family, not just one or more of its members, receives support and services (Allen & Petr, 1996; Epley et al., in press). Policy makers and professionals now recognize that partnerships should not be limited to parents only (especially to mothers only). Partnerships can and should involve relationships between professionals and other family members, such as fathers, grandparents, brothers and sisters, and even close family friends. Each of these people can support and enhance the educational outcomes for students with exceptionalities. You will read in the Together We Can box below about a partnership that produced remarkable outcomes for the student we featured in this chapter, Jay Turnbull.

TOGETHER WE CAN

Being Cool, Defying the Historical Norm, and Shaping the Future

How important is it for a student with a disability to be "cool" in high school? Very. Dressing, walking, and talking "cool" reduces the stigma of disability and increases the student's inclusion into nearly every school activity.

How important is it for the student's parents and teachers to agree that "being cool" is a legitimate educational goal? Very. Without an agreement, neither the parents nor teacher will reinforce the student's "cool" behaviors. Education will not generalize across school and home, and education at school will not be as durable as education in both school and home.

What does it matter in the long run—from the perspective of history—that at least two parents, two younger sisters, and one "with it" teacher agreed to teach a 20-year-old man with an intellectual disability to be "cool"? It matters a great deal.

It matters because an entire family and one teacher entered into a single-minded partnership to secure the maximum inclusion of that young man. They had an outcome in mind, and they pursued it directly, collaboratively, and forcefully.

What difference did it make that Ann and Rud Turnbull, their daughters Amy and Kate, and Mary Morningstar started their partnership by recognizing that Jay Turnbull would not fit into a large high school of very upper-middle-class students unless he dressed, walked, and talked "cool"?

When Jay received his varsity letter for being the assistant manager of the varsity football team, the mothers of the tri-captains approached him and said, "Jay, our sons drew lots to see which of you would wear his letter jacket to school for the rest of the year. You see, you will get one, but not for a few months, and our boys want you to be as cool as you can be, which is very cool."

Take Action!

- Think about the symbolism in the offer of a letter jacket by the coolest of the cool, a football captain, of the competition among each captain to donate something of himself to Jay, and of the lessons the captains and Jay taught their parents and their schoolmates. What lesson do you learn about status, stigma, and symbols, and how will you act on that lesson?
- Think about the letter jacket as a lesson about acceptance, even about welcoming an otherwise different person into the inner circle of coolness. What will you do when you teach a student who is not "cool" enough but can learn to be cool?
- Regard the partnership as purposeful—as wholly committed to integration. Would integration—the welcoming and acceptance—be so possible without the partnership?

Source: Adapted from Turnbull, A., & Morningstar, M. (1993). Family and professional interaction. In M. E. Snell (Ed.), *Instruction of students with severe disabilities* (4th ed., pp. 31–60). New York: Macmillan Publishing Company.

Merriam-Webster's Collegiate Dictionary (2003) defines *partnership* as "a relationship . . . involving close cooperation between parties having specified and joint rights and responsibilities." This definition places families and professionals into a relationship where each has rights and responsibilities toward the other. As you will learn in chapter 7, we elaborate on the dictionary definition and define *partnerships* as follows:

> Partnership refers to a relationship in which families (not just parents) and professionals build on each others' expertise and resources, as appropriate, for the purpose of making and carrying out decisions that will directly benefit students and indirectly benefit family members and professionals.

As you will learn in chapter 7, there are seven principles of partnership: communication, professional competence, respect, commitment, equality, advocacy, and trust.

> Embracing the idea of partnership means moving beyond the recognition that families should be involved in the educational process and moving toward establishing relationships between families and professionals that are firmly rooted in an idea of equal partnership . . . If trust is not present, a partnership will likely not survive. It becomes the shared responsibility of all stakeholders, including practitioners, administrators, policymakers, and university faculty, to ensure that partnerships with families are the standards across schools in America and that these family-professional partnerships not only are sustained but flourish. (Erwin & Soodak, 2008, pp. 58–59)

Family-professional partnerships have two important benefits. First, they benefit the student by bringing together multiple perspectives and resources. Second, they benefit the partners by making available multiple perspectives and resources. For example, a general classroom teacher who is responsible for educating a student with autism is not left alone to solve all the challenges facing the student. Instead, the teacher can rely on a dynamic team of partners to find the most successful solutions to those challenges.

Because partnerships occur in school contexts, we describe in the next chapter the policies that most directly affect students, families, and professionals who are involved in special education.

REVISITING JAY TURNBULL AND HIS FAMILY

Do not for a moment doubt that Rud and Ann Turnbull ever regretted that they played so many roles in Jay's life. They often said, "Jay has been our best teacher. The problem often is that he gives us our final examination before enrolling us in the course he is teaching." By that they mean simply that they followed Jay; he was their guide, insisting on a life of dignity, one that he could not obtain without their support, without laws benefiting him and them, without research that demonstrated effective means of support, and without professional partners and other reliable allies who shared Jay's vision for his life and his parents' and sisters' commitment to follow Jay's lead and support him to have just that life (Turnbull & Turnbull, in press).

When he was failing at group home living, they asked, "Jay, where do you want to live?" He answered, "With Sue and Dom," indicating he wanted to live in a home of his own, with housemates (such as Sue and Dom, who lived with Jay in the residential program in New England) who were deeply devoted to him and not themselves. When they asked, "Jay, where do you want to work?" He answered, "Coat and tie," indicating he wanted to work somewhere else than in a workshop with no one but people with disabilities.

In answering Jay's call to dignity, Ann and Rud played every role except one: They were never blamed for the fact that Jay had disabilities. Instead, professionals often accused them of being unrealistic, of having greater expectations for Jay than were possibly justified given the nature and extent of his disabilities. Still other professionals subscribed to what Jay, Rud, and Ann wanted; they became partners, communicating effectively, advocating for Jay, Rud, and Ann, respecting each of them, treating them with respect and as equal partners in Jay's life, developing their own and other professionals' competence to respond to Jay's needs and choices, and trusting both Jay and his family that the path Jay and they wanted to follow was the right one. In chapter 6, you will learn how the law fosters exactly that kind of partnership by creating rights for Jay and his parents and students and families affected by disability.

SUMMARY

You have learned that parents have played eight roles. Rather than being discrete and occuring only at easily defined points of time, these roles overlap; parents must play some of them simultaneously.

PARENTS AS SOURCE OR CAUSE OF THEIR CHILD'S DISABILITY

- The eugenics movement accused parents of being the source or cause of their child's disability.
- Although the parents-as-cause perspective extended to many different disabilities, historically it has been particularly strong in the field of autism.

PARENTS AS RECIPIENTS OF PROFESSIONALS DECISIONS

- In the early 1900s, professionals strongly encouraged parents to place their children in institutions and resisted parents' efforts to keep their children at home.
- In the 1970s, the prevailing view in special education was that parents should follow professionals' advice about the nature of special education and the child's placement.

PARENTS AS ORGANIZATION MEMBERS

- Parents begin to organize on a local level in the 1930s and on a national level in the 1940s and 1950s to encourage stronger societal support for children with disabilities and to share emotional support with other parents.

PARENTS AS SERVICE DEVELOPERS

- Parents have played a major role in developing services for individuals with disabilities at all life stages.

PARENTS AS TEACHERS

- Especially in the 1970s, the view was that parents should assume a teaching role and work to increase their child's overall development and educational success.

- Parents had a particularly strong role as teachers in early childhood special education programs, and an unintended consequence of parents providing instruction for their children was a negative impact on the child's self-esteem.

PARENTS AS POLITICAL ADVOCATES

- Parents of children with disabilities were particularly influential in their advocacy by bringing court cases on the right-to-education of students with disabilities and in convincing Congress to pass federal legislation pertaining to the education of students with disabilities (IDEA).

PARENTS AS EDUCATIONAL DECISION MAKERS

- Congress regarded parents as persons who could ensure that professionals would provide an appropriate education to children with disabilities.
- The majority of parents participate in educational decision making in a more passive rather than active role.

FAMILIES AS PARTNERS

- Partnerships are relationships in which families (not just parents) and professionals build on each others' expertise and resources, as appropriate, for the purpose of making and carrying out decisions that will directly benefit students and indirectly benefit family members and professionals.
- The most contemporary role for families is to have trusting partnerships with professionals, sharing responsibility for educational success.

LINKING CONTENT TO YOUR LIFE

As a professional, it is particularly important that you know the field's history. If you will be teaching older students, their families will have played many different roles before they have an opportunity to develop a partnership with you. Even if families have younger children, they often have heard the "stories" about when times were different. For these reasons, you should not only be aware of historical roles but also reflect on your own values and opinions that relate to these roles. Let's consider those roles and how you will respond to them.

PARENTS AS THE CAUSE

- What is your responsibility if you know that a friend or acquaintance is pregnant and using alcohol? How will you respond to her if her child has fetal alcohol syndrome?

PARENTS AS ORGANIZATION MEMBERS

- If a father of a young child refuses to join a parent organization, how should you respond when you think he and his child could benefit from joining it?

PARENTS AS SERVICE DEVELOPERS

- When a parent asks you to help develop a service that the child's school does not provide but that research shows will help the child, what role do you want to play?

PARENTS AS RECIPIENTS OF YOUR ADVICE

- When you offer a completely evidence-based recommendation and a student's parents reject it, should you consider reporting them for neglecting their child or should you offer alternative but also professionally defensible recommendations?

PARENTS AS TEACHERS

- When a mother who has no partner to help her at home and has other children to raise tells you she simply can't carry out some at-home training that you are providing at school, how should you respond?

PARENTS AS ADVOCATES

- When you believe your school district should change some of its practices, do you tell the parents what to advocate for and then let them do so alone, or do you join them as a reliable ally?

PARENTS AS EDUCATION DECISION MAKERS

- When parents refuse to defer to your judgment, do you dismiss them as ignorant or uncaring, or do you ask yourself, "What's at the root of the parents' resistance?"

PARENTS AS PARTNERS

- When you consider the many roles parents have had to play, often unwillingly and unnecessarily, which of the seven elements of an effective partnership do you practice most, or do you practice all of them simultaneously?

CHAPTER 6

Policies and Family and Professional Partnerships

JAY, RUD, AND ANN TURNBULL

Congress enacted the predecessor to today's special education law in 1975, when Jay Turnbull was 8 years old. As the 1975–1976 school year approached, Ann and Rud, his parents, enrolled him in school in Chapel Hill, North Carolina, and, on the opening day of school that year, awaited the school bus that would pick him up and take him and other students in his neighborhood to school. They had worked closely with the school superintendent, securing state funding for the school program, recruiting and recommending two well-qualified former students of Ann's, and meeting with the district's special education director and other staff. They expected no problems, for they had been good partners with the district's administrators. On that first day of school, however, they were rudely surprised.

The bus never stopped to let Jay board it.

Later that morning, Rud met with the school district superintendent to ask why Jay had been bypassed. Reluctantly, for he did not want to disrupt the partnership he and Ann had worked to create, Rud mentioned that he had drafted the state's new special education law and that he had had a role in drafting the "due process" regulations of the new federal special education law. Hopefully, he said that he was sure the superintendent knew about both laws. After they talked about Jay's rights, they each affirmed that they were committed to ensuring Jay's rights. Having reached consensus, they shook hands and parted.

The bus stopped the next day, and thus Jay began his free appropriate public education. During the years beginning in 1975 and ending in 1987, Jay was in separate special education programs for students with an intellectual disability, in both Chapel Hill and, later, Lawrence, Kansas. He had only casual interactions with peers who did not have disabilities.

In his last year of school eligibility, 1987–1988, Jay, then age 20, remained in a separate academic program but was fully integrated into extracurricular and other school

activities at Walt Whitman High School, Bethesda, Maryland. By then, he had been classified as having both an intellectual disability and autism. He had begun to learn some, but too few, skills to equip him to work in his community, in a real job.

At Walt Whitman, however, Jay earned his letter in football as a manager of the varsity team. He acquired skills at reading, clerical work, and community transportation that he had never been taught before. And he danced the entire night long, with cheerleaders, pom-pom girls, members of the school band, and his classmates with disabilities at the senior prom.

What made the difference? The law made a difference. Likewise, reforms that were sweeping across special and general education. So, too, research about teaching and learning for students such as Jay.

The biggest change, however, was that one person was highly qualified and deeply value-driven. She was Jay's teacher, Mary Morningstar, who is now a professor at The University of Kansas' Department of Special Education.

think about it

- What are the elements of school reform in special and general education? What reforms benefited Jay and should benefit students these days?
- Given that school reform makes schools accountable for assuring acceptable outcomes for all students, what opportunities exist for parents and professionals to be partners in an era of accountability? What are the alternatives to adversarial confrontation, such as Jay's parents sometimes had to use?
- What are the basic principles of the two federal laws shaping children's education and parents' and professionals' partnerships in an era of accountability? How do those laws benefit today's students and how might they have benefited Jay when he was a student, one of the first cohort of students with disabilities to benefit from the federal special education law?

:: ::

:: INTRODUCTION

In chapter 5, we highlighted eight roles that parents and families of students with disabilities have played, and we concluded that, today, families and educators are expected to be partners with each other to enhance student outcomes. Although we briefly discussed how IDEA has influenced families' roles, we did not explore the most powerful factor that now affects families' roles. That factor is the nation's efforts to reform its schools.

:: SCHOOL REFORM, ACCOUNTABILITY, AND PARTNERSHIPS

Reform for Accountability

Four Major Influences. During the past 50 years, at least four major recurring developments have influenced policy makers, educators, and families as they have sought to improve

America's schools (Berliner & Biddle, 1996; Burello, Lashley, & Beatty, 2001; Fullan, 1999; Goldenberg, 2004; Koret Task Force, 2003; Loveless, 2003; Senge, 2000; Tyack & Cuban, 1995). Those four developments are:

- advances in technology by economic competitors— formerly, Russia, Germany, and Japan, and, recently, Korea, China, and India,
- the low achievement scores of American students when compared to those of students in other nations,
- the need for a well-trained domestic workforce, capable of retaining American economic, technological, and military supremacy in the world, and
- the civil rights movements on behalf of students who are female, who are from culturally and linguistically diverse backgrounds, and who have disabilities.

The Federal-State-Local Relationships. To advance our nation's interests in an increasingly globalized and technology-driven world, our nation looks to its schools to educate the country's youth to lead the country and maintain its world-leading role. But in looking to our schools, our policy makers—those who want to use the federal government to support schools to secure national goals—confront the fact that state and local governments have had a great deal of discretion in how to operate schools. The tradition of local control of schools, subject to state oversight, is as old as our country.

Even today, state laws, the regulations promulgated by each state education agency (SEA) and the policies and procedures of each local education agency (LEA), have a significant role in educators' day-to-day job of educating all children, especially those with disabilities. Nevertheless, federal laws have priority over state and local laws when there is a conflict between the federal and the state/local laws. That is why we emphasize the federal laws.

How did the federal government become so involved in general and special education? The answer requires us to review a history that began more than 55 years ago (as of the date we are revising this book).

Evolving Federal, State, and Local Government Roles in Reforming General Education. The federal government's initial step into public education resulted from the decision of the United States Supreme Court, in *Brown v. Topeka Board of Education* (1954), that racial segregation in education violated the federal constitution by denying equal educational opportunities to African American students. A decade later, Congress responded to *Brown*, emphasizing equity and equality; later, it focused on excellence, outcomes, and accountability. The following are the laws Congress enacted to spur general education reform.

- The Civil Rights Act of 1964 (P. L. 88-352) prohibits SEAs and LEAs from discriminating against students on the basis of their race, color, or national origin.
- Title IX of the Education Amendments of 1972 (P. L. 92-318) prohibits SEAs and LEAs from discriminating on the basis of sex.
- The National Defense Education Act of 1958 (P. L. 85-854) created a loan program for university and college students studying science, mathematics, and foreign languages.
- The Elementary and Secondary Education Act of 1965 (P. L. 89-10) launched a comprehensive set of school reforms, including, under Title 1 of the Act, assistance to schools in which there were large numbers of students living in poverty to attempt to close the performance gap between poor and affluent children.
- The Elementary and Secondary Education Act Amendments of 1988 (P. L. 100-297) required LEAs and SEAs to conform to a new accountability system, using average individual student gains on annual standardized, norm-referenced tests as indicators of their effectiveness or lack of effectiveness and allowing Title 1 funds to be used for school-wide reform in schools where at least 75% of the students were at or below the then-federal poverty level.
- The Goals 2000: Educate America Act of 1993 (P. L. 103-227) responded to critics who charged that the 1988 amendments overemphasized basic skills, isolated poor students from the general curriculum, and caused schools to rely on procedural compliance rather than outcomes. The 1993 amendments rested on a report developed by federal and state government leaders, A Nation at Risk. This report sought excellence and accountability in schools through voluntary "opportunity to learn standards" that address curricula, instruction, assessment of student performance, teacher capability, and nondiscriminatory practices benefiting all students.
- The Improve America's Schools Act of 1994 (P. L. 103-382) reflected a standards-based approach but replaced annual testing with three-year testing in grades 3–5, 6–9, and 10–12. It allowed each SEA to define what constitutes adequate yearly progress for all students and required each to disaggregate data on students by race and disability so that accountability and transparency would exist.
- The No Child Left Behind Act of 2002 (P. L. 107-110) is the current general-education reform law. We discuss it in detail next and refer to it as NCLB.

Bear in mind the obvious trend of these general education reform laws: first, assistance, and, then, insistence on outcome-based education through standards-based approaches. Federal insistence on schools' accountability is not a new fact of life for educators, parents, and students (including those with disabilities). It is, however, especially powerful in NCLB.

The Evolving Federal, State, and Local Government Roles in Special Education. The civil rights movement for African Americans and then the civil rights movement for women set the precedent for a civil rights movement for students with disabilities. Two federal court decisions (*PARC v. Commonwealth*, 1971, 1972) and *Mills v. D.C. Board of Education* (1972) established the rule that state and local education agencies may not discriminate on the basis of disability, which, like race and sex, is an unchosen trait. Further, the state of the science in special education made it clear that all children could learn; there was no justification, then, for a state or local agency to exclude any child with a disability from schools. Congress responded to the courts' decisions and the science by enacting laws benefiting children with disabilities.

- By enacting the Education for All Handicapped Children Act of 1975 (P. L. 94-142), Congress established that all children with disabilities have a right to a free appropriate public education. That law, commonly called P. L. 94-142, is the predecessor to today's Individuals with Disabilities Education Act.
  - ✓ Congress later amended this law by (a) creating incentives for early intervention and early childhood special education and for transition-to-adulthood programs (P. L. 98-199, 1983), (b) establishing a new early intervention program (P. L. 99-457, 1986), (c) strengthening students' rights and renaming the statute to be Individuals with Disabilities Education Act of 1990 (P. L. 101-476), and (d) protecting students against unjustified discipline (P. L. 105-17, 1997).
  - ✓ Congress amended IDEA in 2004 (P. L. 108-446), responding to two reports (Finn, Rotherman, & Hokanson, 2001; President's Commission on Excellence in Special Education, 2002) by (a) strengthening the accountability-for-outcomes provisions, (b) increasing parents' responsibilities to be partners with educators, and (c) granting schools more discretion in disciplining students. The 2004 version of the law is the current one.
- In 1975, Congress enacted Section 504 of the Rehabilitation Act Amendments of 1975 and prohibited any recipient of federal financial assistance, including SEAs and LEAs, from discriminating solely on the basis of disability in schools and other federally assisted programs.
- Finally, in 1990 Congress enacted a broad civil rights law, The Americans with Disabilities Act, and prohibited discrimination solely on the basis of disability in nearly all aspects of the private sector.

As the first decade of the twenty-first century comes to an end, federally driven reforms give two messages: (a) schools must be accountable for educating all students and (b) "all" includes every student with a disability. Accountability is an absolute necessity. And all means all.

Families

Families are the core social units of society. They, not the federal or a state government, have the ultimate—and awesome—responsibility to raise their children. As you learned in chapter 5, families' roles with respect to their children and educators have changed. But families' responsibilities for assuring their children receive and benefit from an effective education have not changed.

Indeed, federal law directly acknowledges that families have significant roles and responsibilities in being partners with educators and that it therefore is proper for federal law to shape and support families' roles. When families are more able to be partners, then the outcomes for their children will be better and in turn our country itself will continue to be a world leader.

The 2004 amendments to IDEA explicitly deal with families and their roles as partners with educators. In those amendments, Congress declared that "almost 30 years of research and experience has demonstrated that the education of children with disabilities can be made more effective by . . . strengthening the role and responsibilities of parents and ensuring that families (of children with disabilities) have meaningful opportunities to participate in the education of their children at school and home" (20 U.S.C. Sec. 1401 (c)(5)(B)). Note the emphasis: Families not only have a role but they also have a responsibility in educating their children. Later in this chapter, we will describe IDEA in detail and emphasize families' roles and responsibilities.

:: INDIVIDUALS WITH DISABILITIES EDUCATION ACT (IDEA)

IDEA requires state education agencies (SEAs) and local education agencies (LEAs) to provide to every student who has a disability a *free appropriate public education* (FAPE). Under IDEA, the U.S. Department of Education allocates federal money to SEAs and LEAs to assist them in educating students with disabilities. One part of the law, called "Part B," provides for the education of students ages 3 through 21. Another part, called "Part C," provides for the education of infants and toddlers, birth to age 3. In order to qualify for Part B and Part C federal money, SEAs and LEAs must adhere to six principles for educating students with disabilities (Turnbull, Stowe, & Huerta, 2007). We will describe those later in this chapter; first, however, we describe the differences between Part B (ages 3 to 21) and Part C (ages birth to 3).

Age Eligibility

Early Intervention. In reenacting IDEA in 2004 and Part C, for infants/toddlers ages birth to 3, Congress declared that there is "an urgent and substantial need" to "enhance" infants' development, "minimize their potential for developmental delays," and "recognize the significant brain development" that occurs in the first three years of their lives. It also stated that it is important to reduce the educational costs that arise from special education, maximize children's potential to live independently, and enhance state and local capacities to meet the needs of very young children (20 U.S.C. Sec. 631(a)(1), (2), (3), and (5)).

Children are eligible for early intervention if they experience significant developmental delays, that is, have a disability resulting in a significant developmental delay or have a diagnosed physical or mental condition that carries a high probability of causing a significant developmental delay (20 U.S.C. Sec. 1432(5)). States may serve children who would be at risk for experiencing those delays if they do not receive early intervention (20 U.S.C. Sec. 1432(1)).

Especially relevant to us in this book is that Congress found an "urgent and substantial need" to "enhance the capacity of families to meet the special needs of their infants and toddlers with disabilities" (20 U.S.C. Sec. 1431(a)(4)).

Consider the language about enhancing families' capacities in light of the other purposes of IDEA. Note how families' capacities to meet their children's needs relate directly to the language about enhancing early development and independent living and reducing special education placement. Then consider that families are the core unit of society and that school reform, accountability for outcomes, and family-school partnerships are linked to each other. Clearly, Congress believed that families must play an important role in the early years of their child's life and must be supported to do so.

Accordingly, Congress provided that parents may consent (or refuse to consent) to any early intervention services, may consent to some but not other services, may participate in developing an individualized plan for their child's education and for their own support in educating their child, and may receive a variety of services even as their child receives other services (20 U.S.C. Sec. 1436). These provisions not only advance families' roles in their children's education but also require families to carry out the two recent roles we described in chapter 5—being educational decision makers and being partners with professionals.

Early Childhood. After a child has qualified for early intervention services, the child's parents and preschool educators may agree that the child will continue to receive early intervention services during ages 3 to 5. Note, early childhood services are not available to a child, aged 3 to 5, who is "at risk" for developmental delays; that kind of eligibility is only available under Part C and does not continue into the child's third and subsequent years of life.

If the child's parents and the child's educators do not agree that the early intervention services will continue when the child is 3, then the child will receive services designed for children ages 3 through 21. These services are authorized by Part B of IDEA. Although IDEA provides that early education, for children ages 3 to 6, is optional (a state may decide to offer it or not), all states offer early education.

Elementary Through Secondary Education. As a consequence of the decision by all states to offer early education, children ages 3 through 21 have a right to a free appropriate public education and are eligible to receive services under Part B if they qualify in 1 of 10 disability categories. The disability categories are: mental retardation (also better known these days as intellectual disability), hearing impairment (including deafness), speech or language impairments, visual impairments (including blindness), emotional disturbance, orthopedic impairments, autism, traumatic brain injury, other health impairments, or specific learning disabilities.

Six principles govern these children's education; we will review those in the next section. Each reflects Congress's intent to make education available to students with disabilities and then to hold schools and parents more responsible for securing acceptable outcomes from the children's education.

Outcomes of a Free Appropriate Public Education

Four Elements of Our Nation's Disability Policy. IDEA (20 U.S.C. Sec. 1401(c)(1)), Section 504 and the Americans with Disabilities Act (ADA) declare that our nation's disability policy includes four elements:

- Equal opportunity—having the same opportunities in life as people without disabilities
- Full participation—having opportunities to be included in all aspects of their community and being free of segregation based on their disabilities
- Independent living—having opportunities to participate fully in decisions about them and to make choices about how to live their lives
- Economic self-sufficiency—having opportunities to work or otherwise contribute to their communities or households.

Three Indicators of Outcomes in Achieving the Four Elements. To what extent are students with disabilities achieving these outcomes? Data are available about three indicators: school completion, post-school employment, and overall satisfaction with life.

Students with disabilities are less likely than their peers without disabilities to complete high school or college (21 percent versus 10 percent) (National Organization on

Disability, 2004). Students with visual impairments, hearing impairments, and traumatic brain injury are more likely than other students with disabilities to earn their high school diplomas; those with emotional/behavioral disabilities, intellectual disability, and multiple disabilities are less likely to do so (U.S. Department of Education, 2007). Students who are American Indian/Alaskan Native and African American and have disabilities are more likely to drop out of school than students with disabilities in any other ethnic group.

Whereas nearly 78 percent of all people without disabilities work full or part time (pre–2008/2009 recession), only 35 percent of adults with disabilities work full or part time (National Organization on Disability, 2004). The more severe the disability the lower the employment rate; and people with significant disabilities who are Latino or African American are also less likely to be employed than their European American counterparts (National Council on Disability, 2000).

Finally, people with disabilities are more likely than those without disabilities to be dissatisfied with their lives. That is so, in part, because people with disabilities are more likely to live in households whose annual income is less than $15,000, more likely to not have accessible transportation, less likely to participate in their communities, and two times more likely not to have health care (National Organization on Disability, 2004). Recently, the National Council on Disability (2009) advocated for beefed-up programs in transition from secondary schools to adult life and increased use of assistive technologies.

You may well be asking: What do IDEA and NCLB have to do with these four elements of our nation's policy and the three indicators showing poor outcomes? Good question; here are the answers.

Six Principles of IDEA Part B

As we said previously, children ages 3 through 21 benefit from the six principles of Part B. Figure 6.1 describes these six principles. With respect to each of IDEA's six principles, we will highlight (a) background problems that persuaded Congress to adopt the principle, (b) major purposes and provisions of the principle (including educators' rights pertaining to each principle), and (c) implications of each principle for family-professional partnerships.

As you read about IDEA and its six principles, you may begin to harbor a suspicion that the law has too much influence on you and your colleagues. You may say, "We are trained to practice" and add, "And we want to be free to practice according to the best professional standards. We don't want Congress telling us what to do."

It is understandable if you respond that way. Many professionals do. But here is the story behind IDEA—a story that relates to your profession. The Council on Exceptional

---

FIGURE 6.1 Six principles of IDEA.

- **Zero reject.** Enroll all children and youth, including all those with disabilities.
- **Nondiscriminatory evaluation.** Determine whether an enrolled student has a disability and, if so, the nature of special education and related services that the student requires.
- **Appropriate education.** Tailor the student's education to address the student's individualized needs and strengths and ensure that education benefits the students.
- **Least restrictive environment.** To the maximum extent appropriate for the student, ensure that every student receives education in the general education environment and do not remove the student from regular education unless the nature or severity of the disability is such that education in general education classes with the use of supplementary aids and services cannot be achieved satisfactorily.
- **Procedural due process.** Implement a system of checks and balances so that parents and professionals may hold each other accountable for providing the student with a free appropriate public education in the least restrictive environment.
- **Parent participation.** Implement the parent participation rights related to every principle and grant parents access to educational records and opportunities to serve on state and local special education advisory committees.

Children (CEC), the nation's special education professional association, profoundly influenced Congress when it enacted IDEA as the Education for All Handicapped Children Act of 1975 (P. L. 94-142). It had lobbied hard for the law and then drafted a Model Statute to assist the states to conform their laws to the new federal law (Higgins, Weintraub, Abeson, & Turnbull, 1977). So, CEC has been involved with special education law from the very beginning. Even now, its code of ethics commands its members to act in ways that align with IDEA. In Figure 6.2, you will find the CEC Code and our commentary relating it to IDEA.

Zero Reject

Background Problems. For many years before 1975, when Congress enacted P. L. 94-142, state and local educational agencies barred many students with disabilities from any kind of education whatsoever. Remember the bus passing by Jay Turnbull? Indeed, Congress found in 1975 that one million

FIGURE **6.2**	CEC Code of Ethics for educators of persons with exceptionalities.

We declare the following principles to be the Code of Ethics for educators of persons with exceptionalities. Members of the special education profession are responsible for upholding and advancing these principles. Members of The Council for Exceptional Children agree to judge and be judged by them in accordance with the spirit and provisions of this Code.

A. Special education professionals are committed to developing the highest educational and quality of life potential of individuals with exceptionalities.

B. Special education professionals promote and maintain a high level of competence and integrity in practicing their profession.

C. Special education professionals engage in professional activities which benefit individuals with exceptionalities, their families, other colleagues, students, or research subjects.

D. Special education professionals exercise objective professional judgment in the practice of their profession.

E. Special education professionals strive to advance their knowledge and skills regarding the education of individuals with exceptionalities.

F. Special education professionals work within the standards and policies of their profession.

G. Special education professionals do not condone or participate in unethical or illegal acts, nor violate professional standards adopted by the Delegate Assembly of CEC.

Source: The Council for Exceptional Children. (1993). *CEC policy manual*, Section Three, part 2, (p. 4). Reston, VA: Author. Retrieved on August 16, 2009, from http://www.cec.sped.org/Content/NavigationMenu/ProfessionalDevelopment/ProfessionalStandards/RedBook

children with disabilities were excluded entirely from schooling, many were not receiving an appropriate education even when they were in school, and too often many were educated in private settings, at great expense and often far away from their parents. To remedy these problems, Congress established the zero-reject principle.

Purposes and Provisions. The principle of zero reject is that no school may exclude any student ages 3 through 21 who has a disability and must educate each such student, without regard to the type or extent of the student's disability. The purpose of the principle is to assure that every student has a chance for the four outcomes described previously: equal opportunity in school and other aspects of life, full participation, independent living, and economic self-sufficiency (20 U.S.C. Sec. 1401 (c)(1)).

Congress stated the zero-reject principle when it declared that the IDEA's purpose is to ensure that all—note the emphasis on *all*—children with disabilities will have a free appropriate public education consisting of special education and related services. All means all. Every child with a disability has the benefit of the zero-reject principle.

Definition of Special Education and Related Services. IDEA defines special education as "specially designed instruction, at no charge to the parents or guardians, to meet the unique needs of a child with a disability" (IDEA, 20 U.S.C. Sec. 1401(a)(16)). Related services are those that "may be required to assist the child with the disability to benefit from special education" (IDEA, 20 U.S.C. Sec. 1401(a)(17)). Figure 6.3 describes the related services for Parts B and C.

Parent counseling and training is one of the related services available when a child is between the ages of 3 and 21 (Part B). It consists of ". . . assisting parents in understanding the special needs of their child, providing parents with information about child development, and helping parents acquire necessary skills that will allow them to support the implementation of their child's IEP" (34 C.F.R. Sec. 300.24 (b)(7)). In addition, counseling and guidance to parents are part of the related services of audiology, psychological services, social work services, and speech pathology.

Parents of children from birth to 3 (Part C) benefit from the related service of "family training, counseling, and home visits" provided by social workers, psychologists, and other qualified personnel "to assist the child's family to understand the child's special needs and to enhance the child's development" (34 C.F.R. Sec. 303.112 (d)(3)). Social work services emphasize parent-child interactions, family-group counseling with parents and other family members, problem solving to enhance the child's development, and mobilizing and coordinating community resources so that the child and the family will receive maximum benefit from early intervention services.

Discipline and School Safety. Many educational agencies have wanted to expel students whose behavior creates discipline problems or violates schools' codes of conduct. On the

FIGURE 6.3	Related services in Part B and Part C of IDEA.

Definitions of Related Services in IDEA
The related services apply to Part B and students ages 3 to 21 unless otherwise indicated.

- *Assistive technology and services:* acquiring and using devices and services to restore lost capacities or improve impaired capacities (Part C, and a "special consideration" for Part B IEPs).
- *Audiology:* determining the range, nature, and degree of hearing loss and operating programs for treatment and prevention of hearing loss.
- *Counseling services:* counseling by social workers, psychologists, guidance counselors, or other qualified professionals.
- *Early identification:* identifying a disability as early as possible in a child's life.
- *Interpreting services:* various means for communicating with children with hearing impairments or who are deaf-blind.
- *Family training, counseling, and home visits:* assisting families to enhance their child's development (Part C only).
- *Health services:* enabling a child to benefit from other early intervention services (Part C only).
- *Medical services:* determining a child's medically related disability that results in the child's need for special education and related services.
- *Occupational therapy:* improving, developing, or restoring functions impaired or lost through illness, injury, or deprivation.
- *Orientation and mobility services:* assisting a visually impaired or blind student to get around within various environments.
- *Parent counseling and training:* providing parents with information about child development.
- *Physical therapy:* services by a physical therapist.
- *Psychological services:* administering and interpreting psychological and educational tests and other assessment procedures and managing a program of psychological services, including psychological counseling for children and parents.
- *Recreation and therapeutic recreation:* assessing leisure function, recreation programs in schools and community agencies, and leisure education.
- *Rehabilitative counseling services:* planning for career development, employment preparation, achieving independence, and integration in the workplace and community.
- *School health services:* attending to educationally related health needs through services provided by a school nurse or other qualified professional.
- *Service coordination services:* assistance and services by a service coordinator to a child and family (Part C only).
- *Social work services in schools:* preparing a social or developmental history on a child, counseling groups and individuals, and mobilizing school and community resources.
- *Speech pathology and speech-language pathology:* diagnosing specific speech or language impairments and giving guidance regarding speech and language impairments.
- *Transportation and related costs:* providing travel to and from services and schools, travel in and around school buildings, and specialized equipment (e.g., special or adapted buses, lifts, and ramps).
- *Vision services:* assessing vision in an infant/toddler (Part C only).

one hand, state-local and federal policies seek to create safe schools. State-local "zero-tolerance" policies, the federal Gun Free Schools Zone Act of 1994, and NCLB favor a policy of safe schools. On the other hand, the zero-reject principle favors a policy of educating all students with disabilities, including those whose behaviors create unsafe conditions.

IDEA strikes a balance between school safety and the zero-reject principle. It requires the student's LEA to determine whether the student's behavior, for which the agency is disciplining the student, is a manifestation of the student's disability. The question is: Did the student's disability cause, or does it have a direct and substantial relationship to, the student's behavior? If the student's behavior is not a manifestation of the disability (the disability does not cause the behavior), then, as a general rule, the school may discipline the student in the same ways and to the same extent that it disciplines students who do not have disabilities. However, the school may not entirely terminate services to a student it has suspended for more than 10 consecutive days; this is the no-cessation rule. Instead, the school must serve the student, either at home, in a different educational setting than the school used before, in a state-operated facility (e.g., psychiatric hospital), or in a private school.

Educators have the following rights and expectations under the zero-reject principle:

- To be safe
- To be a member of decision-making teams
- To participate in a manifestation determination hearing to determine the relationship between the child's disability and the child's behavior
- To benefit from comprehensive programs, such as school-wide positive behavior support, to address problem behavior

Note how educators' rights and expectations support the students' education and carry out the zero-reject principle.

Implications for Family-Professional Partnerships. When students with disabilities teeter on the line between attending school and being suspended or expelled, typically the whole family is vulnerable to the potential for exclusion. Parents generally do not want to invest time and energy in advocating that their child not be disciplined; they are dealing with their child's behavior as well. They usually cannot eagerly enter into a partnership with professionals who only regard their child as needing discipline. Nor do most of them want to be involved in disciplinary hearings—the "manifestation determinations"—or other adversarial meetings about their child and school discipline. When a child is creating discipline problems, the child's teacher should contact the parents and, in partnership with them, try to determine why the child violates school codes or endangers himself or herself, other students, or school staff.

When they exclude students from school, educators often make it necessary for at least one of the child's parents to miss work or forego other commitments so they can stay at home with their child. In the Change Agents Build Capacity box on page 118, you will read how Sheri McMahon struggled and then eventually won policy changes for children in a state's foster care system, many of whom, like her son, have disabilities.

Nondiscriminatory Evaluation

Background Problems. It has not always been easy for schools to determine whether a student has a disability, much less, if the student has one, what kind of education to provide to mitigate the disability's effects. Too often in the past, evaluations and assessment tests were simply not refined enough to identify a disability or its educational consequences. The result was that schools often excluded from special education students who should have been included or placed students into special education programs that were not likely to benefit the students.

Unhappily, there was another problem. For many years, the tests that schools administered arguably discriminated against students who were from culturally and linguistically diverse backgrounds. Indeed, when Congress enacted P. L. 94-142 in 1975, it acknowledged that many students from culturally and linguistically diverse backgrounds have been recommended for services or placed in special education programs, often because there are not enough safeguards around evaluation to (a) protect against any possible bias in the tests or in educators' testing procedures and test interpretations and (b) assure that the students indeed do have a disability that requires special education intervention.

Twenty-nine years later, when it reenacted IDEA (2004), Congress again acknowledged that discrimination in special education still exists. There are two important aspects of the discrimination: (a) mislabeling and high dropout rates among minority students and (b) disproportionate representation in special education of minority children, especially of African American students classified as having intellectual disability and emotional-behavioral disorders (20 U.S.C. Sec. 1401 (c)(10) and (11)).

Purposes and Provisions. The nondiscriminatory evaluation principle assures that each student will have a fair, unbiased evaluation to determine whether he or she has a disability; and, if so, the nature of special education and related services that the student needs. We discuss the evaluation requirements in detail in chapter 10. At this point, we identify only the four major dimensions of evaluation that IDEA addresses and an example of only one of the IDEA requirements within each category:

- *Breadth of the evaluation:* include more than one test,
- *Procedures:* use assessments that are validated for the specific purpose for which they are used,
- *Timing:* reevaluate the student every three years or more frequently if conditions warrant or it is requested by the student's parent or teacher, and
- *Interpretation* of the evaluation data: ensure that a group of persons consisting of educators and parents interprets evaluation data.

The principle of nondiscriminatory evaluation creates a process through which educators and families, in partnership with each other, may understand the student's needs and strengths and then use the evaluation to provide the student

CHANGE AGENTS BUILD CAPACITY

Sheri McMahon—Reforming the Foster Care and Special Education Systems

Sheri McMahon says she has been caught 'twixt and 'tween. The 'twixt is the special education system that has duties to educate her 18-year-old son. The 'tween is the foster care system that had custody of him for 33 months when he was between 10 and 14 years old. He entered the foster care system in the middle of a dispute with his school whether he needed special education services. As soon as he entered that system, he was moved from his current school to one farther away. While in foster care, he attended four different schools in two different states.

When Sheri was able to persuade one school to begin to evaluate him for special education, he would be moved before the evaluation was completed. When an evaluation team determined he was not eligible for special education, Sheri invoked her due process rights and was challenged on the ground that she was not his parent any longer—the foster care system was his parent and she had no right to sue to enforce his rights. By then, he had been moved to yet another school system. "There were so many school and foster-care records but so little education," she wrote. "Our lives were documented, not lived."

For years, Sheri struggled to persuade the state education agency and foster care agency to align their values and systems. What was the problem? It was that the education system values participation in society and individual planning for the child, in partnership with the child's parents. By contrast, the foster care system values the "best interest" of the child and the child's safety and disregards the child's parents' wishes.

Sheri decided to work both inside and outside these systems to reform them. As sort of an insider, she served on the state's mental health planning committee and a regional mental health advisory council. As an outsider, she organized parents who have had children in the foster care system; this ad hoc coalition had the goal of persuading the state legislature to consider creating an ombudsman over the child protective services system. The ombudsman would have power to receive and investigate complaints from parents and others about faults in the system, identify legal and practice barriers to safe care of foster children, and propose system-wide and child-specific solutions. That's all—just a person with power to investigate, analyze, and recommend.

Sheri's efforts paid off when a member of the legislature introduced a bill that would require the legislature and its research staff to study the ombudsman approach. In response to oral testimony from a parent and written testimony from over a dozen parents whose children had been in foster care, the legislature passed and the governor signed Senate Bill 2420. Sheri's work was not finished, however. Next, she needed to persuade the legislature's staff to give high priority to SB 2420. Again, petitions from parents and the publication of an "op-ed" (opinion editorial) in five of the state's newspapers did the job: the bill received high priority.

Meanwhile, Sheri's son still has not been qualified for special education services despite overwhelming evidence that he has a disability. He has qualified to receive Social Security benefits as an adult with a disability. But he is still 'twixt and 'tween foster care and special education—like a ping-pong ball in a world-cup tournament, he is volleyed back and forth, apparently because neither foster care nor special education wants to serve him. Ironically, Sheri's action has benefited nearly everyone except her son.

Take Action!

- Don't let a "Sheri" situation develop for any child you are teaching.
- Identify whether any of your students is in foster care.
- Determine who their biological and foster parents are, and who their foster care case manager is.
- Determine who has legal authority to speak for the child—the case manager, the foster care parent, or the biological parent.
- Involve these people and the student, as appropriate, as you develop the student's IEP, but remember you have to defer to the person legally authorized to give consent for the child to be evaluated and served through special education.

Source: Adapted with permission from "Caught 'Twixt and 'Tween," by Sheri McMahon, in Turnbull, A., Turnbull, R., and Wehmeyer, M. L. (2010), *Exceptional Lives: Special Education in Today's Schools* (6th ed., p. 195). Upper Saddle River, NJ and Columbus, OH: Merrill/Pearson.

with a free appropriate public education. The partnership cannot occur, however, unless the parents know that a school wants to evaluate their child, so IDEA requires schools to give notice to the parents whenever it wants to evaluate the student (whether for the first or any other time) and to get the parents' consent for each evaluation before conducting it and before placing the student into or out of special education.

Educators themselves have to benefit from the nondiscriminatory evaluation principle; after all, the evaluation must help them decide, in partnership with the child's parents, how and where to educate the student. Educators' rights and expectations are as follows:

- To obtain evaluations that provide a relevant basis for appropriate curriculum, instruction, and assessment.
- To have their observations and classroom-based assessments considered as part of the evaluation data.
- To participate on the evaluation team to make sure that results are helpful for planning curriculum, instruction, and assessment.

Implications for Family-Professional Partnerships. The nondiscriminatory evaluation is the foundation for all other education decision making (Turnbull, Stowe, & Huerta, 2007). Unless the evaluation is accurate, the child's education program and placement will be flawed. Because highly technical terms and difficult concepts are involved in evaluations, educators should communicate with parents in clear and understandable language (see chapter 10).

Appropriate Education

Background Problems. Even when students with disabilities were admitted to schools and evaluated fairly, there were no assurances that they would benefit. That was a problem when Congress enacted P. L. 94-142 in 1975; sadly, it still was a problem when Congress reenacted IDEA in 2004. At that time, it found that the children's education has been impeded by "low expectations" and "an insufficient focus" on using research that demonstrates how to teach students with disabilities (20 U.S.C. Sec. 1401 (c)(4)).

To secure better outcomes for the children, Congress admonished educators and parents alike to have "high expectations" for the children, and it required educators to ensure that the children have access to the regular classroom to the maximum extent appropriate for the child so that the students will "meet the developmental goals and, to the maximum extent possible, the challenging expectations that have been established (under NCLB) for all children" (20 U.S.C. Sec. 1401 (c)(5)). Further, Congress encouraged educators to use "whole-school approaches, scientifically based early reading programs, positive behavioral interventions and

supports, and early intervening services" (20 U.S.C. Sec. 1401 (c)(5)).

Major Purposes and Provisions. Appropriate education means that schools must tailor a student's education to the student's individual needs and capacities and thereby benefit the student. These twin demands—*individualization* and *benefit*—are satisfied when professionals and parents (and students, when appropriate) partner with each other in developing and carrying out appropriate, individualized curriculum and instruction for the student, that is, when they *follow the process* that IDEA sets out. When a student is between the ages of 6 and 21, the student is entitled to an individualized education program (IEP). When the child is between the ages of birth and 3, the child and family are entitled to an individualized family services plan (IFSP). When the child is between the ages of 3 and 6, the IFSP may serve as the child's IEP or the child may receive an IEP that replaces the IFSP.

The IEP and IFSP set out the type and extent of special education and related services that the child (and family, in the case of an IFSP) will receive from the school (see chapter 11). The IFSP and IEP specify the content that the student will be taught (curriculum), how the student will be taught (instructional strategies), how the student's progress will be determined (assessment), and where the student will be educated (placement in the least restrictive environment). Parents are members of the IFSP and IEP teams and have the right to be full-fledged educational decision makers. In chapter 11, you will learn how to implement IDEA's "individualization" provisions. Read about Greg Motley in the Together We Can box on page 120 to understand the benefits of partnership.

Educators, too, have rights and expectations around appropriate education:

- To seek and expect to have reliable allies among family members and professional colleagues who assist in instructing the student.
- To secure guidance related to curriculum and instructional modifications and support and to benefit from supplementary aids and services (for example, universally designed curriculum).
- To be a member of the IFSP/IEP team.
- To expect that the school will comply with the required participants and components of an IFSP/IEP.
- To read a copy of their student's IFSP/IEP.

Implications for Family-Professional Partnerships. IDEA sets out both a process (required meetings) and documents (IEP and IFSP) that, together, define the nature and extent of the special education and related services that each student will receive. Chapter 8 teaches you the

TOGETHER WE CAN
Greg Motley and His Team—Away from "F"

Greg Motley, a high school freshman who qualified for IDEA benefits, simply could not stay seated during class, keep his hands to himself, take tests in the same room as other students, or move from the "all-F (failing)" tier of his class into a "passing grade" tier. At least he couldn't until his IEP team decided that he could and that the team would transform *could* into *would* and then into *will*.

Greg himself was the team leader. He acknowledged that he needed various kinds of help "to get better, to do better." His mother, Sherry, his teachers, Stephen D. Kroeger and Donna Owens at Turpin High School in the Forest Hills School District in suburban Cincinnati, other teachers, and administrators at his school were his team players,

Together but following Greg's lead, they agreed on a vision for Greg. It was more than staying in his seat and so on; it was that Greg would work outdoors, perhaps as a forester, perhaps in other jobs. This vision drove the team to specify goals and objectives that would be part of Greg's IEP and would help move him toward his vision. The authentic buy-in from vision, goals, and objectives that Greg, Sherry, Stephen, and Donna made then shaped the response of the rest of the Turpin High School staff.

Promised accommodations in how he tests, who his teachers are, and what supplemental aids and supports he receives, Greg signed off on his IEP. Soon, he climbed out of the "F" category and into the "C" category. As his teachers noted, "The IEP is a useless document unless the student buys it."

Take Action!

- Identify the causes of a student's academic and social failure. It may well be that the student believes his teachers utterly disregard him and his needs.
- Having identified the causes, convene a team to address them. If the student believes his teachers do not respond to him, include the student on the team and pay particular attention to his suggestions.
- Be sure to include the student's parents (they have a legal right to be members of the team) but do not let them dominate the family's perspective. They may not understand as well as the student what happens when teachers and the student interact, and so they may not be as helpful as the student in suggesting a better way to teach and learn.

Source: Adapted from Kroeger, S. D., Leibold, C. K., & Ryan, B. (1999, Sept./Oct.). Creating a sense of ownership in the IEP process. *Teaching Exceptional Children,* 4–9.

---

communication skills that you should use when developing the IFSP/IEP. Chapter 11 teaches you how to be an active participant in the meetings and how to develop the IFSP/IEP document.

Least Restrictive Environment

Background Problems. Historically, local educational agencies segregated children with disabilities from their age-appropriate peers who did not have disabilities; as Congress recognized in enacting P. L. 94-142 in 1975, these children did not have an opportunity to attend school "with their peers" who do not have disabilities (20 U.S.C. Sec. 1400(c)(2)(C) (1997)). That is so because schools assigned students with disabilities to special school districts, or placed them into buildings or classrooms where the only students were those with disabilities, physically separating them from their peers without disabilities. All too often, these settings and programs limited the students' abilities

and opportunities to learn and to use their education outside of school.

Congress continued to be concerned with segregation when it reenacted IDEA in 2004. It declared that children's education can be more effective when the children have access to the general curriculum in the regular classroom; it declared special education should be a service for the children and not a place where children are sent; it acknowledged the benefits of providing special education, related services, and supplementary aids and services in the regular classroom; and it imposed strict requirements on schools to integrate children with disabilities to the maximum extent appropriate for each of them (20 U.S.C. Sec. 1401 (c)(5)).

Major Purposes and Provisions. The principle of least restrictive environment is that schools must educate students with a disability alongside students who do not have disabilities to the "maximum extent appropriate" for each student with a disability. IDEA gives meaning to the concept of "appropriate" by providing that ". . . special classes, separate schooling, or other removal of students with disabilities from the regular education environment (may) occur(s) only when the nature or severity of the disability is such that education in regular classes with the use of supplementary aides and services cannot be achieved satisfactorily" (20 U.S.C. Sec. 1412).

Just how much removal from the regular classroom does IDEA allow? And to what kinds of settings? IDEA is explicit that schools may offer a continuum of placements, from less to more restrictive (e.g., regular education classrooms to home-based, hospital-based, or institutional placements) and may place students in one of these atypical (separate or segregated) settings only if it also provides an appropriate education to them.

Thus, this principle creates a presumption in favor of educating students with a disability with their peers who do not have disabilities. IDEA specifically implements this presumption by requiring that a student's IEP must describe

- the extent to which, if any, a student may not participate in general education.
- the special education, related services, supplementary aids and services, program modifications, and other supports that will enable the student to make progress in the general curriculum and to participate in extracurricular and other school activities.
- the extent to which, if any, the student will or will not be in general education. This provision creates a "full inclusion" and "partial inclusion" option for these IEP team members. A student may fully participate in some of the general curriculum or may partially

participate in it. IDEA defines the general curriculum as consisting of three different elements: the academic curriculum, the extracurricular activities of the school, and the other school activities offered to students without disabilities (20 U.S.C. Sec. 1414(d)(1)(A)). Thus, the IEP team members may decide, for example, that a student should be in some but not all special education classes for some or part of a school day, be in some but not all extracurricular activities for an entire day, and be fully included in all other school activities (dances and field trips). When the student needs related services or his or her teachers can benefit from supplementary aids and supports to include the student, these should be forthcoming.

Figure 6.4 illustrates this "mix and match" approach—mixing full/partial and matching that approach with the three domains of the general curriculum.

The principle of least restrictive environment also affords rights to teachers to

- benefit from a nondiscriminatory evaluation that addresses the student's LRE opportunities and to be members of a team that provides benefits to students in all three domains of the general curriculum,
- benefit from related services and supplementary aids and services and from collaborations with professionals who deliver those services, and
- have the student's IFSP/IEP team plan program modifications and supports to enable teachers to successfully teach students with disabilities.

FIGURE 6.4   **The mix-and-match matrix.**

	Academic	Extracurricular	Other School Activities
Full			
Partial			

Implications for Family-Professional Partnerships.
Because professionals and parents alike are members of the
IFSP and IEP teams that make the placement decisions, the
LRE principle creates an opportunity for professionals and
families to be partners in determining the placement that
constitutes the least restrictive environment for the student.

Procedural Due Process

Background Problems. Traditionally, educators had
nearly unchallenged authority to operate their classrooms
on their own terms. For students with disabilities, that kind
of authority too often resulted in:

- *Exclusion:* violation of the principle of zero reject.
- *Misclassification:* violation of nondiscriminatory
  evaluation.
- *Denial of a genuine individualized education:* violation of
  appropriate education.
- *Segregated placements:* violation of least restrictive
  environment.

Moreover, students and their parents traditionally
lacked the right to protest educators' actions. As you
learned in chapter 5, parents were sometimes obliged to
play the roles of service developers and political advocates
if professionals did not serve their children. The professionals' power, however, was inconsistent with the traditional notion of American law that those who are in public
service must be held accountable to the public for their
decisions.

In reenacting IDEA in 2004, Congress restated its
commitment to procedural due process. IDEA remained
consistent in expressing concerns about schools' accountability (20 U.S.C. Secs. 1401 (c)(5)(C)), and aligned IDEA
with NCLB (Sec. 1414(d)(1)(a)(i)), requiring students to
participate in state and local education agency assessments of
student and school progress. But it also was the intent to
focus education resources more on teaching and learning
and less on paperwork and other requirements that "do not
assist in improving educational results" (20 U.S.C. Sec. 1401
(c)(5)(G)). Similarly, IDEA expressed its commitment to
relieving schools of "irrelevant and unnecessary paperwork
burdens that do not lead to improved educational outcomes"
(20 U.S.C. Sec. 1401 (c)(9)). Although one of the motivations for Congress reenacting IDEA was parents' alleged
overuse of due process to hold schools accountable (Finn,
Rotherham, & Hokanson, 2001; President's Commission on
Excellence in Special Education, 2002), Congress declared
that "(p)arents and schools should be given opportunities to
resolve their disagreements in positive and constructive
ways" (20 U.S.C. Sec. 1401 (c)(8)).

Major Purposes and Provisions. It is inarguable that professionals and parents should be accountable to each other.
From the constitutional perspective, the due process principle codifies the historic rule of governmental accountability to
the public and the constitutional principle of due process—
that is, fair dealing between the government and the gov-
erned. Indeed, Congress, when it reauthorized IDEA in 2004,
intended to strengthen parents' roles and responsibilities for
their children's outcomes (20 U.S.C. Sec. 1401 (c)(5)(B)).

Accordingly, IDEA requires schools to provide parents
with notice concerning the action they want to take concerning a child's evaluation (NDE), program (AE), or placement (LRE) (20 U.S.C. Sec. 1415(b) and (c)). It also gives
parents and educators two procedures for holding each other
accountable for the child's education. They are (a) the due
process hearing and (b) two different forms of alternative
dispute resolution.

The Due Process Hearing. Parents or schools may require each other to "go to a hearing" before an impartial
"hearing officer," who serves as a judge to adjudicate the
parents' and teachers' rights and responsibilities. At the
hearing, the parents or schools may challenge each other's
actions in providing, or failing to provide, the student with
a free appropriate public education in the least restrictive
environment.

The hearing is a mini-trial, with the parents and school
professionals each having the right to introduce evidence,
present and cross-examine witnesses, be represented by a
lawyer, and obtain a written or electronic record of the hearing. Parents also have the right to have their child present at
the hearing. Initially, the hearing is held in front of an individual called the due process hearing officer. The losing party
may appeal an adverse judgment to a federal or state trial
court, go to trial on the case, and then appeal still further to
higher courts, including a state supreme court or the United
States Supreme Court.

There are two disadvantages to the due process provisions. One is that they can cause schools to practice defensive education, being concerned only with protecting
themselves from any form of legal liability rather than with
providing an appropriate education. The other is that they
can create an adversarial process, involving huge financial
and emotional costs to the parties and siphoning schools'
and parents' resources from their major duty to educate and
raise a student (Fiedler, 2000; Lanigan, Audette, Dreier, &
Kobersy, 2000). That's the perspective one parent expressed, as you will read in the My Voice box on page 123.

Two Types of Alternative Dispute Resolution. IDEA
offers parents and professionals two different processes for

MY VOICE

April Bruce-Stewart—It's the Best I Can Do

April Bruce-Stewart has been advocating for her daughter from the moment she enrolled her in the first grade. She requested an evaluation and was told she "just" wanted services. She decided to take the path of least resistance and homeschool her daughter. Six years later, after her daughter had been diagnosed with diabetes and mental health challenges, April tried to get a Section 504, reasonable accommodations plan developed for her. The school refused but still made some accommodations, largely because of the school nurse.

After her daughter entered high school in August 2007, April took a letter from her daughter's physicians to school and unsuccessfully sought accommodations. When her daughter's cell phone rang in class to remind her to take her diabetes medications, the teacher disciplined her by putting her into detention. That discipline provoked April into requesting a "504 plan." Four months later, the school responded: "No," and April next filed a complaint with the Office of Civil Rights (OCR), U.S. Department of Education. Now the school district administrators started stonewalling her. First, they said she had to fill out a particular form; she did. Then they requested a meeting to discuss only one, not all, of April's requests and her daughter's needs. April complained again to the OCR. When the administrators soon thereafter said her daughter might be eligible for accommodations because of her mental health challenges, they also asked for all of her psychiatric-treatment records; April refused, citing privacy concerns, and filed another complaint with OCR. OCR responded by saying it could not act yet because school administrators had not properly completed an OCR form. Knowing that April would pursue her daughter's rights, the school principal called April, met with her, correctly completed the OCR forms but refused to make any accommodations even though April gave him a sheaf of records from her daughter's psychiatrist.

Now the school district's lawyers wanted to meet with April, but not to offer accommodations but rather to persuade her to back off from some, if not all, of her requests. April refused to meet. By that time, she had spent 15 months trying to get to the table with OCR and the school district. The attorneys again pressed her to meet; she finally agreed only to be told the agenda was the process everyone would follow in handling the dispute, not the nature of the accommodations her daughter would have. Meanwhile, her daughter was failing one subject; was not allowed to bring her cell phone to school even though it is programmed to remind her when to take her medication or have her blood sugar checked; and was prohibited from bringing her diabetic stick into school, on the ground that it is a weapon.

"Whatever she needs," writes April, "the school says 'no.' And so the legal process is all I have left for her, and it grinds slowly and ever so finely. I think the idea is to wear me down or have me pull my daughter out of school again. I don't know yet what 'the best I can do is.' I'm still working on it. I hope it's better than I've done so far."

Put yourself in April's shoes. Then try on the shoes of the school administrators. What's your role as an educator—to stonewall or accommodate? What does it take to convince you, a professional, that a child has a disability? Does the legal process—with its slow and fine grinding down of a parent—serve the child well? Or does it really protect the school from doing what the law requires? What should April do—keep advocating and invoking her daughter's rights, or homeschool her daughter again? What are your duties under the CEC ethical code?

Take Action!

- Pay attention to the student's parents; they have information you need.
- Act quickly. The student needs your expertise now, not years later.
- Don't nitpick about which form needs to be filled out; forms don't drive the substance of the action you have to take to benefit the student.
- Try to avoid forcing parents to due process hearings. Use mediation or the IDEA's dispute resolution conference.
- Put yourself in the parent's place and ask: What is the right action for me to take?

Source: Turnbull, A., Turnbull, R., and Wehmeyer, M. L. (2010). *Exceptional lives: Special education in today's schools* (6th ed., p. 105). Upper Saddle River, NJ, and Columbus, OH: Merrill/Pearson.

resolving their disputes other than by a due process hearing and trial.

First, IDEA provides that parents and professionals may agree to engage in mediation before going to a due process hearing. Indeed, IDEA requires the schools to tell parents where they can get information about the benefits of mediation. Schools and parents cannot force each other into mediation, however; both must agree to it.

Mediation engages parents and representatives of the school district in a collaborative problem-solving process, not the formal due process hearing. An impartial mediator leads the process, and the decision of the parents and educators is reduced to writing, remains confidential, and is enforceable in court.

Second, IDEA provides that parents and professionals may agree not to use mediation but instead to engage in a "resolution session" at which members of the student's IEP team and a person from the student's local educational agency with power to make decisions, and the parents, discuss the dispute and how to resolve it (20 U.S.C. Sec. 1415(f)(1)(B)).

Particularly because IDEA assumes that professionals and parents alike are committed to the child's appropriate education and that their disagreements focus on the child, educators also have due process rights to

- Initiate due process against parents who, in the educators' judgment, err in refusing consent to let educators evaluate or recommend their child for special education service.
- Have the same rights in due process hearings, mediation, and resolution sessions as the parents.
- Receive support from school administrators and school lawyers as they participate in these proceedings.

Implications for Family-Professional Partnerships.
IDEA's due process provisions seek mutual accountability. They make it possible for parents to know what educators propose to do (the notice requirements) and to consent to them or to protest through mediation. They also make it possible for educators to seek a hearing in order to protest the parents' refusal to consent to a proposal that educators believe will benefit the child. The purpose of mutual accountability is, of course, to ensure that the student receives a free appropriate public education in the least restrictive environment.

Parent Participation

Background Problems. As you learned in chapter 5, schools often excluded parents from the process of making decisions about students' education. Parents were merely recipients of educators' decisions. The principle of parent participation challenges educators and parents to cast off that subservient and historic role and to become partners in making and carrying out decisions about the students' education.

Major Purposes and Provisions. The principle is that parents have a role and even a responsibility to make decisions about their child's education and that IDEA should strengthen parents' ability to exercise these roles and responsibilities (20 U.S.C. Sec. 1401 (c)(50(B)). In the broadest of ways, this principle legitimizes parents and students as educational decision makers and enables parents, students, and professionals to establish partnerships with each other.

- Parents have rights to participate in disciplinary hearings (e.g., the manifestation determinations) in the zero-reject principle; to be involved in the child's evaluation through the nondiscriminatory evaluation principle; to be members of the team that decides on the child's program (the appropriate education principle) and placement (the least restrictive education principle); and to challenge (or be challenged) concerning the child's IDEA rights (the due process principle).
- Parents have access to school records concerning the student and control over who has access to those records.
- Representatives of parents—themselves parents—must participate on state and local special education advisory committees to ensure that parent perspectives are incorporated into policy and program decisions.

Figure 6.5 sets out tips for educators in providing parents access to their children's education records.

As partners in making decisions, educators, too, have rights and expectations:

- To expect their colleagues to protect the confidentiality of information about students.
- To benefit from the contributions that parents make on local and state advisory committees.
- To form partnerships with parents to assure acceptable special education outcomes.

Implications for Family-Professional Partnerships.
The principle of parent and student participation pervades all aspects of IDEA. It also is the theme of this entire textbook, so, in chapters 8 through 12, we discuss in detail how parents and professionals can be partners in carrying out this principle.

We have described the six principles of IDEA. That law, however, applies to only those students who are qualified as

FIGURE 6.5	Tips for providing access to parents of their children's educational records.

- Comply with parents' requests to read their child's educational records within 45 days of the request.
- Interpret or explain the records to the parents.
- Give copies of their child's records to parents who request it.
- Provide copies at no cost to the parents, if they cannot afford the cost of copies.
- Listen to parents who believe that the educational records contain inaccurate or misleading information. If they request that information in the records be changed, determine if you agree with their position. If you do agree, make the change in the records. If you do not agree, recognize that the parents may initiate a due process hearing to resolve the conflict of opinion.

FIGURE 6.6	Six principles of NCLB.

Accountability for results. Reward school districts and schools that improve student academic achievement and reform those that do not.

School safety. Acknowledge that all children need a safe environment in which to learn and achieve. Require states to report on school safety to the public and districts to establish a plan for keeping the school safe and drug free.

Parental choice. Grant parents the right to transfer their child from a "failing" or "unsafe" school to a better and safer one.

Teacher quality. Acknowledge that learning depends on teaching; students achieve when they have good teachers. Condition federal aid on states' agreement to hire "highly qualified" teachers.

Scientifically based methods of teaching. Acknowledge that teaching and learning depend not just on highly qualified teachers but also on the teachers' use of scientifically based methods of teaching. Grant federal funds to states and school districts that use only those methods.

Local flexibility. Encourage local solutions for local problems and do not hold schools accountable for student outcomes unless the schools also can use federal funds to respond to local problems in particularly local ways.

having one of the disabilities listed in IDEA and therefore needing special education. These students, and other students with disabilities, do not need special education but are still protected against discrimination under Section 504 of the Rehabilitation Act Amendments. They are also covered by the federal general education law, NCLB, which we now describe.

:: GENERAL EDUCATION REFORM: NO CHILD LEFT BEHIND ACT

In signing the No Child Left Behind Act (NCLB), President George Bush declared that "too many children in America are segregated by low expectations, illiteracy, and self-doubt. In a constantly changing world that is demanding increasingly complex skills from its workforce, children are literally being left behind" (Bush, January, 2001). As he put it, "More and more, we are divided into two nations. One that reads, and one that doesn't. One that dreams, and one that doesn't" (Bush, 2001).

Congress intended NCLB to benefit all students, including those with disabilities and those who are exceptionally gifted and talented, in kindergarten through 12th grade. You may recall that IDEA allows a student with a disability to remain in school until age 21, so, if a student is covered by IDEA, NCLB applies to that student until the student graduates from school or leaves school permanently. NCLB does not apply to infant and toddler programs operated under Part C of IDEA, but it does provide incentives for schools to

develop standards and to provide early literacy curricula at the preschool level.

Figure 6.6 describes NCLB's six principles for school reform. Just as we did with IDEA, we will describe (a) the background problems that each principle is intended to address, (b) the major purposes and provisions of each principle, and (c) the implications of each principle for family-professional partnerships.

Congress probably will amend the law in 2010 (and then probably amend IDEA soon thereafter). It is unclear what Congress will do, but it is clear that there is controversy about the effect of NCLB's accountability-and-standards provisions. Some believe they benefit students by ratcheting up expectations, requiring educators to prepare students in the core courses to be proficient on the state and district assessments, and creating more accountability and transparency in education. Others believe that NCLB has forced teachers to "teach to the test" and ignore students' other educational needs, including the need to learn how to solve problems, engage in critical thinking, become entrepreneurs, and develop their creativity.

Those who criticize NCLB for its narrow focus do not want to abandon the quest for proficiency and the requirement for accountability. Instead, they recognize that NCLB does not develop the whole child and therefore insufficiently responds to the country's needs for a citizenry truly capable of leading America and the world in the twenty-first century. Now that you know the background of NCLB and the criticisms it has engendered, you need to know about its six principles. You will find them in Figure 6.6.

Accountability for Results

Background Problems. Congress was aware that many students in general education were academically underprepared relative to students from many other countries, especially in their reading and mathematical skills; that many needed to take a remedial course before beginning college courses, even after they graduated from high school; and that the huge sums of money (approximately $120 billion annually) spent by nearly 39 different agencies within the Department of Education were still producing less than satisfactory student outcomes (U.S. Department of Education, 2001).

Major Purposes and Provisions. One of NCLB's purposes is to "ensure that all children have a fair, equal, and significant opportunity to obtain a high-quality education and reach, at a minimum, proficiency on challenging State academic achievement standards and state academic assessments" (T. I, Sec. 1001). NCLB intends that every child will demonstrate proficiency on state-defined standards in reading-language arts, mathematics, and science by the end of the 2013–2014 school year.

Standards: SEAs must develop standards that
(a) describe what students will know and be able to do; (b) include coherent and rigorous content;
(c) encourage teachers to instruct in advanced skills;
(d) apply to all students (including those with disabilities); (e) describe achievement levels as high/advanced, proficient, and basic; and (f) include competencies within each level.

Assessment: To determine whether SEAs and students are meeting the standards, SEAs must establish statewide assessment systems aligned to the standards. Each school must (a) test at least 95 percent of its student body and (b) report the students' collective scores according to the three levels and each subject.

Students with Disabilities: NCLB applies to the students who (a) have qualified under IDEA and (b) are protected under Section 504. A student's IEP team will determine whether the student is capable of taking the statewide assessment without accommodations or if the student needs an accommodated, modified, or an alternate assessment. Accommodations include any changes in testing materials or procedures that enable the student to perform at his or her level of proficiency (e.g., large print, extended time). When students take an accommodated assessment, they are completing the same assessment as their peers without disabilities; only the format or administration procedures for the test change. Modified assessments are based on grade-level standards, but the breadth or depth of the content students are assessed on is reduced. Alternate assessments are also based on grade-level standards but reflect a significant reduction in the complexity of the skills assessed. Alternate assessments are reserved for students with significant cognitive disabilities who have a modified curriculum that their IEP team has been deemed appropriate for them (20 U.S.C. Secs. 1414(c)(1)(B) and (d)(1)(A)).

Disaggregating Performance Data and Reporting Data on Annual Yearly Progress: Each SEA and LEA must disaggregate the assessment data according to these subgroups of students: (a) those with disabilities, (b) those who are migrants, (c) those who receive free and reduced lunches, (d) those who have limited English-language usage, (e) those who belong to various racial/ethnic groups, and (f) males and females. The SEA may set different targets for adequate yearly progress for each of these groups; if one subgroup does not make adequate yearly progress or if less than 95 percent of the students in a subgroup do not take the assessment, the SEA will not have made adequate yearly progress. The SEA and each LEA must issue "report cards" describing the results of the assessments according to these subgroups.

Annual Yearly Progress: Each SEA must develop a system for determining whether each LEA and school makes annual yearly progress (AYP)—specifically, whether students are progressing toward proficiency in the core academic subjects at the level that the SEA has set as its standard. To ensure that all of their students meet the reading-language arts and mathematics standards by the 2013–2014 school year, the SEA must set specific annual targets for students in these subjects. To measure progress, the SEA must determine what its "starting point" will be; the starting point represents the percentage of students who score "proficient" on the statewide assessment.

Having established a starting point, the SEA then must gradually increase the percentage of students who annually score at the proficient level. The end result is that all students will score at the proficient level by the 2013–2014 school year.

Further, SEAs must establish at least one academic measure to show students' progress. They may set the indicator at the elementary school level (e.g., proficiency in reading) but they must use high school graduation as the indicator for the secondary school level.

SEAs may reward LEAs and schools that make AYP, usually by public recognition or a grant of federal and/or state funds. If, however, a school does not make AYP in one year, the SEA must provide technical assistance to it. If in subsequent years the school does not make AYP: (a) the school must develop an improvement plan, (b) the SEA must continue to provide technical assistance, (c) the SEA may offer supplemental services (including tuition) to students whose families are at or below the federal poverty level, (d) the SEA must offer parents the option to transfer their students to AYP-complying schools, and (e) the SEA must require the school to take corrective action, including restructuring. These stepped-up sanctions begin at the first year and continue into the fifth year during which the school does not make AYP.

Similar stepped-up sanctions apply to entire LEAs (school districts). Likewise, if an entire state does not make AYP for two consecutive years, the U.S. Department of Education must provide technical assistance to the SEA.

Implications for Family-Professional Partnerships.

There are at least two implications of NCLB and IDEA's corresponding student-assessment provisions (remember, the two laws align with each other). First, NCLB requires each school to report the results of each student's academic assessments to the student's parents. Among the assessment reports must be "diagnostic" reports. Parents will be able to use those evaluations in collaborating with teachers to design their children's individualized programs.

Second, schools must inform parents about the performance of the whole school and their options if their child's school is not making AYP. Schools must distribute annual report cards that enable parents, community citizens, and other concerned stakeholders to compare and contrast the performance of schools within their community and across communities in the state. This kind of information sharing can inform parents about their own child's performance relative to other students and about the performance of the whole student body in the school that their child attends.

School Safety

Background Problems. When it enacted NCLB in 2002, Congress responded to data and perceptions that schools are unsafe (Garcia & Kennedy, 2003; Willert & Lenhardt, 2003). The U.S. Department of Education annually reports data about violent deaths, nonfatal student victimization, violence and other crime, nonfatal teacher victimization, and fear-inducing school environments (U.S. Department of Education, National Center for Educational Statistics, 2007). Safety is important for at least three reasons: (a) SEAs and LEAs may be liable in law if they do not take reasonable measures to protect their staff and students from violence and other crime in schools, (b) safety is essential so students may learn, and (c) safety is essential so teachers may teach.

Definition of Principle. The principle is that schools must be safe and drug- and alcohol-free. NCLB has two major strategies for addressing school safety. First, it provides funds to SEAs and LEAs (a) to prevent school-based violence and the illegal use of drugs, alcohol, and tobacco and (b) to foster safe and drug-free teaching and learning environments. To qualify for funds, schools must

- address local needs as established by objective data,
- be grounded in scientifically based prevention activities,
- consult with parent, student, and community organizations,
- measure and evaluate progress on a continuous basis, and
- establish a uniform system for reporting data to parents and other citizens.

Second, parents may transfer their children from a dangerous school setting to a safe school setting. Also, parents of children who are victims of violent crimes at school or who attend "persistently dangerous schools" (as determined by the SEA) may choose to leave the school and attend a safer one. When an SEA identifies a school as being persistently dangerous, it must notify parents of every student in the school and to offer them opportunities to transfer to a safe school. This is a parental choice provision, the third NCLB principle.

Under a different federal law, the Gun-Free School Act of 1994 (P. L. 104-208), SEAs and LEAs must (a) expel for at least one year any student who brings a firearm to school or possesses a firearm in school and (b) report any such student to the criminal justice or juvenile justice system. There are exceptions to the expulsion rule, but, generally, parents have no say about expulsion and reporting. There is no partnership opportunity here, only a duty the schools cannot avoid. The law applies to any student with a disability whose behavior is not a manifestation of the disability. If the behavior is a manifestation, however, IDEA's zero-reject rule comes into play and a student is placed into an interim alternative educational setting and still receives an appropriate education there.

Implications for Family-Professional Partnerships.

NCLB's approach to increasing school safety is to grant parents active decision-making roles. It requires schools to involve parents in designing violence prevention and addictions prevention programs. It also requires schools to give parents full access to reports on the status of school safety and drug use among students. Both of these requirements give parents information and opportunities to assume decision-making roles in contributing to safe school environments. Parents of students with disabilities are entitled to have the same reports as parents of students who do not have disabilities.

Parental Choice

Background Problems. "What's a parent to do?" is a fair question when some of America's schools fail to produce acceptable academic achievement results for students or when schools are found to be persistently dangerous. These two problems—academic underachievement and school violence—are the sources of NCLB's third principle, parental choice. Indeed, NCLB relies on the same strategy that IDEA had proposed over 25 years earlier—parent participation to enable parents to hold schools more accountable for providing an appropriate education.

Major Purposes and Provisions of the Principle. One of NCLB's purposes is related to students' academic achievement but is specifically focused on their parents, namely, "affording parents substantial and meaningful opportunities to participate in the education of their children" (Title I, Sec. 1001(12)). Among those opportunities is the "transfer option" for good cause, and the good cause is the failure of a school to make AYP for three years or to provide a safe environment for teaching and learning. Parents, including those whose children are covered by IDEA, may enroll their child in another public school including a charter school, in the district, or, under limited circumstances, in another district. As a general rule, LEAs must provide transportation for the transferring students. If a parent does not choose to transfer a child, the child should not be penalized by that choice but should receive supplemental educational services in that school. The "transfer" provisions theoretically increase parents' choice and thereby put pressure on the failing or unsafe schools to improve. Recent research suggests that few parents elect the transfer option, and more select to receive supplemental educational services such as tutoring (Petrilli, 2007).

To provide alternatives to existing public schools, NCLB provides funding to help charter schools pay for start-up costs, facilities, and other needs. Charter schools are public schools and must meet the same standards as other public schools, but they are "created" by parents and educators who "charter" them by organizing them, specifying their mission, and controlling their staffing and curriculum. Charter schools may not discriminate against children with disabilities and must comply with the same IDEA rights for students as other public schools.

No parent can make an informed choice without information, so NCLB requires schools periodically to report certain data to parents. Figure 6.7 summarizes NCLB's data-reporting and notice requirements. These provisions also apply to parents whose children receive services under IDEA.

NCLB also authorizes funding for Parental Assistance Information Centers. These centers provide support, training, and information to parents, professionals, and organizations that work with parents. Their goal is to increase parent-professional partnerships that will ultimately lead to improved achievement results for students. You will learn more about these centers in chapter 9.

| **FIGURE 6.7** | **NCLB data-reporting and notice requirements.** |

- The first kind of data relates to the particular student. NCLB requires each school to measure each student's academic achievement in reading and math in each of grades 3 through 8 and at least once during grades 10 through 12 and to report the information to the student's parents.
- The second kind of data relates to the school as a whole. The parent gets a report card about the child's progress. This is the student report card. The parent also receives a report about the overall achievement of students in that school, about the teacher's qualifications, and about school safety. This is the school report card.
- Each school must notify all parents (through the report cards) if their child is eligible to transfer to another school or district because (1) the student's present school or school district needs improvement, corrective action, or restructuring because of poor student outcomes in the assessments of academic achievement, (2) the school is "persistently dangerous," or (3) the student has been the victim of violent crime while on school grounds.

Implications for Family-Professional Partnerships. As an abstract principle, parent choice is appealing. After all, parents are legally responsible for their children until their children reach the age of majority (18) and many thereafter remain financially and otherwise responsible for them, especially if they have disabilities. So, parents should be able to choose how to have their children educated.

But, how much will the principle benefit families who have children with disabilities? Two factors influence the answer to this question. First, parents must know about their choices (and NCLB requires educators to inform them), have the motivation to exercise the choices, have the skills to turn motives into actions, and have the resources to turn actions into reality (Turnbull & Turnbull, 2000). Second, a parent's choice may be limited by the child's disability. The special education services in schools that are making adequate progress may be overtaxed; it may be difficult for them to accommodate more students. In urban districts, transfer from one school to another may be easier than in rural districts where there may be only one elementary school, one middle school, and one senior high school.

Teacher Quality

Background Problems. Congress was acutely aware when it enacted NCLB that schools could not hire enough well-qualified teachers. Indeed, there was a shockingly low percentage of teaches in the hard sciences and in special education who were fully qualified by reason of their training to teach the courses and students they were instructing (Abt Associates, Inc., 2002; U.S. Department of Education, 2002).

Definition of Principle. The teacher quality principle is that learning depends on teaching, and student outcomes depend on teacher competency. It follows that student learning and outcomes will remain unsatisfactory unless there are enough highly qualified teachers. Accordingly, one of NCLB's purposes is to provide grants to state and local educational agencies "to increase student achievement through strategies such as improving teacher and principal quality and increasing the number of highly qualified teachers in the classroom and highly qualified principals and assistant principals in the schools" (T. II, Sec. 2101). Significantly, IDEA also requires SEAs and LEAs to employ highly qualified teachers (20 U.S.C. Sec. 1401(10)).

NCLB advances this principle by requiring every SEA to develop plans to assure that all teachers of core academic subjects in all schools will be "highly qualified" by the end of the 2005–2006 school year and that all teachers of these subjects in Title I schools are highly qualified as of the 2002–2003 school year. The core subjects are English, reading or language arts, mathematics, science, foreign languages, civics and government, arts, history, and geography. A "highly qualified" teacher is one who has a full teacher's certification, a bachelor's degree, and passes a state-administered test on core academic subject knowledge. These requirements apply to teachers in general and special education. Under NCLB, special education teachers may participate in some instructional activities that do not require them to be highly qualified in core academic subjects (e.g., implementing positive behavior support, consulting with teachers who are highly qualified in core academic subjects, selecting appropriate curriculum and instructional accommodations, working with students to teach study skills, and reinforcing instruction that a student has received from a highly qualified teacher). However, if a special education teacher is delivering instruction independently in a core academic area, the teacher must be certified both in special education and in the academic area.

NCLB requires that paraprofessionals who teach in Title I schools must have earned a secondary school diploma or its equivalent. In general, paraprofessionals must have an associate degree or higher, or they must have completed two years of postsecondary study at an institution of higher education. Paraprofessionals also have the option of passing a local or state examination that examines their knowledge related to teaching the core academic subjects.

Each LEA and school must report its progress toward the teacher qualification goal when it issues its annual report cards on adequate yearly progress. The report must be accessible to the public.

Implications for Family-Professional Partnerships. NCLB's requirement for public disclosure enables parents to know whether each teacher is state-certified, is teaching under an emergency or provisional status, and/or has earned a bachelor's or higher degree or certificate. Parents who know the qualifications of their children's teachers presumably know what to expect when they meet with the teachers, what to request in terms of better teachers, and how to approach their partnerships with teachers. Teachers, however, who do not meet the requirements for being fully qualified may feel threatened or intimated when this information is shared with parents.

Scientifically Based Methods

Background Problems. Much of the impetus to use scientifically based methods derived from research about reading achievement and, more to the point, how to teach children to read (U.S. Department of Education, 2002). Congress responded by insisting that schools and their faculty use scientifically based methods to teach students. That is the basic requirement of NCLB. It is also what Congress intends under IDEA: that education agencies use "scientifically based instructional practices, to the maximum extent possible" (20 U.S.C. Sec. 1401 (c)(5)(E)). Sometimes, however, there are no such methods with respect to teaching some students with disabilities, so IDEA provides that state and local educational agencies must, to the extent practical, provide for services that are based on peer-reviewed research (20 U.S.C. Sec. 1414(d)(1)(A)(i)(IV)).

Definition of Principle. The principle is that instruction is most effective when it proceeds from scientifically based research. Accordingly, one of NCLB's purposes to improve student academic achievement is by funding state and local educational agencies "to implement promising education reform programs and school improvement programs based on scientifically based research" (Title V, Sec. 5101). NCLB defines scientifically based research as "research that applies rigorous, systematic, and objective procedures to obtain relevant knowledge" (20 U.S.C. Sec. 6368(6)). Such research occurs when the researchers used empirical methods, applied rigorous data analyses to test their hypotheses and justify their findings, used multiple measures to gather data, and ensured that a peer-review process evaluated the defensibility of the research methods and findings.

Under NCLB, the U.S. Department of Education will provide grants to SEAs and LEAs that use scientifically based methods in reading instruction. Each state is responsible for establishing a Reading Leadership Team comprised of policy makers, educators, and at least one parent of a school-aged student. The Reading Leadership Team is responsible for ensuring that schools that need to improve their reading achievement scores are using scientifically based instructional methods for teaching reading and that a comprehensive, seamless approach to reading instruction occurs in schools throughout all LEAs in the state. In addition, the Department may require "failing" schools or districts to use scientifically based instructional methods in order to remain in business.

Implications for Family-Professional Partnerships. In order for parents to engage in partnerships in making educational decisions, it will increasingly be necessary for parents to be informed about scientifically based instructional methods or peer-reviewed research in special education. Parents may seek that information from their children's schools. If schools do provide that information, they should format it in a family-friendly way so as to inform but not overwhelm or intimidate parents.

Local Flexibility

Background Problems. School reformers had long argued that initiatives such as accountability, teacher quality, and scientifically based instruction fail because different federal, state, and local laws and regulations restrict state and local school administrators' ability to use federal and state dollars in ways that respond effectively to local problems. They argue that there are just too many different federal programs, many of which are inconsistent with each other. Reformers also argue that the federal programs adopt a top-down and one-size-fits-all approach; there is great inflexibility in how educators can administer the federal programs locally. That very same inflexibility inhibits administrators from devising local responses to local needs.

Definition of Principle. The principle of local flexibility is that federal programs should encourage local solutions for local problems. The principle holds that schools should have more discretion to use federal funds, but they should also be accountable for student results. The justification for the principle is that it is inconsistent to hold state and local districts accountable for student results without giving them discretion to respond to local problems in local ways.

Accordingly, NCLB provides that state and local agencies are responsible for administering federal funds and designing programs to comply with NCLB.

NCLB consolidates 55 separate federal general education categorical programs into 45, reduces federal and state red tape and the costs of maintaining large bureaucracies, and allows state and local administrators to transfer money from one federal program to another. IDEA is not one of the federal programs subject to consolidation. Arguably, consolidation increases local control, flexibility, and innovation.

NCLB also permits states and school districts to designate themselves as charter states/charter districts. These states and districts will be relieved of the requirements under the many federal categorical programs if they enter into a five-year performance agreement with the U.S. secretary of education. Under that agreement, these charter states and districts will be subject to especially rigorous standards of accountability and to sanctions (e.g., loss of freedom from federal requirements) if student achievement and other performance indicators do not improve according to the terms of the agreement between the charter state/district and the secretary.

Implications for Family-Professional Partnerships. First, the principle of flexibility should make it easier for parents to know what services their children are receiving. They also should find it easier to coordinate their partnerships with professionals because the professionals will operate under consolidated programs and not a large number of separate programs. Second, parents and professionals may collaborate to create charter schools and thus acquire opportunities for partnership and greater control over students' education.

REVISITING JAY TURNBULL AND PUBLIC POLICY

What differences would IDEA and NCLB make for Jay Turnbull if he were born in 2009 rather than 1967? There would be no arguments about his rights; they would have been established long ago. As a child, he would have access to early intervention and early childhood education and his parents would have a family-centered plan supported by professionals. He would be fully evaluated for his cognitive, behavioral, physical, and developmental needs, and he would have individualized programs that address those needs as well as his strengths. He would have the benefit of related services and supplementary aids and services to participate in the three domains of the general curriculum. He would have highly trained teachers who would use scientifically based or peer-reviewed curricula and instructional strategies. He would be assessed for progress toward his goals. His parents would still have due process rights but would have far more effective means for being partners with his educators.

Ultimately, he would have equal opportunities for independent living, full participation, and a degree of economic self-sufficiency. In the long run, Jay attained those outcomes but at great emotional, physical, and economic cost to his parents and his sisters.

It need not have been so difficult for them from 1975, when he entered school, through 1988, when he left school, or for the 21 years after, when they followed Jay's lead to create a life where Jay could choose his path and be supported to follow it in his own home (independent living); in his community as a full, participating citizen (full participation); and in his employment—Jay worked for 20 consecutive years as a research and clerical aide at The University of Kansas (economic self-sufficiency).

In a word, IDEA and NCLB would have made all the difference for him, just as it would have made for his parents and teachers, as partners with each other in service to him.

SUMMARY

We have discussed the history of school reform, the efforts to achieve accountability, and the implications of the reform and accountability initiatives for parent-professional partnerships. We reviewed IDEA's and NCLB's six principles and the background and parent-professional implications of each:

IDEA six principles. IDEA has six principles related to providing a free appropriate public education.

- **Zero reject.** Enroll all children and youth, including all those with disabilities.
- **Nondiscriminatory evaluation.** Determine whether an enrolled student has a disability and, if so, the nature of special education and related services that the student requires.
- **Appropriate education.** Tailor the student's education to address the student's individualized needs and strengths and ensure that education benefits the student.

- **Least restrictive environment.** To the maximum extent appropriate for the student, ensure that every student receives education in the general education environment and do not remove the student from regular education unless the nature or severity of the disability is such that education in general education classes with the use of supplementary aids and services cannot be achieved satisfactorily.
- **Procedural due process.** Implement a system of checks and balances so that parents and professionals may hold each other accountable for providing the student with a free appropriate public education in the least restrictive environment.
- **Parent participation.** Implement parent participation rights related to every principle and grant parents access to educational records and opportunities to serve on state and local special education advisory committees.

NCLB six principles. NCLB has six principles for school reform for all students.

- **Accountability for results.** Reward school districts and schools that improve student academic achievement and reform those that do not.
- **School safety.** Acknowledge that all children need a safe environment in which to learn and achieve. Require states to report on school safety to the public and districts to establish a plan for keeping schools safe and drug-free.
- **Parental choice.** Grant parents the right to transfer their child from a "failing" school to one that meets annual yearly progress.
- **Teacher quality.** Acknowledge that learning depends on teaching; students achieve when they have good teachers. Condition federal aid on states' agreement to hire "highly qualified" teachers.
- **Scientifically based methods of teaching.** Acknowledge that teaching and learning depend not just on highly qualified teachers but also on the teachers' use of scientifically based methods of teaching. Grant federal funds to states and school districts that use only those methods.
- **Local flexibility.** Encourage local solutions for local problems and do not hold schools accountable for student outcomes unless the schools also can use federal funds to respond to local problems in particularly local ways.

LINKING CONTENT TO YOUR LIFE

As you start or continue working as an educator, ask yourself what you know about IDEA and NCLB's provisions and how you would implement them when providing special education services.

- If you were Jay Turnbull's teacher, could you answer a question about the principles of both laws in ways families would understand? Could your colleagues?
- Why do you think that you and your colleagues owe it to students like Jay and their families to know the laws that govern your practice?
- How well do you and your colleagues adhere to the requirements of both laws? Knowing is one thing; following the law is another, especially in an era of outcome-driven education.
- How else could students like Jay benefit and have some assurance they will have equal opportunities, full participation, independent living, and economic self-sufficiency?

- Are you as qualified as you can be? Are you willing to defend your education and competence if parents were to confront you in a due process hearing?
- Do you have high expectations for your students? Or do you believe that their disabilities really require you to just protect them?
- Are you aware of and do you use scientifically based or peer-reviewed curriculum and instructional strategies when you teach? Can you defend your educational decisions and practices in a due process hearing?
- Do you enter into partnerships with parents that reflect the suggestions you read in the "Implications for Family-Professional Partnerships" sections of this chapter? Just how many of the seven elements of parent-professional partnerships are you adopting?

PART III

Strategies and Processes for Partnerships and Desired Outcomes

S trategies are the tools professionals use to build effective partnerships. When, however, professionals meet challenges in applying strategies and creating trusting and trustworthy partnerships, they need problem-solving processes. The next five chapters identify how professionals can use both evidence-based strategies and problem-solving processes to be partners with parents of children with disabilities.

Chapter 7 describes the seven elements of an effective partnership and advises you on how to implement these elements. It emphasizes that six of the elements (communication, competence, commitment, advocacy, equality, and respect) are necessary for the seventh, which is trust, and that trust underlies effective partnerships and leads to better outcomes for students with disabilities.

Chapter 8 sets out strategies you can use to communicate effectively with families.

Chapter 9 describes how teachers and other professionals can be partners with families when evaluating a student in conformity with IDEA.

Chapter 10 describes how teachers and other professionals can be partners with families and students when developing and implementing a student's individualized plan or program in conformity with IDEA.

Chapter 11 provides strategies for professionals in supporting families to meet their basic needs and how, by helping parents meet those needs, educators are supporting the child, too.

CHAPTER 7

Seven Principles of Partnerships and Trust

CHAD, MARLEY, AND CHANDLER NELMS

There's an adage in the Marine Corps that a Marine never leaves a wounded or fallen Marine on the field of battle. In its most fundamental way, this adage expresses the Corps' motto, Semper Fidelis: Always Faithful. It also articulates the commitment of one Marine to be a partner to another.

"Never leave behind" and Semper Fi are particularly apt for Chad Nelms, the 8-year-old son of Marley and Marine Lt. Col. Chandler Nelms. Chad has autism. Because his father has been assigned to three different duty stations in Chad's short lifetime and because his parents received services from public and private agencies, Chad has had more than three different teams of professionals working for him and his family.

In one of them, "More Than Words," Marley and Chandler, together with other parents of very young children with autism, spent six weeks learning how to elicit language from Chad, then just a few months short of his second birthday. Marley describes the San Diego–based program as "the best" she and Chandler have ever experienced. Why? For two reasons.

First, the professionals there helped them understand how Chad would acquire language and "where he could be in the future." They set high expectations for him and trained his parents so that high expectations became more than a phrase; it was a concrete goal—Chad would have effective and sufficient language. Second, the professionals were "uniquely trained," not just as speech therapists but as specialists in autism. "For me, there's already a level of trust there, that they know something above and beyond the normal person graduating from a speech-language pathology program. They've done specialized training, so I had great confidence in knowing these are people I can trust."

As much as More Than Words benefited Marley and Chandler and then Chad, a preschool program, the Center for Autism and Related Disorders (CARD), also in the San Diego area, was effective in shaping Chad's behaviors. Beginning when he was 2½ and continuing until he was 5 years old, CARD professionals offered applied behavior analysis interventions at both the Nelms' home and in a center-based program. Just as Marley trusted the professionals in More Than Words, she trusted the professionals in CARD, too.

Marley's trust was not misplaced. In both programs, professionals offered highly structured classes for Marley and Chandler or for Chad. They made their objectives clear, they offered concrete strategies, and they answered Marley's and Chandler's questions by offering techniques that they individualized for Chad. While Chandler was deployed to Iraq for two years, professionals in CARD respected Marley's competence and treated her as an equal in developing Chad's language. To confirm their decisions, they consulted with board-certified specialists who had even more training and experience then they. And they measured Chad's progress regularly, holding themselves accountable to him and his parents.

Not all professionals have been like those in More Than Words and CARD. When Marley and Chandler asked Chad's preschool program in the San Diego area to continue the strategies that had benefited him so much the year before, they refused and offered another program instead. Marley and Chandler sued and won a partial victory; by then, they had spent $58,000 for tuition and attorneys' fees.

Marley and Chandler experienced similar resistance after he was transferred to Camp Lejeune, in North Carolina. There, Marley declined to enroll Chad in the county's public schools: "They were too segregated, by disability." Instead, she enrolled him in a Department of Defense school on base. That's where she has encountered some teachers who are hardly the paragons of professional partners, although she has worked with some teachers who are superb partners. The less-than-effective partners are those who, in Marley's words, "give me attitude." When she expressed concerns about Chandler's pragmatic skills—he sits alone at lunch, in silence, not communicating or connecting at all with his classmates who have and do not have disabilities—Chad's teacher asks her for examples of how to increase his social interactions.

When she suggests an intervention not used in the state, professionals tell her, "Well, you're in a different country now," remaining loyal to the one intervention that the state and local educational agencies have adopted. They ask, aloud, why the Marines send their officers to North Carolina instead of retaining them in California.

When she suggests a strategy that benefited Chandler earlier, "they just kind of nod their heads but I don't get a real feeling they are really respecting what I'm saying and valuing my experience."

Who are these dismissive professionals, the ones who "roll their eyes" at Marley? They tend to be the ones who have been working for decades, not the ones who have recently graduated from teacher-training programs. The former have not continued to learn; the latter have recently learned.

think about it

Few—indeed, as the Marine Corps pronounces, only a very few—people will be Marines or Marine wives. Few parents of children with disabilities will be deployed so often and so widely within the country; few know if their spouses will be in potentially mortal combat for more than a year. But most—indeed, all—parents of children with disabilities will have to work with professionals throughout their children's lifetimes.

- If you could choose a professional to be your partner to treat you or your child, what traits would you want that person to have?
- If you had to assign priorities to their traits, which ones would you value over others? Pick from the following: their abilities to communicate, their professional competence, their genuine respect for you and your knowledge about your child, their commitment to you and your child, their sense that they and you have equal talents to bring to bear for the child, their advocacy for your child, or their trustworthiness?

- Do you even accept the premise that you have to choose? Do you say, "That's a false choice—I want them to have all of those traits"?
- What makes it possible for you, as a professional, to earn the trust of the parents whose children are entrusted to you for their education? Is it a combination of traits that you can learn and practice?

:: INTRODUCTION

You have learned about families and how they operate as a system (chapters 1 to 4), about the roles families historically have played (chapter 5), and about the policies that shape today's family-professional partnerships (chapter 6). In this chapter, you will learn about the seven principles of partnerships, including trust and its indispensable role. First, however, you need to know what the word *partnership* means.

Partnership—The Dictionary Definition and the Laws

Among other things, the word *partnership* refers to a relationship involving close cooperation between people who have joint rights and responsibilities (Merriam-Webster's Collegiate Dictionary, 1996). As you learned in chapter 6, IDEA and NCLB set out the rights and responsibilities that families and educators have with respect to each other. And although IDEA's "core" is the "cooperative process" it establishes between parents and schools (*Shaffer v. Weast,* 2004), neither IDEA nor NCLB defines the term *cooperative process;* both assume that a partnership is desirable but neither identifies the specific practices that families and educators should use to be effective partners.

Partnership—Our Definition and Its Logic

To assist you in learning what the "cooperative process" means and to take action to make the process truly meaningful by entering into an active and authentic partnership with parents, we first offer a definition of *partnership;* we then turn to the large body of research on parent-educator relationships to discover and define the seven principles of a partnership; and finally, we explain each principle and offer suggestions that you may follow to be an effective partner with parents, other family members, the student, and your professional colleagues. In chapters 8 through 12, we help you apply these seven principles and best practices as you carry out your duties under IDEA and NCLB.

Here is our definition of *partnership*. Note that we incorporate but enlarge the dictionary's definition that a partnership consists of "joint rights and responsibilities."

> Partnership refers to a relationship in which families (not just parents) and professionals agree to build on each others' expertise and resources, as appropriate, for the purpose of making and implementing decisions that will directly benefit students and indirectly benefit other family members and professionals.

We also define the term *benefit* as it applies to the students, again relying on IDEA and NCLB. Here is our definition:

> Benefit refers to the four national policy goals that IDEA identifies and that will be available to a student when families and professionals perform their respective duties to evaluate a student and then provide the student an appropriate education in the least restrictive environment.

Note that our definition of *benefit* for students has several elements:

- It explicitly acknowledges that the ultimate benefits of a student's education are the four national outcomes: equal opportunity, independent living, full participation, and economic self-sufficiency. We defined each outcome in chapter 6.
- It then holds that students will be poised to achieve these outcomes if families and professionals discharge their IDEA duties to evaluate, provide an appropriate education, and do so in the least restrictive environment, namely, the general curriculum.
- Thus, the ultimate end of special education is the student's achievement of the four goals; the means for achieving them is compliance with the law and the research evidence on effective practices.
- The compliance is far more likely to occur when families and professionals enter into partnerships.

Here, then, is the logic of the definitions of *partnership* and *benefit*:

> Partnerships lead to compliance with the law; and compliance with the law supports the student to achieve the four national outcomes.

As you read this chapter and chapters 8 through 12, you will find that we guide you through the logic, step by step.

You will also note that there are benefits for the student's family/parents and professionals. Those occur because the family systems theory you learned in chapters 1 through 4 holds that any benefit to one member of a family accrues to the other members.

You will also note that there are benefits to the professionals. Those occur because partnership is important, if not essential, for the professional working with the student to attain student benefits. As we said in chapter 5 and here, partnerships bring to bear the multiple perspectives and resources of the professionals and the family members. There is another, and perhaps surprising, benefit of partnerships for professionals. It is the huge psychic gratification that the professional has—a sense that "we" (student, family member/parents, and professional) are "all in this business of education, together!"

Seven Principles of Partnership

There are seven principles of the family/parent and professional partnership: communication, professional competence, respect, commitment, equality, advocacy, and trust. Let's consider, first, the concept of a "principle."

The word *principle* refers to a comprehensive and fundamental law, doctrine, or assumption. Our seven partnership principles do not constitute a law because they do not have the power to command behavior. Nor do they constitute an assumption because they are based on research. Instead, they constitute a *doctrine*, a body of principles in a branch of knowledge. The knowledge derives from the research and recommended practice that you will learn about in this and subsequent chapters.

Now, let's describe the relationship of these seven principles to each other. Figure 7.1 illustrates the seven partnership principles by using the structure of an arch. There are three principles on each side of the arch. The seventh principle, trust, is the keystone. A *keystone* is the wedge-shaped piece at the crown of an arch that locks the other pieces into place (Merriam-Webster's Collegiate Dictionary, 2003). It's now time for you to learn the meaning of each of the seven principles and the research and

FIGURE 7.1 The seven principles of partnership.

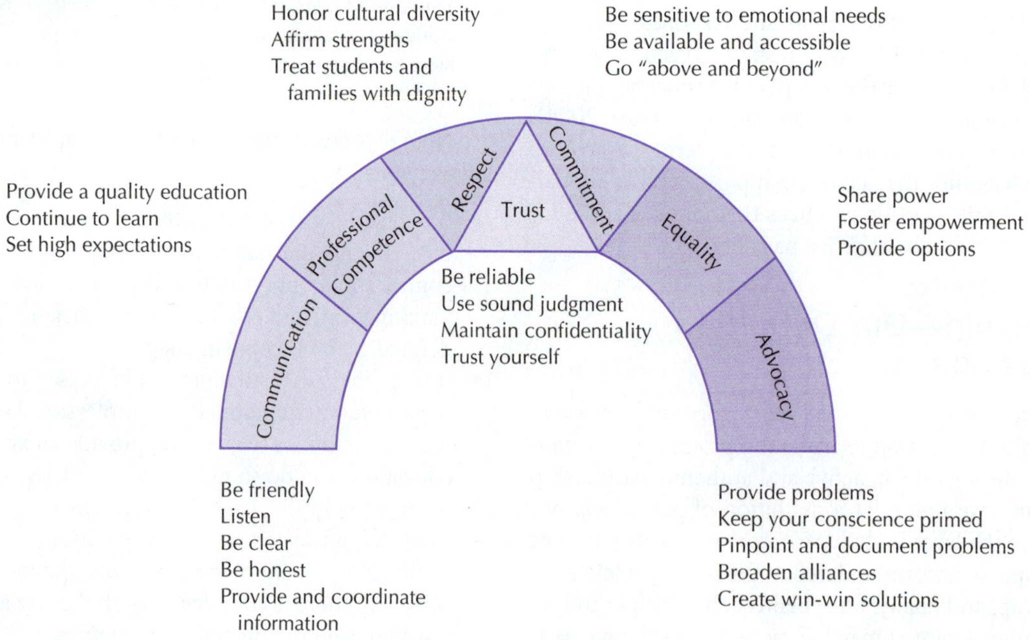
Honor cultural diversity
Affirm strengths
Treat students and families with dignity
Be sensitive to emotional needs
Be available and accessible
Go "above and beyond"
Provide a quality education
Continue to learn
Set high expectations
Share power
Foster empowerment
Provide options
Communication
Professional Competence
Respect
Trust
Commitment
Equality
Advocacy
Be reliable
Use sound judgment
Maintain confidentiality
Trust yourself
Be friendly
Listen
Be clear
Be honest
Provide and coordinate information
Provide problems
Keep your conscience primed
Pinpoint and document problems
Broaden alliances
Create win-win solutions

evidence-based practices that you will want to use as you apply each principle.

:: COMMUNICATION

Effective partnerships require effective communication. That is easy enough to say. What is difficult is to be a good communicator. Effective communication requires that we pay careful attention to both the quality and the quantity of our communication. Quality means that we have to be positive, clear, and respectful of the person with whom we are communicating. Quantity refers to how often we communicate and if we use our own and others' time efficiently. The following five actions almost always are necessary for effective communication between family members on the one hand and professionals on the other (Blue-Banning, Summers, Frankland, Nelson, & Beegle, 2004):

- Be friendly.
- Listen.
- Be clear.
- Be honest.
- Provide and coordinate information.

In chapter 8, we will provide even more strategies for being an effective partner through good communication, but for now it is best for you to learn about those five necessary communication practices.

Be Friendly

Some professionals mistakenly believe that being professional means they must be formal, distant, and even controlling when they communicate with family members. A survey of families and professionals, not limited to those in special education, underscored what professionals believe parents want from them and what parents actually want:

> In a classic example of misunderstood cues, the reported preferences of parents are not what school personnel think they are. School personnel passionately believe that a professional, businesslike manner will win the respect and support of parents. The response of parents to questions about their contacts with the school revealed that they view "professionalism" on the part of teachers, school psychologists, guidance counselors, or principals as undesirable. Parents mention their dissatisfaction with school people who are too businesslike, patronizing, or who talk down to us. . . . Parents reported a "personal touch" as the most enhancing factor in school relations. (Lindle, 1989, p. 13)

What is the "personal touch"? A parent whose child was receiving home-based early intervention services described it this way:

> At first, I was tense with a professional coming to my home. But it was a nice little conversation. The professional's mannerism and the way she asked questions was like we were sitting down for a cup of coffee. She got a lot of information without asking. (Summers et al., 1990, p. 87)

Simply put, the personal touch means being friendly; that is the key to helping parents feel comfortable enough to share information about a child or even about the family. Instead of "interviews," have conversations (Coles, 1989). Here's the advice of an early childhood educator:

> Professionals need to be able to be nice. In a professional meeting, we need to be able to put the family at ease by showing them that we are working together for the good of the family member that's in need. So we need to be able to be nice to each other and joke around a bit. We need to try to get the family to feel like this team is going to work. That they're going to help me. They like each other. They need to get the impression that we like each other and that we know what we're doing. (Frankland, 2001, pp. 107–108)

An early intervention provider who makes home visits to families who have children identified as having a disability or being at risk for a disability describes how she tries to establish a personal touch:

> Well, definitely you have to build a rapport first and you've got to be personable. You've got to . . . they've got to feel that you're an advocate for them and that you are someone they can depend on. And then you can ask those tough questions . . . sometimes, sometimes it takes time. (Friend, 2007, p. 51)

Listen

Listening is the language of acceptance. One of the seven habits of highly effective people, as described by Stephen Covey, is to "seek first to understand, then to be understood" (Covey, 1990, p. 237). When you truly seek to understand the other person before stating your own perspectives, you will find yourself in a listening mode; you will hear the family's "language" and you will incorporate it into your communication with them. Covey (1990) described empathetic listening as "listening with intent to really understand":

> Empathetic listening involves much more than registering, reflecting, or even understanding the words that are

said. . . . In empathetic listening, you listen with your ears, but you also, and more importantly, listen with your eyes and with your heart. You listen for feeling, for meaning. You listen for behavior. You use your right brain as well as your left. You sense, you intuit, you feel. (pp. 240–241)

When you listen empathetically, you do not agree or disagree; instead, you simply try to understand what it means to be in the other person's shoes (sand and all!). You convey genuine interest, understanding, and acceptance of the family's feelings and experiences.

To understand from the family's point of view requires you to be nonjudgmental. That is not easy; we all make judgments about other people and their lives. But you still should try to accept others as they are. Suspend your own judgment of what is right or wrong, and try to relate to families' differences and values. Keep in mind that both you and the families share a common goal, namely, attainment of the four outcomes for their children.

Families want professionals to be empathetic listeners. Indeed, parents have reported that professionals' refusal to listen to them escalates conflicts that, in turn, can lead to formal mediation or even a due process hearing (Lake & Billingsley, 2000). By contrast, empathetic listening can contribute to trusting partnerships and can even de-escalate conflicts, as a father commented:

> The first thing is to LISTEN to us. Because we know our kids better than anybody, ya know, they're our kids. They're part of us! And, ya know, you go to some of those places and they just fill a form, ya know, and that's it. (Blue-Banning et al., 2004, p. 175)

The more empathetic listening becomes a natural part of your communication, the more likely you are to be an effective listener as you interact with families.

Be Clear

As is true of other professions, the discipline of special education is full of complicated concepts and terms. Few of them are readily understandable by people who have not had formal training or extensive experience in special education, even when the terms and concepts are used in full. Acronyms just compound the challenge of being clear in your communications with families. In the following example of how *not* to be clear, a psychologist is explaining the results of an evaluation of a student who has a specific learning disability to the student's mother:

> I gave him a complete battery . . . he had a verbal IQ of 115, performance of 111, and a full scale of 115, so he's a bright child . . . very high scores, in, . . . information which is his long-term memory . . . vocabulary, was, . . . considerably over average, good detail awareness and his, um, picture arrangement scores, he had a seventeen which is very high . . . very superior rating, so . . . his visual sequencing seems to be good and also he has a good grasp of anticipation and awareness of social situations . . . he . . . scored in reading at 4.1, spelling 3.5, and arithmetic 3.0, which gave him a standard score of 100 in, uh, reading, 95 in spelling, and 90 in arithmetic. When compared with his [overall] score, it does put him somewhat ah below his . . . his capabilities. I gave him the Bender Gestalt and he had six errors . . . his test age was 7.0 to 7.5 and his actual age is nine. . . . I gave him the, . . . VADS and . . . both the oral-aural and the visual-written modes of communication were high but the visual oral and the oral written are low, so he, uh, cannot switch channels. . . . I gave him several projective tests . . . he [does] possibly have some fears and anxieties . . . so perhaps he might . . . benefit . . . from special help. He . . . was given the WISC-R and his IQ was slightly lower, full scale of a 93. He was given the ITPA and he had high auditory reception, auditory association, auditory memory. So his auditory skills are good . . . He was given the Leiter and he had an IQ of 96 . . . they concluded that he had a poor mediate recall but . . . they felt . . . some emotional conflicts were . . . interfering with his ability to concentrate. (Mehan, 1993, pp. 251–252)

Little wonder that families would have a hard time understanding such an evaluation report!

Many families have learned the terms and concepts of special education; they may even use this terminology themselves when they communicate with you. Other families will be new to special education and its terminology. Still other families will face the challenge of learning English as a second language. A good way to clearly communicate with a family is to listen and pay attention to the terms that they use. You then will know what level of complexity will help you become a clear communicator with that family.

You may find it helpful to avoid using technical terms; instead, translate your information, using simple synonyms or several words to explain a concept that professionals have reduced to a single word. You will want to introduce this family and others like them—the newcomers to special education—to technical terms by using the term and then clearly explaining its meaning.

The term *jargon* refers to the technical terminology or characteristic idiom of a special activity or group. Jargon impedes communication; it creates obscurity, not clarity. An effective communicator is a "jargon buster." When you hear other professionals using terms you know the family members do not understand, ask questions that help clarify the meaning, or explain the terms yourself. Keep your communication clear and direct.

Be Honest

Being Direct Means Being Honest. Many families want you to be honest and not to "sugarcoat" problems even when you have to give them bad news. But they also need you to be tactful (Sebald & Luckner, 2007). Being tactful involves conveying hard-to-receive information in ways that are sensitive to how a family will react. You can be tactful by sharing information with a family in a private setting; by not blaming family members for problems; and by pointing out the strengths, not just the challenges and concerns, related to the family or the family's child.

Being honest is especially important when disagreements occur among family members, between a family member and one or more professionals, or among professionals, as this teacher pointed out:

> Good communication means that if you disagree on something, you can say that in a tactful way, you can discuss those issues. The conversation will still go on. Everybody will still be there present and discussing and not offended, no one leaves. Everybody can discuss the positives and negatives in a tactful way without hurting someone else's ego or feelings. I think good communication means you can say "No, I don't agree with that, let's talk about that some more or let's try something else." (Frankland, 2001, p. 111)

Another dimension of honesty is being straightforward when you do not know an answer to a question. It is far better to admit you cannot answer a question and commit to securing and communicating a full and accurate answer, as this father noted:

> If she doesn't know anything, she makes sure she finds out. . . . When you ask a question, she makes sure that you get a response to it. And yeah, she's not scared to tell us up front, you know, I don't know. Which is one thing that I appreciate . . . tell me you don't know and get the information back to us. (Beach Center, 2000)

Provide and Coordinate Information

Families want and need information (Jackson, Traub, & Turnbull, 2008; Matuszny, Banda, & Coleman, 2007; Stoner et al., 2005). Key topics include a description of present services, future services, the nature of their child's disability, experiences of other parents who have a child with similar needs, community resources, and legal rights (Sebald & Luckner, 2007). They do not want the runaround from professionals:

> Well I think that the Board of Education has all of these different little programs. And apparently the only way

to know about them is by speaking to other parents. And I think they are selective as to whom it is they tell. (Soodak & Erwin, 2000, p. 36)

Families particularly emphasize the importance of getting relevant and practical information when their child is first identified as having a disability. A parent of a child who was diagnosed with a hearing loss wished that she could have had more emotional and informational support when that news was relayed to her:

> You learn that your child is deaf and you need to talk to somebody. You need to learn more about that, but the audiologist was off to her next appointment. (Jackson et al., 2008, p. 92)

Another mother when reflecting on her experience in receiving the news that her child was deaf stated:

> I felt lost, at first. I felt really, really lost . . . I'm just like—uh, what do I do with this [the list of resources]? (Jackson et al., 2008, p. 92)

This mother's comment reminds you of the importance of not only providing a list of resources but guiding families in which resources are likely to be most helpful and what should they expect to access from each of the suggested resources.

Parents also want their children to be respected and treated with dignity, similar to the way a preschool director acts toward a child:

> She'll stop whatever she is doing if Lena asks her something. She'll stop and get on her knees and say, "Lena, tell me again. I don't hear you. Say it slow." And she'll sit there for five minutes and be late for a meeting until she can figure out what my child wants, and then answer her. (Soodak & Erwin, 2000, p. 37)

Providing information to families is especially important when children and youth, because of the nature of their disability, are not able to communicate on their own with their parents about what is going on at school. A parent of a child with autism described the situation as follows:

> I don't know, I always feel—and it is more my outlook—but I never feel like I know enough about what is going on. And I think that goes from the fact that Pete can't tell me what is going on. You know? I mean I can't ask him. You know, what he did today. What I mean is, I can ask him, but he is not going to tell me. Not specifically. And that is the frustrating part for me. (Stoner et al., 2005, p. 46)

For parents whose children are not able to communicate directly, they often rely on their children's behavior as an indication of how well things are going at school. A parent who relied on her child's behavior described how problem behavior was a trigger for increased communication with her child's teacher.

> He would get easily angered and so I started reviewing notes saying, what is changing at school? Because obviously something is going on because of what I see at home. Oh yeah, oh it was very rosy in the notebook, and then if his behavior hadn't started to kick up, then I would not have known. (Stoner et al., 2005, p. 46)

Sometimes, the very nature of the child's exceptionality can make it more difficult to locate information or make informed decisions. Moreover, there often are competing theories about the causes and appropriate interventions for some exceptionalities; autism and deafness are good examples. Especially when different factions of professionals and families strongly agree or disagree about various interventions, families face additional challenges, beyond how to raise and educate their child. Most families want to know about all the optional interventions (Jackson, Becker, & Schmitendorf, 2002). Families also want professionals to coordinate the information, not just to provide it (Kasahara & Turnbull, 2005).

:: PROFESSIONAL COMPETENCE

In chapter 6, we compared IDEA's and NCLB's "law on the books" about highly qualified teachers with the "law on the streets," namely, the realities about the teacher workforce. What are the implications for "law on the streets"? Being qualified and competent means that you know how to:

- Provide an appropriate education.
- Continue to learn.
- Set high expectations.

Provide an Appropriate Education

What is an appropriate education? As you learned in chapter 6, IDEA approaches that concept by requiring schools to provide an individualized appropriate education to students with disabilities and then defines *appropriate* as an education that offers an equal opportunity to learn. NCLB approaches the concept by requiring schools to enhance students' achievement in core academic subjects, using scientifically based instructional strategies. These two laws aside, however, parents report that an appropriate education begins when professionals recognize their child as an individual and then plan a curriculum, its method of instruction, and its assessment to build on the child's individual strengths (Blue-Banning et al., 2004; Jindal-Snape et al., 2005; Kasahara &

Turnbull, in press). Here is how one parent with a child with Asperger's expressed this perspective:

> I think the special ed teacher is a very key person in Paul's life, but I've never yet met a special ed teacher who had any understanding of Paul's disabilities and it's a long, slow education process. You know, it's probably around January that they're clicking into what he needs, and then next year it's a different [special ed teacher] again. So the lack of education of special ed teachers [about] his disability is a big problem. (Brewin, Renwick, & Schormans, 2008, p. 249)

In a nutshell, parents want educators to have the knowledge and skills to individualize instruction to meet their child's special educational needs and to provide the appropriate supports and services. This means that you must master the content of your undergraduate or graduate program, individualize what you know for the students you teach, and become a lifelong learner, continuing to build on your present strengths.

Continue to Learn

State education agencies require teachers to renew their teaching certificates periodically, believing that mastery of new curriculum and methods of instruction will result in better student outcomes. Teachers generally have formal requirements to participate in continuing education programs.

In addition to these formal opportunities to learn, every interaction you have with a family gives you an opportunity to examine your present skills and to reflect on how you can improve them. In the short run, it may be easier not to take the time for self-reflection or to invite the perspectives of other educators or of families. In the long run, however, it is highly time efficient to learn from every situation. You need not repeat your mistakes and spend additional time correcting them.

To continue to learn, you will need to seek feedback about your work with families and to be nondefensive. Being nondefensive means that you are open to others' perspectives about your performance and feel little, if any, need to defend or justify yourself.

You also may want to ask your students' families and your colleagues—those whom you can trust and who have expertise that you want to acquire—for pointers on how to improve your teaching and your partnerships.

Set High Expectations

As you learned in chapter 4, when families first learn that their child has a disability, they often fear the future, assuming that their child may not be able to make sufficient progress in school, participate in typical experiences with peers, or even enjoy a high quality of life. Similarly, many students may fear the future. Both families and students need to be hopeful about what lies ahead; hope is a powerful motivator for them to take action to get what they need to live the kind of life they want.

You also learned in chapter 6 that Congress found as a fact that one of the barriers to delivering an effective education for students with disabilities (and achieving the four national outcomes) is that educators and families too often have low expectations for the students (20 U.S.C. Sec. 1401 (c)).

To help families and students set high expectations for themselves, you would do well to be skeptical when professionals encourage families to "be realistic." That perspective can limit the family's ambition, goals, and sense of well-being.

A different perspective from being realistic adopts a theory of "positive illusions" (Taylor, 1989). This theory helps to explain how people adapt to threatening situations. Some people tell themselves or others that they have to be realistic and therefore should not have "false hope" about themselves and their world. Others, however, regard themselves, their world, and the future with positive, self-enhancing illusions. We use the term *great expectations*, not *illusions*. But, name aside, such an outlook does not deny the truth; instead, it creates a reality by promoting, rather than undermining, good mental health.

> Overall, the research evidence indicates that self-enhancement, exaggerated beliefs in control, and unrealistic optimism typically lead to higher motivation, greater persistence at tasks, more effective performance, and, ultimately greater success. A chief value of these illusions may be that they help to create self-fulfilling prophecies. They may lead people to try harder in situations that are objectively difficult. Although some failures are certainly inevitable, ultimately the illusions will lead to success more often than will lack of persistence. (Taylor, 1989, p. 64)

When reflecting on his treatment for the cancer that eventually took his life, Norman Cousins (1989), a distinguished editor of a major literary magazine, deplored the fact that many professionals were worried about giving him and others "false hope." Cousins said that these professionals never realized how frequently they gave "false despair" (p. 100) and how false despair can dissuade people from creating any kind of desirable future: "Perhaps the most important of these characteristics (of people who vigorously pursue active treatment) is the refusal to accept the verdict of a grim inevitability. . . . What it means is that any progress in coping . . . involves not denial but a vigorous determination to get the most and the best out of whatever is now possible" (pp. 76, 78).

Many students with disabilities and their families are frequently given false despair. Far too often, it limits their sense of the future and constitutes a major barrier to securing desired outcomes. By contrast, students such as Lanz Powell (chapters 3 and 4), Jay Turnbull (chapters 5 and 6), Dani Gonzales (chapters 9 and 10), and Ryan Frisella (chapters 11 and 12) were not limited by their families or many of the professionals who served them. Given the strong commitment Christine and Eric Lindauer have to Luke and their own education (chapters 1 and 2) and the determination that Marley and Chandler Nelms bring to Chad's education (chapters 7 and 8), it is likely that false despair is an unknown in their lives. Instead, great expectations and the effective use of many of the seven elements of partnership you are learning about will lead (or, in Jay Turnbull's life, did lead) to appropriate education and desirable postsecondary outcomes. These families are not the only ones with great expectations. Janet Vohs, a parent of a daughter with significant disabilities, shared her perspective on the power of a positive vision of the future:

> Families of children with disabilities are not allowed—or at least not encouraged—to have a dream or a vision for their children's future. What the past has given as possible outcomes for people with disabilities is far less than inspiring. If all we have to look forward to is an extension of the past, I should think we would want to avoid the pain of that future as long as possible. But I have a motto: Vision over visibility. Having a vision is not just planning for a future we already know how to get to. It is daring to dream about what is possible. (Vohs, 1993, pp. 62–63)

Having a Vision for the Future Fuels Great Expectations. When you develop and communicate high expectations for students and families, you will be a catalyst for them to develop their own high expectations. When people are enthusiastic about their future, they are far more likely to work hard to achieve their goals.

What if you had high expectations for yourself but found, once you started your teaching career, that you were not as competent as you thought you were? That situation often happens to many professionals, regardless of your particular role or expertise. You may well have that experience one day. In the My Voice box on the next page a teacher describes her self-doubt as a new teacher and its effect on her relationships with her students' families.

:: RESPECT

Respect in partnerships means that families and professionals regard each other with esteem and communicate

MY VOICE

Nina Zuna—First-Year Teaching and Professional Competence

My first year as a teacher was filled with many learning experiences about professional competence. . . . How competent I felt as a teacher had a profound impact on my partnerships, both my peers and with parents of the children I served.

While a student teacher and a beginning teaching professional, I taught several students with rare disabilities. At first, I felt very guilty that I had not heard of their disability . . . Perhaps, I didn't study enough while a student. Why hadn't I heard of these disabilities? Would the parents think I was incompetent to teach their child? Admitting lack of knowledge was my first step, and deep down I knew it was the right thing to do. Upon confiding in the parents, I found my fears were unwarranted. I was not chastised for my ignorance, and oftentimes, the parents were still learning about their child, too. They appreciated my honesty and were eager to share with me knowledge about their child and also their frustrations of sometimes just not knowing what to do. . . .

The partnerships I had with families seemed to click much more easily than those I shared with professionals. I was very comfortable conversing with parents and being an advocate for all of my students, but sometimes this stance negatively impacted my relationships with my peers. . . . My unabashed optimism and willingness to try new things was sometimes met with skepticism from my peers. At times I felt challenged during interchanges to defend my actions, while at other times, I could sense that my peers felt that I challenged their work, too. In this mode, we were no longer focused on producing the best educational outcomes for the child but were, instead, embroiled in a competition of purporting ideas or ideological viewpoints. . . . I had to work on my interpersonal skills, diplomacy, and patience to ensure that my partnerships with my peers were productive and respectful.

Many individuals immediately associate professional competence with earning continuing education credit, but this alone does not ensure professional competence. Professional competence also entails how you view yourself as a professional and the image you project to others as a professional. Ensuring continued professional growth is a daily job. My most valuable learning experience was connecting my academic professional growth with my personal growth.

Take Action!

- Be honest with parents and peers in letting them know when you do not have sufficient knowledge and then seek out that knowledge.
- Recognize that having great expectations for students and being open to new ideas might create conflictual situations with some of your peers. Similar to Nina, seek to develop trusting partnerships with peers who do not agree with you.
- Recognize that you should seek every opportunity for your professional and personal competence to grow on a daily basis.

Source: Nina Zuna, Assistant Professor of Special Education, University of Texas (formerly, Research Scientist, Beach Center, University of Kansas).

---

that esteem through their words and actions (Blue-Banning et al., 2004). A respectful professional will:

- Honor cultural diversity.
- Affirm strengths.
- Treat students and families with dignity.

Honor Cultural Diversity

In chapter 1 you learned how cultural characteristics can influence family-professional partnerships. Take a moment to review chapter 1's information about the racial/ethnic profiles of students in special education, and pay particular attention to the differences that often exist in cultural values. Think how you can best honor each family's cultural beliefs as a way of demonstrating your respect for them. Honoring cultural diversity begins with understanding the family's culture and its related microcultures. Figure 1.2 (in chapter 1) depicts the broad range of family perspectives stemming from cultural and microcultural beliefs.

Where do your beliefs fall? By answering that question, you will know where to focus your attention to honor families' cultural diversity. For example, "equality" reflects a belief that it is important for individuals to have equal rights and opportunities, including the opportunity to be an equal member of a team that makes decisions about a student. Equality is just one example of how practices in the field of special education are rooted in cultural beliefs strongly associated with a European American tradition (Hanson, 2004).

What if you are trying to develop a partnership with a family who does not believe families should have equal rights and responsibilities when working with professionals? Instead, the family may want the professionals to control the decision making and give the family guidance, even directives. Figure 7.2 provides a progressive plan of how you can implement activities to honor cultural diversity throughout the entire school year.

In addition to their cultural values, families also have personal values, such as a preference for communicating with a teacher through e-mail rather than face-to-face meetings. You need to take multicultural issues and personal preferences into account as you develop partnerships with families; the strategies in Figure 7.2 will help you take multicultural issues into account.

Affirm Strengths

Many families find that the professionals who work with them and their children focus on only the family's or the child's weaknesses, not their strengths. Sadly, many families are accustomed to getting bad news about their child or hearing a litany of problems. That emphasis on weaknesses can cause families to feel sad, frustrated, and defensive. In turn, these feelings can impede effective communication. One parent put it this way:

> I often think if [school staff] could do one-on-one instead of [coming] with five people, telling me Susie can't do this, and Susie can't do that, and Susie can't this, and Susie can't that. And I am thinking, "What about "Susie *can* do this and Susie *can* do that"? (Lake & Billingsley, 2000, p. 245)

Parents appreciate hearing about their child's strengths and hearing other positives, as one parent described (Sebald & Luckner, 2007):

> The last two years have been like in a dream world. It is like I want to call them up and say, "You do not have

---

FIGURE 7.2   Tips for honoring cultural diversity.

General Tips

- Gain insight from talking with families, talking with colleagues, reading, and other opportunities provided through the school and community to learn how education is perceived in the cultures of the students in your class related to issues such as teacher authority, discipline, academic success, homework, and peer relationships.
- Tie the content of the general curriculum to the particular skills and knowledge that are especially valued in your students' cultures.
- Incorporate projects into the curriculum that enable students to reflect on their culture, relate their culture to what they are learning, and share information about their culture with their classmates.
- Invite parents of students in your class to share information with the class about their culture.

Specific Tips for Communicating About Cultural Values

- Learn about the family's strengths, needs, and expectations by communicating with families consistent with their preferences (see chapter 9).

- Determine the family's priorities and preferences for their child's nondiscriminatory evaluation (chapter 11) and IFSP/IEP (see chapter 12). Seek to understand and honor the family's cultural values and priorities.
- Talk with the family about the assumptions that underlie their cultural values and priorities. Seek to find out about the reasons for their priorities and preferences.
- As you reflect on their priorities and preferences, identify any disagreements or alternative perspectives that you or other professionals have associated with providing educational supports and services to the student or family. Identify the cultural values that are embedded in your underlying interpretation or in the interpretation of other professionals. Identify how the family's views differ from your own.
- Respectfully acknowledge any cultural differences you have identified and share your perspectives on cultural values related to your and other professionals' assumptions.
- Brainstorm and then determine how you and the family can find "common ground" in your understanding.

nothing (sic) negative to say?" This educational system—this school itself has worked wonders with my son. It has taken a lot of stress off ME, so that when I go home, I do not have to get into it with him and say, "Oh, you know, the school called me today about this and that." They will call me, but they have already worked it out. Or they will call me to praise him and tell me how wonderful and how positive a role model he is now, and it's because they have worked with us. It is like I said, it has been a dream world to me. (Beach Center, 2000)

Note the two important points that this parent makes. The first is that she appreciates the focus on strengths rather than weaknesses. The second is that she finds it helpful when she does not need to "get into it" with her son in the evening by following up on a problem that the school identified. Reflect on the information you learned in chapter 2 about family interaction—especially the parental subsystem—and consider the potential for conflict between parents and children when educators share only negative information.

Just as it is critical to affirm students' strengths, it is also important to affirm the strengths of families. As you learned in chapter 5, at one time professionals regarded families as the source of a child's problems; indeed, some professionals still do and perceive that their parenting is characterized by weaknesses as contrasted to strengths:

> They don't understand or they don't want to understand what Aspergers is. Their whole attitude is that I'm just a crappy mom and I don't know how to raise him. (Brewin et al., 2008, p. 246)

It may be that families with whom you seek to develop a partnership have had the painful experience of being blamed for their child's problem. They may not tell you this directly, but they nevertheless may fear that you will criticize or blame them.

Even families who face special challenges (for example, substance abuse) have strengths. In your communication with all families, try to genuinely affirm their strengths and let them know that you notice and appreciate the positive things they do for their child. Figure 7.3 includes examples of families' strengths.

Treat Students and Families with Dignity

Treating students and families with dignity—treating them as honored, worthy, and esteemed—shows how you respect them. Families want you to regard their child as a person rather than as a diagnosis or a disability label, as this mother says:

> They allow Stephen to be Stephen, they don't try to slot him in with the other kids. . . . And, uh, there are certain

FIGURE 7.3   **Samples of families' strengths.**

- Lots of caring, extended families
- Being very optimistic
- Being very knowledgeable
- Making the child feel loved and accepted
- Maintaining an orderly, well-organized, and safe home
- Having a yard or park for playing
- Encouraging the child to notice, hear, and smell different interesting things around the house
- Encouraging wellness and health in all family members through exercise, balanced diet, and healthy habits
- Seeking out support from friends or counseling as needed
- Finding unique ways to use informal teachable moments as part of a typical home life
- Communicating thoughts and feelings to family members in a supportive and authentic way
- Having a sense of humor
- Being persistent in seeking help and support from others
- Having a strong religious faith
- Having interesting hobbies to share with children

Source: Adapted from Turbiville, V., Lee, I., Turnbull, A., & Murphy, D. (1993). *Handbook for the development of a family friendly individualized service plan (IFSP).* Lawrence, KS: University of Kansas, Beach Center on Families and Disability.

things that, you know, you have to do differently. . . . And I think that in a way, it's a way of showing, the teachers of showing Stephen that they respect him as an individual. (Brewin, 2008, p. 248)

Another aspect of treating a family with dignity is to treat them as decision makers without condescension, as happened to one parent:

> Instead of making accommodations for him, it was just a lot of deception, a lot of manipulation, and a lot of head patting. I felt like I was constantly being just patted on the head and told to go home and everything would be fine. And they hardly ever listened to the concerns with an open ear at all. It was just "go away, you're bothering me." I think they were trying to humor me and they wanted me to just be happy with what they wanted to give. (Lake & Billingsley, 2000, p. 247)

Treating people with dignity involves honoring their cultural diversity; what one family considers appropriate, dignified treatment may be offensive to another family. For example, the formality of the relationships you establish with families and how you address them (first name or last name, title or not), the nature of your eye contact with them, and how you arrange a room when you meet with them should reflect respect but also be shaped by a family's culture. Remember, if you make unintentional mistakes, you can learn from them and avoid them in the future. In this way you can teach yourself to become culturally competent; it is worth the effort!

:: COMMITMENT

Commitment occurs when professionals consider their relationship with a child and family to be more than an obligation incurred through work. It occurs when they feel loyal and are sensitive in working with the child and the family (Blue-Banning et al., 2004). To demonstrate commitment, you should:

- Be sensitive to emotional needs.
- Be available and accessible.
- Go "above and beyond."

Be Sensitive to Emotional Needs

As you have learned in chapters 1 through 4, especially 4, having a child who has a disability can add additional responsibilities to family life as families deal with any stigma their child's disability evokes and seek to navigate at least one and usually more than one service system. Additional responsibilities can take an emotional toll on families and result in their having emotional needs that can be helped or hindered by how professionals respond (Brotherson et al., 2009; Rogers, 2007). The child might be teased, be excluded from educational and community opportunities, or face architectural and other societal barriers. The family often worries greatly about locating resources to meet future needs (Jackson et al., 2008).

Professionals, too, have complicated lives. As many will say, "We're only human." Some professionals interact with students and their families by focusing on only the student's developmental/academic priorities; they distance themselves from any of the extraordinary circumstances that accompany disability. Others invest in a different kind of relationship with students and families. They embrace the full reality of the student's and family's life. That full reality includes the need for emotional as well as academic support.

A parent described a benefit of receiving emotional support from her child's teacher as follows:

> It was such a relief that I didn't have to try to fake my emotions when I was around my son's teacher. If I got

choked up with tears, I knew that it was going to be okay to do that. In most of my relationships with teachers in the past, I have always felt that they expect me to "keep a stiff upper lip" and always be objective when I hear bad news about my son. I can't separate myself from my emotions, and I'm so glad that I finally found a teacher who is comfortable with me expressing my true feelings. (Beach Center, 2000)

There are many ways to demonstrate sensitivity to a family's emotional needs. These include empathetic listening, connecting families to other families who have experienced similar emotional issues (you will learn about the Parent-to-Parent program in chapter 11), and seeking assistance from school counselors or social workers when more emotional support is needed than you as a teacher can provide alone.

Be Available and Accessible

Availability and accessibility occur when professionals arrange their schedules so families can reach and communicate with them. Families often praise professionals who are available for guidance or conversations "off hours"—at those times when parents are free from their work or other responsibilities. A parent described available and accessible educators as follows:

> The teachers here aren't just your 8:30 to 2:30 people. They are involved in the lives of the children and their well-being—not just education. They are interested in their education, but it doesn't stop there. And they have also made themselves available to us as a family that other teachers wouldn't. (Nelson, Summers, & Turnbull, 2004, p. 153)

Being available and accessible means being there. Many parents have expressed frustration about IEP or other school meetings that professionals do not attend; they also become frustrated when professionals come in and out of a meeting. A parent described the situation as follows:

> I had to leave my job to go to the [IEP] conference. . . . Do you want to know how many educators came in and had me sign something and walked out? And I just, I thought that was so rude . . . they do not give me or my daughter the respect that we need. . . . It's like you're just being brushed through like an assembly line. Or they were like scanning you through the grocery line. And then, they leave. (Beach Center, 2000)

Although it is difficult to schedule meetings that are convenient for everyone, the IEP meeting absolutely requires the availability and accessibility of professionals who have responsibility for providing an education to the student. An option that you will learn about in chapter 11 is to hold meetings at times and in locations better suited to parents' needs.

:: GO ABOVE AND BEYOND

When describing the professionals who are effective partners with them, families frequently use the following phrases:

- "More than a job." Professionals undertake an obligation to enter into a reliable alliance with the family.
- "More than a case." Professionals recognize the student and family as real people, not just one more group to which they reluctantly owe a duty.
- "Going the second mile." Professionals provide assistance to the student and family beyond their job description (Blue-Banning et al., 2004; Kasahara & Turnbull, 2005).

Korean American parents expressed the sentiment of going above and beyond as teachers having "special hearts" (Kim, Lee, & Morningstar, 2007, p. 258) and demonstrating genuine care for the students. Some parents even describe professionals going "above and beyond" when professionals speak to them while in community settings other than the school. These professionals demonstrate a genuine interest in the student and family as *persons,* not as *objects* of their job.

Professionals who, themselves, were identified as exemplary collaborators described going above and beyond in these terms:

- "Those who give the sweat equity"
- "Doing the extra step that may not be required"
- "Putting your all into your work"
- "Working outside the parameters of the job description"
- "Taking it to the next level and not just doing what you need to do, but going a little beyond" (Frankland, 2001, p. 130)

In this same study of exemplary professionals, an audiologist described how going above and beyond worked as part of a team effort with educators:

> The team was not trying to squeeze these children into any square pegs. . . . As silly as that may sound, many teams that I have worked with, because of the sheer volume (of students), have to make the child fit the process. My experience was just the opposite with this team. They also followed up with things that were not mandated by any guidelines. They worked through the IEP process, and they advocated for the kids. That is a true sign of commitment, going beyond what is required for compliance. (Frankland, 2001, pp. 130–131)

Going above and beyond within a school context yields "extracurricular" (outside of school) benefits for the professionals. They have the satisfaction of being included in family events such as birthday parties, weddings, and funerals. Listen to what one professional said:

> Parents can really tell when you truly believe in them . . . I mean, we don't just go in, sit down, and start . . . doing paperwork. . . . We may talk about soap operas or . . . one of the kids we're working with, the parents are getting married, we're going to the wedding. We're going to the shower. I mean it's just stuff like that. Because you talk about other stuff that's happening in their lives. I'll tell them about, ya know, I'm doing this, I'm doing that. So it's not just professional. (Nelson et al., 2004, p. 160)

Going above and beyond to participate in family events raises the issue of boundaries in family-professional partnerships. Some human service professions, such as social work and counseling, have explicit guidelines for ethical and unethical practice related to professional-family relationship boundaries (American Counseling Association Foundation, 1995; National Association of Social Workers, 1996). And, although the field of education generally does not (Cobb & Horn, 1989; Keim, Ryan, & Nolan, 1998; Nelson et al., 2004), the Council for Exceptional Children's Code of Ethics guides special educators, as you learned in chapter 6.

Is it appropriate to question the traditional belief that professionals should keep their distance from families? To encourage professionals in education to cross boundaries that professionals in other disciplines must not cross? Yes.

You will remember that one of the indicators of communication is being friendly. Being friendly suggests an informal rather than formal relationship. Schorr (1997) visited many human service programs nationally and synthesized what works for students who face the greatest vulnerabilities—students who experience poverty and the challenges that are associated with it. What works, she wrote, is ". . . a new form of professional practice" (p. 12), going beyond the traditional boundaries of professional norms to establish closer and friendlier relationships with families. She believes that this approach is particularly effective for families from poverty backgrounds who are accustomed to having unequal relationships with professionals.

:: EQUALITY

Equality refers to the condition in which families and professionals feel that each of them has roughly equal power to influence a student's education. They will not feel equal unless they believe that each of them is being fair with the other (Blue-Banning et al., 2004). To establish the condition of equality, effective professionals:

- Share power.
- Foster empowerment.
- Provide options.

Share Power

As you learned in chapter 5, family-professional relationships historically placed the professionals at the top of the relationship and the families at the bottom; you also learned that, nowadays, best-practice partnerships occur when all team members collaborate and enter into trust-building relationships. You also learned in chapter 6 that parent participation is one of IDEA's six principles and that increasing the roles and responsibilities of parents is one of the ways to secure a more effective appropriate education for a student with a disability.

Hierarchies and professional dominance reflect how power is distributed within relationships. Power is the ability and intention to use authority, influence, or control over others. Many forms of power can greatly influence the extent that equality exists in partnerships. Just consider two of them: *power-over* and *power-shared* relationships.

In power-over relationships, professionals typically exert decision-making control over families. These relationships reflect vertical hierarchies, with professionals on top. A mother described what it was like for her to experience power-over relationships in an IEP conference:

> I was told that this is a room full of professionals. All these people have college degrees. She told me, there's an MSW, and there's a Ph.D., and I mean she was naming off more initials than I even know what they mean. . . . And I'm just sitting here, nobody looked at me as the professional of knowing how these boys live. (Wang, Mannan, Poston, Turnbull, & Summers, in press)

One of the major outcomes of a power-over relationship is conflict within the family-professional relationship. Many families feel anger when they find that professionals are relating to them from a hierarchical position of power. Unfortunately, anger often begets still more anger, and anger leads to conflict and can cause partnerships to dissolve. A parent described his anger cycles as follows:

> No matter how angry I got, the angrier they got back. The angrier I got, the worse the response was. I'm sure I was very annoying to them, . . . but they're very good at wearing you down. And I was worn down a number of times. It was fighting, all the time. It was like pushing back the water. No matter where you pushed, you were met with resistance everywhere. (Lake & Billingsley, 2000, p. 247)

In power-over relationships, it is ultimately the student and family that will experience the consequences of decision making. Whenever you are in situations where professionals are forcing their judgments on families, you would do well to remember the perspective that a parent has offered:

> I said, you intend to do this regardless of what I say. I said, if you made the wrong mistake, what will happen to you? Nothing. I said, I have to live with the outcome of any erroneous decision for the rest of my life because I will be caring for my child until I'm gone from this planet and I have to reap the consequences . . . I said, I want to make the decisions about my child and I'll live with the consequences if I happen to make the wrong one. But it's difficult to live with the consequence for the decision you made that I was against. (Beach Center, 2000)

An alternative to power-over is a power-shared partnership. Power-shared partnerships are horizontal, not vertical. Imagine a team of professionals and family members all sharing their talents, time, and resources so that the whole is greater than the sum of the parts. Greater power is generated because everyone is working together toward mutual goals, and individual energy becomes group synergy. Each person's efforts significantly and exponentially advance individual and group goals (Senge, 1990; Turnbull, Turbiville, & Turnbull, 2000). A parent describes the synergistic benefit of power-shared partnerships as follows:

> It has been WONDERFUL. It has absolutely been the best thing. Not only have there been benefits and services that have come, but all of the people that we deal with have got to where there's relationship there with everybody and there's this bonding, and we're getting to where we're on the same page and . . . nobody gets 100% of their way. It's everybody there, you put it in a pile, and it's give and take. (Wang et al., in press)

The Together We Can box on the next page includes the perspectives of a mother from a Los Angeles urban neighborhood. She describes a situation when her son's early intervention teacher shared power with her and another experience when a social worker exercised power over her.

TOGETHER WE CAN

Hortense Walker—Don't Be a Hammer!

Hortense's best experiences came with Eric's teacher in an early intervention program. Before Eric entered the program at age 18 months, Marlene (the teacher) visited the Walker home and with her encouraging attitude, she and Hortense easily bonded.

How was she encouraging? By not being a "hammer" and insisting that Eric should be in the program. Rather, she explained how the program would help Eric and the whole family and then let the family decide whether to enter it. She gave them a reason to enroll Eric and information on which to make a decision. She acknowledged to them that they have the power to make decisions.

How was she able to create a bond? She was considerate of the family, keeping her appointments and gently prompting Hortense and her husband Michael to ask questions they were afraid to ask, questions about Eric and his impact on the family.

"We came to see Marlene as a person whose first objective was to meet the needs of our family as a whole. She emphasized the positives of the program for us and for Eric. We just ate up her time and her knowledge. She felt appreciated by us, and she was. That made the difference." Marlene became a resource to Hortense and Michael and laid the foundation for a trusting partnership.

By contrast, the least effective professional, a social worker at the regional service center, never asked Hortense and Michael what they needed. "Eric was very young, throwing up everything he ate, very skinny, and never asleep. I'd work all day and then sleep just an hour a night," recalled Hortense. But the social worker visited only once and never asked if Hortense needed respite care (child care so Hortense could take a break from caregiving). "She was rationing the respite to families whose children were more severely involved than Eric."

Yet in Hortense's mind. Eric was indeed a child with a severe disability, and Hortense herself was fast approaching the end of her rope.

The result of that interaction with the social worker? "I grew up in a home that respected professionals. I was raised by my grandmother and oldest sister; my mother died at childbirth. They taught me to respect doctors and teachers and to do as they say."

The social worker taught Hortense just the opposite. Now, Hortense questions everyone closely and doesn't let anyone take her or her family lightly.

Well, almost everyone. With Marlene, it's not necessary to question closely. After all, Marlene acknowledges Hortense's and her family's decision-making power. In doing so, she creates a different kind of life for them, one in which they are invited by her to be partners and in which they gladly accept her invitation.

Take Action!

- Avoid being a "hammer" by strongly directing people in terms of what you think is best.
- Take Marlene's approach of providing information and options, emphasizing the positive, and acknowledging the family's decision-making power. Recognize that some families who may initially distrust you and question your intentions may have had very disappointing interactions with professionals in the past.

Compare and contrast these different relationships, identifying the partnership benefits when power is shared and the partnership limitations when it is not.

It is important not to share so much power with families that they feel they have more responsibility than they have the time, energy, or desire to handle. One mother made an incredibly important point about the meaning of an equal partnership:

> In the beginning I was an insignificant member of this team. But as the years go on, I do find myself taking more leadership in this. But that bothers me because I don't want the leadership role. I want an equal partnership. (Soodak & Erwin, 2000, p. 37)

Foster Empowerment

Empowered people strive to have control over their lives; they take action to get what they want and need (Turnbull, Turbiville, & Turnbull, 2000; Van Haren & Fiedler, 2008); they know what action to take to solve the problems they face. Empowerment is the opposite of

SEVEN PRINCIPLES OF PARTNERSHIPS AND TRUST :: **151**

being stuck with a problem and having no motivation or capacity to resolve it.

As you become a partner with families and earn their trust, you will be an agent of their empowerment, demonstrating how you and they can take action to get what both of you want for the student. But you also will be an agent of your own empowerment, learning what you want and how to take action to get it.

A key aspect of taking action is persistence—putting forth sustained effort over time. Persistence requires tenacity. It entails refusing to give up when your initial efforts do not immediately produce the desired results (Scorgie et al., 1999). Sometimes certain goals, such as finding the best medication and diet regimen for a child with diabetes or working through problem behavior for a youngster with an emotional disorder, are especially elusive. Families and professionals will go through periods of trial and error before obtaining a successful solution. Persistence is required to work through seemingly insoluble challenges as well as to solve discrete, time-limited, or relatively short-term challenges. Empowered people typically refuse to give up until they find a solution to a challenge.

We encourage you to empower yourself, your professional colleagues, students, and families by being persistent in seeking the nation's outcomes for people with disabilities—equal opportunity, independent living, full participation, and economic self-sufficiency through an appropriate education (see especially chapter 5 but also chapters 8 through 12). When all the partners in a student's life are more empowered, it is far more likely that each of them will feel relatively equal to the others. Each will correctly regard the others as capable of solving challenges, influencing outcomes, and participating in joint decision-making activities. Among the partners are, of course, the students themselves and the important concept of self-determination (see especially chapter 4 but also chapters 8 through 12).

Provide Options

Solutions to challenges often do not come quickly and easily. One response to a challenging situation is to be inflexible and absolute:

- "I'm sorry but we have never done that at this school."
- "The rules and regulations say that is impossible to consider."
- "You have to be realistic and accept the fact that what we are offering you is all there is."

Another response to a challenging situation is to be flexible and creative. Just because one possible solution has never been tried before is not a good reason not to try it. Indeed, the mere novelty of a possible solution may be just the reason to try it. Committed professionals do not allow their thinking to be restricted. They embrace the complexity of challenges and the contexts in which challenges arise. They thrive on flexibility and creative options.

Equality is promoted when many options are available rather than backing families into a corner with only one alternative. People who have choices are able to be more powerful decision makers.

:: ADVOCACY

Advocacy refers to speaking out and taking action in pursuit of a cause. Advocacy is problem oriented; it identifies the nature of a problem, the barriers to solving it, the resources available for solving it, and the action to be taken (LaRocco & Bruns, 2000). Your advocacy on behalf of a student or family leads to partnerships because it demonstrates your commitment to them. To be an effective advocate and a partner, you should:

- Prevent problems.
- Keep your conscience primed; be alert for opportunities to advocate.
- Pinpoint and document problems.
- Form alliances.
- Seek win-win solutions.

Prevent Problems

In chapter 6, you learned about IDEA's six principles and the problems they address. These problems are worth a closer look in light of the partnership principle of advocacy. A national random-sample survey of over 500 parents of children in special education reported the following results:

- Forty-five percent of parents believe their child's special education program is failing or needs improvement when it comes to preparing them for life in the real world after high school.
- Thirty-five percent believe their child's special education program is failing or needs improvement when it comes to being a good source of information about learning problems and disabilities.
- Thirty-three percent believe their child's current school is doing a fair or poor job when it comes to giving their child the help that they need.

- Thirty-one percent of parents of children with severe disabilities indicated that they have considered suing, as did 13 percent of students with mild disabilities (Johnson, Duffett, Farkas, & Wilson, 2002, p. 23).

Would the survey have reported such discouraging results if professionals regarded themselves as advocates and acted accordingly? Most likely not. As a professional, you will encounter many situations in which you have the opportunity to pass the buck. But you also will have an opportunity to take responsibility. The advocating professional—the one who is a partner to students and families—tries not to pass the buck to someone else. That professional does not want to be labeled as Everybody, Somebody, Anybody, or Nobody:

> This is a story about four people named Everybody, Somebody, Anybody, and Nobody. There was an important job to be done, and Everybody was asked to do it. Anybody could have done it, but Nobody did it. Somebody got angry about that, because it was Everybody's job. Everybody thought Anybody could do it, but Nobody realized that Everybody wouldn't do it. It ended up that Everybody blamed Somebody when Nobody did what Anybody could have done.

Keep Your Conscience Primed; Be Alert for Opportunities to Advocate

Keeping your conscience primed means feeling a sense of concern, irritation, and sometimes even outrage when children and youth with exceptionalities and their families face injustice. The opposite of a primed conscience is indifference to the circumstances of students and families. Try to stand in the shoes of the two parents whose feelings are expressed next. Think about whether your professional duty is to advocate for them as a partner or to be indifferent to their concerns.

> Those of us that have older kids, it was a struggle. You have to basically get on your knees and crawl every step to get one thing (Beach Center, 2000). And they wanted me to sign a paper that he would never talk. I said how do you know he'll never talk—I said I'm not signing anything so I went over the teacher's head to speech therapist and they were very angry with me and I went to the principal and he said—who told you to sign the paper—I said the teacher did—well, she was outraged. But they did reprimand the teacher, and I wish I could find her today now. He's a motor mouth. We call him motor mouth. (Beach Center, 2000)

The more you prime your conscience to these types of injustices, the more likely it is that you will be an effective and motivated advocate.

FIGURE 7.4 Pinpointing and documenting problems.

- Observe the behavior of the people who seem to contribute to the problem and of those who seem to contribute to its solution.
- Keep data charts that reveal the frequency and types of problems that occur.
- Supplement these data charts with notes about what you observe; interview students, families, and colleagues and make notes of your conversations with them.
- Ask your professional colleagues for second and third opinions about the nature of the problem and the possible solutions.

Pinpoint and Document Problems

Effective advocacy requires you to develop a clear and detailed description of the nature of the problem you, a student, and a family face. It is not enough to describe a problem in a general way; you also need evidence about the nature and extent of the problem. Figure 7.4 includes tips for pinpointing and documenting problems.

Broaden Alliances

An old adage advises, "Lone wolves are easy prey." The opposite statement assures, "There is safety in numbers." Effective advocacy occurs when there are alliances among individuals who have similar concerns and interests—teachers, related service providers, principals, families, students, community citizens, and others. You will learn more about the positive outcomes of strong alliances in chapter 12.

A parent described the strength of her child's team, composed of professionals and family members who have formed a strong alliance:

> We're getting strong and what we're doing is we're forming this circle of strength around John and John is in the middle, he can't break through this. He's just surrounded by this wall of togetherness and strength. (Beach Center, 2000)

Create Win-Win Solutions

Advocacy, within a partnership context, emphasizes the creation of win-win solutions; everyone who has a stake in a problem has a way of winning through the particular solution. A win-win satisfies everyone; it solidifies a partnership. The opposite is a win-lose situation. Hardly conducive to partnership, it pits one person against another.

The win-win approach is consistent with conflict resolution programs that focus on using communication skills to prevent, manage, and peacefully resolve conflict (Jones, 2003). When the other five principles of partnership are in place and when trust has evolved, it is much more likely that parties can negotiate to identify solutions everyone can endorse.

Communication can lead to win-win results; and the earlier the win-win results occur, the more likely it is that the final result will satisfy all parties. Consider a situation in which a parent asks the principal of his son's school to place the child into a private school, at public school expense, because the education the child is receiving in the principal's school seems to be inappropriate. As you learned in chapter 6, IDEA provides that a local educational agency must pay for the tuition of a private school placement if the public school does not offer an appropriate education but the private school does. Sometimes it is necessary for the parent to have an administrative or judicial due process hearing to prove that the public system must pay the private school tuition. Few principals want to admit that the school cannot offer an appropriate education; few want to be identified as the chief of a school that costs the public system even one private school tuition. So, what process of communication will enable the parent and professionals to create a win-win situation? A mediator suggested:

> Ask questions. If a parent comes in and says I found this new program down the road 50 miles, and I want that for my child, it's an error to say we don't do that or we're not going to provide that. The best response is, "Come in. Have a cup of coffee. Tell me about it. What did you like about the program? You went and saw it, did your son see it? What did he like? How were you treated? What did you see there that particularly impressed you?" Because it's the answers to those questions that reveal a person's needs and interests. . . . So try to think of our negotiation without walls, without artificial boundaries between what you can do and what you can't do. (Lake & Billingsley, 2000, p. 246)

How might a win-win situation be created by handling the situation this way as contrasted to immediately engaging in a power-over approach? Which approach is most likely to strengthen partnerships and build trust?

:: TRUST

The last principle of effective partnerships is trust. We define trust as having confidence in someone else's reliability, judgment, word, and action to care for and not harm the entrusted person. Trust exists when people believe that the trusted person will act in the best interests of the person extending the trust and will make good faith efforts to keep their word (Baier, 1986; Rotter, 1967; Tschannen-Moran & Hoy, 2000). Four practices will enable you to create trust in your partnerships with families:

- Be reliable.
- Use sound judgment.
- Maintain confidentiality.
- Trust yourself.

Be Reliable

Reliability occurs when you do what you say you will do; it means keeping your word (Blue-Banning et al., 2004). When you are reliable, others can depend on you to act predictably. A parent of a child with a disability put it this way: "If you tell me you're going to do something, do it . . . don't tell me you are going to do this and don't do it; and don't tell me you did it when you didn't—just don't tell me an untruth" (Blue-Banning et al., 2004, p. 179).

To be reliable, you first must believe that it is important to be reliable. Then you must want to be reliable; you must have the desire, energy, and persistence to match your words and behavior, to "walk the talk."

In a teacher's busy life, it may not always be easy to keep your word, even when you deeply want to do so. So much can get in the way; there can be a slip between what you say and what you do. To be reliable, you need to organize your tasks and your time. You may want to keep a "trust me" notebook in which you write down all of your commitments—a list of issues you want to discuss with a parent, a message from a teacher that you promised to give to a student, a phone number for a return phone call, a request from a parent to know about upcoming school holidays. The notebook can help you remember your commitments. It is a good device for combining your values and motivation with your behavior. Also, don't be afraid to be honest with parents about the demands on your time. This can help them understand your life and build your partnership and expectations for each other.

Use Sound Judgment

Teachers make judgment calls in countless situations, often on the spur of the moment. Families will trust you if they can rely on your good judgment in such matters as curriculum, instruction, assessment, discipline, social relationships, and particularly safety. Parents often perceive a sense of betrayal when they have confidence that they are dealing with educators who are "experts" and then they encounter situations when they place belief in the educators' judgment and the outcome was disappointing. A mother of a young child with autism described the situation as follows:

> So, and that was a wake-up call for us, because I personally trusted the school system and I had no clue about these kids. So I put my trust in the school system. That they know these kids, they know what is best for them, and unfortunately it didn't turn out very well. (Stoner et al., 2005, p. 46)

Parents want to be assured that their child will be both physically and emotionally safe. Many parents of children with problem behavior have concerns about some of the extreme measures that schools take to discipline students, especially students with disabilities. Consider trust in light of one parent's experience: "I found out they were keeping my son in the bathroom for an hour at school because of his behavior. So I was very upset because of the time that lapsed without me finding out. I couldn't do anything about it" (Beach Center, 2000). Just how much will that parent trust a teacher or school that isolates a child and then does not tell a parent about that "treatment"?

Using sound judgment involves being competent. Professional competency, you will recall from earlier in the chapter, is one of the principles of partnership. When you show that you know how to provide scientifically based instruction and how to promote positive behavior in scientifically valid ways (not using the "bathroom isolation technique"), it is far more likely that parents will trust you. That is the point of the Change Agents Build Capacity box below.

CHANGE AGENTS BUILD CAPACITY

Leia Holley and Tierney Thompson—Circles of Tears, Circles of Triumphs

Sean Holey challenged everyone. He did not intend to; he just did—his significant autism, epilepsy (for which he had brain surgery), and limited language that caused him to injure himself, frustrated because he could not make himself understood made it difficult for teachers and their administrators. No one seemed to want to teach him; no one seemed to believe in him. No one except his mother, Leia, and his teacher, Tierney.

And even they challenged each other. Leia insisted that Sean be included in academics, extracurricular activities (swim team), and other school events (field trips). Tierney doubted Leia's judgment; school administrators in Bonner Springs, Kansas, thwarted Leia's plans; and soon a circle of tears surrounded Sean. Leia, Tierney, and the administrators battled constantly; anger, sadness, and frustration ensued.

Until the day Leia decided to end the war. "It's a new day, let's start over," she told Tierney. "We can do this if we want to. What do you need from me? You know what I need from you." Leia became the sponsor of Tierney's special education classroom and an intermediary between Tierney and general education teachers. Between them, civility and candor replaced anger; compromise substituted for intransigence; Sean soon began to take some academic subjects with students without disabilities; he joined the swim team (but, by agreement among the coaches in the league, his "time" was discounted in calculating the winner of his event, the back stroke); and Sean's peers entered the circle that previously had included only his mother, teacher, and her administrators. With Leia's and Tierney's sponsorship, they formed a circle of friends around Sean; the circle endured from his years in elementary school through his years in senior high school.

Take Action!

- Listen to the parents and to yourself; and then communicate civilly and candidly.
- Use an expert, such as a student's parent(s) to augment teachers' competence.
- Commit to a vision; don't reject it out of hand.
- Advocate for IDEA's principle of least restrictive environment; the LRE is not automatically foreclosed—indeed, it is presumed to be the right place for students with disabilities.
- Accept what a student's parents know about the child; they can be your equals in understanding how to teach the child.
- Treat the student's parents with respect; listen respectfully to their vision and then work with them to achieve it.
- Trust a student's parents; few do not have their child's best interests at heart.

Maintain Confidentiality

The records of a student with a disability or giftedness will contain information that is highly sensitive. Often, parents will share information with you only if they understand or expect that you will treat the information as confidential and not share it with other professionals.

Some of the information will come from the nondiscriminatory evaluation that IDEA requires. As you learned in chapter 6, the purpose of that evaluation is to determine whether a student has a disability and, if so, the implications for the student's program and placement. Other information will come from conversations with the student's family or other teachers, or from other agencies that provide services to the student (such as a mental health or social service agency). As a general rule, the Federal Educational Rights and Privacy Act (FERPA) requires you to treat all the information as confidential and to disclose it only with the consent of the student's parents or, if necessary, to disclose it to other professionals only in order to benefit the student. FERPA implicitly provides a foundation for trust because it requires you to do exactly what parents trust you to do, which is to maintain their confidentiality. We cannot emphasize enough how important it is to maintain that confidentiality. A teacher described her perspectives as follows:

> It's purely a matter of trust, that they can trust that person so that they can tell them whatever. I have heard all kinds of things ya know, from families and from the children that I work with, and I consider that pretty sacred, actually. It's kind of a compliment, as far as I can see, that they're willing to trust me with those kinds of things. (Blue-Banning et al., 2004, p. 179)

In your many interactions in the school building (including the teachers' lounge and school office) and even outside it, the best approach for trust building is to regard confidential information about students and their families as absolutely off-limits in any discussions. Under FERPA and IDEA, you may share information in team meetings about the individual student when the information is relevant, recent, reliable, and necessary for making decisions about the student's education. As you will learn in more detail in chapter 11, the one exception to this rule is that, in most states, teachers and other educators are "mandated reporters," meaning that they must report to a child protection agency any abuse, neglect, maltreatment, or exploitation the child may be experiencing. If you suspect any of those, you should consult with your immediate supervisor or school principal concerning your duties and the process for reporting. Otherwise, regard information to be held in a sacred trust.

Trust Yourself

Trusting yourself means that:

- You have confidence in your own reliability, judgment, word, and action.
- You know that you have the capacity to care for and not harm what others entrust to you.
- You know that you will act in the best interest of others who trust you and that you will make good efforts to follow through on your word.

Trusting yourself is tied to your self-efficacy. Self-efficacy refers to beliefs in one's capacities to organize and carry out a course of action (Bandura, 1997). In general, self-efficacy influences how people set expectations for themselves, the extent to which they persist in reaching goals, and their commitment to go above and beyond. We encourage you to reflect on people who have achieved important goals. How do you think their self-efficacy played a key role when compared to other characteristics such as intelligence, quality of their educational background, or assistance from others? People with high self-efficacy tend to take on challenging tasks and to persevere in order to achieve desirable outcomes.

Your self-efficacy will influence how much you trust yourself to carry out all the partnership practices related to the seven partnership principles: communication, professional competence, respect, commitment, equality, advocacy, and trust. As you develop your capacities for each of the partnership practices and gain confidence in your own skills, you will be far more likely to believe you can develop successful partnerships, even with families who have a disposition to distrust you.

Self-efficacy is not a static characteristic; rather it can be enhanced through a variety of means. Figure 7.5 includes tips for enhancing your self-efficacy (Hoy & Miskel, 2001). You can develop not only your competence across partnership practices but also confidence in your own competence. You will increasingly evolve in your capacity to trust yourself. When you trust yourself, it will be far more likely that families will trust you as well.

:: TRUST AS THE KEYSTONE OF EFFECTIVE PARTNERSHIPS

As Figure 7.6 shows, trust is the keystone in the arch that illustrates the partnership principles. Take a look at some arches, usually found in campus buildings or houses of worship. You will see that several stones on the left, and the same number of stones on the right, rest on top of each other and lean toward each other. These inclining stones meet at a center point, and the stone at the center is the keystone. Without it, the left and right sides of the arch will not connect. When the left and right sides connect, they do so at the point of the keystone. Figure 7.6 illustrates the central role that trust plays in family-professional partnerships.

What is the practical significance of the arch metaphor? How you carry out each of the six other partnership principles significantly influences the extent to which families trust you. Some examples of trust as the *keystone* of partnerships are as follows (Blue-Banning, Summers, Frankland, Nelson, & Beegle, 2004; Frankland, 2001; Tschannen-Moran & Hoy, 2000):

- *Communication.* You build trust when you exchange information in open and honest ways.
- *Professional competence.* You build trust when you are skilled in providing a quality education to students and quality partnerships with families.
- *Respect.* You build trust when you treat people with dignity and honor their cultural values.
- *Commitment.* You build trust when you go "above and beyond" in meeting the priority needs of students and families.
- *Equality.* You build trust when you share power with families.
- *Advocacy.* You build trust when you take action to seek win-win solutions when students and families experience injustices.

Like the mason who builds the arch, you build trust when you practice each of these six partnership principles, for each leads to the seventh partnership principle, trust.

| **FIGURE 7.5** | Enhancing your self-advocacy. |

- ▩ *Mastery experiences.* The more you incorporate *partnership practices* and refine your skills related to each one, the stronger your self-efficacy will become.
- ▩ *Modeling.* The more you observe successful *partnership practices* of other professionals and families, the more likely you are to believe that you, too, can be successful.
- ▩ *Verbal persuasion.* The more you listen to the advice and experience of others, as well as read current literature on best partnership practices, the more likely you will have a strong knowledge base and greater confidence in your capacities.
- ▩ *Physiological state.* The more you can minimize your stress when engaged in partnership practices and maximize feelings of confidence and enthusiasm, the more likely you are to strengthen your self-efficacy (Hoy & Miskel, 2001).

| **FIGURE 7.6** | The seven principles of partnership. |

Honor cultural diversity
Affirm strengths
Treat students and
   families with dignity

Be sensitive to emotional needs
Be available and accessible
Go "above and beyond"

Provide a quality education
Continue to learn
Set high expectations

Share power
Foster empowerment
Provide options

Be reliable
Use sound judgment
Maintain confidentiality
Trust yourself

Be friendly
Listen
Be clear
Be honest
Provide and coordinate
   information

Provide problems
Keep your conscience primed
Pinpoint and document problems
Broaden alliances
Create win-win solutions

REVISITING CHAD, MARLEY, AND CHANDLER NELMS

Chad is now at his "second duty station," that is, yet another school, having spent his first years in San Diego. As long as his father Chandler remains in the Marine Corps, he and his mother Marley will move from duty station to duty station, from school district to school district. They are the classic intranational migrants, the difference between them and corporate migrants or farm-worker migrants being that Chandler lays his life on the line when doing his job.

Let's make some assumptions about their future. Assume the Nelms remain at Camp Lejeune for another two years; assume Chandler is deployed to and returns unharmed from duty in the Middle East. Assume he then receives an appointment to Marine Corps headquarters in Anacostia, Virginia, and the Pentagon. Finally, assume Marley and he have a choice of school districts in which to live—some in northern Virginia, some in Maryland, and the one in the District of Columbia.

Now, let's make an assumption about you. Assume you have read this book and are the lead special education teacher in the school district to which Chandler, Marley, and Chad have moved. Chandler and Marley bring Chad to interview you before the new school term begins. You have not only read this book, but have re-read this chapter, intending to prepare yourself for the meeting with them.

What will you bring to that meeting? Tape recorders? Pencils, paper, and clipboards? A laptop computer? Anything at all for making notes? Will you bring anything at all, other than yourself? If only yourself, what questions will you want them to answer, and what questions do you think Marley and Chandler will want you to answer? Remember, they, too, have read this chapter.

Are most of the questions likely to be about Chad, or are most likely to be about how you and they will work to be sure that Chad gets the appropriate education to which he has an IDEA right? If you expect most of the questions to be about you and them, not Chad, what is the first question—the very first question (other than, "How are you today?")—you will ask?

How's this for an answer: "Whatever we do together for Chad, we have to trust each other. How do you, Marley and Chandler, want to establish that trust?"

Now assume it's the end of the school term. What have you done to establish the trust you want? Remember, Marley trusts professionals who communicate clearly and candidly and civilly; are competent and committed to her, Chandler, and Chad; respect her and Chandler and work with them as equals; and advocate for each other and for Chad. Remember, too, that she and Chandler are willing to go to the mat—as it were, to war—to be sure Chad receives the best possible services. Where do you begin with them, and what is the course of action you will follow throughout the term and any term thereafter?

SUMMARY

DEFINITION OF PARTNERSHIP

- A partnership refers to a relationship in which families (not just parents) and professionals agree to build on each others' expertise and resources, as appropriate, for the purpose of making and implementing decisions that will directly benefit students and indirectly benefit other family members and professionals.
- An arch (Figure 7.1) illustrates the seven partnership principles with three principles on each side of the arch and the seventh principle, trust, serving as the arch's keystone that locks the other pieces into place.

EFFECTIVE PARTNERSHIPS REQUIRE EFFECTIVE COMMUNICATION

- A professional who has effective communication will be friendly, listen, be clear, be honest, and provide and coordinate information.

PROFESSIONAL COMPETENCE INVOLVES BEING QUALIFIED AND COMPETENT

- A professional who is competent will know how to provide an appropriate education, continue to learn, and set high expectations.

RESPECT INVOLVES EACH OTHER WITH ESTEEM AND COMMUNICATING THAT ESTEEM

- A professional who is respectful will honor cultural diversity, affirm strengths, and treat students and families with dignity.

COMMITMENT IS MORE THAN AN OBLIGATION

- A professional who is committed will be sensitive to emotional needs, be available and accessible, and go "above and beyond."

EQUALITY INVOLVES FAMILIES AND PROFESSIONALS HAVING ROUGHLY EQUAL POWER

- A professional demonstrating equality will share power, foster empowerment, and provide options.

ADVOCACY REFERS TO SPEAKING OUT AND TAKING ACTION

- A professional who is an effective advocate will prevent problems, keep your conscience primed, pinpoint and document problems, form alliances, and seek win-win solutions.

TRUST IS HAVING CONFIDENCE IN SOMEONE ELSE'S RELIABILITY, JUDGMENT, WORD, AND ACTION

- A trusting professional will be reliable, use sound judgment, maintain confidentiality, and trust yourself.

LINKING CONTENT TO YOUR LIFE

In this chapter, we defined partnership and each of its seven elements. Now, let's link them to your life.

- **Communication.** Reflect on your relationships with others and identify the people who bring out the best in your ability to listen empathetically. Who brings out the worst in how you listen? What characteristics are associated with each of those two groups of people? What do your reflections teach you about improving your capacity to listen?
- **Professional Competence.** Describe a situation in which you felt a great deal of pity for a person with a disability. What was the source of that pity, and how could you transform that pity into a sense of high expectations for that person's future?
- **Respect.** Identify a person who seems to you to be without many strengths. What might you do to find a strength of that individual, no matter how many challenges that person faces?
- **Commitment.** How would you react in a situation in which you want to be available and accessible to a family, but the best time for them to meet with you conflicts with a planned get-together with your family

or friends? How should you handle this situation and how can you create a win-win situation?
- **Equality.** Describe a situation in which you have sought help from a professional who ultimately used a power-over approach with you. How did you feel in that relationship? How did it influence the trust you placed in the professional and the extent to which you followed the professional's advice? What implications does this experience have for you in developing your professional skills?
- **Advocacy.** Do you perceive yourself as a loner or as a person who naturally seeks alliances with others to solve problems? How does your own comfort as a team member affect your tendency to broaden alliances in order to be a more successful advocate? What steps can you take to foster your capacity to form alliances with both professionals and families?
- **Trust.** When have you entrusted yourself to another? When has another entrusted himself or herself to you? What factors influenced you and others to give and receive trust? What do you do now to earn another person's trust?

CHAPTER 8

Families as Partners in Communication and Collaboration

CHAD, MARLEY, AND CHANDLER NELMS

When Chad Nelms was just 9 months old, his parents, Marley and Chandler, suspected he might have some delays. Why? Because he was not using words; he had no effective language. Their goal, first and foremost, was language-related. Why is that significant?

Because, for one thing, language is the basis of communication and communication is essential for partnerships. Think about it: When Marine Lt. Col. Chandler Nelms is flying combat missions, he has to communicate with other pilots and with ground controllers and other units. Failing to do so, he jeopardizes himself and others.

The same is true with respect to Chad, Marley, and Chad's teachers. If Chad cannot communicate with words, he will communicate with behavior. And, communicating with behavior could be problematic, for understanding and responding appropriately to a child's behavior is not always easy—that's just one reason Marley and Chandler enrolled Chad in the CARD program for behavior analysis intervention.

Likewise, if Marley and Chandler cannot communicate with each other, they may not always be on the same page as they raise Chad. If Marley cannot communicate with Chad's teachers, they will lose the benefit of her experience with Chad and her recommendations about effective interventions. And when Chad's teachers cannot communicate among themselves, they may deny him the full benefit of their combined talents. Communication connects people to each other.

It is easy to assume we all know how to communicate well, but that assumption is not always valid. When Marley enrolled Chad in kindergarten, she had already established a firm partnership with his language and in-home behavior modification professionals. What she needed, and what she got, was a professional who could mediate between Chad's new teachers in kindergarten, Marley, and the in-home professionals. "There was a responsibility and openness on the part of the school district to allow that to happen."

At the same time, Chad's teacher made it clear to Marley that she had a deep commitment to Chad: "I'm going to work as hard as I can for him this year because I know he didn't get to this point without you and your home team doing a whole lot of work for him." As Marley noted, "What I sensed from her was a commitment to him

to do his best and for her to educate him. You just can't fake that commitment."

By contrast, Marley is too familiar with teachers who are "faking it." Some make it clear they will do "only what the law requires them to do" to educate Chad. Some regard her as "too involved" and decline to collaborate or be creative about solutions that might help Chad, based on what worked for him in the past and on the recommendations of professional associations specializing in child development and autism.

Some nod in apparent agreement or "roll their eyes" when they do not dare disagree explicitly and directly with her. Some ask Marley for suggestions on what to do, unaware of the fact that, by asking Marley, they may reveal their own lack of professional competence.

Others "take offense" when she mentions interventions that have benefited Chad but that are not on the "approved" list in North Carolina—the list of interventions developed by the TEAACH program at the University of North Carolina at Chapel Hill. They do not want Marley to "make waves" about the fact that they are committed to one and only one approach in educating Chad.

think about it

- If you were meeting with a parent as committed and informed as Marley Nelms, what positive response might you offer when she asks you to communicate with professionals from another agency?
- What positive response might you have when she brings data proving that some interventions have greatly helped Chad?
- How would you develop a positive partnership with her if you knew she and her husband had sued a school district and won a partial victory, costing a school district a tidy sum of money?

:: INTRODUCTION

Communication is essential to all interpersonal interactions. Every professional has to communicate with at least two different groups of people. First, there are students and their families. Second, there are the other professionals involved with students, especially those professionals who design and implement each student's Individualized Family Service Plan (IFSP) and Individualized Education Program (IEP).

In this chapter, you will learn about communication and its essential role in establishing effective family-professional partnerships. You will also learn skills that will help you communicate and become a partner with families and other professionals. Note that we emphasize communication with other professionals, not just with families. We do so because professionals need to be partners with each other in educating children and collaborating with their families. In this chapter, you will learn that a "collaborative climate" is essential to partnerships and depends on effective communication. Then you will learn strategies and tools to communicate effectively with families and other professionals.

:: CREATING A COLLABORATIVE CLIMATE

Have you ever been in a situation where the members of a group were working in isolation from one another? Have you ever been in a group where all the members were working cooperatively and collectively toward a mutual goal? Which situation is more likely to engender the mutual respect and equality that advances partnerships? Obviously, the latter because communication is an essential element of partnerships.

Communicating Within a Team Context

Nearly all educators work as members of teams that are responsible for providing effective early intervention and then a free appropriate education to each child with a disability. As members of a team, they evaluate the child and then develop and carry out the child's individualized plan or program. What types of teams do schools use to carry out their IDEA duties and partner with students' parents?

Types of Teams in Schools. Many different types of teams exist. Because their purposes vary, their membership also varies and usually consists of individuals from different disciplines. The team members' disciplines include, but are not limited to, special education, general education, speech-language-communication therapy, occupational therapy, physical therapy, school social work, school psychology, school nursing, audiology, vision and orientation and mobility, applied behavior analysis/positive behavior support, and paraprofessionals. These professionals bring to bear the related services that Figure 6-3 describes. The number of professionals on a team often depends on the student's educational needs. The more needs the student has, the more likely there will be more members of the student's team.

How professionals provide services and interact with one another depends on the type of team approach. One type is the multidisciplinary team approach. This type consists of members from more than one discipline. In a multidisciplinary team, members typically meet to share information with each other; however, members do not tend to work collaboratively and seek to cut across each other's disciplines. Note that the team members confine themselves to their own disciplines. By contrast, other types of teams foster greater levels of interaction and collaboration across disciplines. For example, in the transdisciplinary approach, which is preferred particularly in early childhood special education (Friend & Cook, 2010; Hemmeter, Joseph, Smith, & Sandall, 2001; Snell & Janney, 2000), families and professionals are collectively responsible for planning, implementing, and evaluating services.

A unique attribute of the transdisciplinary approach is the use of *role release*. Role release occurs when team members, including the parents, "step out of their usual roles to become either teachers of other team members or learners taught by other team members" (Snell & Janney, 2000, p. 5). When using the transdisciplinary approach, team members do not allow traditional disciplinary boundaries to guide their work; instead they share their particular information and skills as well as their responsibility for facilitating the student's program.

Other types of teams include collaborative teaming, collaborative consultation, and integrated therapy (Friend & Cook, 2010; Giangreco, 1986; Scott, McWilliam, & Mayhew, 1999). The common thread in each of these approaches is a shared responsibility for planning, implementing, and communicating about the student's services and supports. In chapter 10, you will learn how students can collaborate with teams to develop their own IEPs.

Fostering Communication Within Teams. Establishing open and honest communication is essential to creating effective partnerships. Team members usually start by assessing how the team functions. Figure 8.1 sets out questions that help members determine the extent to which they have developed a positive, collaborative team approach.

Families' Roles on Teams. As you learned in chapter 6, IDEA provides that parents have the right to be members of the team that evaluates a student and develops the child's individualized education plan or program. Data on IDEA's parent participation principle indicate that parents' level of involvement and satisfaction with the team process varies greatly.

Some families feel they are welcomed and important members of the team, but other families feel that they are not part of the team at all (Johnson, 2003; Soodak & Erwin, 2000; Squires, 2000) or that they are taking on more responsibility than they want and prefer instead that the professionals would take more initiative (Erwin, Soodak, Winton, & Turnbull, 2001). When parents perceive they are part of a team, it seems to make all the difference for them, the professionals, and the child. Listen to this parent's perspective:

> It is a team effort, I think because, myself, my husband, the grandparents, aunts, uncles, and the school are working together. It is like everybody is working for the best of Adam. They are all so supportive of me and my husband. It makes such a difference. (Erwin et al., 2001, p. 142)

Ultimately, parents should decide how they want to participate in teams. Some parents may want to be an active participant at every team meeting, but others may prefer a less intensive role. To honor parents' preferences and establish trust with them, you should ask parents what role they want to have as a member of a school team, and then you need to respect their preferences. You should always

FIGURE 8.1   Are we really a team? Worksheet.

Directions: Circle the points to the right of each question only if all group members answer yes to the question. Tally the total number of points circled. The maximum score is 100 points.

	Points			Points
1. Do we meet in a comfortable environment?	4	16. Do we consciously attempt to improve our communication skills (e.g., giving and receiving criticism, perspective taking, creative problem solving, conflict resolution) by:		
2. When we meet, do we arrange ourselves so that we can see each other's faces?	4	a. Setting aside time to discuss our interactions and feelings?		3
3. Is the size of our group manageable (e.g., 7 or fewer members)?	4	b. Developing a plan to improve our interactions next time we meet?		3
4. Do we have regularly scheduled meetings that are held at times and locations agreed on in advance by teammates?	3	c. Arranging for training to improve our skills?		3
5. Do needed members:		17. Do we use a structured agenda format that prescribes that we:		
a. Receive an invitation? (Note: Needed members may change from meeting to meeting based on agenda items.)	2	a. Have identified agenda items for a meeting at the prior meeting?		2
b. Attend?	2	b. Set time limits for each agenda item?		2
c. Arrive on time?	2	c. Rotate leadership roles?		2
d. Stay until the end of the meeting?	2	d. Devote time for positive comments and celebration?		2
6. Do we start our meetings on time?	3	e. Have public minutes?		2
7. Do we end our meetings on time?	3	f. Discuss group effectiveness in accomplishing tasks, communicating, abiding by ground rules, and coordinating actions?		2
8. Do we update tardy members at a break or following the meeting rather than stopping the meeting in midstream?	3			
9. Do we have a communication system for:		18. Do we consciously identify the decision-making process (e.g., majority vote, consensus, unanimous decision) that we will use for making a particular decision?		3
a. Absent members?	2			
b. People who need to know about our decisions but who are not regular members of the team?	2	19. Do we summarize the discussion of each topic before moving on to the next agenda item?		3
10. Have we publicly discussed the group's overall purpose?	3	20. Do we refocus attention when the discussion strays from the agenda?		3
11. Have we each stated what we need from the group to be able to work toward the group's goals?	3	21. Do we generally accomplish the tasks on our agenda?		4
12. Do we distribute leadership responsibility by rotating roles (e.g., recorder, timekeeper, encourager, facilitator)?	3	22. Do we distribute among ourselves the homework/agenda items?		4
13. Have we established norms for behavior during meetings (e.g., all members participate, no "scapegoating")?	3	23. Have we identified ways for "creating" time for meetings?		4
14. Do we explain ground rules to new members?	3	24. Do we have fun at our meetings?		4
15. Do we feel safe to express our genuine feelings (negative and positive) and to acknowledge conflict during meetings?	3			

Our score = _____   Total possible points = __100__

Source: From Thousand, J. S., & Villa, R. A. (2000). Collaborative teaming: A powerful tool in school restructuring. In R. A. Villa & J. S. Thousand (Eds.), *Restructruing for caring and effective deuction: Piecing the puzzle together* (2nd ed., pp. 254–292). Baltimore: Paul H. Brookes Publishing Company. Adapted by permission.

comply with IDEA's provisions about notifying parents of their rights and when teams meet, and, whatever role they want to play, you should always welcome them and value their contributions to the team.

Communicating with Families

As you learned in part 1 (chapters 1 through 4), each family has a unique set of characteristics, interactions, functions, and life cycle experiences. Indeed, no two families are exactly alike, so you will need to tailor your communication to match what each family wants or needs.

In the following section, we describe the skills you can use to communicate positively with families to develop partnerships with them and earn their trust. Then we will discuss how you can tailor your communication to honor families' preferences, cultural values, and linguistic diversity. Bear in mind that communication is just one of the seven principles of partnership and that it connects to others, such as the principle of commitment and how meeting families' basic needs also relates to partnerships:

> I think it's actually talking to them that counts. Some of my parents can't read, and so for me to send home a letter, that is just frustrating for them. So if I can't get in touch with them, I walk to their house because if their phone has been disconnected, maybe I can help out in some way. (Eberly, Joshi, & Konzal, 2007, p. 19)

You may well ask, "So what do I do now that I have the big picture? What strategies should I use to communicate with families and other professionals?" Read on: You'll find the answers in the next section.

:: USING POSITIVE INTERPERSONAL COMMUNICATION SKILLS

The more accurately and constructively you, the family, and the professionals on the team communicate with each other, the more successful your interactions will be and the more you will create partnerships grounded in trust.

We encourage you to incorporate positive communication skills into your personal style so that they become natural and spontaneous. That requires systematic practice. It also requires cultural and disability sensitivity among all team members.

> Language barriers to active participation may exist among native English speakers and in the presence of professional jargon. Whether intended or not, language preferences and practices embedded in each culture can create

a barrier to active parent participation. (Dabkowski, 2004, p. 37)

Refining your nonverbal communication skills with any family is challenging; it is especially challenging when you are developing partnerships with families from cultures different from your own. For example, the European American culture believes a professional (or other person) is being attentive and polite when looking directly at the speaker, looking her "in the eye," as it were (Gollnick & Chinn, 2002). But eye-to-eye contact with members of the opposite sex, people in authority, or elders can be considered disrespectful within an Asian culture (Chan & Lee, 2004).

Like some other professionals, you may be inclined to misinterpret parents' silence or limited responses during meetings or school-related activities. Some parents report they deliberately chose to avoid interaction or play a passive role in meetings because of language barriers (Kim, Lee, & Morningstar, 2007; Lai & Ishiyama, 2004; Salas, 2004). Other parents are deliberately passive, believing they must placate professionals in order to ensure continued services (McHatton, 2007). Obviously, a parent's own disabilities sometimes interfere with communication skills, so you need to make accommodations. For example, a parent or team member who is deaf and communicates through sign language will need an interpreter or professional collaborators who can sign. When communicating with any parents, you need to know about nonverbal and verbal communication skills, how to solve problems creatively, and how to resolve conflicts and misunderstandings.

Nonverbal Communication Skills

Nonverbal communication includes all communication other than the spoken or written word. Each of us communicates nonverbally through gestures, facial expressions, physical proximity to others, and posture. Often, we are unaware of the many nonverbal cues we transmit to others. If you wish to improve your communication with families and other professionals, you will need to be more aware of nonverbal communication skills such as physical attending and listening.

Physical Attending. Physical attending consists of contact, facial expressions, and gestures. The contact component involves both eye contact and the degree of physical contact, or closeness, between people who are communicating with one another.

Because your eyes often may be one of your primary vehicles for communicating, maintaining culturally appropriate eye contact is a way of showing respect for and interest in another person. It is estimated that European

American middle-class people look away from the listener approximately 50% of the time when speaking but make eye contact with the speaker about 80% of the time when listening. By contrast, African Americans tend to make more eye contact when speaking and less eye contact when listening. Native Americans consider it a sign of disrespect to ask direct questions and to make eye contact with people in authority (Joe & Malach, 2004). In South Asian cultures, sustained eye contact between people of different ages, of different social standing, or of the opposite gender is viewed as rude, hostile, or flirtatious (Jacob, 2004).

Adjusting the physical space between yourself and family members with whom you are communicating may also convey a particular message. Proximity between European American individuals engaged in a conversation is typically 21 inches apart. Among other cultural groups, such as Latinos, Arabs, and Southern Europeans, the physical proximity during conversation is often much closer (Gollnick & Chinn, 2002). As you become more culturally aware of the specific traditions of families, observe their interactions with each other and with others and ask for advice from professionals who have worked successfully with them.

Facial expressions are another component of physical attending. Typically, desirable facial expressions are described as being appropriately varied and animated, occasionally smiling, and reflecting warmth and empathy. Cultural groups vary in the emphasis and frequency of smiling. For example, many people from Southeast Asia tend to smile regardless of being happy or sad or even when they are being reprimanded (Chan & Lee, 2004). By contrast, having a stiff facial expression, smiling slightly, or pursing the lips is often considered undesirable within the European American culture.

Even as disability affects verbal communication, so it also affects facial expressions and your accommodations to them. Some have no ability to smile, frown, or otherwise express their feelings through their face or eyes.

> I was born with absolutely no facial expression—smile, frown, wink, etc. Due to the "wonders" of microscopic surgery, I now can "smile," albeit artificially. I have been an elementary school teacher for 20 years. The road to a successful career was not easy. . . . Contrary to the Dean of Students' wishes [when I was an undergraduate majoring in education] I went into teaching (despite the horrific student teaching experience!) and became a well-respected educator. (Beach Center, 2000)

Gestures are the third component of physical attending. The meaning of gestures varies across cultural groups. Some hand gestures mean one thing for one cultural group but a different thing for another group; some groups may regard "thumbs up" or "V for victory" as vulgar signs, whereas other groups may regard them as entirely positive. Just as you do in seeking to understand contact and facial expressions, so you should learn or seek advice from experienced peers about hand gestures.

Listening. To listen with genuine, undivided attention requires diligence, practice, and an awareness of different types of listening (Covey, 1990):

- *Ignoring:* not paying attention at all to the person talking
- *Pretending:* giving the outward appearance you are listening but actually thinking about something entirely different or thinking about what to say in response
- *Selective listening:* listening to only parts of what someone is saying based on your own energy, time, interests, or emotions
- *Attentive passive listening:* listening to what the other person is saying but not using nonverbal attending skills, using silence or minimal encouragement for the speaker to continue, or not communicating any acceptance of what he or she is saying
- *Active listening:* assuming a much more involved and direct role by being animated, making comments, asking questions, and even sharing personal experiences to foster a dialogue
- *Empathetic listening:* standing in the shoes of the person who is talking and attempting to see the world and the situation as he or she sees it

Nearly all parents want professionals to listen carefully, nonjudgmentally, and without predetermined ideas.

> . . . I think some of these people have preconceived notions about everything . . . So if I tried to say, to tell them [professionals] something, it'd be LISTEN TO ME. (Blue-Banning, Summers, Frankland, Nelson, & Beegle, 2004, p. 175)

Although none of us likes to admit it, we all have ignored, pretended to hear, and been highly selective in what we take from what we have heard. Listening takes hard work but can convey our level of interest, commitment, and understanding.

Verbal Communication Skills

Just as important as nonverbal communication skills are your verbal responses. Examples of verbal responses include (1) furthering responses, (2) paraphrasing, (3) responding to affect, (4) questioning, and (5) summarizing.

Furthering Responses. Furthering responses indicate attentive listening and encourage people to continue to speak and examine their thoughts and feelings. There are two types of furthering responses. The first, *minimal encouragers,* includes short but encouraging responses such as "Oh?" "Then?" "Mm-hm," "I see," or "And then?" Minimal encouragers can also be nonverbal and take the form of head nods, facial expressions, and gestures that communicate listening and understanding. The second type of furthering responses, *verbal following,* involves restating the main points or emphasizing a word or phrase from what the family member has said, using the language system of the family. Verbal following not only encourages the family member to go on speaking but also provides the professional with a means of checking his or her own listening accuracy.

Paraphrasing. Paraphrasing involves using your own words to restate the other person's message in a clear manner. In paraphrasing, you are restating the cognitive aspects of the message (such as ideas or objects) but not necessarily the affective state of the speaker. Use language as similar to the family's as possible. You might say something such as, "Let me see if I am understanding this correctly." By paraphrasing, you respond to both the implicit and the explicit meanings of what the speaker has said. You also are checking for accuracy and making sure that you have a clear understanding of the issues you and the speaker have been discussing.

Paraphrasing is extremely useful in clarifying content, tying a number of comments together, highlighting issues by stating them more concisely, and—most important—communicating interest in and empathetic understanding of what the family member or professional is saying.

You can use reframing when paraphrasing; when you do, you are trying to ensure that you maintain a positive point of view. You can reframe problems, issues, and concerns as the goals and dreams that parents hold for their children. For example, you can use reframing by talking about a child as spirited rather than hyperactive or by describing a parent as inquisitive rather than nosy. By reframing, you encourage parents and professionals to join you in regarding a situation constructively, fostering trust, and encouraging parents and professionals to contribute their ideas and efforts to the partnership (Christenson & Sheriden, 2001).

Responding to Affect. Responding to another person's affect involves two skills: (1) perceiving accurately the other person's apparent and underlying feelings and (2) communicating understanding of those feelings in language that is attuned to the other person's experience at that moment. You pay attention to not only what the other person says but also how that person says something. When you use this technique, try to verbalize the other person's feelings and attitudes, and use accurate responses that match the intensity of the other person's affect. Developing a vocabulary of affective words and phrases can be helpful. For example, you might say, "It seems that you are feeling very let down by a family member who you thought would always be there for you." You would be communicating that you are hearing their feelings and perspectives about the situation. Simultaneously, you are checking on the accuracy of your perceptions of the other person's feelings.

Questioning. Questions generally fall into two categories: closed-ended and open-ended. Closed-ended questions are used mostly to ask for specific factual information. Skillful communicators keep their use of closed-ended questions to a minimum because this type of question limits responses to a few words or a simple yes or no. Overuse of closed-ended questions can make an interaction seem like an interrogation. Although closed-ended questions can restrict conversation and often yield limited information, they are appropriate when used sparingly and wisely. Here are some examples of closed-ended questions that are usually appropriate:

- "When did Carlos first start having seizures?"
- "How old is Betty?"
- "Would a ten o'clock meeting be okay for you?"

Unlike closed-ended questions, open-ended questions invite family members and professionals to share and talk more. Some open-ended questions are unstructured. For example, posing the question, "What things seem to be going very well right now?" allows family members and professionals to talk about whatever is on their mind.

Other open-ended questions are more structured and impose boundaries on possible responses by focusing the topic—for example, "What are some of the specific methods you've tried to help Matthew behave more appropriately?" You can formulate open-ended questions in three general ways:

- *Asking a question.* "How is Miko getting along with her new wheelchair?"
- *Giving a polite request.* "Would you please elaborate on your feelings about how Charles is tolerating the new bus schedule?"
- *Using an embedded question.* "I'm interested in finding out more about Angel's toilet training at home."

Open-ended questions generally involve using the words *what* and *how.* We encourage you to be cautious about "why" questions because they can connote disapproval, displeasure, or blame—for example, "Why don't you listen to me?" or "Why are you late?" may provoke a negative or defensive response.

Indeed, we caution you generally about questioning. That is so because you might unintentionally phrase questions in a way that focuses on problems, deficits, and concerns. For example, if you ask the rather simple and usually proper question, "What problems are you experiencing with your child?" a parent may think you are suggesting that the parent is having problems with the child when, in fact, that may not be the case at all. Indeed, the parent's problems may be with the professionals who do not provide sufficient services. So, add the words "or with our work with him" at the end of the sentence, before the question mark. Similarly, when you ask about a family's or child's needs, you might be reinforcing the misconception that families of children with disabilities are overly "needy" but that is not at all what you wish to communicate. If you simply replace the term *needs* with *priorities*, you may very well create a more positive and family-identified picture of what the family really wants.

Try to think of interactions with families as conversations, not interviews. Use open-ended, opportunity-driven questions such as, "What is one of the best experiences that you have had with a professional? What can we learn from that experience about how we might best work together?" or "What would an ideal day be like in the life of your family?" Of course, you can use the same approach when working with your professional colleagues: converse, do not interview them.

We also caution you against intruding too much as you ask questions of family members. Families vary in their comfort about being asked questions. Some believe that most or all questions challenge their competency, invade their privacy, or both. One African American parent said she was raised by her parents and she raised her own children with the firm belief that "What happens in this house stays in this house." It was totally foreign to her to go into a conference with educators and be asked questions about what happens in her house and how she raises her children. Our advice: Respect family boundaries about what is private versus public information.

Summarizing. Summarizing—sometimes called "summarization"—is restating what the other person has said, with an emphasis on the most salient thoughts and feelings. Although similar to paraphrasing, summaries are substantially longer. Summarization is helpful in remembering the highlights of a meeting. For example, you might say, "Let's review our plan. By next week, I will meet with the physical therapist and you will contact the pediatrician." This statement provides a helpful review as well as closure to a meeting. Summarizing can also be

used to clarify complicated or extensive content. For example, you might say, "Let's make sure we are on the same page regarding the ordering of the assistive technology and in our decisions about how it will be used in the classroom."

Whether you are in a school-based management meeting or an IEP conference, communication skills such as empathetic listening, paraphrasing, and summarizing can facilitate the relationships between and among participants. You will be able to use these communication skills frequently in your interactions with families and professionals as you work with them one-on-one. But what about communicating within a meeting of a school team?

Solving Problems Collaboratively and Creatively

You can use the nonverbal and verbal communication skills you have just learned about not only in a two-way relationship between yourself and a family member but also within group discussions, including school-team meetings (Lambie, 2000).

Why would you want to do that? Because many teams waste valuable time by failing to use a dynamic and creative problem-solving process. Some team members approach students' educational programs from isolated perspectives, often contributing to fragmented and inconsistent outcomes. By contrast, other team members share their resources, experiences, and ideas, enhancing the chance that the student will have meaningful and positive outcomes.

Using Cultural Competence to Seek Solutions

As you learned in chapter 1, cultural values influence how families make decisions about their children and themselves. Some cultural groups view professionals as the primary decision maker about their child's education (Lynch & Hanson, 2004). Even when there may be questions or disagreements about the school's approach, some parents are not likely to communicate their perspectives. One Korean parent commented, "You know, our culture totally trusts and obeys school. We do not express even though we have complaints. There are many moms like that" (Park & Turnbull, 2001, p. 137). Betsy, an early interventionist, struggled with wanting to be respectful of the family's culture and at the same time wanting to work in partnership:

> How can I be culturally responsive when I go into the homes of families from cultures that make sharp distinctions between parents and "experts"? Take Karen, for example; she's a single mother from Puerto Rico

whom I see weekly. When I ask her to tell me what she'd like for Maya, she tells me that I am the "expert" and that I should tell her what needs to be done. . . . I know that Karen cares about Maya and is just expressing her respect for my professional skills, but how can I involve her more actively in Maya's activities while I am there? (Barrera & Corso, 2002, pp. 105–106)

As we have pointed out, the partnership principle of respect, particularly the practice of honoring cultural diversity, is necessary at every stage of planning and implementing students' educational plans. How can professionals creatively resolve problems and issues and at the same time honor families' cultural beliefs and practices?

Lamorey (2002) has suggested that instead of trying to persuade families to change their opinions and beliefs, professionals should consider themselves "interpreters or translators of Westernized approaches and resources available within the special education community, and as guides who respectfully offer services that families may or may not choose to embrace" (p. 70). By serving as an interpreter or translator of Westernized practices, professionals can convey American practices and at the same time learn about families' practices and cultural beliefs. Only then can they launch a meaningful dialogue about how to address issues or problems, because they have created a context of equal and respectful sharing of information.

Similarly, Harry (2008) points out that professionals often are not aware that assumptions embedded in special education practices can directly conflict with the beliefs and values of many culturally and linguistically diverse families. Likewise, educators often are not aware of others' histories and cultures; hence, they cannot identify the personal biases that the families might have. Awareness is one thing; an effective strategy, however, moves you from awareness to action.

Skilled dialogue is a strategy that can help you be a more effective partner with families whose cultural perspectives differ from your own (Barrera & Corso, 2002). Two assumptions guide skilled dialogue: (1) cultural diversity is a *relational reality*—everyone is diverse depending on the specific environments, and (2) cultural diversity is a positive attribute and never negative, problematic, or limiting. Skilled dialogue is highly consistent with the cultural reciprocity practices you learned in chapter 7 (Kalyanpur & Harry, 1999).

Skilled dialogue relies on two skills: anchored understanding and third space. Anchored understanding occurs when there is a "compassionate understanding of differences" that comes from truly getting to know individual families (Barrera & Corso, 2002, p. 108). You achieve an anchored understanding when you respect and appreciate the actions, intentions, and beliefs of a particular family, even in situations where you might have acted or thought differently.

"Third space" refers to a situation in which people creatively reframe the diverse perspectives and contradictions of each other so that these perspectives merge to address challenging issues. A third-space perspective occurs when family members and professionals each reach a new perspective without abandoning their individual points of view. You can implement skilled dialogue by asking yourself:

- What is the meaning of this person's actions?
- How does my behavior influence this interaction?
- What can I learn from this person?

Using skills such as paraphrasing or reframing assists you to obtain another's perspective. Think about a time when you might have used skilled dialogue to address a complicated issue with a family (or even within your own family or with a friend). How could you have achieved an anchored understanding of the family's perspective? What third-space alternatives could you have considered? What are some of the challenges and benefits you might personally face using this approach?

Using Creative Group Problem-Solving Approaches.

Disagreements with families or other professionals are opportunities to learn and become a partner; they need not be roadblocks to partnership. Indeed, you can successfully address disagreements by using these problem-solving techniques:

- Develop a vision.
- Agree on a specific goal.
- Brainstorm options for addressing the goal.
- Evaluate benefits and drawbacks of each option.
- Select the most appropriate option.
- Specify an implementation plan, including the person responsible, resources needed, and time line.
- Implement the plan.
- Evaluate how closely the results of the action matched the goals.
- Modify the plan and continue to make progress.

Read the Together We Can box on the next page and consider when and how you might apply group problem-solving techniques. That scenario illustrates how group problem solving can resolve a situation associated with truancy. Resolution depends on a structured framework for documenting next steps, the person responsible, resources needed, and time lines.

The Group Action Plan problem-solving process can be helpful in dealing with minor or major issues, but it is often especially beneficial in times of crisis. Because crisis

TOGETHER WE CAN

James's Team—Solving Problems and Creating Action Plans

Lekia was feeling a bit desperate. It was Monday morning and she had received another phone call about her son, James. James had been picked up by a local police officer when he should have been in school—he obviously was truant. James had been steadily going downhill since the beginning of the school year. It was early October and James had already skipped 20 classes. And, because he was missing so many classes, he was failing every subject. His school team convened each time he skipped. It wrote new behavior plans, rearranged his schedule, and even paired him with different teachers. Lekia believed the school was trying to help James, but she knew nothing was working.

Today, the team was meeting to try a new approach. One of the team members had read about Group Action Planning—an approach that brought together key people in James's and Lekia's lives from school, family, and the community to identify a shared vision and engage creative group problem solving to identify new ways to support James to be successful. The Group Action Planning team included members of James's existing IEP and behavior support team, but also one of his friends from school, his uncle, and a deacon from his church.

The team identified a vision that included a short-term goal of identifying supports to promote James's school attendance and a long-term goal of helping him identify his motivations to learn so he would be able to achieve his goals as an adult. Because the immediate issue was getting James to attend his classes, the team focused on developing strategies to address the short-term goals. Because everyone knew James, but interacted with him in different ways, they identified new and innovative strategies to motivate him to attend classes. They also identified the person responsible for making the strategies happen and devised an e-mail communication strategy and a plan for another face-to-face meeting in one month to evaluate the impact of the interventions put in place. Lekia left the meeting excited for the first time in a long time—she thought that some of the strategies may actually have an impact on James's attendance!

Strategy	Person Responsible
1. Finding an adult buddy who James could spend time with after school on the days he attended school.	The church deacon will solicit volunteers from church to cover different days of the week. He will coordinate with Lekia and the special education teacher to address transportation and scheduling based on James's school attendance plan.
2. Establishing a place where James could go at school and a person he could talk to at school if he felt too much pressure or was thinking about leaving school.	The teacher will involve the school counselor and identify a place in her classroom that James can visit. James's peer also said that he would be willing to talk with James when he was feeling frustrated.
3. Call his uncle every day at lunchtime.	James's uncle will set up his schedule to ensure he is available for a 5-minute phone call at lunchtime; the special education teacher will make her telephone available to James.

Take Action!

- When you and your colleagues run into challenges, enlarge the partnership by bringing in people from a student's family or community. Use the Group Action Approach.

- Support a student's parents by going above and beyond your regular duties, such as by convening at a GAP meeting; in the long run, that approach will pay off for the parents, the student, and yourself.

situations often involve heightened risk, danger, or emotional turmoil, a comprehensive written action plan can help everyone—families, students, and professionals—collaborate and support each other.

Resolving Conflict and Misunderstanding

Communication skills are particularly important during times of crisis. When in crisis, families may respond to you with anger, fear, or resistance, making meaningful communication more difficult to initiate or maintain. Likewise, when a major disagreement occurs between families and professionals, trust becomes an important factor to resolve conflicts respectfully and positively.

During difficult interactions with families, you may need to use the whole spectrum of communication skills. It is particularly helpful to examine your own behaviors and beliefs to be aware of how your actions may or may not have an impact on the misunderstanding. Sometimes, professionals who regard a parent as "high maintenance" simply fail to acknowledge their own biases and insecurities (Stonehouse & Gonzalez-Mena, 2001).

You may encounter parents who appear very angry, even hostile. Kroth and Edge (2007) suggest that if you know you are going to be involved in a potentially aggressive or antagonistic situation, being well prepared is an essential step. They suggest that you consider the following questions:

- Do I have confidence in my ability to conduct the conference?
- Do I know enough about the conference participants?
- Do I clearly understand the problem?
- Have I scheduled sufficient time for the conference?
- Have I developed a plan of action?

Through careful planning and preparation, you have an opportunity to gather the resources and information you need to handle competently a potentially difficult encounter.

Professionals' level of awareness of parents or other professionals will also influence their interactions (Ulrich & Bauer, 2003). A mismatch between a family member and professional could exist because of differences in their feelings about a disability, personal histories, prior experiences, knowledge of related issues, and cultural and personal beliefs (Ulrich & Bauer, 2003). A mismatch in expectations for appropriate classroom behavior also can lead to a conflict. For example, a child who does not actively raise her hand in class to volunteer may be viewed as passive by some professionals, but this behavior might be very appropriate and even expected within the child's culture. When professionals disagree with parents, they should try to understand why the mismatch occurs and how to address it collaboratively. The skilled dialogue approach can be quite helpful.

An effective professional will be aware of the feelings, anxieties, and tensions that families may be experiencing and then will communicate without doing any harm to the family (Montgomery, 2005). One way to avoid doing harm is to be acutely aware of our own ideas, biases, and attitudes about families and that we acquired them from our own family, friends, and colleagues. Self-awareness affects our communication and, in turn, our partnerships with families.

Conflict is a "natural part of collective human experience . . . and [has] the capacity to inform and advance our collective efforts" (Uline, Tschannen-Moran, & Perez, 2003, p. 782). Experiencing conflict need not be negative or harmful. On the other hand, the costs of suppressed conflict can be quite significant (Uline et al., 2003). It is better to engage in a healthy disagreement that moves toward a resolution grounded in trust than not to engage in conflict at all.

Conflict resolution strategies will help you deal with challenges in a respectful and honest manner. In their seminal work on resolving conflict, Fisher and Ury (1991) suggest practical and effective skills for resolving conflicts. They titled their approach, "Getting to Yes." Their win-win approach emphasizes understanding the problem from the other person's perspective and identifying all existing options so everyone wins. There are four basic steps to their win-win approach:

- *Separate people from issues* by understanding the other side's point of view and practicing active listening when other people express their feelings.
- *Focus on interests, not positions* by identifying the interests underlying each side's position.
- *Generate options* by brainstorming all possible solutions.
- *Use objective criteria* by developing and agreeing on principles based on scientific findings, professional standards, or legal precedents.

Conflicts or crises offer unique opportunities to strengthen trust. Approaching a potentially challenging situation with respect is critical. Susan Rocco, a parent who charted new territory by having her son, Jason, included in general education in Hawaii, understood the power of respect and culturally relevant communication skills. Susan knew, "You get more flies with honey than vinegar." Abandoning the mainland confrontational style, she adopted the nonassertive, nonconfrontational mores of Hawaii. She also had to trust professionals in order to secure their trust in her. She was successful, and Jason now owns and operates his own candle-making business.

Another consideration is the power of anger to motivate people. Often, anger leads to transforming events as outrage is channeled into positive action. We encourage you to view conflict as an opportunity to get things moving in a positive direction, sometimes with a sense of urgency that is hard to establish when all is going well.

You can embrace conflict as a unique opportunity to renew and enhance a partnership. You can practice these skills throughout all of your conversations with families and other professionals, during team meetings, and even when communicating in personal relationships. Improving communication requires time, effort, attention, and a genuine desire to be the most effective communicator you can possibly be.

∷ STRATEGIES FOR COMMUNICATING POSITIVELY

In this section you will learn to use the positive communication skills we just described. Before learning them, bear in mind that, despite the fact that IDEA lays out a formal process and specific opportunities for families and professionals to communicate and be partners with each other, parents frequently prefer *informal* rather than *formal* communication (Soodak & Erwin, 2000). Generally, they want their communication with professionals to be frequent, comfortable, nonhierarchical, and positive. In the following section, you will learn how to tailor your communication strategies to individual families.

Identifying and Respecting Family Preferences

To determine a family's preferences, you need to develop a family systems perspective, understand and honor the family's cultural values and traditions, and make accommodations for linguistic diversity.

Gaining a Family Systems Perspective. Your best approach for understanding a family is to develop a comfortable, trusting, authentic partnership that begins informally. The more you genuinely connect with the family, the more its members will be eager to share their family story with you. As you listen to family members, you can begin to fill in the different parts of the family systems framework.

You already know that it is good practice to engage families in conversations rather than interviews. That's so because families are more likely to communicate when conversing than when answering direct questions.

> Telling their story comes much more naturally to parents, and is less intrusive than talking about their "needs" or stress, or being asked only to circle numbers on a questionnaire or fill in blanks on a form. (Bernheimer & Weisner, 2007, p. 200)

The family story paints a contextual portrait of who that family is. "Families' stories offer a window into the way in which families make sense of their worlds" (Bernheimer & Weisner, 2007, p. 198). If you want to understand the child, you must first understand the family. Indeed, as you develop genuine partnerships with families, you will not need to administer so many formal assessments when evaluating the child for special education (see chapters 6 and 9) or have stiff, professionally controlled interviews. The more you think of yourself as a partner and incorporate the partnership practices associated with respect, equality, and commitment, the more your exchanges will be natural and relaxed conversations.

Connecting in a comfortable way is especially important when you work with families from culturally and linguistically diverse backgrounds. The whole special education process can be overwhelming for many families, especially families from diverse backgrounds who may have limited English proficiency or hold values different than those that often guide special education practices. The more formally you present the paperwork and questionnaires, the more intimidating you are likely to be. Remember, too, that some families do not have documented legal-alien status in the United States. Be sensitive to their desire for privacy and understand that paperwork can be a special threat to families who, for whatever reason, do not wish to reveal information about themselves.

You can use the family systems framework, which you learned about in chapters 1 through 4, in your conversations with families. Families, however, do not share their stories all neatly organized according to the family systems framework. But in practically every exchange, information about that family will crisscross the four components of the family systems framework. Listen carefully and without judgment. What components and subcomponents of the family systems framework do you detect in Armando Sellas's description of his daughter, Angelica, who has Down syndrome?

> Our expectations of Angelica have been very, very little different between what we expect from her sister and what we expect from her. We take into account that they are two distinct individuals, and they're each going to have their own identity, but you know we expect Consuelo to do certain things in the way of chores around the house or homework and things like that, then we have the same expectations for Angelica to get up in the morning, make her bed, get freshened up, go to the bathroom, brush her teeth and get ready to go. (Beach Center, 2000)

What did you learn from Armando about sibling interaction, parental expectations, the family function of daily living, or the family cultural characteristics? Now consider a passage from a different parent:

> I was raised up in my own religion, but then just recently I stopped going. My kids already know God is very important, we were all raised that way. They know right from wrong. They also already know that they are going to experience things, and I sit and tell them I know this is wrong, because I've done it. You want to smoke a cigarette, I'll buy the pack. You know, don't do it behind my back. My daughter, if you're pregnant and you're out there, then come to me and we'll talk about it. Don't keep bringing babies because it's too hard. You want to have sexual intercourse, there's birth control. If you want to talk, we can talk. I'll try to be very open about anything you want to talk about. I advise that they learn streets, but be intelligent too. Stay in school, get an education, because that's the only way you're going to get by in this world. (Beach Center, 2000)

What did you learn here about family cultural characteristics, the parental subsystems, family interaction in terms of cohesiveness and adaptability, and life cycle stages and transitions?

A good strategy for understanding a family and its system is to use a *portfolio*. The portfolio is a folder, file, or packet where you can keep notes of your conversations, copies of correspondence, and information. You can organize the portfolio into the family systems framework. Whenever you learn relevant information about a particular component of the framework, make a note in the appropriate place. As the information accumulates, you will increasingly understand and be more able to work in partnership with the family.

Although checklists and surveys can also help you collect family information (as you will learn in chapter 10), conversations offer a more open-ended and friendly way to develop trust in your relationships. Take time to get to know a family. Follow the partnership practices associated with the principle of communication: be honest, be friendly, and listen.

Respecting Family Preferences. To individualize your communication, you need the effective positive communication skills—verbal, nonverbal, and problem solving—that you learned about earlier in this chapter. You also need a keen understanding of the family's preferences for communicating with school personnel. Whenever possible, modify the strategies to suit a family's preferences and your personal style.

How do you learn about a family's preferences for communication? Simply ask. We recommend that you use open-ended questions to begin a conversation. At least three areas of questioning may be useful. First, you may want to ask, "How do you wish to communicate?" You can follow up by asking parents what they have liked or not liked about their past communications with professionals. For example, are telephone calls effective or inconvenient? Are written notices helpful?

Second, you may want to ask, "What information is important to you to communicate about?" Some parents may want to know about their child's health status, whereas others may be interested in school activities or classroom behaviors.

Last, you may ask, "With whom would you like to communicate?" Some parents may wish to be in contact with the paraprofessional who works directly with their child, whereas others prefer to be in contact with their child's teacher.

Think about family preferences as you read the Change Agents Build Capacity box on the next page. How would you gather information about the family's preferred way for staying in touch? What role might you have played if you were one of the student's elementary school teachers? How would you now rebuild the breakdown in communication?

It is not a good idea for school administrators to limit parents to communicating with only some professionals, putting other professionals "off limits." That is so because parents are apt to distrust an administrator who restricts their access to professionals who serve their child (Soodak & Erwin, 2000). One parent recalled the principal's comment to her upon their introduction: "If you have any problems, go to the consultant teacher" (p. 37). To the contrary, asking parents about their preferences respects them and engenders their trust (Zionts, Zionts, Harrison, & Bellinger, 2003).

Creating Supports to Accommodate Linguistic Diversity. You will need to develop proficiency with translations of written communications and with interpretations of oral communications. Some families with whom you will be working will have limited English proficiency, often because they are from diverse cultural and linguistic populations. To communicate with them, you will have to translate or secure translation of written documents into the language in which they are proficient. You will need to talk with your school administrator and other professionals, such as teachers of English as a second language, to explore local and state resources for translation. You also may want to use various software programs, though they may be limited when you are communicating highly technical matter about a child's evaluation and a proposed individualized approach to educating the child.

Some families are unable to read because they are not educated and literate or have disabilities. You should

CHANGE AGENTS BUILD CAPACITY

The Sauer Sage—The Fragility of Inclusion

Earlier in the year, I received a phone call from my son's first grade teacher about dinner time. I saw her nearly every morning when I dropped off my son, and I communicated daily with her or the associate in our communication notebook. She told me that she and the special education teacher had discussed *it*. (His performance? His placement? I didn't know what *it* was). "He should go down to the resource room, for math at least," she suggested. This time, I found my voice and said, "We need a meeting before changing John's placement." I hung up the phone wondering when the school personnel had decided this and why we had not first tried intervention strategies and/or other supports.

Although this was a legal issue, and it was possible that the teacher just did not realize she had not followed the correct process, I was more bothered by the feeling that they had discussed and made decisions without me and my husband. We made it clear from the start how important it was to us that we have our son included (it was our vision statement in the IEP) with his classmates, even if his goals might differ from theirs. I had also shared articles with the team in which the authors described the benefits of inclusion. Now it felt as if our opinions were being disregarded with an unexpected phone call.

For me, it has become ever more apparent how John's teachers' attitudes toward him and toward disability affect their expectations. Their expectations then play a part in how "appropriate" his placement is. Since my son's transition from a fully inclusive preschool to a local public kindergarten class, I have been asking myself the following questions: "Why isn't inclusion the assumed placement for my son? Why do I feel an awkward tension between myself and my child's educational team? Is my situation unique?"

Take Action!

- Don't communicate unexpected and predictably unwelcome information (about a child's program) by an unusual method (a dinner-time telephone call). Doing so indicates you are conniving without a parent's participation and that you don't want that participation. Poor communication, disrespect, and unequal treatment breed distrust.
- Do schedule a face-to-face meeting. Then explain and justify your plan, and ask the parent to comment. Candid, civil, and justified communication, and the invitation for the parent to comment, exemplify respect and equality and, in turn, trust.

Source: Sauer, J. S. (2007). No surprises, please: A mother's story of betrayal and the fragility of inclusion. *Intellectual and Developmental Disabilities, 45,* 273–277.

---

always consider the reading level at which you provide written communication. Try to make it understandable and accessible to the families with whom you are working. And of course you should always accommodate for a person's disabilities.

In face-to-face interactions, consider the occasions when you will need to have an interpreter for families who do not speak English or who are deaf. Again, you can work with your school administrators to identify local and state resources that can be used in meeting this need. Often families have preferences for interpreters with whom they have worked in the past. If those interpreters are not available, you might provide families with choices so that they have some control over who does the interpreting.

Some families may suspect that, when they are in an adversarial situation with their child's educators, the interpreter is "on the side" of the school. In chapter 1, we offered tips for communicating with families through interpreters. In an equal and respectful partnership, families must have confidence that the interpreter will convey both the substantive content and the emotional overtones of their messages. You should not underestimate the importance of having interpreters. One Chinese mother highlighted the difficulty communicating without the support of an interpreter, "Sometimes parents . . . go to school. It's the teacher who talks and I listen. I can only understand about (pause) not even one third of what is said" (Lai & Ishiyama, 2004, p. 102).

Throughout the remainder of this chapter, we will focus on five major strategies for communicating with families: (1) handbooks, handouts, and newsletters; (2) letters, notes, and dialogue journals; (3) telephone contacts; (4) technology options; and (5) face-to-face meetings. Some families will prefer only one or a few of these strategies. They may be illiterate. They may not have a telephone or a computer. They may not have transportation to come to a conference. Obviously, you will need to adapt your communication strategies to respect the family's preferences and capabilities. Frequent, open, and honest communication is key to knowing whether the strategies you select strengthen your partnerships.

Low-Tech Written and Spoken Methods of Communication

Handbooks, Handouts, and Newsletters. Many school *handbooks* for families outline administrative policies and procedures but do not include information about educational services or opportunities for parent involvement. You may want to develop a handbook containing information specific about your class or program, including information about personnel, classroom procedures, classroom supplies, transportation, methods of reporting progress, and topics unique to your program.

Content aside, you must also consider format. Handbooks are more enjoyable to read when they are well organized and inviting. Consider creating or modifying handbooks so they are user-friendly and written in clear, simple language. Including pictures of the different professionals in the classroom and of the classroom layout can also be helpful. If families do not speak English or if they speak it as a second language, consider having the handbook printed in other languages. Translation services are becoming increasingly available, and sometimes bilingual parents may assist in producing the handbook in different languages.

Handouts deal with specific matters such as resources in the community, safety and travel, accessible places of leisure and recreation, sources of college scholarships, drug prevention, responsible online behavior, and summer enrichment programs. To get families to read the handouts and establish communication with you, consider whether the information is useful,, affirming, and relevant.

Consider individualizing the handouts by highlighting or placing stars next to items that are particularly pertinent to specific families or family members. Ask your students to help prepare the handouts by writing, illustrating, or duplicating them; their contributions can be meaningful language arts activities. When you personalize communications that are originally intended for a larger audience, you show your respect for an individual family and treat families as equal members in your partnership with them.

Newsletters can be enjoyable and useful communication techniques. They can be developed by a teacher and class, an entire grade, an entire school, or by families. Any of these groups can contribute, edit, and publish newsletters, submitting drawings, quotations, essays, comic strips,

announcements, updates on ongoing school projects, advice, descriptions of adaptive devices, advertisements for toy swaps, methods of encouraging positive child behaviors, announcements of workshops and seminars, and "bragging" notes. Articles about homework, teacher profiles, "getting to know you" features, reports about special projects, and parenting tips are often well received by parents.

Keep newsletters brief (1 to 2 pages) and present topics that are of interest to families (Hollingsworth, 2001). Try to recruit families to help in publishing the newsletter, thereby showing that their input is valued and needed. Most people like to see their names in print; by sharing good news about families in the program, you affirm their strengths.

School newspapers that include information about exceptionality issues give a positive message about inclusion and can also address substantive family concerns. Box 8.3 contains a letter written by Kate Turnbull for her high school newspaper, expressing her views on using respectful language. This letter reflects her own experiences as the sister of her brother, Jay, who was 11 years older than she. Kate not only expressed her preferences about respectful language, but also educated her peers on the important topic of offensive language, showing them how to become more sensitive about disability discrimination. Consider how you use language in professional and personal situations. Kate raises a call to action by suggesting that our words are a reflection of the choices we are making. What does your language say about your choices?

Letters, Notes, and Dialogue Journals. By contrast to the strategies we just described, which are suitable for wide audiences, letters, notes, and dialogue journals are strategies to exchange information with individual families.

According to parents, written communications, such as school-to-home notebooks, can serve a number of helpful functions, including letting them know what's happening in their child's day, assuring them of their child's participation, and providing opportunities for informal troubleshooting with staff (Davern, 2004). Involve families in deciding how frequently to write, who will write, what kinds of information to exchange, and whether the journal will be open to all family members, not just restricted to parents.

Some professionals and families prefer dialogue journals over notes and letters, which may be more easily lost or misplaced. Dialogue journals offer a record of communication over time and aid in end-of-the-year reports.

As much as possible, use dialogue journals to communicate positive information about the student; keep negative comments to a minimum. Reread your comments to see if the tone or content of your message can be misinterpreted (Davern, 2004). Sensitive information is best shared in

MY VOICE

Kate Turnbull and the "R" Word

The word "retard," unfortunately, has now achieved mainstream status. I have been affected by the word all my life because I have a brother with mental retardation and autism. When I was in elementary school and junior high, I was embarrassed about my brother because people always used "retard" so lightly. Now that I am no longer embarrassed, rather, I am proud of him, I had hoped to escape the word. So far at my school, I have been unable to do so.

I frequently hear "You are such a retard!" or "Gosh, I'm so retarded!" when someone has made a mistake or has said something seemingly stupid. Every time I hear the word, I cringe. I think about my brother, my greatest teacher, and know that someone is making a mockery out of his disability.

Oftentimes the speaker does not realize the effect of their words. What happens when lower school students, walking down the hall to class, hear the word spoken by an upper school student? They are going to think that "retard" isn't a bad word. It is. The word itself is obviously derogatory to people with disabilities because it is never used to describe something or someone that is successful or intelligent.

People with mental retardation are not stupid; they are just slower at processing information. J. T., my brother, leads a completely normal life despite his disabilities. He works at the University of Kansas, rides the campus bus to work everyday, and lives in his own house with two graduate students. No one would want to approach him and call him a retard to his face so why is it O.K. to use the term so loosely behind his back? . . .

Some people might say that if they use "retard" or other offensive words in such a way that they don't mean them in a demeaning way, people should not take them offensively. If you know, however, that the words have the potential to demean someone, why use them and intentionally flare up conflict or hurt someone's feelings?

"Retard" is only one example of the offensive language circulating the halls and classrooms. Our vocabulary is filled with stigmatizing words such as "faggot," "chick," and "retard." These words have the potential to deepen the factions already apparent in the human race. They cannot possibly be doing more good than bad, so why use them?

Our school is only a microcosm for the "real" world. We hear these words from our peers and even our role models everyday, but whether or not we choose to use them is solely up to us. This is a major source of conflict for students in high schools and in our everyday society. But does it have to be?

Kate Turnbull
Editor-in-Chief

---

person when parents can ask questions and seek clarification. One parent sadly described her son's dialogue journal as a "log of sins." Each day when he got home, she dreaded pulling out the notes and reading about the 10 to 15 behavioral infractions that day. You can imagine how painful this was for her and what a strain it created between her and the teacher and even with her son. By failing to affirm the child's strengths, the teacher failed to show respect, the principle that would lead to a partnership with the parent.

Telephone Contacts. The telephone can be an effective means for providing both information and emotional support. Occasional telephone calls to families may even result in improved student performance. Approximately 94% of all children live in homes equipped with telephones (O'Hare, 2001). However, children living in poverty are four times more likely to be living in phoneless households than are children living in homes with income above the poverty line (O'Hare, 2001).

As a general rule, keep your telephone conversations with parents brief and to the point. When you need to have longer, more involved conversations, try to have them face-to-face. There are disadvantages to telephone conversations, such as not being able to see the parents' nonverbal reactions. So, listen carefully and check out your perceptions by asking questions and summarizing. Ask families in advance about convenient times to contact them, and also share with them preferred times for you to receive telephone calls. Before calling a family member at work, ask whether that person wants to receive telephone calls there. Families often appreciate it when teachers share their telephone number with them. This gives families a greater sense of connection; they regard the teacher as a partner in their child's education.

> . . . in all the previous schools, not one teacher gave me their home phone number . . . so I think one of the characteristics of these [collaborative professionals] is that they truly, truly, have a genuine interest into the well-being of that child and they believe that in order to serve the child properly they have to have a close personal relationship with the parent. (Blue-Banning et al., 2004, p. 176)

Also consider when it is convenient for you to receive and have enough time to respond to parents' telephone calls (Lord-Nelson, Summers, & Turnbull, 2004). An answering machine at the school central office or a teacher's own voice mail lets educators receive messages from parents when it is impossible or inconvenient to answer the telephone.

Speakerphones and three-way calling options allow more than two people to participate in a telephone conversation. Involving more than one parent or additional team members on the same telephone conversation may increase participation of key stakeholders and prevent miscommunication (Chaboudy & Jameson, 2001). But not everyone is comfortable with this technology. Ask parents for their permission to bring others into the conversation, and honor their preferences.

The telephone can be an efficient way to get information to several people with relatively little effort. Many schools set up a telephone "chain" whereby you telephone one or two parents with a message. Each of them, in turn, calls two or more other parents and so on until all parents have been contacted. This system has the additional advantage of providing parents with opportunities to interact.

Another way to use the telephone is to record daily messages on an automatic answering machine that parents can access. For example, you can prerecord information about schedule changes or homework assignments.

School receptionists or secretaries frequently take messages from families, handle small decision making on their own, call parents when they need to pick up their child, and relay significant information. Collaborate with these colleagues in discussing family preferences for communication, such as whether parents want to be called at work or which parent to call in families in which a divorce or separation has occurred.

High-Tech Methods of Communication

The Internet provides numerous and ever-expanding ways to communicate with families. Many parents may welcome the opportunity to communicate through e-mail. An e-mail bulletin board system for all parents or a restricted e-mail system for each family may be quite effective, especially if parents are among the 63% of adults with a computer with e-mail or Internet access (Madden, 2003). Of course, you need to be considerate of families without computers or Internet access. You will need to print and mail or otherwise deliver information to them (Johnson, 2000), and you may want to tell these families where they can find free Internet services in their communities (Beghetto, 2001). You should ask parents if they want to receive Internet messages at their places of work, if not also at home.

E-mail messages serve many of the same purposes as other forms of written communication. A middle school in Ohio e-mails a summary of its weekly team meetings to parents and extended family members so that everyone knows what is going on at school (Chaboudy & Jameson, 2001). Be cautious about including confidential information in these e-mails; indeed, it is often best to communicate confidential information about students through more secure methods. Consider the tips for using e-mail correspondence in Figure 8.2. Which strategies already come easily to you? Are there any strategies that might be more challenging for you to use?

Many schools have their own websites. These include information about the school and, often, mini-sites that allow teachers and parents to communicate with each other. Websites also allow family members or even students to raise questions, share ideas, plan class activities, learn about school activities, express their concerns, ask questions, or organize their own meetings or activities (Beghetto, 2001).

Websites that enable users to have a written dialogue often have "delayed" or "asynchronous" communication, giving family members time to reflect, compose, and edit their message before sending it (Walther, 1996).

Websites can provide information in multiple formats. For example, the SPIES website (www.cpd.usu.edu/spies) provides families and professionals information about recommended practices for educating young children with disabilities. It uses both written text and videotapes to describe and model practices (Cook, Rule, & Mariger, 2003). An evaluation study of the website indicated that parents found it to be practical, accessible, and appropriate. Although some parents had difficulty accessing the videos, many noted their usefulness: "If I wasn't sure exactly what

FIGURE 8.2	Tips for using technology to communicate with families.

- Ask parents if this is a preferred method of communication.
- Treat every incoming or outgoing message as important.
- Personalize your conversation by addressing the parents by name.
- If you are using a phone or text message, ask first if this is a good time for the family to communicate or if there is a more convenient time.
- Start out saying something positive about the child and/or family.
- Put in writing only what you would say directly to a person if he or she were in front of you.
- Make sure you provide an opportunity for parents to ask questions.
- Return calls, e-mails, and other communication from families promptly.
- If you are not able to address a parent's question or concern at the moment, let the parent know you received the message and will get back in touch shortly.
- Let parents know you appreciate their time in communicating with you.

the written description was trying to teach, I could look at the visual example" (Cook et al., 2003, p. 26).

Blogging has become another distinctive and widely used way of communicating with families. Blogging is basically online journaling and has become popular because of its many benefits. Within just a few minutes, a blogger can post text, photos, and video and audio clips. A blog's reader can access the blog from any Internet connection. So, blogs allow your professional colleagues to communicate with each other and with one or more families.

Blogging provides an open door into your classroom. You can post a blog at least once a day to showcase highlights of the day's activities and to invite families to have a virtual shared experience with their child. But you should be cautious about blogging about your classroom because you may violate students' privacy and families' confidentiality, especially since any viewer can copy photographs and use them in unauthorized or even surprisingly negative ways. Innes Borstel, a teacher of infants and young toddlers at the Ben Samuels Children's Center at Montclair State University, posts blogs about her inclusive classroom at least once or twice a day to strengthen trust through open communication between the families and staff. Her interactive classroom blog shares a variety of updates and infor-

mation such as sibling news, daily classroom experiences, and child-tested recipes.

Text messaging, also known as texting, is another tool to communicate with families. Texting allows teachers and other professionals and parents to send and receive brief messages instantly. Texting is particularly useful if there are simple exchanges that take place. Keep in mind that not all families are familiar with, have access to, or are interested in texting. Additionally, texting can seem intrusive particularly if an immediate response is expected.

Videotapes (used independently of the computer) are another viable technological medium for communicating with parents. Videotapes can give parents and teachers an understanding of what their children are doing, with whom they are interacting, and what they are learning. A study of videotape use with families of students in three early childhood classrooms found that parents and teachers benefited from this means of communication (Hundt, 2002). One teacher noted:

> The parents have been very positive. It's the only school correspondence that _____ 's family has had in two years. It also shows parents what I am talking about when I conference with them. (Hundt, 2002, p. 42)

Videotapes can be used as picture report cards, progress reports, or illustrations of instructional procedures, particularly for parents for whom English is not their primary language or families who are emerging readers. In addition, videotapes allow families who cannot come into classrooms during the school day to learn what is going on.

Portable digital or microcassette audio recorders allow students, family members, and school personnel to exchange greetings, information, and ideas. Students can listen at home to recorded messages from friends; family members can find out from teachers what happened during the day or what has been assigned for homework. Quicker and less demanding than written communication, portable audio recorders are an inexpensive and quite effective way to make conversations more accessible.

Face-to-Face Interactions

Face-to-face interactions are one of the most effective and commonly used methods of family-professional communication. We will discuss three types of face-to-face interactions: (1) planned meetings, (2) unplanned meetings, and (3) group meetings.

Planned Meetings. Regularly scheduled meetings can help to maintain and enhance family partnerships

(Lambie, 2000). Planned meetings (sometimes called parent-teacher conferences) allow you to discuss a student's progress with the family. They also allow you to meet with your colleagues to make decisions about a student's individualized education. (You will learn more about these particular meetings in chapter 11.) Because of their many potential benefits, you should try to hold these meetings throughout the school year, not just at the beginning and the end of the school year. Review Figure 8.3 for tips on meetings.

Sometimes, a family, because of its culture, will want face-to-face meetings; another family, also because of its culture, will not. Further, some families will attend a meeting but decline to take an active role in it, being intimidated by the formal process and many professionals who attend (Lake & Billingsley, 2000; Lynch & Hanson, 2004). We urge you to think about whether you have what one educator called "Westernized blinders" in your partnerships with families (Lamorey, 2002, p. 68). How do you interpret families' beliefs and practices about participating when they differ from your own? How do you honor their beliefs?

In planning a meeting, you will need to consider three major phases: (1) pre-meeting, (2) meeting, and (3) post-meeting.

Pre-meeting preparation consists of notifying families of the meeting, planning an agenda, and arranging the environment (Kroth & Edge, 1997). Consider whether the family will need translators, either because English is not their primary language or because one or more of them has a hearing impairment. In Figure 8.3, we offer tips on how to do your pre-meeting planning.

When you notify parents about a meeting, ask them who in their family or among their friends they want to bring with them and whether they want their child to attend. When appropriate, involving the student in the discussions and in solving problems can help build the student's confidence and ensure that team decisions reflect student preferences. (You will learn more about student participation in IEP meetings in chapter 10.) Be sure to practice the partnership principles of communication and respect for the family's culture when asking whether to include the student in the meetings.

FIGURE 8.3   **Questions to be considered.**

Notifying Parents
- Have you notified parents of the reason for the meeting in an understandable and nonthreatening manner?
- Did you follow up written notification with a telephone call to be certain that family members understand the reason for the meeting, to answer questions, and to find out if assistance with child care or transportation is needed?
- Did you discuss with family members whether they would like their child to attend the meeting?
- Did you discuss with family members whether they would like to have professionals from specific disciplines or other individuals who are important to them participate in the meeting?
- Did you provide information to parents about what will happen at the meeting and what they might do to prepare for the meeting in advance?
- Have you considered the family's preferences in planning the time and location of the meeting?

Setting the Agenda
- Does the agenda include topics the family has mentioned as important?
- Is the agenda flexible enough to accommodate last-minute additions?

- Does the agenda allow adequate time for discussion with family members?
- Is the family comfortable with a written agenda or would they prefer that a more informal approach be used?

Preparing the Environment
- Would it be preferable to hold the meeting in a setting other than the school, such as the family's home, a coffee shop, or the community library?
- Have you made arrangements to meet in a private, comfortable, well-lighted room that has limited distractions?
- Have you gathered all necessary materials and made arrangements not to be interrupted?
- Does the room contain an adequate number of adult-sized chairs and tables?
- Is the furniture arranged in a manner that reflects equality? (Are the seats arranged to avoid having someone sitting behind a desk or at the head of the table?)
- Are all participants able to locate and access the building, parking lot, meeting room, and nearest restrooms?
- Are tissues, beverages, papers, and pens available for all participants?

You may want to consider meeting at the family's home if that is desired and convenient for the family. Home visits are an effective mode of communicating with families as well as delivering services to their young children with disabilities. Professional communication (i.e., accepting ideas, asking questions, praising) seem to boost family participation in home-based early intervention (Brady, Peters, Gamel-McCormick, & Venuto, 2004). Whether at home or school, professionals want to create individualized and culturally responsive programs for their students. Ridgley and O'Kelley (2004) suggest a process for developing individually responsive home visits that (a) centers on the child and family, (b) considers the family's daily routines to practice skills, and (c) provides an opportunity for the family and home visitor to share information.

Although home visits for students of any age may mean more distractions and logistical coordination, they provide an important opportunity to gather a more complete picture of the child's environment and family life. Figure 8.4 includes tips for making home visits in a friendly, professional, and individually responsive manner.

Your next step in preparing in advance of a meeting is to prepare an agenda. An agenda (1) helps ensure your own preparation, (2) notifies participants about what topics are to be covered, and (3) serves as a guide for structure and sequence during the conference.

Keep in mind that not all families value efficiency in their interactions with others. Often, European American professionals are eager to follow an agenda and to be as time efficient as possible. Some families, particularly from culturally and linguistically diverse backgrounds, may prefer a more indirect approach that leaves room for conversations about tangential issues, humor, and personal stories (Lynch & Hanson, 2004). By honoring families' preferences and providing options, you can foster respect and equality in your partnership with family members.

Your final step is to arrange the physical environment and establish an atmosphere that will enhance communication. Two of the most important considerations are privacy and comfort. Consider the strategies we described in Figure 8.3. How could the environment play a role in your meeting with a family? Effective communication during the pre-meeting phase can build trust in your partnership. Be friendly, be clear, and provide information to prepare families for the meeting. Consider what can happen when there is inadequate communication prior to a meeting:

> When Kristi was first evaluated for a special education program, the school social worker called to say that she was coming to our home for a visit. She did not say why

FIGURE 8.4	**Tips for making home visits.**

- Talk with family members about the home visit before scheduling the appointment.
- Make home visits only if they are scheduled with the family ahead of time.
- Arrive and leave on time.
- Cancel home visits only when absolutely necessary.
- Dress appropriately and comfortably.
- Respond with sensitivity to offers of food and beverages.
- Expect distractions.
- Bring activities for the children.
- Be aware of the environment, and alter the visit if your safety or the safety of the family makes you uncomfortable.
- Leave your schedule and where you will be with someone.
- If part of your visit includes working with the child, take a blanket or tablecloth and spread it on the floor for your work area.
- Parents make choices when home visitors work with their children—some choose participation in the visit, and some use it for a few minutes of respite. Do not be judgmental of their choices.

she was coming, and I did not ask. I only knew that social workers normally visit a home to see if it "passes inspection." I cleaned for days, baked cookies and had coffee, tea, and homemade lemonade ready for her visit. The joke was on me. She had only come for a social history. She did not inspect my home or even eat a cookie. How much easier my life would have been if she would have explained to me why she was making her visit. (Beach Center, 2000)

Having done your planning, you and the family members are better prepared to meet and converse. During the meeting you should focus on (1) building rapport, (2) obtaining information, (3) providing information, and (4) summarizing.

Building rapport is important because rapport affects the tone of the entire meeting. Your genuine interest in and acceptance of the family and its commitment to the student can build rapport. Reflect on the professionals who provide services to you (such as physicians or other therapists) with whom you have a genuine rapport. What contributes to that rapport? How long did it take to develop? What could have been done to facilitate it more readily? By incorporating the seven partnership principles you learned about in chapter 7, you will have a better chance of establishing a positive rapport with families.

Obtaining information gives you a chance to practice many of the nonverbal and verbal communication skills we described earlier in this chapter, such as empathetic listening. Encourage families to share information by asking open-ended questions. When you are unclear about a family member's point of view, ask the person to clarify or give specific examples. Respond empathetically if families have difficulty expressing a thought or a feeling. Provide feedback to the family regarding the ideas, and affirm their strengths and contributions.

To share information effectively, you must use jargon-free language. Jargon limits families' ability to understand information. When you use clear and simple terms, you promote equity in your partnerships. Parents can be made to feel inadequate, as this Mexican parent describes: "I don't like walking into those special education meetings and everybody staring at me. . . . They always use those big words that I can't understand. I try to get there as early as I can so I don't look stupid" (Salas, 2004, p. 188). Another parent wrongly blames herself because she cannot understand professional jargon: "It is the terminology that they carried on between themselves that really I did not understand. I cannot really put any fault on anybody there because I did not understand the terminology that they were using at the IEP" (Childre & Chambers, 2005, p. 224).

Your language can either enhance or hinder partnerships with families. When sharing information, begin on a positive note, pointing out the student's strong points before mentioning topics that concern you or the family. Provide specific examples by telling anecdotes or showing samples of the student's work. Be aware of and respond to the impact of what you are saying on the family. If they are frowning or appear puzzled, stop for a moment to provide an opportunity for questions or comments. Ask the parents what kind of person their child is at home and to share information to assist in understanding the child (Walker-Dalhouse & Dalhouse, 2001). As much as possible, encourage everyone to exchange information and concerns. One mother described the critical role of two-way communication in successful meetings:

> The all-important purpose of home and school meetings should be to facilitate communication between families and schools. . . . Parents need to have a voice and be able to ask questions and receive accurate, up-to-date information. This dispels rumors and builds confidence and trust. . . . With good team work, things get done. (Haviland, 2003, p. 52)

When you are summarizing or planning follow-up activities, review the high points of the meeting and emphasize next-step activities. Restate who is responsible for carrying out those tasks and the date by which they are to be completed. Discuss and agree on options for follow-up strategies. If another meeting is planned, decide on the time and place. End the meeting on a positive note. Thank the family for their interest and contributions, and offer to be available should any questions or issues arise.

After the meeting concludes, take time to share information and reflect on the team process:

- Review the meeting with the student (with parental consent).
- Share the outcome of the meeting with other professionals.
- Record and file minutes of the meeting.
- Evaluate your satisfaction with the meeting and seek reactions, feedback, and suggestions for improvement from other participants.

The more you reflect and invite feedback on planned meetings, the more likely it is that your partnership with families will flourish.

Unplanned Meetings. Unplanned meetings are spontaneous; time and place vary. Parents may unexpectedly drop in at school before, during, and after school hours; you may receive telephone calls or e-mails at home in the evenings and on weekends; or you may be approached by families with child-related concerns at unlikely places, such as a movie theater or a grocery store.

Although it is probably impossible to avoid being caught off guard at such times, you can prepare for these meetings and the likelihood that parents will express their most intense thoughts and feelings.

- Decide in advance what is possible for you to do in response to unplanned conferences.
- Talk with other professionals about their strategies for handling unplanned meetings.
- Identify the topics that are open or closed for discussion at unplanned meetings.
- Have helpful resources readily available for families seeking information (e.g., names, addresses, and phone numbers of other agencies, families, and professionals).
- Seek advice and support from the administrator or other professionals at your school.
- Be flexible and open to unique circumstances that require an immediate meeting.

Of course, you need to inform families of your preferences. Ideally, you should do this at the beginning of the year before any unplanned meetings have occurred. Communicate your preferences both verbally and in writing to avoid misunderstanding and to allow the families to ask questions. Be sure to explain your rationale regarding unplanned meetings in noneducational settings: for example, "I want to be able to meet your needs and answer your questions as well and as completely as possible; however, I am not able to do so without sufficient preparation and access to your child's records."

Practice the positive communication skills discussed earlier in this chapter during unplanned meetings. Without positive communication skills, even the best prepared professionals can fail in their attempts to meet the needs of families.

Group Meetings. Almost all schools have orientation meetings or open houses during the year for families to learn about their child's schedule and curriculum. Although it is difficult to connect with families individually at such large meetings, group meetings provide information to many people at one time and give families an opportunity to meet each other.

Arrange for group meetings to be at a time convenient for families. Consider giving families the option of meeting during the day and or in the evening. Holding the meeting in community locations or at work sites may make transportation and child care easier for some families to arrange. Finally, remember to inform parents of what is to take place during the meeting and how the meeting will be conducted (Lundgren & Morrison, 2003). Pena (2000) described a situation in which a school, composed primarily of Latino families, had planned for parents to move from the cafeteria to their children's classrooms on Back to School Night. Because the procedures were not made clear to parents, many simply exited the building after leaving the cafeteria, unaware that the meeting had not yet ended.

Face-to-face meetings with parents, whether planned, unplanned, or group, provide an opportunity for partnership building. In each situation, the communication practices of honesty, clarity, and friendliness strengthen relationships and build trust.

Before revisiting the Nelms family, let's review this chapter by considering how to build partnerships based on trust by communicating effectively with families. Look at Figure 8.5 for our best-practice suggestions.

REVISITING CHAD, MARLEY, AND CHANDLER NELMS

Marley, Chandler, and Chad have a natural communication loop. They talk and listen to each other. They are not unlike nearly every other family. The challenge for every professional working with them to provide an appropriate education to Chad is to break into this loop and ultimately use communication as the basis for a partnership based on trust. The professionals who accepted data from agencies other than their own demonstrated a commitment to Chad and thus entered the family's communication loop. The professionals who responded to the data that Marley presented and who respected her for bringing those data to the partnership opened the loop still further.

By contrast, the professionals who guarded their own agency's turf and expertise and who casually dismissed Marley and the data she brought not only did not enter the family's communication loop; they also breached the first principle of a trust-based partnership, which is to be an effective communicator.

Which approach is likely to be more promising for Chad? The former. And which is likely to be less provocative of a family who, Marine-like, is not afraid to do combat to secure what it wants for its son? No doubt, the former.

FIGURE 8.5   Creating partnerships through trust-building.

Partnership Principles and Practices	Issues	Actions Leading to Distrust	Actions Leading to Trust
Communication: Listen.	You are participating in a conference with parents who are extremely angry that their gifted child is making poor grades and believe that it is your fault.	Tell the parents that they have not provided proper supervision for homework and that the poor grades are their fault.	Listen empathetically and ask if they would be willing to brainstorm options that would involve them and you collaborating to promote their child's program.
Respect: Honor cultural diversity.	The school handbook is only available in English, yet the parents speak Mandarin.	Tell the parents that maybe their child or some friends can translate parts of the handbook to them.	Talk with your administrator about getting the handbook translated into Mandarin or securing someone to explain it to the parents.
Professional Competence: Set high expectations.	Parents of a student who is failing every subject are not showing any concern about school failure.	Tell the parents that you object to their family priorities and that they are only hurting their son.	Meet with the family and find out, from their perspective, their priorities for their son, both this year and in the future.
Equality: Provide options.	A parent asks if a conference can be arranged before school to accommodate her work schedule.	Tell the parent it is against teacher-union policy.	Ask the parent if it would be possible to talk on the telephone early in the school day rather than to meet at school.
Commitment: Be sensitive to emotional needs.	The family has just moved to a new community, and neither the student nor the parents know anyone at the child's new middle school.	Assume that the parents may be interested in coming to the school open house next year; leave them on their own to make connections in the new community and school.	Call the parents, issue a special invitation to come to the school open house, and arrange with another family to meet the new parents and student and introduce them to others.
Trust: Maintain confidentiality.	The school administration asks parents to contribute to a fund to pay for the classroom newspaper, but the parents do not have money to contribute.	Tell them they'll not be able to get the newspaper, since they have to "pay their own way."	Identify a nonmonetary way for them to contribute to the class; tell them their classroom contribution represents their donation; keep everything confidential.

SUMMARY

You have learned that positive communication is a critical element to developing partnerships with families and professionals. To be an effective communicator, you will want to reflect on and develop your own interpersonal skills and tailor your communication strategies to be consistent with family preferences and cultural influences.

- **Create a collaborative climate** in which the family believes it is an integral and valued member of the team.

- **Use positive interpersonal and communication skills.** Use nonverbal communication, practice cultural competence, and seek creative solutions through problem solving. Rely on culturally responsive strategies to resolve conflicts.
- **Develop strategies for communicating positively.** Respond to family preferences and create supports to accommodate culturally and linguistically diverse families. Ask family members about their preferences for different methods of communication.

LINKING CONTENT TO YOUR LIFE

Effective communication occurs when you use positive strategies to learn about students and their families, share ideas and information with them, and strengthen your partnerships with individual family members. Communication is the one partnership principle that allows you to give expression to the values inherent in the others: equity, respect, competence, advocacy, commitment, and trust.

- How would you characterize your ability to communicate with others? Are you comfortable interacting with all families? Other professionals?
- Do your interactions convey to others that you are a team member worthy of trust? How so? Do you think families and other professionals would agree?
- Think about your nonverbal communication. How do you use gestures and facial expressions to communicate your understanding? When have different

cultural perspectives influenced your nonverbal communication? How do you modify your physical proximity and posture to accommodate the preferences of others?
- Think about a recent conversation with a family member or colleague. What questions were asked that opened up the dialogue? What responses led you or someone else to pull back?
- You can learn a great deal about effective communication and trust building from difficult situations. Consider a time when you held a different position than a family member or colleague. Were your respective positions shared openly? How did yourability to see the issue from the other's perspective affect your ability to seek alternative solutions? Think about what you might have done differently to promote trust and enhance communication.

CHAPTER 9

Families as Partners in Evaluating a Student

MARIA, ELOISA, AND HENRIQUE HERNANDEZ

As Maria Hernandez begins seventh grade in the fall of 2009, she is well-known to the district-wide special needs team in her school district in the suburbs of a large city and to her teachers in her new middle school and in her former middle school. The team and the teachers have a full dossier about her childhood diabetes. Prepared by physicians at a local hospital, it prescribes her insulin dosages and treatment in case she has elevated or depressed blood-sugar levels. The team and teachers also have all the data and recommendations from the full, nondiscriminatory evaluation it performed in the fall of 2006. And the team and her present teachers have to comply with IDEA and seek Maria's parents' consent for the mandatory three-year reevaluation.

So, why are Eloisa and Henrique, Maria's parents, concerned? It's because they have different priorities for Maria than do the special needs team and many of her teachers. They are worried about their daughter's social skills. They know her behaviors are absolutely appropriate; it's just that she lacks confidence with her peers and seems to be lonely. Perhaps it is because she has mild speech-language challenges that she is reticent and shy; perhaps it is because she speaks with a Spanish accent.

Her parents are not especially worried about their daughter's academic skills. She reads somewhat below grade level but still quite satisfactorily; she can read and comprehend the food labels that tell how much carbohydrates a package of food contains. Nor are they too worried about her abilities to use math in her daily life; she can calculate the amount of carbs and then adjust her diabetes pump (implanted into her side) so she will have just the right amount of them.

By contrast, all but one of Maria's teachers are concerned about academic skills. In her school district, students' performance on the statewide assessments required by the No Child Left Behind Act are a critical measure of the school's abilities and a hallmark for its reputation. The higher the scores, the better the district ranks in the state and nationally.

So, even though Maria is now taking an "alternate assessment," as IDEA permits, her teachers and the school team are determined to keep Maria out of general education classes where she would meet and then model peers of her own age. For all but one of the educators, inclusion would impair their ability to teach other students; thus impaired, the other students may not perform as well on the statewide assessments, thereby reducing the district's scores and reputation. In their judgment, academics trumps social skills even though some of them know that Maria's social skills will be more important to her as an adult than her ability to read and calculate at advanced levels.

Only one teacher demurs from her peers' consensus; recently graduated from a nationally top-ranked special education teacher-training program, she concurs with Maria's parents. With them, she wonders: What kind of partnership will exist when Maria has her next full nondiscriminatory evaluation? Will Maria's parents once again be at odds with the other educators? Will this lone-wolf teacher be successful in advocating for more inclusion and for social skills training for Maria?

think about it

- What does IDEA require as families and professionals evaluate a student to determine if the student has a disability and needs special education? How wide in scope must the evaluation be?
- What practices advance family and professional partnerships in a student's nondiscriminatory evaluation, especially where there is a history of disagreement?

(*Authors' Note:* The vignette for this chapter and for chapter 10 portrays a real family and student. Their names and the names of the student's school district and teacher have been changed to assure their privacy.)

:: INTRODUCTION

In this chapter, we describe the requirements of the Individuals with Disabilities Education Act (IDEA) and today's best practices for referral and evaluation of a student for special education services. As you learned when reading chapter 6, IDEA provides that the student's parents have various rights with respect to the student's evaluation. But as you learned when reading chapter 1, the family systems theory comes into play as professionals work with families.

In this chapter, you will learn how partnership in the referral-evaluation process can benefit students, families, and professionals. You will also learn strategies for developing partnerships and especially for fostering trust with families throughout the evaluation process, beginning with the student's initial referral and continuing to when the student receives special education supports and services.

When we describe IDEA, we will use the term *parents*, but when we describe how you may be a partner with not just the parents but also the student and other family members, we will use the term *family*. Likewise, IDEA uses the term *local education agency* to refer to a student's school; we sometimes use that term, or abbreviate it as *LEA*, and we sometimes use a synonym, *school*.

:: IDENTIFYING AND SCREENING STUDENTS

The referral process begins when a parent, teacher, or other professional familiar with a student wants to consider whether the student is eligible for special education services. Sometimes, one or more of these individuals refer the student only after they learn how well or poorly the student performed on tests administered to all students. These all-student tests *screen* students to determine which of them may need further evaluation. If a student does need further evaluation, educators then refer the student for the evaluation. The term *referral* describes the formal request to conduct an evaluation. IDEA defines *evaluation* as the procedure to determine whether a child has a disability and, if so, the child's educational needs (20 U.S.C. Sec. 1414(a)(1)(C)).

As you learned in chapter 6, no student may become eligible for IDEA's special education services unless the student first has been evaluated fairly; that is the principle of nondiscriminatory evaluation. And as you also learned in chapter 6, IDEA provides that parents have a role in the evaluation process, namely, consenting or not to an evaluation or reevaluation and securing an independent evaluation that the student's school must consider. IDEA does not specify whether parents are members of the evaluation team; indeed, it provides only that the student's local education agency shall conduct the evaluation and does not specify the members of the agency team. But IDEA does require the agency to use strategies to gather information from the student's parents concerning the student's functional, developmental, and academic status (20 U.S.C. Sec. 1414(b)(1)(A)).

IDEA thus lays the foundation for partnerships that can yield a full understanding of what the student needs by way of special education. That understanding becomes the foundation for the documents that set out the services the student will receive. The documents are (1) an Individualized Family Support Plan—IFSP—for children from their birth to age 3, and (2) an Individualized Education Program—IEP—for children and students ages 3 to 21. The evaluation also depends on partnerships among the professionals, family, and student as they implement the IFSP/IEP. Finally, the evaluation anticipates and is the basis for long-term outcomes for the student, especially those that IDEA identifies: equal opportunity, full participation, independent living, and economic self-sufficiency.

Figure 9.1 outlines eight steps in the referral and evaluation process. In this chapter, you will learn about each step in the referral and evaluation process. You also will learn about practices that, throughout this process, promote partnerships and trust with the families of your students. We urge you to learn about and comply with policies and guidelines that your state department of education and local school board have adopted; these may include requirements above and beyond IDEA's.

:: IMPLEMENTING PREREFERRAL AND RESPONSE TO INTERVENTION STRATEGIES

Implementing Prereferral Interventions

Prereferral intervention occurs before professionals request a student's parents to consent to a full, nondiscriminatory evaluation of their child. Its primary purposes are to analyze the student's strengths and needs and provide additional assistance to the student or teacher so that the student is able to achieve without needing a formal evaluation for special education services (Bahr, Fuchs, & Fuchs, 1999; Bahr, Whitten, Dieker, Kocarek, & Manson, 1999; Papalia-Berardi & Hall, 2007).

Prereferral teams are known by different names, including intervention assistance teams (Ortiz, Wilkinson, Robertson-Courtney, & Kushner, 2006), teacher assistance teams (Chalfant & Pysh, 1989), and instructional consultation teams (Gravois & Rosenfield, 2006). These teams may consist of general and special educators, school psychologists, and other professionals. They typically are responsible for recommending and implementing supports, strategies, and services to address a student's academic or behavioral challenges within the general education setting.

Prereferral intervention sometimes can prevent students from being unnecessarily referred for special education evaluation and placement (Buck, Polloway, Smith-Thomas, & Cook, 2003; Gravois & Rosenfield, 2006; Green, 2005). These interventions are particularly promising in the education of students from culturally and linguistically diverse backgrounds, who continue to be at greatest risk of being inappropriately referred for special education services. For example, schools using instructional consultation teams for two years had fewer students from minority backgrounds who were referred to and received special education services than schools without these teams (Gravois & Rosenfield, 2006). These teams help teachers to plan and deliver instruction for all students in their general education classes. Culturally responsive instruction in general education reduces the number of students inappropriately referred for evaluation (Garcia & Ortiz, 2004; Green, 2005; Ortiz, 2002).

FIGURE 9.1   Referral and evaluation process.

Responsible Agent	Function	Actions
Teachers and other school-based professionals, family members	Identifying and screening students	■ Observe student. ■ Analyze test results to identify struggling learners. ■ Discuss concerns with family.
School-based professionals in collaboration with family members	Implementing prereferral and response to intervention strategies	■ Observe student in general education. ■ Revise instruction. ■ Provide ancillary supports. ■ Provide consultation to teacher. ■ Discuss concerns with and elicit input from family member. ■ Monitor student progress.
Special services team	Initiating and reviewing a referral	■ Complete and submit referral form including description of prereferral strategies. ■ Examine information and determine if referral is necessary. ■ Review questions from team. ■ Determine need for evaluation. ■ Appoint a multidisciplinary team. ■ Discuss concerns with family.
Multidisciplinary team	Providing notice; obtaining consent	■ Inform parents of rights and proposed action. ■ Obtain parental consent for evaluation.
Multidisciplinary team; additional individuals as needed	Collecting evaluation information	■ Share information on each team member's resources, priorities, and concerns. ■ Identify appropriate evaluation instruments and procedures. ■ Assign responsibilities for obtaining evaluation. ■ Match option for family collaboration with family preferences. ■ Provide ancillary supports. ■ Schedule and complete evaluations. ■ Receive and review evaluation summaries. ■ Document any biasing factors during evaluations.
Multidisciplinary team	Analyzing evaluation information	■ Score and interpret meaning of evaluation results. ■ Analyze and synthesize all evaluations.
Multidisciplinary team; additional individuals as needed	Discussing evaluation results with families	■ Inform family of meeting and invite members to attend. ■ Discuss all obtained information. ■ Identify needs related to program planning. ■ Provide family with a written summary of evaluation results.

Most prereferral practices do not include active parent or student participation (Truscott, Cohen, Sams, Sanborn, & Frank, 2005). However, unnecessary referrals can be avoided if educators and family members share information about changes at school or at home and exchange ideas to support learning. Family members can provide valuable information about the social, linguistic, and cultural experiences of students from diverse backgrounds (Ortiz et al., 2006). To develop trust through the partnership principles of communication and respect, inform families about your concerns and seek their perspective before launching a prereferral intervention.

Considering Response to Intervention Strategies

Response to Intervention (RTI) is a process used to determine whether a student who is struggling to learn would benefit from more specialized or intensive instruction. Similar to the prereferral interventions, RTI is a problem-solving approach in which teams design and implement interventions to help students succeed (National Joint Committee on Learning Disabilities, 2005). RTI uses a systematic approach to identifying and addressing students' learning difficulties before referring a student for special education evaluation. RTI calls for ongoing monitoring of a student's progress and for the use of high-quality, research-based instruction and behavioral support (Klotz & Canter, 2007).

RTI also involves multiple "tiers" of increasingly more intensive interventions for a student. As the student's needs for support in learning increase, the amount of resources and instructional supports also increase (Harris-Murri, King, & Rostenberg, 2006). Under an RTI approach, only those students who do not adequately respond to research-validated interventions within general education are referred for a nondiscriminatory evaluation.

RTI can help to reduce the overall number of students referred to special education (Fuchs & Fuchs, 2007). The presumption that learning difficulties arise from inadequate instruction can help to diminish the unjust placement of students from culturally and linguistically diverse backgrounds in special education. Rather than immediately looking for "deficits" within the student who is struggling, educators will look for more effective ways to teach that student.

The RTI approach especially benefits students from diverse backgrounds because they are more likely to achieve when provided with high-quality instruction that responds to their cultural background and language proficiency (Klinger & Harry, 2006; Linan-Thompson, Cirino, & Vaughn, 2007; McMaster, Kung, Han, & Cao, 2008). Under this approach, "a child's language and culture are never viewed as liabilities but rather as strengths upon which to build an education" (Brown & Doolittle, 2008, p. 67). Unfortunately, not all struggling learners have access to high-quality, culturally and linguistically appropriate instruction in general education (Liu, Ortiz, Wilkinson, Robertson, & Kushner, 2008).

IDEA gives local education agencies the option of using RTI procedures as part of the evaluation process related to a student who may have a specific learning disability (20 U.S.C. 1414(b)(6)(B)), but it does not specify how the agencies must carry out RTI, nor does it restrict the agencies from using RTI for students who may have a disability other than a specific learning disability.

As you learned in chapter 6, IDEA provides that parents have important roles in the nondiscriminatory evaluation of their child; so, it makes sense for them to be partners with educators using RTI. The partnership practices of open communication and respect should underlie the professional-parent relationship when educators are using RTI. Think about the following questions, as you consider your school's partnership with parents when using RTI:

- How do you inform parents about RTI and its use in your school?
- How do you include them in developing instructional plans and time lines for determining RTI's effectiveness?
- Do you provide parents with regular progress reports?
- How and at what point do you inform parents of their due process rights, including the right to request a special education evaluation (Klotz & Canter, 2007)?

When parents and professionals work together to find ways for students to succeed, everyone benefits. In the My Voice box on the next page you can read how one teacher built trust with a student's parents by welcoming their ideas for ensuring the child's success within general education.

:: INITIATING AND REVIEWING A REFERRAL

Nature, Purpose, and Sources of a Referral

A referral consists of a formal request, made to the appropriate administrator of the student's school (e.g., principal or special-services/education director), to evaluate a

MY VOICE
Carrie and Ms. Ross—Laying the Foundation for Trust

Raising twin daughters has taught me that life is full of surprises. Since giving birth six years ago, it still amazes me that Sara and Carrie are so alike in their energies and so different in their interests. Even when I think I have everything figured out, I can be surprised by something they will say or do. With the girls around I can always count on the unexpected to happen! That's why it was important to me to be told early on about the challenges Carrie was having in first grade.

Carrie's teacher, Ms. Ross, first told me of her concerns during the fall parent-teacher conference. She spoke of Carrie's developing friendships and ability to persevere. She also told me that Carrie was having difficulty learning letter sounds. She explained that she was going to work with Carrie on a special "phonics-based" reading program and would ask for a consult from the school's speech therapist. She asked me how Carrie responded when I read to her at home and suggested books we could read together. The next week Ms. Ross called to let me know that the speech therapist would be working with Carrie several times a week.

When we met again after the winter school break, Ms. Ross shared with me information about Carrie's progress. She told me that while Carrie was doing better, she still had difficulty distinguishing similar sounds and sounding out unfamiliar words. She showed me Carrie's written work and a chart of the sounds she could identify. She shared with me a report she was given by Carrie's speech therapist. The therapist was seeing small gains in Carrie's listening ability. We agreed to have Carrie continue with the reading program and speech intervention. We also discussed the options that were available if

Carrie needed greater assistance in the future. We both agreed that a formal referral to special education remained a possibility.

The end-of-year conference with Ms. Ross came around more quickly than I expected. I knew that Carrie had made progress in first grade, but was still not reading as well as her sister. I was concerned a referral to special education would accentuate the differences between the girls.

As I entered the meeting, I knew that there would be a difficult decision to make, but I also knew there would be no surprises. I felt I could be open with Ms. Ross about my hopes and fears and that together we would decide how best to help Carrie. And for that I was very, very, grateful.

Take Action!

- Model Ms. Ross's approach of telling Carrie's mother about her daughter's abilities and limitations. Play up a child's strengths even as you talk about her needs.
- Follow Ms. Ross's example of bringing a specialist to consult. When you are not sure what, if any, limitations a child faces, don't evaluate the student on your own; bring in a specialist.
- Remember that Carrie's mother was prepared to make a decision about Carrie receiving special education services largely because Ms. Ross prepared the way. As Carrie's mother said, "I felt . . . that together we would decide how best to help Carrie." Ms. Ross had laid the foundation for the trust that this sentence reveals.

student to determine whether he or she has a disability and, if so, to determine the student's educational needs. A referral not only signals concern but also begins a process through which educators, parents, and other family members or individuals can fully evaluate the student.

A referral can be made by the student's parents or anyone who is concerned about the student's education. A random national survey of parents of students referred for evaluation found that 40% of the recommendations were initiated by teachers, 33% by parents, and 13% by the student's physician (Johnson & Duffett, 2002).

Referral and Response to Intervention

Referral may occur because educators, other professionals, or parents suspect that a student needs specially designed instruction or services that are not otherwise available to general education students. Often the student is performing significantly below expectation levels or has atypical behaviors. Referral may also occur because the school system is ineffective. Class size, teachers' lack of knowledge, and inappropriate instructional materials may lead staff to think that a student has special needs. Sadly, efforts designed to rule out the role of ineffective instruction in student performance *prior* to referral have not yet been fully successful (Harry, Klingner, Sturges, & Moore, 2002).

Usually referral takes place after a prereferral intervention. In schools using RTI, the referral will determine the student's eligibility for special education services after the student has failed to make adequate progress with interventions provided at lower tiers. Typically, educators or other professionals identify children with moderate and severe disabilities during infancy or during the early years when developmental milestones, such as walking, talking, and interacting typically occur. Children identified during their school years may achieve developmental milestones in early childhood but begin to demonstrate symptoms in school-based instructional settings.

Parents and Referral

Although IDEA does not require a child's parents to consent for referral, some state and local educational agencies do. Even if the parents' consent is not required where you work, we encourage you to tell parents that their child may need specially designed instruction. In so doing, you will enhance the parents' understanding of their child's performance and grade-level expectations, reinforce benefits of evaluation and intervention, and establish the foundation for an effective partnership and ongoing trust.

Parents respond in different ways when they learn that their child is referred. Some express relief: "It was clear to us that there was something wrong. . . . What was even better was we could get some early intervention and get started while he was young" (Nissenbaum, Tollefson, & Reese, 2002, p. 37). Some experience anxiety in learning of their child's referral: "Just the word 'evaluation' has a strong impact on a parent, because you realize that if everything's okay, there's no need to go to an evaluation. Your anxiety starts building at this point" (Lytel, Lopez-Garcia, & Stacey, 2008, p. 49).

Other parents may object to the formal referral and evaluation process. They may feel that the negative effects of having their child labeled outweigh the benefits of the services the child will receive. Some may fear that others will have low expectations of their child; others worry that being labeled as having a disability will interfere with their child leading a "typical life."

The partnership principles of communication, respect, and commitment are particularly important when you discuss a referral with the child's parents and other family members. The more you communicate honestly, show genuine interest in the student and family, affirm the student's strengths, and talk about your great expectations for the student, the more the family will be able to understand how referral can benefit their child and that the teachers are genuinely concerned about and are advocating for the child. Once the parents know that professionals care about their child and respect their opinions, parents may approach evaluation in partnership with educators.

If, however, families strongly object to a referral, listen to their concerns and respect their reasons. Assume that their perspectives are valid (Barrera & Corso, 2002; Chamberlain, 2005). Most important, avoid being defensive. Ask them, "What would you like to have happen?" rather than "Don't you want what is best for your child?" In the spirit of partnership, try to see the situation from their point of view; they may be right that a referral will not be in the student's best interest. A true partnership enables you and your evaluation team colleagues to benefit from a very important perspective, the family's.

The student's school special services team is responsible for addressing concerns that surface with a referral. The team may decide to gather more information, wait several months in case the student's problem is temporary, provide individualized general education rather than evaluate the student for special education, or pursue evaluation. The vast majority of those students who are referred for evaluation ultimately are later determined to be eligible for special education (Christensen, Ysseldyke, & Algozzine, 1982; Hosp & Reschly, 2003; Ysseldyke, Vanderwood, & Shriner, 1997).

:: NOTIFYING AND OBTAINING PARENTS' CONSENT

As you learned in chapter 6, parents have the right to be informed of the team's decision to evaluate their child for special education services and to provide or withhold consent for the school to evaluate their child (20 U.S.C. Sec. 1414(a)). Typically, one member of the special services team is responsible for communicating with the student's parents throughout the evaluation process, including providing notice and seeking consent.

Often referred to as the service coordinator (or case manager), this person should already have established a partnership with the parents, having already discussed the mutual concerns that preceded referral and intervention. The service coordinator provides ongoing support to the student's parents, guides them through the referral and evaluation process, and helps develop the IFSP/IEP. You will learn more about the service coordinator's role in chapter 11. At this point, you should recognize that the service coordinator must establish and maintain a trusting partnership with the parents and, as they designate, other family members. Ideally, the service coordinator will have had frequent contact with the parents, share values or communication styles that complement the parents', and have sufficient time to work with the parents and school-team members.

Notifying

IDEA requires a local education agency (the student's school) to provide written, timely notice to the student's parents in their native language whenever the school proposes or refuses to initiate or change the student's identification, evaluation, educational placement, or services (20 U.S.C. Sec. 1414(a)). The written notice must include:

1. A description of what the school proposes or refuses to do.
2. A description of each evaluation procedure, assessment, record, or report the agency used as a basis for its action.
3. A description of any other options that the school considered and the reasons why it rejected those options.
4. A description of other factors that influenced the proposed or refused actions.
5. A full explanation of parents' due process rights and, if this notice is not seeking consent for an initial referral for evaluation, how they may obtain a copy of a description of their legal rights (which are referred to as procedural safeguards).
6. A description of sources that parents can contact to obtain assistance in understanding information provided in the notice.

The notice must also be in the parents' native language or other form of communication (e.g., Braille if the parents are blind or by interpreters for the deaf if the parents are deaf or hearing impaired).

The information in the notice must be clear, accurate, and easily understood by the general public, otherwise the notice fails in its purpose and may be legally indefensible. Review your school's notice to ensure that the parents with whom you work can easily understand it. Don't be surprised by what you find. One study of the readability of parents' rights documents found that 20% to 50% of the documents were at or above a college reading level (Fitzgerald & Watkins, 2006).

You may want to share your school's document with several parents with varying levels of education and invite their suggestions on how to make the notice clear, relevant, and jargon-free. If it is unclear to you, your colleagues, or family members, assume that it is not an effective way to foster communication and build trust. An excellent resource for information about parents' rights is the Parent Training and Information Center (PTI) in your state. You and the families you serve may want to attend the center's workshops on IDEA and student and parent education rights.

The overall purpose of the notice is to inform the student's parents why educators want to evaluate their child. Best practices are for educators to summarize information from the prereferral intervention or from the team's discussion and include names and purposes of the recommended tests. If the teacher or service coordinator has already contacted the student's parents to discuss educators' concerns and options, information in the notice will seem less intimidating and legalistic.

Notification presents educators with an excellent opportunity to communicate positively with the student's parents and to practice the partnership principles of respect and equality in their relationships with families. Consider this father's response to the preschool teacher's suggestion that his child be evaluated:

> . . . they pulled my wife to the side and said "You know, we notice a couple of things here. I think you should have him evaluated further." Another tough thing to hear, because even though you're involved; even though you take steps; even though your conscious of a challenge, of a problem you need to address, every time you hear it, it just brings it home a little bit more. It's never something you want to hear. (Lytel, Lopez-Garcia, & Stacey, 2008)

Although IDEA provides only that the agency must inform the parents where they may obtain assistance in understanding the provisions of the notice, it is good practice for educators to tell the student's parents about resources from which they learn more about the nondiscriminatory evaluation, such as by referring them to the state PTI, Parent to Parent programs, or websites and books that focus specifically on the disability the educators think the student may have.

If parents do not respond to notices, do not presume a reason. Consider the partnership elements of respect and commitment and learn how the parents want you to communicate. Express yourself in a friendly, clear, and honest way by phoning, making a home visit, or consulting with other professionals involved with the family. The more you work to build a partnership, the more likely it is that parents will respond to written notices.

Obtaining Parents' Consent

To protect parents' and children's rights and to secure their participation in evaluation, IDEA requires educators to secure parents' consent for each proposed evaluation, reevaluation, or special education placement (20 U.S.C. Sec. 1414(a)). As a general rule, consent consists of three components:

1. *Information/Knowledge:* The parent has been fully informed of all information relevant to the evaluation in his or her native language or other mode of communication.
2. *Voluntariness:* The parent understands that the consent may be revoked at any time but not retroactively.
3. *Competence:* The parent is legally competent to give consent.

It is good practice to communicate clearly, even repeatedly, how an evaluation will help determine whether the student has a disability and, if so, how the student might benefit from special education and related services. If you believe that an evaluation will not help the student, it is also good and ethical practice to state your viewpoint. Listen carefully to the student's parents; understand and acknowledge their thinking and feelings about the proposed evaluation. Parents who refuse consent may be right! Their son or daughter may be harmed rather than helped by an evaluation and possible placement in a special education class or program. You yourself should be alert to the inadequacy of evaluation data; some may be old, incomplete, and inaccurate. After all, students change. When you begin to be suspicious of evaluation data, bear in mind your legal obligations (and the CEC Code of Ethics) and the story you will read in the Together We Can box on the next page.

If the student's parents do not consent to the evaluation and if school personnel refuse to seek alternatives to a full evaluation, the school and the parents must first attempt to resolve the conflict (see chapter 6) (20 U.S.C. Sec. 1415). They may use mediation, the mandatory dispute resolution process, or, with mutual consent, waive both and go directly to a due process hearing. Both the parents and the school may initiate a due process hearing.

If the hearing officer rules in the school's favor, the school may proceed with evaluation. The parents may decide to appeal the hearing officer's decision to a state-level hearing officer or a state or federal court (according to the procedure in the state's special education plan). If the hearing officer rules in favor of the parents, the school may not proceed with the evaluation unless the school successfully appeals the decision.

Supplementing Written Notices and Consent

Although the notice to the parents and their consent must be in writing, face-to-face communications at this early stage of the evaluation process are important opportunities to build partnerships and trust. It is not good practice to offer only one way of providing notice and requesting consent. You might send parents the written notice and request consent, then follow up with a face-to-face meeting to discuss your request and answer questions. Or you might share information with the parents in person, either before or when you provide written notification. Ask them which option they prefer. This shows parents that you value their preferences and want to build a trusting partnership.

:: COLLECTING EVALUATION INFORMATION

As you learned in chapter 6 and as you are learning in this chapter, a student's evaluation for special education services has two purposes: to determine whether the child has a disability and, if so, what the student's special education and related services will be. Beyond determining eligibility and the nature of services, the evaluation data also inform educators and the student's parents about the student's placement in the least restrictive environment (the general curriculum). That is so because IDEA requires the local educational agency to "gather relevant functional, developmental, and academic information, including information provided by the parent," that may assist the agency in "enabling" the student to be "involved in and progress in the general education curriculum" (20 U.S.C. Sec. 1414(b)(2)(A)). Figure 9.2 describes the IDEA requirements for nondiscriminatory evaluation.

As you read earlier in this chapter, IDEA requires the agency to gather information from the student's parents about the student's functional, developmental, and academic status (20 U.S.C. Sec. 1414(b)(1)(AA)). That is an important provision because parents are members of the team—the IEP team that you learned about in chapter 6 and will learn more about in chapter 11—that makes decisions about the student's program and placement (20 U.S.C. Sec. 1414(a)(1)(D)).

You already know that families are systems (chapter 1), so whatever happens to one tends to happen to all. Although IDEA mentions only the student's parents as a source of information about the student, it is good practice to include other family members (designated by the parents) in gathering information about the student. These other family members can include the student. Their input can be useful in understanding teachers' concerns and validating evaluation results (Wilkinson, Ortiz, Robertson, & Kushner, 2006).

Unfortunately, although family members can give valuable information from a unique perspective, professionals do

TOGETHER WE CAN
Maria's Teacher—the "Legal Rebel"

I have known Maria for several years. I was a reading specialist and she was in my class during elementary school. I was not on her evaluation team; but I was on her IEP team. I consulted often with her parents about her strengths and needs—I had all the data from her evaluation—and became their and Maria's very close friend. I did that mostly by communicating often with them, going to their home, and taking Maria out to eat or go to a movie with me. The more time I spent with her, not just at school but at her home and in the community, the more I realized that the evaluation revealed only some of her abilities. I suspect that such close and informal contact was irregular and perhaps disapproved at the school district level. But Maria and her parents appreciated what I was doing; they trusted me and believed in me, and I was determined to prove to my colleagues that Maria was "more" than the evaluation data said she was—more able, of course.

I could not let Eloisa, Henrique, and Maria down so, in IEP and transition meetings, I broke the "informal understanding"—a school "custom" or "norm"—that new teachers such as me would not "go up against" the district's standard policies on inclusion, and that I would always defer to the judgments of long-established general and special education teachers, almost all of whom invariably said that the standard policies would fit Maria well, as they fit everyone else well. I didn't buy the "one size fits all"—I knew Maria aside from the evaluation data.

It's not just that Maria's parents trusted me, or that I obviously challenged the status quo. It's also that what I did was consistent with IDEA. That law provides that a student should be in the least restrictive setting to the maximum extent appropriate for the student. The law permits full and partial inclusion; it targets the academic, extracurricular, and other school activities as the environments for full or partial inclusion. Further, "appropriate" means that the student will have a genuine opportunity to learn. And learning leads to the four national outcomes—equal opportunity, independent living, full participation, and economic self-sufficiency.

I relied on my understanding of IDEA when I partnered with Eloisa and Henrique for Maria. They wanted her to have those outcomes; unless she were included, even partially, in her school's academic, extracurricular, and other activities, I wondered: How will she become the person her parents want her to be, and how can she become the person she wants to be and the citizen the law wants her to be if she is not included to the fullest extent possible? I concluded: none of that will happen without me. So, I became a "rebel," but I was at least a "legal rebel"—one who insisted on stricter compliance with the letter and spirit of IDEA.

Take Action!

- Maria's teacher grounded the IEP on the outcomes the family had in mind. She respected them, treated them as equals, and advocated for them. She used three of the principles of partnership. She's a fine model for you.

- Maria's teacher also befriended Maria and then developed a firm commitment to her, used her knowledge of the law to prove her professional competence to her district and more-seasoned teachers, and communicated to everyone by referring to IDEA itself. Here, too, she used three of the principles of partnership. You could do far worse than follow her example.

- Trust abounds—at least among Eloisa, Henrique, Maria, and her teacher. It rests on those six other principles of partnership. In time, Maria's other teachers may understand that they can benefit Maria and other students by doing as Maria's teacher did. Don't let the opportunities pass you by to use the IEP process to drive toward outcomes through inclusion.

not regularly seek their input (Crais, Roy, & Free, 2006; Klingner & Harry, 2006). One mother described what she experienced in the absence of collaboration:

> And then when they called me, they're like "we need a meeting, we need to do this, we need to do that." And I

sat there and I'm like "okay, what's wrong?" Well, "this is wrong, and this is wrong, and he doesn't do this" . . . and I was like "well, why wasn't I called before? Why wasn't I informed before? Why didn't anybody tell me?" . . . I came in at the end and was told at the end. (Hess, Molina, & Kozleski, 2006, p. 152)

FIGURE 9.2	IDEA nondiscriminatory evaluation requirements in brief.

Who evaluates? The student's local educational agency appoints a team. The evaluators must be trained and must administer tests in accordance with the instructions governing the tests.

Are the parents involved? Yes, but not as members of the team. The team must consider information from them and any independent evaluation they offer.

What tests must the team use? It must use standardized and validated tests.

How does the team avoid cultural bias? It must use tests that are not discriminatory on the basis of race or culture and must administer all tests in the student's native language.

Are there other rules about bias? Yes. The team may not determine the student is eligible for special education if the student has not had appropriate instruction in reading, has not had instruction in mathematics, or has limited English proficiency (but not a disability).

Are there special rules about specific learning disability? Yes. The team may not classify a student as having such a disability if the student's learning problem is primarily the result of visual; hearing or motor disabilities; intellectual disability (mental retardation); emotional disturbance; or environmental, cultural, or economic disadvantage. The team may classify the student if the student has failed to respond to intervention (RTI) or has a severe discrepancy between ability and performance.

What procedures must the team follow? It must (a) use a variety of assessment tools and strategies, (b) use technically sound instruments to assess the student in four domains (cognitive, behavioral, physical, and developmental), (c) use tools and strategies that directly help the team satisfy the student's education needs, and (d) review existing evaluation data, including those from parents, teacher observations, state and local assessments, and other sources. It may not rely on any single measure or assessment.

When must the team act? It must do an initial evaluation within 60 days after the student's parents consent.

How often must it reevaluate the student? It must reevaluate the student at least once every three years unless the parents waive that evaluation, and not more than once a year unless there are reasons to suspect a change in the student's eligibility or need for special education.

Listening to and valuing parents' and other family members' perspectives fosters communication, respect, and equality—elements of effective partnerships.

Partnership Practices in Evaluation

If you want to create a context for shared decision making with families, think about how your evaluation practices hinder or foster trust. Approaching evaluation as a partnership means that you will involve the student's parents and other family members in decisions about whether and how the evaluation will be conducted and how its results will be used. You can enhance the partnership principles of respect and equality when you honor the family's cultural diversity, treat all family members respectfully, and give them options during evaluation.

A family's preferences and concerns should guide decisions about the evaluation process. Sometimes a family's concerns should be addressed even before the evaluation begins. For example, one team intervened to address the challenges a mother experienced with her preschool child, who had been adopted at age 2 (Prelock, Beatson, Contompasis, & Bishop, 1999). Instead of proceeding with a formal evaluation, the team arranged for a speech-language pathologist, developmental pediatrician, and nutritionist to assist the child and family. In addition, all team members were given information about attachment disorders and adoption so that they would better understand the child's feelings and behavior.

In this situation, the evaluation team deferred decisions about the child's diagnosis. Instead, it responded to the mother's concerns about her son and identified supports and services to foster his development.

It is particularly important to ground evaluation in an understanding of the family's culture when the educators' approach to evaluation differs from the family's ideas about

| FIGURE **9.3** | **Partnering with families.** |

1. Recognize family members as individuals with preferred learning styles, values/opinions on education, child-rearing practices, and parenting roles.
2. Recognize families as partners in the process and as ultimate decision makers.
3. Provide families partnership opportunities regarding the evaluation process, contexts, and participants.
4. Share information in a reciprocal, sensitive, and timely manner.
   - Provide program, state, and federal rules and regulations; community resources; and evaluation process information.
   - Explain the advantages and limitations of various evaluation and assessment measures.
   - Ask the family to describe the student's abilities/interests and their concerns/priorities.
   - Continue to share information throughout the evaluation process.
   - Present the evaluation results in a strengths-based, family-friendly, program-planning approach.
   - Provide time for the family members to ask questions and review the evaluation with team members.

   - Avoid professional jargon and acronyms.
   - Present information in the family's language, using interpreters.
   - Give information in formats and quantities that match the family's preferences and skills.
5. View evaluation as a teaching/intervention opportunity.
   - Explain the purpose of your evaluations.
   - Provide information about their child's development and the possible impact of the disability.
   - Encourage family members to demonstrate/describe their child's skills/behaviors that occur in other settings.
   - Identify the strategies you want to use to observe the child's optimal performance.
6. Identify supports for a family member's participation.
   - Provide information about their child's development, disability, or legislation.
   - Provide information about community resources (e.g., respite, utilities).
   - Encourage the participation of extended family or other family support individuals.

their child's learning and development (Schuman, 2002). Equally important is the need for bilingual assessors to fully participate in the evaluation of students who have limited use of English by gathering information from families and attending meetings in which evaluation information is discussed (Klinger & Harry, 2006).

How can you create partnerships with parents and other family members? Include them in decisions about the time and place of the evaluation. Identify the aspects of the student's learning and development that need evaluation. Help gather information. Confirm and interpret test results. Figure 9.3 provides strategies for conducting evaluations with parents and other family members within a partnership framework.

Consider how you introduce parents and other family members to the evaluation process. They may enter the evaluation with limited knowledge about schools, schooling, special education, or evaluation. They may be inexperienced in procedures, terminology, and their options for participation, and unfamiliar with a team-based

approach to decision making. Include someone who knows them well, perhaps the service coordinator or a teacher, in your initial discussions about the evaluation process.

This designated person can use information in videos, flowcharts, pamphlets, and contacts with other parents to explain the steps that will be followed in conducting the evaluation and options for sharing information. Consider how you learned about referrals and evaluations. What explanations, images, and experiences helped you understand the process? The same might help the family.

Professionals, parents, and other family members generally agree on evaluation practices that promote partnership (Crais, Roy, & Free, 2006). They also agree that many highly valued practices have been underused, such as pre-assessment planning. How effectively does your program or school incorporate good partnership practices in evaluating children? To answer that question, use the self-rating tool in Figure 9.4.

FIGURE 9.4	Partnering with families to evaluate culturally and linguistically diverse students.

IDEA requires a nondiscriminatory evaluation of all students referred to special education. Why then do educators need to go "the extra mile" to determine whether students from culturally and linguistically diverse backgrounds are struggling to learn for reasons other than a disability? The reasons are both simple and complex: First, there is overwhelming evidence that students from linguistically and culturally diverse backgrounds are disproportionately referred to special education and identified as disabled (U.S. Department of Education, 2007). Second, overreferral and misidentification have been linked to biases in the referral to evaluation process (Klingner & Harry, 2006).

What can you do to facilitate fairness in the evaluation of students from culturally and linguistically diverse families? We encourage you to use the following strategies for enhancing equity in student evaluation:

■ Reflect on all possibilities that might explain students' poor performance, including cultural incongruence in instruction and second-language acquisition; avoid blaming students and families for underachievement.

■ Implement prereferral strategies with commitment and fidelity; use performance data to guide instructional decisions and future recommendations.

■ Meaningfully include parents and other family members in the evaluation process by inviting them to participate in all assessment procedures; elicit and respect their preferences for participating in and scheduling meetings.

■ Ensure that students are evaluated in their native language and that assessment instruments are congruent with their cultural background.

■ Use multiple and different sources of information in the evaluation; rely more on curriculum-based and performance-based measures than on norm-referenced assessments to enable students to demonstrate their capabilities, strengths, and needs.

■ Provide extended time for explaining results to families who may hold very different values and beliefs about the meaning of disability; listen carefully to understand families' perspectives and respond to their concerns, and expectations.

■ Invite an independent person who is familiar with the family's culture to interpret during the conference; encourage families to bring friends or advocates who share their cultural beliefs with them to the conference.

Tapping into a family's knowledge about the student enhances their confidence and ability to participate, builds trust among team members, and increases the likelihood that valid information will be gathered (Woods & McCormick, 2002). Not all parents and other family members enter the evaluation process with the same expectations, priorities, or resources. Some may choose a quieter role in their child's evaluation and may have specific preferences for how and with whom they exchange information. One mother explained her initial feelings about communicating openly with the team in this way. "It was against my nature to let other people look at us so closely. It was very hard for me to do, but I did it" (Kincaid, Chapman, Shannon, Schall, & Harrower, 2002, p. 314).

When parents opt out of the evaluation process, respect their choice but encourage them to give their perspectives about their child in another way. Establish trust by providing information and options that enable parents to share what they know about their child in ways that meet the parents' preferences. This is the partnership practice of fostering empowerment, which is part of the partnership principle called equality.

Parents' and Other Family Members' Participation in Collecting Evaluation Information

To create partnerships that promote trust and lead to shared decision making about evaluation and to comply with IDEA's requirement to gather information from the student's parents, invite the student, the student's parents, and other family members designated by the parents to (1) share their family story, (2) express preferences and great expectations and describe their child's strengths and needs, (3) help professionals evaluate and administer evaluations, (4) collaborate with professionals to construct portfolio assessments, and (5) work with professionals to conduct a transdisciplinary evaluation. (For the sake of brevity, we will refer to the parents, student, and designated family members as *the family*.)

Sharing the Family Story. Often the most relevant information evolves from informal conversations in which the family members express their hopes, worries, successes, and questions. By telling stories in their own words, families bring the student to "life" and authenticate the evaluation. During an initial evaluation of a preschool child, one mother spoke of her daughter's pride in learning to ride a bicycle, her delight in having a first playdate, her growth in learning to share, and the fright of her daughter's first asthma attack (Woods & McCormick, 2002). Think how the daughter would seem had she been described simply (and rather clinically) as "a child with autism or child with a health impairment."

Stories unfold in different ways, so it is good practice to give the family choices about how to contribute to the evaluation. Some families will want to talk openly, whereas others will prefer to prepare a memo or letter for professionals. Some even feel more comfortable demonstrating their routines, interactions, and activities by showing a video or DVD of the family in action (Thompson, Meadan, Fansler, Alber, & Balogh, 2007).

Expressing Preferences, Great Expectations, Strengths, and Needs. Giving the family members an opportunity to share their preferences, great expectations, strengths, and needs during evaluation contributes significantly to partnerships. They can convey their preferences about school subjects, hobbies, peer relationships, future aspirations, and other relevant matters. Team members should pay attention to such clearly expressed preferences from the family, especially at the outset of the evaluation process. Listen carefully to what they say about their preferences and expectations so that you come away with a richer understanding of their cultural beliefs, interests, and traditions. This information will be useful in developing the student's appropriate education program and placement and in identifying priorities, goals, and objectives for the student, as you will learn in chapter 11.

Professionals can help the family share information by using probe questions and through active listening. Questions should be open-ended, nonjudgmental requests for information. For example, ask, "Tell me more about . . ." rather than simply "What do you mean?" (Woods & McCormick, 2002). Effective probe questions spark conversation. You might ask family members, "What makes your child smile and laugh?" "What brings out the best in your child?" "What is your child especially good at doing?" or "What gets your child to try new things?" (Dunst, Herter, & Shields, 2000). Consider how you would use, modify, or add to these questions to help parents express insights into a child's strengths, challenges, and successes. Remember

that you enhance the partnership principle of respect by honoring their culture and beliefs.

You also can offer them the option of completing checklists. Among the several checklists for evaluation in early childhood are the Family Interest Survey (Cripe & Bricker, 1993), Parent Needs Survey (Seligman & Darling, 1997), Family Needs Survey (Bailey & Simeonsson, 1988), and Family Needs Scale (Dunst, Cooper, Weeldreyer, Snyder, & Chase, 1988). Families use checklists by rating how items apply to their situation.

These scales, however, do not focus on the family's strengths, priorities, and resources as much as they do on the family's needs. These checklists are not an interactive or personal communication.

Consider whether checklists are appropriate for all families, especially those from culturally and linguistically diverse backgrounds or those in nontraditional arrangements (Barrera & Corso, 2002). For families with limited English proficiency, a checklist can be not only daunting but a professional misstep.

Evaluating and Administering Evaluation Instruments. Family participation may occur in many ways. Before the evaluation takes place, families can and should help identify strategies to be used, such as how and when to administer evaluations to their children. Families can help identify tools or strategies that are congruent with the child's preferred cultural background or language proficiency (Harris-Murri et al., 2006).

During the evaluation, family members may observe and even administer evaluations. Although some evaluation and evaluation procedures feature standardized instructions, others are more flexible and can be adapted for family participation. Family members may join the professional who is evaluating their child or administering the evaluation. This is a common practice particularly in the evaluation of infants and toddlers.

Family members may also be asked to gather information by recording or describing observations of their child, completing an evaluation tool, or commenting on an evaluation they have completed. Families' contributions will help to develop a richer understanding of the child and strengthen their partnerships with professionals. Despite awareness of their importance, many of the preassessment and evaluation strategies just described are used infrequently (Crais et al., 2006).

If you were the parent of a child with disabilities, would you rather discover the exact nature of your child's disability through your own observation and collaboration, or would you prefer to sit in the waiting room and receive the experts' verdict? The more you involve families in collecting evaluation information, the more likely you are to develop accurate information and establish partnerships with them.

Some educators believe that families cannot assess their own child's performance accurately. A number of research studies, however, have compared professional and parental ratings of child performance. Generally, parent versus teacher reports were similar in adaptive and social behavior assessments (Gagnon, Nagle, & Nickerson, 2007; Voelker, Shore, Hakim-Larson, & Bruner, 1997), communication assessments (Diamond & LeFurgy, 1992), and cognitive ability assessments (Oliver, Dale, Saudino, Petrill, Pike, & Plomin, 2002). When differences occurred, teachers typically rated the children as more skilled than did the family members. There is good evidence that parental involvement in collecting evaluation information will lead to accurate rather than subjective profiles of their children.

Constructing Portfolio Assessments. In contrast to traditional evaluations that provide a "snapshot" of a student at a specific time, portfolio assessments document a student's progress over an extended period (Demchak & Greenfield, 2003). Portfolio items may include drafts of a student's written work, pictures of projects, excerpts from a reflective journal, a chart of student progress, videotape demonstrations, artwork, homework, essays, and open-ended problems. Portfolios can also include a student's personal reflections on his or her own strengths, preferences, and challenges, as well as other information they wish to share (Kelly, Siegel, & Allinder, 2001).

A Family Assessment Portfolio uses technology to create a broad picture of the child and family (Thompson, Meadan, Fansler, Alber, & Balogh, 2007). The portfolio can be presented as a scrapbook, home movie, or web-based profile that links to video clips, pictures, and text. You can assist families in creating their portfolio by providing them access to equipment, technical support, and the opportunity to share their completed portfolio with the evaluation team.

Because portfolio assessments showcase typical experiences, family partnership assumes a much greater role (Demchak & Greenfield, 2003; Lynch & Struewing, 2001; Thompson et al., 2007). Family input presents a different and often more well-rounded picture of the child's development and the method itself encourages communication, affirms the child's strengths, and fosters effective partnerships. Encouraging input from parents is essential when you evaluate students from diverse cultural and linguistic backgrounds to ensure that they gain equal access to special and gifted education services (Baldwin, 2002; Klingner & Harry, 2006).

Conducting Transdisciplinary Evaluation. You learned about transdisciplinary approaches in chapter 8 and about the benefits of that approach. One benefit is that the transdisciplinary team is particularly useful when evaluating a student because the team consists of professionals who evaluate a child across multiple domains or areas (Kilgo, 2006; Ogletree, 2001).

Professionals and family members sometimes carry out the evaluation together, from planning to implementation. In the transdisciplinary approach, a service coordinator or facilitator explains the process and asks the family to state their goals and priorities. The professionals and family observe the student in an array of play-based activities across a variety of settings and reach consensus about the child's strengths and needs (Grisham-Brown, 2000). The evaluation follows the student's lead to elicit his or her best performance. In this way, the evaluation process is sensitive to the family's recommendations on how to obtain the most accurate picture possible of the student's skills and behavior. In addition, when educators use information from family interviews and naturalistic observations, they secure a richer understanding of the student because their understanding is contextualized and then can lead to context-specific functional goals (Jung & Grisham-Brown, 2006).

Transdisciplinary teams also gather anecdotal data to develop comprehensive understanding of the student's behavior within a variety of contexts (Rogers, 2001), including, when appropriate, the family home. In that case, and also as a general rule, the transdisciplinary evaluation usually places the family at the center of decision making (Kilgo, 2006). Overall, a transdisciplinary approach promotes partnership principles of respect and equality by treating families with dignity and fostering their empowerment.

Each of the five ways for involving families in collecting evaluation information can build partnerships. They also produce robust understanding of the student. Rather than having a limited view of the child's skills and abilities on a given evaluation day, the team secures a comprehensive understanding of the student's and family's lives.

Incorporating Person-Centered Planning

An effective method of involving parents, the student, other family members, and others who care about the student is called person-centered planning. Person-centered planning elicits their great expectations and then develops plans on how to support those expectations. It advances the partnership principles of respect, commitment, equality, and advocacy.

- Person-centered planning strategies include Personal Futures Planning (Mount, 1995), Making Action Plans (Falvey, Forest, Pearpoint, & Rosenberg, 1997; Forest & Lusthaus, 1990), Essential Lifestyle Planning (Smull & Harrison, 1992), Planning Alternative Tomorrows with Hope (Falvey, Forest, Pearpoint, & Rosenberg, 1994), and Group Action Planning (Turnbull, Turbiville, Schaffer, & Schaffer, 1996; Turnbull & Turnbull, 1996; Turnbull, Turnbull, & Blue-Banning, 1994). Each focuses on the dreams, interests, preferences, strengths, and capacities of the student and thus provides a foundation for special education, related services, and supplementary aids and supports.
- Person-centered planning usually involves the family, professionals, and others invited by them; together, these individuals form a circle of support for the student.
- Person-centered planning also identifies the settings, services, supports, and routines available in the community; it seeks to maximize the individual's full participation in typical activities and to minimize the student's use of disability-specific settings, services, and supports.
- Person-centered planning also values and uses personal knowledge of the person's history and desired futures, not just data from formal evaluations (Bui & Turnbull, 2003; Schwartz, Holburn, & Jacobson, 2000).
- Person-centered planning enables professionals and families to approach the ideal IFSP/IEP process by reframing their thinking about what they are trying to achieve: to affirm the student's strengths and have high expectations.

Researchers have found that mothers often favor a person-centered approach to evaluation because it allows them to partner with people who appreciate their children to imagine great opportunities and envision bright futures for their children (Rocco, Metzer, Zangerle, & Skouge, 2002). When families and professionals use person-centered planning effectively, there are two major outcomes: positive changes in the lives of the focus persons (Holburn, 2002; O'Brien, 2002) and satisfaction with the process (Everson & Zhang, 2000). In contrast to goals derived from need-based evaluations, the vision of person-centered planning centers on seeking inclusive educational programs and opportunities for more friendships and social activities.

Most writing about person-centered planning has focused on European American families. This does not mean that the planning process does not respond to families and individuals from culturally and linguistically diverse backgrounds. In one study using focus groups to gather Hispanic parents' perspectives on Group Action Planning, parents emphasized the benefits of teamwork and flexibility (Blue-Banning et al., 2000). The parents also identified disadvantages of vulnerability in being so open with a group of people and the time commitment that is involved. Professionals report that families and students benefit when they facilitate person-centered planning with flexibility and cultural sensitivity (Callicott, 2003; Trainor, 2007). A facilitator of person-centered planning spoke of how this approach enhanced her partnership with a parent who had been reluctant to participate at other times:

> One of my students, the parent doesn't know English, undocumented, but just a real nice person, comes always to all the [IEP] meetings . . . he just stays really quiet . . . When we did the [PCP] meeting, it was different. It was informal. It was in Spanish. It was in his territory. He didn't have to dress up, you know, he just gotten home from work, and you don't talk about academics so much. (Trainor, 2007, pp. 97–98)

Person-centered planning creates a context of belonging and reciprocity beneficial to all group members. But neither occurs without trust. One professional said that person-centered planning "challenges everyone involved to think about themselves critically, related to how they interact with [the student]. You need to trust everybody on your team to open yourself up to that level" (Kincaid et al., 2002, p. 318).

Right of Parents to Obtain Independent Evaluations

Under IDEA, parents have the right to obtain an independent evaluation of their child (20 U.S.C. Sec. 1415(b)(1)) and to have that evaluation and other information taken into account (20 U.S.C. Sec. 1414(b)(2)(A)). This right applies even if the school's evaluation has already been completed.

Why would parents seek independent evaluation? They may be concerned about the appropriateness, accuracy, completeness, or timeliness of the school's evaluation; or they may be concerned about the implications of the evaluation. In either case, IDEA requires the student's evaluation team to consider the independent evaluation; that evaluation is as important as any other evaluation. You should acknowledge that parents may have a very good reason for securing an independent evaluation, and you should treat them and regard their reasons respectfully.

:: ANALYZING EVALUATION INFORMATION

As you have learned, the evaluation team must determine whether the student has a disability and qualifies for special education services and, if so, the student's educational needs. To make these decisions, the team first scores, analyzes, and interprets results of each evaluation instrument or procedure and then synthesizes and evaluates all the separate evaluations. The team members usually do the first task individually or collaboratively among those members who administered the evaluation procedures; by contrast, they usually do the second task at a full team meeting.

Family members are rarely involved in analyzing evaluation information. Many professionals assume that scoring, analyzing, and synthesizing evaluations require technical expertise that most families do not have. Family members, however, can gather information and provide perspectives on what the information means in the student's daily life. Although some evaluation procedures, such as an IQ test, must be administered and scored only by people with special training, many evaluation procedures can be carried out collaboratively with family members (provided that procedures and their administration comply with the instructions of the developers of the evaluation instruments, as IDEA requires).

Some families participate by analyzing evaluation information, but others prefer not to be involved. Some families appreciate being present at any discussion related to their child, perhaps because they think that is the best way to ensure that their perspective is considered. Others will opt out of the process. However, professionals should not consider interpretations of evaluation information final until families have a chance to review and comment. If you want to create partnerships with families, you need to respect their perspectives and be careful to reach conclusions only when you have their input.

:: DISCUSSING EVALUATION RESULTS

You should adhere to these four good professional practices when you discuss the results of the student's evaluation with the student's parents, the student, and other family members: (1) notify the parents, (2) take into account the family's perspective, (3) consider the student's role in discussing evaluation results, and (4) follow an agenda for the discussion.

Notifying Parents

As you learned earlier, IDEA requires a local educational agency (a school) to notify parents in writing anytime it proposes or refuses to change a student's identification, evaluation, or educational placement or the provision of free appropriate education, and why it proposes or refuses to take certain action. Schools can comply with these requirements by providing a summary or full copy of all evaluation information to the student's parents and others, including family members, whom they designate.

Full disclosure frequently enhances a family's trust in professionals and increases probability of informed decisions. In addition, because evaluation information can be highly technical and written explanations may not be fully informative, it is good practice to explain the results face-to-face with the parents. These discussions can elicit the family's perspectives to validate or dispel tentative interpretations. Parents can share information about their son's or daughter's special needs, confirm whether the performance that professionals describe is typical, and make connections between the independent evaluations that the family offers.

One option is to hold a separate conference with the parents; another is to review the evaluation information during the IEP/IFSP. By holding a separate conference, particularly for the initial evaluation, professionals on the evaluation team allow more time to discuss their findings and for parents to assimilate information before making program and placement decisions (assuming the student is eligible for special education). It is usually difficult to review and discuss evaluation data and also plan an IFSP/IEP in just one meeting. It is better practice to invite the parents to a separate conference to discuss the initial evaluation and all subsequent reevaluations.

Taking the Family's Perspective

How do families respond to evaluation results? From relief to pain, the gamut of their responses is long and varied. However sensitively you convey the information, many families—particularly those who strongly value academic achievement, success, and conformity—may be sorely disappointed by the confirmation of a disability. As we mentioned in chapter 8, many parents want and benefit from hopeful information. One mother noted that hope was "why we wake up every day. There is nothing that any of us cannot go through if we believe that there is hope for progress" (Nissenbaum et al., 2002, p. 36). Presenting information optimistically can enhance families' motivation, just as negative expectations can diminish or even quash families' hope:

> I was totally stunned. Very upset . . . it took me back a great deal . . . I wanted to hold on to what I knew . . . about him, his abilities, you know, rather than someone coming in and pulling all that apart . . . throwing it all up in the air. (Rogers, 2007, p. 139)

Some parents may feel they have contributed to their child's disability or that they should have attended to it earlier. They may worry about their child's future and fear that the child's and the family's challenges will inevitably escalate. They may doubt the credibility or expertise of the evaluation team, and they may need time to come to grips with the reality of the evaluation results.

You must be extremely sensitive about reverting to an earlier model (referred to in chapter 5) in which many parents were mistakenly blamed for their child's disabilities: For example, one parent said that he felt guilt when a professional used the expression "children bring their lifestyle to school" in the discussion of his child's evaluation (Rocco et al., 2002, p. 78).

Other families feel justified and relieved to learn the results of their child's evaluation; justified because they, perhaps unlike the school, believed all along that their child had real needs, and relieved because at last they have an evaluation that can lead to effective intervention. In the words of one mother, "I spent 24/7 with my daughter, still they didn't take my concerns seriously until the diagnosis was in writing" (Beach Center, 2000). Relief also comes from knowing that the school staff may finally understand their child as they do. One parent explained, "They recognize the disability so he is not being blamed for being a child as he knows being a child" (Brewin, Renwick, & Schormans, 2008, p. 247).

Perhaps most sadly, relief for some families comes from ending their long struggle to be heard. This is the story of one mother's description of learning of her son's diagnosis:

> It was a difficult year. It was a year that required much work. She had just arrived to the United States from the Dominican Republic on her own without knowing the language. She had to deal with several agencies, which in her opinion were very slow to assist her. She said, "I cried, I begged, I asked." She was very concerned because she saw how the months would pass without any services being provided to her son. (Hughes, Valle-Riestara, Arguelles, 2008, p. 251)

Parents' perspectives are likely to reflect their culture and beliefs. Families from different cultures ascribe different meanings to the concept of disability and even to standard terminology (Harry, 2008). For example, a Puerto Rican mother described the distinction, from her cultural and language perspective, between *retarded* and *handicapped*:

> For me, retarded is crazy; in Spanish that's "retardado." For me, the word "handicapped" means a person who is incapacitated, like mentally, or missing a leg, or who is blind or deaf, who cannot work and cannot do anything . . . a person who is invalid, useless. . . . But for Americans, it is a different thing—for them "handicapped" is everybody! (Harry, 1992, p. 31)

Many traditional Native American languages do not have words for disability or handicap (Siantz & Keltner, 2004). In fact, the overall concept for disability is different in some American Indian communities than it is in the mainstream culture. For example, a Navajo child who is diagnosed with Down syndrome may not be considered disabled if the child functions well at home (Saintz & Keltner, 2004). American Indian families value "balance" and "harmony" in their lives. One parent said of his family's experience: "you just accept it and both grow" (Nichols & Keltner, 2005, p. 34).

At no time are partnership practices of sensitivity, availability, accessibility, respect, and honesty more important than when you share evaluation information. We encourage you to reflect on your communication with families, particularly those from culturally and linguistically diverse backgrounds. As you examine the strategies for evaluating students from diverse cultures listed in Figure 9.5, ask yourself, "How do each of these strategies contribute to the partnership principle of trust?"

In chapter 7, we emphasized the importance of empathetic listening, expression, and reciprocity to build effective partnerships. You should display empathy in all your communications. Linda Mitchell, a parent and speech-language pathologist whose son experiences a developmental disability, characterizes the critically important role of empathy:

> I don't want someone to feel sorry for me. Sorrow sets me up to grieve for a loss, but I don't feel that my son, John, is any kind of a loss. He is truly a source of great happiness and a huge contributor to our family. Empathy says I feel for you because I care about you. Sympathy says I feel sorry for you. Empathy connects, sympathy disconnects. If you want to really begin to build a relationship with me, empathize with me, and then help me move on. (Beach Center, 2000)

Considering the Student's Role in Discussing Evaluation Results

Sharing evaluation results with students can help them decide about their education and other activities, provide them with accurate estimates about their abilities, and

FIGURE 9.5	**Sharing findings with family members.**

Imagine this: You are the parent of a child who has been evaluated for special education services and you are about learn the results of your child's evaluation and his or her diagnosis. How might professionals share their findings to help you accept and understand the information you are about to hear?

Review the following list and consider how you would implement these practices to facilitate trust when sharing evaluation findings:

- Create a setting that makes all participants comfortable.
- Convey the message that you have the student's and family's best interests in mind.
- Be concrete and precise in your presentation of the findings.
- Identify the developmental or content area assessed before presenting test results.
- Explain the text results in everyday language.
- Provide specific examples of skills the student can and cannot perform.
- Stay focused on the whole child.
- Present the diagnosis and explain terms using clear and understandable language.
- Discuss possibilities and provide hope.
- Take time to listen and respond to parent's verbal and nonverbal responses.
- Provide a list of resources and offer suggestions for follow-up reading material.
- Be available and responsive to families in their requests for information.
- Schedule a follow-up meeting if you or the family needs time to reflect on or gather information.

contribute to their self-esteem (Sattler, 2001). There are a number of ways to share information with students. First, parents may share evaluation results and recommendations with their son or daughter. Second, the student may participate at the end of a conference held initially only with parents. Third, one or more members of the evaluation team may hold a separate conference with the student. This approach may prevent the student from becoming overpowered by the presence of many adults. Finally, the student can participate in the regular evaluation team meeting. In that event, prepare the student in advance, be sure the discussion at the conference is clear to the student, and explicitly affirm the student's strengths.

Whatever the approach, remain sensitive to the family's and student's preferences and needs about how they want to receive evaluation information:

> Definitely it was better not to have [my son] there because [the diagnosis of autism] is a real big blow to give parents. They need to deal with their emotions, or at least in our case, we needed to deal with our emotions and kind of get figured out how we were going to think about this and how we were going to deal with it. We needed time. (Nissenbaum et al., 2002, p. 35)

Sharing the Evaluation Results with Parents

You will have at least three goals as you discuss the evaluation results with families:

1. Ensure that they have a clear understanding of the student's strengths, preferences, great expectations, and needs.
2. Support them to adjust emotionally to the evaluation information.
3. Interpret and communicate information to lay the foundation for the student's appropriate education and for partnership among the student, family, and professionals.

You are likely to meet these goals when you follow partnership practices leading to trust. Specifically, convey information clearly; treat the parents, student, and other family members with respect; and respond to their emotional needs as you discuss results, your diagnosis, and recommendations.

You will want to follow an agenda for discussing evaluation results with families. Organize the meeting into four components: (1) opening dialogue, (2) presentation of findings, (3) discussion of recommendations, and (4) summary. The opening dialogue should inform the family of the purpose of the conference and convey that you desire and value their contributions. Families should have the opportunity to describe their perspectives about their child's functioning, to offer their views, and to react to and reflect on others' input. Their comments will reveal their understanding about their child and even allow you to incorporate some of the words they use (such as "lagging behind") in your subsequent explanations.

Most of the conference will be devoted to sharing results of the evaluation and discussing recommendations, which we cover in the next section of this chapter.

The final agenda item is providing a clear and concise summary of the information discussed. Describe any consensus about information or other discussions. In the spirit of partnership, end the meeting by affirming that you will continue to be accessible to the parents.

Presenting the Findings. When you communicate evaluation findings, be as concrete, precise, accurate, and complete as possible. First, identify the subject or developmental area that you assessed (such as reading, social skills, communication, or mathematics) and then present your findings. Be very clear about the meaning of specific test scores. For example, if a student scored at the 60th percentile on a standardized test, explain that he or she scored higher than 60% of all other test takers. Give examples of skills the student could and could not perform accurately. Link these skills to real-life activities whenever possible. These examples should help identify skills in which the student excels and skills for which supports may be needed. There are several sources for clear, accurate, and informative descriptions of tests and test scores. For example, *Straight Talk About Psychological Testing for Kids* is a useful guide to testing written by two psychologists, Ellen Braaten and Gretchen Felopulos (2004).

You and your colleagues should present a composite of the student's strengths, preferences, great expectations, and needs, not just list separate and isolated discipline-specific reports. The family sees the whole child, not a child segmented into discrete parts:

> Specialists see [my daughter] from their own point of view. I guess the hardest thing is that I want answers. I wanted them to say she is going to make it or she isn't going to make it. I guess the hardest thing is not getting answers and everyone looking at their particular area and no one giving me the whole picture. Everyone is just looking at one area and forgetting she is a whole child. (Beach Center, 2000)

The presentation of findings should not be one-sided; you should stimulate discussion and address the priorities and concerns of the family and other team members. Whenever practicable, include a member of the same cultural group as the student, in addition to the family, in the discussion of the findings (Harris-Murri et al., 2006). Be careful to affirm the student's and family's strengths throughout the discussion. If you leave families without hope and optimism, they will be poorly motivated to develop partnerships with you.

When sharing findings with families, listen actively so that you can provide useful, personalized feedback. Different families will have different responses, perspectives, and schedules (Nissenbaum et al., 2002). Most will need time to absorb evaluation information and develop new understandings about their child. Think about how you might incorporate the communication skills you learned in chapter 8 as you share evaluation findings with families. Figure 9.5 offers tips for sharing findings with families. Because most families appreciate direct yet sensitive communication, consider the partnership principles of communication, competence, and commitment when presenting evaluation findings.

Discussing the Diagnosis. You and other members of the evaluation team should discuss the student's performance and the type and extent of any disability. Consider the family's personal and cultural perspectives about labeling when you present the child's potential diagnosis. Some parents may find categorical labels painful or demeaning. Others are relieved to have a name attached to a condition that has created so many concerns. When they have a diagnosis of their child, many parents begin to take forward-looking action.

> I will never forget how numb I felt when they told me that [my son] was on the "Autistic Spectrum." I went outside and threw up. Then I started my battle plan. (Fleischmann, 2004, p. 39)

Sometimes professionals mistakenly assume that it is best to offer services to the child without making the child's diagnosis explicit. They think that by avoiding the use of disability labels they will be able to communicate better with parents. Unfortunately, ambiguity does not enhance a family's understanding and contributes to inequity in the relationship with the family. The partnership principle of communication and related practices of clarity and honesty are crucial to building trust with families.

The key is to explain categorical labels to family members in a straightforward manner. Before the meeting, think about the language you will use. When you are uncomfortable using specific terminology, you may jumble words, ramble, or rush through your comments, creating tension for families and professionals alike.

> [Parents] can sense the tension in our voices and I think they react to it. They know that something is wrong with their child just by our behavior. Our anxiety brings out their own anxiety. (Nissenbaum et al., 2002, p. 36)

Explain what the label or diagnosis means using clear and nontechnical language. For example, you might say that *intellectual disability*—the current term for mental retardation—means that the child has lower-than-average scores on assessments of intellectual and adaptive behavior. Because many families associate that particular disability and others with negative stereotypes, you should talk about the different degrees of intellectual disability and the positive outcomes that many individuals with that disability experience when they have access to an appropriate education in the least restrictive environment. Connect parents to local or regional parent organizations that you learned about in chapter 7, such as a PTI center, a Parent to Parent group, or other disability-specific groups. Encourage them to talk to other parents whose children experience similar disabilities, to learn about services, and to get emotional support.

Many information sources (such as parent support groups, Internet sites, blogs, listservs, books, and criteria for access to funding) are organized by category of disability. When families have a label for the condition, they are likely to get information about their child's strengths and needs more easily.

Sometimes, parents will not immediately accept your evaluation results and may criticize your diagnosis. Take into account the parents' perspectives. Realize how much they love their child and how much they need to "stack the deck" in their child's favor. Your support and patience will pay off in the end.

Some parents seek additional information, perhaps from one specialist and then another, searching for answers to their questions. These parents have been unkindly labeled as "shoppers" who have failed to accept their child's exceptionality. But consider this: They may be investigating the widest possible range of professional resources so that they can make an informed decision about their child and about the professionals with whom they might want to form a partnership.

Unfortunately, some professionals interpret families' desire to get a second opinion as a personal challenge to their expertise. Any family who wants additional information or resources deserves immediate referrals. If you support rather than criticize their actions, you will strengthen your partnership with the family and serve as a catalyst for their empowerment.

Making Recommendations. After discussing the evaluation results, you must make recommendations. The more parents and other family members have been partners in the evaluation process, the more they are apt to trust and follow through on these recommendations.

Traditionally, professionals agree in advance of the conference about their recommendations and then present them to families. A partnership model, however, encourages families and professionals to reflect together about evaluation data and then generate recommendations for action. The recommendations should, at the very least, enhance the student's appropriate education in the least restrictive environment (general curriculum) and, at best, help both the child and family. When professionals, family members, and students work together to identify priorities and set goals, great expectations for achieving equal opportunity, independent living, economic self-sufficiency, and full participation are more likely to be realized. You will learn more about developing life enhancing educational plans with students and families in chapter 11.

The recommendations must provide families, general and special education teachers, and related service providers with detailed information about the child's participation and progress in all aspects of school, including the general curriculum. They should also show how best to promote preferences, build on the student's strengths, and address the student's education-related needs.

Parents are most apt to carry out recommendations that they have helped develop and that they believe to be beneficial to their children (Eccles & Harold, 1996; Stoner, Bock, Thompson, Angell, Heyl, & Crowley, 2005). To ensure that all recommendations are implemented, develop a specific plan of action. Specify who is responsible for following through on each recommendation, when those people will begin and finish their duties, the necessary resources they need to perform their duties, and how everyone will know when work is completed. It also is useful to continuously reflect in subsequent evaluations or IFSP/IEP conferences about how the partnership is maturing and how professionals interact with each other and with families.

As we conclude this section on discussing evaluation results, we underscore what a formative moment it is for most parents when they first learn about the nature of their child's disability (Jackson, Traub, & Turnbull, 2008; Stoner et al., 2005). Bear in mind that the parents' expectations for the future, great or small, may be largely determined by words and messages you convey at this crucial time.

:: FOSTERING TRUST

There are many opportunities throughout the evaluation process to build trust with families. You can build trust by using the partnership practices that support it, such as communicating by responding to parents' questions honestly and clearly, demonstrating your professional competence by describing and giving concrete examples of their child's performance, proving your commitment to the child by talking about outcomes you envision, and respecting the family and child by affirming their child's and their own strengths and abilities. You can also build trust by keeping

CHANGE AGENTS BUILD CAPACITY
Facing an Ethical Challenge

Although IDEA requires a nondiscriminatory evaluation, unintentional biases may creep into the evaluation process. What might you do if you recognize that the evaluation data underestimated a student's abilities?

Assume you are a member of an evaluation team. You and other team members are meeting with the child's parents to discuss the results of the nondiscriminatory evaluation. The student and his family had moved from South America two years earlier. A translator was also present at the meeting to assist in translating for the team and the parents, whose primary language was Spanish. As members of the team presented the data and their conclusions, the student's parents expressed, through the translator, their surprise at how poorly their son had done. You, too, were skeptical about the accuracy of the results since you knew that this student was achieving satisfactorily in your class in some of the areas in which the team reported deficits. You suspected that some of the team members may have

been unconsciously biased against an immigrant who does not speak English. What do you do about your concerns?

Take Action!

- Share what you know about the student's achievement; be clear and honest in your description of the student's progress in your class.
- Ask questions that will encourage the team to explore why the assessment results differ from how the parents and you see the student.
- Suggest that additional information be considered before decisions about the student's education are made.
- Respect all team members; wait until after the meeting to discuss with the evaluation team why you may have concerns about the selection of assessment instruments.

your conscience primed at times when parents' interests in the evaluation process are overlooked, such as in the situation described in the Change Agents Build Capacity box above.

More than that, you can be the catalyst for long-term positive outcomes, as this mother experienced through her partnership with professionals in the evaluation process:

> At the beginning we were unsure. "How could we do it?" But the more you learn, the more you realize how rewarding it is that you can see your child move forward. So you try to balance all these things out and it is

very difficult. We realized with every child, and with every family dynamic, it's different. We were very lucky, in also having a therapist that was helping us through the process, explained it to us and sat down at a human level. They understood the uniqueness of everybody's situation. (Lytel, Lopez-Garcia, & Stacey, 2008)

Before revisiting Eloisa and her family, let's wrap up the chapter by considering how to create partnerships through trust building. Figure 9.6 gives you our best-practice suggestions.

FIGURE 9.6   Creating partnerships through trust building.

	never	sometimes		always

TRUST

1. Do you offer parents a choice as to with whom and how the evaluation information will be shared? 1 2 3 4 5

2. Do you honor parents' decisions even when you are not in agreement with them? 1 2 3 4 5

COMMUNICATION

3. Do you offer parents opportunities to share their stories, dreams, and priorities and do you actively listen as they share this information? 1 2 3 4 5

4. Do you clearly explain evaluation results to parents using terms that are readily understood and meaningful to them? 1 2 3 4 5

5. Do you give parents copies of all evaluation reports before meeting with them? 1 2 3 4 5

RESPECT

6. Do you conduct evaluations and hold meetings at times that are convenient to parents? 1 2 3 4 5

7. Do you ask parents to help determine if a test is fair (i.e., if their child is familiar with the language or content of the test)? 1 2 3 4 5

8. Do you include in evaluation reports only information that has been discussed with and agreed upon by parents? 1 2 3 4 5

EQUALITY

9. Do you provide parents with options for gathering and sharing information about their child or family? 1 2 3 4 5

10. Do you ask parents which professionals or disciplines they want involved in the evaluation of their children? 1 2 3 4 5

11. Do you offer parents the opportunity to be present at all discussions about planning their child's evaluation and the results? 1 2 3 4 5

COMMITMENT

12. Do you notice and respond to how parents feel about information they receive about their child's evaluation? 1 2 3 4 5

13. Do you make yourself available to parents throughout the evaluation process? 1 2 3 4 5

ADVOCACY

14. Do you let parents know that they may have anyone else whey want present at or involved in the evaluation of their child? 1 2 3 4 5

15. Do you think that parents would consider you to be their advocate in the evaluation process? 1 2 3 4 5

PROFESSIONAL SKILLS

16. Do you have knowledge of and access to resources for parents? 1 2 3 4 5

17. Do you have the skills, knowledge, and resources to contribute meaningfully to the evaluation process? 1 2 3 4 5

FIGURE 9.7 Partnership practices in evaluation: questions for self-reflections.

Partnership Principles and Practices	Issues	Actions Leading to Distrust	Actions Leading to Trust
Communication: Be honest.	In your noncategorical program, parents ask you what "functional placement" means. You know that the professional interpretation is "severe disability," but the school district forbids you to use that classification.	Tell parents that "functional placement" really does not have a meaning, and that the professionals do not associate any kind of diagnostic label with it.	Explain to the parents the rationale for noncategorical programming and share your own value. Also tell them that sometimes noncategorical labels have other connotations, and honestly share those connotations with them.
Respect: Honor cultural diversity.	Asian family members tell you that they believe their son's leaning disability is a punishment to him for not adequately honoring their ancestors.	Tell the family to discount nonscientific interpretations as groundless and foolish.	Listen empathetically to the family's perspectives and ask members what information or support you could provide that they might find helpful.
Professional Competence: Set high expectations.	Parents have just received the diagnosis that their infant is legally blind.	Encourage the parents to be realistic and to recognize that it is too much of a burden for community preschools to adapt their programs.	Ask the parents what information would be especially helpful for them as they consider their next steps. Let them know that you look forward to collaborating with them and watching their child grow and develop. Tell them that you are available to help make their dreams for their child come true.
Equality: Share power.	In the evaluation conference, the parents seem to want to "kill the messenger." They are angry at the professionals for "creating their child's problem."	Point out to the parents that they have displaced anger and that you and other professionals are doing all that you know how to help them.	Listen empathically to the parents' perspectives and reflect on whether any of the communication used in the conference could unintentionally come across as representing a "we-they" orientation.
Commitment: Be sensitive to emotional needs.	A mother with AIDS comes to a diagnostic conference to hear the latest educational report on her child, who also has AIDS.	Tell the mother that nothing would make you feel as guilty as giving AIDS to your child.	Share with the mother one or more things that she has done that has made a difference in the child's educational progress and tell her you appreciate her efforts.
Advocacy: Create win-win solutions.	Parents are highly dissatisfied with the evaluation that you believe has been done very appropriately. They request an independent evaluation, but you do not believe one is needed.	Defend the school's evaluation and tell the parents that their request is unwarranted.	Encourage the parents to discuss with you their concerns, and ask them to describe an evaluation process that they would find satisfactory. Inform them of the process for initiating an independent evaluation.

REVISITING ELOISA, HENRIQUE, AND MARIA HERNANDEZ

IDEA requires educators to evaluate each child not only fairly (without bias) but also broadly (a whole-child approach). Eloisa, Henrique, and Maria's former teacher—the one who has demurred from her colleagues' recommendations about separating Maria from her age-equivalent peers—know that IDEA requires the evaluation team, whether in an initial or a subsequent evaluation, to "gather relevant functional, developmental, and academic information, including information provided by the parent, that may assist in determining the content of the child's individualized education program, including . . . information related to enabling the child to be involved in and progress in the general education curriculum" (20 U.S.C. Sec. 1414(b)(2)(A)). They also know that IDEA defines "general education" as including the academic, extracurricular, and other nonacademic activities (20 U.S.C. Sec. 1414(d)(a)(1)(IV)(bb)).

When Maria was in elementary school, she was included in academics and the rest of the school life; she made friends; she was happy. She and her friends moved together from that school to another for her sixth grade year; her friendship network was intact and her social skills expanded. Moved to yet another middle school for her seventh grade year, her network has been dissolved and her social skills are not growing—if anything, they are at risk to deteriorate.

Which of the six partnership principles will Eloisa, Henrique, and Maria's former teacher bring to bear when the district's special education team reevaluates her and develops a new IEP based on the evaluation results? When faced with objections, what are they to do? What, indeed, should the educators do? After all, it's Maria's and the family's life, not the educators.

SUMMARY

Collaborating with families throughout the referral and evaluation process enriches the team's understanding of the student and provides the foundation for a trusting partnership between families and professionals. The referral and evaluation process has many component parts, each with opportunities to practice the partnership principles:

- Identify and screen students.
- Implement prereferral and response to intervention strategies.
- Initiate and review the referral.
- Provide notice and obtain consent.
- Collect evaluation information.
- Analyze evaluation information.
- Discuss evaluation results with the family.

We encourage you to consider how the partnership practices leading to trust can be used throughout the referral and evaluation process. Review your partnership practices using the self-reflection guide in Figure 9.7. Remember, the actions you take will help you build and maintain trusting partnerships with families. Upon this strong foundation, you can develop the student's individualized education program.

LINKING CONTENT TO YOUR LIFE

We have identified practices you can use to promote partnerships in student evaluation, potentially empowering families by emphasizing their perspectives and preferences.

- What would you do if you identified practices in your school or district that inhibited partnership?
- Which of the principles of partnership will be more effective than others in situations such as Maria's

reevaluation—communication, competence, commitment, advocacy, respect, or equality?
- When in your life have you confronted indispensable professionals who dismissed your concerns about yourself? What did you do, remembering you needed them (they were indispensable to your health) and needed to be partners with them?

Families as Partners in Developing Individualized Plans

MARIA, ELOISA, AND HENRIQUE HERNANDEZ

As you know from reading chapter 9, Eloisa and Henrique Hernandez have not been totally pleased with the special education team in Maria's school district and some of her teachers. Ever since Maria entered school, they have asserted her IDEA right to be included, to the maximum extent appropriate for her, in the general education curriculum, extracurricular activities, and other nonacademic activities in her schools. They have recognized that Maria has some academic challenges—especially in reading, in which her elementary school reading teacher tried to help her by using evidence-based interventions during their teach-learn sessions. They also know she has a good deal of trouble with mathematics. So they do not object as much to her not being in the academic general education curriculum as much as they object to some of the attitudes and rigidity they encounter.

When, for example, they were in an IEP meeting to plan Maria's transition from elementary to middle school and its general education program, they were surprised when the middle school reading teacher—without having given more than a cursory review of Maria's records—said Maria should be in a separate self-contained reading program. They have finally acknowledged that the district would have its way, no matter what. "They gave us no choice, they had their minds made up. We feel we are forced to take the district's decision."

It has not always been that way, and they hope it won't always be that way. They remember fondly the partnership they had with Maria's elementary school special education and reading teacher. That teacher adapted the district's evidence-based reading and math programs, giving Maria a chance to read to students less capable than she and teaching her to do the functional math of knowing how many carbohydrates to ingest daily.

She visited their home and told them about Maria's progress, and she always asked them for their consent before making any modifications in the curriculum. Beyond this communication and respect, that teacher took Maria out to dinner or movies weekly and taught her social skills where she would need them—in her neighborhood settings. That commitment mirrored her advocacy when Maria was leaving elementary and entering middle school—advocacy for as much academic and social inclusion as could possibly be designed. Seeing the difference that this one teacher was making in Maria's life, Eloisa and Henrique trusted her judgment about what is best for Maria.

Now, as Eloisa and Henrique prepare for Maria's three-year mandatory reevaluation and annual IEP, they ask themselves: What kind of progress will our daughter make this year, and what teacher or teachers will be the ones who help her make that progress? They have to wait for the IEP conference for an answer; while waiting, they hope that another authentic partner will step forward—one like that elementary school special educator and reading teacher.

think about it

- What are the IDEA requirements with respect to individualized education?
- What factors contribute to successful partnerships as professionals and families develop an individualized education program (IEP) and an individualized family service plan (IFSP)?
- What are the major differences between the IEP and the IFSP documents and processes?
- What effect might these differences have on professionals and families?
- What role does culture play for professionals and families?

:: INTRODUCTION

As you learned in chapter 9, professionals and families can be partners when evaluating a student to determine whether the student has a disability and needs special education. You also learned that the student's evaluation is the basis on which professionals and families begin to develop an appropriate education plan, one that supports the student to achieve, in the long term, the four IDEA outcomes you first learned about in chapter 6: (1) equal opportunity, (2) independent living, (3) economic self-sufficiency, and (4) full participation.

In this chapter, we connect chapters 6 and 9 and describe not only the IDEA requirements but also the recommended practices for developing the student's individualized education program or plan.

:: UNDERSTANDING THE INDIVIDUALIZED PROGRAM AND PLAN

IDEA Requirements

In chapter 6, you learned that Part B of IDEA regulates the appropriate education of (1) children in early childhood education who are between the ages of 3 and 5 years and (2) students in elementary, middle, and secondary school programs who are between the ages of 6 and 21. Part C of IDEA regulates the education of infants and toddlers (birth to 3 years). We begin by describing Part B's individualization requirements.

Part B, Ages 3 to 21 Years. Every student receiving special education has a right to an individualized education program (IEP) (20 U.S.C. Sec. 1414(d)). The IEP itself is a road map that leads professionals, families, and students toward the four outcomes we just described; bear in mind that it does so by using the six principles of partnership we described in chapter 7. As a document, the IEP describes what families and professionals have agreed they will do to make sure the student has an appropriate education and thus attain the four outcomes. But the IEP is more than just a document of agreement toward a result, as we will now explain.

The IEP as a Means for Communication and Self-Advocacy. The process for developing a student's IEP and the IEP itself have long been regarded as vehicles for communication between parents and school personnel (U.S. Department of Education, 1981). Likewise, the process and the document itself can be vehicles for communication by and to the student. That is so because IDEA permits the student to be a member of the IEP team and to participate in developing his or her IEP when appropriate. The student's parents and educators often agree when it is appropriate for the student to attend the meeting in which others develop the IEP and when it is appropriate for the student to participate actively in that meeting. They normally take into account the student's chronological age and developmental stage.

By participating as a member of the IEP team, the student also learns how to self-advocate (Arndt, Konrad, & Test, 2006; Mason, McGahee-Kovac, & Johnson, 2004; Van Dycke, Martin, & Lovett, 2006; Wood, Karvonen, Test, Browder, & Algozzine, 2004). We explain the concept called *self-advocacy* later in this chapter. For now, bear in mind that students will need to know how to represent themselves in order to attain IDEA's four outcomes because their parents and teachers will not always be available to them. At some point, they may be on their own.

Legal Liability and Good Faith.
Although IDEA exempts schools, teachers, or other professionals from legal liability if a student does not achieve the annual goals set forth in the IEP, these professionals must make good-faith efforts to help students master IEP goals and objectives. What constitutes a good-faith effort in developing and implementing an IEP? Good faith occurs when members of the team follow precisely IDEA's provisions governing the process for developing an IEP. When the IEP complies with the IDEA, then the document is rightly the basis for the process of educating the student. The document prescribes the process. And a fair process—complying with IDEA—tends to produce fair and acceptable results.

Documenting Parent Participation.
IDEA acknowledges that parents are valued, integral participants in developing their child's IEP. It does so by requiring educators to document their efforts to secure parent participation. Educators may comply with the documentation rule by keeping copies of letters to or from the parents and detailed records of telephone calls and visits to parents' homes or workplaces and the results of those visits.

Required Components.
Educators must also build the IEP on the basis of the nondiscriminatory evaluation of the student (20 U.S.C. Sec. 1414(d)). They must take into account the student's strengths and the parents' concerns. They should also take into account the student's performance on prereferral interventions and the results of the student's performance on general state or district-wide assessments. The IEP must contain statements concerning each factor described in Figure 10.1.

Required Participants.
The following individuals are the required members of each student's IEP team:

- The student's parents
- Not less than one general education teacher with expertise related to the student's educational performance
- Not less than one special education teacher
- A representative of the local educational agency
- An individual who can interpret the instructional implications of the student evaluation results
- At the discretion of the parent or agency, other individuals with expertise regarding the student's educational needs, including related service personnel as appropriate
- The student, when appropriate (see our previous discussion concerning "when appropriate")

Part C, Ages Birth to 3 Years.
Part C authorizes federal assistance to state and local education agencies so they may achieve four different outcomes: (1) enhance the infants' and toddlers' development and minimize their potential for developmental delays, (2) reduce the costs of special education by minimizing the need for that service, (3) minimize the need for institutionalization of people with disabilities and maximize their potential for independent living, and (4) enhance the capacity of state and local agencies to meet the needs of "under-represented populations, particularly minority, low-income, inner-city and rural populations" (20 U.S.C. Sec. 1431).

To achieve these outcomes, Part C uses a similar approach as Part B, namely, an individualized approach. Instead of an IEP, however, Part C provides for an IFSP, the document that describes the process that families and professionals will follow as they seek to achieve those outcomes.

Note the outcome differences between the IEP and IFSP. Unlike the IEP, the IFSP includes family outcomes. The IFSP enhances the child's development while simultaneously enhancing the family's capacity to meet the child's unique needs. Figure 10.2 lists the required components of an IFSP.

Timing.
The initial meeting to develop the IFSP must take place within 45 days after the child or family is referred for early intervention services. Thereafter, periodic review is available in two ways: (1) The IFSP team must review the IFSP every six months to determine whether the young child is making progress toward IFSP goals and whether to amend the IFSP, and (2) the team must meet annually to evaluate the IFSP and revise it as needed.

Pre-evaluation Services.
If the parents agree, early intervention services may start before their child has been fully

FIGURE 10.1 Required components of the IEP.

The IEP is a written statement for each student, ages 3 to 21. Whenever it is developed or revised, it must contain statements about the following:

- **The student's present levels of academic achievement and functional performance, including:**
  - how the disability affects his or her involvement and progress in the general education curriculum
  - how the disability of a preschooler (ages 3 through 5) affects his or her participation in appropriate activities
  - a statement of benchmarks or short-term objectives if the student is to take alternate assessments
- **Measurable annual goals, including academic and functional goals, designed to:**
  - meet the student's needs that result from the disability, in order to enable the student to be involved in and make progress in the general education curriculum
  - meet each of the student's other disability-related educational needs
- **Measurement of annual goals:**
  - how the school will measure the student's progress toward annual goals
  - how often the school will report the student's progress
- **Special education, related services, and supplementary aids and services, based on peer-reviewed research to the extent practicable,** that will be provided to the student or on the student's behalf, and the program modifications or supports for school personnel that will be provided so that the student can:
  - advance appropriately toward attaining the annual goals
  - be involved in and make progress in the general education curriculum, and participate in extra-curricular and other nonacademic activities, and

- be educated and participate with other students with disabilities and with students who do not have disabilities in the general education curriculum and extracurricular and other nonacademic activities
- **The extent, if any, to which the student will not participate with students without disabilities** in the regular class and in the general education curriculum and extracurricular and other nonacademic activities.
- **Any individual appropriate accommodations necessary to measure the student's academic achievement and functional performance on state and local assessments** of student achievement. If the IEP team determines that the student will take an alternate assessment on a particular state- or districtwide assessment, the IEP must document why the student cannot participate in the regular assessment and what alternate assessment is appropriate.
- **Projected date** for beginning services and program modifications, and the anticipated frequency, location, and duration of each service and modification.
- **Transition plans, including:**
  - beginning not later than the first IEP to be in effect after the student is 16, and annually thereafter
  - appropriate measurable postsecondary goals
    - based on age-appropriate transition assessments
    - related to training, education, employment, and, where appropriate, independent living skills
  - the transition services, including courses of study, needed to assist the student to reach those goals
  - beginning at least one year before the student reaches the age of majority under state law (usually at age 18), a statement that the student has been informed of those rights under IDEA that will transfer to the student from the parents when the student becomes of age

---

evaluated. In that case, parents and the appropriate professionals develop an interim IFSP (naming the service coordinator and demonstrating that the child and family need services immediately), and then complete the child's evaluation within the 45-day period.

Parents' Consent for Evaluation and Service. Early intervention providers must explain to families what the IFSP contains and obtain families' informed, written consent for those services. Families may consent to and

receive some services but object to other services and decline them.

Required Participants. As you read a few paragraphs above, the IFSP uses the term *family*, whereas the IEP uses the term *parent*. This difference reflects evolving recognition of the importance of the family systems perspective you learned about in chapters 1 through 4.

The required participants in the initial and in each annual IFSP meeting must include the child's parent or parents

FIGURE 10.2   Required components of the IFSP.

The IFSP is a written statement for each infant or toddler, ages birth through 2, and the family. It must contain a statement of the following:

- Child's present levels of physical, cognitive, communication, social or emotional, and adaptive development, based on objective criteria.
- Family's resources, priorities, and concerns related to enhancing their child's development.
- Measurable outcomes for the child and family, including preliteracy and language skills, and criteria, procedures, and timelines used to determine progress and need for modifying outcomes.
- Specific early intervention services based on peer-reviewed research, to the extent practicable, to meet the child's and family's unique needs, including the frequency, intensity, location, and service delivery method.
- Natural environments in which early intervention services are provided, and why services will not be provided in those environments if the plan so provides.
- Projected dates for initiating services and the expected length, duration, and frequency of each.
- Name of the service coordinator, from the profession most immediately relevant to the child's or family's needs, responsible to implement and coordinate the IFSP with other agencies and persons, including transition services.
- Transition plan to support the child's transition from early intervention to preschool or other appropriate services.

and professionals from more than one discipline. This type of membership ensures that the IFSP will reflect perspectives and assessments from a variety of disciplines, the child's unique strengths and needs, a family-directed assessment of family resources, priorities and concerns, the services appropriate to meet the child's needs, and the services and supports necessary to enhance the family's capacity to meet their child's developmental needs. If a required person is not available for a meeting, other means for participation are required—for example, telephone conference calls, attendance by a knowledgeable representative, or access to pertinent records at the meeting. In keeping with the partnership approach, all meetings must be at times and places convenient to the family and must be arranged to allow them enough time to plan to attend. All notices to the family must be in their native language or other mode of communication. (If you are in doubt about what language to use, ask the family members.)

Transition Plans

Transition involves passage from one place to another or from one time to another; they are elements of each family's life cycle stages that you learned about in chapter 4. Students with disabilities and their families experience several transition stages. In early childhood, an infant or toddler with disabilities transitions from receiving early intervention services to preschool special education services; the young child then transitions from receiving preschool services to school-age services; finally, when a student is older, he or she begins a transition to adulthood.

Transition Services and IEPs—Leaving Secondary and Entering Postsecondary Services. To ease the difficulties of transition and assure effective services in the "receiving" service system—the one to which a student transitions—IDEA also requires the parents, the student when appropriate, and the professional members of the student's IEP team to develop transition plans to prepare the student for adult life and to include these transition plans in the student's IEP. Transition planning must occur no later than the first IEP that will be in effect when the child is 16 years old (20 U.S.C. 1414(d)(1)(A)). The plan must consider the student's preferences for postsecondary activities.

One year before the student reaches the age of majority (typically 18 years), the student's LEA must notify the student that he or she will attain the age of majority at age 18 and will have the right to make decisions for himself or herself about the IEP's content (20 U.S.C. Sec. 1414(d)(1)(A)). When the student attains the age of majority, all of the parents' rights transfer to the student (20 U.S.C. Sec. 1415(m)), assuming the student is competent to exercise those rights. If the student is not, the student's parents or another adult will do so consistent with procedures the SEA must establish (20 U.S.C. Sec. 1415(m)). The significance of these provisions for professionals is this: The student must be included in the IEP process from the earliest time when the student can make useful contributions to the process.

Transition Statements and IFSPs—Leaving Early Intervention and Entering Early Childhood Education. For the same reasons it requires transition planning for students leaving secondary and entering postsecondary services, IDEA requires early intervention programs to develop transition plans for all children receiving early intervention services before they reach age 3. These programs help children adjust to new services and settings, prepare service providers who will support the transition, and identify individuals responsible for helping children and families make a smooth transition.

Partnerships and Collaboration: The Core of the IFSP and IEP.

You may notice many similarities as well as differences between the IFSP and the IEP. There is, however, a primary common theme, regardless of the student's age. It is that both documents and the processes they launch involve partnerships between families, students, and professionals. Having considered IDEA itself, let's pay attention to the research about these individualized approaches, beginning with a still-valid statement from the U.S. Department of Education concerning the intent behind the IFSP.

The U.S. Department of Education (1999) clearly states IDEA's original intent with respect to children from birth to age 3 and the IFSP:

> Throughout the process of developing and implementing IFSPs for an eligible child and the child's family, it is important for agencies to recognize the variety of roles that family members play in enhancing the child's development. It also is important that the degree to which the needs of the family are addressed in the IFSP process is determined in a collaborative manner, with the full agreement and participation of the parents of the child. Parents retain the ultimate decision in determining whether they, their child, or other family members will accept or decline services under this part. (U.S. Department of Education, 1999)

Note the language in this policy interpretation: ". . . collaborative manner with the full agreement and participation of the parents. . . ."

As you learned in chapter 6, the Supreme Court regards the "collaborative process" between parents and professionals to be the "core" of the law (*Schaffer v. Weast*, 2004). In that case, the Court addressed IDEA's intent as applied to students not in early intervention but, instead, in early childhood and elementary, middle, and secondary school; it applied to the participants developing a student's IEP, not those developing an IFSP.

IDEA clearly expects a solid family-professional partnership, grounded in trust. Further, IDEA's provisions granting parents and the student a right to be a member of the IEP team simply carry forward the principle of partnership. There is evidence, however, that the ideal and the reality in today's schools do not match.

Research on Partnerships.

Since the 1980s, the research literature has been fairly consistent in acknowledging that IEP/IFSP conferences often fail to honor partnership practices. In a summary of the IEP literature from IDEA's initial enactment in 1975 through 1990, Smith (1990) concluded, "After more than a decade of implementation, research, and subsequent recommendations for improvement, substantive IEP change has not ensued" (p. 11).

Current Research.

Although two decades have passed since Smith's analysis, a pressing need still exists for the IEP to reflect adequately the priorities of children with disabilities and their families. For example, IEP conferences still do not typically allow enough time to plan appropriate educational programs; moreover, parents tend to have limited roles in these meetings (Harry, Allen, & McLaughlin, 1995; Lo, 2008; Soodak & Erwin, 2000; Stroggilos & Xanthacou, 2006; Vaughn, Bos, Harrell, & Lasky, 1988). Conferences usually end at a previously set time regardless of whether the participants have fully completed an IEP. In violation of the spirit and often the exact provisions of IDEA, the main activity within conferences too frequently consists of obtaining parents' signatures on IEP documents and following a preset agenda, not encouraging parents' genuine participation (Childre & Chambers, 2005; Harry et al., 1995). One parent describes it this way:

> When they have the goals set, it is just like the parents just have to agree to whatever the [professionals] have on the papers that are already written up . . . We are just there to put our signatures on paper . . . I felt like a lot of times they pretty well had the agenda set before we got there . . . The few things we would mention, it was like "Well, that is great," then they would go back into the set agenda. It just kind of seemed like it was kind of a cut and dry thing basically before we got there. (Childre & Chambers, 2005, p. 224)

Another parent echoes a similar frustration that the team had completed all the planning and decision making before the parent ever set foot in the meeting.

> . . . We walk into a meeting with a stack of papers already completed—and they read it and we are asked to sign it. So, all of the decisions have been made without parental input. (Fish, 2006, p. 63)

Soodak and Erwin (2000) noted a similar theme in their research: Although some parents were involved in a series of collaborative meetings to develop their child's IEP, the majority of parents were asked to attend only one IEP meeting and to simply agree with decisions that professionals had previously made.

Many parents have also complained that LEAs developed computer-generated IEPs before the IEP meeting took place. It is proper for you to ask: How can a student's plan be individualized or reflect meaningful parent input if developed by a commercially available computer program without family and student input? Before concluding that a computerized IEP is indefensible, you may want to bear in mind that LEAs use computerized IEPs for administrative/ efficiency purposes. Then, take into account that computerizing an IEP can limit the choices of services available to parents and their professional allies on the IEP team.

In IEP conferences, professionals are the primary decision makers, and parents often feel neither heard nor comfortable with sharing their ideas (Childre & Chambers, 2005; Hanson et al., 2000; Salas, 2004). When the IEP process thwarts parents' participation, it is debatable whether the resulting IEP is genuinely individualized and likely to benefit the student (Etscheidt, 2003; Pretti-Frontczak & Bricker, 2000). Further, how can families regard themselves as equal partners when they are denied adequate time and opportunity to participate meaningfully? Parents are still viewed as participants, not as trusted partners in important educational planning.

Research on Transition Planning. Similar challenges to partnership persist for students and families as they transition from one program to another. Although IDEA transition mandates have had a positive impact, progress remains inconsistent and slow-moving (Hasazi, Furney, & Destefano, 1999; Johnson, Stodden, Emanuel, Luecking, & Mack, 2002). For example, students with disabilities still lack access to a full range of curricular options and learning experiences in general education, and to community-based work and vocational education (Johnson et al., 2002).

Research on Student Participation. Further, given that students routinely do not have opportunities to participate in a meaningful way in their own IEP planning (Martin, Marshall, & Sale, 2004), you should ask yourself: How can we expect students to be independent and responsible for their lives once they graduate high school if they are not actively involved in the planning of their own IEP?

In recent years, student participation in IEP meetings and transition planning has received increased attention. Evidence suggests that middle and high school students need specific instruction about how to participate effectively in their own IEP meetings (Martin et al., 2006). Research also shows that effective curricula and interventions are available for increasing meaningful student participation in IEP meetings (Hammer, 2004; Test, Mason, Hughes, Konrad, Neale, & Wood, 2004; Van Dycke, Martin, & Lovett, 2006). The use of strategies to promote student-directed IEPs have been successful in increasing student participation as well as family satisfaction and collaboration between team members (Arndt, Konrad, & Test, 2006; Childre & Chambers, 2005; Martin, Van Dycke,

Christensen, Greene, Gardner, & Lovett, 2006; Myers & Eisenman, 2005; Snyder, 2002). One high school student said, after learning how to lead his own IEP meeting, "I've been to my IEP meeting, but didn't really understand all that stuff. I know more now" (Arndt, Konrad, & Test, 2006, p. 198). One special educator reflected on her experience with Henry, a 16-year-old African American student and his student-directed IEP:

> As special educators, it is important to teach our students skills that they can apply to post school situations. By teaching students the skills necessary to conduct their own IEPs, they learn a set of skills that can be applied to a variety of situations . . . Students learn how to choose, develop and assess goals. By developing goals and learning how to manage goals, students will learn skills necessary to become successful adults. (Myers & Eisenman, 2005. p. 58)

There is also growing attention directed to young students' participation in the transition process from Part C to early childhood education and from that stage to elementary school, and then from that to the next (middle school) and then the next still (secondary school). Given the necessary tools and support, students with disabilities achieve positive outcomes when they and their families take part in important IEP and transition planning.

For example, there are practical strategies for fostering the transition from elementary to middle school for children with significant disabilities and their families (Carter, Clark, Cushing, & Kennedy, 2005). One model, True Directions, uses specific forms that facilitate participation and identifies critical information across all team members (Chambers & Childre, 2006). BEGINNINGS is a tool used in neonatal intensive care nurseries and adapts the components of the IFSP to the unique needs of the newborn and his or her family (Browne, Langlois, Ross, & Smith-Sharp, 2001).

Early Intervention and IFSPs. Despite the available resources, choices and options remain limited for young children with disabilities and their families (Hanson et al., 2000). For some, there is still a disconnect between family-identified priorities and the outcomes and supports written on the IFSP (Ridgley & Hallam, 2006).

In addition, a dramatic shift occurs in the values of service delivery as young children and their families move from early intervention, which adopts a supportive, family-centered approach, to school-based services, which tend to focus more narrowly on child- and school-centered practices (Hanson et al., 2000).

Challenges related to IEP implementation have also been identified for the IFSP; these include issues of time, scheduling, and collaboration with other professionals (Zhang, Fowler, & Bennett, 2004). Although experience and research indicate that the IFSP process comes closer than the IEP to fostering partnerships, the IFSP process still generally fails to fulfill the seven elements of partnerships.

Cultural Influences. You know (from reading chapter 6 and this chapter) that compliance with the IEP process is essential—fair process yields fair results (appropriate education) for the student. You also know, from chapter 1, that many students receiving special education services are members of a cultural, ethnic, or linguistic minority group. Does that fact make a difference? Yes.

Indeed, "how one defines 'successful adulthood,' the end goal of transition planning, is determined by culture-specific values and expectations such as work, community integration, role expectations, and social functioning" (Geenen, Powers, & Lopez-Vasquez, 2001, p. 266). As you learned in chapter 4, each family has its own visions about the future that cultures and microcultures shape. Culture is the lens through which each of us "sees" and understands the world (Turnbull, Turnbull, & Wehmeyer, 2010). Given that culture is an essential part of one's identify, let's explore how culture is understood within the IEP/IFSP process.

Although there is a substantial body of research on families and the IEP/IFSP process, professionals do not consistently or widely use practices to support families who are members of cultural, ethnic, or linguistic minority populations.

> Three decades of literature on the involvement of CLD [culturally and linguistically diverse] families in the special education process underscores the continuing challenging of collaboration across perceived barriers of race, culture, language and social class. . . . yet attainment of these goals [a vision of collaborative partnership] remains elusive for many CLD families. (Harry, 2008, p. 385)

Families from these diverse backgrounds often experience the IEP meeting as upsetting, confusing, or isolating—the exact opposite of a partnership grounded in trust! In a study on Chinese parents' perceptions and experiences at the IEP meeting, Lo (2008) noted there was minimal interaction between parents and professionals, and the majority of parents left the meeting dissatisfied. The differences between families of culturally and linguistically diverse backgrounds are significant, and yet many families have faced similar challenges in the IEP meeting such as language alienation, perceptions of limited time, limited or no access to information, and lack of respect or unresponsiveness to families' needs (Kim, Lee, & Morningstar, 2007; Lo, 2008; Salas, 2004; Zhang & Bennett, 2003). Here is one Mexican

American parent's negative and isolating experience of the IEP meeting:

> I don't like walking into those special meetings and everybody staring at me. All those people. They pretend to care about us, but they don't know us. They don't ask us what we need or want. They always use those big words that I can't understand. (Salas, 2004, p. 189)

A Korean parent shares her story about her worst IEP experience:

> My worst IEP meeting lasted almost 5 hours. It was my worst IEP meeting for so many reasons, but the main underlying reason was the teacher was not ready to partner with parents in order to develop the most appropriate IEP that met my son's educational needs. I was told I was the first parent to question any of the goals and objectives that were recommended by the teacher. It was very difficult to ask anything because with any and every question, the teacher took parent questions as a critique of her teaching ability and parent dissatisfaction, when in actuality, my questions were for my own understanding of how my son is learning. (Beach Center on Disability, 2000)

Notice the misunderstanding and missed opportunities in this parent's experience . . . and this lasted for five hours! Can you identify how many of the partnership principles are noticeably absent?

Here's another, more positive IEP experience, also from a Korean parent, "What made it my best IEP meeting was that my son's new teacher was very open to discussion and willing to hear out my concerns for my son's educational progress and needs" (Beach Center, 2000).

The voices from families from culturally, ethnically, and linguistically diverse families are more present than ever, and yet effective and responsive practices to promote partnerships during their IEP/IFSP meetings are the exception in practice, not the rule. Given what you learned in chapter 10, it seems that many of the issues that arise for families during the evaluation process persist long after a recommendation for services is made.

Research, Culture, and Partnerships. In summary, the dominant theme of the IEP research over the past two decades is that schools try to comply with IDEA and with state and local regulations and procedures, but seldom strive to foster trusting partnerships (Childre & Chambers, 2005; Coots, 2007; Smith, 1990; Smith & Brownell, 1995; Soodak & Erwin, 2000). Indeed, one of the most common reasons for disputes between families and schools has been disagreement concerning how professionals develop and implement students' IEPs (U.S. Department of Education, 2003).

Partnerships make a difference when they do occur. A mother of a young child with a disability summed up her family's positive, empowering experiences with team members after creating their child's IFSP: "[They] recognized our concern, saw it as part of our long-term vision for our child and family, and helped us work out ways to achieve our goal" (Squires, 2000, p. 11). In the next section, we offer practical suggestions for developing an IEP/IFSP in a collaborative way, creating partnerships and fostering trust.

:: CREATING AND STRENGTHENING TRUST DURING THE PLANNING PROCESS

It bears repeating that many families and professionals regard the IEP/IFSP planning process and the IEP/IFSP meeting as a "meaningless ritual in which teachers dictate the prescribed educational program and then pass the ceremonial pen to parents to secure their signatures" (Rock, 2000). You, however, should regard the process and meeting as an exciting, creative opportunity to generate fresh ideas, dream, and find resourceful solutions. In short, the planning process and meeting should be occasions for creating or strengthening the mutual trust between the professionals on the one hand and the parents and student on the other.

As you learned in chapter 7, progressive educators are moving beyond family-centered practices to professional-family partnerships grounded in trust. Hanson and Lynch (2004) acknowledge that a "cluster of practices" are essential for healthy collaboration between families and professionals. How can you adhere to the partnership approach and engender trust? Start by paying careful attention to how you and families develop an IEP/IFSP. If you comply with IDEA and simultaneously practice the partnership principles you are leaning in this book, you can create great expectations for students and their families.

Developing the Individualized Program or Plan

The process for developing a student's individualized plan is as important as the final product. The IEP/IFSP can be developed over time in a series of conferences. One mother pointed out, "because all along I've been involved, . . . we reached consensus by the time we came to the meeting" (Soodak & Erwin, 2000, p. 35).

Because of time and other constraints, however, some schools may choose to develop the plan in a single conference. Whatever the type or number of meetings, spend the allotted time as efficiently as possible. If only one conference

occurs in which yearlong recommendations are made, you should conscientiously use all partnership elements—communication, respect, commitment, advocacy, professional skills, and trust. All conferences should consist of these ten components:

1. Prepare in advance.
2. Connect and start.
3. Review the student's nondiscriminatory evaluation and current levels of performance.
4. Share your thoughts and take into account the parents' and student's thoughts about resources, priorities, and concerns.
5. Share each others' visions and great expectations and attainment of equal opportunity, independent living, full participation, and economic self-sufficiency.
6. Consider the interaction of the proposed and prioritized goals, services, and placement.
7. Translate priorities into written goals or outcomes.
8. Determine the nature of special education, related services, least restrictive placement, and supplementary aids and services.
9. Determine appropriate modifications in assessment and take into account the five special factors that we described in chapter 6 (positive behavior supports, limited English proficiency, visual impairment and the use of Braille, hearing impairment and the benefits of learning from and with others with hearing impairments, and assistive technology).
10. Conclude the conference.

Look at Figure 10.3, summarizing these suggestions, and ask yourself: Does the school you work in, or are familiar with, follow these practices? If so, how would you describe the quality and consistency of these practices? If your school does not implement these practices, what suggestions do you have for how to foster family-professional partnerships?

Let's review briefly what you learned about families in chapters 1 through 4. There, you learned about the four components of the family system—characteristics, interactions, functions, and life cycle. You learned that each of the four components influences families' preferences for participation. You will want to bear each in mind as you prepare for and carry out a meeting with families to develop their children's individualized plans. Remember especially that culture plays an important role in influencing family preferences for the planning process (Geenen et al., 2001; Harry, 2008; Kalyanpur & Harry, 1999; Zhang & Bennett, 2003). We urge you to apply the partnership practice of *respecting* and *honoring diversity* when working with parents to make IEP/IFSP plans.

Prepare in Advance

- Appoint a service coordinator to organize the conference.
- Make sure evaluation has included all relevant areas, is complete, and has clearly synthesized results.
- Ask the family's preferences regarding the conference. Reflect on what you know according to the family systems consideration. Find out whom the family wants to invite.
- Arrange for a translator to attend the conference, if needed.
- Decide who should attend the conference, and include the student if appropriate. Discuss with the student his or her preferences about who should attend.
- Arrange a convenient time and location for the conference, based on family preferences.
- Help the family with logistical needs such as transportation and child care.
- Inform the family and students who are at least 14 years of age (in jargon-free language) orally and/or in writing about the following:
    - Purpose of the conference
    - Time and location of the conference
    - Names and roles of participants
    - Option to invite people with special expertise
- Exchange information in advance by giving the family and student the information they want before the conference.
- Encourage and arrange for the student, family members, and their advocates to visit optional educational placements for the student before the conference.
- Review the student's previous IFSP/IEP and document the extent to which each goal has been met. Identify factors and barriers that contributed most to these results.
- Request an informal meeting with any teachers or related service providers who will not attend the conference. Document and report their perspectives at the conference.
- Consider whether providing snacks is appropriate and possible, and make arrangements accordingly.

Connect and Start

- Greet the student, family, and their advocates.
- Share informal conversation in a comfortable and relaxed way.
- Serve snacks, if available.
- Share an experience about the student that was particularly positive or one that reflects the student's best work.

- Provide a list of all participants or use name tags if there are several people who have not met before.
- Introduce each participant, briefly describing his or her role in the conference.
- State the conference's purpose, review its agenda, and ask if additional issues need to be covered.
- Ask the participants how long they can stay, discuss the conference time frame, and, if needed to complete the agenda, offer to schedule a follow-up conference.
- Ask if family members want you to clarify their legal rights, and do so, if they request.

Review Formal Evaluation and Current Levels of Performance

- Give family members written copies of all evaluation results.
- Avoid educational jargon and clarify terms that puzzle the family, student, or their advocates.
- If a separate evaluation conference has not been scheduled, discuss evaluation procedures and tests and the results and implications of each.
- Invite families and other conference participants to agree or disagree with evaluation results and to state their reasons.
- Review the student's developmental progress and current levels of performance in each subject area or domain.
- Ask families if they agree or disagree with the stated progress and performance levels.
- Strive to resolve disagreements among participants using the Skilled Dialogue or other strategy, as discussed in Chapter 9.
- Proceed with the IFSP/IEP only after all participants agree about the student's current levels of performance.

Sharing Thoughts about Resources, Priorities, and Concerns

- Plan how all participants can share expertise and resources to create the most comprehensive support system possible in addressing priorities and responding to concerns.
- Ask participants to share their priorities.
- Encourage all participants to express their concerns about their own roles in supporting the student, especially in areas where they believe they will need support or assistance.
- Note the resources that all committee members can contribute.

FIGURE 10.3 (Continued).

Share Visions and Great Expectations

- If a MAPs process has been completed, share the results with everyone.
- If a MAPs process has not been completed, consider incorporating it into the conference.
- Encourage the student and family members to share their visions and great expectations for the future, as well as the student's strengths, gifts, and interests.
- Identify the student's and family's visions and great expectations as well as those of the professionals (those attending and absent).
- Express excitement about the visions and great expectations, and about commitment to goals and objectives (or outcomes) that will be planned at the conference.

Consider Interaction of Proposed Student Goals, Placement, and Services

- Assure the family that the decisions about the student's IFSP or IEP will be made together.
- State that interactive factors between the student's proposed goals, placement, and services will be examined carefully before final decisions are made.

Translate Priorities into Written Goals or Outcomes

- Discuss and prioritize the student's needs in light of the student's and family's visions, great expectations, strengths, interests, and preferences.
- Generate appropriate goals for all academic and functional areas that require specially designed instruction, consistent with stated great expectations, priorities, and MAPs process.
- Determine the evaluation criteria, procedures, and schedules for measuring the goals and how parents will be regularly informed.

Determine Nature of Services

- Identify placement options that reflect the least restrictive environment (e.g., regular class with necessary supports in the first option considered; close to student's home).
- Consider characteristics of placement options (e.g., building characteristics, staff and student characteristics).
- Specify supplementary aids/services and related services the student will receive to ensure appropriateness of the educational placement.
- Explain the extent to which the child will not participate in the general education program.

- Identify the supplementary aids/supports and related services the student will need to access education and achieve goals and objectives.
- Document and record the timeline for providing supplementary aids/services and related services.
- Discuss benefits and drawbacks of types, schedules, and modes of providing related services the student needs.
- Specify dates for initiating supplementary aids/services and related services, frequency, and anticipated duration.
- Share names and qualifications of all personnel who will provide instruction, supplementary aids/services, and related services.

Determine Modifications in Assessments and Special Factors

- Determine necessary modifications for the student to participate in state or districtwide assessments of student achievement.
- If the student is not able to participate in state or district assessment, provide a rationale and specify how the student will be assessed.
- Consider the five special factors identified in IDEA (for example, positive behavioral support, limited English proficiency, use of Braille, language and communication modes for people who are deaf or hard of hearing, and assistive technology), and make plans as needed for the student.
- Identify any other modifications or special factors that apply to the student, and develop appropriate plans to address those.

Conclude the Conference

- Assign follow-up responsibility for any task requiring attention.
- Summarize orally and on paper the major decisions and follow-up responsibilities of all participants.
- Set a tentative date for reviewing IFSP/IEP implementation.
- Identify preferred options for ongoing communication among all participants.
- Reach a consensus decision with parents on how they will be regularly informed of the student's progress toward the annual goals and the extent to which that progress is sufficient in achieving the goals by the end of the year.
- Express appreciation to all team members for their collaborative decision making.
- Affirm the value of partnership, and cite specific examples of how having a trusting atmosphere enhanced the quality of decision making.

Prepare in Advance. Families and educators frequently fail to prepare adequately for conferences. As we noted, the real work usually does not begin until everyone convenes, and even then parents are expected to sign pre-prepared IEPs.

When preparing for the conference, implement our suggestions from chapter 7 for building partnerships with families. Establishing trust at the outset is the foundation for all other partnership practices. Begin by communicating positively with families. Create a climate of respect, commitment, and equality from the start. By creating partnerships with families, you set the stage for meaningful preconference preparation.

Some schools convene a preconference meeting to share the results of the student's nondiscriminatory evaluation with families and to establish meaningful dialogue about the family's priorities for their child. Although sometimes informal, this preconference meeting respects the family's right to state their priorities and enables professionals and families to gather and consider relevant information before making any final decisions.

Before you attend an IEP conference, you may refer families to Parent to Parent and to Parent Training and Information Centers so they may acquire the emotional and informational resources they may need to feel confident and empowered at their conferences. The more you incorporate partnership practices—communicating effectively with families and respecting their preferences—during referral and evaluation, especially when the student is being evaluated for the first time for special education services, the more likely it is that partnerships will coalesce before the conference meeting.

Everything you have learned from chapters 1 through 10 can become part of your preconference preparation. But you should also consider four additional issues when preparing in advance:

- Designate a service coordinator.
- Invite and prepare participants (and students when appropriate).
- Take care of logistical considerations.
- Exchange information in advance.

Designate a Service Coordinator. Even though a service coordinator is required only for the IFSP, having a service coordinator can be just as useful when developing an IEP. The service coordinator's main responsibility at this stage is to ensure that preconference preparation is carried out and guided by students' and families' strengths, preferences, great expectations, and priorities. The service coordinator should also help other professionals monitor how they implement the student's IEP. Some families find that service coordinators block access to other professionals, which is not good practice. The coordinator should ensure access and communication.

Invite and Prepare Participants, Including the Student, when Appropriate. Give families information early so they can be prepared. Provide them with access to evaluation reports, including a report of prereferral interventions, a summary of the student's strengths and needs in each subject area, information on their and their child's legal rights, descriptions of various placement options and related services, student priorities and draft goals from the professionals' perspective, options for extracurricular activities, and information on transition services. Gather this information early so there is time to make needed arrangements or changes.

Consistent with IDEA and the practices we have described, you should learn a family's preferences for who should attend the conference, convenient times and places for scheduling, whether assistance with transportation or child care would be helpful, and the kinds of information the family wants in advance. Consult with the family in a face-to-face conference or by telephone. Do not rely on others to tell you what the family wants; others may contribute, but families are the experts.

Learn which family members want to participate—fathers, grandparents, brothers and sisters, cousins, live-in significant others, godparents, or other people who have family-like relationships. Remember that friends of the student or family, people who can foster community membership (such as soccer coaches, scout leaders, and religious education teachers), and people who can mentor the student to explore hobbies or career choices (such as musicians, business leaders, and mechanics) could participate and enhance the quality of education (Turbiville, Turnbull, Garland, & Lee, 1996). Urge families to identify not just those people they usually include in conferences, but also others with unique resources and expertise.

When determining whether a student should participate in the IEP meeting, consider the partnership principle of equality. Equality involves sharing power and fostering empowerment, especially a student's choice of whether to participate in the conference. In chapter 4, we discussed self-determination and adolescents. As you learned previously, IDEA provides that a student may participate in IEP meetings "whenever appropriate," transition planning begins no later than age 16, and parents' IDEA rights transfer to students when they are 18 (age of majority). IDEA presumes that transition-age students will participate in their IEP conferences.

Although some parents feel their child should be involved in school-to-adulthood transition planning wherever possible

(Goupil, Tasse, Garcin, & Dore, 2002), past experiences may discourage the students from participating:

> When I go to them meetings, I get really frustrated because it seems like if you do something wrong, you know, which everybody does, they exaggerate it. I mean you tell them the basic of what happened, but they, like, exaggerate it. Teachers are good at that. They should be salesmen. (Morningstar, Turnbull, & Turnbull, 1995)

There have been efforts to encourage student participation at their IEP meeting (Hammer, 2004; Martin et al., 2006; Test et al., 2004; Wood et al., 2004), and there is recent movement to encourage students to lead the meeting (Arndt, Konrad, & Test, 2006; Barrie & McDonald, 2002; Childre & Chambers, 2005; Mason et al., 2004). When older students attend their own IEP meetings, parents report that they themselves understand significantly more and feel more comfortable contributing (Martin, Marshall, & Sale, 2004). There is a significant body of research demonstrating how educators can develop the self-determination skills of students with disabilities (Algozinne, Browder, Karvonen, Test, & Wood, 2001).

You will find many ways to involve students in educational decision making and transition planning (Martin et al, 2006; Mason et al., 2004; Van Dycke, Martin, & Lovett, 2006). As you learned in chapter 9, a student's or family's cultural values may be inconsistent with special education practices, including student involvement in conferences. Cultures differ in the value they place on child and adolescent autonomy. For example, the Taiwanese mother of a junior high school student was frustrated at the IEP conference because the professionals were more concerned with her daughter's preferences than with the mother's viewpoint:

> During the meeting [the education counselor] only asked my daughter what she wanted to do in the next year, and she didn't ask me. After she asked my daughter, then she gave me the papers and said, "Okay, sign your name." That was really frustrating. (Beach Center, 2000)

A Hispanic mother agreed with this view when she added her comments:

> I think that basically the cultural differences are not being considered in these IEP meetings. And here in the United States it is like you always ask the child first, and for us it's very important for us as a parent to participate . . . I know that it's not on their mind, but it really hurts our feelings . . . why we were one way at home (in asserting parental authority) and the teachers treated them in a different way (offering them more choices). (Beach Center, 2000)

You should consider cultural appropriateness of involving students in conferences and help students develop participation skills. By honoring the partnership practice of cultural diversity throughout the planning process, you earn trust from parents and students.

Take Care of Logistical Considerations. Every conference requires logistical considerations such as scheduling, committee size, transportation, and child care. Consider the size of the student's IEP/IFSP team. Some parents prefer a limited number of people at the conference, but others want everyone with a stake in their child's education to attend. Smaller conferences can be less intimidating and more focused. Larger conferences include wider ranges of expertise and provide opportunities for all professionals to develop the student plans for which they are responsible.

Time is another major logistical issue. As you learned previously, there usually is not enough time for making decisions about the student's program and placement. Clearly, the place to cut corners is not during the conference itself. You and other professionals might ask your school to (1) hire a permanent floating substitute so teachers are free to address conference tasks, (2) use administrators and other school staff to provide educators with additional release time, (3) assign weekly shared prep periods for staff collaboration, (4) create early-release days reserved only for collaborative activities, or (5) purchase laptop computers for all teachers to use in developing an IEP/IFSP (Johnson, Proctor, & Corey, 1995; Snell & Janney, 2000; Walther-Thomas, Korinek, McLaughlin, & Williams, 2000; West, 1990). You may want to hold a series of planning meetings so teachers and families feel no pressure to "get everything in" during a single meeting.

Attendance and punctuality are important elements of an effective IEP meeting. There may be a good reason if professionals are absent, arrive late, or leave early from meetings, but these behaviors may lead families to believe that the professionals disrespect them (Lo, 2008; Salas, 2004). When preparing for the IEP/IFSP meeting, make sure that all the required and important participants are available for the entire meeting and that there is ample time to plan and make decisions.

Exchange Information in Advance. By exchanging information in advance, you and your IEP partners can use conference time to clarify issues and make decisions. Without advance information, you may spend most of your time reviewing information, generating ideas, and perhaps rushing decisions. Be careful to distinguish between preparation and predetermination. Parents are dissatisfied with educators who predetermine decisions and interfere with their ability to make decisions for their children.

Exchange information in advance to minimize cultural differences between families and professionals. A family's religious beliefs are sometimes overlooked as a component of cultural difference, as one teacher noted:

> Sam's expression was wide-eyed when the psychologist who was to test him walked through the door. Sam was not going to perform well for this man, I could tell. I was teaching in a private Christian school, and Sam's parents were fundamentalist Christians. The psychologist was dressed, to put it kindly, casually and very differently from the dress code we had at our school. . . . A simple phone call to Sam's administrator, myself, or his parents to ask what might prove offensive to the family's religious beliefs would have established a better rapport with all concerned and provided Sam with an opportunity to perform to his capacity during assessment. (Beach Center, 2000)

Connect with the Parents and Student, and Then Start.

It is important to attend to the partnership principles in all of your work, but especially to the principle of communication. When you practice effective communication (chapter 8), you can direct a team toward the shared, and IDEA-required, goal of creating a program for the student's appropriate education in the least restrictive environment.

It is both polite and important to introduce everyone and describe the conference format and time line. Be sure to establish that each professional values the family's contributions and wants to form a partnership. Doing so will emphasize equality, an important partnership principle. Key practices of equality are avoiding hierarchies, sharing power, and fostering empowerment. To equalize power, start by creating a warm, relaxed atmosphere defined by the positive communication skills we discussed in chapter 8. Betsy Santelli, the parent of two daughters enrolled in a gifted program, described the importance of informal sharing:

> Although anxious at first about what our roles might be, Jim and I were delighted to find a real willingness and genuine interest on the part of the staffing team to learn from us about Maren and Tami's unique and special qualities as well as those of our family. Before any assessment results were shared or questions were asked, time was allowed for informal sharing among all of us as people—not professionals, not parents—just people. Those few minutes helped set the stage for the comfortable sharing of information that followed and continues to this day. By starting with a climate of trust, you will make great progress toward establishing partnership with families. If you genuinely connect with families,

you all but guarantee a successful conference. (Beach Center, 2000)

Review the Student's Nondiscriminatory Evaluation and Current Levels of Performance.

As we pointed out previously, IDEA requires that each IFSP and IEP describe the present level of academic achievement and functional performance (20 U.S.C. Sec. 1414 (d)(1)(A)). This information should come directly from the student's nondiscriminatory evaluation and is the foundation for the student's individualized plan for an appropriate education (20 U.S.C. Sec. 1414(c)(1)(A) and (B)).

You can proceed in two ways. First, you can use the conference to review the formal evaluation results and develop the actual plan. Of course, you will want the family and other team members to agree to this approach. Second, you can hold a separate meeting (before the conference) to review evaluation results.

When you share evaluation information, you have an opportunity to practice the partnership principles of communication, respect, and commitment. Parents may feel vulnerable or overwhelmed when hearing the information and its educational implications. Your sharing must establish or maintain the highest levels of trust. Decisions about when and how to report evaluation results should be based on family and professional preferences.

Share Your Thoughts and Take into Account the Parents' and Student's Thoughts About Resources, Priorities, and Concerns.

The referral and evaluation process can be a time for families, teachers, related service providers, friends, and other interested people (such as physicians) to identify their resources, priorities, and concerns. Identifying and agreeing to share resources, priorities, and concerns should start during the evaluation process and continue during the conference. The goal is to link evaluation information with outcomes for students and families.

How can you ensure that parents do not feel brushed aside or rushed during conferences? After reviewing the evaluation and performance information, offer family members adequate time to express their ideas fully. Be sure to offer them and the other participants a genuine opportunity to make their respective special contributions.

Next, identify the general priorities for the student before identifying specific goals and objectives. By doing so, all participants will help ensure that the student's goals and objectives reflect the team's individual and collective priorities.

Then discuss the participants' general concerns or potential barriers to the goals and objectives—for example, are there resources available within the team or from the family, school, or community to satisfy agreed-upon priorities? A general educator who is concerned about individualizing the curriculum for a student with a learning disability may need support from a consulting special education teacher. Similarly, teachers anxious about attending to the needs of students who are supported by medical equipment may receive instruction and support from parents, the school nurse, and other specialists. By discussing special and common resources and concerns, team members can support each other. Partnership means that no one on the team must address concerns in isolation.

Share Each Other's Visions and Great Expectations and Attainment of Equal Opportunity, Independent Living, Full Participation, and Economic Self-Sufficiency.

Typically, people are more excited and motivated when working for something that genuinely sparks their hopes and dreams. A vision statement allows families and their children to express their hopes and concerns for the future; it helps generate enthusiasm and inspiration for the future; and it is a valuable investment of time because it helps determine priorities, shape decisions, and generate priority goals for a student's IEP and the child's and family's IFSP.

As you share your visions and great expectations, do so in light of the four outcomes that IDEA declares as the nation's goals for people with disabilities: equal opportunity, independent living, full participation, and economic self-sufficiency.

And remember to agree on a plan for following up and holding each other accountable. The group is only as strong as its weakest link; when everyone on the team supports everyone else and expects everyone else to do as they agree, then there is a sort of peer-support and peer-monitoring that will keep everyone working in the same direction and for the same outcomes.

The Process of Making Action Plans and Vision Statements.

The making action plans (MAPs) process is one of the most effective ways to develop vision statements. MAPs is a practical, positive way to provide open-ended, intimate, and personalized views of the student and family. The process portrays the student within the full context of his or her life at home and school and within the community. The MAPs process is used frequently for students with severe disabilities (Mount & O'Brien, 2002; Thousand, Villa, & Nevin, 2002).

Those attending MAPs meetings should include the student, parents, other family members, student and family friends, educators, and others interested in making the school and community as close to the student's preferences

as possible. MAPs gatherings are usually held in comfortable surroundings—often the student's home or some other community setting—to encourage connections and relationships. The My Voice box on the next page illustrates these seven questions that guide the MAPs process.

The order of the questions can vary, but their purpose remains consistent: to stimulate dynamic, open-ended discussion among everyone concerned about the student's well-being. As you learned in chapter 6, the IEP content should directly relate to the four outcomes in IDEA: equality of opportunity, independent living, full participation, and economic self-sufficiency.

In a MAPs gathering, experienced facilitators guide discussion and encourage brainstorming to generate as many creative ideas as possible. As ideas are shared, facilitators record them on a large poster board.

Ideally, the MAPs process should be complete before holding an IEP/IFSP conference. If the family has already completed a MAPs process, you may want to devote the initial portion of the conference to reviewing the MAPs plan. If the family has not engaged in a MAPs process, you might offer to incorporate it into the initial conference, recognizing that you cannot complete that activity and develop a full IEP/IFSP at the same time. If the family and professionals mutually decide to forgo the complete MAPs process, they still need to make time for sharing visions, great expectations, and strengths. One student described the benefits of sharing:

> I have never in my life heard a group of adults sit around and say anything positive about me. That list is exactly right. (Kroeger, Leibold, & Ryan, 1999, p. 6)

As we discussed in chapters 4 and 9, if it is consistent with family preferences, you can promote opportunities for self-determination when you encourage older students to take an active role in this process.

The MAPs process can strengthen the partnership among professionals and family members. When everyone works as partners, dreams can indeed come true. One parent, Sara, recalled that church was a focal point in her family's life. It was important for Kimberley, her daughter with cerebral palsy and visual impairments, to go to the toddler class in the church program with her twin sister, Abigail.

> By identifying this church activity as being of prime importance to our family's happiness and well-being . . . our family was able to shape the attitudes and obtain the tools necessary to make this dream a reality. The service providers recognized our concern, saw it as part of our long-term vision for our child and family, and helped us work out ways to achieve our goals. (Squires, 2000, p. 11)

MY VOICE
A Teacher Speaks Out and Recommends MAPs

As a special education teacher, I have attended many team meetings. Unfortunately, many of these meetings have not focused on identifying a vision that is shaped by the student and family's values. I think of one of my first IEP meetings as a student teacher. The meeting started with the special education teacher handing the parents a copy of a "tentative" IEP and asking, before the parents had even had a chance to review the IEP, "Do you have any concerns about enhancing your child's education?" It seemed as though this was the parents' only chance to present their vision—and they seemed noticeably flustered and uncertain of how to respond. And, as the meeting progressed, it seemed that even if the parents could articulate their vision on such short notice, they would not have much influence. It was communicated to the parents that they were expected to just sign off on the IEP the way it was. Any concerns that were brought up were either answered with, "Well he's been doing really well with that," or "Yes, that's in there."

When I took a class on family-professional partnerships, I learned about the making action plans (MAPs) process. I was so excited about how MAPs could be used to develop a vision to guide the IEP and ensure that the team came together to articulate their vision and that this vision could be used to guide the student's IEP. I now use the MAPs process with all of my students— I try to schedule a time with each family to go through this process. It helps me learn more about my students and their families. And, it also helps build trusting partnerships with families because they know that I want to learn about their hopes and dreams. And, it seems like we all achieve better outcomes—better relationships and outcomes for students. Sometimes it can be time consuming, but I think it is more important to invest the time up front!

Questions to guide the MAPs process:

- What is the student's history or story?
- Who is the student?
- What are the student's strengths, interests, gifts, and talents?
- What are the student's priorities?
- What are the dreams for this student?
- What are the nightmares for this student?
- What is the plan of action?

Take Action!

- Use the MAPs process to build trusting partnerships with families, a shared vision for the team, and to guide the development of the IEP and student goals. Disregard how busy you are; instead, think about how investing the time to build trusting partnerships up front can lead to better outcomes for everyone.
- Consider how you would feel if you went into an IEP meeting and it was not clear that your vision was respected or would be used to guide your child's education. Remember that communication and collaboration are essential to building a team— MAPs is a way to facilitate this communication and collaboration.

As the team's visions and great expectations become more concrete, the next step is to identify goals or outcomes that can transform the vision into a reality.

Consider the Interaction of Proposed and Prioritized Goals, Services, and Placement. Few aspects of educational decision making are more important than determining student outcomes, related services, supplementary aids/services, and placement. However, the sequence that some educators follow in determining services and placement may jeopardize development of appropriate, individualized plans for the student, sometimes excluding parents from decision making (Giangreco, 2001).

Once again, we urge you, as you and the parents and student consider goals, services, and placement, to keep in mind IDEA's four main outcomes—equality of opportunity, independent living, full participation, and economic self-sufficiency. It is not always apparent how a student's IEP relates to these "big" outcomes. That is so because many professionals now use computerized IEPs and because professionals and parents alike tend to focus on the "smaller" goals and objectives. Nonetheless, you and your parent partners need to keep them in mind and use "smaller" goals and objectives, decide about services, and determine placements in light of these four outcomes.

The immediate question is this: How can you ensure that parents feel like partners in planning and making decisions about their child's education, especially about these four outcomes and the lesser, subsumed ones? Giangreco (2001) proposes the following process in which families and professionals work together to discuss the child's goals, placement, and services:

- Determine the student's educational program by identifying student learning outcomes as well as supports needed to achieve these outcomes or goals.
- Discuss proposed educational placement options by examining how the placement conforms to the least restrictive environment requirements and the specific characteristics of the location (i.e., building accessibility).
- Determine services needed to support the proposed placement including nonspecialized support (i.e., paraprofessional) and specialized support (i.e., occupational therapy, school psychology services).
- Consider interactions between placement and services and discuss the impact and any implications.
- Finalize placement and services by comparing advantages and disadvantages of the different options.

Through this process, families and professionals work as partners, identifying and examining options and making final decisions. They can follow the process when (1) translating student priorities into written goals and objectives that constitute the student's individualized appropriate education and that can be justified as leading to the four overarching outcomes, (2) identifying what related services the student needs, (3) specifying the student's least restrictive placement, (4) specifying the supplementary aids and services that the student and his teachers will receive so he can participate in the general curriculum, (5) describing any necessary modifications to state and local assessments, and (6) addressing IDEA's five special considerations.

Translate Priorities into Written Goals or Outcomes.

IDEA requires the IEP to describe the student's present levels of academic achievement and functional performance (20 U.S.C. Sec. 1414 (d)(1)(A)(i)(I)). Only if the student takes alternate assessments that are aligned to alternate achievement standards must the student's IEP describe the benchmarks or short-term objectives that the IEP team prescribes. The IEPs of students who do not take the alternate assessments are not required to contain benchmarks or short-term objectives. IDEA does not prohibit the IEPs of these students from containing them; it simply does not require it to contain them.

In addition, the IEP of every student, including those in preschool and those who take the alternate assessment, must describe the student's measurable annual goals, including academic and functional goals (and others as the IEP team determines). In addition, the IEP of every student must describe how the student's progress toward meeting these annual goals will be measured and when periodic reports on the student's progress will be provided (20 U.S.C. Sec. 1414 (d)(1)(A)).

The measurable annual goals (and benchmarks and short-term objectives for students who will be using alternate assessments) shape the student's involvement and progress in the general curriculum; the way the school will respond to the student's academic and functional goals and other educational needs that result from the child's disability; the related services and supplementary aids and services that the student will receive; the extent, if any, that the student will not participate in the regular class and extracurricular and other nonacademic activities; and the nature and reason for alternate assessments (20 U.S.C. Sec. 1414 (d)(1)(A)).

Before discussing the student's goals, team members should identify their own priorities for the student. Those discussions will reflect the individual and collective priorities of the team. One mother, Sherry, described the IEP meeting of her high school son:

> We discussed as a group the goals we wanted my son to achieve. As a group, we came to the same conclusions as far as strategies to implement the goals we wanted my son to attain. The whole process was very beneficial to me as a parent. We all know what our role would be to help my son attain his goals. The program was a complete success as far as I am concerned. (Beach Center, 2000)

To begin translating the student's needs into measurable annual goals, the parents and other team members must ask: What are the most meaningful goals for this student? The question is shaped by the student's and family preferences; nondiscriminatory evaluation data related to the student's academic, developmental, and functional needs; the student's strengths and interests; and the team's visions, great expectations, and priorities. In partnership with families, you can begin translating the evaluation information, including the MAPs or vision statement, into meaningful goals for the student.

Before writing those goals, the IEP team would do well to ask, with respect to each goal, whether the goal represents

- Student and family visions and great expectations?
- Access to the general education curriculum and active participation in inclusive settings?
- The family's culture, values, and priorities?
- The student's interests, strengths, priorities, and challenges?
- Chronological age-appropriateness?
- A strong generalization probability?

- Enhancement of friendships, social opportunities, and membership?
- Enhancement of the child's and family's quality of life?
- A strong connection to future outcomes (e.g., lifelong habits, career, or other postsecondary opportunities) and to the general outcomes of equal opportunity, independent living, full participation, and economic self-sufficiency?

Answers to these questions will assist the team members in identifying the student's highest- and next-highest-priority goals. Team members may add to or modify these questions as they believe are desirable to secure the student's appropriate education in the least restrictive environment. They also may rank draft goals, discuss the rankings, and then set priorities.

The student's goals must be closely related to the general curriculum, which consists of three domains: academic, extracurricular, and other school activities (for example, field trips and dances). The team must consider access to and full or partial participation in each of the three domains of the general curriculum when formulating goals and objectives; it may not focus solely on academic skills. Areas often neglected in formulating student goals include peer group membership, friendships and other social relationships, and participation in extracurricular activities (Turnbull, Blue-Banning, & Pereira, 2000). Nonacademic opportunities related to a student's hobbies or leisure skills are equally important.

> Tony is a 17-year-old student with autism. He believes that "music is magic." Music was identified as an important subject to include on Tony's IEP. One of the objectives was to teach Tony to play a guitar. As the year progressed the music program and the guitar, as contrasted to the independent living and career-education programs, provided the spark for Tony to turn off the alarm clock and get out of bed every morning. (Beach Center, 2000)

If the goals are specific and personally relevant, the team members will be more accountable to each other for student progress.

Having discussed IEP goals for students, let's now turn our attention to IFSP and family (not infant-toddler) outcomes (Part C). IDEA requires that each family whose infant-toddler receives services must have an IFSP. The IFSP must describe the family's resources, priorities, and concerns relating to enhancing the infant-toddler's development (20 U.S.C. Sec. 1436(d)(2)).

The purpose of identifying family outcomes is not for professionals to assign duties to families but to guide professionals as they provide culturally (and personally) relevant supports and services to families and their infants and toddlers. Some family outcomes may be addressed during the family's typical routines such as enhancing the quality of family meals by teaching the young child how to eat independently. Ridgley and O'Kelley (2008) suggest that some family-identified outcomes cannot be addressed during the family's typical routines because they may require gathering information or obtaining additional resources and services. For example, one family's priority may be to explore child care options for their toddler and another family's priority may be to ensure a smooth transition during the grandparents' impending divorce.

Developing an IFSP is as important as specifying its outcomes. To partner with families to identify outcomes related to their quality of life, early intervention program planners almost invariably need to work with other professionals and agencies. The outcomes that educators and related service providers are prepared to address may differ from those requiring expertise or training from physicians and other health care providers, social workers, audiologists, psychologists, and occupational or physical therapists. Early educators should inform families about other agencies or service providers who could help them meet their outcomes. By referring families, you will demonstrate the partnership practice of professional competence. You do not need to have all the answers, but you should know where to find someone who does.

You should especially keep in mind the partnership principles entitled communication and respect. They will be particularly useful in addressing any discrepancies between family and professional opinions about goals, placement, and outcomes. By using communication skills from chapter 8 to resolve disagreements, you help families and professionals understand discrepancies and perhaps find common ground.

Determine the Nature of Special Education, Related Services, Least Restrictive Placement, and Supplementary Aids and Services. As you learned in chapter 6, the IDEA principle of the *least restrictive environment* presumes that each student with a disability will be educated with peers without disabilities to the maximum extent appropriate for the student (20 U.S.C. Secs. 1412 and 1414(d)). Indeed, IDEA provides that special education is a service, not a setting (20 U.S.C. Sec. 1400(c)). IDEA thus requires that students with disabilities have opportunities to participate in the same general curriculum that is available to their nondisabled peers. This academic general curriculum is based on content and performance standards that individual states develop for students at different grade levels.

Further, IDEA makes it clear that students also have a right to participate in extracurricular and other school activities, not just in the academic general education curriculum (20 U.S.C. Sec. 1414(d)(1)(A)(i)(bb)). And it makes it clear that the IEP team must document the extent, if any, that the student will not participate in these three domains (academics, extracurricular, and other school activities) (20 U.S.C. Sec. 144(d)(1)(A)). As we pointed out in chapter 6, this is the "mix and match" approach.

As you learned in chapter 7, support for inclusion by families varies (Duhaney & Salend, 2000; Erwin, Soodak, Winton, & Turnbull, 2001). Although more placement options are available now than ever before, many disagreements persist between parents and professionals over placement decisions. Consider the "wall" one parent faced when discussing her child's placement with professionals:

> They claimed that her disability was so severe that she could not make it anywhere else. So they have all the children with disabilities in this one classroom. And then they have an adjoining door to another classroom where typical children are. And they tried to convince me how wonderful the program was. They said, "look, there is a door that is open between children with disabilities and children that are typical." And my response was "you see the open door. But I see the wall between my child and the typical children." (Soodak & Erwin, 2000, p. 38)

Families do not always believe they have access to inclusive educational environments (Erwin & Soodak, 1995; Erwin et al., 2001; Hanson et al., 2000; Hanson et al., 2001). A study of experiences of parents of children with significant disabilities across three states showed that only two out of ten parents were offered inclusive placements for their children, and one of those parents was responsible for paying the tuition (the school district offered to pay tuition if the parent chose a self-contained placement) (Soodak & Erwin, 2000). Sadly, district or school personnel often send parents the message that their children are unwanted.

However, you have a legal duty to include and a professional duty to welcome students and their families into general education settings. They have a right to be there unless they cannot benefit from academic, extracurricular, or other general curriculum activities even with related services and supplementary aids and services. Ensuring that special education supports and services are provided is not enough. You should show parents as well as their children that they are valued members of the school community. Families hope to hear that their children are accepted. They are understandably alienated by professionals who consider their children burdens on teachers and classmates. It is not hard for families to perceive teachers' negative attitudes even if teachers do not give voice to them.

By acknowledging your own and others' professional competence while you, a family, and other professionals are discussing a student's educational placement, you can use the partnership practices of continuing to learn, setting great expectations, and providing a high-quality education. Together with families, the team can share and then make informed decisions about placement. During a conference you may be called upon to take into account another partnership principle, advocacy. Consider the real-life scenario in the Together We Can box on the next page.

IDEA requires a student's IEP to list supplementary aids and services the school will provide so the student will be able to participate in the general curriculum (academic, extracurricular, and other school activities) to the maximum extent appropriate for the student. This requirement reflects professionals' and families' concerns about securing program modifications and ensuring teacher competency for children's success in the least restrictive setting (Erwin et al., 2001; Fisher et al., 1998). See Figure 10.4 on p. 229.

Universal design for learning and positive behavioral supports are examples of aproaches that you will want to consider as these supports provide opportunities for partnership across the disciplines that they represent. Figure 10.4 defines and provides examples of supplementary aids and services. The student's IEP also must identify the individuals who will provide the supplementary aids and services.

Consider, for example, a high school freshman who has difficulty with English and math but not with science or social studies. When he is in English and has difficulty reading, the student can ask permission to leave class and go to the resource room to read, often with one-on-one support from his English teacher. The student knows what accommodations he needs and asks for them; they are clearly documented in his IEP. The result? The student's failing grades have become passing grades. He is successful in school and proud of his accomplishments. Given the fast-paced development of new technologies, families and educators will discover even more ways to provide individualized options for supplementary aids and services.

Many students may also require additional services and supports. IDEA requires the IEP team to identify the related services a student needs to benefit from special education. We identified those related services in Figure 6.3 in chapter 6. The IEP or IFSP must specify how often and in what way the related services will be provided. Team members may choose among a variety of service delivery models. These might include consulting with general education teachers, providing therapy within general education classrooms, and working with students in one-to-one arrangements or small groups (Thousand et al., 2002; Walther-Thomas et al., 2000).

If parents choose related services not included in the IEP/IFSP, they must pay for them and may use any insurance or federal benefits to which they are entitled. For example, if they qualify for Medicaid (health-related services for parents who meet federal low-income standards, and whose children qualify for Medicaid because of their disabilities), parents may seek reimbursement from the state Medicaid agency if services are not provided for in their child's IEP.

TOGETHER WE CAN
Gabe DeCicco Remains Included

At the Ben Samuels Children's Center at Montclair State University, a fully inclusive center serving children with and without disabilities from 3 months to 6 years of age, the DeCicco family had formed a strong partnership with their son Gabe's teacher, Erin Clark. Gabe, who was diagnosed with autism, had been a full-time member in Erin's class over the past three years. When it was time to transition to kindergarten, Gabe's parents wanted him to attend the same public school where his older sister would be starting sixth grade. Given his highly positive experiences at the Children's Center, both parents unquestionably wanted an inclusive kindergarten classroom with appropriate supports. But given the district's track record and previous conversations, the DeCiccos weren't so sure that their district team would be in agreement. To secure the result they wanted was going to require some advocacy work by Gabe's teachers on behalf of Gabe's parents.

Erin and the rest of the team worked closely with Gabe's parents to build their confidence and competence in being vocal advocates. Through coaching and conversations, the team worked closely with the DeCicco family to help them anticipate the district's likely objectives and be ready to offer evidence-based strategies to meet those objections. Some of the strategies were from the research literature; others were based on experience, such as finding Gabe a quiet space when noise was too overwhelming. Gabe's parents were successful and their son entered a full-time inclusive kindergarten class with the appropriate supports and services in the public school.

Take Action!

- Don't hesitate to advocate for the child and family. By agreeing to advocate with Gabe's parents, Gabe's teachers demonstrated the partnership element known as advocacy.
- Treat the family as equals. By providing Gabe's parents with knowledge of evidence-based strategies, Gabe's teachers demonstrated the partnership element known as equality.
- Respect the family's preferences. Gabe's family had good reason to want another full-inclusion program for him. Their preferences were reasonable and Gabe's educators properly honored them.
- Commit yourself to the child and family. That's what the teachers had been doing all along; it would have been a violation of the commitment element of partnership for them to back down in the face of a school district objection to integration.

Determine What, If Any, Appropriate Modifications the Student Needs to Participate in State and District Assessment and Take into Account the Five Special Factors. As we noted in chapter 6, the general academic curriculum sets performance standards for all students, and NCLB requires periodic state or local assessments of all students to determine how well they have mastered the curriculum. The purpose of including students with disabilities in these assessments is to hold schools accountable for improving educational results.

Accordingly, each student's IEP must describe all individual appropriate accommodations that are necessary to measure the student's academic achievement and functional performance (20 U.S.C. Sec. 1414(d)(1)(A)(VI)). If the student's IEP team determines that the student should take an alternate assessment, the IEP must state why the student cannot participate in the regular assessment and why the alternate assessment that the team selects is appropriate for the student.

Teachers of students with severe disabilities have suggested ways to carry out alternate assessments (Ysseldyke & Olsen, 1999). These include observations, interviews or surveys, record reviews, and tests. For example, you can assess students' academic or functional literacy skills by interviewing or surveying people who are regularly involved with them, using checklists of functional skills. You should relate your assessment to meaningful community settings, to a student's progress, measured across time, in those settings, and then provide integration rather than testing discrete, isolated skills. Parents report satisfaction with the use of alternative assessments for their children with severe disabilities, with satisfaction being the strongest among parents of young children and when academic goals are being addressed (Roach, 2006).

During a conference you may be called on to apply many of the partnership practices. This is more likely to occur when service providers and educators disagree about who pays for related services. The Change Agents Build Capacity box on page 229 illustrates the advocacy principle

| FIGURE **10.4** | **Supplementary aids and services.** |

Domain	Definition	Examples
Universal design for learning	Modifications to how curriculum is presented or represented or to the ways in which students respond to the curriculum	Digital Talking Book formats, advance organizers, video or audio input/output
Access	Modifications to the community, campus building, or classroom to ensure physical and cognitive access	Curb cuts, wide doors, clear aisles, non-print signs
Classroom ecology	Modifications to and arrangements of features of the classroom environment that impact learning	Seating arrangement, types of seating, acoustics, lighting
Educational and assistive technology	Technology that reduces the impact of a person's impairment on his or her capacity	Calculator, augmentative communication device, computer
Assessment and task modifications	Modifications to time or task requirements (but not content or material) to assist in participation in assessment or educational task	Extended time, scribe, note taker, oral presentation
Teacher, paraprofessional, or peer support	Support from another person to participate in instructional activities	Peer buddy, paraeducator, teacher

CHANGE AGENTS BUILD CAPACITY

Ethical Duties and Partnership Principles

When you are a teacher you may be confronted with difficult situations. You may find yourself in situations with school or district personnel who may not share your value of creating a partnership with families. Torn between the child and your employer, you may confront an ethical challenge.

You have learned in chapters 6 and 9, IDEA provides that a student has rights to a special education, related services, supplementary aids and services, all to be delivered in the least restrictive environment. You also learned in chapter 6 that the Council for Exceptional Children has a code of ethics. Those are powerful tools if you confront an ethical challenge.

Assume you are working in a school in which your 3-year-old student had not received occupational therapy for a couple of months because a therapist could not be found to replace one who has been on maternity leave. The child had been making steady progress when occupational therapy was provided in your classroom during cooking, art, and other daily activities. The school administrators maintain that it is difficult and costly to find a substitute occupational therapist. They become mulish. You want to

stand up for the child but you also don't want to become adversarial; you need and like your job and want to be around next year to carry on your work. What do you do?

Take Action!

- Begin by reminding the district's personnel that their primary obligation is to the child. Call attention to IDEA and the CEC Code of Ethics. Now you are demonstrating the partnership principle of commitment.
- Advise the child's parents that you are taking that stand. Now you are communicating with the parents and advocating for the child and family.
- Offer to call the therapist who is on leave to learn some strategies you can use while she is away from her duties. Now you are enlarging your professional competence.
- Acknowledge that the school district faces various challenges. Now you are treating your colleagues with respect without conceding that it is agreeable for the child to be without a necessary related service.

FIGURE **10.5**   Creating partnerships through trust building.

Partnership Principles and Practices	Issues	Actions Leading to Distrust	Actions Leading to Trust
Communication: Listen.	You are working with parents who have had past negative professional interactions; they're angry.	Tell parents that you are not the one who committed past mistakes, and you do not appreciate their taking it out on you.	Listen emphatically to their experiences; invite suggestions on making the IEP conference as supportive as possible.
Respect: Affirm family strengths.	You are developing an IFSP with parents whom you believe emotionally neglect their toddler.	Ask the parents to explain why they don't say kind things about their child and blame the parents indirectly at the conference for being the cause of their child's low self-esteem.	Highlight one or more positive contributions that the parents make to their child; alert them to community resources (including Parent to Parent) that provide parenting support and information.
Professional Competence: Set High Expectations.	A gifted student says her goal in to get a scholarship to Harvard.	Discourage the student by emphasizing the excess expense that the scholarship is unlikely to cover.	Collaborate with the student and family to research scholarship options; locate a community mentor who graduated from Harvard to provide admissions advice.
Equality: Foster empowerment.	A family wants an adolescent with mental retardation to attend a community college. You and other team members do not think it is a feasible transition goal.	Redirect the conversation and ignore family members' preferences; talk with them about vocational training.	Contact community colleges and find out about their admissions policies and accommodations for persons with disabilities.
Commitment: Be sensitive to emotional needs.	The parents are very worried and sad that their child with multiple disabilities has no friends.	Inform the parents that the IEP focuses on skill development and then consider adding a specific goal, such as turn taking to the child's IEP.	Have all IEP team members share vision, goals, and strategies for increasing the child's social connections and friendships.
Advocacy: Prevent problems.	A grandparent and mother (who has a history of chronic drug abuse) attend the IEP meeting; the grandmother criticizes her daughter and preempts her contributions.	Minimize the mother's role in the IEP process. Address your comments to the child's grandmother. Assume that a mother with a history of drug abuse probably does not care about her child and is not capable of making worthwhile contributions.	Reflect on the mother's strengths and let her know the positive things that she is doing or can do. Point out the grandmother's strengths and express your desire to work together as a team.

and related practices of preventing problems, keeping your conscience primed, and pinpointing and documenting problems. Remember, the student's priorities are the primary consideration, not the availability or cost of related services.

Conclude the Conference. To conclude the conference, you should synthesize the family's and professionals' recommendations and develop an action plan for follow-up responsibility, as shown in Figure 10.3.

Acknowledge and affirm contributions from the family and others, express great expectations for ongoing collaboration in implementing the plan, and encourage the family to contact other members with follow-up questions or suggestions. You should do all this because you want to end the conference with enhanced appreciation for the team's shared commitment and hard work. In the end, what counts is what you do for the student and the family and, equally important, how you do it. That's the point of Figure 10.5.

REVISITING MARIA, ELOISA, AND HENRIQUE HERNANDEZ

Let's assume that, at Maria's forthcoming IEP meeting, all the individuals required to attend are there, they are not rushed, and they have taken the first three of the ten steps we recommend for an effective IEP conference. Let's also assume that Maria herself attends.

Finally, let's assume there has been a significant change in the attitudes of district personnel and their values. Instead of concentrating so much on the academic outcomes for Maria, they are now much more concerned about her social skills. Instead of having one approach that must fit all students, they are flexible and truly individualize for her. How will a disinterested outside observer know there has been a change, and how will the change make a difference for Maria?

The change will be obvious when the educators ask Maria's parents to state their thoughts about how the district will use its resources, set priorities, and respond to Maria's and her parents' concerns. It will be obvious when the educators, Maria, and her parents share their visions for her future—her years in middle school, secondary school, and beyond. It will be obvious when everyone suggests and then agrees

on priorities, develop goals to implement the priorities, determine the services Maria will receive, and confirm the modifications in statewide assessments.

What difference will all that make for Maria? She will be enrolled in at least one general education academic class (English), with support; she will be invited to participate in at least one extracurricular activity; and she will be paired with students who don't have disabilities so she can participate with them in other school activities. In a word, she will have full and partial inclusion in each of the three domains of school life.

At the end of the school year, her social skills will be well polished, her self-confidence strong, her friendship networks robust, and her academic skills improved to the point that she may not need to have an alternate assessment of her progress.

Looking into the future, Maria will have been prepared so that she can take advantage of the equal opportunities she has a right to and the outcomes that IDEA declares: independent living, full participation, and economic self-sufficiency. Her team and her IEP will deliberately point to those outcomes; there will be a partnership now that will secure the long-term results that Maria and her parents rightfully expect.

SUMMARY

After describing and distinguishing the differences in IDEA's requirements related to an IEP and IFSP, we described how you can create and enhance a trusting partnership with parents by applying recommended practices, keeping in mind IDEA's four overarching outcomes, and taking into account any cultural differences that might exist.

IDEA REQUIREMENTS

- Part B, ages 3 through 21
- Part C, birth to 3
- Transition services and IEPs
- Transition services and IFSPs
- Research on partnerships
- IDEA's original intent
- Research on partnerships
- Cultural influences
- Research, culture, and partnerships

CREATING AND STRENGTHENING TRUST: TEN STEPS

- Prepare in advance.
- Connect and start.
- Review the student's nondiscriminatory evaluation and current levels of performance.
- Share your thoughts and take into account the parents' and students' thoughts about resources, priorities, and concerns.
- Share each others' visions and great expectations and attainment of equal opportunity, independent living, full participation, and economic self-sufficiency.
- Consider the interaction of proposed and prioritized goals, services, and placement.
- Translate priorities in written goals or outcomes.
- Determine the nature of special education, related services, least restrictive placement, and supplementary aids and services.
- Determine appropriate modifications in assessments and take into account five special factors.
- Conclude the conference.

LINKING CONTENT TO YOUR LIFE

Your contributions in the IEP or IFSP process may be one of the most important and lasting activities that shape your role as a professional. There is no better time to strengthen the partnership you are creating with families. Think about the following questions and consider the qualities and skills you could bring to this process. One of the best ways to reflect on these questions is to think about goal setting and transitions in your own life.

- What was a significant life transition that you experienced and how did it impact your life? How did planning and goal setting (or the lack of these factors) influence the outcome?
- How would you want parents to describe your participation and support during the individualized planning process for their child?
- What do you think might be challenging for you during IEP or IFSP meetings and why?

CHAPTER 11

Meeting Families' Basic Needs

RYAN, MARY, AND JOHN FRISELLA

You may have heard the proverb, "It takes a village to raise a child." The proverb teaches that a child's family, alone, does not and indeed cannot do everything their child needs. The family needs support, too.

Mary and John Frisella could well have adopted that proverb as they raised their son, Ryan. Ryan was born with cerebral palsy. It has impaired his mobility and fine motor skills, but not his spirit nor his mind. It also has not altered his family's high expectations for him and need to marshal a vast network of "villagers."

It has not been inexpensive to address Ryan's medical needs. Within the last half-decade, he has had surgery on both legs and received physical therapy and occupational therapy. Although he had some physical therapy in school, he had most of it, and most occupational therapy, outside of Pershing Middle School and Patrick Henry High School. Although the state-funded California Children's Services program paid for those therapies, thus relieving his parents of a tremendous and continuous burden, his school counselors and teachers had to accommodate to him according to the protocols from Ryan's therapists. Meeting Ryan's basic physical-health needs meant that his therapists, educators, and parents had to be partners in and outside of school.

So, what did his schools do to meet his and his family's basic needs? It is unclear whether any of his primary school teachers told him about Wheelchair Sports, operated by the city's park and recreation agency, but he obtained a flyer from that agency, joined the program, and soon became a trophy winner. His parents also participated in that program, deriving much emotional happiness from his delight in racing and learning more about his capacities and about accommodations. His high school counselor, Nancy Regas, advised him about his academic courses and especially about how to transfer from one class to another. Together with Mary and Ryan and other teachers, Nancy helped develop an IEP that allowed him additional time to go from one class to another. Sometimes, he walked from class to class, and sometimes he used his wheelchair. But he always needed some extra time and Nancy made sure all of his teachers knew about that accommodation. Similarly, his high school's nurse, Susan Efting, was been more than willing to let Ryan use the restroom in her

office when a more-distant restroom was occupied or difficult for Ryan to get to in the short amount of time he had between classes. These professionals reduced any feelings of anxiety Ryan's parents had about his high school years and offered information on learning and mobility skills that would benefit Ryan at college and in his community.

Although each of these educators formed "the village" that helped Mary, John, and Ryan as he spent four years at Patrick Henry High School, Mary believes, and Ryan concurs, that one program in school and one out of school have made a huge difference in his life.

Ryan's teachers knew that their resources—time and money—were limited; they knew Ryan could benefit from services outside of school, so they referred him to a community-based program entitled What's Next? It is a "peer mentoring" program operated by older adults with disabilities for younger adults and teenagers. Transition from school entails a range of challenges: transportation around a large, spread-out metropolis; attendance at any one of the many excellent universities in San Diego; interviewing for and landing a job; and knowing your rights against disability-based discrimination and to the federal and state benefits you learned about in chapter 6. Despite all Ryan received in school, he benefited from a program that operated outside of his school and addressed challenges Ryan would face after he graduated. By combining school-based and community-based programs, Ryan's teachers solidified their partnership with him and his parents—they treated them as equals and with respect, giving them choices about what to do; they advocated for him and helped him learn to advocate for himself; and they proved they were committed to his life after high school.

think about it

- Do educators' have a professional or ethical duty to help families meet their own basic needs?
- Is this duty inconsistent with their roles in educating students to be successful in academic, extracurricular, and other school activities?
- Or is this duty—assuming it exists, as Ryan's teachers, counselors, and health assistants believe it does—entirely consistent with their duty to "educate" him?
- Who is in your "village" and what benefit do you receive when other villagers help you or your family meet your basic needs?

:: INTRODUCTION

You learned in chapters 1 through 4 that many families face such difficult challenges that it is very hard for them to concentrate as much on their child's education as educators do and want them to do. These challenges can range from loneliness, isolation, and a general lack of knowledge of community resources to systemic challenges associated with family finances and abuse and neglect of their children. As a teacher, what is your role in addressing these family difficulties that are not *directly* related to education but are *indirectly* related to the success of children and youth in their school experiences?

Although your job is focused on children's education, you can be a partner with families by also knowing and communicating with them about helpful community, state, and national resources. In this chapter, you will learn that, to support families as they support their children, you will want to have resources at your fingertips to support families' basic needs—emotional, informational, financial, and safety. You will learn how you can be a partner with other educators, including social workers, school psychologists, and counselors, who can help families meet their basic needs by also applying the seven partnership principles. We encourage you to build trust with families by considering each family's individual needs, strengths, and preferences, particularly in situations that differ from your own. When providing resources to address families' basic needs, remember the partnership principle of commitment and, in particular, (1) being sensitive to families' emotional needs, (2) being available and accessible, and (3) going above and beyond.

Before addressing these three strategies, we want to provide one caveat. You can best use them if, first, you determine whether a family either prefers to address their basic needs from support within their family system or is open and even eager to receive support from others, including educators such as yourself. Although some families look outside their family system for support, others seek this kind of support from within their own family. In chapter 2, you learned about the importance of all family subsystems. Think about how different family members could be rich sources of support, particularly because they are familiar with and part of the family context. Within-family support is an essential source of problem solving, especially when caregiving expectations and practices are culturally determined.

We especially encourage you to recall what you learned about cohesion in chapter 2. Some families have very close emotional bonds; their family relationships are tight and their resistance to assistance by people outside the family may be high. You will do well not to assume what is right or helpful for a particular family but rather to ask families whether it might be helpful to them to have access to outside resources. Our experience is that many families are open to and eager to secure support from outside the family. When families are interested in receiving information about resources, you can cultivate trusting partnerships with them by providing resources to address their unmet basic needs related to (1) emotional support, (2) informational support, (3) economic support, and (4) support to address abuse and neglect.

:: RESOURCES FOR EMOTIONAL SUPPORT

Emotional support involves spending time with others, feeling cared about by others, feeling encouraged, and having a sense of being understood. You will probably encounter families who express needs to talk with other families who have a child with a disability in order to address needs such as:

- Feeling as if they are not alone
- Having hope for the future
- Sharing feelings about the "trials and triumphs" related to their child's special needs
- Getting practical guidance about how to resolve challenges
- Finding out about community resources (i.e., physicians, dentists, religious organizations, recreational options) that welcome children and youth with disabilities and their families

Two types of programs—Parent to Parent programs and parent support groups—are uniquely geared to addressing the emotional needs of families. Although these programs are especially helpful in addressing emotional needs, they also provide information, as you will learn later in this chapter.

Parent to Parent Programs. An excellent way to enable families to obtain emotional support is to connect them with other families who share similar experiences (Ainbinder et al., 1998; Irey et al., 2001; Singer et al., 1999). A widespread and valued type of one-to-one emotional support is called *Parent to Parent*. Statured programs are run by parents for parents. No two statewide programs are exactly alike. There are 34 statewide programs and hundreds of substate programs; there is at least one Parent to Parent program in every state. Approximately 155,000 parents are matched annually with more than 7,000 trained support parents (DiVenere, 2009). A manual that describes best practices in statewide programs is available in the Parent to Parent section of the Beach Center's website (www.beachcenter.org).

Parent to Parent programs establish one-to-one matches between a trained "support parent"—someone with experience as a parent of a child with a disability and who receives training related to the support parent role—and a "referred parent" who has a child with a disability and requests to talk to a parent with similar experience for the purpose of gaining support. The veteran parent provides emotional support (and information) to the referred parent. Consider how one parent who had a child with extensive medical needs (requiring 24-hour nursing support) benefited from the advice of another parent who "had been there":

> When Janelle was first born, I was overwhelmed. I was referred to Parent to Parent through our early intervention program. I knew I needed the medical professionals, but I didn't know how talking with Parent to Parent would benefit my family. . . . I connected with Nancy whenever I was having a particularly hard day. Nancy started attending our quarterly high-tech program care conferences during which Janelle's pediatrician, respite provider, nursing agency director and her care coordinator (assigned by the nursing agency) and Neal and I reported in on how Janelle was doing. We always reported that shifts were not being covered and that our filling-in was greatly affecting our family life. Parent to Parent's presence at these meetings were critical. Neal and I felt state Medicaid staff behaved differently when Parent to Parent was at the table . . . Nancy was open-minded which was way different from what we were experiencing with the nursing agencies. We had confidence in Nancy, she listened, and we as a family felt validated. (Beach Center transcript, 2008)

Typically, Parent to Parent programs serve parents without regard for the type of disability their children have. The matches between the "veteran" and the "new" parent are usually made on the basis of six factors: (1) a similar disability, (2) a family facing similar problems, (3) a veteran parent who can respond within 24 hours, (4) children with disabilities who are close to the same age, (5) families who live close by, and (6) families with a similar family structure (i.e., single parent).

The match often occurs just after the initial diagnosis that the child has a disability, usually within the neonatal intensive care unit of the hospital or shortly after the family begins exploring community services and supports. Most parents who are matched during the child's early years testify to the value of such early support, as this parent indicates:

> When our son with Down syndrome was born three years ago, my husband and I were shocked and devastated. . . . The couple that our Parent to Parent program sent us were such warm, optimistic, "normal" people, they gave us hope. About a year later, my husband and I were trained by our program to be support parents. The Parent-to-Parent office has many requests for visits from both father and mother. My husband was one of very few men willing to go through formal training. I have also found that support for non-English speaking families is hard to come by. It has been satisfying to me to be able to serve the Spanish-speaking community. (Beach Center on Disability, 2001)

Many referred parents become support parents as they share insights and practical know-how with newly referred parents. Support parents have not only the benefit of knowing they are helping others but also an opportunity to reinforce their own learning.

As contrasted to all the resource networks that you will learn about in this chapter, Parent to Parent is the one that has been most extensively researched in terms of identifying the outcomes for families and the specific evidence-based practices that lead to these outcomes. University researchers and members of Parent to Parent organizations have interviewed 400 parents nationally (Santelli, Singer, DiVenere, Ginsberg, & Powers, 1998; Singer et al., 1999). More than 80% of the parents found Parent to Parent programs to be helpful. Specifically, parents who used Parent to Parent services reported feeling better able to deal positively with their child and family situation, view their circumstances in a more positive light, and make progress on goals that were important to them. Two evidence-based practices derived from the research: The support parent makes at least four contacts within the first eight weeks of receiving the match, and the support parents receive training on topics such as communication skills, cultural diversity, and confidentiality (Parent to Parent USA, 2006).

Parent to Parent is also a resource for professionals. Listen to what a school administrator said about the unexpected impact of Parent to Parent on his staff:

> When the Parent to Parent program was established, we knew that it would be helpful for families, but we didn't realize until later that it would also be helpful to our staff. As professionals, we often feel inadequate because we cannot understand what families are going through because we haven't actually experienced what they have. Our staff became aware that the Parent to Parent program could fulfill a need for families that they could not. (Santelli et al., 2001, p. 66)

In order to find out about local and state Parent to Parent resources in your state, we encourage you to visit the Parent to Parent website (www.p2pusa.org) and click on the map at the bottom of the home page to get a national directory of programs. You will be able to get contact information as well as an overview of resources offered by various state programs. If a state or local program is not available in your area, send an e-mail to the Parent to Parent website to ask if the national leaders know of parents in your state who might be good resources for helping to arrange individualized matches among parents of children with disabilities when no programs are available. Once you have these resources at your fingertips, you will be ready to offer them to parents who share with you that they would like to talk with other parents as a way of gaining emotional support. If there are no parent support groups in your community, you might consider partnering with families and professionals to create and provide ongoing organizational assistance for a support group. Figure 11.1 identifies some of the steps

| FIGURE **11.1** | Theory into practice: Working with families to start a Parent to Parent program. |

- **Identify a small group of parents who are interested in developing a Parent to Parent program.** Parent leadership, energy, and commitment are keys to the program's success. Professionals can be important guides and offer a newly developing program many important resources.
- **Determine roles and responsibilities.** Decide whether your program is going to be entirely staffed by volunteers or sponsored by a service provider agency, disability organization, existing parent group, or other group. If you take the volunteer route, you may find it useful to ask people in the community for advice and assistance. Also consider asking banks, religious organizations, libraries, and other places to donate space for your meetings or office needs.
- **Connect with established Parent to Parent programs** who might be able to offer excellent information and training materials. You can get information on local programs by visiting the Parent to Parent website (www.p2pusa.org) or the Beach Center on Disability website (www.beachcenter.org).
- **Establish a system to connect parents.** You will need a local telephone number, preferably available at all times, that potential program parents can call. Use an answering machine if necessary. Appoint someone to coordinate incoming referrals and establish matches.
- **Develop a record-keeping system** for keeping track of referrals and matches.
- **Let people know what you are doing.** Use flyers, brochures, word of mouth, parent speeches, radio, newspapers, doctor offices, and Internet—anything you can to promote the program.
- **Offer optional support activities,** such as ongoing consultation for veteran parents, informational group activities, social gatherings, advocacy training, and instruction for others in the community.

Source: Beach Center on Disability, University of Kansas, Lawrence.

that you can take. You can also read research that identifies key issues for ensuring that support groups are not only developed but also continue year after year (King, Stewart, King, & Law, 2000).

Parent Support Groups. Unlike the one-to-one support of Parent to Parent, parent support groups bring many families, similar needs together in group meetings. Support groups can be led by parents and/or professionals, and members of the group can include parents only or a combination of parents and professionals. Parent support groups are helpful to families of children with disabilities; their positive impact does not vary significantly on account of the child's gender or age (Hudson, Reece, Cameron, & Matthews, 2009). Parents report these groups develop a sense of belonging, a sense of "normalcy" about feelings, an opportunity to share family stories, experiences, and accomplishments, and a sense of empowerment and commitment (Huws, Jones, & Ingledew, 2001; Jones & Lewis, 2001; Law, King, Stewart, & King, 2001; Solomon, Pistrang, & Barker, 2001). Parents often first participate in support groups to gain emotional support.

> I feel more comfortable talking about things that I'm dealing with that might be really upsetting at the time. I feel more comfortable talking to these people than I do to my family or other friends outside of the group. I feel like I'm being heard.
>
> This is our lifeline, like sometimes it's the only thing that keeps you going till the next month to be able to talk to the mothers. It's just not the same when you talk to your own husband, who's full with his own problems of the same sort, or you're just getting on each other's nerves—it's a different thing to talk to someone who is not emotionally involved with you. It's absolutely essential. (Law, King, Stewart, & King, 2001, p. 38)

As participants experience a sense of belonging, they also benefit from the experiential knowledge of other families, learning how they resolved their own challenges. With that knowledge comes confidence in being a partner in educational decision making:

> When you have a normal child you know what the best is—the best school, etc. When you have a child with special needs, you don't know—the best services, the best care, etc. You get that information from the group. . . .
>
> If you go into the [special education] process ignorant, you'll end up with what professionals want to give you, whereas if you go in with the right level of knowledge because you've talked to parents who've been through it already, then hopefully you'll come out with what's best for you and your child. You learn that through other people's mistakes. (Solomon, Pistrang, & Barker, 2001, p. 121)

CHANGE AGENTS BUILD CAPACITY

Izzie Hodge—A Marine Wife Comes to the Aid of Marine Families

You read about Marley, Chandler, and Chad Nelms in chapters 7 and 8. You will remember that they are a Marine family with a child with autism. There's another Marine family you should know about. It's the family of Isabel Hodge. You should know about her because she built a family support program for Marine mothers at the Marines' basic training base at Parris Island, South Carolina.

Like other Marine mothers who have children with disabilities, "Izzie" was searching for "survival strategies, a few helpful resources, and the trust and companionship of others who could relate to our life as parents of a child with a disability and a military family living a mobile lifestyle."

Consider carefully what Izzie and other families wanted. First, they wanted survival skills—sounds like a warrior in combat, doesn't it? Next, they wanted just a "few helpful resources"—not everything, just a few need-to-have resources—traveling light in combat, aren't they? Finally, they wanted trust and companionship—a partnership with others that would carry them though the battles ahead, don't you agree?

So what did Izzie do? She identified the need, scouring Parris Island for families such as hers. Then she and the other families established ground rules, rules of engagement having to do with location, equipment, and supplies,

contact information, child care, and refreshment. Next, they marketed themselves, soliciting other families to join. Then they sought funding, through community outreach. They spent a great deal of time providing emotional support and information to new parents. They established ground rules for meetings, such as absolute confidentiality. And then they set goals for their group, for in that way they also helped families set goals for themselves.

Take Action!

- When you learn about unmet needs, be bold. Never underestimate the power of a single person or a small group to make a positive change.
- Be clear about your needs. Start with the result you want (to satisfy certain needs) or else you'll not end up where you want to end up.
- Be smart. Organize. Perspire (work at it). Inspiration will follow—inspired ways to satisfy your needs.
- Work with others. A single warrior is less powerful than a small band, and a small band is less powerful than a battalion.

Source: Adapted from Hodge, I. (June, 2007). Establishing a support group for military families with special needs. *Exceptional Parent Magazine*, 86–88.

There is no single website for you to learn about whether parent support groups are available in your community; and, if so, for you to access the name of the contact person and the meeting schedule. You might start by asking the director of special education at your school district to let you know what parent support groups are available. You can also ask senior special education teachers, contact your local mental health center to find out if they offer support groups, and/or look on community websites for the list of support groups. Support groups are typically organized around types of disability. For example, there may be a support group for parents of children with autism and/or children with attention-deficit/hyperactivity disorder (AD/HD).

As an alternative to organizing support groups around specific types of disabilities, sometimes support groups are organized around particular shared issues of families. The Change Agents Build Capacity box above describes how

parents partnered to create a support group for military families who have children with special needs. In this case, the "tie that binds" among group members was not the type of the child's disability but rather the fact that all the families were in the military and were dealing with the special issues that are associated with military life such as frequent moves and deployments to combat duty.

:: RESOURCES FOR INFORMATIONAL SUPPORT

In addition to seeking emotional support, most families at one time or another need information and information-based support to make informed decisions about their child's education and overall well-being. Families may

- Have questions about their child's diagnosis, as well as what to expect in the future.

- Be unsure about their rights and responsibilities tied to IDEA.
- Feel intimidated in an IEP/IFSP conference and not understand how to participate.
- Wonder about the benefits and drawbacks of inclusion.
- Be unsure about what type of assistive technology might help their child.
- Need help in disciplining their child at home and in the community.

Families need access to knowledge that is current, accurate, family-friendly, and accessible. Knowledge is power, and shared power—a practice related to the partnership principle of equity—is central to every partnership. Research reveals that families want information

- from a single person who coordinates information and services across systems (Mitchell & Sloper, 2002);
- from another parent who has faced similar challenges and found successful solutions (Ireys et al., 2001; Ruef & Turnbull, 2001; Shapiro, Monzo, Rueda, Gomez, & Blacher, 2004);
- in a user-friendly style using a variety of formats (especially stories) and providing for varying degrees of detail (Edinippulige, 2007; Ruef & Turnbull, 2001; Turnbull et al., in press);
- in their primary language and with flexible levels of literacy (Shapiro et al., 2004); and
- through technology enabling immediate access (Margalit & Raskind, 2009; Skinner & Schaffer, 2006; Turnbull et al., 2009).

The partnership principle of communication helps match families' informational needs to specific resources. By providing and coordinating information for families who want information but do not know where or how to get it, you meet one of their basic needs. Of course, there will be questions that neither you nor anyone else seems able to answer.

Even though there are more resources available to families than ever before, many families still have limited access to the knowledge that they need in order to be an informed educational decision maker. Sometimes the information that a family does have is not in a format that is helpful to them. One parent summed it up this way:

> It's not simply that people aren't getting the information, it's why are they not getting it when they want it or in the form that they can absorb it, or in a way that they can act on it?. . . . So it's not enough for services to simply chuck the leaflets across and say there you are,

there's the information, because it doesn't work. (Mitchell & Sloper, 2002, p. 78)

When you realize that your school is giving out information that is not presented in a useful and readily accessible format, you will need to consider how to use the partnership principle of advocacy and the corresponding practices of preventing problems, keeping your conscience primed, and pinpointing and documenting problems. Consider how effective the professional quoted below has been:

> . . . I give them so much information. . . . They're really grateful about that because no one else really gives them that much information. . . . They trust me now, you know, and I can help them better if they trust me . . . I build a lot of relationships through a lot of talking and giving them information and that's important to them. (Blue-Banning et al., 2004, p. 175)

The partnership principle of trust is the key to positive partnerships with families. Having access to information enables families to make informed decisions affecting their child and the rest of the family. You are a rich source of information, particularly for parents who are new to the special education system or who do not understand how the system works.

There are several options for acquiring and sharing informational resources that families want. You have already learned about two types of programs that provide emotional support—Parent to Parent programs and parent support groups. These also are rich resources of information for families (Ireys et al., 2001; Santelli, Turnbull, Sergeant, Lerner, & Marquis, 1996; Santelli et al., 2001). Other resources for informational support include (1) federally funded Parent Centers, (2) family organizations, (3) technology, (4) books and magazines, and (5) local neighborhood resources.

Federally Funded Parent Centers

Recognizing that parents need knowledge to help their children develop to their fullest potential and secure their rights under federal and state laws, Congress began authorizing and funding parent coalitions in the late 1960s. Parent Centers still are authorized by IDEA and are funded by the U.S. Department of Education to provide informational support to families of children and young adults with the full range of disabilities from birth to age 22. These Parent Centers are categorized into two types—Parent Training and Information Centers (PTIs) and Community Parent Resource Centers (CPRCs).

Parent Training and Information Centers. PTIs support parents to:

- Understand the nature and needs of their children's disabling conditions.
- Provide follow-up support for their children's educational programs.
- Communicate with special and general educators, administrators, related services personnel, and other relevant professionals.
- Participate in decision-making processes, including development of the child or youth's IEP and IFSP.
- Obtain information about programs, services, and resources available at national, state, and local levels and the degree to which they are appropriate to their children's needs.
- Understand IDEA's provisions for educating infants, toddlers, children, and youth with disabilities.

There are approximately 73 PTIs; there is at least one in each state. When there is only one PTI in a state, it generally has the mandate to serve the entire state. When there is more than one PTI in a state, then the multiple PTIs divide the state into regions for their catchment area. Connie Zienkewicz, director of the Kansas Parent Training Center, Families Together, says that the most valuable service her organization provides is getting families through the maze of educational and community services. She explains that "families [are] standing by who have the experience and expertise to help other families, one-on-one, in navigating the maze. They can address a myriad of informational needs, such as finding an expert to treat an unusual medical condition, accessing information on a child's school program, or locating a specialist in challenging behavior."

Community Parent Resource Centers. CPRCs have the specific mission of providing support to families in traditionally underserved communities, that is, families who are characterized by cultural and linguistic diversity. There are approximately 30 CPRCs; each must

- Provide one-on-one assistance.
- Distribute family-friendly materials (including materials translated into languages other than English).
- Engage in outreach to families in their communities.
- Prepare new family leaders.

Unlike PTIs that have a state or regional focus, CPRCs target a community catchment area. In the Together We Can box on the next page, you will read about a parent who receives support from a CPRC in Brooklyn New York,

United We Stand. As reflected in her story the role of CPRCs is to know who the families are, where they are, what they need, what language and customs they use, and what approaches work in involving them. Even though CPRCs are funded to provide support to families, their conferences, newsletters, and other resources are often available to educators as well. If you are fortunate enough to be in a community where there is a CPRC, we encourage you to make contact and to find out how your own competence in cultural responsiveness can grow through your affiliation with them.

Technical Assistance for Parent Centers. All the Parent Centers across the nation are connected to a network called the Technical Assistance ALLIANCE for Parent Centers (www.taalliance.org), generally referred to as "the ALLIANCE." The ALLIANCE coordinates technical assistance for PTIs and CPRCs and is located in Minneapolis, Minnesota. It is affiliated with the Parent Advocacy Coalition for Educational Rights (PACER) Center (www.pacer.org), which is the PTI for the state of Minnesota. The ALLIANCE has six regional centers. Each regional center is administered by a state PTI that provides technical assistance and conferences for all PTIs within the region.

You can locate the PTI in your state and check to see if there is a CPRC in your community by linking to www.taalliance.org and then linking to your state on the map. You will get contact information for all of the Parent Centers in your state as well as a link to each center's website. (When you view the list of programs on this website, the CPRCs are distinguished by having the following notation after the name of the program—[CPRC]. The programs without any notation after their name are PTIs.) Both PTIs and CPRCs are helpful sources of knowledge for families and educators. We encourage you to first and foremost take advantage of this helpful resource so that, in turn, you will be in a position to describe to families the helpful resources within the broad Parent Center network.

Outcome Data on Parent Centers. On an annual basis, Parent Centers, composed of all PTIs and CPRCs, provide *direct* assistance to approximately 1.2 million parents, professionals, and families through telephone calls, e-mails, letters, home visits, and meetings. Another approximately 20 million parents and professionals receive *indirect* assistance through newsletters and websites. Parent Centers also provide more extensive services of attending IEP meetings, facilitating IEP meetings, and engaging in conflict resolution with approximately 10,000 parents and professionals (Technical Assistance ALLIANCE for Parent Centers, 2009).

TOGETHER WE CAN

United We Stand of New York—Being at Home When Away from Home

Imagine that you are a licensed professional in another country where English is not the primary language; you speak only Spanish. There are no resources for you and your newly born child, who has an intellectual disability and other impairments. You immigrate to America with your daughter and mother, and you start life over here, in New York City.

Seeking services for your daughter, you visit various hospitals. There, the staff turn their backs on you because you have no health insurance. Those who do spend time with you don't speak Spanish, and, instinctively, you do not trust their interpreter to be accurate.

When you enroll your daughter in school, the city board of education puts her into a special school, one that serves only children with disabilities. You distrust the board, believe it does not have your daughter's best interests at heart, and struggle in vain to justify your decision. Before long, you are embroiled in adversary hearings against the board of education.

Where's your help?

It comes from United We Stand of New York (UWSNY), a CPRC that serves Latino and other culturally and linguistically diverse families throughout New York's five boroughs. Lourdes Putz directs UWSNY; she is fluent in Spanish and English and has children with disabilities; so do all of her staff and all of the thousands of families she serves.

Reflecting on your experiences with Lourdes, UWSNY, and its families, you write:

With them, I was able to receive the support and information I needed. With them, I felt protected. When I was hindered by language barriers or for any reason, those parents were there to help me and Nicole (my daughter). With their assistance, I have gotten my daughter enrolled in a special education program that is meeting her needs. . . . With them, I feel I am at home. They are like family.

Take Action!

- Imagine yourself as the families of the children you teach.
- Don't let families' poverty, such as not having insurance, and diversity, such as speaking only a language other than English, impede their children's appropriate education.
- Refer them to the networks created to help them—a CPRC, a Parent Information and Training Center, a Parent to Parent program, or a disability-specific association. Help them take advantage of these resources; it costs you and your school nothing to support them emotionally and with information.

Source: Adapted from Fields, J. (Summer/Fall, 1999). Home is where the heart is. *Tapestry, III* (1), 4. (*Tapestry* is the magazine of the Grassroots Consortium on Disability, a national not-for-profit association of and for families from ethnic, cultural, and linguistic diverse backgrounds.)

A national report documented outcomes of the Parent Centers from 2007 to 2008 (Technical Assistance ALLIANCE for Parent Centers, 2009):

- Ninety-four percent of parents indicated the information learned during training was useful.
- Ninety percent of parents reported that they were better able to work with the school to address one of their child's critical education needs.
- Eighty-six percent of parents reported that they shared the information that they received from the Parent Center with other families.

- Eighty-three percent of parents reported that their child received more appropriate services because of the information they learned.
- Eighty-three percent of parents reported that information received from Parent Centers helped resolve disagreements with schools.

Of the many comments collected through the national survey, one that particularly points out the power of information is as follows: "I gained not only information, but the courage to proceed" (Technical Assistance ALLIANCE for Parent Centers, 2009, p. 15).

Data from the national report also indicate several trends in providing support to families. For example, the commitment of Parent Centers to serving families from culturally diverse backgrounds is growing. In 2007–2008, approximately 34% of the families that Parent Centers served were from culturally diverse backgrounds, compared to only 22% in 1997–1998.

Family Organizations

There is no way to accurately know how many family organizations exist nationally and have the specific purpose of addressing the needs of families of children with disabilities, but (based on our extensive work with families nationally, for over 30 years) we predict there are thousands of them. These organizations vary in size, scope, and operating budgets. Most focus on specific disabilities. Some address large-population categories of disabilities such as learning disabilities and attention-deficit/hyperactivity disorder, and others address a relatively rare syndrome such as Trisomy 13 (www.livingwithtrisomy13.org).

One of the largest family organizations, The Arc of the United States, is the world's largest community organization that focuses on individuals with intellectual and developmental disabilities. The Arc has approximately 140,000 members affiliated with 780 state and local chapters. In chapter 5, you read about The Arc's critical role in advocating for individuals with intellectual disabilities and their families and in stimulating state-of-the-art programs and support systems. The Arc at national, state, and local levels is an extremely valuable source of information on topics relevant to intellectual and developmental disabilities including public policy, state-of-the-art supports and services, and funding opportunities for individuals with intellectual and developmental disabilities and their families.

The best way to locate family organizations in your state is to go to the NICHCY website (www.nichcy.org) and click on the State Specific Info link on the home page. You will learn about this website later in the chapter. It will enable you to locate the disability organizations and parent groups in your state. You can provide contact information about these programs directly to families or you can contact these programs yourself to gain information that you need in carrying out your job duties and also that families need in order to make informed decisions.

Technology

Technology, particularly the Internet, vastly expands families' access to information. A longitudinal research study followed families who have children with a genetic diagnosis, documenting how they use the Internet to locate information (Skinner & Schaffer, 2006). Interestingly, 83% of the families used the Internet for some purpose related to their child's disability; the majority of the parents "went online" themselves, whereas a much smaller number asked others to search the Internet for them. Across racial/ethnic groups, Internet usage was 94% for European American families, 86% for Native American families, 65% for African American families, and 55% for Latino families. Families with lower educational levels and lower income were less likely to use the Internet, but still 69% of the families with incomes below $30,000 reported using the Internet. Typically mothers in families were the ones who conducted the Internet searches. These mothers indicated their reasons for Internet use were to gain more information in family-friendly terms about their child's diagnosis, as well as to connect with other families through online support and advocacy groups.

Research has documented that families who have access to state-of-the-art knowledge about their children with disabilities are more confident and empowered to partner with professionals in making complex decisions (Skinner & Schaffer, 2006). A mother of a child with an intellectual disability described the negative effects of not having access to essential knowledge to make careful decisions as follows:

> Oh my gosh. I cannot even imagine. I think I'd be taking what the doctor said more at face value . . . I don't think he would have the advantage of me being able to sound assertive or aggressive, of going armed with information. I mean, it could make a major difference in his medical care. (Skinner & Schaffer, 2006, p. 23)

The researchers described the families as viewing themselves as ". . . critical information managers who were the arbitrators of that knowledge" (Skinner & Schaffer, 2006, p. 21).

In this section we will briefly highlight three types of technology that offer vast informational resources for families: (1) federally funded clearinghouses, (2) websites of family organizations, and (3) online support groups and chat rooms.

Federally Funded Clearinghouses. Two online clearinghouses are funded by the U.S. Department of Education to distribute information to families and educators: the National Dissemination Center for Children with Disabilities (NICHCY) and the Family Center on Technology and Disability (FCTD).

NICHCY prepares and disseminates free information (downloadable from the Internet) about children and youth with disabilities and disability-related issues to families, educators, and other professionals. NICHCY is a *central* source of information on the nature of disabilities, IDEA, NCLB, and research-based information on effective educational practices.

A unique resource on the NICHCY website is referred to on its home page as "State Specific Info" and can be found at www.nichcy.org/Pages/StateSpecificInfo.aspx. You can go to your state and locate the names and contact information for dozens of state resources related to disability including state agencies, disability-specific organizations, and parent organizations. This list can be especially valuable when you are looking for specific information for a family because of the comprehensiveness of state resources presented—for example, the names of state parent organizations that provide local support groups for families.

Another especially useful feature of the NICHCY website is that it includes succinct research summaries that inform educators and families about evidence-based practices on a range of topics related to providing an appropriate education to students with disabilities. Given that both IDEA and NCLB require you as an educator to provide research-based interventions, these research summaries can help you stay current in knowing the best available research results.

The second online clearinghouse, the Family Center on Technology and Disability, specializes in providing information on assistive technology related to the needs of children and youth with disabilities. Their website (www.fctd.info) includes a searchable database with hundreds of books, research articles, and other resources, information on disability organizations focusing on assistive technology, monthly newsletters, brief fact sheets on resources, and success stories. A helpful feature of this clearinghouse is a searchable database that enables you to indicate content topics (i.e., funding, computer software, writing aids), material types (i.e., booklets, fact sheets, videos), and the full range of disability categories. Once keywords are identified, you are able to link to the informational resources that match your keywords.

When families want more information on various topics in order to make informed educational decisions, these two clearinghouses can be extremely helpful to them. Additionally, these clearinghouses can provide you with relevant information in English and Spanish that you can distribute to families.

Websites of Family Organizations. You learned about family organizations previously and how you can locate family organizations from the "State Specific Info" on the NICHCY website. From the NICHCY website, you will be able to link to the websites of the state organizations. As you become familiar with the resources at the state level, you will find links to the national organizations with which these state programs are affiliated. Websites of the national organizations are especially rich with information on a wide variety of topics and in a range of formats including downloadable pamphlets, fact sheets, articles, and videos.

We encourage you to become familiar with the websites of the leading state and national organizations in the area of special education in which you are specializing. As you become familiar with the content of these websites, you will be able to help families match their questions with the particular website that can provide them with useful and family-friendly information. Many organizations will enable you to sign up for an online newsletter. This is a good way to stay current with new resources that they post.

Online Support Groups and Chat Rooms. In addition to having technology-mediated clearinghouses and extensive websites developed by family organizations, many parents of children with disabilities also participate in online support groups and chat rooms. One of the most comprehensive research studies carried out on this topic focused on Australian parents of children who are deaf and documented their participation in various technology-mediated options in order to identify helpful information to make educational and health decisions (Edirippulige, 2007). Highlights of this study's findings are as follows:

- Mothers of the family member typically do the majority of Internet searching.
- Approximately half of the respondents had participated in an online support group or e-mail listserv for people interested in hearing loss.
- Approximately one third had signed up for at least one electronic newsletter.
- The most frequent methods of searching included a generic search engine (87%), visiting websites with a specialty in hearing loss (44%), and following the recommendations of parents who have children with similar needs (31%).
- The rate of access varied daily (12%), several times a month (31%), and to less than every few months (17%).
- The most common reasons for searching the Internet were to find parent support groups (55%) and information about educational options (54%).
- Participants expressed interest in locating success stories as well as stories that focus on challenges.

Similar to other face-to-face forms of parent support, parents who participate in discussions with other families' online experience:

- Emotional support—"I have met cyberfriends, yes. But I've also met real life friends . . . these social connections provided a shoulder to cry on when you need [it]" (Margalit & Raskind, 2009, p. 44).

• Informational support—"You help me write letters. You help me develop my son's IEP. You help me request additional services. You helped me let go of services that really weren't necessary. As much as you helped my son, you helped me too" (Margalit & Raskind, 2009, p. 44).

In research on the outcomes of technology-based parent support focused on parent support groups of children with special health care needs (Baum, 2004), the three most frequently identified outcomes included finding people with similar challenges (79%), receiving information and advice (59%), and feeling understood and accepted (50%).

How do you locate the most useful and reliable support groups and chat rooms for your own benefit as well as for the benefit of families with whom you work? We recommend that you go to the websites of established national organizations within the disability field and review their links. These organizations often provide links for both families and professionals to opportunities to interact online with others who share similar priorities and experiences. As you and the families with whom you are partnering participate in these various groups and chat rooms, you can gather feedback on satisfaction and, perhaps, develop a handout that you can give to families who are interested in online resources of the particular links that have been recommended to you.

Books and Magazines

Families, individuals with disabilities, and professionals are prolific authors of books and articles about disability, education, and families. A recent search of www.amazon.com using the words *disability* and *family* produced a list of approximately 175,000 books. This number is approximately 5½ times what it was six years ago. These books vary from focusing broadly on all types of disabilities and many issues to focusing on only one disability and a very narrow issue. You might consider partnering with your school librarian to set up a library of disability-related books from which both professionals and parents could benefit (Williams & Coles, 2007).

Despite the large market for disability-related books and how-to guides (especially those by families for families), disability information is not widely incorporated into popular magazines (although there has been an increase in coverage, especially on the topic of autism, in the last several years).

Exceptional Parent (www.eparent.com) is a magazine specifically aimed at parents who have a child with an exceptionality. Published since 1971, this monthly magazine offers practical information about the day-to-day issues of living and working with a child who has a disability or special health care need. *Exceptional Parent* also has a library that provides easy access to a broad range of books on disability topics. We encourage you to visit the website and become familiar with its resources. Perhaps your school library could subscribe to this magazine and make it available to families.

Local Resources

Countless untapped resources can be found in our own communities. Local resources can be essential sources of support and information because parents have a history within their own communities and may have already established comfort zones and trust.

For example, children and youth with exceptionalities and their families can connect with and learn from neighbors and community members with disabilities who have "insider" knowledge. Vicki Turbiville, who contracted polio when she was 3½ years old, maintains that students with disabilities should have opportunities to be with other children and adults who have disabilities.

> They also need to have an opportunity to learn from adults who have disabilities and to see us in responsible and desirable positions. Getting information directly from us also affirms our own skills and abilities.
>
> We all value competence and helpfulness. When you ask for help or information from an adult with a disability, you are affirming our contribution to the well-being of others and our place in the community.

Consider adults with exceptionalities in your community as possible mentors, guides, and sources of information and advocacy. You can contact them through a local or state independent living center, which is a community advocacy program for adults with disabilities. You can get contact information for independent living centers from the NICHCY website under State Specific Info.

Likewise, a doctor's office might be a valuable resource for disability-related information because of its familiar atmosphere. The local library is a rich, sometimes underused source for informational resources. That is the point made by a parent who felt that information could be more accessible if it were in everyday, familiar places:

> We said we'd like to see information more in places like the post office, doctors' surgeries (clinics), because some people find clinics intimidating places to just walk in. We shouldn't really have to search out information, it should be readily available in places that you go into every day. (Mitchell & Sloper, 2002, p. 74)

As we noted earlier, information is not always reaching families when they need it. As you check out the resources we are recommending, you will expand your own knowledge that can benefit you in your teaching. Additionally, you will enhance your familiarity with these resources so that you can be in a position to recommend them to families at just the right time and in just the right way when they have major questions that they need to answer.

:: RESOURCES FOR ECONOMIC SUPPORT

As you learned in chapter 1, family characteristics related to socioeconomic status, employment, and opportunities to earn income vary. Relative to families who do not have children with disabilities, families who have children with disabilities typically experience greater economic vulnerability.

- Over one third of students with disabilities live in households with incomes of $25,000 or less as compared to approximately one fourth of students in the general population (Wagner, Marder, Blackorby, & Cardeso, 2002).
- Almost twice as many students in the general population, as compared to students with disabilities, live in households with incomes of more than $75,000 (Wagner et al., 2002).
- Forty percent of families caring for children with special health care needs have financial concerns related to needing additional income for their child's care, terminating or reducing employment because of caregiving, and/or experiencing other child-related financial problems (Kuhlthau, Hill, Yucel, & Perrin, 2005).
- Children with the most limited functional abilities, children in poverty, and Hispanic children are at much higher risk for not having adequate health care insurance (Honberg et al., 2005).

All families require adequate economic resources to meet their members' basic needs. Given the higher rate of economic challenges for families who have children with disabilities, as contrasted to families who have children without disabilities, you can count on encountering families at some point who experience difficulty in concentrating on educational issues because of their worry about finances, including some of the following needs:

- Worrying about how to provide food and shelter for their children.
- Forgoing health care and medication because they cannot afford it.

- Being unable to get necessary disability-related equipment such as a wheelchair, hearing aid, assistive technology, and other educationally relevant resources.
- Wanting to provide tutoring and enrichment activities for their child but not being able to afford it.
- Having no respite care (child care to provide a break from continual caregiving).

The major sources of financial assistance (sometimes called "income support" or "cash transfers") for families who have children with disabilities derive from the federal Social Security Act, although there are other resources for families (Turnbull, Stowe, Agosta, Turnbull, Schrandt, & Muller, 2007). In this section, we describe the two most significant Social Security Act programs that address families' needs.

Federal Programs: Supplemental Security Income and Medicaid

Supplementary Security Income (SSI). The SSI program is funded from the federal income tax and administered by the Social Security Administration. SSI pays monthly benefits to individuals with limited incomes who are 65 years of age or older, individuals age 18 and older who have a disability or who are blind, and children under 18 who have significant disabilities. The SSI program is "means-tested"; that is, a person is not eligible unless he or she meets the federal standards for poverty and thus does not have the means to meet his or her basic needs. A person who meets this means test must then prove to the Social Security Administration that he or she has a significant disability. As of January 2009, an individual eligible for SSI receives $674 per month.

To meet the disability criteria, children must meet Social Security's definition of disability: a physical or mental impairment or a combination of impairments that results in *marked* and *severe* functional limitations. The definition of *marked* is performing at a rate of less than 70% of childhood functioning in areas including motor skills; self-care; persistence, concentration, and pace; and social-emotional skills. The definition of *severe* is a developmental rate of one half or less and is considered to be extreme. The criterion of functional disability is met when the child has one marked delay or one extreme delay. The child's disabling condition must last or be expected to last for a continuous period of at least 12 months or be expected to result in the child's death. Furthermore, the child must not be engaged in any "substantial gainful activity" (a job that pays more than about $980 per month in 2009).

A disability evaluation team collects evidence about the disability and makes a determination of eligibility. The team examines information to compare the functioning of a child with a disability to other children of the same age. Some disability categories entail a presumption of disability, and payments can start before the evaluation is completed. Examples of these categories include total blindness, Down syndrome, and severe intellectual disability.

When a youth with a disability reaches 18 years of age, he or she must requalify for Social Security benefits, using adult disability criteria. These criteria focus on impairment that restrict individuals from doing any substantial gainful activity (work) for more than a year, has already lasted more than 12 months, or that is expected to result in death. Only the income of the young adult with a disability is counted; the person's family's income is not counted. A useful source of information for you, a teacher, is an article entitled "The Facts Ma'am, Just the Facts: Social Security Disability Benefit Programs and Work Incentives" by Brooke and McDonough (2008); you may want to share it with your students' families. It provides a teacher-friendly description of the additional employment-related incentives that are available for adults with disability through the Social Security program.

Although SSI can be extremely helpful to families in addressing their basic economic needs, only a small portion of families who are eligible for SSI are receiving benefits (Msall, Bobis, & Field, 2006). For example, slightly less than one third of families with low income headed by a single mother in which both the mother and the child have a disability receive SSI benefits (Lee, Sills, & Oh, 2002). Furthermore, only 20% of the single-headed families with a child with a severe disability receive SSI, which indicates that the severity of the child's disability does not increase the likelihood of receiving SSI.

The Social Security Administration's website (www.ssa.gov) provides helpful information about eligibility. There is even an opportunity for families to enter demographic information and find out whether they qualify for SSI and other benefits. We encourage you to review this website, become knowledgeable about SSI, and be prepared to provide information on SSI to families who can substantially benefit from additional economic resources.

The Social Security Administration has over 1,300 local offices, organized into 10 regional programs. You can visit your local office to obtain copies of pamphlets and booklets written specifically for parents who have children with disabilities. Some of these resources are available in multiple languages. You can give one of these pamphlets/booklets to families who might qualify and encourage them to check out their eligibility. When families do apply, another way that you can be a partner is to assist them in documenting the nature and extent of their child's disability. Families will need to provide information concerning physicians, medical treatment, and educational records. Families will also need to have their child's Social Security number and birth certificate.

Medicaid. Medicaid is a program of medical and health care assistance for low-income people, including those with disabilities. Children who get SSI payments qualify in most states for Medicaid; often Medicaid eligibility comes automatically once a child has qualified for SSI. In some states, however, it is necessary to go through a separate application process for Medicaid, even after receiving SSI. In order to find out the procedures in your state, we encourage you to ask about the process for qualifying for Medicaid in your state at the local Social Security office, your state's Medicaid agency, or at a social services office (state or county).

Medicaid is commonly known as the Title XIX program, referring to the portion of the Social Security Act that authorizes Medicaid. Title XIX was first authorized in 1965 to provide funds for the health care of individuals who are poor and who have disabilities. Congress amended Title XIX in 1971 to allow federal funding for states to improve conditions in state institutions for people with intellectual disabilities and related developmental disabilities. These funds, however, created a federal bias in favor of institutions, whereas other federal and state policy was directed at deinstitutionalization (discharging people from institutions and preventing them from being placed there).

Accordingly, in 1981, Congress authorized a new program within the Medicaid program, called the Home and Community-Based Services (HCBS) waiver program. The HCBS program changed the pro-institutional bias by allowing states to use Medicaid funds to provide community-based residential and employment supports and services to individuals who would otherwise require institutional or nursing facilities (CMS, 2009). The major impact of the HCBS waiver was to reverse the bias toward institutional placement and to provide a catalyst for family and community supports (Turnbull et al., 2007).

Currently, all 50 states and the District of Columbia have a waiver program; the waiver participation has grown from approximately 1,400 recipients in 1982 to 501,500 recipients in 2007 (Lakin, Prouty, Alba, & Scott, 2008). Although HCBS programs vary greatly from state to state, typically, services financed by the waiver include "management, homemaker assistance, home health aids, personal care, residential and day habilitation, transportation, supported employment, home modifications, respite care, and therapies" (Research and Training Center on Community Living, 2009, p. 4). These services are frequently referred to as "family support."

Family support policy and programs seek to build on the strengths and resources of families, enable them to stay intact, and provide caregiving for their member with a disability. As of 2006, 24 states provide cash subsidies to families (Braddock, Hemp, & Rizzolo, 2008). In 2006, $2.3 billion was spent on family support for 426,782 families (Research and Training Center on Community Living, 2009). Seventy percent of all the family support services were financed through the HCBS waiver. You can find the amount your state spends per family and how it compares with other states in a research brief by the Research and Training Center on Community Living (2009).

An exciting new development for adults with disabilities, including students moving from high school into adulthood, is variously called consumer control, individualized budgeting, self-determination, or participant direction. We use the term *participant direction* to refer to this HCBS program. Under participant direction, the person with a disability or his or her representatives (such as family members or a guardian), rather than a local service-provider agency, decide whom to hire as support staff and how to spend the person's HCBS funds (Mosley, 2005; Walker, Hewitt, Bogenschulz, & Hall-Lande, 2009). The individual or a representative develops a budget to hire staff and fit the individual's particular needs. Individuals with disabilities, in partnership with their chosen reliable allies, are able to hire and fire support staff and purchase services that will enable them to meet their individual goals. The My Voice box below provides the perspective of a mother of an adult with Down syndrome, Ryan. Ryan is able to live in his own home and have his own vending machine business, largely due to the fact that he is a recipient of an HCBS Medicaid waiver through the participant direction option.

MY VOICE
Ryan Banning—"It's My Life, Not Yours"

Ryan Banning is a self-determined man: He knows what he wants and lets everyone know he knows, and he often knows how to get what he wants.

More than anything else, he (and his parents Martha and Bob) wanted to live on his own, work and make money, and fully participate in his community with support. Those goals, however, were simply subsidiaries of Ryan's and his parents' ultimate goal: Ryan would be responsible for his life and have control over his own life. Responsibility and control are mutually necessary; neither can exist without the other.

Even when Ryan's teachers, friends, and his parents' friends and professional allies agreed on the ultimate and intermediate goals, they encountered two huge obstacles. First, they had to have financial support; they simply did not have the resources to "go it alone." Second, they had to control the finances; unless they did, they had no assurances they would be allowed to choose what they thought would be best for Ryan.

Fortunately, they lived in Kansas. There, a pilot program demonstrated that "participant direction" made it possible for nearly 100 individuals receiving SSI and Medicaid to have control over their lives, with support. When that pilot program expired, the state Medicaid and developmental disabilities agencies decided to continue, albeit in a highly modified way, the "participant direction" option.

What did that mean to Ryan? It meant he—supported by his family and a "fiscal intermediary" (an accountant who kept track of Ryan's Medicaid funds and how he used them)—was able to live in a house his parents owned, hire two roommates to live with him and support him there; to start his own business, supplying vending machines; to hire staff to help him drive from one business to another, putting soft drinks and candy into the machines, taking the cash and depositing it in a bank, and investing his profits into getting more and more customers.

Ryan has about a dozen customers; he's well known in each place of business; he and his employees have baseball caps and polo shirts emblazoned "Ryan's Vending Business": and he is responsible—and receives help—for living his life as he wants to. "It's my life, not yours," is how he describes it. He would not have it but for the Medicaid participant direction policy. He's the participant, and he's directing his life.

Take Action!

- As your students reach the age of 16, if not before then, tell them and their parents about federal benefits such as Medicaid and SSI.
- Tell them to go to the local Social Security Administration office to learn about the programs and apply to be eligible for them.
- Encourage them to dream big, tell them about Ryan Banning, and let them know, "It's your life, not someone else's."

Research on participant direction indicates higher levels of choice and control for individuals with disabilities and their families in creating supports, as well as higher quality of life outcomes as a result (Caldwell & Heller, 2007; Neely-Barnes, Graff, Marcenko, & Weber, 2008; Stancliffe & Lakin, 2005). The public policy goal of the HCBS participant direction program is to maximize opportunities that a person with a disability will have to determine how to achieve the outcomes that IDEA stipulates (see chapter 6): equality of opportunity, full participation, independent living, and economic self-sufficiency.

States vary on the amount of family support payments and on the extent to which family support payments are provided to families of children versus adults. Payments in 2006 ranged from $931 in Connecticut to $13,815 in Illinois; the average across the states was $3,046 per family (Research and Training Center on Community Living, 2009). An analysis of payments in six states in 2006 indicated that 56% of the families receiving payments had children under the age of 18 and 44% were families supporting adults 18 years and older (Braddock & Hemp, 2008).

Access to family support results in a wide range of benefits; they include fewer placements in nursing homes and institutions (Caldwell, 2007), increased satisfaction with services (Caldwell & Heller, 2003), and increased self-efficacy (Heller, Miller, & Hsieh, 1999). Families who received family support in Illinois reported having approximately $2,000 less in out-of-pocket expenses as compared to families on the waiting list for this program (Caldwell, 2006). When families had greater out-of-pocket expenses, they tended to decrease the access of family caregivers to health care in order to cover family expenses. This finding is consistent with other research showing that approximately half of family caregivers forego their own medical care because of economic restraints (Ho, Collins, Davis, & Doty, 2005).

On the whole, families approve of family support services, and the services effectively carry out the purposes for which they were created. Because families define their own needs and spend the cash to satisfy those needs, they believe that they experience less stress and have improved quality of life. Figure 11.2 includes quotations from families in Iowa, Illinois, and Louisiana who participate in their states' family support programs.

Your Role in Meeting Families' Basic Needs

As you develop partnerships with families, especially in the transition-to-adulthood years (ages 16 and older, under IDEA—see chapter 6), you should know how families can

| FIGURE **11.2** | What family support means to us. |

- Having a child who is quadriplegic is very expensive. I am a single mother and this money helps us get through everyday living.
- [We appreicate] the fact that we are able to spend the money on our child without being told what to buy. We feel that we are being trusted to meet the needs of our child.
- It is like a breath of fresh air to a drowning person.
- It is the only program that has been willing to help us financially and recognize our needs.
- The extra money helps us to keep our child at home.
- Our family member was able to get high-quality hearing aids that we would not have been able to afford.
- It gave us an opportunity to build a ramp which increased our child's safety and lessened physical stress on us.

Source: Agosta, J., & Melda, K. (1995). *Supplemental Security Income for Children.* Boston, MA, and Salem, OR: Human Services Research Institute.

access and benefit from SSI and Medicaid/HCBS option, especially participant direction. However, these programs have complicated regulations and are implemented in somewhat different ways by each state. Again, we urge you to contact your local Social Security office for printed information and assistance in learning about funding availability in your state and community. We also encourage you to partner with other professionals in your school building or school district including counselors and school social workers who can be helpful in linking families to resources to address economic needs. You likely will also find some experts at your state PTI center. You should share with families everything you know about these programs and refer them to the Social Security Administration and the PTI for more in-depth information.

:: RESOURCES FOR SUPPORT TO ADDRESS CHILD ABUSE AND NEGLECT

A fourth way to support families to meet their basic needs is to partner with them in ways that build trust while ensuring their children's safety. In this section, we provide strategies for interacting responsibly with children and their families to prevent situations that jeopardize children's health and well-being. You are likely to be in situations in which families express needs similar to the following:

- Feeling exceedingly frustrated and even angry about their child's behavior problems.
- Expressing exhaustion that they have no time for themselves and are overextended with caregiving.
- Being vague and nonresponsive when you inquire about a child's bruises or injury.
- Being unusually secretive about what goes on at home.
- Humiliating their child through ridicule and bullying.
- Expressing that they are at their wit's end in addressing their child's problems.

In this last section, you will learn about (1) definitions and types of maltreatment, (2) prevalence, (3) identifying and reporting, and preventing maltreatment.

Definitions and Types of Child Abuse and Neglect

As defined by the Federal Child Abuse Prevention and Treatment Act as amended by the Keeping Children and Families Safe Act of 2003, the term *child abuse* and *neglect* is defined as, at a minimum:

- Any recent act or failure to act on the part of a parent or caretaker that results in death, serious physical or emotional harm, sexual abuse, or exploitation; or
- An act or failure to act that presents an imminent risk of serious harm (Child Welfare Information Gateway, 2008).

Although the Federal Child Abuse Prevention and Treatment Act defines this minimum definition, each state has the responsibility of identifying types of child abuse and neglect and definitions for each. Four major types of abuse and neglect recognized across states include physical abuse, neglect, sexual abuse, and emotional abuse. Sexual abuse is defined by the legislation rather than by states. Figure 11.3 highlights definitions of these four types of child maltreatment that are generally recognized across states, although variation does exist.

Prevalence of Child Abuse and Neglect

According to a national child abuse and neglect database, 10.6 per 1,000 children were victims of child abuse and neglect in 2007 (U.S. Department of Health & Human Services, 2009). Neglect is by far the most frequent category followed by physical abuse, sexual abuse, and emotional abuse. The prevalence of neglect is about 13 times more frequent than the prevalence of emotional abuse; whereas the least frequent is sexual abuse, experienced by 7.6%. Additional trends include the following:

- Younger children, especially those under the age of 1, are victims of child abuse and neglect more frequently than older children.
- Black children have the highest rate of substantiated child abuse and neglect, followed by American Indian/Alaska Native children, children of two or more races, native Hawaiian/other Pacific Islander children, Hispanic children, White children, and Asian children. The rate for Black children is 8½ times greater than it is for Asian children.
- Types of maltreatment vary across the age span. For example, 21% of abuse for adolescence ages 16–17 involves physical abuse as contrasted to 13% for children birth–3.

Given this overall rate of child abuse and neglect, what are your predictions about how the occurrence of child abuse and neglect of children with disabilities compares to the occurrences of child abuse and neglect of children without disabilities? The most comprehensive and scientific comparison of the rates of abuse of children without and children with a disability focused on more than 50,000 children in Nebraska; the study analyzed school, foster care, and police records (Sullivan & Knutson, 2000). When compared to children without disabilities:

- Children with disabilities are 3.4 times more likely to be maltreated.
- Children with disabilities are significantly more likely to experience maltreatment multiple times and in multiple ways.

In addition, this study showed that:

- There were no significant relationships between disability type and type of abuse and neglect.
- The prevalence of type of disability from highest to lowest was neglect, physical abuse, emotional abuse, and sexual abuse.
- Lower socioeconomic levels were significantly associated with multiple forms of maltreatment, especially neglect. The age range of 6–9 was the time that a significant number of children were maltreated for the first time as compared to other age groups.

| FIGURE 11.3 | Definitions of major forms of child abuse and neglect. |

Physical abuse is nonaccidental physical injury (ranging from minor bruises to severe fractures or death) as a result of punching, beating, kicking, biting, shaking, throwing, stabbing, choking, hitting (with a hand, stick, strap, or other object), burning, or otherwise harming a child, that is inflicted by a parent, caregiver, or other person who has responsibility for the child [nonaccidental injury that is inflicted by someone other than a parent, guardian, relative, or other caregiver (i.e., a stranger), is considered a criminal act that is not addressed by Child Protective Services]. Such injury is considered abuse regardless of whether the caregiver intended to hurt the child. Physical discipline, such as spanking or paddling, is not considered abuse as long as it is reasonable and causes no bodily injury to the child.

Neglect is the failure of a parent, guardian, or other caregivers to provide for a child's basic needs. Neglect may be:

- Physical (e.g., failure to provide necessary food or shelter, or lack of appropriate supervision)
- Medical (e.g., failure to provide necessary medical or mental health treatment)
- Educational (e.g., failure to educate a child or attend to special education needs)
- Emotional (e.g., inattention to a child's emotional needs, failure to provide psychological care, or permitting the child to use alcohol or other drugs)

These situations do not always mean a child is neglected. Sometimes cultural values, the standards of care in the community, and poverty may be contributing factors, indicating the family is in need of information or assistance. When a family fails to use information and resources, and the child's health or safety is at risk, then child welfare intervention may be required. In addition, many states provide an exception to the definition of neglect for parents who choose not to seek medical care for their children due to religious beliefs that may prohibit medical intervention.

Sexual abuse includes activities by a parent or caregiver such as fondling a child's genitals, penetration, incest, rape, sodomy, indecent exposure, and exploitation through prostitution or the production of pornographic materials.

Emotional abuse (or psychological abuse) is a pattern of behavior that impairs a child's emotional development or sense of self-worth. This may include constant criticism, threats, or rejection, as well as withholding love, support, or guidance. Emotional abuse is often difficult to prove and, therefore, child protective services may not be able to intervene without evidence of harm or mental injury to the child. Emotional abuse is almost always present when other forms are identified.

Source: Child Welfare Information Gateway. (2008). What is child abuse and neglect? Retrieved August 18, 2009 from www.childwelfare.gov/pubs/factsheets/whatiscan.cfm.

- Males with a disability had a higher prevalence rate as contrasted to females having a higher rate among individuals without disabilities.
- Females with disabilities are more likely to experience sexual abuse, and males are more likely to experience physical abuse.
- Children with behavior disorders, autism, and intellectual disabilities were the most likely to experience child abuse and neglect.

A range of child and family risk factors contribute to the fact that 31% of children receiving special education services experience abuse and neglect—one in three children. Characteristics of children with disabilities that contribute to this higher incidence include communication problems, problem behavior, and inability to defend themselves or escape from harm.

Family risk factors have been associated with child abuse and neglect; they include substance abuse, domestic violence, family isolation, and low parental self-esteem (Gore & Janssen, 2007). Clearly the interaction of family characteristics and child characteristics increase the maltreatment vulnerability of children with disabilities. In addition to being more vulnerable to abuse and neglect, children with disabilities are least likely to have their stories believed or investigated, and are least likely to experience justice in having their abusers prosecuted (Oregon Institute on Disability and Development, 2000).

States are not required to collect data on disability status under the Child Abuse and Prevention Treatment Act, and 12 states do not (U.S. Department of Health and Human Services, 2007). In addition, states that do collect data typically do so through records of Child Protective Services, and often this agency does not require that a child with disability be diagnosed and reported (U.S. Department of Health and Human Services, 2007). For example, the most recent U.S. Department of Health and Human Services (2007) report from states on child abuse reported a rate of 8.1% of children who had a disability; whereas the comprehensive research study described earlier reported the rate of 31%.

In addition, states do not typically document the number of children whose disabilities were found to be caused by maltreatment. Child abuse leading to the diagnosis of traumatic brain injury accounts for approximately one third of hospital admissions of children younger than 3 years of age and one fifth of hospital admissions in children younger than 6½ years of age (Reece & Sege, 2000). Shaken Baby Syndrome is a cause of traumatic brain injury that results when a caregiver has shaken a baby violently, often in response to a child's crying, with the result being that the child has traumatic brain injury (Michaud et al., 2007).

Identifying and Reporting Abuse and Neglect

One of your major obligations as a teacher is recognizing and reporting situations in which you suspect maltreatment of a child. A teacher, Susan Pass (2007), developed three helpful decision-making matrices to guide teachers in knowing the type of action that is needed in a given situation related to three of the four types of maltreatment— physical abuse, sexual abuse, and neglect. These matrices are provided in Figures 11.4, 11.5, and 11.6. Based on your own observation of symptoms related to each form of

FIGURE 11.4 Decision-making matrix for physical abuse.

Directions

☐ File notes for future reference.

▨ Consult with child, parent or guardian, school nurse, principal, and school counselor, as appropriate. After consultation, if possible abuse was indicated, call local child protective services agency.

▨ When a physical symptom intersects with a behavioral symptom, call local child protective services agency.

	Wary of adult contact	Apprehensive when other kids cry	Behavioral extremes	Frightened of parents
Internal injuries				
Bruises/Welts				
Dry burns/Rope burns				
Round burns/Immersion burns				
Fractures				
Difficulty in walking/sitting				

FIGURE 11.5 Decision-making matrix for sexual abuse.

Directions

☐ File notes for future reference.

▨ Consult with child, parent or guardian, school nurse, principal, and school counselor, as appropriate. After consultation, if possible abuse was indicated, call local child protective services agency.

▨ When a physical symptom intersects with a behavioral symptom, call local child protective services agency.

	Won't change clothes	Withdrawal	Fantasizes with infantile behavior	Poor peer relations	Bizarre or unusual sexual behavior	Itching in genital area
Difficulty in walking/sitting						
Torn/bloody underclothing						
Venereal diseases						
Delinquent/Truant/Runaway						
Pregnancy						
Bleeding/Bruises in genital area						

FIGURE **11.6** Decision-making matrix for neglect abuse.

Directions

	Begging for or stealing food	Constant fatigue	Drug or alcohol abuse	Falling asleep in class/Listless	Voluntary extended stays at school
☐ File notes for future reference.					
☐ Consult with child, parent or guardian, school nurse, principal, and school counselor, as appropriate. After consultation, if possible abuse was indicated, call local child protective services agency.					
☐ When a physical symptom intersects with a behavioral symptom, call local child protective services agency.					
Abandonment					
Consistent lack of supervision					
Consistent hunger					
Delinquent/Truant/Runaway					
Inappropriate dress					
Poor hygiene					
Unattended medical or physical needs					

abuse, these matrices will enable you to assess which of three actions you should take:

- When only behavioral symptoms are observed, file notes about the observations for future reference.
- When only physical symptoms are observed, immediately consult with the child as well as the parent or guardian. Also consult the school nurse, principal, and school counselor, as appropriate. After consultation, if possible abuse was indicated, call the local child protective services agency.
- When a child displays a combination of physical and behavioral symptoms, an educator has a legal obligation to inform the local child protective services agency about a possible case of child abuse or neglect (Pass, 2007, p. 135).

Pass (2007) spent two years developing these matrices and worked through 12 drafts. She obtained feedback and affirmation of the matrices' validity from 126 administrators, teachers, counselors, police officers, and social workers, as well as from two state agencies—Illinois State Department of Child Services and Texas State Department of Child Protective Services. Pass (2007) describes the process of using the charts as follows:

- Note observations of questionable behaviors or dispositions on the yellow vertical bars.
- Document their occurrence for future consideration.
- Observe physical appearance or conditions that are more concrete noted in the blue horizontal bars.
- Inquire with the child and the child's parent or guardian what the rationale is for these observations; notify the principal, school counselor, school social worker, and/or school nurse to communicate your observations.
- If you observe a combination of symptoms from the yellow, vertical bar and the blue, horizontal bar (intersecting in the light blue boxes), immediately notify the local government agency responsible for child protection.

These three matrices provide excellent guidance for you in reporting physical abuse, sexual abuse, and neglect; but what about emotional abuse? Some of the different types of emotional abuse include:

- Parent requiring a child to engage in illegal behaviors or degrading acts
- Destroying personal property
- Withholding or threatening to withhold required adaptive equipment (such as a wheelchair)
- Calling the child names, bullying, or swearing at the child
- Threatening to have the child removed from the home through institutionalization or other arrangements (Fitzsimons, 2009).

When children are experiencing emotional abuse, you might observe them as being withdrawn or acting out, overly rigid or passive, destructive to them or others, as well as having learning problems.

Every state requires educators to report suspected maltreatment. You can read your state's specific policies about reporting maltreatment by going to the Child Welfare Information Gateway's website at www.childwelfare.gov/systemwide/laws_policies. In addition to being legally and ethically required, it is noteworthy that if you fail to report child abuse, depending on your state laws, you could lose your teaching license, be sued for damages, fined, and even imprisoned (in two states the length of imprisonment is six months) (Kirk, 2007). Perhaps, the most compelling reason to report is suggested by the following perspective:

> A wait-and-see approach is not an option. In most cases of fatal child abuse . . . a professional has at some point decided to wait or trust the carer. (Selby, 2008, p. 34)

It is disturbing that a national study reported that 84% of all suspected maltreatment in schools are not reported (Dombrowski & Gischlar, 2006).

What should you do if you suspect a child has been maltreated?

1. Make sure that your suspicions are based on facts and that you have reasonable grounds for concern.
2. Follow your school's procedures for reporting within the school. You may be required to report to the school social worker, counselor, nurse, or principal, depending on school procedures.
3. Call the local or state child protection agency; if you do not know what agency to call, a toll-free number to find out who to call in your state to report child abuse is 1-800-4A-CHILD (1-800-422-4453); contact your school social worker, counselor, or principal, or call your local district or county attorney.
4. Be prepared to provide the names and addresses of the child and parent, or other perpetrator, type and degree of injury/condition, prior observations related to injury/condition, actions you or others have taken, the location of where you think the injury/condition occurred, and your name and contact information (Pass, 2007).

It is important for you to know that the names of mandated reporters are kept confidential; and if your report eventually is not documented as accurate, you will be protected as long as you made the report in good faith.

We encourage you to inquire with your principal about whether or not your school district has a policy on reporting maltreatment; if not, you can become an advocate in encouraging your school district to develop a comprehensive policy and to conduct in-service training for all educators to enhance the likelihood that children will be safe and healthy (Dombrowski & Gischlar, 2006).

Preventing Abuse and Neglect

Your efforts to prevent maltreatment should focus on both the child and the family. Concrete actions that you can take to contribute to prevention include the following (Kirk, 2007; Gore & Janssen, 2007):

- Ensure that students have communication skills related to the names of body parts, appropriate and

inappropriate touching, how to identify people with whom they can have honest communication, and self-advocacy skills.
- If children have a pattern of being absent for no apparent reason, partner with your school counselor or social worker to monitor their absences.
- For children with a problem behavior, share PBS strategies with parents and seek to be helpful in improving the child's behavior at home as well as at school.
- Partner with your school psychologist, counselor, social worker, and/or nurse to find out about community resources through agencies such as your local mental health center and hospital that provides training and support for parents related to enhancing safety and preventing maltreatment.
- For children who could especially benefit from an adult mentor, consider how you might locate resources for a big brother/big sister program or a community mentor through other community service programs.
- Communicate each child's strengths to parents and invite parents to let you know what strengths they perceive.
- Ask parents who you suspect might be at risk for engaging in maltreatment if they would find it helpful to be linked through a Parent to Parent program to another parent who has a child with a similar disability and has found successful solutions to address challenges.
- Provide sexuality training, in line with your school's policy regarding sexuality education, to address assertiveness and self-protection.
- Do not blame parents or get angry at them, but seek to be nonjudgmental and to recognize that they need help rather than judgment.
- Teach and encourage children to describe their feelings both verbally and nonverbally. Listen to children when they describe incidences that could be related to abuse and neglect and let them know that communication about maltreatment is difficult but necessary.

You face a dilemma when confronted with abuse and neglect, your obligation to report it, and your desire to collaborate with a family. It is particularly challenging but necessary to use partnership practices to seek to maintain trust with families. If you communicate honestly rather than placing blame on the family, you may be able to help them access the supports they need. As you discuss these sensitive issues with parents, you must disclose your responsibility to their children and the possible consequences to them if you know or suspect that abuse or neglect has occurred (Child Welfare Information Gateways). Remember, the goal is establishing trust with the family so you can help them access resources for themselves and protect their child. You already are aware of the importance of including the seven elements of an effective partnership in your interactions with families. Helping families meet their basic needs creates a powerful context where trust is created and maintained. Our best-practice tips are in Figure 11.7.

FIGURE 11.7 Creating partnerships through trust building.

Partnership Principles and Practices	Issues	Actions Leading to Distrust	Actions Leading to Trust
Respect: Honor cultural diversity.	A parent wants her young daughter with intellectual disability to learn Spanish as well as English, but the speech-language pathologist at another agency says that two languages will be too confusing.	Advise the parent to be realistic about the fact that her child will be lucky to learn English.	Network to locate the most current information on bilingual education for children with disabilities. Review the information with the parent and plan next steps.
Communication: Provide and coordinate information.	Parents of a child with spina bifida who is in an early intervention program believe that their child will have no future.	Warn the parents that they'd better make sure that their marriage is not torn apart by the child.	Suggest to the parents that they contact the local Parent to Parent program to be matched with parents of older children with spina bifida.
Equality: Foster empowerment.	A family has just been informed that their child has been diagnosed with Attention-Deficit/Hyperactivity Disorder and is invited to an IEP conference; they do not know what this is or have any relevant information.	Send the parents a list of their legal rights even though you know the information is practically incomprehensible.	Ask the family about their preferences for information, and review a wide range of resources with them. Respond to their priorities.
Advocacy: Keep your conscience primed.	A student comes to school with unexplained bruises and cuts. He has a communication impairment and will not or cannot explain why he is so frequently injured.	Call the parents, accuse them of abuse, and threaten to call the police if their son ever shows any more signs of maltreatment.	Ask the school social worker to join you in gathering more information, filing a report if appropriate, and informing the parents.

REVISITING RYAN, MARY, AND JOHN FRISELLA

As you read about Ryan Frisella and his parents Mary and John, you may have thought that none of them has any "basic needs." How right or wrong were you? They clearly had an emotional need; they were anxious about Ryan's academic performance in high school and then in college and about the accommodations he would need in college. They had needs for information about mobility in the city and at college and about academic support in college.

They did not express any needs related to their finances, but in time Ryan may consider whether he is eligible for any federal financial assistance and would be prepped for that time if he had been in touch with the local Social Services Administration office while in high school. And, because the Frisella family is a close-knit and loving one, they had no needs related to abuse and neglect.

As you read about the Frisellas, you may have noticed how educators involved with Ryan responded to his and his family's needs, especially his counselor, Nancy Regas, and the school nurse, Susan Efting. The adage about "a village" as the essential factor in "raising a child" is a metaphor for educators: When educators take into account and then respond to a family's and child's basic needs, even when those needs are not directly related to their duty to educate the child, they basically "raise" a different child. They help create a Ryan Frisella—a young man headed confidently to college.

SUMMARY

In this chapter, we asked you to consider your role as an educator in helping families meet their basic needs. We acknowledged that you have a role that relates to the child's education; this is your direct role with respect to the child and family. But we said that families have basic needs that they must satisfy while, and sometimes even before, they can be your partner in satisfying their child's educational needs. That's where you come in, playing an indirect role to help them satisfy their basic needs. Those needs and your ability to respond include the following.

Emotional Needs. Support the family by referring them to
- Parent to Parent
- Parent support groups

Informational Needs. Support the family by helping them locate
- Federally funded parent support centers (PTIs, CPRCs, and the Technical Assistance Center)
- Family organizations
- Technological-based resources (clearinghouses, websites, and online support/chat groups)
- Books and magazines (such as *Exceptional Parent*)
- Local and neighborhood resources

Financial Needs. There are two major Social Security programs for families
- SSI
- Medicaid

Safety Needs. You have a duty to protect a child from abuse and neglect
- Defining abuse and neglect
- Knowing its prevalence
- Identifying and reporting it
- Preventing it

LINKING CONTENT TO YOUR LIFE

When you were a student in elementary, middle, or secondary school, your parents undoubtedly needed some support at home or in the community so they could carry out their functions for you and other members of your family (chapter 3). Or, as a parent, brother, or sister of a student in school, you may have recognized that you or your family needed support over and beyond what educators normally offered.

- What support did your parents, you, or your brothers and sisters need?
- Did they ask educators to assist them to find that support, and, if so, how and why did the educators respond as they did?

- Knowing now about the family systems theory (chapters 1–4), the policies and law that are the foundations for your work (chapters 5 and 6), and the principles of partnership (chapter 7) and how they bear on a student's evaluation (chapter 9) and individualized program (chapter 10), what do you believe are your duties and opportunities to support families to meet their basic needs?

CHAPTER 12

Professionals and Families as Partners for Student Outcomes

RYAN, MARY, AND JOHN FRISELLA

When you first read about Ryan Frisella, in chapter 11, you learned he was a "villager" and that his and his family's village consisted of people in and outside of his schools. These other villagers helped Ryan and his mother and father, Mary and John, meet some of Ryan's basic needs; some were directly related to his education, especially his successful retaking of a course in calculus; and all supported him in one way or another as he proceeded through junior and senior high school.

You learned that Ryan graduated from Patrick Henry High School in 2009. You did not learn, however, that he had a cumulative grade point average in the B range and enrolled at San Diego State University (SDSU) in the fall of 2009. There, he lives in a dormitory and has a college life like any other student, save for the fact that (as you read in chapter 6) he has a right under Section 504 of the Rehabilitation Act not to experience discrimination solely on account of his disability and to receive reasonable accommodations. As Mary noted just a week before he graduated from high school: "No more IEPs." But, still many challenges lie ahead.

Is Ryan ready for college academics? It is safe to answer, "Yes." His father, John, helped him with some of his math homework, but that was in the early years of his high school experience; Ryan's teachers had no objections to John's assistance because Ryan still had to prove that he had mastered his subjects.

Is he ready to be out from under the fairly constant scrutiny and support of his teachers at Patrick Henry High School and his family? That's harder to answer because his teachers monitored his progress through regular tests and observations. As they did for every other student, they posted his test grades on the school's website (the scores were available only by sign-in using a personalized code). But then they called Mary, John, and Ryan to comment on his performance and explain why he performed as he did and how he could improve his performance. Will college instructors give so much feedback? They will, to Ryan; but not to his parents because, as you learned in chapter 6, the federal Family Education Rights and Privacy Act entitles him, but not his parents, to have access to his college records.

Will there be a school-sponsored Circle of Friends at SDSU? Perhaps there will be a similar organization, but it will be up to Ryan to reach out to peers with disabilities even as he makes friends with students who do not have disabilities. Will there be service coordinators to assist him as he receives health-related care? Probably not; Ryan probably will have to

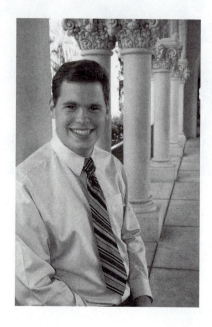

negotiate the college health care maze without a case manager. Will he have access to staff who support students with disabilities? Yes, but he will be solely responsible for reaching out to them and determining the nature and extent of support he wants to receive (within the boundaries of what the college staff offer).

think about it

Ryan has a lot going for him. But think about this:

- What if Ryan's father, with support from Ryan's teachers, had not helped him with his homework?
- What if Ryan's high school teachers had not been so willing to post more than just his grades on his personal site at high school?
- What if a speech teacher had not encouraged him to join the Circle of Friends?
- What if he had not been supported outside of school by peers with disabilities in the program entitled What's Next?
- What kind of "village" can you create for your students, supporting them to move from one program to another while they are in school and then from school to postsecondary lives?
- Just what does it take, besides highly qualified teachers using scientifically based instructional methods and curricula, to make it possible for all the "Ryans" to have an equal opportunity to learn, to be independent in their adult lives, to participate in their communities, and to receive the training that will lead to economic self-sufficiency?

:: INTRODUCTION

In the preceding chapters you have learned how to be a partner with families in planning for their child's education and in meeting the family's basic needs. The partnership that begins as families and professionals develop an infant-toddler's individualized family service plan (IFSP) or a student's individualized education program (IEP). The partnership continues as they implement the plan to advance a student's learning and development. Learning and development should support the student to achieve each of IDEA's outcomes—equal opportunity, independent living, full participation, and economic self-sufficiency. In this chapter, let's consider how you can partner with families so their children can attain those outcomes.

:: BENEFITS OF PARTNERSHIPS

Before discussing *how* families may be involved in their child's learning, let's consider why family-professional partnerships are important in promoting students' outcomes (Christenson & Sheridan, 2001). One reason is that families and school professionals have already discussed and agreed on the educational outcomes by including them in the student's IEP/IFSP; they already have a mutual commitment to the student. Another reason is that effective partnerships honor and encourage families' contributions to their child's learning and development. A third is that partnerships respect families' preferences for participation in their child's education. A fourth reason is that, when parents engage with students in learning activities at home and in the community, children tend to perform better and achieve more at school. Parent involvement in their child's learning contributes to

- Reading achievement (Bailey, Silvern, Brabham, & Ross, 2004; Chavkin, Gonzalez, & Rader, 2002; Jeynes, 2005; Simpkins, Weiss, Kreider, McCartney, & Dearing, 2006)
- Math achievement (Chavkin et al., 2002; Simpkins, Weiss, Kreider, McCartney, & Dearing, 2006; Sheldon & Epstein, 2005)
- Positive attitudes toward school (Shumow & Miller, 2001)

- Attendance and retention (Anguiano, 2003; Bernard, 2004)
- Homework completion (Van Voorhis, 2003; Patall, Cooper & Robinson, 2008)
- Positive behavior at home and at school (Simkins et al., 2006)

The benefits of family involvement endure over time (Barnard, 2004; Jeynes, 2005). Studies of the children of parents who participated in Chicago's Child-Parent Centers found that these children were better prepared for kindergarten, less likely to be referred to special education, and had higher levels of reading achievement and high school completion (Barnard, 2004; Clements, Reynolds, & Hickey, 2004). Family participation in the early years sets the stage for sustained family involvement and positive student outcomes in the later grades (Ou, 2005).

Partnership Preferences. Children from all backgrounds and income levels benefit from family-professional partnerships. Yet, the advantages of family involvement may vary, based on the family's cultural, linguistic, and economic background. For example, volunteering is associated with a greater reduction in behavior problems for children in low-income families than those in middle-class families (Domina, 2005). Also, parents' attendance at school functions has a positive effect on the increased academic achievement for African American students but not for other ethnic groups (Jeynes, 2005). These differences may reflect the different ways in which parents choose to support their child's education and the influence of family characteristics on these choices.

As an educator, you are responsible for ensuring that all parents have opportunities to participate in their child's education; that's your duty under IDEA. You also have a professional ethical obligation under the CEC Code of Ethics to try to assure that students and families will benefit from these partnerships.

Do not assume that a lack of family involvement means that parents are not committed to their child's educational progress. Try to understand the reasons for their level of involvement. As you learned from reading other chapters in this book, parents may not be aware of the options for their participation, they may be reluctant to participate because of their limited English proficiency, or they may hold views of education that differ from those of American educators (Barrera & Liu, 2006). In fact, parents who have recently immigrated perceive the greatest barriers to participation in their child's education (Turney & Kao, 2009).

The partnership principles of commitment and professional competence are particularly important as you

work with all families to promote student learning. Setting high expectations for students and being accessible to families are key partnership practices. As you learned in chapter 6, these practices also are consistent with IDEA and its finding that high expectations and enhanced parent participation can lead to better educational outcomes for students.

Although most research on how parent involvement affects student learning has taken place in general education settings, these findings can inform how professionals and families of children with disabilities can work together to support student learning. Students with cognitive or behavioral challenges often have difficulty generalizing what they learn at school to home and community settings, making the home-school partnership even more vital.

> If I do it alone, by myself at home, he is not going to get it. If [the teacher] does it at school by herself, alone, he is not going to get it. It has to be together and in the same direction. That is really, really important for Scott, that we are going in the same direction, that we are not pulling him apart by going in two different directions. And I think she knows that. (Stoner & Angell, 2006, p. 183)

We will discuss the five opportunities that parents and professionals have for working together to promote student learning in school, at home, and in the community: (1) fostering homework collaboration, (2) sharing information about student progress, (3) using assistive technology, (4) promoting friendships and community membership, and (5) providing positive behavior support.

:: PARTNERSHIPS IN HOMEWORK

Traditionally, homework has been one of the activities that families, students, and schools have shared most often. School reform efforts such as No Child Left Behind (NCLB) have raised expectations for homework. As more and more students with disabilities participate in the general education curriculum, they are expected to complete work at home. For students with and without disabilities, homework is generally assigned to enhance achievement, promote study skills, and, in some cases, keep parents informed of their children's progress.

Many studies have focused on parents' involvement as their children do their homework. A meta-analysis of 14 studies of parents trained to work with their children to complete homework (Patall et al., 2008) found that students benefitted most from having their parents assist them by setting rules and communicating expectations.

The benefits of having parents involved in homework are not limited to gains on achievement tests. An earlier review of the research concluded that when parents support and become involved in their child's homework, students (1) are more likely to develop positive attitudes toward homework and learning, (2) feel more self-confident, and (3) take greater responsibility for completing their work (Hoover-Dempsey et al., 2001).

In general, students who have mild disabilities and those at risk of failing academically benefit from completing their homework because of its relationship with academic achievement (Bailey, 2006; Bailey et al., 2004; Hoover-Dempsey et al., 2001). However, there is little research on the role of homework for students with severe disabilities, particularly those who are in inclusive, general education settings.

Although homework can support a student to learn, students with disabilities often have more problems with homework than classmates who do not have special needs (Bryan, Burstein, & Bryan, 2001). Students with disabilities may receive homework less consistently, but spend approximately 20 minutes more per night completing assignments than their peers without disabilities (Harniss, Epstein, Bursuck, Nelson, & Jayanthi, 2001). According to the Brown Center on Education Policy (2003), 83% of elementary students spend up to 1 hour on homework, and most secondary students spend between 1 and 2 hours each night on homework. The time demands associated with even usual homework assignments can be challenging for students with disabilities who often have difficulty sustaining attention and organizing time.

Key Issues Regarding Homework

Think about how homework completion can affect families. In chapter 3, you learned about the numerous functions that already require time and attention in families' busy lives. Mindful of the demands on parents' time, you can enhance your partnership with families when you carefully take into account families' preferences and resources. In the following section, we will discuss (1) family concerns about homework and (2) practical suggestions for homework collaboration.

Family Concerns About Homework. Students with disabilities are more likely to require their families' assistance in completing homework than are children without disabilities (Harniss, Epstein, Bursuck, Neslon, & Jayanthi, 2001). In this section, we will focus on the concerns of families who have children with disabilities. Because homework is rarely given to students with severe disabilities, the existing research focuses on the concerns of parents of students with mild disabilities.

Particularly if they lack knowledge about the topic or information about teachers' expectations, parents may feel inadequate in helping their children with homework, (Kay, Fitzgerald, Paradee, & Mellencamp, 1994). Indeed, Latino families tend to want schools to provide specific suggestions for assisting their children at home, especially in topics that are challenging to their children (Hughes, Valle-Riestra, & Arguelles, 2008). Problems may arise when the homework is too difficult for a child or the child has not acquired the skills needed to complete the assignment. Children may become frustrated by the complexity of the assignment, and parents may feel pressure to teach, rather than assist, their child. This situation can place undue stress on families and cause parent-child conflicts (Bryan, Burstein, & Bryan, 2001).

What partnership practices can you draw on to respond to some of these concerns? Think back to chapter 8 on communication and chapters 2 and 3 on family interaction and family functions. What impact does the stress associated with homework have on parental and sibling interactions, on marital and extended family interactions, and on family functions?

Parents want comprehensive, two-way communication with teachers. They want assignments given to their children to be practical and individualized (Margolis & McCabe, 2004). Parents know that if homework is too difficult for their children to complete or the children consider it to be busy work, their children are likely to lose any motivation to complete the homework (Margolis, 2005). Parents and students prefer homework that involves concrete, hands-on projects that are interesting and engaging (Bryan & Sullivan-Burstein, 1998). Students complete their homework more often when assignments are tailored to reflect their individual interests and abilities. Assignments should not be too difficult or take excessive time to complete.

Effective teachers make reasonable modifications in homework assignments (ERIC/OSEP Special Project, 2001). You can offer accommodations by adjusting questions, allowing alternative response formats, modifying the length of the assignment, providing peer tutors or study groups, providing learning tools, and giving fewer assignments. You also can provide tiered assignments targeted at a student's ability or interest level. For example, you can ask students to practice map-reading skills by using maps that contain more or less detail. In the following section, we will describe how you can collaborate with families on homework to foster partnerships based on trust.

Practical Suggestions for Partnerships in Homework

There are at least three ways to enhance partnerships in homework: (1) create more opportunities for students, parents, general education teachers, and special education teachers to communicate with each other; (2) minimize family responsibility for homework; and (3) use strategies to improve homework practices (Epstein, Munk, Bursuck, Polloway, & Jayanthi, 1999; Harniss et al., 2001). Figure 12.1 provides suggestions for promoting positive homework experiences.

Create Opportunities to Communicate. Both teachers and parents want timely and consistent communication (Nelson, Jayanthi, Brittain, Epstein, & Bursuck, 2002). Each of the communication strategies you learned in chapter 8 has relevance for homework collaboration.

Some elementary schools use communication notebooks so students can carry information between their school and home (Bos, Nahmias, & Urban, 1999; Stoner & Angell, 2006).

The notebooks contain announcements, notes, weekly school newsletters, and weekly homework packets. Often, teachers adapt the homework packets for students with disabilities according to each student's strengths and needs. When you first discuss homework policies and practices with them, you may want to ask parents if they want to review and sign homework packets early in the school year (Margolis, 2005).

In upper grades, some students with disabilities meet with a homework "coach" to address organizational, study, time-management, and self-advocacy skills. The coach helps the student communicate with the various content teachers as well as with parents. "Contracts" for longer assignments are also helpful in planning timelines and responsibilities.

Internet-based homework assistance centers may provide a unique opportunity for promoting communication between students, families, and professionals (Salend, Duhaney, Anderson, & Gottschalk, 2004). Websites can be designed and used to suggest activities, explain assignments, offer resources, and provide guidelines on effective homework practices. The Internet can assist students and families

---

FIGURE 12.1   Promoting positive homework experiences for students and families.

How often do you use the following practices?	Always Practice	Sometimes Practice	Will Practice in the Future
1. Encourage families to designate a study area and regular time for homework.			
2. Provide parents with suggestions they may use to help their children with homework.			
3. Provide students and parents with a list of assignments at the beginning of the school year.			
4. Use homework assignments that involve families and students in carrying out projects at home.			
5. Send home all texts and materials needed to complete the work.			
6. Send home assistive technology devices the student uses in school.			
7. Discuss homework expectations and modifications at a student's IEP meeting and include them in the document.			
8. Post information about homework assignments on a class or school website or record assignment information as an outgoing message on a telephone answering machine.			
9. Share homework expectations with students and families and agree on the consequences for incomplete homework.			
10. Encourage families to reward their child's reasonable efforts to complete homework.			
11. Discuss with families how they can recognize and avoid their child's frustration in completing homework.			
12. Communicate regularly with parents about homework assignments and student progress.			

in forming online cooperative homework groups or peer tutoring sessions. You may also designate a time that you will be online to answer questions from students and parents.

One approach to facilitating homework partnerships with families involves training family members to support homework completion. Parent training increases students' rate of homework completion and reduces the frequency of problems with homework (Pattall et al., 2008).

For example, a comprehensive approach to homework partnerships provided an opportunity for parents and middle-school students with emotional and behavioral disorders to learn about self-management skills (Cancio, West, & Young, 2004). This approach required students to complete daily math assignments by using self-monitoring, self-recording, self-reinforcement, and self-instruction. The training for parents and students contributed to gains in homework completion and accuracy and a reduction in perceived homework problems for the students.

In another study, parents of second graders who were at risk of failure participated in a four-week training program in which they were given strategies for promoting their child's reading skills (Bailey, 2006). By the end of the training, parents were spending more time interacting with their children on homework activities, and their children showed gains in their ability to answer inferential questions.

Finally, you can communicate with parents about how they can help their children at home by providing them with brief videotaped demonstrations of specific activities, such as paired reading or dictation (Ganske, Monroe, & Strickland, 2003).

Create Options to Minimize Family Responsibility for Homework. Sometimes you may want to find ways for students to complete homework outside the home or to otherwise minimize the role of parents in its completion. Research tells us that parents should not be responsible for acting as teachers or feel the need to police homework completion (Marzano & Pickering, 2007). Struggling learners can become frustrated by assignments they find difficult or explanations that differ from what they have been taught in school. As a teacher, you can help families avoid conflicts related to homework by clarifying a parent's role in homework completion.

Your first option is to limit the amount of homework you assign. There has been no firm conclusion about the optimal amount of time spent on homework (Marzon & Pickering, 2007). However, it does appear that benefits decrease when students spend too much time on homework or when they are unable to complete the assignments.

To avoid assigning too much homework, ask parents to record how long their children spend on homework (Margolis, 2005). Also, ask both the student and their parents about the assistance that was needed to complete the work. Use this information to adjust the length or difficulty level of future assignments.

Your second option is to provide alternate settings in which students can complete homework. In a growing number of communities, public libraries are offering homework assistance to students, with benefits ranging from improved study habits and grades to learning to cooperate with adults (Mediavilla, 2001). Homework assistance and tutoring may also be available in community centers. A study of after-school programs for immigrant Hmong students held in community centers within low-income housing projects found that successful programs were less structured than school and were led by community members (Lee & Hawkins, 2008).

Other options to minimize parents' responsibility for supporting homework completion include arranging for peer tutoring, and providing homework assistance in study hall or after-school programs (Harniss et al., 2001).

Think about times when it may be most effective to reduce the amount of homework a student is required to complete. Be particularly mindful whether your motivations to reduce the amount of homework respect the families' strengths and preferences and whether your actions reinforce trusting partnerships. These questions are especially relevant when you are working with a family whose skills or resources are limited when it comes to helping their child with homework. You can affirm how such a family values learning in a number of ways, including by assisting the family in finding someone to provide homework assistance or locating free materials in the local library or on the Internet.

Use Strategies to Improve Homework Practices. Students spend approximately one fifth of all homework time at home. You can help ensure positive homework experiences for students and their families by providing meaningful and individualized assignments, teaching students study skills, and providing parents with suggestions for setting up useful routines and practices (Bryan & Sullivan-Burstein, 1998; Epstein et al., 1999; Harniss et al., 2001; Salend, Elhoweris, & Van Garderen, 2003). Similarly, you can:

- Ensure that your students record assignments and take home the necessary materials.
- Teach your students to use homework planners.
- Teach your students to manage their time effectively.
- Enter into "contracts" with your students to monitor their completion of long assignments.
- Collaborate with other teachers to avoid overloading your students with homework.

We encourage you to ask families about their experiences with their child's homework. This is a perfect opportunity to be aware of the partnership principle of communication and apply the practice of listening. When you can actively listen and then respond to parents' experiences and concerns regarding homework, you are honoring and strengthening the partnership. To create a responsive context around homework issues, you will need to individualize your approach for each family. Your respect for the family's preferences will build trust and support student achievement and performance.

Report Progress and Other Information. You also should maintain ongoing communication about their child's achievement and performance and progress toward measurable annual goals from the child's IEP. Reports cards, grading, and progress reports are strategies for sharing that kind of information. As you learned in chapter 6, NCLB requires schools to provide all parents with frequent reports on their child's progress and to specify when and how reports will be provided. IDEA requires schools to report the student's progress toward the measurable annual goals that are set out in the student's IEP through the use of quarterly or other periodic reports, issued concurrently with school's distribution of report cards.

Because growing numbers of students with disabilities receive services in general education, general and special educators alike are paying a great deal of attention to their grading practices and methods of reporting grades. Grading the performance of students with disabilities in inclusive settings can be a stressful process for teachers (Silva, Munk, & Bursck, 2005). You may want to consider factors other than performance in the assignment of grades. However, if you do, recognize that you may de-emphasize mastery of the curriculum and confuse parents and students about the meaning of the grades (Guskey, 2009). At the same time, bear in mind that personalizing or adapting grading systems can improve motivation in students who have received low or failing grades (Munk & Bursuck, 2004).

Given that grading is often at the discretion of general educators, partnership among special educators, general educators, and families is necessary to determine grading criteria (sometimes called rubrics), grading adaptations, and methods for reporting student progress. The first step for these professionals is to develop a shared understanding about the purpose of grading and then communicate it to the student and parents, who may have different ideas about what grades mean (Munk & Bursuck, 2003).

One study asked parents of secondary students with and without disabilities to indicate how effectively report card grades met a set of specific purposes (Munk & Bursuck, 2001). Both groups of parents believed that grades were important in communicating information about students' achievement, effort, and work habits. At the same time, both groups were skeptical about how effectively report cards met these purposes. Compared to parents of students without disabilities, parents of students with disabilities assigned more importance to grades as indicators of their child's strengths and needs and assigned less importance to the role of grades in conveying information to postsecondary schools or employers.

We encourage you to ask parents their thoughts about the purpose of report cards. For example, ask them if they feel grades should reflect how much their child improved or how their child's performance compares to the performance of other children. Also ask them whether they expect their child's grades to convey information about their child's interests, effort, level of independence, or his or her ability to work with other students (Munk, 2003). Use this information as you develop grading policies and make decisions about individual grading adaptations.

Grading adaptations communicate information about a particular student's accomplishments. Because adapted or personalized grades are individualized to meet a student's needs, they provide a more precise measure of progress for that individual (Silva et al., 2005). If you use grading adaptations, you should describe them in a student's IEP, explain the basis of grading to students and parents early in the school year, and review your method throughout the year.

You have a choice in how you adapt grading and discuss grading with your students' parents (Munk & Bursuck, 2004; Silva et al., 2005). Consider how the following adaptations relate to your own thinking about the purpose of grading:

- Prioritize and limit the number of assignments to be graded.
- Weight some assignments more heavily than others.
- Assign greater weight to effort.
- Base part of the grade on the processes or strategies the student uses to complete the assignment.
- Grade students on their progress toward IEP goals.
- Grade on the basis of the student's improvement over time.

By working with other professionals to create an open dialogue with families about grading, you will promote partnerships that can lead to a high-quality education for a child.

In addition to setting out a student's grades on assignments and report cards, progress reports can also provide families with timely feedback. Your progress reports can be comprehensive or simple; you can send them home once a day, once a week, or once every few weeks; you can use them to communicate about a single subject of area of development or about multiple areas. One Hmong mother of a 10-year-old child with multiple disabilities spoke of what she had learned about her daughter's progress from a teacher she trusted:

> The teachers say that when they speak she could understand more now. Like for example colors, red, green orange, white, black, she knows which are which. If the teachers ask which color is which she is able to point that out. When they give her toy to play with they first give her one specific toy and ask her to give them the same one back, she can now pick the same one and give that toy to them. About writing, she still can't write well. She can only read a few words because her brain is that way. (Barrera & Liu, 2006, p. 48)

When working with some families of different cultures, you may find it helpful to provide information about their child's progress through cultural mediators or parent liaisons, and to use photographs or videotapes to show the child's performance in a real and concrete context (Lynch & Hanson, 2004; Sanders, 2008). Remember to obtain the parents' permission before videotaping their child.

By sharing information about student progress in ways that respect families' preferences, you put into practice several partnership principles, including respect, communication, and equality. In the Change Agents Build Capacity box below, you will read how a white teacher, newly graduated from a

---

CHANGE AGENTS BUILD CAPACITY

Mike Lamb—The Four-R Approach

Eighth-grade students and their families in Chicago's rough and tumble South Side had plenty of reasons to be cautious about Mike Lamb. He wasn't educated in the city's schools but in a private school associated with the University of Chicago. He graduated from Duke University. He is white; most of the students are African or Latino Americans. And he was a rookie teacher. Mike says, "On good days, I faced skepticism; on bad, defiance."

Mike met his concern by looking inward: ". . . to communicate with my students, I had to ask myself: Why am I here? Is it about me or them? Who am I and where did I come from? What do I bring to them? What strengths do they bring to the table?"

Then he required himself to see his students in a different light. "I needed to make my respect for my students, families, and their lives clear. . . and to show them that I respected their essential humanity, their innate goodness. . . . I had to affirm that each could become a better reader, regardless of their scores."

Next, he had to establish relationships with the students' families. "I had determined that my students' families were essential for both me and their children's education. I called all of them the first day of school, seeking their trust. At the first parent-teacher conference, I said I was all about power and opportunity for our students. From then on, they were major resources for me. I do not remember one interaction that ended negatively that year. But I couldn't get my students to buy in."

So, Mike worked on his relationships with them. He brought his mother to school and let his students see him through her eyes . . . once as a boy, now as a man. He then brought rigor to his curriculum: "We would become

critical thinkers together, whether reading *Much Ado About Nothing* or *Fahrenheit 451.*" His demanding approach caused his students to understand that he respected them.

Because not all students could achieve as he wanted them or as they wanted, some would get into trouble or fail academically. Issues would spiral out of control. "They were uncertain of forgiveness and lacked strategies to resolve routine problems. . . . But I talked with them about overcoming obstacles."

Mike's Four-R Approach—respect, relationships, rigor, and resilience—worked. At the beginning of the school year, only 12% of his students passed the state's reading examination. At the end of the school year, 71% passed. The next year, same result, but with different students.

Take Action!

- Show that you respect your students and their families; it is not enough to respect them unless you show them you do.
- Seek relationships with your students' families, offering to be a partner.
- Don't compromise your students or their families, for if you do, you compromise yourself. Rigor is a two-way street.
- Hang tough and teach your students to do likewise. Resilience is important because learning is hard work.

Source: Lamb, M. (2010). My voice: The Four-R approach. In A. Turnbull, R. Turnbull, & M. L. Wehmeyer, *Exceptional lives: Special education in today's schools* (6th ed., pp. 78–79). Upper Saddle River, NJ and Columbus, OH: Merrill/Pearson.

top-20 university, worked with his middle-school students and their parents, nearly all of whom were African American; pay close attention to his "Four-R" rule—it's not about reading, writing, arithmetic, or rules of the school.

:: PARTNERING TO USE ASSISTIVE TECHNOLOGY

A third opportunity for collaborating with families to support student learning and development relates to assistive technology. IDEA (20 U.S.C. Sec. 1402(1)) classifies assistive technology as a related service and defines *assistive technology device* as any item, piece of equipment, or product system—whether acquired off the shelf, modified, or customized—that is used to increase, maintain, or improve a student's functional capabilities. (IDEA excludes any medical implant from the definition of *related service* and *assistive technology*.) For example, if a student has difficulty holding objects, an adapted spoon becomes an assistive technology device. Assistive technology devices also include typing telephones for people who are deaf or hard of hearing and motorized wheelchairs for students who cannot walk.

Assistive technology is similar to and different from instructional technologies such as calculators and interactive whiteboards. Both assistive and instructional technologies foster students' access to and progress in the academic curriculum (Peterson-Karlan & Parette, 2008). However, instructional technologies have the purpose of developing a student's skills or supplement the student's learning, whereas assistive technologies have the purpose of enhancing the student's life functioning over the life span by enabling them to participate in everyday activities in school, at home, and in the community (Edyburn, 2002).

The successful use of assistive technology rests largely on how families are involved in decisions about their child's use of assistive technology. In the following section, you will learn how to reach decisions about technology that are consistent with the family's goals, values, and lifestyle.

Accessing Assistive Technology

Assistive technology can be low-tech, such as communication boards or cards, or high-tech, such as a computerized speech recognition system. The IDEA definition includes off-the-shelf, adapted, or customized devices, thus creating many choices for parents, the student, and teachers. Selecting a device is an important decision. They will have already considered whether to use assistive technology when they are evaluating the student (chapter 9) or developing an IEP (chapter 10). If they include assistive technology in the

student's IEP, the school must provide it, as it must provide all other related services listed in the IEP.

IDEA (20 U.S.C. Sec. 1402(2)) defines *assistive technology service* as a related service that assists the student in the selection, acquisition, or use of an assistive technology device. If the student, the family, or the school staff need training to use the device and the IEP includes the training as a related service, the school must provide the training or make sure that an appropriate person or organization provides it.

As a teacher, you will observe when a student is unable to fully participate in or benefit from instruction. As a trusted partner, you can be instrumental in helping parents identify situations at home in which the student might benefit from the use of an assistive device.

Using Assistive Technology at Home

Assistive technology can make a significant positive impact on the lives of students with disabilities and their families (Angelo, 2000; Weikle & Hadadian, 2003). Unfortunately, students and families do not always benefit from assistive technology (Parette, Brotherson, & Huer, 2000; Parette, Peterson-Karlan, & Wojcik, 2005). Acquired devices are often underused or abandoned, particularly when the student is expected to use the device outside of school (Judge, 2002; Lahm & Sizemore, 2002). Rather than bringing the intended joy and independence to family life, assistive devices sometimes leave families feeling frustrated and dissatisfied (Bailey, Parette, Stoner, Angell, & Carroll, 2006; Parette & McMahon, 2002).

Why does this occur? Usually, it is because parents do not have a meaningful voice in decisions about technology and because teachers accordingly make inappropriate recommendations. Think about what can happen when a teacher or other professional disregards the partnership practices of communication, respect, and trust.

> It turned out to be more than I thought it would be—more demanding and a little more difficult. I take some of the responsibility for not having it up and running, but I just expected more support from the school district . . . I don't mean to disparage [the teacher] at all. She's a great lady, but she sort of seems hands off, kind of. She wants it up and running, but she doesn't really want to get involved in how to program it, although she's interested in how to integrate it into the school day . . . So she sort of passed that off to me and to the school speech therapist. (Bailey et al., 2006, p. 55)

There are two main reasons why parents may not use the assistive technology at home. First, some parents are unprepared or unable to carry out the responsibilities that teachers assign to them; they already have ordinary care-giving duties (Bailey et al., 2006). These responsibilities include training to use and maintain the device, providing ongoing care and maintenance, helping their child use the device, and transporting the device to new locations.

Your expectations about parent participation must be consistent with the family's resources and comfort in taking on the additional learning and responsibilities (Kemp & Parette, 2000; Long, Huang, Woodbridge, Woolverton, & Minkel, 2003). Some parents do not have the time, child care, or other resources needed to attend training; other parents feel overwhelmed by the expecta-tions imposed on them to support their child's use of technology. For one mother, simply handling the device posed a challenge: "The biggest concern I have right now is the weight of the device [Dynovox] . . . I couldn't have begun to even push the thing across the table, more or less carry it from room to room" (Parette, Brotherson, & Huer, 2000, p. 186).

The second reason parents may experience difficulties is that they may perceive the technology to be incompatible with the family's values, cultural background, and lifestyle (Jeffs & Morrison, 2005; Parette, Brotherson, & Huer, 2000). Sensitivity and respect for a student's background is important in all interactions with families, but decisions about technology raise a particular set of issues:

- *Parents' desires for their children to fit in:* In studies involving African American families, some family members spoke of their concern about drawing negative attention to their child's disability through use of a device (Parette, Brotherson, & Huer, 2000).
- *Families' preferences about how their children communicate:* In a study of Mexican American families, many parents said they prefer that their children use sign language and speech instead of an augmentative device (Huer, Parette, & Saenz, 2001). Another study revealed that parents of African American children may prefer that communication systems with speech output reflect the vocabulary and dialects of the family (Parette, Huer, & Wyatt, 2002).
- *The value families place on their children's independence:* Some parents place greater value on interdependence than do some professionals who reflect typical European American perspectives that emphasize independence. For example, some Asian and Hispanic families do not necessarily support the use of technology to encourage their child's independence (Parette & McMahan, 2002).

- *The role of other family and community members:* Parents report that decisions about assistive technology need to consider with whom the student will want to communicate and socialize at home and in the community, as well as how the technology will be received by family and community members (Parette et al., 2002).
- *Family's expectations about the immediacy of the benefits of the technology:* Families differ in how quickly they expect to have access to the device or how quickly they expect to see changes in their child's functioning once the device is used (Bailey et al., 2006; Huer et al., 2001).

In the absence of ongoing communication with pro-fessionals, parents may feel frustrated and disappointed, abandon the technology, and begin to distrust the profes-sionals. You must involve families in decision making from the outset and provide ongoing support to them to use the technology.

Involving Families to Make Decisions. Although pro-fessionals and parents agree that it is important for them to be partners in making decisions about technology, partner-ship does not always occur. In one study of 16 professionals, all participants indicated they worked as a decision-making team, but not one indicated that a family member was part of the team (Lahm & Sizemore, 2002).

Your initial discussions with parents about assistive technology give you an opportunity to support their prefer-ences as well as understand and respect the influence of their cultural and linguistic backgrounds as they make decisions. Your initial discussions with families should provide you with an understanding of the family's knowledge, interest, and expectations related to the use of assistive technology (Parette & McMahan, 2002). You may also want to ask family members about any concerns they may have in using assis-tive technology at home or in the community. The questions you ask should reflect the communication strategies you learned about in chapter 8.

It is good practice to provide opportunities for families to see and use the technology being considered. Try to arrange for them to observe children using the device, and try out different devices with their children in the settings in which they will use the device (Judge, 2002). Encourage practice or trial sessions so they may select the device that best meets their child's needs and be most readily accept-able to them (Long et al., 2003). You can create these opportunities when you conduct a nondiscriminatory eval-uation of the student (chapter 9). The partnership practice of empowering families, which is linked closely with the partnership principle of equality, provides families with a sound basis for making decisions about assistive technology that further solidifies their trust in you.

Supporting Families to Use the Technology. Families need information, training, and other supports to enable them to use assistive devices at home. Families want information about the types of devices available, features of different devices, availability of vendor support, funding, and warranties (Bailey et al., 2006; Parette, Brotherson, & Huer, 2000). They want that information in user-friendly formats in their native language, and they like demonstrations and hands-on learning (Parette, Brotherson, & Huer, 2000). Support groups made up of families who have experience with specific devices are helpful resources. Parents also need training, particularly in using, programming, and maintaining assistive devices (Long et al., 2003). Parents may also want extended family members to receive training (Parette, Brotherson, & Huer, 2000).

To ensure the student uses assistive technology at home, you may need to give families ongoing support and guidance (Long et al., 2003). Take the time to ask periodically whether students and family members have questions or concerns about the device. Find out if the device continues to be useful and appropriate as the child matures or whether adjustments need to be made. Check to see whether the student avoids using a device he or she deems "uncool" (Parette et al., 2005). Remember, "if the child is to be truly successful using the technology, the delivery day actually marks just the beginning" (Long et al., 2003, p. 281).

Even when you make decisions with families with careful consideration of their personal and cultural preferences, it is likely that changes in the student, family, or technology will require you to continue to be available to families. When families trust you and other professionals to support them in decision making as well as in their use of technology, a unique opportunity exists to reinforce partnerships with families and to support student learning.

:: PROMOTING FRIENDSHIPS AND COMMUNITY MEMBERSHIP

As you learned in chapter 3, families want their children to have social relationships and are deeply concerned about the lack of friends or possible rejection in their children's lives. Recreational experiences and community environments are important to families. Fostering friendships and a sense of community for students and their families is yet another opportunity for parent-professional partnerships.

Enhancing Friendships

Parents clearly want their children to be accepted and valued members of a group, whether in home, school, or community life. Parents of all backgrounds and cultures want their children to lead "normal" lives regardless of the child's strengths and disabilities (Hughes et al., 2008). They want their children to "fit in," and they believe that schools should facilitate friendships among children. One parent stated that her son who was diagnosed with Asperger's syndrome "needs opportunities to play with other children . . . he needs to learn how to make friends" (Brewin, Renwick, & Schormans, 2008).

It is not enough merely to place students with and without disabilities together and expect that everyone will feel included and make friends. How do educators work with families to create meaningful connections for students with disabilities within their classrooms, recreational activities, and neighborhoods? How can friendships develop and peers naturally advocate for each other when someone is not included?

One way is to embrace the partnership principle of professional competence. By providing a quality education, continuing to learn, and setting high expectations, you will be able to explore with families the importance of friendship and discuss with them how friendships can best be achieved. Refer to chapter 3, particularly Figure 3.4, to review several strategies for being a partner with families to promote friendships among students. Then consider how you could use the following approaches and examples to promote friendships in your classroom:

- *Provide opportunities for friendships to develop:* Encourage and support student participation in activities that are fun, engaging, and accessible and use cooperative grouping during instruction to enable students to work together (Meadan & Monda-Amaya, 2008; Sapon-Shevin, 1999).
- *Teach about diversity:* Teach using an antibias curriculum, incorporate materials that are culturally diverse, and teach students how to identify and respond to stereotyping and discrimination (Harriott & Martin, 2004; Salend, 2001).
- *Teach about friendships:* Use children's literature to teach about friendships and embed the themes of friendship and social skills in your literacy or social studies curriculum (Anderson, 2000; Forgan & Gonzalez-DeHass, 2004).
- *Encourage students to participate in extracurricular activities:* Make information about after-school clubs, events, teams, and volunteer activities available to

students and families and collaborate with other professionals to adapt activities to enhance participation (Kleinert, Miracle, & Sheppard-Jones, 2007).

- *Provide social skills instruction:* Ask students to role-play possible responses to social situations or listen to and interpret carefully constructed situations presented as "social stories" (Rogers & Myles, 2001; Spencer, Simpson, & Lynch, 2008).
- *Use peer support:* Prepare students to support each other as peer-tutors through peer-mediated learning or help each other as "buddies" during noninstructional time (Copeland et al., 2002; Dion, Fuchs, & Fuchs, 2005; Turnbull, Pereira, & Blue-Banning, 2000).

Inclusive general education classrooms provide a particularly rich opportunity for friendships between children with and without disabilities to occur. In one study of typically developing middle-school students, the majority of students spoke of the importance of inclusive schooling in the development of friendships with students with disabilities (Chadsey & Han, 2005). One seventh grader noted, "If [students with disabilities are] not in your classes with you then you're probably not going to meet them and you're not going to talk to them, or anything" (p. 53).

Although inclusive settings provide the opportunity for children to interact, interaction is not automatic. You can, however, use three strategies to ensure that meaningful relationships develop and grow in these settings. First, select the classrooms and supports so that all students in the class may experience acceptance, independence, and success (Boutot, 2007). Second, model effective collaboration and encourage positive interactions among students. Third, provide information to all families about inclusive education and encourage them to foster inclusive values in their children (Salend, 2006). For example, you can recommend books about diversity for families to read at home or suggest ways they can use language or engage in behaviors that communicate their acceptance of individual differences (Salend, 2004).

Instructional practices that promote friendships are those that instill a culture of acceptance. We encourage you to use the partnership practices associated with the principles of respect and commitment to facilitate students' friendships in school and in the community.

Fostering Parent Participation

Families also need to feel that they are an important part of the school community. Think about the families you have known or worked with in the past. Would they say they felt like valued members of their child's school community? Why or why not?

There are many ways to enhance families' participation and sense of community in their child's school. First, you might consider helping families connect with other families at school. As you learned in chapter 11, the support that families find in one another is immeasurable. You might also review school policies or mission statements to see how building-level expectations contribute to families' perception of inclusion or exclusion. If you make membership a priority for children as well as their families, you are creating a powerful context for trust to flourish.

Providing meaningful opportunities for parents to attend and volunteer in school activities fosters partnerships with families and enhances their sense of community within the school. Are parents invited a couple of times each year for a conference or school play or are they encouraged to participate in a variety of meaningful activities throughout the school year? Meaningful involvement builds trust between families and teachers.

> The teachers know that [they can call on me] if they need any kind of help, let's say they need somebody to laminate things for them or do copying. There is a lot of stuff that I have at home that the Board of Education doesn't have in their classrooms. If they ask me, I will not even hesitate. I will send it right away. (Stoner & Angell, 2006, p. 183)

By providing families with choices, you demonstrate your respect for families' preferences for participating in school activities and events. Specifically, you can create partnerships when families (1) attend school events, (2) contribute to classroom instruction, (3) contribute to other school tasks, (4) attend classes of their own, (5) participate in the parent-teacher organization, and (6) participate in family resource centers. Figure 12.2 lists examples of strategies that can be used within each of these options.

You should always bear in mind that the family, not you, makes the choice whether to be involved. You may encourage the family to be involved, but be cautious about causing embarrassment or shame. Families may differ from you and your professional colleagues in the value they place on involvement in school activities, and cultural or language differences may make it difficult for families to be involved. Some families may lack the economic resources to participate. This includes resources for child care and transportation (Reglin, King, Losike-Seimo, & Ketterer, 2003). Two researchers provide a sobering assessment of the experiences of some families:

> Parental involvement at school is certainly important to children's academic progress, but not all parents are equally equipped to participate at school. Minority immigrant parents face additional barriers that prevent them from participating in their children's school at

FIGURE **12.2**	Opportunities for parent participation in school activities.

Opportunity for Participation	Illustrative Examples
Attending School Events	Attending an open house or back-to-school night
	Attending the school-sponsored book fair
	Attending season parties
	Attending school performances or concerts
	Attending school-run ball games
Contributing to Classroom Instruction	Developing instructional materials or equipment
	Tutoring individual students
	Participating in field trips
	Making a guest presentation in an area of expertise
Contributing to Other School Tasks	Supervising students in after-school activities
	Helping to organize school events, such as book sales or career days
Attending Classes	Attending evening classes for self-enhancement (for example, computer literacy, English as a second language, grant writing, cooking)
	Attending classes as a family
	Attending classes on child development
Participating in the Parent-Teacher Organization	Attending school- or districtwide meetings
	Participating on a committee (for example, the special education parent committee)
Participating in Family Resource Centers	Accessing information or resources
	Participating in parent support networks

comparable levels, and their children seem to suffer the consequences not only through their actual levels of participation but by virtue of the obstacles themselves that likely represent general domestic hardships. (Turney & Kao, 2009, p. 257)

The basic point of this quotation and the text before it is simply this: Communicate with families to learn how much they want to be involved and how each family defines involvement.

You would do well to bear in mind that families of children with disabilities who attend general school events may not know many of the other families. Often, families come to know other families because their children are friends. You can welcome families into the school by increasing membership opportunities for them and their children. Consider the ideas presented earlier in this chapter as well as the strategies presented in chapter 3. Introduce the families of students with disabilities to other families, highlight their children's meaningful contributions to the class, and create opportunities for students and their families to make friends

within the school and community. By using the practices associated with the partnership principle of commitment, you contribute to trust among families and professionals.

:: USING POSITIVE BEHAVIOR SUPPORT

Partnerships with families that are well grounded in trust are particularly important to prevent situations in which students' behavior impedes their participation in school, at home, or in the community. In this section, we turn to the fifth opportunity for professionals to collaborate with families: partnerships in using positive behavior support (PBS).

As you learned in chapter 6, one of NCLB's principles is school safety; PBS advances school safety. And as you also learned in chapter 6, IDEA requires educators to consider using positive behavior supports and other strategies when a student's behavior impedes his/hers or others' learning. What is PBS and why do these laws favor it?

Positive behavior support is a problem-solving, data-based, and proactive approach to changing students' challenging behaviors. It uses systemic and individual strategies to modify the environment, especially the interactions between the student and other individuals, including educators and peers, to prevent problem behavior and maximize students' behavioral and learning outcomes.

The outcomes of comprehensive PBS can be supportive school systems, responsive classrooms, and student skill development (Horner, Sugai, Todd, & Lewis-Palmer, 2005; Sugai et al., 2000). Whereas the traditional behavior management approach views students as the problem, PBS views systems, settings, and skill deficiencies as areas of concern. Thus, PBS shifts the focus from "fixing" the individual to changing systems, settings, and skills.

Family-professional partnerships are essential to implementing and maximizing the outcomes of PBS (Lucyshyn, Horner, Dunlap, Albin, & Ben, 2002). The features of effective family-centered PBS (Buschbacher, Fox, & Clarke, 2004; Lucyshyn et al., 2002) include:

- Partnerships with families
- Functional assessment to understand the purpose of the behavior and to develop support strategies
- Attention to family priorities, values, and resources to ensure that support strategies have a good "contextual fit" with the student, family, and environment
- Multicomponent support plans that are both preventative and instructive
- Family setting as unit of analysis and intervention

PBS is an approach to maximize expectations of the student and affirm the student's strengths while simultaneously responding to the needs of the students and the family. One mother wrote of her family's experience in a home-school partnership to implement PBS:

> The sweetest fruit of this successful partnership was that Samantha had gotten beyond violence . . . As Sam's life blossomed, our life together as a family began to open up as well. We purchased, for the first time in years, new furniture. We started to take Sam out with us. We went out to dinner, included her on shopping trips, and took her on a five-day vacation to California. It was fun to be with Sam. For the first time, we felt that we were becoming a family. (Fake, 2002, p. 214)

School-Wide Positive Behavior Support

In recent years, a school-wide approach has emerged as an effective way to create an environment that benefits all students, not just those with disabilities (Horner et al.,

2005; Sailor, Zuna, Choi, Thomas, McCart, & Roger, in press; Turnbull et al., 2002). The National Center for Positive Behavioral Interventions and Supports (www.pbis.org) is taking the lead nationally in creating successful school-wide models. Visit the website to learn about the latest research.

As Figure 12.3 illustrates, school-wide models generally offer three levels of positive behavior support: (1) universal support, (2) group support, and (3) individual support. The three levels provide a continuum of interventions that vary in the intensity of services, with far fewer students receiving the more intensive supports.

Level 1—Universal Support. Universal support provides clear expectations and positive feedback for all students across all classrooms and nonclassroom settings (for example, halls, cafeteria, playgrounds, buses). There are four key elements of universal support (Horner, 2000; Sugai, Horner et al., 2000; Sugai et al., 2000):

- *Behavioral expectations are clearly defined:* These expectations are typically simple, positively framed, and few in number.
- *Behavioral expectations are taught:* Each of the behaviorally stated expectations must be explicitly taught so that students will know exactly what is expected of them.
- *Appropriate behaviors are acknowledged:* Schools need to build a positive culture in which students are positively affirmed at least four times as often as they are negatively sanctioned.
- *Program evaluations and adaptations are made by a positive behavior support team:* School-wide systems need guidance, and that guidance can best come from a collaborative team composed of administrators, teachers, parents, students, and community representatives.

Families are important members of the school's PBS team in helping to develop, teach, and monitor school-wide behavioral expectations. Parents are also important collaborators in following through at home with the school's expectations. The more students receive consistent expectations across home, school, and community settings, the more likely they are to incorporate behavioral expectations across all aspects of their lives.

Community representatives can also serve on the school-based team, incorporating the same behavioral expectations in various community environments in which students participate—recreation programs, scouting, restaurants, religious organizations, and others. Ursula and DJ Markey, parents of two children with

FIGURE 12.3	School-wide framework for positive behavioral support.

Key Features	Universal Support	Group Support	Individual Support
Target group	All students	Some students	Fewer students
Settings	Classrooms and other school settings	Classrooms and other school settings	Classrooms, other school settings Multiple environments, including home and community
Data gathering	Interview school staff Observations across school settings Descriptive group statistics	Interview specific students Observe targeted behavior of specific students in school settings	Functional behavior assessment of individual students in multiple settings Person-centered planning Interviews with student and family
Focus of interventions	Define, disseminate, and teach universal behavioral expectations	Implement self-management for targeted students	Provide individual support across multiple settings Develop collaborative partnerships with stake-holders to implement supports and leverage resources
Intensity	Limited	Moderate	Pervasive

disabilities and founders of the Pyramid Parent Training Community Parent Resource Center in New Orleans, remind us of the importance of PBS to families in communities in crisis:

> PBS raises the bar for everyone. There is a commonality that professionals, community members, families, and schools work towards—common positive expectations and language. PBS is a different way of being in the world; it offers and reinforces support rather than control. In an urban community, especially one in crisis, teaching parents and families the skills to become leaders in addition to PBS strategies is critical so that they can help the communities' efforts to move forward more successfully. (DJ & U. Markey, 2007 as cited in McCart, Wolf, Sweeny, Markey, & Markey, 2009)

Universal support is meeting the needs of a substantial number of students by increasing successful behavioral and academic outcomes (Horner et al., 2005; Lassen, Steele, & Sailor, 2006; Luiselli, Putnam, & Handler, 2005). For example, school-wide implementation of positive behavior support in an urban middle school in Kansas City, Kansas (Turnbull et al., 2002) involved these practices:

- Codes of conduct that are consistent with specific shared behavioral expectations.
- Students' explicit learning to use these behaviors.
- A referral/ticket system to reinforce desirable behavior.

After two years of implementing school-wide supports, office discipline referrals decreased by 23%, time-outs went down by 30%, in-school suspensions were reduced by 12%, and 1- to 5-day suspensions decreased by 60%.

Level 2—Group Support. Group support moves beyond universal support to interventions for a specific group of students in classroom or nonclassroom settings. Level 2 support can involve group interventions at the classroom level.

Typically, educators gather information about the group through observations and interviews and then use the information to discern the patterns of behaviors within the group of students. For example, a teacher may ask: "When does my class have the most and least difficulty attending to schoolwork? Why do problems tend to occur during transitions?" Interventions are aimed at benefiting multiple students. For example, you may reteach a group of students how to meet behavioral expectations or you may rearrange the classroom to enhance communication or peer support.

How do family-professional partnerships enhance group support? Family members can contribute to the understanding of their child's behavior, offer suggestions for change, and help students work on generalizing the skills they are learning in school to community settings. The more you and other educators and families can agree on expectations, rewards, and other important elements of positive behavioral support, the more successful students will be in overcoming their behavioral challenges. Draw on your partnership practices to enhance understanding of a student's behavior and promote a shared commitment to effect change.

Level 3—Individual Support. Educators provide individual support to students who can benefit from greater support than that provided through universal or group interventions. Individual support can occur solely in school or across multiple settings. Team decision making is at the core of individual support, and families are key collaborators.

Typically, the first step in providing individual support is for the student's IEP team and, if not already present, a specialist in PBS to conduct a functional behavioral assessment. A functional behavioral assessment usually involves collecting information through direct observation and interviews with the student and others who spend significant amounts of time with the student. The purpose of the observations and interviews is to understand the purpose of the problem behaviors, by considering the situations in which they occur and the consequences that maintain the behaviors (Crone & Horner, 2003; Sugai, Lewis-Palmer, & Hagan-Burke, 2000). It is good practice to incorporate a functional behavioral assessment into the student's nondiscriminatory evaluation (see chapter 9) and IEP (see chapter 10).

Information drawn from the functional behavioral assessment becomes the foundation for planning individualized interventions. There are numerous ways to support individual students, including changing conditions within the environment and teaching students effective ways to communicate or interact with others. Figure 12.4 sets out several suggestions for providing individual supports. Consider how they foster empowerment of students and families and demonstrate your respect for their individuality.

FIGURE 12.4 PBS support strategies.

- Alter the environment.
  - Accommodate students' environmental needs (e.g., attend to noises, light, and other sensory stimuli that may be distracting; provide quiet learning area).
  - Consider room arrangements and traffic patterns.
- Increase predictability and scheduling.
  - Use visual or written schedules to provide structure.
  - Prepare students in advance for changes and transitions.
- Increase choice making.
  - Encourage students to express their preferences and take them into account in planning instruction and environment supports.
  - Teach students specific skills in decision making and self-determination.
- Make curricular adaptations.
  - Adjust tasks and activities so that they are presented in formats that are consistent with students' strengths, needs, and preferences.

- Appreciate positive behaviors.
  - "Catch the student being good," and provide affirmation to students and families.
  - Teach student to use self-monitoring as a way to track their own success.
  - Maintain a 4-to-1 ratio of positive to negative statements.
  - Embed rewards within difficult activities.
- Teach replacement skills.
  - Teach students a different way to accomplish their purpose without needing to engage in the impeding behavior.
  - Teach students problem-solving skills so that they will know how to generate appropriate alternatives when they encounter problems.
- Change systems.
  - Work with other educators and families to develop state-of-the-art services and supports.
  - Work within your community to create inclusive opportunities in which students with impeding behavior can participate in a successful way.

Family-professional partnerships are essential in carrying out a functional assessment and in developing, implementing, and monitoring a behavior intervention plan (Peck-Peterson, Derby, Berg, & Horner, 2002; Rao & Kalyanpur, 2002). Family members have unique insights about the student, the situation, and the problem behavior. Just as parents know what brings out the best in their child, they also are likely to know what might trigger a problem behavior. In addition, many families already know ways to prevent problem behavior. This a perfect opportunity to use the partnership practices to affirm the families' strengths and foster their empowerment.

Family participation not only enriches understanding of the student's behavior, but also ensures that the selected interventions are consistent with the family's priorities, culture, values, and preferences. By honoring cultural diversity, you can achieve a fuller and clearer understanding of a student's behavior. For example, Chen and colleagues (2002) described a situation in which a misunderstanding occurred when a teacher made an erroneous assumption about a student's refusal to eat lunch at school. Not until the teacher visited the child at home and observed the family eating sticky rice with their fingers did she realize that a change in school rules, not a behavior plan, was warranted.

You will want to remember that it may take time and respect for the PBS team to build trust when working with families whose beliefs differ from their own. Wang, McCart, and Turnbull (2007) described how one team exercised cross-cultural competence, an important practice you learned about in chapter 8, to support a young middle-school girl who had recently moved from China. Initially the family "did not think that [their daughter's] nighttime issue (bedwetting) was a serious problem to be addressed by so-called intervention strategies" (Wang et al., 2007, p. 44). However, by using informal communication, involving teachers familiar to the family, and continually honoring the families' beliefs about discipline and meaningful lifestyle, the family began to understand that they could and should address their daughter's challenge as a behavioral (not medical) issue.

Of course, it helps families to understand teachers' perspectives about any intervention (including PBS). Just as Mike Lamb presented himself to his students as a person who was at one time a "child" and student like them (p. 264), so Ryan Frisella describes his partnership with Nancy Regas in the Together We Can box on the next page and Nancy describes hers in the My Voice box on page 277.

To involve families and community members in collecting information and decision making, consider using person-centered planning, which you learned about in chapter 9. Person-centered planning is a tool for engaging families, community members, educators, and students in developing a vision plan to actively support students in achieving their dreams. PBS becomes a strategy for activating the vision and advancing toward it.

The use of PBSs with families leads to positive outcomes for individual families and their children (Lucyshyn, Kayser, Irvin, & Blumber, 2002; Moes & Frea, 2002; Vaughn, White, Johnston, & Dunlap, 2005; Vaughn, Wilson, & Dunlap, 2002). This approach has been shown to decrease a wide range of problem behaviors in children (including preschoolers to adolescents). Partnerships with parents have led to children's improved participation in home and community activities and have enhanced family quality of life. In addition, the positive outcomes of family implementation of PBS endure over time (Luchyshyn et al., 2007).

Many students benefit from individualized supports in school, at home, and in the community. However, for some children, change cannot occur unless the environment in which they live also changes. Conditions such as poverty, family health challenges, and impoverished neighborhoods play a powerful role in shaping students' behaviors. Supports and services for families impacted by social, economic, and health issues must be comprehensive and coordinated. Integrated services provide an ideal context in which to embed individualized behavior support. Models are emerging that incorporate person-centered planning, positive behavior support, and coordinated supports and services to address issues impacting family life (for example, see Becker-Cottrill, McFarland, & Anderson, 2003; McCart et al., 2009).

Unfortunately, most schools still do not have comprehensive services. You can use the partnership practices associated with the principle of advocacy to think about how you can support the transformation of discrete, segmented programs into ones that meet the holistic needs of students and families. In the final section of this chapter, you will learn about best practices in integrating services across numerous sectors. But first we will explore how professionals enhance students' learning and development within schools.

∷ PARTNERING WITH COLLEAGUES

You have just learned about five opportunities for professionals to collaborate with families to support student learning and development. Professionals are also partners with each other, especially because students' IEP and IFSP teams must consist of various professionals who are from different disciplines. In addition, collaboration and co-teaching have become prevalent practices as more students are educated in

TOGETHER WE CAN

Ryan and Mrs. Regas—Respect, Advocacy, Communication, Commitment, and Trust

Although I would occasionally talk to my teachers or sometimes the Circle of Friends advisor Mrs. Goren (as the club Circle of Friends was a large part of my extracurricular activity at school), the person I most often relied on was my counselor Mrs. Regas. Even though I'm sure she tells all her students to contact her at any time to talk, I felt like we had an especially strong relationship.

First, she never treated me differently because of my physical disability. She always thought of me as a kind, intelligent, hard-working, and determined student and overall just a good person. Mrs. Regas respected and trusted all my judgments after she gave her advice. To give an example, I had an extremely difficult math class in my junior year. Mrs. Regas suggested that I take the class over again with a different teacher although it was challenging for me so that it would look good on my transcript if I tried again. Although Mrs. Regas was very strong about this suggestion, she reminded me that in the end it was completely my decision and she would support whatever I decided. I tried the class again this last year and did much better.

Second, I appreciate all the times she advocated for me including contacting my teachers, writing recommendation letters as part of my scholarship applications, and attending as many school functions that I was involved in as she could. If there were ever a problem that she needed to ask about, she made a point to find me at school or contact my parents.

Third, she was very easy to communicate with through a meeting or e-mail. Even when I didn't have an urgent issue to discuss with her, she was willing just to have a conversation about my personal life and didn't rush me. I could tell she was very well liked by other students as well probably because she developed a friendly relationship with them also.

Finally, Mrs. Regas gave many tips about the upcoming college years as far as what I need to be successful and recommended a book, which gave even more tips (partly because her daughter is featured in it). She was very sad and happy for me at the same time when I graduated and made sure she kept me as her student and that she was the counselor who announced my name at the ceremony even though her alphabet was supposed to change! I could tell she also developed a strong relationship with my parents and I thank her for everything she did for me.

Take Action!

- Trust a student and you'll engender trust, not just by the student but also by the student's parents.
- Remember that you will not trust and earn trust unless you, like Mrs. Regas, respect your students, advocate for them, communicate clearly with them, and demonstrate your commitment to them.

---

inclusive general education settings. We now turn our attention to the critical role of partnerships among professionals in coordinating and implementing a student's IFSP or IEP.

Professional-professional partnerships are not fundamentally different than family-professional partnerships. In both relationships, individuals work together to reach a mutual goal. The partnership principles shape the interactions among team members. Whether professionals are providing services to students directly or indirectly or whether they are co-teaching or supporting students at different times or in different settings, professional partnerships need to be grounded in trust. Trust evolves as team members adhere to the principles of communication, respect, commitment, advocacy, equality, and professional competence. All members of the team need to rely on each other and themselves.

Think for a moment how the partnership principles apply to your own professional partnerships. For example, have you achieved parity in decision making with other professionals with whom you have worked? Or have you experienced the inequity described by this professional:

> . . . One person on the team . . . saw his [the student's] issues as much more behavior than everyone else and she was basically consequencing behaviors instead of understanding the underlying mental illness . . . There was no one on that team who could convince her any differently. She just got very dug in and she felt she was the expert . . . So one of the things that makes a team function poorly is when somebody gets very territorial or very proprietary. (Blue-Banning, Summers, Frankland, Nelson, & Beegle, 2004, p. 177)

A key question in the implementation of an IFSP or IEP is how best to coordinate services to support the student's learning and development and to minimize the fragmentation or duplication of services and supports. According to teachers, service providers, and parents, the answer lies in effective professional-professional partnerships (Giangreco, Prelock, Reid, Dennis, & Edelman, 2000; Snell & Janney, 2000; Soodak & Erwin, 2000).

Three critical strategies for maintaining effective partnerships include (1) ensuring adequate time for planning; (2) regularly assessing team roles, responsibilities, and functioning; and (3) providing services to students in the classroom and other natural contexts (Friend & Cook, 2003; Giangreco et al., 2000; Thousand, Villa, & Nevin, 2002).

Ensure Adequate Planning Time

Professionals need face-to-face communication to work within a common framework to benefit the student. However, it is often difficult for professionals to find the time to meet (Friend, 2007; York-Barr, Ghere, & Sommerness, 2007). Because related service personnel may support students in more than one class or divide their time across schools, they have few opportunities for a common meeting time. Although it is critical for all team members to meet regularly, some teachers find it useful to meet individually with related service providers (Snell & Janney, 2000).

An alternative is for service providers to schedule themselves for longer blocks of time within a particular school to allow greater flexibility in their scheduling or to provide time for meetings within the schedule. This is difficult to do when therapists' schedules are developed after the school year begins. Thus, many administrators start the scheduling process several months before the start of a new school year to ensure that there is adequate planning time between professionals from various disciplines.

Another way to create time to meet is to have assigned planning times overlap. Effective implementation of the student's IEP cannot occur unless everyone working with the student is on the same page. You may find it necessary to advocate for collaborative planning time in your school.

Assess Team Roles, Responsibilities, and Functioning

Team members bring different skills and knowledge to the partnership. Effective teams recognize these unique contributions and use them to benefit students. They are not limited by rigid disciplinary boundaries imposed within an "expert" model of service delivery. When team members trust each other, they can share their expertise and learn from each other. Research on teacher collaboration to support English language learners in an elementary school discovered the mutual benefits of shared expertise:

> The teachers came to understand that relationships were the means by which their collective wisdom of practice could be realized. Creating an environment in which taking risks to experiment with new ways of practice is encouraged and in which unsuccessful attempts are not unduly punished but viewed as opportunities to learn, fosters trust. (York-Barr et al., 2007, p. 329)

Paraprofessionals frequently play an important role in the education of students with disabilities. You will want to consider carefully how they will participate in implementing instruction and in communicating with other team members, including families. That careful consideration is particularly necessary because school administrators seem to rely too much on paraprofessionals and do not offer them sufficient training to support students (Giangreco & Doyle (2002). It may be difficult, but nonetheless essential, to ensure a balance between the use of paraprofessional support and teacher, service provider, peer, and other support (Giangreco & Broer, 2007).

Provide Services Within the Classroom and Other Naturally Occurring Activities and Contexts

In chapter 3, you learned that providing services in naturally occurring contexts gives the students opportunities to participate in inclusive recreational activities. Providing related services within the context of the student's class, school, and home routines also enhances service integration and professional-professional partnerships (Dunst & Bruder, 2002). When related service providers work alongside teachers, everyone can share instructional decision making, model practices that can be used at other times, and modify instruction to address real-life situations (Giangreco et al., 2000).

In situations where services are poorly coordinated, teachers, parents, and students are left with the task of making sense of a fragmented educational program. Poor coordination and lack of communication can affect students' learning and motivation and often impacts students most in need of assistance.

One approach that has been used to support students in a general education classroom is the integrated comprehensive service delivery model (Frattura & Capper, 2007). This approach calls for multiple team structures that are organized according to the needs of students so that they can benefit from comprehensive services provided in integrated settings. Three of the teams function at the school level: a planning team, a service delivery team, and a grade-level team; the fourth team functions at the district level (Frattura & Capper, 2007).

Parents suffer when coordination among teachers and service providers is poor or nonexistent. Some parents of young children with disabilities have had to assume roles that should have been carried out by professionals, largely due to poor coordination and the absence of trust (Soodak & Erwin, 2000). These roles included sharing information among teachers, therapists, and other team members to ensure consistency in their child's education, and arranging for specialized equipment and consultants. Where there is a lack of trust and poor coordination of services, parents may feel obliged to monitor their child's education to make sure it complies with the IEP. Professionals must honor their responsibilities and develop trusting partnerships with each other and with parents.

All service providers within and across programs need to work together in partnerships characterized by a commitment to students and families and trust in each other. We now turn our attention to those partnerships that extend beyond the school walls.

:: INTEGRATING SCHOOL AND COMMUNITY SERVICES

Throughout this book you have learned about the importance of partnerships among individuals—primarily families and school professionals. Partnerships also occur at the systems level among agencies providing different types of services to children and their families.

There are two reasons schools and communities need to form partnerships. First, education is a community responsibility. With an increasing number of children entering school with complex challenges and risks (Federal Interagency Forum on Child and Family Statistics, 2000) and children with disabilities being disproportionately exposed to conditions such as poverty and neglect (Emerson, 2007; Fujiura & Yamaki, 2000), it has become ineffective for schools to work alone in meeting the needs of students and their families.

Second, it is unreasonable to require family members to spend the often inordinate amount of time it takes to identify and access services within a fragmented system, to navigate several service systems and coordinate each with the other, and to drive powerfully toward IDEA's four overarching outcomes. But families do whatever it takes, often with the support of teachers such as yourself, other professionals, and friends.

Full-Service and Community Schools. Service integration provides comprehensive, seamless support for children and their families. The general education literature has described various models of service integration. Two of the most frequently used terms are *full-service schools* and *community schools*. Other terms include *interprofessional collaboration, coordinated services, community-linked services,* and *school-linked services* (Adelman & Taylor, 1997; Blank, Melaville, & Shah, 2003; Blank & Berg, 2006; Calfee, Wittwer, & Meredith, 1998; Dryfoos, 2004; Maguire, 2000). These approaches are substantial improvements over the typical situation of having services spread throughout the entire community and requiring families to access and coordinate services on their own.

Full-service or community schools seek to provide quality education (for example, school-based management, individualized instruction, and team teaching). They link their students and staff to a vast array of other services provided by the school (for example, comprehensive health education and social skills training) and by community agencies within a school-based location (for example, immunizations, social services, and substance abuse treatment) (Dryfoos, 2004).

> In community schools, educators do not operate on the assumption that the school has all the assets and expertise necessary to improve student learning. Instead, they collaborate with partners who demonstrate that they are committed to results that are important to the school system and the community. Schools are transformed into much more than just a portfolio of programs and services. They become a powerful agent for change in the lives of young people and their families and improve the climate of the entire school. (Blank & Berg, 2006, p. 12)

Full-service or community schools have a single point of delivery, meet the holistic needs of the students within the context of their families, and provide whatever services are needed to enhance a child's success in school and in the community (Dryfoos, 2004). The schools and agencies providing integrated services do not merge; instead, they have mutually increased collaboration and coordination.

Community or full-service schools are growing throughout the United States (Blank et al., 2003). Although each school develops in response to the needs and preferences of its community, each strives to be a one-stop center for all education and community services. For example, one full-service or community school located in rural Vermont serves over 400 students, with more than half of them living in poverty (Maguire, 2000). In addition to a solid curriculum and high instructional expectations, multiple other services are available at the school, including after-school, early childhood, health and wellness (e.g., medical care,

MY VOICE

Nancy Regas—"Seeing My Melissa in Ryan"

"I see so much of my daughter Melissa in Ryan Frisella. I see things many people don't. Consequently, many times I can anticipate a student's needs."

So says Nancy Regas, the school counselor at Patrick Henry High School who worked with Ryan Frisella for four years. Who is Melissa, what does Nancy see, and what does she do as a result?

Melissa is Nancy's 30-year-old daughter. She has Ehlers-Danlos syndrome, a disorder of the connective tissue that affects her joints and skin, causing her to bruise easily, have skin that lacerates easily, and inflicts daily pain. She also has bilateral hearing loss. Despite that, she graduated from high school with a 4.24 average, earned her college degree, and is working part-time as a visual artist.

"Melissa inspires me in my career, even with students without physical challenges," says Nancy. "We all have trials and challenges."

Ryan's struggles were never about his spirit. "When he graduated, he brought me flowers to say thank you. I cried. He has a spirit that says, 'I'll try this on my own.' He doesn't know anything about 'learned helplessness.'"

Nancy had an easy time of it in working with Ryan on personal-social matters. "He has intrinsic bravery, fostered from 'day one' by his family. They encouraged him to interact with adults. Adults, more than students, brought out Ryan's innate courage. He savors life, and adults latch on to that."

But Ryan did have one big academic challenge. He struggled in his pre-calculus class in his junior year. Nancy encouraged him to retake the class in his senior year. He did, he mastered it, and he gained a great deal of self-confidence.

Notice that Nancy said she "encouraged" him. She didn't instruct, demand, or order him to retake the class. Nor did she use a commanding approach when counseling him about his academics in school and after he graduated.

"I wanted to know his interests. I believed he had the ability to do college work. But Ryan was hesitant. So I talked with him about his options and about finding his niche. I helped him explore and never told him what to do. I helped him discover his options and ability levels. I asked him, 'What is your passion?' and then I helped him find ways to play it out. We talked about college and work. He wanted college, and I helped him as he applied. He's going to San Diego State University and will live in the dorms. He's putting himself out there."

Take Action!

- Carefully consider how Nancy counseled Ryan so that he, not she, would make the decisions. Notice how she was subtly advancing Ryan's "self-determination"—never passing up an opportunity to encourage and guide his goals, with support when he needs it.
- Use your own life experiences as you work with your students. Nancy's daughter, Melissa, obviously is a powerful reference point when Nancy works with her students. Don't compartmentalize yourself; try to bring your personal experiences to bear in your work.

healthy snack cart), parental involvement, and literacy programs. There are also two mentoring programs. One provides credit to high school students for spending quality time with a younger student, and the other involves local business owners mentoring a student every week.

The emerging research on the effectiveness of community schools is quite promising. All the participants in a study examining 49 community school programs reported positive results on at least one outcome, including academic achievement, attendance, student behavior, or family well-being (Dryfoos, 2004). Another report concluded that full-service schools increase the use of services for children and their families and positively affect developmental outcomes for students living in high-risk situations (ERIC/OSEP Topical Brief, 2002).

What can teachers and other professionals do to make integrated services available to all students and their families? School-community partnerships are based on the same principles that promote trust within parent-professional and professional-professional partnerships.

First, effective school-community partnerships require all individuals to communicate openly and to learn about each other's needs and preferences. Professional competence is also important in establishing school-community partnerships.

Teachers need to know and understand the community in which they work and the families of the students they teach (Blank, 2004; Blank et al., 2003; Park & Turnbull, 2003). In addition, teachers must be familiar with the services, supports, regulations, and funding available to families. At the very least, they need to know where to refer families to access information.

Full-service and community schools provide unique opportunities to partner with service providers throughout the community. The partnership principles of respect and equality should guide the development of these new relationships. Although locating integrated services on school grounds enables collaboration among the various professionals, issues of role clarification, space, and confidentiality can arise.

Be mindful of power and equity as you move toward collaborative relationships with professionals in agencies that have a history of working independently. This is particularly true in early intervention where the integration of services required for coordination and implementation of IFSP goals has been particularly challenging (Summers, Steeples et al., 2001; Zhang, Schwartz, & Lee, 2006). Formal and informal approaches to interagency collaboration are needed to ensure that families of children dually enrolled in Early Head Start and Part C early intervention programs are supported through partnerships among the agencies (Zhang et al., 2006).

Wraparound. A similar approach to comprehensive, well-integrated service delivery is called *wraparound*. Wraparound is a planning process that is designed to coordinate school and community services for students with complex mental health needs (Eber, Breen, Rose, Unizycki, & London, 2008). A strengths-based planning process is used to identify and coordinate services that reflect the perspectives of the student, family, and other key adults.

Wraparound helps the student and family by blending natural supports, such as friends, extended family and neighbors, and community-based services. These services may include mental health therapy, special education, substance abuse treatment, public assistance, health care, and caregiver support (Pullman et al., 2006). Thus, this systemic intervention aims to "wrap" services around students and their families in a respectful and comprehensive way (Stambaugh, Mustillo, Burn, Stephens, Baxter, Edwars, & Dekraai, 2007).

The wraparound process generally involves four steps. In the first step, called the engagement phase, the family is introduced to the wraparound process. A facilitator will guide a discussion of the family's story as well as a discussion of the family's concerns, hopes, dreams, and great expectations. During the planning phase, team members learn about the family's strengths and expectations and together decide what to work on and how the work will be accomplished. A plan to manage crises that may arise is also developed. In the third phase the plan is implemented. During this phase, the family and team meet regularly to review accomplishments and make adjustments. In the fourth phase, preparations are made for the family to transition out of formal wraparound and plans for accessing future support, if needed, are developed.

Wraparound is a relatively new approach to supporting students with complex needs and their families. It draws on multiagency support to prevent students from being excluded from school or being placed in restrictive settings (Eber et al., 2008). However, evidence of the effectiveness of this approach is beginning to emerge. Research suggests that wraparound services may improve the clinical symptoms of students receiving mental health services as well as reduce the rate of recidivism of those in the juvenile justice system (Pullman et al., 2006; Stambaugh et al., 2007).

The partnership practices of effective communication, competence, and respect are as important in the implementation of wraparound services as they are in other collaborative endeavors. Teachers and other professionals also need to embrace the practices associated with the principle of advocacy when collaborating with families to integrate services within or across agencies.

School-community partnerships are emerging in response to a need to support families and enhance student learning and development. Keep your conscience primed to make sure the services and supports match the needs and preferences of the families, students, and the community. Broaden your alliances when different services or partnerships are warranted. Perhaps most important, advocate for systems change so that integrated rather than discrete services are provided to the families and students in your school.

Whether working with individuals from different disciplines within the same school, or across different agencies, working in partnership to implement the child's individualized education can bring positive and meaningful outcomes for everyone involved, particularly families.

REVISITING RYAN, MARY, AND JOHN FRISELLA

Never doubt the power of great expectations held by a student, the family, teachers, and counselors. Great expectations fuel ambition, and ambition—in Ryan's and his parents' case, ambition to be fully the person he is capable of being—spurred Ryan, his parents, and his counselor, Nancy Regas. To be fully himself, Ryan had to face his own limitations; interestingly, they did not relate so much to his disability as to his academic challenges in mathematics. Indeed, Ryan barely acknowledges any disability-related challenges. By facing his academic challenge and receiving support from Nancy to do so, Ryan had to make a choice. The choice was his and his alone to make: whether to retake the course or not. The process he followed, however, exemplified partnership—the one he and Nancy had. Moreover, he also benefited from the partnership he and his father had around homework—a partnership that his teachers approved.

Reread the first sentence of the first paragraph. Note that it mentions great expectations held by three people—the student, the family, and the teachers. These three form a partnership. Ryan's graduation with a B average and his entry into college are the result of partnerships combined with great expectations.

When children are young, it is not likely that they will be partners with their parents and teachers, but as they grow older, it is likely that many of them will be, even as Ryan was. Would Ryan have graduated with a good average and be headed to college without a partnership and great expectation? Probably not. Both were essential to the outcomes he achieved. And both will be essential for him as a college student and then in his life after college.

Good early habits—having great expectations and achieving them through partnerships—really are good life-long skills.

SUMMARY

In this final chapter, we focused on the outcomes of parent-professional partnerships, telling how partnerships can lead—as they did for Ryan Frisella—to the four national policy outcomes that IDEA envisions: equal opportunities (especially in education), independent living, full participation, and economic self-sufficiency.

Benefits of Partnership. These are essentially academic

Partnerships in Homework
- Key issues and family concerns
- Practical suggestions
  - Create opportunities to communicate
  - Create options to minimize family responsibility
  - Use strategies to improve family homework practices
  - Report progress and other information

Partnerships in Using Assistive Technology
- Accessing assistive technology
- Using assistive technology at home

Promoting Friendships and Community Participation (Including Fostering Parent Participation)

Using Positive Behavior Supports

Partnering with Colleagues
- Ensuring adequate planning time
- Assessing team members' roles
- Providing services in appropriate environments

Integrating School and Community Activities
- Full-service and community schools
- Wraparound services

Figure 12.5 summarizes the partnership practices we have recommended.

FIGURE 12.5

Creating partnerships through trust building: selected actions leading to trust and distrust in supporting students' learning and development.

Partnership Principles and Practices	Issues	Actions Leading to Distrust	Actions Leading to Trust
Communication: Listen.	Family members share with you that they feel very embarrassed when they are in public and their child with problem behavior goes up to strangers and makes inappropriate remarks.	Tell the family that you are not embarrassed, and they should not be either.	Listen empathetically to what they are saying and ask what they think would be helpful in becoming more comfortable; ask if they have ever had the opportunity to talk with other families who face similar situations.
Respect: Honor cultural diversity.	A family who has been contacted to be involved in integrated services will not answer the door when someone makes a home visit, fearing loss of family privacy.	Decide that the family has "lost its chance" and drop them from a list of potential participants.	Arrange for someone from the family members' own cultural group to make contact with them, and recognize that building a trusting relationship may take significant time and effort.
Professional Competence: Provide a quality education.	A mother's partner (who is gay) is interested in helping the student in your class with homework, but she doesn't know the best way to go about it.	Ignore the partner because of your own values related to gay lifestyles.	Set up a dialogue journal with homework suggestions.
Equality: Foster empowerment.	The parent of one of your students has a chronic mental illness, and you are hesitant to include her as a classroom volunteer.	You ask the student if he thinks his mother is up to coming to school.	You call the mother, invite her perspectives on the kinds of school activities that would be especially meaningful to her, and make arrangements to respond to her priorities.
Commitment: Be sensitive to emotional needs.	Parents refuse to allow their teenager to go out during evenings or weekends because they are afraid of the impeding behavior that might occur.	Consider out-of-school issues to be outside the realm of your professional responsibility.	Facilitate friendships at school with peers, support the parents in using positive behavioral support with the student, and encourage them to include the student in evening and weekend classes.
Advocacy: Prevent problems.	Parents of a student with AD/HD are worried about the problems their child is having during after-school hours when they both are working and there is no one to provide child care.	Tell them that you strongly encourage them to take action before there is a serious problem with neighbors or others who live close by.	Provide them with information on the comprehensive school-linked services program and ask if they would like to receive information on community resources for after-school child care.

LINKING CONTENT TO YOUR LIFE

Understanding the assumptions, skills, and knowledge you have about your own teaching and learning will help you form partnerships with families. How would you describe your learning experiences in and outside of school? How do your own experiences help you find meaningful ways to involve families in their children's learning?

- As a student, how do you complete academic assignments outside of school? What person or environmental supports do you need? How do you access help?
- Reflecting on your own school experiences, did you always consider yourself to be a valued member of the class? What did teachers do to help your relationships with other students?
- In this chapter, we addressed the importance of family membership. To what extent did your family consider themselves to be members of the school and community? What contributed to their feelings of membership?
- Think back to a time when you worked collaboratively with others to accomplish a difficult task. Did you have sufficient opportunities to communicate with other individuals? Were the perspectives of all team members heard and respected?

REFERENCES

Abbott, D. A., & Meredith, W. H. (1986). Strengths of parents with retarded children. *Family Relations, 35*, 371–375.

Abt Associates, Inc. (2002). *Study of state and local implementation of impact of the Individuals with Disabilities Education Act.* Report on focus study I. Bethesda, MD: Abt Associates, Inc.

ACOG Committee on Practice Bulletins. (2007). ACOG Practice Bulletin No. 77: Screening for fetal chromosomal abnormalities. *Obstetrics & Gynecology, 109*(1), 217–227.

Adelman, H. S., & Taylor, L. (1997). Addressing barriers to learning: Beyond school-linked services and full-service schools. *American Journal of Orthopsychiatry, 67*(3), 408–419.

Agran, M., Blanchard, C., Wehmeyer, M., & Hughes, C. (2002). Increasing the problem-solving skills of students with developmental disabilities participating in general education. *Remedial and Special Education, 23*, 279–288.

Ainbinder, J., Blanchard, L., Singer, G. H. S., Sullivan, M., Powers, L. K., Marquis, J., & Santelli, B. (1998). A qualitative study of parent to parent support for parents of children with special needs. *Journal of Pediatric Psychology, 23*, 99–109.

Ainge, D., Colvin, G., & Baker, S. (1998). Analysis of perceptions of parents who have children with intellectual disabilities: Implications for service providers. *Education and Training in Mental Retardation and Developmental Disabilities, 33*(4), 331–341.

Alan Guttmacher Institute (2006). U.S. teenage pregnancy statistics: National and state trends and trends by ethnicity. Retrieved on August 1, 2009, from http://www.guttmacher.org/pubs/2006/09/12/USTPstats.pdf

Alan Guttmacher Institute. (2009). *State policies in brief: Sex and STI/HIV education.* Washington, DC: Author.

Algozzine, B., Browder, D., Karvonen, M., Test, D. W., & Wood, W. M. (2001). Effects of interventions to promote self-determination for individuals with disabilities. *Review of Educational Research, 71*(2), 219–277.

Al-Hassan, S., & Gardner, R. (2002). Involving immigrant parents of students with disabilities in the educational process. *Teaching Exceptional Children, 34*(5), 52–58.

Allen, R. I., & Petr, C. G. (1996). Toward developing standards and measurements for family-centered practice in family support programs. In G. H. S. Singer, L. E. Powers, & A. L. Olson (Eds.), *Redefining family support: Innovations in public-private partnerships* (pp. 57–89). Baltimore, MD: Paul H. Brookes.

Alpern, C. S., & Zager, D. (2007). Addressing the communication needs of young adults with autism in a college-based inclusion program. *Education and Training in Developmental Disabilities, 42*(4), 428–436.

Altshuler, S. J. (1997). A reveille for school social workers: Children in foster care need our help! *Social Work in Education, 19*(2), 121–127.

American Counseling Association Foundation. (1995). *The ACA code of ethics and standards of practice.* Retrieved on December 9, 2009, from http://www.AmericanCounselingAssociationFoundation/Resources/Ethics/CodeofEthics

American Psychiatric Association. (2000). *Diagnostic and statistical manual of mental disorders* (4th ed., rev.). Washington, DC: Author.

Anderson, P. L. (2000). Using literature to teach social skills to adolescents with LD. *Intervention in School and Clinic, 35*(5), 271–279.

Angelo, D. H. (2000). Impact of augmentative and alternative communication devices on families. *Augmentative and Alternative Communication, 16*(1), 37–47.

Anguiano, R. P. V. (2003). Families and schools: The effect of parental involvement on high school completion. *Journal of Family Issues, 25*(1), 61–85.

Ankeny, E. M., Wilkins, J., & Spain, J. (2009). Mothers' experiences of transition planning for their children with disabilities. *Teaching Exceptional Children, 41*(6), 28–36.

Arndt, S. A., Konrad, M., & Test, D. W. (2006). Effects of the self-directed IEP on student participation in planning meetings. *Remedial and Special Education, 27*(4), 194–207.

Avis, D. W. (1985). *Deinstitutionalization jet lag* (2nd ed.). Upper Saddle River, NJ: Merrill/Pearson Education.

Bahr, M. W., Fuchs, D., & Fuchs, L. S. (1999). Mainstream assistance teams: A consultation-based approach to prereferral intervention. In S. Graham & K. Harris (Eds.), *Teachers working together: Enhancing the performance of students with special needs* (pp. 87–116). Cambridge, MA: Brookline Books.

Bahr, M. W., Whitten, E., Dieker, L., Kocarek, C. E., & Manson, D. (1999). A comparison of school-based intervention teams: Implications for educational and legal reform. *Exceptional Children, 66*(1), 67–83.

Baier, A. C. (1986). Trust and antitrust. *Ethics, 96*, 231–260.

Bailey, D. B., Hebbeler, K., Scarborough, A., Spiker, D., & Mallik, S. (2004). First experiences with early intervention: A national perspective. *Pediatrics, 113*(4), 887–896.

Bailey, D. B., Hebbeler, K., Spikeer, D., Scarborough, A., Mallik, S., & Nelson, L. (2005). Thirty-six-month outcomes for families of children who have disabilities and participated in early intervention. *Pediatrics, 11*(6), 1346–1352.

Bailey, D. B., & Simeonsson, R. J. (1988). Assessing needs of families with handicapped infants. *Journal of Special Education, 22*(1), 117–127.

Bailey, D. B., Skinner, D., Correa, V., Arcia, E., Reyes-Blanes, M. E., Rodriguez, P., & Skinner, M. (1999). Needs and supports reported by Latino families of young children with developmental disabilities. *American Journal on Mental Retardation, 104*(5), 437–451.

Bailey, D. B., Skinner, D., & Sparkman, K. L. (2003). Discovering Fragile X syndrome: Family experiences and perceptions. *Pediatrics, 111*(2), 407–416.

Bailey, D. B., Skinner, D., & Warren, S. F. (2005). Newborn screening for developmental disabilities: Reframing presumptive benefit. *American Journal of Public Health, 95*(11), 1889–1893.

Bailey, L. B. (2006). Interactive homework: A tool for fostering parent-child interactions and improving learning outcomes for at-risk young children. *Early Childhood Education Journal, 34*(2), 155–167.

Bailey, L. B., Silvern, S. B., Brabham, E., & Ross, M. (2004). The effects of interactive reading homework and parent involvement on children's inference responses. *Early Childhood Education Journal, 32*(3), 173–178.

Bailey, R. L., Parette, H. P., Stoner, J. B., Angell, M. E., & Carroll, K. (2006). Family members' perceptions of augmentative and alternative communication device use. *Language, Speech, and Hearing Services in School, 37,* 50–60.

Baker, B. L., Ambrose, S. A., & Anderson, S. R. (1989). Parent training and developmental disabilities [special issue]. *Monographs of American Association on Mental Retardation, 13.*

Baker, B. L., & Blacher, J. (2002). For better or worse? Impact of residential placement on families. *American Association on Mental Retardation, 1,* 1–13.

Baker, B. L., McIntyre, L. L., Blacher, J., Crnic, K., Edelbrock, C., & Low, C. (2003). Pre-school children with and without developmental delay: Behaviour problems and parenting stress over time. *Journal of Intellectual & Developmental Disability, 47*(4/5), 217–230.

Baker-Erizcen, M. J., Brookman-Frazee, A., & Stahmer, A. (2005). Stress selves and adaptability in parents of toddlers with and without autism spectrum disorders. *Research and Practice for Persons with Severe Disabilities, 30*(4), 194–204.

Baldwin, A. Y. (2002). Culturally diverse students who are gifted. *Exceptionality, 10*(2), 139–147.

Bambara, L. M., Wilson, B. A., & McKenzie, M. (2007). Transition and quality of life. In S. L. Odom, R. H. Horner, M. E. Snell, & J. Blacher (Eds.), *Handbook of developmental disabilities* (pp. 371–389). New York: Guilford Press.

Bandura, A. (1997). *Self-efficacy: The exercise of control.* New York: W. H. Freeman.

Banks, S. (2009, May 9). These moms know true love. *Los Angeles Times.* Retrieved August 25, 2009, from http://articles.latimes.com/2009/may/09/local/me-banks9

Barlow, J., & Coren, E. (2000). Parenting programmes for improving maternal psychosocial health (Cochrane Review). In *Issue 3, Oxford: Update Software. Cochrane Library.*

Barlow, J., & Stewart-Brown, S. (2000). Behaviour problems and group-based parent education programs. *Developmental and Behavioral Pediatrics, 21*(5), 356–370.

Barnard, W. M. (2004). Parent involvement in elementary school and educational attainment. *Children & Youth Services Review, 26*(1), 39–62.

Barr, M. W. (1913). *Mental defectives: Their history, treatment, and training.* Philadelphia: Blakiston.

Barrera, I., & Corso, R. M. (2002). Cultural competency as skilled dialogue. *Topics in Early Childhood Special Education, 22*(2), 103–113.

Barrie, W., & McDonald, J. (2002). Administrative support for student-led individualized education programs. *Remedial and Special Education, 23*(2), 116–121.

Batshaw, M. L. (2002). *Children with disabilities.* Baltimore, MD: Paul H. Brookes.

Batshaw, M. L., Pellegrino, L., & Roizen, N. J. (2007). *Children with disabilities* (6th ed.). Baltimore, MD: Paul H. Brooks.

Baum, L. S. (2004). Internet parent support groups for primary caregivers of a child with special health care needs. *Pediatric Nursing, 34*(5), 381–401.

Bayat, M. (2007). Evidence of resilience in families of children with autism. *Journal of Intellectual Disability Research, 51*(9), 702–214.

Beach Center. (1999). Unpublished transcripts. Lawrence, KS: Beach Center on Disability.

Beach Center. (2000). *Unpublished research transcripts of focus groups.* Lawrence, KS: Beach Center on Disability.

Beach Center. (1999). *Unpublished transcripts.* University of Kansas, Lawrence, KS: Beach Center on Disability.

Becker-Cottrill, B., McFarland, J., & Anderson, V. (2003). A model of positive behavioral support for individuals with autism and their families: The family focus process. *Focus on Autism and Other Developmental Disabilities, 18*(2), 113–123.

Beghetto, R. A. (2001). Virtually in the middle: Alternative avenues for parental involvement in middle-level schools. *Clearing House, 75*(1), 21–25.

Behr, S. K., & Murphy, D. L. (1993). Research progress and promise: The role of perceptions in cognitive adaptation to disability. In A. P. Turnbull, J. M. Patterson, S. K. Behr, D. L. Murphy, J. G. Marquis, & M. J. Blue-Banning (Eds.), *Cognitive coping, families, and disability* (pp. 151–164). Baltimore, MD: Paul H. Brookes.

Behrman, R. E. (Ed.). (2004). *The future of children: Children, families, and foster care.* Los Altos, CA: David and Lucile Packard Foundation.

Bell, M., & Stoneman, Z. (2000). Reactions to prenatal testing: Reflection of religiosity and attitudes toward abortion and people with disabilities. *American Journal on Mental Retardation, 105,* 1–13.

Bell, M. J. (2007). Infections and the fetus. In M. L. Batshaw, L. Pellegrino, & N. J. Roizen (Eds.), *Children with disabilities* (6th ed., pp. 71–82). Baltimore, MD: Paul H. Brooks.

Belle, D. (2003). Poverty, inequality, and discrimination as sources of depression among U.S. women. *Psychology of Women Quarterly, 27*(2), 101–113.

Benn, P. A. (2002). Advances in prenatal testing for Down syndrome: I. General principles and second trimester testing. *Clinica Chimca Acta, 323*(1–2), 1–16.

Benn, P. A., & Chapman, A. R. (2009). Practical and ethical considerations of noninvasive prenatal diagnosis. *JAMA, 301*(20), 2154–2156.

Bennett, J. M. (1985). Company, halt! In H. R. Turnbull & A. P. Turnbull (Eds.), *Parents speak out: Then and now* (2nd ed., pp. 159–173). Upper Saddle River, NJ: Merrill/Pearson Education.

Benson, B. A., & Gross, A. M. (1989). The effect of a congenitally handicapped child upon the marital dyad: A review of the literature. *Clinical Psychology Review, 9*(6), 747–758.

Benson, P., Karlof, K. L., & Siperstein, G. N. (2008). Maternal involvement in the education of young children with autism spectrum disorders. *Autism, 12*(1), 47–63.

Benton Foundation. (1998). *About foster care, take this heart: The foster care project.* Retrieved August 14, 2004, from http://www.benton.org/pub library/mtm/pages/aagtth.html

Berliner, D. C., & Biddle, B. J. (1996). *Manufactured crisis: Myths, fraud, and the attacks on America's public schools.* New York: HarperCollins.

Bernheimer, L. P., & Weisner, T. (2007). "Let me just tell you what I do all day. . ." The family story at the center of intervention research and practice. *Infants and Young Children, 20*(3), 192–201.

Berrera, M., & Liu, K. K. (2006). Involving parents of English language learners with disabilities through instructional dialogues. *Journal of Special Education Leadership, 19*(1), 43–51.

Bettelheim, B. (1950). *Love is not enough.* Glencoe, NY: Free Press.

Bettelheim, B. (1967). *The empty fortress: Infantile autism and the birth of the self.* London: Collier-Macmillan.

Bezdek, J., Summers, J. A., & Turnbull, A. (in press). Professionals' attitudes in partnering with families of children and youth with disabilities. *Education and Training in Developmental Disabilities.*

Birenbaum, A. (2002). Poverty, welfare reform, and disproportionate rates of disability among children. *Mental Retardation, 40*(3), 212, 218.

Bishop, S. L., Richler, J., Cain, A. C., & Lord, C. (2007). Predictors of perceived negative impact in mothers of children with autism spectrum disorders. *American Journal on Mental Retardation, 112*(6), 450–461.

Blacher, J. (1984a). Sequential stages of adjustment to the birth of a child with handicaps: Fact or artifact? *Mental Retardation, 22*, 55–68.

Blacher, J. (1984b). *Severely handicapped young children and their families: Research in review.* New York: Academic Press.

Blacher, J., & Baker B. L. (2007). Positive impact of intellectual disability on families. *American Journal on Mental Retardation, 112*(5), 330–348.

Blacher, J., & Hatton, C. (2001). Current perspectives on family research in mental retardation. *Current Opinion in Psychiatry, 14*, 477–482.

Blanchett, W. J. (2002). Voices from a TASH forum on meeting the needs of gay, lesbian, and bisexual adolescents and adults with severe disabilities. *Research and Practice for Persons with Severe Disabilities, 27*(1), 82–86.

Blanchett, W. J., & Wolfe, P. S. (2002). A review of sexuality education curricula: Meeting the sexuality education needs of individuals with moderate and severe intellectual disabilities. *Journal of the Association for Persons with Severe Handicaps, 27*(1), 43–57.

Blank, M., & Berg, A. (2006). All together now: Sharing responsibility for the whole child. Washington, DC: Association for Supervision and Curriculum Development.

Blank, M., Melaville, A., & Shah, B. (2003). *Making the difference: Research and practice in community schools.* Washington, DC: Coalition for Community Schools, Institute for Educational Leadership.

Blank, M. J. (2004). How community schools make a difference. *Educational Leadership, 61*(8), 62–65.

Blue-Banning, M., Turnbull, A. P., & Pereira, L. (2000). Group Action Planning as a support strategy for Hispanic families: Parent and professional perspectives. *Mental Retardation, 38*(2), 262–275.

Blue-Banning, M. J., Santelli, B., Guy, B., & Wallace, E. (1994). *Cognitive coping project: Coping with the challenges of disability.* Lawrence: University of Kansas, Beach Center on Families and Disability.

Blue-Banning, M. J., Summers, J. A., Frankland, H. C., Nelson, L. L., & Beegle, G. (2004). Dimensions of family and professional partnerships: Constructive guidelines for collaboration. *Exceptional Children, 70*(2), 167–184.

Boggs, E. M. (1985). Who is putting whose head in the sand? (Or in the clouds, as the case may be). In H. R. Turnbull & A. P. Turnbull (Eds.), *Parents speak out: Then and now* (2nd ed., pp. 39–55). Upper Saddle River, NJ: Merrill/Pearson Education.

Booth, T., & Booth, W. (2000). Against the odds: Growing up with parents who have learning difficulties. *Mental Retardation, 38*(1), 1–14.

Booth-LaForce, C., & Kelly, J. F. (2004). Childcare patterns for families of preschool children with disabilities. *Infants and Young Children, 17*(1), 5–16.

Bos, C. S., Nahmias, M. L., & Urban, M. A. (1999). Targeting home-school collaboration for students with ADHD. *Teaching Exceptional Children, 31*(6), 4–11.

Boutot, E. A. (2007). Fitting in: Tips for promoting acceptance and friendships for students with autism spectrum disorders in inclusive classrooms. *Intervention in School and Clinic, 42*(3), 156–161.

Braaten, E., & Felopulos, G. (2004). *Straight talk about psychological testing for kids.* New York: Guilford Press.

Braddock, D., Hemp, R., & Rizzolo, M. (2008). *The state of the states in developmental disabilities: 2008.* Boulder, CO: University of Colorado, Department of Psychiatry and Coleman Institute for Cognitive Disabilities.

Braddock, D., Rizzolo, M. C., & Hemp, R. (2004). Most employment services growth in developmental disabilities during 1988–2002 was in segregated settings. *Mental Retardation, 42*(4), 317–320.

Brady, S. J., Peters, D. L., Gamel-McCormick, M., & Venuto, N. (2004). Types and patterns of professional-family talk in home-based early intervention. *Journal of Early Intervention, 26*(2), 146–159.

Brantlinger, E. (1992). Professionals' attitudes toward the sterilization of people with disabilities. *Journal of the Association for Persons with Severe Handicaps, 17*(1), 4–18.

Brewin, B. J., Renwick, R., & Schormans, A. F. (2008). Parental perspectives of the quality of life in school environments for children with Asperger syndrome. *Focus on Autism and Other Developmental Disorders, 23*(4), 242–252.

Bricker, W. A., & Bricker D. D. (1976). The infant, toddler, and preschool research and intervention project. In T. D. Tjossem (Ed.), *Intervention strategies for high risk infants and young children* (pp. 545–572). Baltimore, MD: University Park Press.

Brobst, J. B., Clopton, J. R., & Hendrick, S. S. (2009). Parenting children with autism spectrum disorders: The couple's relationship. *Focus on Autism and Other Developmental Disabilities, 24*(1), 38–49.

Broderick, C., & Smith, J. (1979). The general systems approach to the family. In W. R. Burr, R. Hill, F. I. Nye, & I. L. Reiss (Eds.), *Contemporary theories about the family* (Vol. 2, pp. 112–129). New York: Free Press.

Bronfenbrenner, U. (1990). Discovering what families do. In D. Blankenhorn, S. B. Ayme, & J. B. Elshtain (Eds.), *Rebuilding the nest: A new commitment to the American family* (pp. 27–38). Milwaukee, WI: Family Service American.

Brooke, V., & McDonough, J. T. (2008). The facts ma'am, just the facts: Social security disability benefit programs and work incentives. *TEACHING Exceptional Children, 41*(1), 58–65.

Brotherson, M. J., Cook, C., Erwin, E. J., & Weigel, C. J. (2008). Understanding self-determination and families of young children with disabilities in home environments. *Journal of Early Intervention, 31*(1), 22–43.

Brotherson, M. J., Cook, C., Erwin, E., & Weigel, C. (2008). Understanding self-determination and families of young children with disabilities in home. *Journal of Early Intervention, 31*, 22–43.

Brotherson, M. J., & Goldstein, B. L. (1992). Time as a resource and constraint for parents of young children with disabilities: Implications for early intervention services. *Topics in Early Childhood Special Education, 12*(4), 508–527.

Brotherson, M. J., Summers, J. A., Naig, L., Kyzar, K., Friend, A., Epley, P., & Gotto, G. (in press). Partnership patterns: Addressing emotional needs in early intervention. *Topics in Early Childhood Special Education.*

Brown Center on Education Policy. (2003). *The 2003 Brown Center Report on American Education: How well are American students learning?* Washington, DC: Brookings Institution.

Brown v. Topeka Board of Education, 349 U.S. 886 (1954).

Brown, I., Anand, S., Fung, W. L. A., Isaacs, B., & Baum, N. (2003). Family quality of life: Canadian results from an international study. *Journal of Developmental and Physical Disabilities, 15*(3), 207–229.

Brown, J. E., & Doolittle, J. (2008). A cultural, linguistic, and ecological framework for response to intervention with English language learners. *Teaching Exceptional Children, 40*(5), 66–72.

Browne, J. V., Langlois, A., Ross, E. S., & Smith-Sharp, S. (2001). BEGINNINGS: An interim individualized family service plan for use in the intensive care nursery. *Infants and Young Children, 14*(2), 19–32.

Bryan, T., & Sullivan-Burstein, K. (1998). Teacher-selected strategies for improving homework completion. *Remedial and Special Education, 19*(5), 263–275.

Bryan, T., Burstein, K., & Bryan, J. (2001). Students with learning disabilities: Homework problems and promising practices. *Educational Psychologist, 36*, 167–180.

Buck v. Bell, 274 (1927).

Buck, G., Polloway, E. A., Smith-Thomas, A., & Cook, K. W. (2003). Prereferral intervention processes: A survey of state practices. *Exceptional Children, 69*(3), 349–360.

Bui, Y. N., & Turnbull, A. (2003). East meets west: Analysis of person-centered planning in the context of Asian American values. *Exceptional Children, 38*(1), 18–31.

Burello, L., Lashley, C., & Beatty, E. (2001). *Educating all students together: How school leaders create unified systems.* Thousand Oaks, CA: Corwin Press.

Buschbacher, P., Fox, L., & Clarke, S. (2004). Recapturing desired family routines: A parent-professional behavioral collaboration. *Research and Practice for Persons with Severe Disabilities, 29*, 25–39.

Bush, G. W. (2001). Foreword: No Child Left Behind. Retrieved on February 23, 2004, from http://www.whitehouse.gov/news/reports/no-child-left-behind.html

Bush, G. W. (2001). Overview: No Child Left Behind, President Bush's education reform plan. Retrieved on February 23, 2004, from http://www.ed.gov/nclb/overview/intro/presidentplan/page_pg3.html#execsumm

Butera, G. (2005). Collaboration in the context of Appalachia: The case of Cassie. *The Journal of Special Education, 39*(2), 106–116.

Caldwell, J. (2007). Experiences of families with relatives with intellectual and developmental disabilities in a consumer-directed support program. *Disability & Society, 22*(6), 549–562.

Caldwell, J., & Heller, T. (2003). Management of respite and personal assistance services in a consumer-directed family support programme. *Journal of Intellectual Disability Research, 47*(4/5), 352–366.

Caldwell, J., & Heller, T. (2007). Longitudinal outcomes of a consumer-directed program supporting adults with developmental disabilities and their families. *Intellectual and Developmental Disabilities, 45*(3), 161–173.

Calfee, C., Wittwer, F., & Meredith, M. (1998). Why build a full-service school? In C. Calfee, F. Wittwer, & M. Meredith (Eds.), *Building a full-service school* (pp. 6–24). San Francisco: Jossey-Bass.

Callicott, K. J. (2003). Culturally sensitive collaboration within person-centered planning. *Focus on Autism and other Developmental Disabilities, 18*(1), 60–68.

Calloway, C. (1999). 20 ways to promote friendship in the inclusive classroom. *Intervention in School and Clinic, 34*(3), 176–177.

Camarota, S. A. (2001). Immigrants in the United States—2000. *Spectrum, 74*(2), 1–5.

Campbell, P. H., Milbourne, S., & Wilcox, M. J. (2008). Adaptation interventions to promote participation in natural settings. *Infants and Young Children, 21*(2), 94–106.

Cancio, E. J., West, R. P., & Young, K. R. (2004). Improving mathematics homework completion and accuracy of students with EBD through self-management and parent participation. *Journal of Emotional and Behavioral Disorders, 12*(1), 9–22.

Canda, E. R. (1999). Spiritually sensitive social work: Key concepts and ideals. *Journal of Social work Theory and Practice, 1*(1), 1–15.

Caplan, P. J., & Hall-McCorquodale, I. (1985). Mother-blaming in major clinical journals. *American Journal of Orthopsychiatry, 55*(3), 345–353.

Carnes, P. (1981). *Family development I: Understanding us.* Minneapolis, MN: Interpersonal Communications Programs.

Carnevale, F. A., Rehm, R. S., Kirk., S., K., & McKeever, P. (2008). What we know (and do not know) about raising children with complex continuing care needs. *Journal of Health Care, 12*(1), 4–6.

Carroll, S. Z., Blumberg, E. R., & Petroff, J. G. (2008). The promise of liberal learning: Crating a challenging postsecondary curriculum for youth with intellectual disabilities. *Focus on Exceptional Children, 4*(9), 1–9.

Carter, B., & McGoldrick, M. (Eds.). (2005). *The expanded family life cycle* (3rd ed.). Needham Heights, MA: Allyn & Bacon.

Carter, E. A., & McGoldrick, M. (1999). *Changing family life cycle: Individual, family, and social perspectives* (3rd ed.). Boston, MA: Allyn & Bacon.

Carter, E. W., Clark, N. M., Cushing, L. S., & Kennedy, C. H. (2005). Moving from elementary to middle school: Supporting a smooth transition for students with severe disabilities. *Teaching Exceptional Children, 37*(3), 8–14.

Cauthen, N. K., & Fass, S. (2009). *Ten important questions about child poverty and family economic hardship.* National Center for Children in Poverty. Retrieved on June 23, 2009, from http://www.nccp.org/publications/pub_829.html

Certo, N. J., Mautz, D., Pumpian, I., Sax, C., Smalley, K., Wade, H. A., Noyes, D., Luecking, R., Wechsler, J., & Batterman, N. (2003). Review and discussion of a model for seamless transition to adulthood. *Education and Training in Developmental Disabilities, 38*(1), 3–17.

Chaboudy, R., & Jameson, P. (2001 September/October). Connecting families and schools through technology. *Book Report*, 52–56.

Chadsey, J., & Han, K. G. (2005). Friendship-facilitation strategies: What do students in middle school tell us? *Teaching Exceptional Children, 38*(2), 52–57.

Chalfant, J. C., & Pysh, M. V. (1989). Teacher assistance teams: Five descriptive studies on 96 teams. *Remedial and Special Education, 10*(6), 49–58.

Chamberlain, S. P. (2005). Recognizing and responding to cultural differences in the education of culturally and linguistically diverse learners. *Intervention in School and Clinic, 40*(4), 195–211.

Chambers, C. R., & Childre, A. L. (2006). Fostering family-professional collaboration through person-centered IEP meetings: The "True Directions" Model. *Young Exceptional Children, 8*(3), 20–28.

Chan, S., & Lee, E. (2004). Families with Asian roots. In E. W. Lynch & M. J. Hanson (Eds.), *Developing cross-cultural competence: A guide for working with children and their families* (3rd ed., pp. 219–298). Baltimore, MD: Paul H. Brookes.

Chavkin, N. F., Gonzalez, J., & Rader, R. (2002). A home-school program in Texas-Mexico border school: Voices from parents, students, and school staff. *School Community Journal, 10*(2), 127–137.

Chen, D., Downing, J. E., & Peckham-Hardin, K. D. (2002). Working with families of diverse cultural and linguistic backgrounds: Considerations for culturally responsive positive behavior support. In J. M. Lucyshyn,

G. Dunlap, & R. W. Albin (Eds.), *Families and positive behavior support* (pp. 133–151). Baltimore, MD: Paul H. Brookes.

Child Welfare Information Gateway. (2008). What is child abuse and neglect? Retrieved on August 18, 2009, from http://www.childwelfare.gov/pubs/factsheets/whatiscan.cfm

Child Welfare League of America. (2002). *Improving educational outcomes for youth in care: A national collaboration.* Washington, DC: Author.

Childre, A., & Chambers, C. R. (2005). Family perceptions of student centered planning and IEP meetings. *Education and Training in Developmental Disabilities, 40*(3), 217–233.

Children's Defense Fund. (2008). *Children in the United States.* Retrieved on June 16, 2009, from http://www.childrensdefense.org/child-research-data-publications/data/state-data-repository/cits/children-in-the-states-2008-all.pdf

Christensen, S., Ysseldyke, J. E., & Algozzine, B. (1982, July). Institutional constraints and external pressures influencing referral decision. *Psychology in the School, 19*(3), 341–345.

Christenson, S. L., & Sheridan, S. M. (2001). *Schools and families: Creating essential connections for learning.* New York: Guilford Press.

Clausen, J. M., Landsverk, J., Ganger, W., Chadwick, D., & Litrownik, A. (1998). Mental health problems of children in foster care. *Journal of Child and Family Studies, 7*(3), 283–296.

Clements, M. A., Reynolds, A. J., & Hickey, E. (2004). Site-level predictors of children's school and social competence in the Chicago Child-Parent Centers. *Early Childhood Research Quarterly, 19,* 273–296.

Cobb, H. B., & Horn, C. J. (1989, November). *Implementation of professional standards in special education: A national study.* Paper presented at the meeting of the Council for Exceptional Children, Birmingham, AL.

Coles, R. (1989). *The call of stories.* Boston: Houghton Mifflin.

Coles, R. L. (2003). Black single custodial fathers: Factors influencing the decision to parent. *Families in Society: The Journal of Contemporary Human Services, 84*(2), 247–258.

Collier, B., McGhie-Richmond, D., Odette, F., & Pyne, J. (2006, March). Reducing the risk of sexual abuse for people who use augmentative and alternative communication. *Augmentative and Alternative Communication, 22*(1), 62–75.

Cook, R. S., Rule, S., & Mariger, H. (2003). Parents' evaluation of the usability of a web site on recommended practices. *Topics in Early Childhood Special Education, 23*(1), 19–27.

Coonrod, E. E., & Stone, W. L. (2004). Early concerns of parents of children with autistic and nonautistic disorders. *Infants and Young Children, 17*(5), 258–268.

Coots, J. J. (2007). Building bridges with families: Honoring the mandates of IDEA. *Issues in Teacher Education, 16*(2), 33–40.

Copeland, S. R., & Hughes, C. (2002). Effects of goal setting on task performance of individuals with mental retardation. *Education and Training in Mental Retardation and Developmental Disabilities, 37,* 40–54.

Copeland, S., McCall, J., Williams, C. R., Guth, C., Carter, E. W., Presley, J. A., et al. (2002). High school peer buddies: A win-win situation. *Teaching Exceptional Children, 35*(1), 16–21.

Coren, E., Barlow, J., & Stewart-Brown, S. (2003). The effectiveness of individual and group-based parenting programmes in improving outcomes for teenage mothers and their children: A systematic review. *Journal of Adolescence, 26,* 79–103.

The Council for Exceptional Children (1993). *CEC policy manual,* Section Three, part 2, (p 4). Reston, VA: Author. Retrieved on August 16, 2009, from http://www.cec.sped.org/Content/NavigationMenu/Professional Development/ProfessionalStandards/RedBook

Cousins, N. (1989). *Head first: The biology of hope.* New York: Dutton.

Covey, S. R. (1990). *The seven habits of highly effective people: Restoring the character ethic.* New York: Fireside/Simon & Schuster.

Crais, E. R., Roy, V. P., & Free, K. (2006). Parents' perceptions of the implementation of family-centered practices in child assessments. *American Journal of Speech-Language Pathology, 15,* 356–377.

Cripe, J., & Bricker, D. (1993). Family interest survey. In D. Bricker (Ed.), *Assessment, evaluation, and programming system (AEPS) for infants and children* (pp. 1–6). Baltimore, MD: Paul H. Brookes.

Crnic, K., Hoffman, C., Gaze, C., & Edelbrock, C. (2004). Understanding the emergence of behavior problems in young children with developmental delays. *Infants and Young Children, 17*(3), 223–235.

Crone, D. A., & Horner, R. H. (2003). *Building positive behavior support systems in schools: Functional behavioral assessment.* New York: Guilford Press.

Dabkowski, D. M. (2004). Encouraging active parent participation in IEP team meetings. *Teaching Exceptional Children, 36*(3), 34–39.

Darling, S. M., & Gallagher, P. A. (2004). Needs and supports for African American and European American caregivers of young children with special needs in urban and rural settings. *Topics in Early Childhood Special Education, 24*(2), 98–109.

Davern, L. (2004). School-to-home notebooks: What parents have to say. *Teaching Exceptional Children, 36*(5), 22–27.

Davey, T., Penuel, W., Allison-Tant, E., & Rosner, A. (2000). The HERO program: A case for school social work services. *Social Work in Education, 22*(3), 177–190.

DeJong, L. (2003). Using Erikson to work more effectively with teenage parents. *Young Children, 58*(2), 87–95.

Demchak, M., & Greenfield, R. (2003). *Transition portfolios for students with disabilities; How to help students, teachers and families handle new situations.* Thousand Oaks, CA: Corwin Press.

Denny, M. K., Okamoto, Y., Singer, G. H., Brenner, M. E., & Barkley, S. C. (2006). Maternal stress and efficacy for Latina mothers with infants in neonatal intensive care. *Research and Practice for Persons with Severe Disabilities, 31*(3), 255–266.

Department of Child and Family Services. (2009). *Quinceañera Program: Description, objectives, overview & criteria.* DCF: Harford, CT. Retrieved on July 30, 2009, from http://www.ct.gov/dcf/lib/dcf/adolescent_services/pdf/2009_quinceparticipation_memo.pdf

Deyhle, D., & LeCompte, M. (1994). Cultural differences in child development: Navajo adolescents in middle schools. *Theory into Practice, 33*(3), 156–166.

Diamond, K. E., & LeFurgy, W. G. (1992). Relations between mothers' expectations and the performance of their infants who have developmental handicaps. *American Journal on Mental Retardation, 97*(1), 11–20.

Diamond, S. (1981). Growing up with parents of a handicapped child: A handicapped person's perspective. In J. L. Paul (Ed.), *Understanding and working with parents of children with special needs* (pp. 23–50). New York: Holt, Rinehart, & Winston.

Dion, E., Fuchs, D., & Fuchs, L. (2005). Differential effects of peer-assisted learning strategies on students' social preference and friendship making. *Behavior Disorders, 30,* 421–429.

DiVenere, N. (2009, August). *Design for success: Everything you need to know about establishing a peer support program*. Paper presented at the meeting of the Institute for Family-Centered Care 4th International Conference on Patient and Family-Centered Care, Philadelphia, PA.

Dombrowski, S. C., & Gischlar, K. L. (2006). Supporting school professionals through the establishment of a school district policy on child maltreatment. *Education, 127*(2), 234–243.

Domina, T. (2005). Leveling the home advantage: Assessing the effectiveness of parental involvement in elementary school. *Sociology of Education, 78*, 233–249.

Douglas-Hall, A., & Chau, M. (2007). *Most low-income parents are employed*. National Center for Children in Poverty. Retrieved on June 30, 2009, from http://www.nccp.org/publications/pub847.html

Douglas-Hall, A., & Chau, M. (2008). *Basic facts about low-income children birth to age 6*. National Center for Children in Poverty. Retrieved on June 23, 2009, from http://www.nccp.org/publications/pub847.html

Dryfoos, J. (2004). *Evaluation of community schools: Findings to date. Coalition for Community Schools*. Retrieved on July 3, 2004, from http://www.communityschools.org/evaluation/evalprint.html#effect

Dugan, L. M., Cambell, P. H., & Wilcox, M. J. (2006). Making decisions about assistive technology with infants and toddlers. *Topics in Early Childhood Special Education, 26*(1), 25–32.

Duhaney, L. M. G., & Salend, S. J. (2000). Parental perceptions of inclusive educational placements. *Remedial and Special Education, 21*(2), 121–128.

Dunst, C. J. (2002). Family-centered practices: Birth through high school. *Journal of Special Education, 36*(3), 139–149.

Dunst, C. J., & Bruder., M. B. (2002). Valued outcomes of service coordination, early intervention, and natural environments. *Exceptional Children, 68*(3), 361–375.

Dunst, C. J., Bruder, M. B., Trivette, C. M., & Hamby, D. W. (2006). Everyday activity settings, natural learning environments, and early intervention practices. *Journal of Policy and Practice in Intellectual Disabilities, 3*(1), 3–10.

Dunst, C. J., Bruder, M. B., Trivette, C. M., Hamby, D., Raab, M., & McLean, M. (2001). Characteristics and consequences of everyday natural learning opportunities. *TECSE, 21*(2), 68–92.

Dunst, C. J., Cooper, C. S., Weeldreyer, J. C., Snyder, K. D., & Chase, J. H. (1988). Family needs scale. In C. J. Dunst, C. M. Trivette, & A. G. Deal (Eds.), *Enabling and empowering families: Principles and guidelines for practice*. Cambridge, MA: Brookline.

Dunst, C. J., Hamby, D., Trivette, C. M., Raab, M., & Bruder, M. B. (2000). Everyday family and community life and children's naturally occurring learning opportunities. *Journal of Early Intervention, 23*(3), 151–164.

Dunst, C. J., Herter, S., & Shields, H. (2000). Interest-based natural learning opportunities. *Young Exceptional Children Monograph Series, 2*, 37–48.

Dunst, C. J., Trivette, C., & Deal, A. (1988). *Enabling & empowering families: Principles and guidelines for practice*. Cambridge, MA: Brookline.

Dyer, W. J., McBride, B. A., Santos, R. M., & Jeans, L. M. (2009). A longitudinal examination of father involvement with children with developmental delays. *Journal of Early Intervention, 31*(3), 265–281.

Dykens, E. M. (2005). Happiness, well-being, and character strengths: Outcomes for families and siblings of persons with mental retardation. *Mental Retardation, 43*(5), 360–364.

Dyson, L. L. (1993). Responding to the presence of a child with disabilities: Parental stress and family functioning over time. *American Journal on Mental Retardation, 98*, 207–218.

Dyson, L. L. (1997). Fathers and mothers of school-age children with developmental disabilities: Parental stress, family functioning, and social support. *American Journal on Mental Retardation, 102*, 267–279.

Dyson, L. L. (2003). Children with learning disabilities within the family context: A comparison with siblings in global self-concept, academic self-perception, and social competence. *Learning Disabilities Research & Practice, 18*(1), 1–9.

Eber, L., Breen, K., Rose, J., Unizycki, R. M., & London, T. H. (2008). Wraparound as a tertiary level intervention for students with emotional/behavioral needs. *Teaching Exceptional Children, 40*(6), 16–22.

Eberly, J. L., Joshi, A., & Konzal, J. (2007). Communicating with families across cultures: An investigation of teacher perceptions and practices. *The School Community Journal, 17*(2), 7–26.

Eccles, J. L., & Harold, R. D. (1996). Family involvement in children's and adolescents' schooling. In A. Booth & J. F. Dunn (Eds.), *Family-school links: How do they affect educational outcomes?* (pp. 3–34). Mahwah, NJ: Erlbaum.

Edinippulige, A. P. S. (2007). Parents of deaf children seeking hearing loss-related information on the Internet: The Australian experience. *Journal of Deaf Studies and Deaf Education, 12*(4), 518–529.

Edyburn, D. L. (2002). Remediation vs. compensation: A critical decision point in assistive technology consideration. Retrieved on May 26, 2009, from http://www.connsensebulletin.com/edyburnv4n3.html

Einam, M., & Cuskelly, M. (2002). Paid employment of mothers and fathers of an adult child with multiple disabilities. *Journal of Intellectual Disability Research, 46*(2), 158–167.

Eisenberg, J. D. (2000). Chronic Respiratory Disorders. In R. E. Nickel & L. W. Desch (Eds.), *The physician's guide to caring for children with disabilities and chronic conditions*. Baltimore, MD: Paul H. Brookes.

Emerson, E. (2007). Poverty and people with intellectual disabilities. *Mental Retardation/Developmental Research Review, 13*, 107–113.

Emerson, J., & Lovitt, T. (2003). The educational plight of foster children in schools and what can be done about it. *Remedial and Special Education, 24*(4), 199–203.

Enrich, S., Leung, P., Kindle, P., & Carter, S. (2005). Gay and Lesbian adoptive families: An exploratory study of family functioning, adoptive child's behavior, and familial support networks. *Journal of Family Social Work, 9*(1), 17–32.

Epley, P., Summers, J. A., & Turnbull, A. (in press). Characteristics and trends in family-centered conceptualizations. *Journal of Social Work Education.*

Epstein, M. H., Munk, D. D., Bursuck, W. D., Polloway, E. A., & Jayanthi, M. M. (1999). Strategies for improving home-school communication about homework for students with disabilities. *Journal of Special Education, 33*(3), 166–176.

ERIC/OSEP Special Project. (2001, Spring). *Homework practices that support students with disabilities. Research connections in special education* (no. 8). Reston, VA: ERIC Clearinghouse on Disabilities and Gifted Education.

ERIC/OSEP Topical Brief. (2002, September). *Full-service schools' potential for special education*. Reston, VA: ERIC Clearinghouse on Disabilities and Gifted Education and the Council for Exceptional Children.

Erickson, W., & Lee, C. (2008). *2007 Disability status report: United States*. Ithaca, NY: Cornell University Rehabilitation Research and Training Center on Disability Demographics and Statistics.

Erwin, E., & Brown, F. (2003). From theory to practice: A contextual framework for understanding self-determination in early childhood environments. *Infants and Young Children, 16*(1), 77–87.

Erwin, E., Soodak, L., Winton, P., & Turnbull, A. (2001). "I wish it wouldn't all depend upon me": Research on families and early childhood inclusion. In M. J. Guralnick (Ed.), *Early childhood inclusion: Focus on change* (pp. 127–158). Baltimore, MD: Paul H. Brookes.

Erwin, E. J., Brotherson, M. J., Palmer, S. B., Cook, C. C., Weiger, C. J., & Summers, J. A. (2009). How to promote self-determination for young children with disabilities: Evidence-based strategies for early childhood practitioners and families. *Young Exceptional Children, 12*(2), 27–37.

Erwin, E. J., & Soodak, L. C. (1995). I never knew I could stand up to the system: Families' perspectives on pursuing inclusive education. *Journal of the Association for Persons with Severe Handicaps, 20*(2), 136–146.

Erwin, E. J., & Soodak, L. C. (2008). The evolving relationship between families of children with disabilities and professionals. In T. C. Jiménez & V. L. Graf (Eds.), *Education for all: Critical issues in the education of children and youth with disabilities*. San Francisco: Jossey-Bass/John Wiley & Sons.

Etscheidt, S. (2003). An analysis of legal hearings and cases related to individualized education programs for children with autism. *Research and Practice for Persons with Severe Disabilities, 28*, 51–69.

Everson, J. M., & Zhang, D. (2000). Person-centered planning: Characteristics, inhibitors, and supports. *Education and Training in Mental Retardation and Developmental Disabilities, 35*(1), 36–43.

Fagan, J. (1999). *Predictors of father and father figure involvement in pre-kindergarten Head Start* (Whitepaper). National Center for Children and Families. New York.

Fake, S. (2002). Learning to collaborate as colleagues: Our key to success. In J. M. Lucyshyn, G. Dunlap, & R. W. Albin (Eds.), *Families & positive behavior support* (pp. 209–218). Baltimore, MD: Paul H. Brookes.

Falicov, C. J. (1988). *Family transitions: Continuity & change over the life cycle*. New York: Guilford Press.

Falicov, C. J. (1996). Mexican families. In M. McGoldrick, J. Giordano, & J. K. Pearce (Eds.), *Ethnicity & family therapy*. New York: Guilford Press.

Falvey, M. A., Forest, M. S., Pearpoint, J., & Rosenberg, R. L. (2002). Building connections. In J. S. Thousand, A. I. Nevin, & R. A. Villa (Eds.), *Creativity & collaborative learning*. Baltimore, MD: Paul H. Brookes.

Falvey, M. A., Forest, M., Pearpoint, J., & Rosenberg, R. (1994). Building connections. In J. S. Thousand, R. A. Villa, & A. I. Nevin (Eds.), *Creativity and collaborative learning: A practical guide to empowering students and teachers* (pp. 347–368). Baltimore, MD: Paul H. Brookes.

Falvey, M. A., Forest, M., Pearpoint, J., & Rosenberg, R. L. (1997). *All my life's a circle*. Toronto, Ontario: Inclusion.

Families and Work Institute. (2002). *When work works: Summary of Families and Work Institute research findings*. New York: Author.

Fass, S., & Cauthen, N. K. (2008). Who are America's poor children? The official story. National Center for children in poverty. Retrieved on June 23, 2009, from http://www.nccp.org/publications/pub_843.html

Featherstone, H. (1980). *A difference in the family: Living with a disabled child*. New York: Basic Books.

Federal Interagency Forum on Child and Family Statistics. (2000). *America's children: Key national indicators of well-being*. Washington, DC: Author. (ERIC Document Reproduction Service No. ED18816)

Feldman, M. A. (2004). Self-directed learning of child-care skills by parents with intellectual disabilities. *Infants and Young Children, 17*(1), 17–31.

Fenning, R. M., Baker, J. K., Baker, B. L., & Crnic, K. A. (2007). Parenting children with borderline intellectual functioning: A unique risk population. *Americal Journal on Mental Retardation, 112*(2), 107–121.

Ferguson, P. M. (1994). *Abandoned to their fate: Social policy and practice toward severely retarded people in America*. Philadelphia: Temple University Press.

Ferguson, P. M. (2008). The doubting dance: contributions to a history of parent/professional interactions in early 20th century America. *Research & Practice for Persons with Severe Disabilities, 33*(1–2), 48–58.

Ferguson, P. M., & Ferguson, D. L. (2006). The promise of adulthood. In M. Snell & F. Brown (Eds.), *Instruction of students with severe disabilities* (6th ed., pp. 610–637). Upper Saddle River, NJ: Merrill/Pearson Education.

Fidler, D. J., Hodapp, R. M., & Dykens, E. M. (2000). Stress in families of young children with Down syndrome, Williams syndrome, and Smith-Magenis syndrome. *Early Childhood Education Journal, 11*, 395–406.

Fiedler, C. R. (2000). *Making a difference: Advocacy competencies for special education professionals*. Boston: Allyn & Bacon.

Fiedler, C. R., Chiang, B., Van Haren, B., Jorgensen, J., Halberg, S., & Boreson, L. (2008). Culturally responsive practices in schools: A checklist to address disproportionality in special education. *Teaching Exceptional Children, 40*(5), 52–59.

Field, S., & Hoffman, A. (2002). Lessons learned from implementing the steps to self-determination curriculum. *Remedial and Special Education, 23*(2), 90–98.

Fields, J. (Summer/Fall, 1999). Home is where the heart is. *Tapestry, III*(1), 4.

File, N. (2001). Family-professional partnership: Practice that matches philosophy. *Young Children*, 70–74.

Finn, C., Rotherman, A., & Hokanson, C. (2001). *Rethinking special education for a new century*. Washington, DC: Fordham Foundation.

Fish, W. W. (2006). Perceptions of parents of students with autism toward the IEP meeting: A case study of one family support group chapter. *Education, 127*(1), 56–68.

Fisher, D., Pumpian, I., & Sax, C. (1998). Parent and caregiver impressions of different educational models. *Remedial and Special Education, 19*(3), 173–180.

Fisher, R., & Ury, W. (1991). *Getting to yes: Negotiating agreement without giving in*. New York: Penguin Books.

Fisman, S., Wolf, L., Ellison, D., & Freeman, T. (2000). A longitudinal study of siblings of children with chronic disabilities. *Canadian Journal of Psychiatry, 45*, 369–375.

Fitzgerald, B. (1999). Children of lesbian and gay parents: A review of the literature. *Marriage & Family Review, 29*(1), 57–75.

Fitzgerald, J. (1997). Reclaiming the whole: Self, spirit, and society. *Disability and Rehabilitation, 19*, 407–413.

Fitzgerald, J. L., & Watkins, M. W. (2006). Parents' rights in special education: The readability of procedural safeguards. *Exceptional Children, 72*(4), 497–510.

Fitzsimons, N. M. (2009). *Combating violence & abuse of people with disabilities*. Baltimore, MD: Paul H. Brookes.

Fleischmann, A. (2004). Narratives published on the Internet by parents of children with autism: What do they reveal and why is it important. *Focus on Autism and Other Developmental Disabilities, 19*(1), 35–43.

Flouri, E., & Buchanan, A. (2003). The role of father involvement in children's later mental health. *Journal of Adolescence, 26*, 63–78.

Force, L. T., Botsford, A., Pisano, P. A., & Holbert, A. (2000). Grandparents raising children with and without a developmental disability: Preliminary comparisons. *Journal of Gerontological Social Work, 33*(45), 5–21.

Forest, M., & Lusthaus, E. (1990). Everyone belongs with the MAPs action planning system. *Teaching Exceptional Children, 22*(2), 32–35.

Forgan, J. W., & Gonzalez-DeHass, A. (2004). How to infuse social skills training into literacy instruction. *Teaching Exceptional Children, 36*(6), 24–30.

Fowler, C. H., Konrad, M., Walker, A. R., Test, D. W., & Wood, W. M. (2007). Self-determination interventions' effects on the academic performance of students with developmental disabilities. *Education and Training in Developmental Disabilities, 43,* 270–285.

Frankland, H. C. (2001). *Professional collaboration and family-professional partnerships: A qualitative analysis of indicators and influencing factors.* Unpublished doctoral dissertation, University of Kansas, Lawrence.

Frankland, H. C., Turnbull, A. P., Wehmeyer, M. L., & Blackmountain, L. (2004). An exploration of the self-determination construct and disability as it relates to the Diné (Navajo) culture. *Education and Training in Developmental Disabilities, 39*(3), 191–205.

Frattura, E. M., & Caper, C. A. (2007). New teacher teams to support integrated comprehensive services. *Teaching Exceptional Children, 39*(4), 16–21.

Fredrickson, N., Dunsmuir, S., Land, J., & Monsen, J. J. (2004). Mainstream-special school inclusion partnerships: Pupil, parent and teacher perspectives. *International Journal of Inclusive Education, 8*(1), 37–57.

Frederickson, N., & Turner, J. (2003). Utilizing the classroom peer group to address children's social needs: An evaluation of the circle of friends intervention approach. *Journal of Special Education, 36*(4), 234–245.

Frederickson, N., Warren, L, & Turner, J. (2005). "Circle of Friends"—An exploration of impact over time. *Educational Psychology in Practice, 21*(3), 197–217.

Frieman, B. B., & Berkeley, T. R. (2002). Encouraging fathers to participate in the school experiences of young children: The teacher's role. *Early Childhood Education Journal, 29*(3), 209–213.

Friend, A. (2007). *Challenged by families with challenges: An investigation of family supports in early intervention.* Unpublished doctoral dissertation, University of Kansas, Lawrence.

Friend, M. (2007). The coteaching partnership. *Educational Leadership, 64*(5), 48–52.

Friend, M., & Cook, L. (2003). *Interactions: Collaboration skills for school professionals.* Boston: Allyn & Bacon.

Friend, M., & Cook, L. (2010). *Interactions: Collaboration skills for school professionals* (6th ed.). Upper Saddle River, NJ: Merrill/Pearson Education.

Fuchs, L., & Fuchs, D. (2007). A model for implementing responsiveness to intervention. *Teaching Exceptional Children, 39*(5), 14–20.

Fujiura, G. T., & Yamaki, K. (2000). Trends in demography of childhood poverty and disability. *Exceptional Children, 66*(2), 187–200.

Fullan, M. (1999). *Change forces: The sequel.* London: Falmer Press.

Furey, E. M. (1994). Sexual abuse of adults with mental retardation: Who and where. *Mental Retardation, 32*(3), 173–180.

Furstenberg, F. F. (2003). Teenage childbearing as a public issue and private concern. *Annual Review Sociology, 29,* 23–39.

Gagnon, S. G., Nagle, R. J., & Nickerson, A. B. (2007). Parent and teacher ratings of peer interactive play and social-emotional development of preschool children at risk. *Journal of Early Intervention, 29*(3), 228–242.

Gallagher, J. J., & Gallagher, G. G. (1985). Family adaptation to a handicapped child and assorted professionals. In H. R. Turnbull & A. P. Turnbull (Eds.), *Parents speak out: Then and now* (pp. 233–244). Upper Saddle River, NJ: Merrill/ Pearson Education.

Gallagher, P. A., Fialka, J., Rhodes, C., & Arceneaux, C. (2001). Working with families: Rethinking denial. *Young Exceptional Children, 5*(2), 11–17.

Gallagher, P. A., Floyd, J. H., Stafford, A. M., Taber, T. A., Brozovic, S. A., & Alberto, P. A. (2000). Inclusion of students with moderate or severe disabilities in educational and community settings: Perspectives from parents and siblings. *Education and Training in Mental Retardation and Developmental Disabilities, 35*(2), 135–147.

Gans, A. M., Kenny, M. C., & Ghany, D. L. (2003). Comparing the self concept of students with and without learning disabilities. *Journal of Learning Disabilities, 36,* 287–295.

Gans, L. (1997). *Sisters, brothers, and disability.* Minneapolis, MN: Fairview Press.

Ganske, K., Monroe, J. K., & Strickland, D. S. (2003). Questions teachers ask about struggling readers and writers. *The Reading Teacher, 57,* 118–128.

Garay, S. V. (2003). Listening to the voices of deaf students: Essential transition issues. *Teaching Exceptional Children, 35*(4), 44–48.

Garcia, C. A., & Kennedy, S. S. (2003). Back to school: Technology, school safety and the disappearing Fourth Amendment. *Kansas Journal of Law and Public Policy 12*(2), 273–288.

Garcia, S. B., & Ortiz, A. A. (2004). *Preventing disproportionate representation: Culturally and linguistically responsive pre-referral interventions.* Tempe, AZ: National Center for Culturally Responsive Educational Systems (NCCRESt).

Gardner, R., Cartledge, G., Seidl, B., Woolsey, M. L., Schley, G. S., & Utley, C. A. (2001). Peer-mediated interventions for at-risk students. *Remedial and Special Education, 22,* 22.

Gargiulo, R. M. (2006). Homeless and disabled: Rights, responsibilities, and recommendations for serving young children with special needs. *Early Childhood Education Journal, 33*(5), 357–362.

Gates, G., Badgett, L., Macomber, J. E., & Chambers, K. (2007). *Adoption and foster care by Lesbian and Gay parents in the United States.* Urban Institute. Retrieved July 20, 2009, from http://urban.org

Gath, A. (1977). The impact of an abnormal child upon the parents. *British Journal of Psychiatry, 130,* 405–410.

Gaventa, B. (2008). Spiritual and religious supports: What difference do they make? *Exceptional Parent, 38*(3), 66–69.

Gaventa, W. C. (2001). Defining and assessing spirituality and spiritual supports: A rationale for inclusion in theory and practice. *Journal of Religion, Disability, and Health, 5*(2 & 3), 29–48.

Gavidia-Payne, S., & Stoneman, Z. (1997). Family predictors of maternal and paternal involvement in programs for young children with disabilities. *Child Development, 68*(4), 701–717.

Geenen, S., Powers, L., & Lopez-Vasquez, A. (2001). Multicultural aspects of parent involvement in transition planning. *Exceptional Children, 67,* 265–282.

Getzel, E. E., Stodden, R. A., & Briel, L. W. (2001). Pursuing postsecondary education opportunities for individuals with disabilities. In P. Wehman (Ed.), *Life beyond the classroom: Transition strategies for young people with disabilities.* Baltimore, MD: Paul H. Brookes.

Giangreco, M. (2001). Interactions among program, placement and services in educational planning for students with disabilities. *Mental Retardation, 39,* 341–350.

Giangreco, M. F. (1986). Delivery of therapeutic services in special education programs for learners with severe handicaps. *Physical and Occupational Therapy in Pediatrics, 6,* 5–15.

Giangreco, M. F., & Broer, S. M. (2007). School-based screening to determine overreliance on paraprofessionals. *Focus on Autism and Other Developmental Disabilities, 22*(3), 149–158.

Giangreco, M. F., & Doyle, M. B. (2002). Students with disabilities and paraprofessional supports: Benefits, balance, and Band-Aids. *Focus on Exceptional Children, 34*(7), 1–12.

Giangreco, M. F., Prelock, P. A., Reid, R. R., Dennis, R. E., & Edelman, S. W. (2000). Role of related services personnel in inclusive schools. In R. A. Villa & J. S. Thousand (Eds.), *Restructuring for caring and effective education* (2nd ed., pp. 293–327). Baltimore, MD: Paul H. Brookes.

Gill, B. (1997). *Changed by a child.* New York: Doubleday.

Gilmore, S., Bose, J., & Hart, D. (2001). Postsecondary education as a critical step toward meaningful employment: Vocational rehabilitation's role. *Research to Practice, 7*(4), 1–4.

Glidden, L. M. (1989). *Parents for children, children for parents: The adoption alternative.* Washington, DC: American Association on Mental Retardation.

Glidden, L. M., Billings, F. J., & Jobe, B. M. (2006). Personality, coping style and well-being of parents rearing children with developmental disabilities. *Journal of Intellectual Disability Research, 50*(12), 949–962.

Glidden, L. M., & Johnson, V. E. (1999). Twelve years later: Adjustment in families who adopted children with developmental disabilities. *Mental Retardation, 37*(1), 16–24.

Glidden, L. M., Kiphart, M. J., Willoughby, J. C., & Bush, B. A. (1993). Family functioning when rearing children with developmental disabilities. In A. P. Turnbull, J. M. Patterson, S. K. Behr, D. L. Murphy, J. G. Marquis, & M. J. Blue-Banning (Eds.), *Cognitive coping, families, and disability* (pp. 173–182). Baltimore, MD: Paul H. Brookes.

Goals 2000: Educate America Act of 1994, P. L. 103–227, 20 U.S.C. § 5801 *et seq.*

Goddard, H. H. (1912). *The Kallikak family: A study in the heredity of feeblemindedness.* New York: Macmillan.

Goldenberg, C. (2004) *Successful school change: Creating settings to improve teaching and learning.* New York: Teachers College Press.

Goldenson, L. H. (1965). Remarks on the occasion of United Cerebral Palsy Associations' 15th anniversary. In. Los Angeles: Paper presented at the 15th annual meeting of the United Cerebral Palsy Associations.

Gollnick, D. M., & Chinn, P. C. (2002). *Multicultural education in a pluralistic society* (6th ed.). Upper Saddle River, NJ: Merrill/Pearson Education.

Gomby, D. S., Culross, P. L., & Behrman, R. E. (1999). Home visiting: Recent program evaluations—Analysis and recommendations. *The Future of Children, 9*(1), 4–26.

Gordon, P. A., Feldman, D., & Chiriboga, J. (2005). Helping children with disabilities develop and maintain friendships. *Teacher Education and Special Education, 28*(1), 1–9.

Gore, M. T., & Janssen, K.G. (2007). What educators need to know about abused children with disabilities. *Preventing School Failure, 52*(1), 49–54.

Gould, S. J. (1981). *The mismeasure of man.* New York: W.W. Norton & Co.

Goupil, G., Tasse, M. J., Garcin, N., & Dore, C. (2002). Parent and teacher perceptions of individualized transition planning. *British Journal of Special Education, 29,* 127–135.

Government Accounting Office (2003). *Special education: Federal actions can assist states in improving post secondary outcomes for youth.* (GAO-03-773). Washington, DC: GAO.

Gowen, J. W., Johnson-Martin, N., Goldman, B. D., & Appelbaum, M. (1989). Feelings of depression and parenting competence of mothers of handicapped and nonhandicapped infants: A longitudinal study. *American Journal on Mental Retardation, 94*(3), 259–271.

Gravois, T. A., & Rosenfield, S. A. (2006). Impact of instructional consultation teams on the disproportionate referral and placement of minority students in special education. *Remedial and Special Education, 27*(1), 42–52.

Green, S. E. (2001). Grandma's hands: Parental perceptions of the importance of grandparents as secondary caregivers in families of children with disabilities. *International Journal of Aging and Human Development, 53*(1), 11–33.

Green, S. E. (2007). "We're tired, not sad": Benefits and burdens of mothering a child with a disability. *Social Science & Medicine, 64*(1), 150–163.

Green, T. D. (2005). Promising prevention and early intervention strategies to reduce overrepresentation of African American students in special education. *Preventing School Failure, 49*(3), 33–41.

Grigal, M., Nuebert, D. A., Moon, M. S., & Graham, S. (2003). Self-determination for students with disabilities: Views of parents and teachers. *Exceptional Children, 70*(1), 97–112.

Grisham-Brown, J. (2000). Transdisciplinary activity-based assessment for young children with multiple disabilities: A program planning approach. *Young Exceptional Children, 3*(2), 3–10.

Grossman, K., Grossman, K. E., Fremmer-Bombik, E., Kindler, H., Scheuerer-Englisch, H., & Zimmerman, P. (2002). The uniqueness of the child-father attachment relationship: Fathers' sensitive and challenging play as a pivotal variable in a 16-year longitudinal study. *Social Development, 11,* 307–331.

Guidry, J., van den Pol, R. Keeley, E., & Neilsen, S. (1996). Augmenting traditional assessment and information: The video share model. *Topics in Early Childhood Special Education, 16*(1), 51–65.

Guskey, T. (2009) Grading and reporting in a standards-based environment: Implications for students with special needs. *Theory into Practice, 48*(1), 53–62.

Haffner, W. H. J. (2007). Development before birth. In M. L. Batshaw, L. Pellegrino, & N. J. Roizen (Eds.), *Children with disabilities* (6th ed., pp. 23–33). Baltimore, MD: Paul H. Brooks.

Hall-Laude as told to C. Johnson. (Fall/Winter 2005–2006). Growing up in foster care: Carolyn's story. *Impact, 19*(1), 1, 35. University of Minnesota: Institute on Community Integration.

Halpern, R. (2002). A different kind of child development institution: The history of after-school programs for low-income children. *Teachers College Record, 104*(2), 178–211.

Hamm, E. M., Mistrett, S. G., & Ruffino, A. G. (2006). Play outcomes and satisfaction with toys and technology of young children with special needs. *Journal of Educational Technology, 21*(1), 29–35.

Hammel, J., Magasi, S., Heinemann, A., Whiteneck, G., Bogner, J., & Rodriguez, E. (2008). What does participation mean? An insider perspective from people with disabilities. *Disability & Rehabilitation, 30*(19), 1145–1460.

Hammer, M. R. (2004). Using the self-advocacy strategy to increase student participation in the IEP conference. *Intervention in School and Clinic, 39*(5), 295–300.

Hanlon, K. (2008). Sometimes getting there is half the fun. *Exceptional Parent, 38*(6), 38.

Hanson, M. J. (1998). Families with Anglo-European roots. In E. W. Lynch & M. J. Hanson (Eds.), *Developing cross-cultural competence: A guide for working with young children and their families* (2nd ed., pp. 65–87, 93–126). Baltimore, MD: Paul H. Brookes.

Hanson, M. J. (2004). Families with Anglo-European roots. In E. W. Lynch & M. J. Hanson (Eds.), *Developing cross-cultural competence: A guide for working with children and their families* (3rd ed.). Baltimore, MD: Paul H. Brookes.

Hanson, M. J., Beckman, P. J., Horn, E., Marquart, J., Sandall, S. R., Greig, D., & Brennan, E. (2000). Entering preschool: Family and professional experiences in this transition process. *Journal of Early Intervention, 23*(4), 279–293.

Hanson, M. J., Horn, E., Sandall, S., Beckman, P., Morgan, M., Marquart, J., et al. (2001). After preschool inclusion: Children's educational pathways over the early school years. *Journal of Early Intervention, 68*(1), 65–83.

Hanson, M. J., & Lynch, E. W. (2004). *Understanding families: Approaches to diversity, disability and risk*. Baltimore, MD: Paul H. Brookes.

Harden, B. J. (1997). You cannot do it alone: Home visitation with psychologically vulnerable families and children. *Bulletin of Zero to Three: National Center for Infants, Toddlers, and Families, 17*(4), 10–16.

Hardman, M. L., & Clark, C. (2006). Promoting friendship through best buddies: A national survey of college program participants. *Mental Retardation, 44*(1), 56–63.

Harniss, M. K., Epstein, M. H., Bursuck, W. D., Nelson, J., & Jayanthi, M. (2001). Resolving homework-related communication problems: Recommendations of parents of children with and without disabilities. *Reading and Writing Quarterly, 17*(3), 205–225.

Harriott, W., & Martin, S. A. (2004). Using culturally responsive activities to promote social competence and classroom community. *Teaching Exceptional Children, 37*, 48–54.

Harris, V. S., & McHale, S. M. (1989). Family life problems, daily caregiving activities, and the psychological well-being of mothers of mentally retarded children. *American Journal on Mental Retardation, 94*(3), 231–239.

Harris-Murri, N., King, K., & Rostenberg, D. (2006). Reducing disproportionate minority representation in special education programs for students with emotional disturbances: Toward a culturally responsive response to intervention model. *Education and Treatment of Children, 29*(4), 779–799.

Harry, B. (2008). Collaboration with culturally and linguistically diverse families: Ideal vs. reality. *Exceptional Children, 74*(3), 372–388.

Harry, B., Allen, N., & McLaughlin, M. (1995). Communication versus compliance: African-American parents' involvement in special education. *Exceptional Children, 61*(4), 364–377.

Harry, B., & Klingner, J. (2006). *Why are so many minority students in special education? Understanding race and disability in schools*. New York: Teachers College Press.

Harry, B., Klingner, J. K., Sturges, K. M., & Moore, R. F. (2002). Of rocks and soft places: Using qualitative methods to investigate disproportionality. In D. J. Losen & G. Orfields (Eds.), *Racial inequality in special education*. Cambridge, MA: Harvard Education Press.

Hart, D., Mele-McCarthy, J., Pasternack, R. H., Zimbrich, K., & Parker, D. R. (2004). Community college: A pathway to success for youth with learning, cognitive, and intellectual disabilities in secondary settings. *Education and Training in Developmental Disabilities, 39*(1), 54–66.

Hasazi, S. B., Furney, K. S., & Destefano, L. (1999). Implementing the IDEA transition mandates. *Exceptional Children, 65*(4), 555–566.

Hasazi, S., Gordon, L., & Roe, C. (1985). Factors associated with the employment status of handicapped youth exiting from high school from 1979 to 1983. *Exceptional Children, 51*(6), 455–469.

Hastings, R. P. (2003). Child behavior problems and partner mental health as correlates of stress in mothers and fathers of children with autism. *Journal of Intellectual Disability Research, 47*(4/5), 231–237.

Hastings, R. P., Beck, A., & Hill, C. (2005). Positive contributions made by children with an intellectual disability in the family: Mothers' and fathers' perceptions. *Journal of Intellectual Disabilities, 9*(2), 155–165.

Hastings, R. P., & Brown, T. (2002). Behavior problems of children with autism, parental self-efficacy, and mental health. *American Journal on Mental Retardation, 107*(3), 222–232.

Hastings, R. P., Daley, D., Burns, C., & Beck, A. (2006). Maternal distress and expressed emotion: Cross-sectional and longitudinal relationships with behavior problems of children with intellectual disabilities. *American Journal of Mental Retardation, 111*, 48–61.

Hastings, R. P., Kovshoff, H., Ward, N. J., Epinosa, F. D., Brown, T., & Remintson, B. (2005). Systems analysis of stress and positive perceptions in mothers and fathers on pre-school children with autism. *Journal of Autism and Developmental Disorders, 35*(5), 635–644.

Hastings, R. P., & Taunt, H. M. (2002). Positive perceptions in families of children with developmental disabilities. *American Journal on Mental Retardation, 107*(2), 116–127.

Hastings, R. P., Thomas, H., & Delwiche, N. (2002). Grandparent support for families of children with Down syndrome. *Journal of Applied Research in Intellectual Disabilities, 15*(1), 97–104.

Hauser-Cram, P., Ericson-Warfield, M., Shonkoff, J. P., Wyngaarden-Krauss, M., Upshur, C. C., & Sayer, A. (1999). Family influences on adaptive development in young children with Down syndrome. *Child Development, 70*(4), 979–989.

Haviland, J. (2003). Time well spent: Determining what parents want in a parent meeting. *Principal Leadership, 3*(5), 50–53.

Hebbeler, K., Spiker, D., Bailey, D. Scarborough, A., Mallik, S., Simeonsson, R., Singer, M., & Nelson, L. (2007). *Early intervention for infants and toddlers with disabilities and their families: participants, services and outcomes*. Final report for the National Early Intervention Longitudinal Study (NEILS). Retrieved on July 21, 2009, from http://www.sri.com/neils/pdfs/NEILS_Report_02_07_Final2.pdf

Heller, T., Hsieh, K., & Rowitz, L. (2000). Grandparents as supports to mothers of persons with intellectual disability. *Journal of Gerontological Social Work, 33*(4), 23–34.

Heller, T., Miller, A. B., & Hsieh, K. (1999). Impact of a consumer-directed family support program on adults with disabilities. *Family Relations, 48*, 419–427.

Helm, D. T., Miranda, S., & Angoff-Chedd, N. (1998). Prenatal diagnosis of Down syndrome: Mothers' reflections on supports needed from diagnosis to birth. *Mental Retardation, 36*(1), 55–61.

Helsel, E. (1985). The Helsels' story of Robin. In H. R. Turnbull & A. P. Turnbull (Eds.), *Parents speak out: Then and now* (2nd ed., pp. 81–100). Upper Saddle River, NJ: Merrill/Pearson Education.

Hemmeter, M. L., Joseph, G. E., Smith, B. J., & Sandall, S. (2001). *DEC recommended practices program assessment: Improving practices for young children with special needs and their families*. Denver, CO: Division for Early Childhood.

Herbert, M. J. (2009, September 18). There's something in the family. *Albany Times Union.* Retrieved August, 25, 2009, from http://www.timesunion.com/AspStories/story.asp?storyID=791282&category=LIFE&BCCode&TextPage=2

Hess, S. R., Molina, A. M., & Kozleski, E. B. (2006). Until somebody hears me: Parent voice and advocacy in special educational decision making. *British Journal of Special Education, 33*(3), 148–157.

Heumann, J. (1997, Spring). Assistant secretary Judith E. Heumann. The parent movement: Reflections and directions. *Coalition Quarterly, 14*(1).

Hewitt, B. (2000). House divided. *People Weekly, 54,* 138–144.

Higgins, S. T., Weintraub, F. J., Abeson, A. R., & Turnbull, H. R. (1977). *Development of a comprehensive state statute for the education of exceptional children.* Washington, DC: Council for Exceptional Children.

Ho, A., Collins, S., Davis, K., & Doty, M. (2005). *A look at working-age caregivers' roles, health concerns, and need for support.* New York: The Commonwealth Fund.

Hodapp, R., Glidden, L. M., & Kaiser, A. P. (2005). Siblings of persons with disabilities: Toward a research agenda. *Mental Retardation, 41*(5). 334–338.

Hodapp, R. M., & Krasner, D. V. (1995). Families of children with disabilities: Findings from a national sample of eighth-grade students. *Exceptionality, 5*(2), 71–81.

Hodge, I. (June, 2007). Establishing a support group for military families with special needs. *Exceptional Parent Magazine,* 86–88.

Holburn, S. (2002). How science can evaluate and enhance person-centered planning. *Research and Practice for Persons with Severe Disabilities, 27*(4), 250–260.

Holburn, S., Perkins, T., & Vietze, P. (2001). The parent with mental retardation. In L. M. Glidden (Ed.), *International review of research in mental retardation* (Vol. 24). San Diego, CA: Academic Press.

Hollingsworth, H. L. (2001). We need to talk: Communication strategies for effective communication. *Teaching Exceptional Children, 33*(5), 4–8.

Honberg, L., McPherson, M., Strickland, B., Gage, J. C., & Newacheck, P. W. (2005). Assuring adequate health insurance: Results of the national survey of children with special health care needs. *Pediatrics, 115*(5), 1233–1239.

Hoover-Dempsey, K. V., Battiato, A. C., Walker, J. M. T., Reed, R. P., DeJong, J. M., & Jones, K. P. (2001). Parental involvement in homework. *Educational Psychologist, 36*(3), 195–209.

Horn, L., Berktold, J., & Bobbitt, L. (1999). Students with disabilities in postsecondary education: A profile of preparation, participation, and outcomes. National Center for Education Statistics, U.S. Department of Education, Office of Educational Research and Improvement.

Horner, R. H. (2000). Positive behavior supports. In M. L. Wehmeyer & J. R. Patton (Eds.), *Mental retardation in the 21st century* (pp. 181–196). Austin, TX: Pro-Ed.

Horner, R. H., Sugai, G., Todd, A. W., & Lewis-Palmer, T. (2005). School-wide positive behavior support. In L. Bambara & L. Kern (Eds.), *Individualized supports for students with problem behaviors: Designing positive behavior plans* (pp. 359–390). New York: Guilford Press.

Horner-Johnson, W., & Drum, C. E. (2006). Prevalence of maltreatment of people with intellectual disabilities: A review of recently published research. *Mental Retardation and Developmental Disabilities Research Reviews. 12,* 57–69.

Hosp, J. L., & Reschly, D. J. (2003). Referral rates of intervention or assessment: A meta-analysis of racial differences. *Journal of Special Education, 37*(2), 67–80.

Hoy, W. K., & Miskel, C. G. (2001). *Educational administration: Theory, research, and practice* (6th ed.). New York: McGraw-Hill. http://www.nlts2.org/reports/2005_06/index.html

Hudson, A., Reece, J., Cameron, C., & Matthews, J. (2009). Effects of child characteristics on the outcomes of a parent support program. *Journal of Intellectual & Developmental Disability, 34*(2), 123–132.

Huer, M. B., Parette, H. P., & Saenz, T. I. (2001). Conversations with Mexican-Americans regarding children with disabilities and augmentative and alternative communication. *Communication Disorders Quarterly, 22*(4), 197–206.

Hughes, C., & Carter, E. W. (2006). *Success for all students: Promoting inclusion in secondary schools through peer buddy programs.* Boston: Allyn & Bacon/Pearson Education.

Hughes, M. T., Valle-Riestra, D. M., & Arguelles, M. E. (2008). The voices of Latino families raising children with special needs. *Journal of Latinos and Education, 7,* 241–257.

Humphrey, K. R., Turnbull, A. P., & Turnbull, H. R. (2006). Impact of the Adoption and Safe Families Act on youth and their families: Perspectives of foster care providers, youth with emotional disorders, service providers, and judges. *Children and Youth Services Review, 28*(2), 113–132.

Humphrey, K. R., Turnbull, A. P., & Turnbull, H. R. (2006). Perspectives of foster-care providers, service-providers, and judges regarding privatized foster-care services. *Research and Practice for Persons with Severe Handicaps, 31*(4), 1–4.

Hundt, T. A. (2002). Videotaping young children in the classroom: Parents as partners. *Teaching Exceptional Children, 34*(3), 38–43.

Hunt, J. (1972). *Human intelligence.* New Brunswick, NJ: Transaction Books.

Hutton, A. M., & Caron, S. L. (2005). Experiences of families with children with autism in rural New England. *Focus on Autism and Other Developmental Disabilities, 20*(3), 180–189.

Huws, J., Jones, R. S., & Ingledew, D. K. (2001). Parents of children with autism using an email group: A grounded theory study. *Journal of Pediatric Psychology, 23*(2), 99–109.

Iceland, J. (2000). *The "family/couple/household" unit of analysis in poverty measurement.* Retrieved September 27, 2001, from http://www.census.gov/hhes/poverty/povmeas/papers/famhh3.html#2

Individuals with Disabilities Education Act, 20 U.S.C. § 1400 et seq.

Inge, K. J., Wehman, P., Revell, G., Erickson, D., Butterworth, J., & Gilmore, D. (2009). Survey results from a national survey of community rehabilitation providers holding special wage certificates. *Journal of Vocational Rehabilitation, 30,* 67–85.

Institute for Children and Poverty. (2001). *Deja vu: Family homelessness in New York City.* New York: Author.

Ireys, H. T., Chernoff, R., Stein, R. E. K., DeVet, K. A., & Silver, E. J. (2001). Outcomes of community-based family-to-family support: Lessons learned from a decade of randomized trials. *Children's Services: Social Policy, Research, and Practice, 4*(4), 203–216.

Itkonen, T. (2007). PL 94–142: Policy, evolution, and landscape shift. *Issues in Teacher Education, 16*(2), 7–17.

Itkonen, T. (2009). Stories of hope and decline: Interest group effectiveness in national special education policy. *Educational Policy, 23,* 43–65.

Ivey, J. K. (2004). What do parents expect? A study of likelihood and importance issues for children with autism spectrum disorders. *Focus on Autism and Other Developmental Disabilities, 19*(1), 27–33.

Jackson, C., Becker, S., & Schmitendorf, K. (2002). *Survey of satisfaction with resources related to deafness in Kansas.* Unpublished manuscript, University of Kansas, Lawrence.

Jackson, C. W., Traub, R. J., & Turnbull, A. P. (2008). Parents' experiences with childhood deafness: Implications for family-centered services. *Communication Disorders Quarterly, 29*(2), 82–98.

Jackson, C. W., & Turnbull, A. (in press). Impact of deafness on family life: A literature review. *Topics in Early Childhood Special Education.*

Jackson, T. (2004). *Homelessness and students with disabilities: Educational rights and challenges.* Alexandria, VA: Project Forum, National Association of State Directors of Special Education.

Jacob, N. (2004). Families with South Asian roots. In E. W. Lynch & M. J. Kay (Eds.), *Developing cross-cultural competence* (3rd ed., pp. 415–439). Baltimore, MD: Paul H. Brookes.

Janicky, M. P., McCallion, P., Grant-Griffin, L., & Kolomer, S. R. (2000). Grandparent caregivers I: Characteristics of the grandparents and the children with disabilities for whom they care. *Journal of Gerontological Social Work, 33,* 35–55.

Jeffs, T., & Morrison, W. F. (2005). Special education technology addressing diversity: A synthesis of the literature. *Journal of Special Education Technology, 20,* 19–25.

Jeynes, W. H. (2005). A meta-analysis of the relation of parent involvement to urban elementary school student academic achievement. *Urban Education, 40*(3), 237–269.

Jindal-Snape, D., Douglas, W., Topping. K. J., Kerr, C., & Smith, E. F. (2005). Effective education for children with autistic spectrum disorder: Perceptions of parents and professionals. *International Journal of Special Education, 20*(1), 77–87.

Joe, J. R., & Malach, R. S. (2004). Families with American Indian roots. In E. W. Lynch & M. J. Hanson (Eds.), *Developing cross-cultural competence.* (3rd ed., pp. 109–139). Baltimore MD: Paul H. Brookes.

Johnson, D. (2000). Teacher web pages that build parent partnerships. *Multimedia Schools, 7*(4), 48–51.

Johnson, D. R., Stodden, R. A., Emanuel, E. J., Luecking, R., & Mack, M. (2002). Current challenges facing secondary education and transition services: What research tells us. *Exceptional Children, 68*(4), 519–531.

Johnson, J. (2003). When it's your own child. *Educational Leadership, 61*(2), 30–34.

Johnson, J., & Duffett, A. (2002). *When it's your own child: A report on special education from the families who use it.* New York: Public Agenda Foundation. (ERIC Document Reproduction Service No. ED471033)

Johnson, S. D., Proctor, W. A., & Corey, S. E. (1995). A new partner in the IEP process: The laptop computer. *Teaching Exceptional Children, 28*(1), 46–56.

Jones, M. H., Pearl, R., Van Acker, R., Farmer, T. W., & Rodkin, P. C. (2008). Peer groups, popularity, and social preferences: Trajectories of social functioning among students with and without learning disabilities. *Journal of Learning Disabilities, 41*(1), 5–14.

Jones, T. (2003). *Conflict resolution quarterly,* no. 3. Indianapolis, IN: John Wiley.

Jordan, L., Reyes-Blanes, M. E., Peel, B. B., Peel, H. A., & Lane, H. B. (1998). Developing teacher-parent partnerships across cultures: Effective parent conferences. *Intervention in School and Clinic, 33*(3), 141–147.

Judge, S. (2002). Family-centered assistive technology assessment and intervention practices for early intervention. *Infants and Young Children, 15*(1), 60–68.

Judge, S. L., & Parette, H. P. (Eds.). (1998). *Assistive technology for young children with disabilities.* Cambridge, MA: Brookline Books.

Jung, L. A., & Grisham-Brown, J. (2006). Moving from assessment information to IFSPs: Guidelines for a family-centered process. *Young Exceptional Children, 9*(2), 2–11.

Kalyanpur, M., & Harry, B. (1999). *Culture in special education: Building reciprocal family-professional relationships.* Baltimore, MD: Paul H. Brookes.

Kanner, L. (1949). Problems of nosology and psychodynamica of early infantile autism. *American Journal of Orthopsychiatry, 19,* 416–426.

Karnes, M. B., & Teska, J. A. (1980). Toward successful parent involvement in programs for handicapped children. In J. J. Gallagher (Ed.), *New directions for exceptional children: Parents and families of handicapped children* (Vol. 4, pp. 85–109). San Francisco: Jossey-Bass.

Kasahara, M., & Turnbull, A. P. (in press). Meaning of partnerships: Qualitative inquiry of desirable family-professional partnerships. *Exceptional Children.*

Kasahara, M., & Turnbull, A.P. (2005). Meaning of family-professional partnerships: Japanese mothers' perspectives. *Exceptional Children, 71*(3), 249–265.

Kay, P., Fitzgerald, M., Paradee, C., & Mellencamp, A. (1994). Making homework work at home: The parent's perspective. *Journal of Learning Disabilities, 27*(9), 550–561.

Kazak, A. E., & Marvin, R. S. (1984). Differences, difficulties and adaptation: Stress and social networks in families with a handicapped child. *Family Relations, 33,* 67–77.

Keim, J., Ryan, A. G., & Nolan, B. F. (1998). Dilemmas faced when working with learning disabilities in post-secondary education. *Annals of Dyslexia, 48,* 273–291.

Keller, D., & Honig, A. S. (2004). Maternal and paternal stress in families with school-aged children with disabilities. *American Journal of Orthopsychiatry, 74*(3), 337–348.

Kelly, J. F., Buehlman, K., & Caldwell, K. (2000). Training personnel to promote quality parent-child interaction in families who are homeless. *Topics in Early Childhood Special Education, 20*(3), 174–185.

Kelly, K. M., Siegel, E. B., & Allinder, R. M. (2001). Personal profile assessment summary: Creating windows into the worlds of children with special needs. *Intervention in the School & Clinic, 36*(4), 202–211.

Kemp, C. E., & Parette, H. P. (2000). Barriers to minority family involvement in assistive technology decision-making processes. *Education and Training in Mental Retardation and Developmental Disabilities, 35*(4), 384–392.

Kilgo, J. L. (Ed.). (2006). *Transdisciplinary teaming in early intervention/early childhood special education.* Olney, MD: Association for Childhood Education International.

Kim, H. W., Greenberg, J. S., Seltzer, M. M., & Krauss, M. W. (2003). The role of coping in maintaining the psychological well-being of mothers of adults with intellectual disability and mental illness. *Journal of Intellectual Disability Research, 47*(4), 313–327.

Kim, K., & Morningstar, M. E. (2005). Transition planning involving culturally and linguistically diverse families. *Career Development for Exceptional Individuals, 28,* 92–103.

Kim, K. H., Lee, Y., & Morningstar, M. E. (2007). An unheard voice: Korean American parents' expectations, hopes, and experiences concerning their adolescent child's future. *Research & Practice for Persons with Severe Disabilities, 32*(4), 253–264.

Kincaid, D., Chapman, C., Shannon, P., Schall, C., & Harrower, J. K. (2002). Families and the tri-state consortium for positive behavior support. In J. M. Lucyshyn, G. Dunlap, & R. W. Albin (Eds.), *Families & positive behavior support* (pp. 309–328). Baltimore, MD: Paul H. Brookes.

King, G., Baxter, D., Rosenbaum, P., Zwaigenbaum, L., & Bates, A. (2009). Belief systems of famlies of children with autism spectrum disorders or Down syndrome. *Focus on Autsim and Other Developmental Disabilities, 24*(1), 50–64.

King, G., Stewart, D., King, S., & Law, M. (2000). Organizational characteristics and issues affecting the longevity of self-help groups for parents of children with special needs. *Qualitative Health Research, 10*(2), 225–241.

Kirby, D. (2000). What does the research say about sexuality education. *Educational Leadership, 58*(2), 72–76.

Kirk, R. (Spring, 2007). Q&A on child abuse. *Kappa Delta Pi Record*.

Kirk, S. A. (1984). Introspection and prophecy. In B. Blatt & R. J. Morris (Eds.), *Perspectives in special education: Personal orientations* (pp. 25–55). Glenview, IL: Scott Foresman.

Klein, S. D., & Kemp, J. D. (2004). *Reflections from a different journey: What adults with disabilities wish all parents knew.* New York: McGraw-Hill.

Kleinert, H. L., Miracle, S. A., & Sheppard-Jones, K. (2007). Including students with moderate and severe disabilities in extracurricular and community recreation activities: Steps to success. *Teaching Exceptional Children, 39*(6), 33–38.

Klingner, J. K., & Harry, B. (2006). The special education referral and decision-making process for English language learners: Child study team meetings and placement conferences. *Teachers College Record, 108*(11), 2247–2281.

Klotz, M. B., & Canter, A. (2007). Response to intervention (RTI): A primer for parents. Washington, DC: National Association of School Psychologists.

Kolstoe, O. P. (1970). *Teaching educable mentally retarded children.* New York: Holt, Rinehart, & Winston.

Koret Task Force. (2003). A report. *Education Next, 3*(2), 9–15.

Kozol, J. (2005). *Shame of a nation: The restoration of apartheid in America.* New York: Random House.

Krauss, M. W., Wells, N., Gulley, S., & Anderson, B. (2001). Navigating systems of care: Results from a national survey of families of children with special health care needs. *Children's Services: Social Policy, Research, and Practice, 4*(4), 165–187.

Kregel, J., & Dean, D. H. (2002). *Sheltered vs. supported employment: A direct comparison of long-term earnings outcomes for individuals with cognitive disabilities in achievements and challenges in employment services for people with disabilities: The longitudinal impact of workplace supports.* Virginia Commonwealth University, pp. 63–84.

Kroeger, K. A., Schultz, J. R., & Newsom, C. (2007). A comparison of two group-delivered social skills programs for young children with autism. *Journal of Autism and Developmental Disorders, 37*(5), 808–817.

Kroeger, S. D., Leibold, C. K., & Ryan, B. (1999, September/October). Creating a sense of ownership in the IEP process. *Teaching Exceptional Children, 32*(1), 4–9.

Kroth, R. L., & Edge, D. (2007). Parent-teacher conferences. *Focus on Exceptional Children, 40*(2), 1–8. Denver, CO: Love.

Kroth, R. L., & Edge, D. (1997). *Strategies for communicating with parents and families of exceptional children* (3rd ed.). Denver, CO: Love.

Kübler-Ross, E. (1969). *On death and dying.* New York: Macmillan.

Kuhlthau, K., Hill, K. S., Yucel, R., & Perrin, J. M. (2005). Financial burden for families of children with special health care needs. *Maternal Child Health Journal, 9*(2), 207–218.

Kuhn, J. C., & Carter, A. S. (2006). Maternal self-efficacy and associated parenting cognitions among mothers of children with autism. *American Journal of Orthopsychiatry, 76*(4), 564–575.

La Paro, K. M., Kraft-Sayre, M., & Pianta, R. C. (2003). Preschool to kindergarten transition activities: Involvement and satisfaction of families and teachers. *Journal of Research in Childhood Education, 17*(2), 147–158.

Lackaye, T., Margalit, M., Ziv, O., & Ziman, T. (2006). Comparisons of self-efficacy, mood, effort and hope between students with learning disabilities and their non-LD-matched peers. *Learning Disabilities Research and Practice, 21*(2), 111–121.

Lahm, E. A., & Sizemore, L. (2002). Factors that influence assistive technology decision making. *Journal of Special Education Technology, 17*(1), 15–25.

Lai, Y., & Ishiyama, F. I. (2004). Involvement of immigrant Chinese Canadian mothers of children with disabilities. *Exceptional Children, 71*(1), 97–108.

Lake, J. F., & Billingsley B. S. (2000). An analysis of factors that contribute to parent-school conflict in special education. *Exceptional Children, 21*(4), 240–251.

Lakin, K.C., Prouty, R., Alba, K., & Scott, N. (2008). Twenty-five years of Medicaid Home and Community Based Services (HCBS): Significant milestones reached in 2007. *Intellectual and Developmental Disabilities, 46*(4), 325–328.

Lalvani, P. (2008). Mothers of children with Down syndrome: Constructing the sociocultural meaning of disability. *Intellectual and Developmental Disabilities, 46*(6), 436–445.

Lalvani, P. (2009). *Ten fingers and ten toes: Mothers of children with Down syndrome: Constructing the sociocultural meaning of disability and motherhood.* Unpublished dissertation, City University of New York.

Lambie, R. (2000). *Family systems within educational contexts* (2nd ed.). Denver, CO: Love.

Lamme, L. L., & Lamme, L. A. (2001). Welcoming children from gay families into our schools. *Educational Leadership, 59*, 65–69.

Lamme, L. L., & Lamme, L. A. (2003). *Welcoming children from sexual-minority families into our schools.* Bloomington, IN: Phi Delta Kappa Educational Foundation.

Lamorey, S. (2002). The effects of culture on special education services: Evil eyes, prayer meetings, and IEPs. *Teaching Exceptional Children, 34*(5), 67–71.

LandAdam, L. J., Zhang, D. D., & Montoya, L. (2007). Culturally diverse parents' experiences in their children's transition: Knowledge and involvement. *Career Development for Exceptional Individuals, 30*, 68–79.

Landman, J. H. (1932). *Human sterilization: The history of the sexual sterilization movement.* New York: Macmillan.

Lanigan, K. J., Audette, R. M. L., Dreier, A. E., & Kobersy, M. R. (2000). Nasty, brutish . . . and often not very short: The attorney perspective on due process. In C. E. Finn, A. J. Rotherham, & C. R. Hokanson (Eds.), *Rethinking special education for a new century* (pp. 213–232). Washington, DC: Thomas B. Fordham Foundation/Progressive Policy Institute.

Lardieri, L. A., Blacher, J., & Swanson, H. L. (2000). Sibling relationships and parent stress in families of children with and without learning disabilities. *Learning Disability Quarterly, 23*(2), 105–116.

LaRocco, D. J., & Bruns, D. A. (2000). Advocacy is only a phone call away: Strategies to make a difference on behalf of children and their families. *Young Exceptional Children, 8*(4), 11–18.

Lassen, S., Steele, M., & Sailor, W. (2006). The relationship of school-wide positive behavior support to academic achievement in an urban middle school. *Psychology in Schools, 43*(6), 701–712.

Law, M., King, S., Stewart, D., & King, G. (2001). The perceived effects of parent-led support groups for parents of children with disabilities. *Physical and Occupational Therapy in Pediatrics, 21*(2/3), 29–48.

Lazarus, C., Evans, J. N., Glidden, L. M., & Flaherty, E. M. (2002). Transracial adoption of children with developmental disabilities: A focus on parental and family adjustment. *Adoption Quarterly, 6*(1), 8–24.

Lee, I. M. (1994). *Collaboration: What do families and physicians want?* Paper presented at the International Conference on the Family on the Threshold of the 21st Century Jerusalem: Trends and Implications.

Lee, S., Sills, M., & Oh, T. (2002). *Disabilities among children and mothers in low-income families* (IWPR Publication #D449) [Electronic version]. Washington, DC: Institute for Women's Policy Research.

Lee, S. J., & Hawkins, M. R. (2008). "Family is here": Learning in community-based after-school programs. *Theory into Practice, 47*(1), 51–58.

Lee, Y. K., & Tang, C. S. (1998). Evaluation of a sexual abuse prevention program for female Chinese adolescents with mild mental retardation. *American Journal on Mental Retardation, 103*(4), 105–116.

Leff, P. T., & Walizer, E. H. (1992). *Building the healing partnership: Parents, professionals, and children with chronic illnesses and disabilities.* Cambridge, MA: Brookline Books.

Leiter, V., Krauss, M. W., Anderson, B., & Wells, N. (2004, April). The consequences of mothering a child with special needs. *Journal of Family Issues, 25*(3), 379–403.

Lenhard, W., Breitenbach, E., Ebert, H. Schindelhauer-Deutscher, H. J., Zang, K. D., & Henn, W. (2007). Attitudes of mothers towards their child with Down syndrome before and after the introduction of prenatal diagnosis. *Intellectual and Developmental Disabilities, 45*(2), 98–102.

Leslie, L. K., Landsverk, J., Ezzet-Lofstrom, R., Tschann, J. M., Slymen, D. J., & Garland, A. F. (2000). Children in foster care: Factors influencing outpatient mental health service use. *Child Abuse and Neglect, 24*(4), 465–476.

Lesseliers, J., & Van Hove, G. (2002). Barriers to the development of intimate relationships and the expression of sexuality among people with developmental disabilities: Their perceptions. *Research and Practice for Persons with Severe Disabilities, 27*(1), 69–81.

Leyser, Y., & Kirk, R. (2004). Evaluating inclusion: An examination of parent views and factors influencing their perspectives. *International Journal of Disability, Development, and Education, 51*(3), 271–285.

Lian, M. G. J., & Fontanez-Phelan, S. M. (2001). Perceptions of Latino parents regarding cultural and linguistic issues and advocacy for children with disabilities. *Journal of the Association for Persons with Severe Handicaps, 26*(3), 189–194.

Lightsey, O. R., & Sweeney, J. (2008). Meaning of life, emotion-oriented coping, generalized self efficacy and family cohesion as predictors of family satisfaction among mothers of children with disabilities, *The Family Journal, 16*(3), 212–221.

Lin, S. (2000). Coping and adaptation in families of children with cerebral palsy. *Exceptional Children, 66*(2), 201–218.

Linan-Thompson, S., Cirino, P. T., & Vaughn, S. (2007). Determining English language learners' response to intervention: Questions and some answers. *Learning Disability Quarterly, 30*(3), 185–195.

Lindle, J. C. (1989). What do parents want from principals? *Educational Leadership, 47*(2), 8–10.

Lindsay, G., & Dockrell, J. E. (2004). Whose job is it? Parents' concerns about the needs of their children with language problems. *Journal of Special Education, 34*(4), 225–235.

Lindstrom, L., Doren, B., Metheny, J., Johnson, P., & Zane, C. (2007). Transition to employment: Role of the family in career development. *Exceptional Children, 73*(3), 348–396.

Liu, Y., Ortiz, A. A., Wilkinson, C., Robertson, P., & Kushner, M. (2008). From early childhood special education to special education resource rooms: Identification, assessment and eligibility determination for English language learners with reading-related disabilities. *Assessment for Effective Intervention, 33*(3), 177–187.

Lo, L. (2008). Chinese families' level of participation and experiences in IEP meetings. *Preventing School Failure, 53*(1), 21–27.

Logan, S. L. (2001). *The black family: Strengths, self-help, and positive change* (2nd ed.). Boulder, CO: Westview Press.

Long, T., Huang, L., Woodbridge, M., Woolverton, M., & Minkel, J. (2003). Integrating assistive technology into an outcome-driven model of service delivery. *Infants and Young Children, 16,* 272–283.

Lord-Nelson, L. G., Summers, J. A., & Turnbull, A. P. (2004). Boundaries in family-professional relationships: Implications for special education. *Remedial and Special Education, 25*(3), 153–165.

Loveless, T. (2003) The *Brown Center report on American education.* Washington, DC: Brookings Institution.

Luchyshyn, J. M., Albin, R.W., Horner, R. H., Mann, J. C., Mann, J. A., & Wadsworth, G. (2007). Family implementation of positive behavior support for a child with autism: Longitudinal, single-case, experimental, and descriptive replication and extension. *Journal of Positive Behavioral Interventions, 9*(3), 131–150.

Lucyshyn, J. M., Dunlap, G. D., & Albin, R. W. (2002). *Families and positive behavior support: Addressing problem behavior in family contexts.* Baltimore, MD: Paul H. Brookes.

Lucyshyn, J. M., Horner, R. H., Dunlap, G., Albin, R. W., & Ben, K. R. (2002). Positive behavior support with families: In J. M. Lucyshyn, G. Dunlap, & R. W. Albin (Eds.), *Families and positive behavior support: Addressing problem behavior in family contexts* (pp. 2–43). Baltimore, MD: Paul H. Brookes.

Lucyschyn, J. M., Kayser, A. T., Irvin, L. R., & Blumberg, E. R. (2002). Functional assessment and positive behavior support plan development at home with families: Designing effective and contextually appropriate plans. In J. M. Lucyshyn, G. Dunlap, & R. W. Albin (Eds.), *Families and positive behavior support: Addressing problem behavior in family contexts* (pp. 97–132). Baltimore, MD: Paul H. Brookes.

Luiselli, J. K., Putnam, R. F., & Handler, M. W. (2005). Whole-school positive behavior support: Effects on discipline problems and academic performance. *Educational Psychology, 25*(2–3), 183–198.

Lundgren, D., & Morrison, J. W. (2003, May). Involving Spanish-speaking families in early education programs. *Young Children*, 88–95.

Lustig, D. C., & Akey, T. (1999). Adaptation in families with adult children with mental retardation: Impact of family strengths and appraisal. *Education and Training in Mental Retardation and Developmental Disabilities, 34*(3), 260–270.

Lyer, M., & Mitchell, Z. (2009, March). Best Buddies creates lasting friendships. Oakton Outlook. Vienna PA: Oakton High Schools. Retrieved June 21, 2009, from http://www.oaktonoutlook.com/?c=121

Lynch, E. W. (1998). Developing cross-cultural competence. In E. W. Lynch & M. J. Hanson (Eds.), *Developing cross-cultural competence* (2nd ed. ed., pp. 47–86). Baltimore, MD: Paul H. Brookes.

Lynch, E. W., & Hanson, M. J. (2004). *Developing cross-cultural competence: A guide for working with children and their families* (3rd ed.). Baltimore, MD: Paul H. Brookes.

Lynch, E., & Struewing, N. (2001). Children in context: Portfolio assessment in the inclusive early childhood classroom. *Young Exceptional Children, 5*(1), 2–10.

Lytel, J., Lopez, Garica, J., & Stacey, P. (2008, March). Listening to parents: Understanding the impact of autism on families. *Zero to Three*.

MacMaster, K., Donovan, L.A., & MacIntyre, P. D. (2002). The effects of being diagnosed with a learning disability on children's self-esteem. *Child Study Journal, 32*(2), 101–108.

MacMurphy, H. (1916). The relation of feeblemindedness to other social problems. *Journal of Psycho-Asthenics, 21*, 58–63.

Mactavish, J. B., & Schleien, S. J. (2004). Re-injecting spontaneity and balance in family life: Parents' perspectives on recreation in families that include children with developmental disability. *Journal of Intellectual Disability Research, 48*(2), 123–141.

Madden, M. (22 December 2003). *The changing picture of who's on line and what they do*. Pew Internet & American Life Project. Retrieved on June 16, 2004, from http://www.pewtrusts.com/pdf/pew_internet_yearend_2003.pdf

Maddux, C. D., & Cummings, R. E. (1983). Parental home tutoring: Aids and cautions. *Exceptional Parent, 13*(4), 30–33.

Magana, S. M. (1999). Puerto Rican families caring for an adult with mental retardation: The role of familism. *American Journal on Mental Retardation, 104*(5), 466–482.

Magliore, A., Grossi, T., Mank, D., & Rogan, P. (2008). Why do adults with intellectual disabilities work in sheltered workshops? *Journal of Vocational Rehabilitation, 28*, 29–40.

Maguire, S. (2000). A community school. *Educational Leadership, 57*(6), 18–21.

Mahon, M. J., Mactavish, J., & Bockstael, E. (2000). Social integration, leisure, and individuals with intellectual disability. *Parks & Recreation, 35*(4), 25–40.

Malach, R. S., Segal, N., & Thomas, R. (1989). *Overcoming obstacles and improving outcomes: Early intervention service for Indian children with special needs*. Bernalillo, NM: Southwest Communication Resources.

Mank, D. (2007). Employment. In S. L. Odom, R. H. Horner, M. E. Snell, & J. Blacher (Eds.), *Handbook of developmental disabilities* (pp. 390–409). New York: Guilford Press.

Mank, D., Cioffi, A., & Yovanoff, P. (1997). Patterns of support for employees with severe disabilities. *Mental Retardation, 35*, 433–447.

Mank, D., Cioffi, A., & Yovanoff, P. (1998). Employment outcomes for people with severe disabilities: Opportunities for improvement. *Mental Retardation, 36*, 205–216.

Mank, D., Cioffi, A., & Yovanoff, P. (1999). The impact of coworker involvement with supported employees on wage and integration outcomes. *Mental Retardation, 37*, 383–394.

Mank, D., Cioffi, A., & Yovanoff, P. (2000). Direct support in supported employment and its relation to job typicalness, coworker involvement, and employment outcomes. *Mental Retardation, 38*, 506–516.

Mank, D., Cioffi, A., & Yovanoff, P. (2003). Supported employment outcomes across a decade: Is there evidence of improvement in the quality of implementation? *Mental Retardation, 41*(3), 188–197.

Marcus, L. M. (1977). Patterns of coping in families of psychotic children. *American Journal of Orthopsychiatry, 47*(3), 388–399.

Margalit, M., Al-Yagon, M., & Kelitman, T. (2006). Family subtyping and early intervention. *Journal of Policy and Practice in Intellectual Disabilities, 3*(1), 33–41.

Margalit, M., & Raskind, M.H. (2009). Mothers of children with LD and ADHD: Empowerment through online communication. *Journal of Special Education Technology, 24*(1), 39–49.

Margolis, H. (2005). Resolving struggling learner's homework difficulties: Working with elementary school learners and parents. *Preventing School Failure, 50*(1), 5–12.

Margolis, H., & McCabe P. P. (2004). Resolving struggling readers' homework difficulties: A social cognitive perspective. *Reading Psychology, 25*, 225–260.

Marks, S. U., Matson, A., & Barraza, L. (2005). The impact of siblings with disabilities on their brothers and sisters pursuing a career in special education. *Research and Practice for Persons with Severe Disabilities, 30*(4), 205–218.

Markward, M., & Biros, E. (2001). McKinney revisited: Implications for social work. *Children and Schools, 23*(3), 182–187.

Martin, J. E., Marshall, H. M., & Sale, P. (2004). A 3-year study of middle, junior high and high school IEP meetings. *Exceptional Children, 70*(3), 285–297.

Martin, J. E., Van Dycke, J. L., Greene, B. A., Gardner, J. E., Christensen, W. R., Woods, L. L., & Lovell, D. L. (2006). Direct observation of teacher-directed IEP Meetings: Establishing the need for student IEP meeting instruction. *Exceptional Children, 72*(2), 187–200.

Marvin, R. S., & Pianta, R. C. (1992). A relationship-based approach to self-reliance in young children with motor impairments. *Infants and Young Children, 4*(4), 33–45.

Marzano, R. J., & Pickering, D. J. (2007). The case for and against homework. *Educational Leadership, 64*(6), 74–79.

Mason, C., Field, S, & Sawilowsky, S. (2004). Implementation of self-determination activities and student participation in IEPs. *Exceptional Children, 70*, 441–451.

Mason, C. Y., McGahee-Kovac, M., & Johnson, L. (2004). How to help students lead their IEP meetings. *Teaching Exceptional Children, 36*, 18–24.

Matson, J. L., Matson, M. L., & Rivet, T. T. (2007). Social-skills treatments for children with autism spectrum disorders: An overview. *Behavior Modification, 31*(5), 682.

Matuszny, R. M., Banda, D. R., & Coleman, T. J. (2007). A progressive plan for building collaborative relationships with parents from diverse backgrounds. *Teaching Exceptional Children, 39*(4), 24–31.

Maxwell, E. (1998). "I can do it myself!" Reflections on early self-efficacy. *Roeper Review, 20*(3), 183–187.

McCart, A.,'Wolf, N., Sweeny, H. M., Markey, U., & Markey, D. J. (2009). Families facing extraordinary challenges in urban communities: Systems level application of positive behavior support. In M. C. Roberts (Series, Ed.), W. Sailor, G. Dunlap, G. Sugai, & R. Horner (Vol. Eds.). *Handbook of clinical and child psychology: Positive behavior support.* New York: Springer Verlag.

McGill, D. W., & Pearce, J. K. (1996). American families with English ancestors from the colonial era: Anglo Americans. In M. McGoldrick & J. Giordano (Eds.), *Ethnicity and family therapy* (2nd ed., pp. 451–466). New York: Guilford Press.

McHatton, P. A. (2007). Listening and leaning from Mexican and Puerto Rican single mothers of children with disabilities. *Teacher Education and Special Education, 30*(4), 237–248.

McMahon, C. R., Malesa, E. E., Yoder, P. J., & Stone, W. L. (2007). Parents of children with autism spectrum disorders have merited concerns about their later-born infants. *Research and Practice for Persons with Severe Disabilities, 32*(2), 154–160.

McMaster, K. L., Kung, S., Han, I., & Cao, M. (2008). Peer-assisted learning strategies: A "tier I" approach to promoting English learners' response to intervention. *Exceptional Children, 74*(2), 194–214.

McWilliam, R. A., & Scott, S. (2001). Integrating therapy into the classroom. *Individualizing Inclusion in Child Care.* http://www.fpg.unc.edu/*inclusion

McWilliam, R. A., Snyder, P., Harbin, G. L., Porter, P., & Munn, D. (2000). Professionals' and families' perceptions of family-centered practices in infant-toddler services. *Early Education and Development, 11*(4), 519–538.

Meadan, H., & Monda-Amaya, L. (2008). Collaboration to promote social competence for students with mild disabilities in the general classroom: A structure for providing social support. *Intervention in School and Clinic, 43*(3), 158–187.

Mediavilla, C. (2001). Why library homework centers extend society's safety net. *American Libraries, 32*(11), 40–42.

Mehan, H. (1993). Beneath the skin and between the ears: A case study in the politics of representation. In S. Chaiklin & J. Lave (Eds.), *Understanding perspectives on activity and context.* Cambridge, MA: Cambridge University Press.

Melnick, R. S. (1995). Separation of powers and the strategy of rights: The expansion of special education. In M. K. Landy & M. A. Levin (Eds.), *The new politics of public policy* (pp. 23–46). Baltimore, MD: The John Hopkins University Press.

Merriam-Webster's collegiate dictionary (10th ed.) (1996). Springfield, MA: Merriam-Webster, Incorporated.

Merriam-Webster's collegiate dictionary (11th ed.). (2003). Springfield, MA: Merriam-Webster.

Meyer, D. (Ed.). (2009). *Thicker than water: Essays by adult siblings of people with disabilities.* Bethesda, MD: Woodbine House.

Meyer, D., & Vadasy, P. (2007). *Sibshops: Workshops for siblings of children with special needs* (rev. ed.). Baltimore, MD: Paul H. Brookes.

Meyer, L. H., Park, H. S., Grenot-Scheyer, M., Schwartz, I. S., & Harry, B. (Eds.). (1998). *Making friends.* Baltimore, MD: Paul H. Brookes.

Michaud, L. F., Semel-Concepcíon, J., Duhaime, A. C., & Lazar, M. F. (2002). Traumatic brain injury. In M. L. Batshaw (Ed.), *Children with disabilities.* Baltimore, MD: Paul H. Brookes.

Michaud, L. J., Duhaime, A. C., Wade, S. L., Rabin, J. P., Jones, D. O., & Lazar, M. F. (2007). Traumatic brain injury. In M. L. Batshaw, L., Pellegrino, & N. J. Roizen (Eds.), *Children with disabilities* (pp. 461–476). Baltimore, MD: Paul H. Brookes.

Miller, N. B. (1994). *Nobody's perfect: Living and growing with children who have special needs.* Baltimore, MD: Paul H. Brookes.

Mills v. District of Columbia Bd. of Ed., 348 F. Supp. 866 (D.D.C., 1972).

Minuchin, S., & Fishman, H. C. (1981). *Family therapy techniques.* Cambridge, MA: Harvard University Press.

Mitchell, W., & Sloper, P. (2002). Information that informs rather than alienates families with disabled children: Developing a model of good practice. *Health and Social Care in the Community, 10*(2), 74–81.

Moes, D. R., & Frea, W. D. (2002). Contextualized behavioral support in early intervention for children with autism and their families. *Journal of Autism and Developmental Disabilities, 23*, 521–534.

Mokuau, N., & Tauiliili, P. (2004). Families with native Hawaiian and Samoan roots. In E. W. Lynch & M. J. Hanson (Eds.), *Developing cross-cultural competence: A guide for working with children and their families.* Baltimore: Paul H. Brookes.

Montgomery, D. J. (2005). Communicating without harm: Strategies to enhance parent-teacher communication. *Teaching Exceptional Children, 37*(5), 50–55.

Moore, K. A., & Vandivere, S. (2000). *Stressful family lives: Child and parent well-being* (B–17). Washington, DC: Urban Institute.

Morningstar, M. E., Turnbull, A. P., & Turnbull, H. R. (1995). What do students with disabilities tell us about the importance of family involvement in the transition from school to adult life? *Exceptional Children, 62*(3), 249–260.

Mortorana, P., Bove, K., & Scarcelli, M. (2008). Families and paediatric feeding problems. *Exceptional Parent, 38*(10), 58–59.

Moses, K. I. (1983). The impact of initial diagnosis: Mobilizing family resources. In J. A. Mulick & S. M. Pueschel (Eds.), *Parent-professional partnerships in developmental disability services* (pp. 11–34). Cambridge, MA: Ware.

Mosley, C. R. (2005). Individual budgeting in state-financed development disabilities services in the United States. *Journal of Intellectual & Developmental Disability, 30*(3), 165–170.

Mount, B. (1995). *Capacity works.* New York: Graphic Futures.

Mount, B., & O'Brien, C. L. (2002). *Exploring new worlds for students with disabilities in transition from high school to adult life.* New York: Job Path.

Msall, M. E., Bobis, F., & Field, S. (200). Children with disabilities and supplemental security income: Guidelines for appropriate access in early childhood. *Infants and Young Children, 19*(1), 2–15.

Mull, C., Sitlington, P. L., & Alper, S. (2001). Postsecondary education for students with learning disabilities: A synthesis of literature. *Council for Exceptional Children, 68*(1), 97–118.

Munk, D. D. (2003). *Solving the grading puzzle for students with disabilities.* Whitefish Bay, WI: Knowledge by Design.

Munk, D. D., & Bursuck, W. D. (2004). Personalized grading plans: A systematic approach to making the grades of included students more accurate and meaningful. *Focus on Exceptional Children, 36*(9), 1–11.

Murphy, A. T. (1982). The family with a handicapped child: A review of the literature. *Developmental and Behavioral Pediatrics, 3*(2), 73–82.

Murphy, N. A., & Elias, E. R. (2006). Sexuality of children and adolescents with developmental disabilities. *Pediatrics, 118*(1), 398–403.

Murray, C., Goldstein, D. E., Nourse, S., & Edgar, E. (2000). The post-secondary school attendance and completion rates of high school graduates with learning disabilities. *Learning Disabilities Research, 15*, 119–127.

Mutua, N. K. (2001). Importance of parents' expectations and beliefs in the educational participation of children with mental retardation in Kenya. *Education and Training in Mental Retardation and Developmental Disabilities, 36*(2), 148–159.

Myers, A., & Eisenman, L. (2005). Student-led IEPs: Taking the first step. *Teaching Exceptional Children, 37*(4), 52–58.

NARC. (1954). Blueprint for a Crusade. In *Publicity and Publications Manual*. Washington DC: The ARC.

National Association of Social Workers. (1996). *Code of ethics of the National Association of Social Workers*. Retrieved on June 8, 2001, from http://www.naswdc.org/ode/ethics.htm

National Coalition for the Homeless. (2002, September). *How many people experience homelessness?* Retrieved August 2, 2004, from http://www.nationalhomeless.org/numbers.html

National Council on Disability. (2000). *Federal policy barriers to assistive technology*. Washington DC: Author.

National Council on Disability. (2009). *National disability policy: A progress report*. Washington: Author.

National Council on Disability and Social Security Administration. (2000). *Transition and post-school outcomes for youth with disabilities: Closing the gaps to post-secondary education and employment*. Washington, DC: Authors.

National Joint Committee on Learning Disabilities. (2005). Responsiveness to intervention and learning disabilities. *Learning Disabilities Quarterly, 28*, 249–260.

National Law Center on Homeless and Poverty (2000). *Program: Children and youth*. Retrieved on June 29, 2009, from http://www.nlchp.org/program.ofm?prog=2

National Longitudinal Transition Study-2. (2005). *Changes over time in the early postsecondary outcomes of Youth with disabilities*. Retrieved on July 30, 2009, from http://www.nlts2.org/reports/2005_06/nlts2_report_2005_06_complete.pdf

National Organization on Disability. (2004). *N.O.D./Harris survey of Americans with disabilities*. New York: Aetna, JM Foundation and Harris Interactive.

National Research Council. (2001). *Educating children with autism*. Washington, DC: National Academy Press.

National Research Council. (2002). *Minority students in special and gifted education*. Washington, DC: National Academy Press.

National Society for Autistic Children. (1977). *A short definition of autism*. Albany, NY: Author.

National Survey of Children with Special Health Care Needs. (2005/2006). Retrieved June 18, 2009, from http://mchb.hrsa.gov/cshcn05/

Neely-Barnes, S., Graff, J. C., Marcenko, M., & Weber, L. (2008). Family decision making: Benefits to persons with developmental disabilities and their family members. *Intellectual and Developmental Disabilities, 46*(2), 93–105.

Nelson, J. S., Jayanthi, M., Brittain, C. S., Epstein, M. H., & Bursuck, W. D. (2002). Using the nominal group technique for homework communication decisions: An exploratory study. *Remedial and Special Education, 23*(6), 379–386.

Nelson, L. G. L., Summers, J. A., & Turnbull, A. P. (2004). Boundaries in family-professional relationships: Implications for special education. *Remedial and Special Education, 25*(3), 153–165.

Newacheck, P. W., & Kim, S. E. (2005). A national profile of health care utilization and expenditures for children with special health care needs. *Archives of Pediatrics and Adolescent Medicine, 159*, 10–18.

Newman, L. (2005a). *Family expectations and involvement for youth and disabilities*. National Center on Secondary Education and Transition, NLTS2 Data Brief. Retrieved June 23, 2009, from http://www.ncset.org/publications/nlts2/NCSETNLTS2Brief_4.2.pdf

Newman, L. (2005b, June). *Parents' satisfaction with their children's schooling*. Facts from OSEP's National Longitudinal Studies. Retrieved June 23, 2009, from http://www.nlts2.org/fact_sheets/nlts2_fact_sheet_2005_06-1.pdf

Newman, L., Wagner, M., Cameto, R., & Knokey, A.-M.(2009). *The post-high school outcomes of youth with disabilities up to 4 years after high school. A report of findings from the National Longitudinal Transition Study-2 (NLTS2) (NCSER 2009–3017)*. Menlo Park, CA: SRI International. Retrieved on July 30, 2009, from http://www.nlts2.org/reports/2009_04/index.html

New York State. Commission to Investigate Provision for the Mentally Deficient. (1915/1976). *Report of the state commission to investigate provision for the mentally deficient*. New York: Arno Press. (Original work published 1915).

Nichols, L. A., & Keltner, B. (2005). Indian American Adjustment to children with disabilities. American Indian and Alaska native mental health research: *Journal of the National Center, 12*(1), 22–48.

Nissenbaum, M. S., Tollefson, N., & Reese, M. R. (2002). The interpretative conference: Sharing a diagnosis of autism with families. *Focus on Autism and Other Developmental Disabilities, 17*(1), 30–43.

Nowicki, E. A. (2003). A meta-analysis of the social competence of children with learning disabilities compared to classmates of low and average to high achievement. *Learning Disabilities Quarterly, 25*, 171–188.

O'Brien, J. (2002). Person-centered planning as a contributing factor in organizational and social change. *Research and Practice for Persons with Severe Disabilities, 27*(4), 261–264.

O'Hare, W. (2001). *Disconnected kids: Children without a phone a home*. Ann E. Casey Foundation Kids Count Snapshot, Retrieved on June 15, 2004, from http://www.aecf.org/kidscount/snapshot.pdf

Obeng, C. S. (2007). Immigrant families and childcare preferences: Do immigrants' cultures influence their childcare decisions? *Early Childhood Education Journal, 34*(4), 259–264.

Ogletree, B. (2001). Team-based service delivery for students with disabilities. *Intervention in School & Clinic, 36*(3), 138–146.

Oliver, B., Dale, P., Saudino, K., Petrill, S., Pike, A., & Plomin, R. (2002). The validity of a parent-based assessment of cognitive abilities in three-year olds. *Early Child Development and Care, 172*(4), 337–348.

Oliver, J. M., Cole, N. H., & Hollingsworth, H. (1991). Learning disabilities as functions of familial learning problems and developmental problems. *Exceptional Children, 57*(5), 427–440.

Olson, D. H. (1988). Family assessment and intervention: The Circumplex Model of Family Systems. *Child and Youth Services, 11*, 9–48.

Olson, D. H. (1988). Family types, family stress, and family satisfaction: A family development perspective. In C. J. Falicov (Ed.), *Family transitions: Continuity and change over the life cycle* (pp. 55–79). New York: Guilford Press.

Olson, D. H., & Gorall, D. M. (2006). FACES IV & the Circumplex model. Retrieved May 5, 2009, from http://www.facesiv.com/pdf/3.innovations.pdf

Olson, D. H., Gorall, D. M., & Tiesel, J. W. (2007). FACES IV & the Circumplex model: Validation study. Retrieved May 5, 2009, from http://www.facesiv.com/pdf/2.development.pdf

Olson, D. H., McCubbin, H. I., Barnes, H., Larsen, A., Muxen, M., & Wilson, M. (1983). *Families: What makes them work?* Beverly Hills, CA: Sage.

Olson, D. H., Russell, C. S., & Sprenkle, D. H. (1980). Circumplex model of marital and family systems II: Empirical studies and clinical intervention. *Advances in Family Intervention Assessment and Theory, 1,* 129–179.

Olson, D. H., Sprenkle, D. H., & Russell, C. S. (1979). Circumplex model of marital and family systems I: Cohesion and adaptability dimensions, family types, and clinical applications. *Family Process, 18,* 3–28.

Olsson, M. B., & Hwang, C. P. (2001). Depression in mothers and fathers of children with intellectual disability. *Journal of Intellectual Disability Research, 45*(6), 535–543.

Oregon Institute on Disability and Development. (2000). *Every child special—every child safe: Protecting children with disabilities from maltreatment: A call to action.* Oregon Institute on Disability and Development. Retrieved on July 12, 2004, from http://www.ohsu.edu/research/oidd/oakspublication.cfm?style=moreaccess

Orsmond, G. I., & Seltzer, M. M. (2000). Brothers and sisters of adults with mental retardation: Gendered nature of the sibling relationship. *American Journal on Mental Retardation, 105*(6), 486–508.

Orsmond, G. I., Lin, L., & Seltzer, M. M. (2007). Mothers of adolescents and adults with autism: Parenting multiple children with disabilities. *Intellectual and Developmental Disabilities, 45*(4), 257–270.

Ortiz, A. A. (2002). Prevention and early intervention. In A. J. Artiles & A. A. Ortiz (Eds.), *English language learners with special needs: Identification, assessment and instruction* (pp. 31–48). Washington, DC: Center for Applied Linguistics and Delta Systems.

Ortiz, A. A., Wilkinson, C. Y., Robertson-Courtney, P., & Kushner, M. (2006). Considerations in implementing intervention assistance teams to support English language learners. *Remedial and Special Education, 27*(1), 53–63.

Orton, S. T. (1930). Familial occurrence of disorders in the acquisition of language. *Eugenics, 3,* 140–147.

Osofsky, J. D., & Thompson, D. (2000). Adaptive and maladaptive parenting: Perspectives on risk and protective factors. In J. Shonkoff & S. J. Meisels (Eds.), *Handbook of Early Childhood Intervention* (2nd ed.). Cambridge, United Kingdom: Cambridge University Press.

Ou, S. (2005). Pathways of long-term effects of an early intervention program on educational attainment: Findings from the Chicago longitudinal study. *Applied Developmental Psychology, 26*(5), 578–611.

Overton, S., & Rausch, J. (2002). Peer relationships as support for children with disabilities: An analysis of mothers' goals and indicators of friendship. *Focus on Autism and Other Developmental Disabilities, 17*(1), 11–29.

Owen-DeSchryver, J. S., Carr, E. G., Cale, S. I., & Blakley-Smith, A. (2008). Promoting social interactions between students with autism spectrum disorders and their peers in inclusive school settings. *Focus on Autism and Other Developmental Disabilities, 23,* 15–28.

Palmer, D. S., Fuller, K., Aurora, T., & Nelson, M. (2001). Taking sides: Parent views on inclusion for their children with severe disabilities. *Exceptional Children, 67,* 467–484.

Palmer, S. B., & Wehymeyer, M. (2003). Promoting self-determination in early elementary school: Teaching self-regulated problem solving and goal setting skills. *Remedial and Special Education, 24,* 115–126.

Palmer, S. B., & Wehmeyer, M. L. (2002). *Self-determined learning model for early elementary students: Parent's guide.* Lawrence, KS: Beach Center on Disability.

Palmer, S. B., Wehmeyer, M., Gipson, K., & Agran, M. (2004). Promoting access to the general education curriculum by teaching self-determination skills. *Exceptional Children, 70,* 427–439.

Papalia-Berardi, A., & Hall, T. E. (2007). Teacher assistance team social validity: A perspective from general education teachers. *Education & Treatment of Children, 30*(2), 89–110.

PARC v. Commonwealth, 1971, 1972, p. 6.

Parent to Parent USA. (2009, August 14). Evidence-based practices for Parent to Parent support summary document. Retrieved on August 14, 2009, from http://www.p2pusa.org/EBPdocumentP2PUSAsummary.pdf

Parette, H. P., Brotherson, M. J., & Huer, M. B. (2000). Giving families a voice in augmentative and alternative communication decision-making. *Education and Training in Mental Retardation and Developmental Disabilities, 35*(2), 177–190.

Parette, H. P., Peterson-Karlan, G., & Wojcik, B. W. (2005). Assistive technology for students with mild disabilities: What's cool and what's not. *Education and Training in Developmental Disabilities, 40,* 320–332.

Parette, P., Huer, M. B., & Wyatt, T. A. (2002). Young African American children with disabilities and augmentative and alternative communication issues. *Early Childhood Education Journal, 29*(3), 201–207.

Parette, P., & McMahan, G. A. (2002). What should we expect of assistive technology? Being sensitive to family goals. *Teaching Exceptional Children, 35*(1), 56–61.

Parish, S. L. (2006). Juggling and struggling: A preliminary work-life study of mothers with adolescents who have developmental disabilities. *Mental Retardation, 44,* 393–404.

Parish, S. L., & Cloud, J. M. (2006). Financial well-being of young children with disabilities and their families. *Social Work, 51*(3), 223–232.

Parish, S. L., Rose, R. A., Grinstein-Weiss, M., Richman, E. L., & Andrews, M. E. (2008). Material hardship in U.S. families raising children with disabilities, *Exceptional Children, 75*(1), 71–93.

Park, J., & Turnbull, A. P. (2001). Cross-cultural competency and special education: Perceptions and experiences of Korean parents of children with special needs. *Education and Training in Mental Retardation and Developmental Disabilities, 36*(2), 133–147.

Park, J., & Turnbull, A. P. (2003). Service integration in early intervention: Determining interpersonal and structural factors for its success. *Infants and Young Children, 16*(1), 48–58.

Pass, S. (2007). Child abuse and neglect: Knowing when to intervene. *Kappa Delta Pi Record, 43*(3), 133–138.

Patall, E. A., Cooper, H., & Robinson, J. C. (2008). Parent involvement in homework: A research synthesis. *Review of Educational Research, 78*(4), 1039–1101.

Peck, C. A., Staub, D., Gallucci, C., & Schwartz, I. (2004). Parent perception of the impacts of inclusion on their nondisabled child. *Research and Practice for Persons with Severe Disabilities, 29*(2), 135–143.

Peck-Peterson, S. M., Derby, K. M., Berg, W. K., & Horner, R. H. (2002). Collaboration with families in the functional behavior assessment of and intervention for severe behavior problems. *Education and Treatment of Children, 25*(1), 5–25.

Pena, D. (2000). Parent involvement: Influencing factors and implications. *Journal of Educational Research, 94*(1), 42–54.

Pennsylvania Association for Retarded Citizens (PARC) v. Commonwealth of Pennsylvania (1971, 1972).

Petersilia, J. (2001). Crime victims with developmental disabilities. *Criminal Justice and Behavior, 28*(6), 655–694.

Peterson-Karlan, G. R., & Parette, H. (2008). Integrating assistive technology into the curriculum. In H. P. Parette & G. R. Peterson-Karlan, (Eds.), *Research-based practices in developmental disabilities* (pp. 183–212). Austin, TX: Pro-Ed.

Petosa, R., & Wessinger, J. (1990). The AIDS education needs of adolescents: A theory-based approach. *AIDS-Education and Prevention, 2*(2), 127–136.

Petrilli, M. J. (2007). Testing the limits of NCLB. *Education Next, 7*(4), 52–56.

Place, F. (2008). Motherhood and genetic screening: A personal perspective. *Down Syndrome Research and Practice, 12*(2), 118–126.

Planty, M., Hussar, W., Snyder, T., Kena, G., KewalRamani, A., Kemp, J. et al. (2009). The *condition of education 2009 (NCES 2009-081)*. Washington, DC: National Center for Education Statistics, Institute of Education Sciences, United States.

Poston, D. J. (2002). *A qualitative analysis of the conceptualization and domains of family quality of life for families of children with disabilities*. Unpublished doctoral dissertation. Lawrence, KS: University of Kansas.

Poston, D. J., & Turnbull, A. P. (2004). Role of spirituality and religion in family quality of life for families of children with disabilities. *Education and Training in Developmental Disabilities, 39*(2), 95–108.

Poston, D., Turnbull, A., Park, J., Mannan, H., Marquis, J., & Wang, M. (2003). Family quality of life: A qualitative inquiry. *Mental Retardation, 41*(5), 313–328.

Potvin, M. C., Prelock, P. A., & Snider, L. (2008). Collaborating to support meaningful participation in recreational activities of children with autism spectrum disorder. *Topics in Language Disorders, 28*(4), 365–374.

Prelock, P. A., Beatson, J., Contompasis, S. H., & Bishop, K. K. (1999). A model for family-centered interdisciplinary practice in the community. *Topics in Language Disorders, 19*(3), 36–51.

President's Commission on Excellence in Special Education. (2002). A new era: Revitalizing special education for children and their families. Retrieved on April 24, 2009, from http://www.ed/gov/inits/commissionsboards/whspecialeducation/reports/letter.html

Preto, N. G. (1999). Transformation of the family system during adolescence. In B. Carter & M. McGoldrick (Eds.), *The expanded family life cycle: Individual, family, and social perspectives* (3rd ed.). Needham Heights, MA: Allyn & Bacon.

Pretti-Frontczak, K., & Bricker, D. (2000). Enhancing the quality of individualized education plan (IEP) goals and objectives. *Journal of Early Intervention, 23*, 92–105.

Protection and Advocacy, Inc. (2003). *Abuse and neglect of adults with developmental disabilities: a public health priority for the state of California*.

Pullman, M. D., Kerbs, J., Koroloff, N., Veach-White, E., Gaylor, R., & Sieler, D. (2006). Juvenile offenders with mental health needs: Reducing recidivism using wraparound. *Crime & Delinquency, 52*, 375–397.

Ray, V., & Gregory, R. (2001). School experiences of the children of lesbian and gay parents. *Family Matters, 59*, 28–34.

Reece, R. M., & Sege, R. (2000). Childhood head injuries: Accidental or inflicted? *Archives of Pediatric and Adolescent Medicine, 154*, 11–15.

Reeves, R. (Fall/Winter 2005–2006). Caring for children with special needs: The Reeves family's experience. *Impact, 19*(1), 20–21. University of Minnesota: Institute on Community Integration.

Reglin, G. L., King, S., & Losike-Sedimo, N., & Ketterer, A. (2003). Barriers to school involvement and strategies to enhance involvement from parents of low-performing urban schools. *Journal of At-Risk Issues, 9*(2), 424–433.

Rehm, R. S., & Bradley, J. F. (2005). Normalization in families raising a child who is medically fragile/technology dependent and developmentally delayed. *Qualitative Health Research, 15*(6), 807–820.

Renwick, R., Brown, I., & Raphael, D. (1998). *The family quality of life project* (Final Report). Toronto: University of Toronto.

Research and Training Center on Community Living. (2009). *Family support services in the United States: 2008*. Minneapolis, MN: University of Minnesota, Institute on Community Integration.

Ricci, L. A., & Hodapp, R. M. (2003). Fathers of children with Down syndrome versus other types of intellectual disability: Perceptions, stress, and involvement. *Journal of Intellectual Disability Research, 47*(4/5), 273–284.

Ridgley, R., & Hallam, R. (2006). Examining the IFSPs of rural, low income families: Are they reflective of family concerns? *Journal of Research in Childhood Education, 21*(2), 149–162.

Ridgley, R., & O'Kelley, K. (2008). Providing individually responsive home visits. *Young Exceptional Children, 11*(3), 17–26.

Rieger, A. (2004). Explorations of the functions of humor and other types of fun among families of children with disabilities. *Research and Practice for Persons with Severe Disabilities, 29*(3), 194–209.

Risdal, D., & Singer, G. H. (2004). Marital adjustment in parents of children with disabilities: A historical review of meta-analysis. *Research and Practice for Persons with Severe Disabilities, 29*(2), 95–103.

Roach, A. (2006). Influences on parent perceptions of an alternate assessment for students with severe cognitive disabilities. *Research & Practice for Persons with Severe Disabilities, 31*(3), 267–274.

Roach, M. A., Orsmond, G. I., & Barratt, M. S. (1999). Mothers and fathers of children with Down syndrome: Parental stress and involvement in childcare. *American Journal on Mental Retardation, 104*(5), 422–434.

Roberts, C. D., Stough, L. M., & Parrish, L. H. (2002). The role of genetic counseling in the elective termination of pregnancies involving fetuses with disabilities. *Journal of Special Education, 36*(1), 48–55.

Roberts, R. (2000). Seizure disorders. In R. E. Nickel & L.W. Desch (Eds.), *The physician's guide to caring for children with disabilities and chronic conditions*. Baltimore, MD: Paul H. Brookes.

Rocco, S., Metzer, J., Zangerle, A., & Skouge, J. R. (2002). Three families' perspectives on assessment, intervention, and parent-professional partnerships. In J. M. Lucyshyn, G. Dunlap, & R. W. Albin (Eds.), *Families & positive behavior support* (pp. 75–91). Baltimore, MD: Paul H. Brookes.

Rock, M. L. (2000). Parents as equals: Balancing the scales in IEP development. *Teaching Exceptional Children, 32*, 30–37.

Rodgers, R. H., & White, J. M. (1993). Family development theory. In P. J. Boss, W. J. Doherty, R. LaRossa, W. R. Schumm, & S. K. Steinmetz (Eds.), *Sources of family theories and methods: A contextual approach* (pp. 225–254). New York: Plenum.

Roehlkepartain, E. C., King, P. E., & Wagener, L. (2005). *The handbook of spiritual development in childhood and adolescence*. Thousand Oaks, CA: Sage Publishing.

Rogers, C. (2007). Disabling a family? Emotional dilemmas experienced in becoming a parent of a child with learning disabilities. *British Journal of Special Education, 34*(3), 136–143.

Rogers, E. (2001). Functional behavioral assessment and children with autism: Working as a team. *Focus on Autism & Other Developmental Disabilities, 16*(4), 228–232.

Rogers, M. F., & Myles, B. S. (2001). Using social stories and comic strip conversations to interpret social situations for an adolescent with Asperger syndrome. *Intervention in School and Clinic, 36*(5), 310–313.

Roggman, L. A., Boyce, L. K., Cook, G. A., Christiansen, K., & Jones, D. (2004). Playing with daddy and toys: Father-toddler social toy play, developmental outcomes, and Early Head Start. *Fathering, 2*(1), 83–108.

Romer, L. T., Richardson, M. L., Nahom, D., Aigbe, E., & Porter, A. (2002). Providing family support through community guides. *Mental Retardation, 40*(3), 191–200.

Rose, L. C., & Gallup, A. M. (1998). The 30th annual Phi Delta Kappa Gallup poll of the public attitudes toward the public schools. *Phi Delta Kappan, 80*(1), 41–55.

Rosenkoetter, S., Schroeder, C., Hains, A., Rous, B., & Shaw, J. (2008). A review of the research in early childhood transition: Child and family based studies. Lexington: University of Kentucky, Human Development Institute, National Early Childhood Transition Center.

Rosentein, D. (2008). *Adapting to the possibilities of life.* Essay written for the series This I Believe on National Public Radio (original airdate: April 27, 2008). Text retrieved August, 25, 2009, from http://thisi-believe.org/essay/39519

Rosenzweig, J. M., Brennan, E. M., Huffstutter, K. J., & Bradley, J. R. (2008). Child care and employed parents of children with emotional or behavioral disorders. *Journal of Emotional and Behavioral Disorders, 16*(2), 78–89.

Rosenzweig, J. M., & Huffstutter, K. (2004). On the job strategies for taking care of business and family. *Focal Point: A National Bulletin on Family Support and Children's Mental Health, 18*(1), 1, 3–5.

Rotter, J. B. (1967). A new scale for the measurement of interpersonal trust. *Journal of Personality, 35,* 651–665.

Rous, B., Myers, C. T., & Stricklin, S. B. (2007). Strategies for supporting transitions of young children with special needs and their families. *Journal of Early Intervention, 30*(1), 1–8.

Rous, B., Schroeder, C., Stricklin, S. B., Hains, A., & Cox, M. (2007). Transition issues and barriers for children with significant disabilities and from culturally and linguistically diverse backgrounds. Lexington: University of Kentucky, Human Development Institute, National Early Childhood Transition Center.

Rousso, H. (1984). Fostering healthy self-esteem. *Exceptional Parent, 8*(14), 9–14.

Rueda, R., Monzo, L. Shipiro, J., Gomez, J., & Blacher, J. (2005). *Cultural models of transition: Latina mothers of young adults with developmental disabilities.*

Ruef, M. B., & Turnbull, A. P. (2001). Stakeholder opinions on accessible informational products helpful in building positive, practical solutions to behavioral challenges of individuals with mental retardation and/or autism. *Education and Training in Mental Retardation and Developmental Disabilities, 36*(4), 441–456.

Rump, M. L. (2002). Involving fathers of young children with special needs. *Young Children, 57*(6), 18–20.

Ryan, S., Murphy, B., Harvey, S., Nygren, K., Kinavey, E., & Ongtooguk, P. (2006). The way of the human being: Supporting Alaska Native families who have a child with a disability. *Young Exceptional Children, 9*(2), 12–19.

Sailor, W., Zuna, N., Choi, J., Thomas, J., McCart, A., & Roger, B. (2006). Anchoring schoolwide positive behavior support in structural school reform. *Research and Practice for Persons with Severe Disabilities, 31*(1), 18–30.

Salas, L. (2004). Individualized Education Plan (IEP) meetings and Mexican American Parents: Let's talk about it. *Journal of Latinos and Education, 3*(3), 181–192.

Salend, S. J. (2001). *Creating inclusive classrooms: Effective and reflective practices* (4th ed.). Upper Saddle River, NJ: Merrill/Pearson Education.

Salend, S. J. (2004). Fostering inclusive values in children: What famines can do. *Teaching Exceptional Children, 37*(1), 64–69.

Salend, S. J. (2006). Explaining your inclusion program to families. *Teaching Exceptional Children, 38,* 6–11.

Salend, S. J., Duhaney, D., Anderson, D. J., & Gottschalk, C. (2004). Using the Internet to improve homework communication and completion. *Teaching Exceptional Children, 36*(3), 64–73.

Salend, S. J., Elhoweris, H., & Van Garderen, D. (2003). Educational interventions for students with ADD. *Intervention in School and Clinic, 38*(5), 280–288.

Saloviita, T., Italinna, M., & Leinonen, E. (2003). Explaining the parental stress of fathers and mothers caring for a child with intellectual disability: A double ABCX model. *Journal of Intellectual Disability Research, 47*(4/5), 300–312.

Sameroff, A. (2009). The transactional model of development: How children and contexts shape each other. Washington, DC: American Psychological Association.

Sanders, M. G. (2008). How parent liaisons can help bridge the home-school gap. *Journal of Educational Research, 101*(5), 287–296.

Santelli, B., Poyadue, F. S., & Young, J. L. (2001). *The Parent to Parent handbook: Connecting families of children with special needs.* Baltimore, MD: Paul H. Brookes.

Santelli, B., Singer, G. H. S., DiVenere, N., Ginsberg, C., & Powers, L. (1998). Participatory action research: Reflections on critical incidents in a PAR project. *Journal of the Association for Persons with Severe Handicaps, 23*(3), 211–222.

Santelli, B., Turnbull, A., Sergeant, J., Lerner, E., & Marquis, J. (1996). Parent to Parent programs: Parent preferences for support. *Infants and Young Children, 9*(1), 53–62.

Sapon-Shevin, M. (1999). *Because we can change the world: A practical guide to building cooperative, inclusive classroom communities.* Boston: Allyn & Bacon.

Satir, V. (1972). *Peoplemaking.* Palo Alto, CA: Science and Behavior Books.

Sattler, J. M. (2001). *Assessment of children: Cognitive applications* (4th ed.). La Mesa, CA: Jerome M. Sattler.

Sauer, J. S. (2007). No surprises, please: A mother's story of betrayal and the fragility of inclusion. *Intellectual and Developmental Disabilities, 45,* 273–277.

Schaffer v. Weast (2005). 126 S. Ct. 528.

Scheerenberger, R. C. (1983). *A history of mental retardation.* Baltimore, MD: Paul H. Brookes.

Scheetz, N. A. (2004). *Psychosocial aspects of deafness.* Boston: Allyn & Bacon/Pearson.

Schleien, S. J., & Heyne, L. (1998, March/April). Can I play too? Choosing a community recreation program. *Tuesday's Child Magazine,* 10–11.

Scholl, K., McAvoy, L., Rynders, J., & Smith, J. (2003). The influence of inclusive outdoor recreation experience on families that have a child with a disability. *Therapeutic Recreation Journal, 37*(1), 38–57.

Schonberg, R. L., & Tifft, C. F. (2002). Birth defects, prenatal diagnosis, and fetal therapy. In M. L. Batshaw (Ed.), *Children with disabilities* (5th ed.). Baltimore, MD: Paul H. Brookes.

Schorr, L. B. (1997). *Common purpose: Strengthening families and neighborhoods to rebuild America.* New York: Anchor Books Doubleday.

Schuman, A. (2002). Help or hindrance? Staff perspectives on developmental assessment in multicultural early childhood settings. *Mental Retardation, 40*(4), 313–320.

Schwartz, A. A., Holburn, S. C., & Jacobson, J. W. (2000). Defining person-centeredness: Results of two consensus methods. *Education and Training in Mental Retardation and Developmental Disabilities, 35*(3), 235–249.

Scorgie, K., & Sobsey, D. (2000). Transformational outcomes associated with parenting children who have disabilities. *Mental Retardation, 38*(3), 195–206.

Scorgie, K., & Wilgosh, L. (2008). Reflections on an uncommon journey: A follow-up study of life management of six mothers of children with diverse disabilities. *International Journal of Special Education, 23*(1), 103–114.

Scorgie, K., Wilgosh, L., & McDonald, L. (1999). Transforming partnerships: Parent life management issues when a child has mental retardation. *Education and Training in Mental Retardation and Developmental Disabilities, 34*(4), 395–405.

Scott, S. M., McWilliam, R. A., & Mayhew, L. (1999). Integrating therapies into the classroom. *Young Exceptional Children, 2*(3), 15–24.

Scotti, J. R., Nangle, D. W., Masia, C. L., Ellis, J. T., Ujcich, K. J., Giacoletti, A. M., Vittimberga, G. L., & Carr, R. (1997). Providing an AIDS education and skills training program to persons with mild developmental disabilities. *Education and Training in Mental Retardation and Developmental Disabilities, 32*(2), 113–128.

Sebald, A., & Luckner, J. (2007). Successful partnerships with families of children who are deaf. *Teaching Exceptional Children, 39*(3), 54–60.

Selby, M. (2008). Recognising signs of child abuse and neglect. *Practice Nurse, 36*(2), 32–35.

Seligman, M., & Darling, R. B. (1997). *Ordinary families, special children* (2nd ed.). New York: Guilford Press.

Seltzer, M. M., & Krauss, M. W. (1989). Aging parents with adult mentally retarded children: Family risk factors and sources of support. *American Journal of Mental Retardation, 94*(3), 303–312.

Senge, P. M. (1990). *The fifth discipline: The art & practice of the learning organization.* New York: Doubleday Currency.

Senge, P. M. (2000). *Schools that learn: A fifth discipline fieldbook for educators, parents, and everyone who cares about education.* New York: Doubleday.

Shafer, M. S., & Rangasamy, R. (1995). Transition and Native American youth: A follow-up study of school leavers on the Fort Apache Indian Reservation. *Journal of Rehabilitation, 61*(1), 60–65.

Shank, M. S., & Turnbull, A. P. (1993). Cooperative family problem solving: An intervention for single-parent families of children with disabilities. In G. H. S. Singer & L. E. Powers (Eds.), *Families, disability, and empowerment: Active coping skills and strategies for family interventions* (pp. 231–254). Baltimore, MD: Paul H. Brookes.

Shapiro, B. K., Church, R. P., & Lewis, M. E. B. (2002). Specific learning disabilities. In M. L. Batshaw (Ed.), *Children with disabilities* (5th ed., pp. 417–442). Baltimore, MD: Paul H. Brookes.

Shapiro, J., Monzo, L. D., Rueda, R., Gomez, J. A., & Blacher, J. (2004). Alienated advocacy: Perspectives of Latina mothers of young adults with developmental disabilities on service systems. *Mental Retardation, 42*(1), 37–54.

Sharifzadeh, J. (2004). Families with Middle Eastern roots. In E. W. Lynch & M. J. Hanson (Eds.), *Developing cross-cultural competence: A guide for working with children and their families.* Baltimore: Paul H. Brookes.

Shattuck, P. T., & Parish, S. L. (2008). Financial burden in families of children with special health care needs: Variability among states. *Pediatrics, 122*, 13–18.

Shearer, M. S., & Shearer, D. E. (1977). Parent involvement. In J. B. Jordan, A. H. Hayden, M. B. Karnes, & M. M. Wood (Eds.), *Early childhood education for exceptional children* (pp. 208–235). Reston, VA: Council for Exceptional Children.

Sheldon, S. B., & Epstein, J. L. (2005). Involvement counts: Family and community partnerships and mathematics achievement. *Journal of Educational Research, 98*(4), 196–206.

Shogren, K. A., & Rye, M. S. (2004). *Religion and individuals with intellectual disabilities: An exploratory study of self-reported perspectives.* Unpublished manuscript, Dayton, OH.

Shogren, K. A., & Turnbull, A. P. (2006). Promoting self-determination in young children with disabilities: The critical role of families. *Infants and Young Children, 19*(4), 338–352.

Shumow, L., & Miller, J. D. (2001). Parents' at-home and at-school academic involvement with young adolescents. *Journal of Early Adolescence, 21*(1), 68–91.

Siantz, M. L. D., & Keltner, B. K., (2004). Mental health and disabilities: What we know about racial and ethnic minority children. *Annual Review of Nursing Research, 22*, 265–281.

Sibshops. (2009). *About Sibshops.* Retrieved on July 27, 2009, from http://www.siblingsupport.org/sibshops/index_html

Silva, M., Munk, D. D., & Bursuck, W. D. (2005). Grading adaptations for students with disabilities. *Intervention in School and Clinic, 41*(2), 87–98.

Silverstein, M., Lamberto, J., DePeau, K., & Grossman, D.C. (2008). "You get what you get": Unexpected findings about low-income parents' negative experiences with community resources. *Pediatrics, 122*(6), 1141–1148.

Simmerman, S., Blacher, J., & Baker, B. (2001). Fathers' and mothers' perceptions of father involvement in families with young children with a disability. *Journal of Intellectual & Developmental Disability, 26*(4), 325–338.

Simpkins, S., Weiss, H. B., Kreider, H., McCartney, K., & Dearing, E. (2006). Mother-child relationship as a moderator of the relation between family educational involvement and child achievement. *Parenting Science, 6*(3), 49–57.

Singer, G. (2006). Meta-analysis of comparative studies of depression in mothers of children with and without developmental disabilities. *American Journal on Mental Retardation, 111*(3), 155–169.

Singer, G. H. S. (2004). *A meta-analysis of depression in mothers of children with and without developmental disabilities.* Manuscript submitted for publication.

Singer, G. H. S. (2006). A meta-analysis of comparative studies of depression in mothers of children with and without developmental disabilities. *American Journal on Mental Retardation, 111*(3), 155–169.

Singer, G. H. S., Marquis, J., Powers, L., Blanchard, L., DiVenere, N., Santelli, B., et al. (1999). A multi-site evaluation of Parent to Parent programs for parents of children with disabilities. *Journal of Early Intervention, 22*(3), 217–219.

Singer, G. H. S., & Nixon, C. (1996). A report on the concerns of parents of children with acquired brain injury. In G. H. S. Singer, A. Glang, & J. Williams (Eds.), *Children with acquired brain injury: Educating and supporting families* (pp. 23–52). Baltimore, MD: Paul H. Brookes.

Sipes, D. S. B. (1993). Cultural values and American Indian families. In N. F. Chavkin (Ed.), *Families and schools in a pluralistic society* (pp. 157–174). Albany, NY: State University of New York Press.

Skinner, D., Bailey, D. B., Correa, V., & Rodriguez, P. (1999). Narrating self and disability: Latino mothers' construction of identities vis-a-vis their child with special needs. *Exceptional Children, 65*(4), 481–495.

Skinner, D., & Schaffer, R. (2006). Families and genetic diagnoses in the genomic and Internet age. *Infants & Young Children, 19*(1), 16–24.

Skinner, D. G., Correa, V., Skinner, M., & Bailey, D. B. (2001). Role of religion in the lives of Latino families of young children with developmental delays. *American Journal on Mental Retardation, 106*(4), 297–313.

Skotko, B. (2005). Mothers of children with Down syndrome reflect on their postnatal support. *Pediatrics, 115*(1), 64–77.

Smith, J. D. (1985). *Minds made feeble: The myth and legacy of the Kallikaks.* Rockville, MD: Aspen Publications.

Smith, S. W. (1990, September). Individualized education programs (IEPs) in special education—From intent to acquiescence. *Exceptional Children, 57*(1), 6–14.

Smith, S. W., & Brownell, M. T. (1995). Individualized education program: Considering the broad context of reform. *Focus on Exceptional Children, 28*(1), 1–12.

Smull, M. W., & Harrison, S. B. (1992). *Supporting people with severe retardation in the community.* Alexandria, VA: National Association of State Mental Retardation Program Directors.

Snell, M. E., & Janney, R. (2000). *Teachers' guides to inclusive practices: Collaborative teaming.* Baltimore, MD: Paul H. Brookes.

Snyder, E. P. (2002). Teaching students with combined behavior disorders and mental retardation to lead their own IEP meetings. *Behavioral Disorders, 27*(4), 340–357.

Solomon, M., Pistrang, N., & Barker, C. (2001). The benefits of mutual support groups for parents of children with disabilities. *American Journal of Community Psychology, 29*(1), 113–132.

Soodak, L. C., & Erwin, E. J. (1995). I never knew I could stand up to the system: Families' perspectives on pursuing inclusive education. *Journal of the Association for Persons with Severe Handicaps, 20*(2), 136–146.

Soodak, L. C., & Erwin, E. J. (2000). Valued member or tolerated participant: Parents' experiences in inclusive early childhood settings. *Journal of the Association for Persons with Severe Handicaps, 25*(1), 29–41.

Soodak, L. C., Erwin, E. J., Winton, P., Brotherson, M. J., Turnbull, A. P., Hanson, M. J., & Brault, L. M. J. (2002). Implementing inclusive early childhood education: A call for professional empowerment. *Topics in Early Childhood Special Education, 22*(2), 91–102.

Spencer, V. G., Simpson, C. G., & Lynch, S. (2008). Using social stories to increase positive behaviors for children with autism spectrum disorders. *Intervention in School and Clinic, 44*(1), 58–61.

Spinelli, C. G. (1999). Home-school collaboration at the early childhood level: Making it work. *Young Exceptional Children, 2,* 20–26.

Squires, S. (2000). Our family's experiences: An important outcome achieved. *Young Exceptional Children, 4,* 9–11.

Stainton, T., & Besser, H. (1998). The positive impact of children with an intellectual disability on the family. *Journal of Intellectual & Developmental Disability, 23,* 57–70.

Stambaugh, L. F., Mustillo, S. A., Burns, B. J., Stephens, R. L., Baxter, B., Edwards, D., & Dekraai, M. (2007). Outcome from wraparound and multisystemic therapy in a center for mental health services system-of-care demonstration site. *Journal of Emotional and Behavioral Disorders, 15,* 143–155.

Stancliffe, R. J., & Lakin, K. C. (2005). Individual budgets and freedom from staff control. In R. J. Stancliffe & K. C. Lakin (Eds.), *Costs and outcomes of community services for people with intellectual disabilities* (pp. 203–218). Baltimore, MD: Paul H. Brookes.

Stein, M. A., Efron, L. A., Schiff, W. B., & Glanzman, M. (2002). Attention deficits and hyperactivity. In M. L. Batshaw (Ed.), *Children with disabilities.* Baltimore, MD: Paul H. Brookes.

Stodden, R. A., & Whelley, T. (2004). Postsecondary education and persons with intellectual disabilities: An introduction. *Education and Training in Developmental Disabilities, 39*(1), 6–15.

Stonehouse, A., & Gonzalez-Mena, J. (2001). Working with a high-maintenance parent. *Child Care Information Exchange, 142,* 57–59.

Stoneman, Z. (2005). Siblings of children with disabilities: Research themes. *Mental Retardation, 43*(5), 339–350.

Stoneman, Z., & Gavidia-Payne, S. (2006). Marital adjustment in families of young children with disabilities: Associations with daily hassles and problem-focused coping. *American Journal on Mental Retardation, 111*(1), 1–14.

Stoner, J. B., & Angell, M. E. (2006). Parent perspectives on role engagement: An investigating of parents of children with ASD and their self-reported roles with educational professional. *Focus on Autism and Other Developmental Disabilities, 21*(3), 177–189.

Stoner, J. B., & Bock, S. J., Thompson, J. R., Angell, M. E., Heyl, B. S., & Crowley, E. P. (2005). Welcome to our world: Parents' perception of interactions between parents of young children with ASD and education professionals. *Focus on Autism and Other Developmental Disabilities, 20*(1), 39–51.

Stowe, M. J., & Turnbull, H. R. (2001). Legal considerations of inclusion for infants and toddlers and for preschool-age children. In M. J. Guralnick (Ed.), *Early childhood inclusion: Focus on change.* Baltimore, MD: Paul H. Brookes.

Strawser, S., Markos, P., Yamaguchi, B., & Higgins, K. (2000). A new challenge for school counselors: Children who are homeless. *Professional School Counseling, 3*(3), 162–171.

Strip, C., & Hirsch, G. (2000). Trust and teamwork: The parent-teacher partnership for helping the gifted child. *Gifted Child Today, 24*(2), 26–30.

Stroggilos, V., & Xanthacou, Y. (2006). Collaborative IEPs for the education of pupils with profound and multiple learning difficulties. *European Journal of Special Education, 21*(3), 339–349.

Sugai, G., Horner, R. H., Dunlap, G., Hieneman, M., Lewis, T., Nelson, C., et al. (2000). Applying positive behavioral support and functional behavior assessment in the schools. *Journal of Positive Behavior Intervention, 2*(3), 131–143.

Sugai, G., Lewis-Palmer, T., & Hagan-Burke, S. (2000). Overview of the functional behavioral assessment process. *Exceptionality, 8*(3), 149–160.

Sullivan, P. M., & Knutson, J. F. (2000). Maltreatment and disabilities: A population-based epidemiological study. *Child Abuse & Neglect: The International Journal, 24*(10), 1257–1273.

Summers, J. A. (1987). *Defining successful family life in families with and without children with disabilities: A qualitative study.* Unpublished doctoral dissertation, University of Kansas, Lawrence.

Summers, J. A., Behr, S. K., & Turnbull, A. P. (1989). Positive adaptation and coping strengths in families who have children with disabilities. In G. Singer & L. Irvin (Eds.), *Family support services.* Baltimore, MD: Paul H. Brookes.

Summers, J. A., Boller, K., & Raikes, H. H. (2004). Preferences and perceptions about getting support expressed by low income fathers. *Fathering: A Journal of Theory, Research, and Practice About Men as Fathers, 2*(1), 61–82.

Summers, J. A., Dell'Oliver, C., Turnbull, A. P., Benson, H., Santelli, B., Campbell, M., & Siegel-Causey, E. (1990). Examining the individualized family service plan process: What are family preferences? *Topics in Early Childhood Special Education, 10*(1), 78–99.

Summers, J. A., Steeples, T., Peterson, C., Naig, L., McBride, S., Wall, S., Liebow, H., Swanson, M., & Stowitschek, J. (2001). Policy and management supports for effective service integration in Early Head Start and Part C programs. *Topics in Early Childhood Special Education, 21,* 16–30.

Summers, J. A., Templeton-McMann, O., & Fuger, K. L. (1997). Critical thinking: A method to guide staff in serving families with multiple challenges. In J. J. Carta (Ed.), *Topics in early childhood education* (pp. 27–52). Austin, TX: Pro-Ed.

Surís, J. C., Resnick, M. D., Cassuto, N., & Blum, R. W. M. (1996). Sexual behavior of adolescents with chronic disease and disability. *Journal of Adolescent Health, 19*(2), 124–131.

Swinton, J. (2004). Restoring the image: Spirituality, faith, and cognitive disability. *Journal of Religion and Health, 36*(1), 21–28.

Taanila, A., Järvelin, M. R., & Kokkonen, J. (1999). Cohesion and parents' social relations in families with a child with disability or chronic illness. *International Journal of Rehabilitation Research, 22*(2), 101–109.

Tasker, F. (1999). Children in lesbian-led families: A review. *Clinical Child Psychology and Psychiatry, 4*(2), 153–166.

Taub, D. J. (2006). Understanding the concerns of parents of students with disabilities: Challenges and roles for school counselors. *Professional School Counseling, 10*(1), 52–57.

Taylor, S. E. (1989). *Positive illusions: Creative self-deception and the healthy mind.* New York: Basic Books.

Technical Assistance ALLIANCE for Parent Centers. (2009). Parent Centers helping families: Outcome data 2007–2008. Minneapolis, MN: PACER Center.

Tekin, E., & Kircaali-Iftar, G. (2002). Comparison of the effectiveness and efficiency of two response prompting procedures delivered by sibling tutors. *Education and Training in Mental Retardation and Developmental Disabilities, 37*(3), 283–299.

Terman, L. (1916). *The measurement of intelligence.* Cambridge, MA: Riverside.

Test, D. W., Fowler, C. H., Brewer, D. M., & Wood, W. M. (2005). A content and methodological review of self-advocacy intervention studies. *Exceptional Children, 72*(1), 101–125.

Test, D. W., Mason, C., Hughes, C., Konrad, M., Neale, M., & Wood, W. W. (2004). Student involvement in Individualized Education Program meetings. *Exceptional Children, 70*(4), 391–412.

Tew, B. J., Payne, E. H., & Lawrence, K. M. (1974). Must a family with a handicapped child be a handicapped family? *Developmental Medicine and Child Neurology, 18*(Suppl. 32), 95–98.

Thoma, C. A., Rogan, P., & Baker, S. R. (2001). Student involvement in transition planning: Unheard voices. *Education and Training in Developmental Disabilities, 36*(1), 16–29.

Thomas, C. J. (1905). Congenital "word-blindness" and its treatment. *Ophthalmoscope, 3,* 380–385.

Thompson, J. R., Meadan, H., Fansler, K. W., Alber, S. B., & Balogh, P. A. (2007). Family assessment portfolios: A new way to jumpstart family/school collaboration. *Teaching Exceptional Children, 39*(6), 19–25.

Thousand, J. S., & Villa, R. A. (2000). Collaborative teaming: A powerful tool in school restructuring. In R. A. Villa & J. S. Thousand (Eds.), *Restructuring for caring and effective education: Piecing the puzzle* (pp. 254–292). Baltimore, MD: Paul H. Brookes.

Thousand, J. S., Villa, R. A., & Nevin, A. I. (2002). *Creativity and collaborative learning* (2nd ed.). Baltimore, MD: Paul H. Brookes.

Titiev, M. (1972). *The Hopi Indians of Old Oraibi: Change and continuity.* Ann Arbor: University of Michigan Press.

Tjosvold, D. (1997). Conflict within interdependence: Its value for productivity and individuality. In C. K. W. DeDreu & E. Van de Vliert (Eds.), *Using conflict in organizations* (pp. 23–37). Thousand Oaks, CA: Sage.

Todd, S. (2007). Silenced grief: Living with the death of a child with intellectual disabilities. *Journal of Intellectual Disability Research, 51*(8), 637–648.

Todis, B., Irvin, L. K., Singer, G. H. S., & Yovanoff, P. (1993). The self-esteem parent program: Quantitative and qualitative evaluation of a cognitive-behavioral intervention. In G. H. S. Singer & L. K. Irvin (Eds.), *Support for caregiving families: Enabling positive adaptation to disability* (pp. 203–229). Baltimore, MD: Paul H. Brookes.

Todis, B., & Singer, G. (1991). Stress and stress management in families with adopted children who have severe disabilities. *Journal of the Association for Persons with Severe Handicaps, 16*(1), 3–13.

Trainor, A. A. (2007). Person-centered planning in two culturally distinct communities. *Career Develop for Exceptional Individuals, 30*(2), 92–103.

Traustadottir, R. (1995). A mother's work is never done: Constructing a "normal" life. In S. J. Taylor, R. Bogdan, & Z. M. Lutfiyya (Eds.), *The variety of community experience: Qualitative studies of family and community life* (pp. 47–65). Baltimore, MD: Paul H. Brookes.

Truscott, S. D., Cohen, C. E., Sams, D. P., Sanborn, K. J., & Frank, A. J. (2005). The current state(s) of prereferral intervention teams. *Remedial and Special Education, 26*(3), 130–140.

Trute, B. (1995). Gender differences in the psychological adjustment of parents of young, developmentally disabled children. *Journal of Child Psychology and Psychiatry, 36*(7), 1225–1242.

Tschannen-Moran, M., & Hoy W. (2000). A multidisciplinary analysis of the nature, meaning, and measurement of trust. *Review of Educational Research, 70*(4), 547–593.

Turbiville, V., Lee, I., Turnbull, A., & Murphy, D. (1993). *Handbook for the development of a family friendly individualized service plan (IFSP).* Lawrence: University of Kansas, Beach Center on Families and Disability.

Turbiville, V. P., Turnbull, A. P., Garland, C. W., & Lee, I. M. (1996). Development and implementation of IFSPs and IEPs: Opportunities for empowerment. In S. L. Odom & M. E. McLean (Eds.), *Early intervention/early childhood special education: Recommended practices* (pp. 77–100). Austin, TX: Pro-Ed.

Turnbull, A., Edmonson, H., Griggs, P., Wickham, D., Sailor, W., Freeman, R., et al. (2002). A blueprint for schoolwide positive behavior support:

Implementation of three components. *Council for Exceptional Children, 68*(3), 377–402.

Turnbull, A., & Morningstar, M. (1993). Family and professional interaction. In M. E. Snell (Ed.), *Instruction of students with severe disabilities* (4th ed., pp. 31–60). Upper Saddle River, NJ: Merrill/Pearson Education.

Turnbull, A., Stowe, M., Zuna, N., Hong, J. Y., Hu, X., Kyzar, K., Obremski, S., et al. (in press). Knowledge-to-action guides for preparing families to be partners in making educational decisions. *Teaching Exceptional Children.*

Turnbull, A., Turnbull, R., & Wehmeyer, M. L. (2010). *Exceptional lives: Special education in today's schools* (6th ed.). Upper Saddle River, NJ: Merrill/Pearson Education.

Turnbull, A. P. (1988). Accepting the challenge of providing comprehensive support to families. *Education and Training in Mental Retardation, 23*(4), 261–272.

Turnbull, A. P., Blue-Banning, M., & Pereira, L. (2000). Successful friendships of Hispanic children and youth with disabilities: An exploratory study. *Mental Retardation, 38*(2), 138–153.

Turnbull, A. P., Blue-Banning, M., Turbiville, V., & Park, J. (1999). From parent education to partnership education: A call for a transformed focus. *Topics in Early Childhood Special Education, 19*(3), 164–171.

Turnbull, A. P., Guess, D., & Turnbull, H. R. (1988). Implications of biobehavioral states for the education and treatment of students with the most profoundly handicapping conditions. *Journal of the Association for Persons with Severe Handicaps, 13*(3), 163–174.

Turnbull, A. P., Pereira, L., & Blue-Banning, M. (1999). Parents' facilitation of friendships between their children with a disability and friends without a disability. *Journal of the Association for Persons with Severe Handicaps, 24*(2), 85–99.

Turnbull, A. P., Pereira, L., & Blue-Banning, M. (2000). Successful friendships of Hispanic children and youth with disabilities: An exploratory study. *Mental Retardation, 38*(2), 138–153.

Turnbull, A. P., & Ruef, M. (1997). Family perspectives on inclusive lifestyle issues for people with problem behavior. *Exceptional Children, 63*(2), 211–227.

Turnbull, A. P., Summers, J. A., & Brotherson, M. J. (1984). *Working with families with disabled members: A family systems approach.* Lawrence: University of Kansas, Kansas University Affiliated Facility.

Turnbull, A. P., Summers, J. A., & Brotherson, M. J. (1986). Family life cycle: Theoretical and empirical implications and future directions for families with mentally retarded members. In J. J. Gallagher & P. M. Vietze (Ed.), *Families of handicapped persons: Research, programs, and policy issues* (pp. 25–44). Baltimore, MD: Paul H. Brookes.

Turnbull, A. P., Turbiville, V., Schaffer, R., & Schaffer, V. (1996, June/July). "Getting a shot at life" through group action planning. *Zero to Three, 16*(6), 33–40.

Turnbull, A. P., Turbiville, V., & Turnbull, H. R. (2000). Evolution of family-professional partnerships: Collective empowerment as the model for the early twenty-first century. In J. P. Shonkoff & S. J. Meisels (Eds.), *Handbook of early childhood intervention* (pp. 630–648). Cambridge, England: Cambridge University Press.

Turnbull, A. P., & Turnbull, H. R. (1996). Group action planning as a strategy for providing comprehensive family support. In L. K. Koegel, R. L. Koegel, & G. Dunlap (Eds.), *Community, school, family, and social inclusion through positive behavioral support* (pp. 99–114). Baltimore, MD: Paul H. Brookes.

Turnbull, A. P., & Turnbull, H. R. (1996). Self-determination within a culturally responsive family systems perspective: Balancing the family mobile. In L. E. Powers, G. H. S. Singer, & J. A. Sowers (Eds.), *On the road to autonomy: Promoting self-competence among children and youth with disabilities.* Baltimore, MD: Paul H. Brookes.

Turnbull, A. P., & Turnbull, H. R. (1999). Comprehensive lifestyle support for adults with challenging behavior: From rhetoric to reality. *Education and Training in Mental Retardation and Developmental Disabilities, 34*(4), 373–394.

Turnbull, A. P., & Turnbull, H. R. (2001). Self-determination for individuals with significant cognitive disabilities and their families. *Journal of the Association for Persons with Severe Handicaps, 26*(1), 56–62.

Turnbull, A. P., & Turnbull, H. R. (2006). Self-determination: Is a rose by any other name still a rose? *Research and Practice for Persons with Severe Disabilities, 31*, 83–88.

Turnbull, A. P., Turnbull, H. R., Agosta, J., Erwin, E., Fujiura, G., Singer, G., & Soodak, L. (2005). Support of families and family life across the life span. In C. Lakin & A. P. Turnbull (Eds.), *National goals and research for persons with intellectual and developmental disabilities* (pp. 217–256). Washington, DC: American Association on Mental Retardation.

Turnbull, A. P., Turnbull, H. R., Agosta, J., Erwin, E., Fujiura, G., Singer, G., et al. (2004). "Leaving no family behind": National goals, current knowledge, and future reserach. In C. Lakin (Ed.), *Keeping the promises: National goals, state-of-knowledge, and a national agenda for research on intellectual and developmental disabilities.* Washington, DC: The Arc of the U.S.

Turnbull, A. P., Turnbull, H. R., & Blue-Banning, M. J. (1994). Enhancing inclusion of infants and toddlers with disabilities and their families: A theoretical and programmatic analysis. *Infants and Young Children, 72*(2), 1–14.

Turnbull, A. P., & Turnbull, R. (in press). Honoring Jay Turnbull's contributions to quality of life: Ten take-home lessons for professional development providers and early childhood practitioners. *Young Exceptional Children.*

Turnbull, A. P., & Winton, P. J. (1984). Parent involvement policy and practice: Current research and implications for families of young severely handicapped children. In J. Blacher (Ed.), *Severely handicapped children and their families: Research in review* (pp. 377–397). New York: Academic Press.

Turnbull, A. P., Winton, P. J., Blacher, J. B., & Salkind, N. (1983). Mainstreaming in the kindergarten classroom: Perspectives of parents of handicapped and nonhandicapped children. *Journal of the Division of Early Childhood, 6*, 14–20.

Turnbull, A. P., Zuna, N., Turnbull, H. R., Poston, D., & Summers, J. A. (2007). Families as partners in educational decision making. In S. L. Odom, R. H. Horner, M. E. Snell, & J. Blacher (Eds.), *Handbook of developmental disabilities* (pp. 3570–590). New York: Guilford Press.

Turnbull, H. R., & Stowe, M. J. (2001). A taxonomy for organizing the core concepts according to their underlying principles. *Journal of Disability Policy Studies, 12*(3), 177–197.

Turnbull, H. R., Stowe, M. J., Agosta, J., Turnbull, A. P., Schrandt, M. S., & Muller, J. F. (2007). Federal family and disability policy: Special relevance for developmental disabilities. *Mental Retardation and Developmental Disabilities Research Reviews, 13*, 114–120.

Turnbull, H. R., Stowe, M. J., & Huerta, N. E. (2007). *Free appropriate public education* (7th ed., revised printing). Denver: Love.

Turnbull, H. R., & Turnbull, A. P. (1978). *Parents speak out.* Upper Saddle River, NJ: Merrill/Pearson Education.

Turnbull, H. R., & Turnbull, A. P. (1996). The synchrony of stakeholders: Lessons from the disabilities rights movement. In S. K. Kagen and N. Cohen (Eds.), *Reinventing early care and education: A vision for a quality system.* (pp. 290–305). San Francisco: Jossey-Bass.

Turnbull, H. R., & Turnbull, A. P. (2000). *Free appropriate public education: The law and children with disabilities* (6th ed.). Denver, CO: Love Publishing Co.

Turnbull, H. R., Turnbull, A. P., & Wheat, M. (1982). Assumptions about parental participation: A legislative history. *Exceptional Education Quarterly, 3*(2), 1–8.

Turnbull, R. (2009). In memory of Jay Turnbull. *Exceptional Parent, 39*(5), 36–37.

Turnbull, R., & Turnbull, A. (2007). Belonging, believing, and becoming. In E. W. Carter (Ed.), *Including people with disabilities in faith communities.* Baltimore, MD: Paul H. Brookes.

Turnbull, R., Turnbull, A., Turnbull, A., & Turnbull, K. (May, 2009). In memory of Jay Turnbull. *Exceptional Parent magazine.* Retrieved on June 29, 2009, from http://www.eparent.com

Turney, K., & Kao, G. (2009). Barriers to school involvement: Are immigrant parents disadvantaged. *Journal of Educational Research, 102*(4), 257–270.

Tyack, D., & Cuban, L. (1995). *Tinkering toward Utopia: A century of public school reform.* Cambridge, MA: Harvard University Press.

U.S. Department of Education. (1981). *Assistance to states for education of handicapped children: Interpretation of the Individualized Education Program (IEP).* Washington, DC: U.S. Government Printing Office.

U.S. Department of Education. (1999). *To assure the free appropriate public education of all children with disabilities.* Washington, DC: U.S. Department of Education.

U.S. Department of Education. (2001). *National assessment of educational progress.* Washington, DC: National Center for Education Statistics.

U.S. Department of Education. (2001). *To assure the free appropriate public education of all children with disabilities: Twenty-third annual report to Congress on the implementation of the Individuals with Disabilities Education Act.* Washington, DC: Author.

U.S. Department of Education. (2002). *To assure the free appropriate public education of all children with disabilities: Individuals with Disabilities Act, Section 618.* Washington, DC: Author.

U.S. Department of Education. (2003). *More local freedom: Questions and answers on No Child Left Behind.* Retrieved on October 30, 2003, from http://www.ed.gov/nclb/freedom/safety/creating.html#1

U.S. Department of Education. (2006). *Public elementary and secondary students, staff, schools, and school districts. School year 2003–04.*

U.S. Department of Education. (2006). *Twenty-eighth annual report to Congress on the implementation of the Individuals with Disabilities Education Act.* Washington, DC: Author.

U.S. Department of Education. (2007). *National Center for Educational Statistics: Indicators of School Crime and Safety* (NCES Report # 2008021). Washington, DC: Author.

U.S. Department of Education. (2007). *To assure the free appropriate public education of all children with disabilities: Individuals with Disabilities Education Act.* Washington, DC: Author.

U.S. Department of Education. (2007). *The 26th annual report to Congress on the implementation of the Individuals with Disabilities Education Act, 2004.* Vol. 1. Washington, DC: Author.

U.S. Department of Education, Office of Special Education Programs, Data Analysis System (DANS). (2006). *Children with disabilities receiving special education under part B of the Individuals with Disabilities Education Act.*

U.S. Department Education, Office of Special Education Programs. (2007). Memorandum to State Directors of Special Education on the Disproportionality of Racial and Ethnic Groups in Special Education. Retrieved on September 22, 2009, from http://www.ed.gov/policy/speced/guid/idea/letters/2007-2/osep0709disproportionality2q2007.pdf

U.S. Department of Health and Human Services. (2006). Health Resources and Services Administration, Maternal and Child Health Bureau. *Child Health USA 2006.* Rockville, MD: U.S. Department of Health and Human Services.

U.S. Department of Health and Human Services. (2009). *Child maltreatment 2007.* Washington, DC: U.S. Government Printing Office.

Uline, C. L., Tschannen-Moran, M., & Perez, L. (2003). Constructive conflict: How controversy can contribute to school improvement. *Teachers College Record, 105*(5), 782–816.

Ulrich, M. E., & Bauer, A. M. (2003). Levels of awareness: A closer look at communication between parents and professionals. *Teaching Exceptional Children, 35*(6), 20–23.

Urbano, R. C., & Hodapp, R. M. (2007). Divorce in families of children with Down syndrome: A populations-based study. *American Journal on Mental Retardation, 112*(4), 261–274.

Van der Klift, E., & Kunc, N. (2002). Beyond benevolence: Supporting genuine friendships in inclusive schools. In J. S. Thousand, R. A. Villa, & A. I. Nevin (Eds.), *Creativity & collaborative learning: The practical guide to empowering stud nets, teachers, and families.* Baltimore, MD: Paul H. Brookes.

Van Dycke, J. L., Martin, J. E., & Lovett, D. L. (2006). Why is this cake on fire? Inviting students into the IEP process. *Teaching Exceptional Children, 38*(3), 42–47.

Van Haren, B., & Fiedler, C. R. (2008). Support and empower families of children with disabilities. *Intervention in School and Clinic, 43*(4), 231–235.

Van Voorhis, F. (2003). Interactive homework in middle school: Effects on family involvement and science achievement. *Journal of Educational Research, 96*, 323–338.

Vaughn, B. J., White, R., Johnston, S., & Dunlap, G. (2005). Positive behavior support as a family-centered endeavor. *Journal of Positive Behavior Interventions, 7*(1), 55–58.

Vaughn, B. J., Wilson, D., & Dunlap, G. (2002). Family-centered interventions to resolve problem behaviors in a fast food restaurant. *Journal of Positive Behavior Interventions, 4*(10), 38–45.

Vaughn, S., Bos, C., Harrell, J., & Lasky, F. (1988). Parent participation in the initial placement/IEP conference ten years after mandated involvement. *Journal of Learning Disabilities, 21*(2), 82–89.

Vega, W., Hough, R., & Romero, A. (1983). *Family life patterns of Mexican Americans.* New York: Brunner/Mazel.

Veisson, M. (1999). Depression symptoms and emotional states in parents of disabled and non-disabled children. *Social Behavior and Personality, 27*, 87–98.

Voelker, S., Shore, D., Hakim-Larson, J., & Bruner, D. (1997). Discrepancies in parent and teacher rating of adaptive behavior of children with multiple disabilities. *Mental Retardation 35*(1), 10–17.

Vogel, G., & Retier, S. (2004). Significance of a bar/bat mitvah ceremony for parents of Jewish children with developmental disabilities. *Mental*

Retardation: A Journal of Practices, Policy and Perspectives, 42(4), 294–303.

Vohs, J. R. (1993). On belonging: A place to stand, a gift to give. In A. P. Turnbull, J. M. Patterson, S. K. Behr, D. L. Murphy, J. G. Marquis, & M. J. Blue-Banning (Eds.), *Cognitive coping, families, and disability* (pp. 51–66). Baltimore, MD: Paul H. Brookes.

Voydanoff, P., & Donnelly, B. (1999). The intersection of time in activities and perceived unfairness in relation to psychological distress and marital quality. *Journal of Marriage and the Family, 61,* 739–751.

Vyas, P. (1983). Getting on with it. In T. Dougan, L. Isbell, & P. Vyas (Eds.), *We have been there* (pp. 17–19). Nashville, TN: Abingdon.

Wade, S. L., Stancin, T., Taylor, G. H., Drotar, D., & Yeates, K. O. (2004). Interpersonal stressors and resources as predictors of parental adaptation following pediatric traumatic injury. *Journal of Counseling and Clinical Psychology, 72*(3), 776–784.

Wagner, M., Marder, C., Blackorby, J., & Cardeso, D. (2002). *The children we serve: The demographic characteristics of elementary and middle school students with disabilities and their households.* Menlo Park, CA: SRI International.

Wagner, M., Newman, L., Cameto, R., Levine, P., & Marder, C. (2007). *Perceptions and expectations of youth with disabilities.* A special topic report of findings from the National Longitudinal Transition Study-2 (NLTS-2). Menlo Park, CA: SRI International.

Walker, P., Hewitt, A., Bogenschulz, M., & Hall-Lande, J. (2009, January). Implementation of consumer-directed services for persons with intellectual or developmental disabilities: A national study. *Policy Research Brief, 20*(1).

Walker-Dalhouse, D., & Dalhouse, A. D. (2001). Parent-school relations: Communicating more effectively with African American parents. *Young Children, 56*(4), 75–80.

Walker-Dalhouse, D., & Dalhouse, A. D. (2001). Parent-school relations: Communicating more effectively with African American parents. *Young Children,* 75–80.

Wall, S., Kisker, E. E., Peterson, C. A., Carta, J. J., & Jeon, H. (2006). Child care for low-income children with disabilities: Access, quality and parental satisfaction. *Journal of Early Intervention, 28*(4), 283–298.

Walther, J. B. (1996). Computer-mediated communication: Impersonal, interpersonal, and hyperpersonal interaction. *Communication Research, 23*(1), 3–44.

Walther-Thomas, C., Korinek, L., McLaughlin, V. L., & Williams, B. T. (2000). *Collaboration for inclusive education: Developing successful programs.* Boston: Allyn & Bacon.

Wang, M., Mannan, H., Poston, D., Turnbull, A. P., & Summers, J. A. (2004). Parents' perceptions of advocacy activities and their impact on family quality of life. *Research and Practice for Persons with Severe Disabilities, 29*(2), 144–155.

Wang, M., McCart, A., & Turnbull, A. P. (2007). Implementing positive behavior support with Chinese American families: Enhancing cultural competence. *Journal of Positive Behavior Interventions, 9*(1), 38–51.

Wang, M., Turnbull, A. P., Summers, J. A., Little, T. D., Poston, D., Mannan, H., & Turnbull, R. (2004). Severity of disability and income as predictors of parents' satisfaction with their family quality of life during early childhood years. *Research and Practice for Persons with Severe Disabilities, 29*(2), 82–94.

Wang, Q. (July, 2005). *Disability and American families: 2000.* Census 2000 Special Reports. Washington, DC: U.S. Department of Commerce.

Warfield, M. E. (2001). Employment, parenting, and well-being among mothers of children with disabilities. *Mental Retardation, 39*(4), 297–309.

Warfield, M. E., Krauss, M., Hauser-Cram, P., Upshur, C., & Shonkoff, J. (1999). Adaptation during early childhood among mothers of children with disabilities. *Journal of Developmental and Behavioral Pediatrics, 43,* 112–118.

Warren, F. (1985). A society that is going to kill your children. In H. R. Turnbull & A. P. Turnbull (Eds.), *Parents speak out: Then and now* (2nd ed., pp. 201–232). Upper Saddle River, NJ: Merrill/Pearson Education.

Webster's Ninth New Collegiate Dictionary. (1990). Springfield, MA: Merriam-Webster, Inc.

Wehman, P., Bricout, J., & Kregel, J. (2000). Supported employment in 2000: Changing the locus of control from agency to consumer. In M. Wehmeyer & J. R. Patton (Eds.), *Mental retardation in the year 2000.* Austin, TX: PRO-ED.

Wehman, P., Mank, D., Rogan, P., Luna, J., Kregel, J., Kiernan, W., et al. (2004). *Employment, productive life roles and income maintenance.* Baltimore, MD: Paul H. Brookes.

Wehmeyer, M., & Palmer, S. (2003). Adult outcomes for students with cognitive disabilities three-years after high school: The impact of self-determination. *Education and Training in Developmental Disabilities, 38,* 131–144.

Wehmeyer, M. L. (2002). *Teaching students with mental retardation: Providing access to the general curriculum.* Baltimore, MD: Paul H. Brookes.

Wehmeyer, M. L. (2003). Perspectives. *American Association on Mental Retardation, 41*(1), 57–60.

Wehmeyer, M. L. (2007). *Promoting self-determination in students with developmental disabilities.* New York: Guilford Press.

Wehmeyer, M. L., Abery, B. H., Mithaug, D. E., & Stancliffe, R. J. (2003). *Theory in self-determination: Foundations for educational practice.* Springfield, IL: Charles C. Thomas.

Wehmeyer, M. L., Agran, M., & Hughes, C. (2000). A national survey of teachers' promotion of self-determination and student-directed learning. *Journal of Special Education, 34,* 58–68.

Wehmeyer, M. L., Agran, M., Palmer, S. B., Martin, J. E., & Mithuag, D. E. (2003). The effects of problem-solving instruction on the self-determined learning of secondary students with disabilities. In D. E. Mithaug, M. Agran, J. Martin, & M. L. Wehmeyer (Eds.), *Self-determined learning theory construction, verification, and evaluation.* Mahwah, NJ: Lawrence Erlbaum Associates.

Wehmeyer, M. L., Palmer, S. B., Agran, M., Mithaug, D. E., & Martin, J. (2000). Promoting causal agency: The self-determined learning model of instruction. *Exceptional Children, 66*(4), 439–453.

Weicker, L. (1985). Sonny and public policy. In H. R. Turnbull & A. P. Turnbull (Eds.), *Parents speak out: Then and now* (2nd ed., pp. 281–287). Upper Saddle River, NJ: Merrill/Pearson Education.

Weikle, B., & Hadadian, A. (2003). Can assistive technology help us to not leave any child behind? *Preventing School Failure, 47,* 181–190.

Werner, E. E., & Smith, R. S. (1992). *Overcoming the odds: High risk children from birth to adulthood.* Ithaca, NY: Cornell University Press.

West, J. S. (1990). Educational collaboration in the restructuring of schools. *Journal of Educational and Psychological Consultation, 1*(1), 23–40.

White, J. M., & Klein, D. M. (2008). *Family theories* (3rd ed.). Thousand Oaks, CA: Sage Publications.

Whitechurch, G. G., & Constantine, L. L. (1993). Systems theory. In P. G. Boss, W. J. Doherty, R. LaRossa, W. R. Schumm, & S. K. Steinmetz (Eds.), *Sourcebook of family theories and methods: A contextual approach* (pp. 325–352). New York: Plenum.

Wilkinson, C. Y., Ortiz, A. A., Robertson, P. M., & Kushner, M. I. (2006). English language learners with reading-related LD: Linking data from multiple sources to make eligibility decisions. *Journal of Learning Disabilities, 39*(2), 129–141.

Willert, H. J., & Lenhardt, A. M. C. (2003). Tackling school violence does take the whole village. *The Educational Forum, 67*(2), 110–118.

Williams, D., & Coles, L. (2007). Teachers' approaches to finding and using research evidence: An information literacy perspective. *Educational Research, 49*(2), 185–206.

Williams, V. I., & Cartledge, G. (1997, Sept./Oct. 1997). Passing notes—To parents. *The Council for Exceptional Children—Family Involvement in Learning,* 30–34.

Willis, W. (2004). Families with African American roots. In E. W. Lynch & M. J. Hanson (Eds.), *Developing cross-cultural competence: A guide for working with children and their families* (pp. 141–177). Baltimore: Paul H. Brookes.

Winerip, M. (2008, October 23). The love that shines through. *New York Times.* Retrieved on August 25, 2009, from http://www.nytimes.com/2008/10/26/nyregion/long-island/26Rparent.html?_r=4&em&oref=slogin&oref=slogin&oref=slogin

Winn, S., & Hay, I. (2009). Transition from school for youths with a disability: Issues and challenges. *Disability & Society, 24*(1), 103–115.

Wolfbiss, D. (2009). Happy tears. *Exceptional Parent, 39*(3), 58.

Wood, W. M., Karvonen, M., Test, D. W., Browder, D., & Algozzine, B. (2004). Promoting student self-determination skills in IEP planning. *Teaching Exceptional Children, 36*(3), 8–16.

Woodland, M. H. (2008). Whatcha doin' aftr school? A review of the literature on the influence of after-school programs on young black males. *Urban Education, 43*(5), 537–560.

Woods, J. J., & McCormick, K. M. (2002). Toward an integration of child- and family-centered practices in the assessment of preschool children: Welcoming the family. *Young Exceptional Children, 5*(3), 2–11.

York-Barr, J., Ghere, G., & Sommerness, J. (2007). Collaborative teaching to increase ELL student learning: A three-year urban elementary case study. *Journal of Education for Students Placed at Risk, 12*(3), 301–335.

Young, D. M., & Roopnarine, J. L. (1994). Fathers' childcare involvement with children with and without disabilities. *Topics in Early Childhood Special Education, 14*(4), 488–502.

Ysseldyke, J., & Olsen, K. (1999). Putting alternate assessments into practice: What to measure and possible sources of data. *Exceptional Children, 65*(2), 175–186.

Ysseldyke, J. E., Vanderwood, M. L., & Shriner, J. (1997). Changes over the past decade in special education referral to placement probability: An incredibly reliable practice. *Diagnostique, 23*(1), 193–201.

Ytterhus, B., Wendelborg, C., & Lundeby, H. (2008). Managing turning points and transitions in childhood and parenthood—Insights from families with disabled children in Norway. *Disability & Society, 23*(6), 625–636.

Zafft, C., Hart, D., & Zimbrich, K. (2004). College career connection: A study of youth with intellectual disabilities and the impact of postsecondary education. *Education and Training in Developmental Disabilities, 39*(1), 45–53.

Zeleke, S. (2004). Self-concepts of students with learning disabilities and their normally achieving peers: A review. *European Journal of Special Needs Education, 19*(2), 145–170.

Zhang, C., & Bennett, T. (2001). Multicultural views of disability: Implications for early intervention professionals. *Infant-Toddler Intervention, 11,* 143–154.

Zhang, C., & Bennett, T. (2003). Facilitating the meaningful participation of culturally and linguistically diverse families in the IFSP and IEP process. *Focus on Autism and Other Developmental Disabilities, 18*(1), 51–59.

Zhang, C., Fowler, S., & Bennett, T. (2004). Experiences and perceptions of EHS Staff with the IFSP process: Implications for practice and policy. *Early Childhood Education Journal, 32*(3), 179–186.

Zhang, C., Schwartz, B., & Lee, H. (2006). Collaborative services for infants and toddlers with disabilities: Perspectives from professionals in an urban setting. *Early Child Development and Care, 176*(3 & 4), 299–311.

Zhang, D. (2005). Parent practices in facilitating self-determination skills: The influences of culture, socioeconomic status, and children's special education status. *Research and Practice for Persons with Severe Disabilities, 30*(3), 154–162.

Zhang, D., & Rusch, F. R. (2005). Spiritual dimensions in living with disabilities. *Journal of Religion, Disability, and Health, 9,* 83–98.

Zigler, E., & Muenchow, S. (1992). *Head Start: The inside story of America's most successful educational experiment.* New York: Basic Books.

Zionts, L. T., Zionts, P., Harrison, S., & Bellinger, O. (2003). Urban African American families' perceptions of cultural sensitivity within the special education system. *Focus on Autism and Other Developmental Disabilities, 18,* 41–50.

Zirpoli, T. J., Wieck, C., Hancox, D., & Skarnulis, E. R. (1994). Partners in policymaking: The first five years. *Mental Retardation, 32*(6), 422–425.

Zoints, L. T., Zoints, P., Harrison, S., & Bellinger, O. (2003). Urban African American family's perceptions of cultural sensitivity within the special education system. *Focus on Autism and Other Developmental Disabilities, 18*(1), 41–50.

Zuna, N., Turnbull, A. P., & Turnbull, H. R. (in press). Family-professional partnerships. In M. E. Snell, & F. Brown (Eds.), *Instruction of students with severe disabilities* (7th ed.). Upper Saddle River, NJ: Merrill/Pearson Education.

Zuniga, M. E. (2004). Families with Latino roots. In E. W. Lynch & M. J. Hanson (Eds.), *Developing cross-cultural competence: A guide for working with children and their families* (pp. 179–217). Baltimore: Paul H. Brookes.

NAME INDEX

Abbott, D.A., 30
Abery, B.H., 76
Abeson, A., 114
Adelman, H.S., 276
Agosta, J., 49, 103, 245
Agran, M., 82
Aigbe, E., 19
Ainbinder, J., 235
Ainge, D., 34
Akey, T., 43
Alba, K., 246
Alber, S.B., 196, 197
Albin, R.W., 270
Algozzine, B., 82, 189, 211, 221
Al-Hassan, S., 12
Allen, N., 214
Allen, R.I., 104, 105
Allinder, R.M., 197
Allison-Tant, E., 20
Alper, S., 84
Alpern, C.S., 85
Altshuler, S.J., 32
Al-Yagon, M., 42
Anand, S., 19, 49
Anderson, B., 58, 60
Anderson, D.J., 261
Anderson, P.L., 267
Anderson, V., 273
Andrews, M.E., 20
Angell, M.E., 203, 259, 261, 265, 268
Angelo, D.H., 265
Angoff-Chedd, N., 74
Anguiano, R.P.V., 259
Ankeny, E.M., 89
Appelbaum, M., 31
Arceneaux, C., 74
Arguelles, M.E., 77, 200, 260
Arndt, S.A., 211, 215, 221
Audette, R.M.L., 122
Aurora, T., 79
Avis, D.W., 19

Badgett, L., 33
Bahr, M.W., 185
Baier, A.C., 153
Bailey, D.B., 19, 40, 55, 72, 75, 196, 260
Bailey, L.B., 51, 258, 260, 262
Bailey, R.L., 265, 266, 267
Baker, B., 30
Baker, B.L., 17, 50, 58, 91, 102
Baker, J.K., 17
Baker, S., 34
Baker, S.R., 89
Baker-Erizcen, M.J., 31

Baldwin, A.Y., 197
Balogh, P.A., 196, 197
Bambara, L.M., 89
Banda, D.R., 141
Bandura, A., 155
Banks, S., 52
Barkley, S.C., 36
Barlow, J., 22
Barnard, W.M., 259
Barr, M.W., 97
Barratt, M.S., 34
Barraza, L., 37
Barrera, I., 167, 189, 196, 259
Barrie, W., 221
Bates, A., 17, 34, 50
Batshaw, M.L., 17, 98
Bauer, A.M., 169
Baum, L.S., 244
Baum, N., 19, 49
Baxter, B., 278
Baxter, D., 17, 34, 50
Bayat, M., 50, 51, 55
Beatson, J., 193
Beatty, E., 110
Beck, A, 50, 58
Becker, S., 142
Becker-Cottrill, B., 273
Beegle, G., 139, 156, 164, 274
Beghetto, R.A., 175
Behr, S.K., 42, 51
Behrman, R.E., 32
Bell, M., 72
Bell, M.J., 98
Belle, D., 51
Bellinger, O., 19, 171
Ben, K.R., 270
Benefit, 119, 137–138
Benn, P.A., 72, 73
Bennett, J.M., 63, 101
Bennett, T., 13, 36, 55, 216, 217
Benson, B.A., 30
Benson, P., 65
Berg, A., 276
Berg, W.K., 273
Berkeley, T.R., 35
Berktold, J., 84
Berliner, D.C., 110
Bernheimer, L.P., 65, 170
Besser, H., 42
Bettleheim, B., 98
Bezdek, J., 99
Biddle, B.J., 110
Billings, F.J., 32, 43
Billingsley, B.S., 140, 145, 146, 149, 153, 177

Birenbaum, A., 7
Biros, E., 20
Bishop, K.K., 193
Bishop, S.L., 36
Blacher, J., 11, 17, 30, 38, 49, 50, 58, 74, 88, 91, 239
Blackmountain, L., 12
Blackorby, J., 245
Blakley-Smith, A., 61
Blanchard, C., 82
Blanchett, W.J., 81
Blank, M., 276
Blank, M.J., 278
Blogging, 176
Blue-Banning, M.J. 18, 61, 62, 103, 139, 140, 142, 144, 147–149, 153, 155, 156, 164, 175, 198, 226, 239, 268, 274
Blum, R.W.M., 81
Blumberg, E.R., 85, 273
Bobbit, L., 84
Bobis, F., 246
Bock, S.J., 203
Bockstael, E., 62
Bogenschulz, M., 247
Boggs, E., 101
Bogner, J., 65
Boldman, B.D., 31
Booth, T., 21
Booth, W., 21
Booth-LaForce, C., 58
Bos, C., 214
Bos, C.S., 261
Bose, J., 84
Boutot, E.A., 268
Bove, K., 59
Boyce, L.K., 35
Brabham, E., 258
Braddock, D., 87, 98, 247, 248
Bradley, J., 58
Bradley, J.F., 59, 63
Brady, S.J., 178
Brantlinger, E., 81
Breen, K., 278
Brennan, E.M., 58
Brenner, M.E., 36
Brewer, D.M., 76
Brewin, B.J., 60, 61, 142, 146, 200, 267
Bricker, D., 196, 215
Bricker, D.D., 102
Bricker, W.A., 102
Bricout, J., 87
Briel, L.W., 84
Brittain, C.S., 261
Brobst, J.B., 30

SUBJECT INDEX